SUPPLEMENT IV, Part 1
Maya Angelou to Linda Hogan

AMERICAN WRITERS
A Collection of Literary Biographies

A. WALTON LITZ

Editor in Chief

MOLLY WEIGEL

Assistant Editor

SUPPLEMENT IV, Part 1
Maya Angelou to Linda Hogan

Charles Scribner's Sons
Macmillan Library Reference USA
Simon & Schuster Macmillan
New York

Simon & Schuster and Prentice Hall International
London   Mexico City   New Delhi   Singapore   Sydney   Toronto

Charles Scribner's Sons
An Imprint of Simon & Schuster Macmillan
1633 Broadway
New York, New York 10019

1 3 5 7 9 11 13 15 17 19   20 18 16 14 12 10 8 6 4 2

Library of Congress Cataloging-in-Publication Data

American writers: a collection of literary biographies.

Suppl. 4 edited by A. Walton Litz and Molly Weigel.
The 4-vol. main set consists of 97 of the pamphlets originally published as the
University of Minnesota pamphlets on American writers; some have been rev. and
updated. The supplements cover writers not included in the original series.
Includes bibliographies.
Contents: v. 1. Henry Adams to T. S. Eliot — v. 2. Ralph Waldo Emerson to
Carson McCullers — [etc.] — Supplement[s] — [etc.] — 4, pt. 1. Maya Angelou to
Linda Hogan. 4, pt. 2. Susan Howe to Gore Vidal.
1. American Literature — History and criticism.   2. American literature — Bio-
bibliography.   3. Authors, American — Biography.   I. Unger, Leonard, ed. II. Baechler,
Lea. III. Litz, A. Walton. IV. Weigel, Molly. V. University of Minnesota. Pamphlets on
American writers.

PS129.A55   810'.9   73-1759

ISBN 0-684-19785-5 (Set)
ISBN 0-684-19786-3 (Part 1)
ISBN 0-684-19787-1 (Part 2)

The paper in this publication meets the requirements of ANSI/NISO Z39.48-1992 (Permanence of Paper).

Acknowledgment is gratefully made to those publishers and individuals who have permitted the use of the following materials in copyright.
"Louis Auchincloss"
Excerpt from "The Fabbri Tape, from *Narcissa and Other Fables* by Louis Auchincloss. Copyright © 1983 by Louis Auchincloss. Reprinted by permission of Houghton Mifflin Company. All rights reserved. Reprinted by permission of Curtis Brown, Ltd.
"Donald Barthelme"
Excerpts from *The Dead Father* by Donald Barthelme. Copyright © 1975 by Donald Barthelme. Reprinted by permission of Farrar, Straus & Giroux, Inc. Excerpt from *Guilty Pleasure* by Donald Barthelme. Copyright © 1963 by Donald Barthelme. Reprinted with permission of Wylie, Aitken & Stone, Inc. Excerpt from *Snow White* by Donald Barthelme reprinted with the permission of Scribner, an imprint of Simon and Schuster. Copyright © 1967 by Donald Barthelme.
"Paul Bowles"
Excerpt from Jane Bowles, *My Sister's Hand in Mine: The Collected Works of Jane Bowles,* Ecco Press, 1978.
"Ray Bradbury"
Excerpt from "Death Warmed Over" originally appeared in *Playboy* magazine. Reprinted by permission of Don Congdon Associates, Inc. Copyright © 1967, renewed 1995 by Ray Bradbury.
"Robert Creeley"
Excerpt from "Fathers" by Robert Creeley, from *Memory Gardens.* Copyright © 1986 by Robert Creeley. Reprinted by permission of New Directions Publishing Corp. Published in Britain by Marion Boyars Publishers Ltd., London. Excerpt from "If" by Robert Creeley, from *Windows.* Copyright © 1990 by Robert Creeley. Reprinted by permission of New Directions Publishing Corp. Published in Britain by Marion Boyars Publishers Ltd., London. Excerpts from "Poem for D. H. Lawrence," "Still Life Or," and "Alba" in *The Charm: Early and Uncollected Poems,* University of California Press, 1969.
"Countee Cullen"
Excerpt from *Caroling at Dusk: An Anthology of Verse by Negro Poets,* © James Rhone, 1927. Excerpts from "The Black Christ" and "Tribute (To My Mother)" in *The Black Christ and Other Poems,* © James Rhone, 1929. Excerpt from "The Shroud of Color" in *Color,* © James Rhone, 1925.

"E. L. Doctorow"

Excerpt from *Jack London, and the Constitution: Selected Essays, 1977–1992,* Random House, 1993. Excerpt from *World's Fair,* Random House, 1985.

"Rita Dove"

Excerpt from "Anti-Father" from Rita Dove, *Museum,* Carnegie Mellon University Press, copyright © 1983 by Rita Dove. Excerpt from "In the Old Neighborhood," from Rita Dove, *Selected Poems,* © 1993 by Rita Dove, used by permission of the author. Excerpt from "The Event" from Rita Dove, *Thomas & Beulah,* Carnegie Mellon University Press, copyright © 1986 by Rita Dove. Excerpt from "After Reading *Mickey in the Night Kitchen* for the Third Time before Bed" from *Grace Notes,* W. W. Norton & Company, 1989. Excerpt from "The Bistro Styx" in *Mother Love,* W. W. Norton & Company, 1995.

"Paula Gunn Allen"

Excerpt from *Coyote's Daylight Trip,* La Confluencia Press, 1978.

"Dashiell Hammett"

Excerpt from *The Thin Man* by Dashiell Hammett. Copyright 1933, 1934 by Alfred A Knopf, Inc., and renewed 1961, 1962 by Dashiell Hammett. Reprinted by permission of the publisher.

"Joseph Heller"

Excerpts from *Catch-22* by Joseph Heller reprinted with permission of Simon & Schuster. Copyright © 1955, 1961 by Joseph Heller, copyright renewed © 1989 by Joseph Heller. Excerpts from *Closing Time* by Joseph Heller reprinted with permission of Simon & Schuster. Copyright © 1994 by Skimton, Inc. Excerpts from *Something Happened* by Joseph Heller. Copyright © 1966, 1974 by Scapegoat Productions, Inc. Reprinted by permission of Alfred A. Knopf, Inc. Copyright © 1974 Scapegoat Productions, Inc. Reprinted by permission of Donadio & Ashworth, Inc.

"Susan Howe"

Excerpt from "Defenestration of Prague" by Susan Howe, 1983, The Kulchur Foundation. Excerpt from "The Last First People" from *Secret History of the Dividing Line,* 1978, Telephone Books, Maureen Owen, ed. Excerpt from *The Europe of Trusts: Selected Poems,* Sun & Moon Press, 1990.

"N. Scott Momaday"

Excerpts from *House Made of Dawn* by N. Scott Momaday. Copyright © 1966, 1967, 1968 by N. Scott Momaday. Reprinted by permission of HarperCollins Publishers, Inc. Excerpt from "A Gathering of Shields" from *In the Presence of the Sun* By Scott Momaday, St. Martin's Press, Inc., New York, New York. Copyright © 1992 Scott Momaday. Excerpt from *The Way to Rainy Mountain* by N. Scott Momaday, University of New Mexico Press, 1969. Excerpt from "An American Land Ethic" in *Ecotactics: The Sierra Club Handbook for Environmental Activists,* Simon & Schuster/Trident Press, 1970.

"Simon Ortiz"

Fight Back: For the Sake of the People, for the Sake of the Land, 1980. Permission granted by the author, Simon J. Ortiz.

"Alberto Ríos"

Excerpts from "The Used Side of the Sofa," "Marvella, for Borrowing," "A Dish of Green Pears," from *Teodoro Luna's Two Kisses* by Alberto Ríos. Copyright © 1990 by Alberto Ríos. Reprinted by permission of W. W. Norton & Company, Inc. Excerpts from "The Friday Morning Trial of Mrs. Solano," "The Lime Orchard Woman," "The Industry of Hard Kissing," "Mason Jars by the Window," "Secret Prune," and "One Winter I Devise a Plan of My Own" in *The Lime Orchard Woman,* 1988; "Kino Viejo," "El Molino Rojo," and "Sundays Visiting" in *Whispering to Fool the Wind,* 1982; and "Taking Away the Name of a Nephew," "Her Dream Is of the Sea," "The Scent of Unbought Flowers," and "I Held His Hand" in *Five Indiscretions,* 1985, reprinted with permission of the author.

"Leslie Marmon Silko"

Excerpts from *The Delicacy and Strength of Lace: Letters Between Leslie Marmon Silko and James Wright,* 1986, reprinted with permission from Anne Wright. Excerpt from *Almanac of the Dead,* Simon & Schuster, Inc., 1991. Excerpt from *Ceremony,* Viking Press, 1977.

"Mark Strand"

Excerpt from *Dark Harbor: A Poem* by Mark Strand. Copyright © 1993 by Mark Strand. Reprinted by permission of Alfred A. Knopf, Inc. Excerpt from *The Continuous Life* by Mark Strand. Copyright © 1990 by Mark Strand. Reprinted by permission of Alfred A. Knopf, Inc. Excerpt from *Darker,* Atheneum, 1970. Excerpt from *Reason for Moving,* Atheneum, 1968. Excerpt from *The Late Hour,* Atheneum, 1978. Excerpt from *The Story of Our Lives,* Atheneum, 1973.

"May Swenson"

Excerpt from "Questions" from *The Complete Poems to Solve* by May Swenson reprinted with the permission of Simon & Schuster Books for Young Readers. Copyright 1954 May Swenson; copyright renewed © 1982 May Swenson. Excerpt from *In Other Words* by May Swenson. Copyright © 1987 by May Swenson. Reprinted by permission of Alfred A. Knopf, Inc. Excerpts from "I Will Lie Down" in *Another Animal: Poems,* 1954; "I Look at My Hand" from *Iconographs: Poems,* 1970; and *To Mix with Time: New and Selected Poems,* 1963, used with permission of the Literary Estate of May Swenson.

"Gore Vidal"

Excerpt from *At Home: Essays 1982–1988,* Random House, 1988. Excerpt from *Empire: A Novel,* Random House, 1987. Excerpt from *United States—Essays 1951–1991,* Random House, 1992.

Editorial and Production Staff

List of Subjects

Part 1

Introduction

The original four volumes of *American Writers: A Collection of Literary Biographies* (1974) assembled the ninety-seven essays that had first appeared between 1959 and 1972 as the University of Minnesota Pamphlets on American Writers. The idea of collecting the essays in a set came to Charles Scribner Jr. (1921–1995) when his dear friend Louis Auchincloss sent him his Minnesota pamphlet on Henry Adams. The pamphlets made up a series of "introductory essays . . . aimed at people (general readers here and abroad, college students, etc.) . . . interested in the writers concerned, but not highly familiar with their work." Characteristically, however, the essays of the initial series and the subsequent supplementary volumes successfully integrated criticism with biographical detail in such a way as to address and to inform both the general reader and the specialist.

Like the essays in *Supplement I* (2 vols., 1979), *Supplement II* (2 vols., 1981), and *Supplement III* (2 vols., 1991), the thirty-five essays in this fourth supplement maintain the original goals of the series: providing—for students in secondary and advanced education, librarians, scholars, critics, and teachers—a comprehensive treatment of the work and life of each author. The essay on Susan Howe bears special mention as the first intensive examination of that poet's literary life and canon, but a number of other essays in *Supplement IV* offer the fullest biographical-critical accounts of their subjects to date. This feature of the present supplement is, to

some extent, the result of the editors' attention to contemporary writers who in the late twentieth century clearly established the lasting import of their literary contributions.

Written by recognized experts, young scholars, and poet-critics, the essays collected here also reflect the range and variety of approaches exhibited in the literary study of the 1980s and 1990s: balancing cultural history and literary biography with thorough analyses of individual major works, these essays are characterized, where appropriate, by their engagement of literary theory; feminist, African American, and Native American interpretations; and the political or aesthetic ideologies of their subjects. These two volumes extend the tradition of diversity set forth in the original four volumes and the previous three supplements. Like the earlier supplements, the present volumes are attentive to women and African American writers, emphasizing both writers who have enjoyed revived critical and popular attention—Maya Angelou, Countee Cullen, May Swenson—and contemporary authors who have established their reputations as writers and maintained that status with continued and significant literary output, among them Anne Tyler and Rita Dove. In addition, these volumes feature a number of significant Native American and Hispanic American authors, including Paula Gunn Allen, N. Scott Momaday, Louise Erdrich, Linda Hogan, Simon Ortiz, Alberto Ríos, and Leslie Marmon Silko. Writers who have produced masterful works in "popular" genres such as detective fiction and science fiction—Ray Bradbury, Raymond Chandler, Dashiell Hammett, and Ross Macdonald—are also included.

In fact, *Supplement IV* is distinguished by a table of contents that includes writers and critics as diverse as Joan Didion and Gore Vidal, Paul Bowles and Neil Simon, Donald Barthelme and E. L. Doctorow, Mary Gordon and Joseph Heller, Ayn Rand and Wallace Stegner. An eclectic collection, these two volumes are also notable for the number of essays devoted to established writers, such as Louis Auchincloss and William Gaddis, whose reputations have not been fully recognized, and to contemporary poets. The poets' presence here reflects the richly various poetic undertakings of writers from the second half of the century. Besides those already mentioned, the poets presented in these two volumes include

a number who came to wide notice between 1975 and 1996, among them Robert Bly, Robert Creeley, James Dickey, Maxine Kumin, and Mark Strand.

As with the essays of the original series, *Supplement IV* offers expertly conceived and informative essays on writers who portray the rich diversity of our literary heritage. These writers remind us, by their disparate yet bold endeavors of the literary life, that the readers of each generation must continue to reevaluate the impact and influence of particular writers and their major works in order to maintain the vitality of that heritage.

A. WALTON LITZ
MOLLY WEIGEL

Contributors

Ronald Baughman. Director of Graduate Studies, Media Arts, University of South Carolina, Columbia. Author of *Undersanding James Dickey;* editor of and contributor of article on Dickey to *Contemporary Authors Bibliographical Series,* volume 2: *American Poets*; editor of *The Voiced Connections of James Dickey: Interviews and Conversations.* JAMES DICKEY

Alma Bennett. Assistant Professor of Humanities and English, Clemson University. Author of *Mary Gordon* and of reviews in various journals. MARY GORDON

Mark S. Braley. Assistant Professor of English, U.S. Air Force Academy. WALLACE STEGNER

Anna Carew-Miller. Professor of English, Swiss Hospitality Institute. Author of articles on Crèvecoeur and on Linda Hogan. LINDA HOGAN

Steven R. Carter. Associate Professor of English, Salem State College. Author of *Hansberry's Drama: Commitment amid Complexity* and numerous articles. LORRAINE HANSBERRY

Peter L. Cooper. Senior Examiner, Educational Testing Service. Author of *Signs and Symptoms.* RAYMOND CHANDLER

Gwen Crane. Assistant Professor of English, State University of New York College at Oneonta. DONALD BARTHELME.

William V. Davis. Professor of English and Writer-in-Residence, Baylor University. Author of *One Way to Reconstruct the Scene; Understanding Robert Bly; Robert Bly: The Poet and His Critics; Miraculous Simplicity: Essays on R. S. Thomas;* numerous critical essays on American and British literature; and hundreds of poems. ROBERT BLY

Jeffery Donaldson. Associate Professor of English, McMaster University. Poet and author of *Once Out of Nature;* author of articles on Richard Howard, James Merrill, Geoffrey Hill, W. H. Auden, and Mark Strand. MARK STRAND.

C. K. Doreski. Teacher of writing, Boston University, Emmanuel College, University of Massachusetts, Boston. Author of *How to Read and Interpret Poetry; Elizabeth Bishop: The Restraints of Language;* and *Writing America Black: Race, Rhetoric, and the Public Sphere.* JOAN DIDION

William Doreski. Professor of English, Keene State College. Author of *The Modern Voice in American Poetry* and *The Years of Our Friendship: Robert Lowell and Allen Tate.* WILLIAM GADDIS

Gerald Early. Merle S. Kling Professor of Modern Letters and Director, African and Afro-American Studies, Washington University. Author of *Tuxedo Junction: Essays on American Culture; The Culture of Bruising: Essays on Prizefighting, Literature, and Modern American Culture; Daughters: On Family and Fatherhood.* COUNTEE CULLEN

J. Ellen Gainor. Associate Professor of Theatre Arts, Cornell University. Author of *Shaw's Daughters: Dramatic and Narrative Constructions of Gender;* editor of *Imperialism and The-*

atre; author of numerous essays and reviews. NEIL SIMON

Carol Gelderman. Distinguished Professor of English, University of New Orleans. Author of *Henry Ford: The Wayward Capitalist; Mary McCarthy: A Life; Louis Auchincloss: A Writer's Life;* and *Conversations with Mary McCarthy.* LOUIS AUCHINCLOSS

Celeste Goodridge. Associate Professor and Chair of English, Bowdoin College. Author of *Hints and Disguises: Marianne Moore and Her Contemporaries.* LESLIE MARMON SILKO

Janet Gray. Lecturer in English, Princeton University; Lecturer in Women's Studies, Trenton State College. Editor of *She Wields a Pen: American Women's Poetry of the Nineteenth Century;* author of *A Hundred Flowers* and of essays on Alice Walker, Elizabeth Hardwick, and Louise Bogan. ROSS MACDONALD

Allen Hibbard. Assistant Professor of English, Middle Tennessee State University. Author of *Paul Bowles: A Study of the Short Fiction;* and numerous articles, translations, and reviews. PAUL BOWLES

Sally L. Joyce. Associate Professor of English and Coordinator of English Composition, Keene State College. Editor of *Cornwall: The Records of Early English Drama.* N. SCOTT MOMADAY

Mary Jane Lupton. Professor of English and Coordinator of the Graduate Program in English, Morgan State University. Author of *Menstruation and Psychoanalysis;* coauthor of *The Curse: A Cultural History of Menstruation;* author of numerous essays on African American women writers. MAYA ANGELOU

Randy Malamud. Associate Professor of English, Georgia State University. Senior Editor,

South Atlantic Review; author of *Where the Words Are Valid: T. S. Eliot's Communities of Drama; T. S. Eliot's Drama: A Research and Production Sourcebook;* and *The Language of Modernism.* E. L. DOCTOROW

Jane Eldridge Miller. Author of *Rebel Women: Feminism, Modernism, and the Edwardian Novel* and numerous articles and reviews. MAY SWENSON

Lauren Muller. Doctoral candidate, Department of English, University of California, Berkeley; Instructor in Native American Studies, African American Studies, and Women's Studies, University of California, Berkeley. Editor of *June Jordan's Poetry for the the People: A Revolutionary Blueprint.* PAULA GUNN ALLEN.

Jacqueline Shea Murphy. Graduate student, Department of English, University of California, Berkeley. Coeditor of *Bodies of the Text: Dance as Theory, Literature as Dance;* author of articles on Leslie Marmon Silko and Sylvia Plath. PAULA GUNN ALLEN

Steven A. Nardi. Doctoral candidate in English, Princeton University. MAXINE KUMIN

Jay Parini. Axinn Professor of English, Middlebury College. Author of four novels, including *The Last Station* and *Bay of Arrows,* and three volumes of poetry; a critical study of Theodore Roethke; and *John Steinbeck: A Biography.* GORE VIDAL.

Adrián Peréz Melgosa. Assistant Professor of Spanish, Seton Hill College. ALBERTO ÁLVARO RÍOS.

Sanford Pinsker. Shadek Professor of Humanities, Franklin and Marshall College. Author of *The Catcher in the Rye: Innocence under Pressure; Jewish American Fiction; Understanding*

Joseph Heller; and numerous articles, reviews, poems, and stories. JOSEPH HELLER

Bill Piper. Teacher of English as a second language and programs coordinator, Counterpoint Language Consultants. ROBERT CREELEY.

Mary Margaret Richards. Associate Professor of English, Wofford College. Author of articles on T. S. Eliot, Edith Wharton, and Alice Walker. ANNE TYLER

Chris Matthew Sciabarra. Visiting Scholar, Department of Politics, New York University. Author of *Ayn Rand: The Russian Radical* and *Marx, Hayek, and Utopia.* AYN RAND

Patricia Clark Smith. Professor of English Language and Literature, University of New Mexico. Author of *Changing Your Story;* coeditor of *Western Literature in a World Context* and *As Long as the River Flows: The Stories of Nine Native Americans.* SIMON J. ORTIZ

William F. Touponce. Associate Professor of English, Indiana University/Purdue University at Indianapolis. Author of *Ray Bradbury and the Poetics of Reverie; Frank Herbert;* and *Isaac Asimov.* RAY BRADBURY

Molly Weigel. Recent Ph.D. in English, Princeton University; freelance writer, editor, and translator. SUSAN HOWE

Lesley Wheeler. Assistant Professor of English, Washington and Lee University. Poet. RITA DOVE

Pauline Groetz Woodward. Associate Professor of Humanities, Endicott College; Instructor, University of Massachusetts, Boston. LOUISE ERDRICH

Robert Worth. Lecturer, Department of English, Princeton University. DASHIELL HAMMETT

Maya Angelou
1928–

MAYA ANGELOU SHARES with the readers of her autobiographies an incredible journey that begins in a small town in Arkansas and stretches to the West Coast of Africa. Although Angelou is most familiar to her international audience for her series of autobiographies, she has excelled in other literary and personal modes as well. Reynolds Professor of American Studies at Wake Forest University in North Carolina since 1981, Angelou has been a poet, a filmmaker, an actress, a cabaret singer, a scholar, a dynamic lecturer, a nominee for both the Pulitzer Prize and the National Book Award—a woman so versatile that she belongs as much to popular culture as to the world of letters. Her poetic force is so widely recognized by African Americans that she was invited to read one of her poems at the Million Man March on October 16, 1995. This essay, while it occasionally touches on her connections with the media, is primarily concerned with the part Angelou has played in the American literary tradition.

It is as an autobiographer that Angelou has made her greatest impact on American literature, joining Richard Wright, Lillian Hellman, James Baldwin, Maxine Hong Kingston, Frederick Douglass, and other writers whose life stories have challenged and enriched the American ethos. So bewitching is Angelou's life-telling that Nancy Chick has called her a ''twentieth-century

Scheherazade,'' after the legendary storyteller who would each night tell the king a new story. By halting before each story's conclusion, Scheherazade kept the king in suspense and forestalled her execution. Like the thousand and one stories collected in the *Arabian Nights*, Angelou's five autobiographies are vivid and episodic narratives that accelerate or reduce their pace as the life winds and unwinds. By the mid-1990s, many of her admirers, anticipating that the pace would continue, suspected that a sixth volume was in the wings.

In her autobiographies Angelou proves to be an astute observer of self and society. Her recollections are grounded in the visual—in sights of shattered dolls, of filmy veils, and of Klansmen riding in the night. Her autobiographies are like a series of snapshots taken at different times from different angles that focus on major themes. For Angelou herself, life and work evoke another visual image, one derived from painting. In a 1977 *Black Scholar* interview, she told Robert Chrisman, then editor of *Ebony* magazine, ''I try to live my life as a poetic adventure . . . , everything is part of a large canvas I am creating, I am living beneath.''

Maya Angelou's poetic adventure began April 4, 1928, when she was born in St. Louis as Marguerite Johnson, daughter of Vivian (Baxter) Johnson and Bailey Johnson Sr. Soon after, the family moved to Long Beach, California, where her parents' troubled marriage ended in divorce. When she was three her father put Maya and her four-year-old brother Bailey on a train from California to Stamps, Arkansas, home of their paternal grandmother, Annie Henderson (generally called ''Momma'' in the narratives). For students of African American literature, these nearly abandoned children and this mighty grandmother are ingrained in the imagination by way of Angelou's first published autobiography, *I Know Why the Caged Bird Sings.*

As Angelou's life is best understood from her own autobiographical writings, this essay will reconstruct Angelou's story as she herself revealed it in *I Know Why the Caged Bird Sings* (1970), *Gather Together in My Name* (1974), *Singin' and Swingin' and Gettin' Merry Like Christmas* (1976), *The Heart of a Woman* (1981), and *All God's Children Need Traveling Shoes* (1986). These volumes, although disparate, are unified through a number of artistic features. While they follow conventional autobiographical technique in tracing the activities of the narrator, they also stretch over time and place to contain detailed portraits of other significant characters: Maya's first husband, Tosh Angelos; the Ghanaian chief and educator, Nana Nketisia; the Stamps ''aristocrat,'' Mrs. Bertha Flowers; the American statesman, Malcolm X; the blues singer, Billie Holiday; her roommate, Alice Windom; and many other characters. Because of the vastness of her canvas, Angelou tends to underplay the traditional autobiographical device of individual development in favor of a more generalized technique; as Dolly McPherson has observed in her 1990 book, *Order Out of Chaos*, Angelou creates ''rich portraits of a wide assortment of people, including description of the rhythms of their lives and the patterns of different environments.''

This multiplicity of rhythms requires the reader to travel through several books to understand, for example, Maya's full attitude toward her mother or the entirety of her feelings about men. As an autobiographer, Angelou echoes in her structure the flexibility of the life processes. She constantly, although perhaps not always consciously, interrelates ideas, images, and characters within the five-volume structure. In her revision of traditional African American autobiography, Maya Angelou sets herself apart by extending the form, incorporating personal and historical materials into a continuing narrative that becomes a record of one black woman's life in America and Africa. From volume to volume there is a sense of historical change: in Jim Crow laws; in the Pan-African and civil rights movements; in black participation in theater; and countless other areas. By focusing on certain themes not ordinarily explored in more impersonal African American autobiographies such as those of Frederick Douglass or Gwendolyn Brooks, Angelou presents one of the closest looks in print at what it is to be an African American woman. She explores her womanhood in meticulous detail, finding both personal and cultural relevance in such diverse events as visiting her son's elementary school, preparing a dinner, or conversing with an African woman at a campfire. Sondra O'Neale writes that Angelou's attention to these ''mundane, though essential, ordinary moments of life'' are aspects of ''superior autobiography.'' As we examine Angelou's autobiographies, their superior quality will become recognizable.

I Know Why the Caged Bird Sings is the first and still best-loved volume in the autobiographical series. *Caged Bird* begins with a symbolic prelude concerning Maya's fears of being stared at in church. Her emotions in this introductory section focus on her contempt for her black skin; like Pecola Breedlove in Toni Morrison's *The Bluest Eye*, she wishes for the privileges that come with being white. Jon Zlotnik Schmidt isolates this opening incident as one of several in which Maya feels abused and devalued because she is a black child who perceives herself as the "other" in a white world. Her "black ugly dream" introduces a motif which sets up the theme of racial displacement that occupies much of *Caged Bird* and of the subsequent volume, *Gather Together in My Name*.

The formal autobiography begins with Maya's recollection of traveling with her brother by train from California to Arkansas. Because Maya was three and Bailey was four they had tags around their wrists with notes "To Whom It May Concern" explaining their names and destination. These children, along with their stern grandmother, Annie Henderson, form an emotional pulse at the heart of *I Know Why the Caged Bird Sings*, a pulse which vibrates from the extended family into the community of Stamps, into its religious, social, and educational institutions. Uncle Willie, Annie Henderson's crippled son, is another key figure at the core of this narrative. In an early episode Uncle Willie is hidden in a potato bin to escape the attention of a white lynching mob; his humiliation gives Maya her first knowledge of racism.

Throughout much of *Caged Bird* Maya remains displaced, rejected in a racist society and all but abandoned by her mother, Vivian Baxter. In one of several reflective fantasies, the child imagines her mother lying in a coffin, dead, faceless: "since I couldn't fill in the features I printed M O T H E R across the O, and tears would fall down my cheeks like warm milk." The empty face of the mother is perceived through the imagination of a child who prints, who writes, who stares back. In the gap left by the absent mother Maya erects Momma Henderson: "I saw only her power and strength. She was taller than any woman in my personal world, and her hands were so large they could span my head from ear to ear."

I Know Why the Caged Bird Sings abounds in such moments of verbal force, where the meta-phors perfectly correspond to the emotion, as in Momma's encompassing hands, as in the Christmas misery when Maya destroys the blond-haired doll her mother had sent her but preserves the other gift, a tea set, "because any day or night she might come riding up." The doll and the tea set seem to represent Maya's torn self, the angry child versus the ungrateful child—the doll destroyed in anger but the tea set saved in the hope of Vivian's return.

Another striking use of metaphor occurs in the confrontation between Annie Henderson and three "powhitetrash" girls who taunt her. The oldest of the girls brazenly performs a pantyless handstand before Momma's eyes. Symbolically, the white child unveils the power of her white sexuality in front of a woman who, though morally superior, is defenseless, being black, being the "other." Momma responds to her situation by quietly singing a hymn, her eyes toward Heaven. In his interpretation of this episode, Stephen Butterfield views Momma's silence as a victory in self-control, although, given the racist underpinnings of her response, her victory is ultimately a "consolation prize." McPherson reads this confrontation scene from Maya's perspective, seeing an example of "the kind of spiritual death and regeneration Angelou experienced during the shaping of her development."

Angelou presents a similar death of the spirit in describing her visit, with Momma, to a white dentist who would rather put his "hand in a dog's mouth than in a nigger's." The horrendous equation between "dog" and "nigger" recounts the history of dehumanization recorded by African American writers, from the first slave narratives to the "mad and hungry dogs" of Claude McKay's famous sonnet, "If We Must Die." Humiliated for herself, for her grandmother, for her culture, Maya retaliates silently in a fantasy of power where Momma's eyes burn "like live coals" and her arms grow to twice their length.

The most powerful emotional response in the

first autobiography, however, is Maya's negation of speech after being raped during a stay with her mother in St. Louis. The beautiful Vivian has a lover, Mr. Freeman, who befriends Maya and later rapes her. Angelou describes the episode in language that has been broadly acclaimed for its candor:

> Then there was the pain. A breaking and entering when even the senses are torn apart. The act of rape on an eight-year-old body is a matter of the needle giving because the camel can't. The child gives, because the body can, and the mind of the violator cannot.

After the rape Maya, ill from the shock and from the pain, is sent to the hospital, where she tells Bailey the rapist's identity. Mr. Freeman is tried and found guilty but inexplicably released the very day of his sentencing. Not long afterward Mr. Freeman's corpse is found behind a slaughterhouse, apparently kicked to death. Although the text suggests that Maya's uncles and grandmother were involved in Mr. Freeman's murder, this is never stated explicitly. After the trial and subsequent murder Maya, who has lied about her earlier sexual contact with Mr. Freeman, becomes mute so that the "poison" in her breath will not damage anyone else. Like Momma in the "powhite-trash" episode, the victimized child experiences a self-imposed "perfect silence."

Vivian Baxter, unable to charm her daughter into speech, sends both children back to Arkansas. Once again in the sanctuary of her grandmother's general store, Maya gathers strength from the African American community, whose values of self-determination and personal dignity help her to overcome her muteness. Maya gains special strength from Bailey and from Mrs. Bertha Flowers, a genteel black woman whose passion for reading helps Maya recover her speech—although Angelou, in a 1990 interview with Dolly McPherson, admitted that her "vol-

untary mutism" actually lasted "almost five years." Maya is eventually restored to speech, regaining her language through self-education and through formal training. Despite her crisis, Maya is able to graduate with top honors from the Lafayette County Training School in Stamps. Four years later she graduates from George Washington, a predominantly white high school in San Francisco, where she studies under Miss Kirwin, a "rare educator who was in love with information" and who had no "teacher's pets." While still in high school she receives a scholarship to study dance and theater at the California Labor School, also called the Mission School. Maya nonetheless remains insecure about her sexuality, so damaged has she been from the psychological consequences of the rape and the ensuing trial and murder. She develops negative images about her body; she thinks that her large bones, small breasts, and deep voice indicate that she is a lesbian. In order to disprove this notion she seduces a handsome neighborhood boy and becomes pregnant. At the end of *I Know Why the Caged Bird Sings*, Maya is a single mother, yet still herself a child, a mother afraid she might harm her baby. Maya's mother, Vivian Baxter, assuages this fear by firmly placing the infant in her daughter's arms.

In *Gather Together in My Name* (1974), Maya is a young mother pessimistic about her place in the American economy, and must face the disruptions that followed the Second World War. Her own tenuous world is steadied through caring for her son, Clyde. As *Gather Together in My Name* opens, Maya and Clyde (who will throughout this essay be known by his chosen name, Guy) are living in San Francisco with Vivian Baxter and her new husband. Maya seems unfocussed: "I was seventeen, very old, embarrassingly young, with a son of two months, and I still lived with my mother and stepfather."

In need of an income, Maya tries her skills at

several low-level jobs, including being a busgirl and a cook at a Creole restaurant. The tedium is alleviated when she falls in love with a man named Curly and experiences sexual pleasure for the first time in her life. The affair ends abruptly when Curly's girlfriend returns from San Diego.

Bailey, the beloved brother of *Caged Bird*, returns to San Francisco from merchant seaman's service and again plays a major role in Maya's life. He encourages her to go to Los Angeles, where she tries without success to live with relatives. At this stage Angelou fantasizes about "a juicy melodrama in which I was to be the star." Instead, she becomes a nightclub waitress and meets two lesbians, Johnnie Mae and Beatrice. In a dramatic scene Maya and the two women, acknowledged prostitutes, spend an afternoon smoking marijuana, dancing, and drinking Dubonnet. Maya convinces them to turn their house into a whorehouse, with Maya as madam. The partnership, so successful that Maya is able to buy a used Chrysler convertible, collapses when Johnnie Mae and Beatrice disobey the house rules.

Returning again to her mother, Maya applies for Officer's Candidate School and is accepted until the Army discovers that she had attended the California Labor School, which was "Communist." Maya then takes yet another minimal job, this time as a waitress at the Chicken Shack, where she meets a dancer, R. L. Poole, and auditions to be his partner. Although they become lovers and partners, the affair is over, as it was with Curly, when Poole's original woman returns.

The string of bad luck continues, next in Stockton, California, where Maya has yet another relationship with a man who manipulates her. L. D. Tolbrook is her father's age, married, and as Maya eventually discovers, a pimp. To please him Maya takes on her most degrading job; she becomes a prostitute. Through the language and the content of the whorehouse sequence, Angelou captures the essence of a subculture of sex and drugs, thus being autobiographically faithful to the self she has become. In doing so she also, as a writer, observes areas of life that rarely find their way into mainstream American literature.

Angelou's arrangement with Tolbrook is interrupted when she learns that her mother is in the hospital and that her brother is deteriorating after his girlfriend's death from tuberculosis. In a reunion that recalls the intensity of *I Know Why the Caged Bird Sings*, Bailey and Maya promise to take care of one another. She feeds and nurtures him; he orders her to quit the business of being a prostitute.

But Bailey's dissipation seems to upset Maya. Although he is mentioned briefly in *Singin' and Swingin' and Gettin' Merry Like Christmas* for supporting Maya's decision to marry, the revered brother gradually disappears from the autobiographies and is rarely mentioned by the literary critics. In *The Heart of a Woman* one learns that Bailey, now aged thirty-three, is in prison for fencing stolen items. Maya's friend Martin Luther King Jr. consoles her: "We must save the Baileys of the world. And Maya, never stop loving him. Never give up on him. Never deny him." This compassionate advice appears to be the last reference to Bailey in the narratives.

Toward the end of *Gather Together in My Name* Maya nearly loses her son when the babysitter, Big Mary Dawson, kidnaps Guy and carries him off to Bakersfield. When Tolbrook refuses to help, Maya takes a bus, retrieves Guy, and returns to San Francisco.

Angelou's distressing second volume reflects the dangers faced by a young black teenager who attempts to take care of a baby in an economy that honors neither poor blacks nor unmarried women. In its explicitness, her self-portrait challenges the more general trend in American autobiography: to project the subject as a model of virtue and achievement, as in the self-righteous *Autobiography of Benjamin Franklin*; or, as in

Zora Neale Hurston's *Dust Tracks on a Road*, which, according to her biographer Robert Hemenway, "sacrifices truth to the politics of racial harmony."

It would have been difficult to predict that the author of *Gather Together in My Name* would become the Maya Angelou of the 1990s, regaled as a prototype for the empowerment of African American women. The early critics of *Gather Together in My Name* were mostly disheartened by this unexpected sequel to *Caged Bird*. Selwyn Cudjoe, for instance, was troubled by its shaky construction, while Lynn Z. Bloom objected to the less-suitable narrator, who lacked the "intuitive good judgment" displayed in *Caged Bird*. In its defense, Dolly McPherson argued that *Gather Together in My Name* is "an artistically more mature work than *Caged Bird*," and that its fragmentations reflect the "alienated fragmented nature of Angelou's life."

To a certain degree, the alienation in *Gather Together* is related to the geographical and spiritual absence of Annie Henderson, whose influence recedes as Maya's life becomes increasingly urban. Near the middle of the autobiography, Maya takes Guy to Stamps for a visit and discovers that she has become too racially liberated to accept Momma's protective regulations concerning whites. After Maya gets in trouble for talking impudently to two saleswomen, Momma slaps her and orders her to leave Stamps for Maya's and the baby's safety. It is to be their final meeting in the autobiographical series.

The climax of *Gather Together in My Name* occurs when an unexpectedly compassionate boyfriend, Troubador Martin, takes Maya, now smoking a lot of marijuana, on an unnerving tour of the underworld of heroin addiction. Troub makes her watch while he shoots up, makes her watch as the needle punctures a scab and "rich yellow pus flowed out and down his arm to the wrist." Maya's refusal, at Troub's advice, to do hard drugs marks the end of her irresponsibility

and her inauguration of new standards that will help safeguard her and her son's survival. The book ends with a vow: "I had no idea what I was going to make of my life, but I had given a promise and found my innocence. I swore I'd never lose it again."

Despite its wildly celebratory title, *Singin' and Swingin' and Gettin' Merry Like Christmas* is fraught with conflicts: Maya's temporary separation from her son; her confused feelings about Vivian Baxter; her failed marriage to Tosh Angelos; her ambiguous assessment of her own motives and behavior; and the irrevocable loss of Annie Henderson.

Maya meets her husband-to-be, Tosh Angelos, when she is working as a salesgirl in a record store. Impressed by the young sailor's enthusiasm for jazz, she introduces him to Guy, who is immediately won over. Vivian Baxter, though, is opposed to Maya's marriage to a "poor white man." The marriage is initially satisfying until Maya begins to resent Tosh's demands that she stay at home and be the perfect housewife, the provider of suitable meals and "fabulous jello deserts." She is also bothered by what she senses to be the disapproval from others because of the interracial marriage.

When Tosh tells Guy that there is no God, Maya is furious. She retaliates by going on a secret quest that ends in her conversion at the Evening Star Baptist Church. Their differences grow until one day Tosh says he's "tired of being married." At this point Maya loses her affection for him, and the marriage of three years collapses.

Much of Maya's struggle in this third and most complex of the autobiographies concerns her private role as single mother versus her public role as a committed actress, one whose career makes it necessary to leave Guy for long stretches of time. Chosen to perform in a European tour of *Porgy and Bess*, Maya faces the realization that in leaving Guy with Vivian, she will repeat the hateful pattern established by her parents when they left her and Bailey in the hands of Momma Henderson. Her feelings are compounded by the fact that, as a young, black, single mother, she bears the ultimate responsibility for her son, whom she wants to support both emotionally (by being home) and economically (by being in Europe). In so concisely identifying the conflicts between working and mothering, Angelou offers her readers a model for understanding the problems that may arise when a woman attempts to fulfill both roles.

Maya returns from Europe to find her lonely son suffering from a skin disease that has psychosomatic origins. Promising never to leave him again, she takes Guy with her to Hawaii, where she has a singing engagement. The autobiography thus concludes with a reaffirmation of the mother-son bond that ended *I Know Why the Caged Bird Sings*.

Discreetly hidden in *Singin' and Swingin' and Gettin' Merry Like Christmas* is another narrative thread to which critics have paid little attention: the definitive separation from Momma Henderson. In the third autobiography, Momma, once the leading influence in Maya's development, vanishes from the texts. The powerful grandmother is dead, no longer able to comfort Maya with her strong hands or to influence Maya's actions. The record of Annie Henderson's death is perhaps the strongest emotional revelation of the five autobiographies. I emphasize the death of the grandmother now, as I did in my 1990 essay, ''Singing the Black Mother,'' to underscore a problem that Angelou never comes fully to terms with in the autobiographical series: her ambivalent feelings toward those she loves, especially Annie Henderson. In her reminiscence about her grandmother's death, Angelou's style shifts from its usual conversational tone and becomes intense, religious, and emotional: ''Ah, Momma. I had never looked at death before,

peered into its yawning chasm for the face of a beloved. . . . If I were as good as God's angels and as pure as the Mother of Christ, I could never have Momma's rough slow hands pat my cheek or braid my hair.'' This moving farewell, untypical of Angelou's more worldly autobiographical style, is overlooked by most critics.

Maya's elegy for her grandmother, which relies on gospel tradition, on the language of Bible stories, and on certain African American literary texts, especially on James Weldon Johnson's ''Go Down Death—A Funeral Sermon,'' is related to a religious conversion previously experienced in *Singin' and Swingin'*. To Angelou the African American spirituals were ''sweeter than sugar. I wanted to keep my mouth full of them . . .''; this image counters the negative images of the empty mother and wordless mouth depicted in *I Know Why the Caged Bird Sings*. Angelou's ''singing'' of the black grandmother in this extraordinary passage suggests a liberation from guilt and a loving reconciliation with Momma, an attempt, through religion, to mollify her ambivalence toward Annie Henderson by identifying with her traditions.

At the beginning of *The Heart of a Woman* Maya, amused by her beatnik appearance, is living with her son and four whites on a houseboat commune near San Francisco. When the situation wearies her, she manages to rent, through the intervention of white friends, a house in a segregated neighborhood. In this house she entertains the legendary Billie Holiday a few months before the singer's death. The record of their four-day friendship, with its portrayal of Holiday's moody anger and vivid language (both of which Guy dislikes), is one of the most memorable vignettes of the series.

After Guy experiences discrimination from the staff of the white school he is attending, he and Maya move to a mixed neighborhood. It is here that she starts to write: ''At first I limited myself to short sketches, then to song lyrics, then I dared short stories.'' Following her decision to leave California for Brooklyn, New York, Maya joins the Harlem Writer's Guild. Through the encouragement and criticism of other African Americans—John Killens, John Clarke, Sarah Wright, and Paule Marshall among others—she begins to define herself as a writer. The act of writing contributes to her increasing maturity: ''If I wanted to write, I had to be willing to develop a kind of concentration found mostly in people awaiting execution. I had to learn technique and surrender my ignorance.''

Maya further expands her potential when she joins the off-Broadway cast of Jean Genet's play *The Blacks*. After hearing a sermon by Martin Luther King Jr., she and Godfrey Cambridge, also playing in *The Blacks*, plan a fund-raiser at New York's Village Gate. Called the Cabaret for Freedom, the fund-raiser is so successful that she is asked to be northern coordinator of King's organization, the Southern Christian Leadership Conference.

Several episodes, though, jar against these successes and recall the anxious motherhood of the earlier volumes. In the most striking of these, Maya returns from an engagement in Chicago to learn that Guy has gotten in trouble with a Brooklyn street gang. In order to protect her son, she confronts the gang leader and threatens to shoot his entire family if Guy is harmed. This confrontation represents the consummation of her maternal strength as she powerfully performs the role of mother and protector.

In *The Heart of a Woman* Maya finds power and happiness through her sexual experiences with Vusumzi Make, but becomes vulnerable to his male authority, as she had with Curly, L. D. Tolbrook, and other men in her past. She marries Make and they eventually move to Cairo, where he expects her to be the perfect African wife and homemaker. Against Make's wishes and Egyptian custom, Maya asserts her woman's will by

taking a job as an associate editor with the *Arab Observer*. The enlightened Angelou soon realizes that the marriage is unstable, that Make is too careless with money and too congenial with other women. The marriage ends bitterly when she becomes convinced of his infidelity.

With the heightened sensitivity that writing brings, Angelou becomes fully aware, for the first time, of her African heritage. As she begins to analyze the ambiguous relationship between being an African and being an African American, she discovers her connection with the African slaves who had been ''tied with ropes, shackled with chains, forced to march for weeks carrying the double burden of neck irons and abysmal fear.''

The problematic relationship with Vus Make; the commitment to Martin Luther King; the identification with the sorrows of Africa; the anguish she endures on realizing that her brother Bailey is in prison: these are some of the features that make *The Heart of a Woman* one of the most sensitive of her books. In it, claims Dolly McPherson, Angelou withholds nothing. ''Her writing here, describing her longings, doubts, and shortcomings, is raw, bare honesty.'' Yet *The Heart of a Woman* is at the same time a very public statement, informed by Angelou's affiliations with the Harlem Writer's Guild, the Cultural Association for Women of African Heritage, the Cabaret for Freedom, the Southern Christian Leadership Conference, and by her work as a political journalist.

Near the end of *The Heart of a Woman* the more private theme of motherhood is tragically reintroduced when Guy's car is hit by a truck outside of Accra, Ghana. As Maya stares at her son's pale face, she sees him ''stretched before me, stiff as a pine board, in a strange country, blood caked on his face and clotted on his clothes.'' Guy suffers a broken arm and leg but gradually recovers and during the act of physical healing grows toward a greater autonomy. In the last two paragraphs we find Angelou alone, testing her independence. She recognizes within herself an emergent new Maya, one emancipated from the role restrictions that had confined her in the earlier volumes.

Through the dramatic repetition of Guy's accident, Angelou ties the end of *The Heart of a Woman* to the beginning of her fifth autobiography, *All God's Children Need Traveling Shoes*. While her major concerns are Guy and his recovery from the car accident, she continues to explore the process of learning to give up her son, a process that accelerates when she discovers that Guy is having an affair with an American woman older than herself. When Maya threatens to punish him, Guy, in a reversal of roles, affectionately pats her head and says, ''Yes, little mother. I'm sure you will.'' Maya herself has a few flirtations in *All God's Children Need Traveling Shoes,* although she is more cautious than she had been with Vus Make. She has the wisdom to refuse the proposal of Sheikali, a wealthy importer from Mali, when he asks her to be wife number two and teacher to his eight children. Although she rejects Sheikali's offer, and despite her unhappiness with Tosh Angelos and Vus Make, Angelou does later remarry. Her third husband is Paul de Feu, a construction worker whom she met in England. In a 1990 essay Carol E. Neubauer mentions the third marriage, stating that the couple spent most of their seven years together on the West Coast.

One also finds, in *Traveling Shoes,* an increasing affirmation of sisterhood, a new respect for women that coincides with the vast political and social changes taking place around the world. She has two roommates, Vicki Garvin and Alice Windom, both of them businesswomen with master's degrees. Angelou also forms a very close friendship with Efua Sutherland, a flamboyant woman who founded the Ghanaian Society of Writers and who wrote tales of strong women such as Foruwa, the royal heroine of ''New Life at Kyerefaso.'' In one touching vignette, Angelou

recounts befriending Comfort Adday, a hairdresser and the victim of a voodoo spell put on her by a jealous woman. Maya loans Comfort the money to go to Sierra Leone, where she is promised a cure. Later Maya learns that Comfort is dead.

Initially alienated from Ghanaians by culture, language, and beliefs, Maya seeks solidarity by joining the fragile African American community. These expatriates, far from the United States, remain committed enough to stage a protest at the American Embassy in Accra as a show of solidarity with the spring 1963 March on Washington. The demonstration, which begins in a restrained, political manner, is soon transformed into ''Ole Time Religious stuff'' when the crowd learns of the death of W. E. B. Du Bois. Angelou writes, ''We were singing Dr. Du Bois' spirit, for the invaluable contributions he made, for his shining intellect and his courage. To many of us he was the first American Negro intellectual.'' The poignantly depicted reaction to the death of Du Bois is both an affirmation of Angelou's inherent attachment to the United States and an evocation of the eulogy to her grandmother in *Singin' and Swingin' and Gettin' Merry Like Christmas.*

All God's Children Need Traveling Shoes and, to a lesser degree, *The Heart of a Woman* seem to vacillate between a retained devotion to African American culture and a desire for commitment to the reincarnated African image—a desire to explore the language and customs of people who, while recognizably ancestors, neither welcome nor admire Americans. Maya first bridges the gap between these two cultures when, under pressure, she and her two roommates take in a young African boy named Kojo. This lovely child, with his dark skin and beautifully shaped head, reminds Maya of her brother Bailey. The three women assume Kojo is poor until, in one charming episode, his entire family, elegantly dressed, introduce themselves with gifts of yams and eggs from their prosperous farm. The encounter with

Kojo's family enables Angelou to move beyond her own concerns for Guy to a larger, almost cosmic theme—her affinity with mother Africa. Linda A. Myers describes this transformation from an American past to a Ghanaian present: Angelou is "able to be a spectator viewing her own past as a complex happening which has ended. Africa provides a renewal for a new pulse of life for her continuing journey."

Determined to immerse herself in the Ghanaian atmosphere of racial pride, Maya rents a car and ventures out alone to contemplate her newly discovered West African heritage. In her travels past Cape Coast and Dunkwa, she recognizes certain connections between her own traditions and those of her African ancestors, including their subjection to slavery, symbolized by the forts of Elmina Castle. She is both proud and amused when she is mistaken for a Bambara from Liberia. She makes friends with a Ghanaian woman, Patience Aduah, whose hospitality reminds her of Annie Henderson, who had aided African American travelers denied food and lodging in the Jim Crow era of segregation in Arkansas.

In Ghana, Angelou also encounters many of the African leaders and intellectuals who had come into power following the liberation: the dancer Grace Nuamah, the scholar J. H. Nketia, the poet Kwesi Brew, and the Ahanta Chief Nana Nketsia. Her initial meeting with Nana Nketsia is delightfully narrated, from the moment when his hesitant driver arrives at Maya's house to the moment when Nana, in a "passion of self-appreciation," affirms the superiority of his blackness. But the most memorable occasion of the volume is the meeting with Malcolm X, who had come to Ghana to speak against American racism following his historic trip to Mecca. Angelou's use of conversational dialogue in the Malcolm X segment lends an immediacy and humanity to a figure so often treated with reverential abstraction. Malcolm stresses the unity of all black people and chides Maya for her intolerance toward middle-class black groups: "When you hear that the Urban League or the NAACP is giving a formal banquet at the Waldorf Astoria, I know you won't go, but don't knock them. They give scholarships to poor Black children."

Angelou's breadth of experience with both people and places in *All God's Children Need Traveling Shoes* surely justifies the title, for she travels through major capitals and small villages, in Egypt and Ghana, in Italy and Germany. As her friend James Baldwin had done in his 1953 essay, "Stranger in the Village," so Angelou investigates the ambivalent role of the educated African American in Europe, offering a series of racially charged anecdotes that are softened by her tolerant humor. This combination of astute observer and experienced traveler has contributed tremendously to Angelou's success as an autobiographer.

Yet despite Angelou's commitment to the journey, *All God's Children Need Traveling Shoes* concludes in a leave-taking; she is leaving both the vigorous rhythms of Africa and her son, Guy, who remains in Accra to finish his degree. The final traveling scene is at the airport, as Maya prepares for her departure from Ghana and her return to the United States. Joyously celebrating her African and her American ancestries, Angelou reaches forth at journey's end to embrace the blues, gospel, and dance, and to bridge the distance between Ghana and the States. These positive fusions of African and American cultures inform much of Angelou's other work—the television scripts; her reflections on being a grandmother; her prose meditation, *Wouldn't Take Nothing for My Journey Now* (1993); and finally, the poems that illustrate the sweep of her literary interests.

In a 1986 essay published in *Woman's Day*, Angelou continues her narrative from the perspective of a grandmother. Her grandson, Colin,

MAYA ANGELOU / 11

had been kidnapped by Guy's ex-wife. The essay recalls Maya's anxiety as she had tried to recover her missing son from his kidnapper, Big Mary, in *Gather Together in My Name.* One of the most interesting aspects of the essay is the feeling of autobiographical continuity as Angelou, now herself a protective grandmother, looks back to Momma Henderson. When Angelou reads Colin the *Brer Rabbit* tales and teaches him spirituals, she identifies with Momma Henderson: "My grandmother had done that for me and I wished to pass these treasures on to Colin." Later, in a moment of panic, Angelou writes, "I reached inside myself all the way back to my own grandmother and found enough reserve to keep from screaming." As in the first three volumes of her autobiography, Angelou, in the 1986 essay, still recognizes in the grandmother the cornerstone of the black community and the keeper of folk tradition.

As an autobiographer Angelou shares in a rich literary tradition of African American autobiography arguably initiated with the 1814 publication of *Gustavus Vassa, the African.* At the same time, however, she occupies a unique place within that tradition, as a number of critics observed in their enthusiastic response to *I Know Why the Caged Bird Sings.* In his 1975 essay George Kent, while he listed her affinities with Richard Wright, Anne Moody, Malcolm X, and others, argued that Angelou's narrative is singular in its distinctive attitude toward self, community, and imaginative form. Both Sidonie Ann Smith in 1973 and Stephen Butterfield in 1974 have compared *Caged Bird* to Richard Wright's *Black Boy,* finding similarities in those works' rendering of life in a small segregated southern town. Butterfield, however, ascribed Angelou's uniqueness as an autobiographer to her creation of a community where women support and respect one another. In a similar vein, Dolly McPherson, two decades later, credits Angelou's

originality to a "preoccupation with the effect of the community on the individual's achievement and retention of an integrated, acceptable self."

While each of these assessments is valid, the uniqueness of Angelou's voice can be further attributed to a number of additional factors, among them her intense examination of her own motives and desires; the complex relationship between her narrative structure and its re-envisioning of earlier forms such as the sermon, the spiritual, and the slave narrative; her singing of the black mother; and her unprecedented success in improvising the single-volume form into an extended, serial autobiography.

It is imperative to distinguish between the serial autobiography—practiced by Angelou, James Weldon Johnson, James Baldwin, and a few other African American autobiographers—with the more standard, single-volume autobiography produced by Zora Neale Hurston in *Dust Tracks on a Road;* or by Anne Moody in *Coming of Age in Mississippi;* or even by Richard Wright, whose 1945 *Black Boy* tells of childhood and adolescence, but whose 1944 political autobiography, *American Hunger,* is so distinct from his account of youth that the two works can hardly be considered parts of a series. And, while one could compare the autobiographical themes of Maya Angelou and Nikki Giovanni, with their emphasis on childbirth, black motherhood, and the family, Giovanni's *Gemini: an extended autobiographical statement on my first twenty-five years of being a black poet* is too brief a piece to convey the breadth that Angelou achieves in her series.

In the serial mode, with its prolonged and continuous narrative, problems arise that are not encountered in single-volume books, with their more ordered chronologies and established endings—although there are exceptions among modern writers, for instance Gertrude Stein, whose 1923 *The Autobiography of Alice B. Toklas* inverted the rules of standard autobiography. As a multivolumed autobiographer, Angelou had to face the technical challenges posed by that genre: when to convert present tense into past or future; how to orchestrate cross-references; how to preserve continuity without lapsing into repetition; how to sustain the theatrical tone; how to find the discipline to continue; where to let the texts die out; and where to begin again.

The serial biographer Angelou perhaps most closely resembles artistically is the dramatist Lillian Hellman, whose autobiographical sequence consists of four volumes: *An Unfinished Woman* (1970); *Pentimento* (1973); *Scoundrel Time* (1976); and *Maybe* (1980). The first of the series, *An Unfinished Woman,* won the 1970 National Book Award for Arts and Letters, the same year that *I Know Why the Caged Bird Sings* was published in a Book-of-the-Month Club edition. The likenesses proliferate. Both women rely on the language of theater as a method for staging first-person episodes. Both women emphasize the painting metaphor to describe their autobiographical method: Angelou's "large canvas" versus Hellman's "pentimento," a layering produced when a painter covers one image with another. Both are strong, independent, political writers who situate their biographies within both American and international settings. Both write with lucidity about the racial "other." Both have experienced enormous public recognition in their lifetimes.

Yet the parallels between Angelou and Hellman, delineated by Stephanie A. Demetrakopoulous in 1980 and by Ekaterini Georgoudaki in 1990, are disavowed by Angelou in an interview with Dolly McPherson in *Order Out of Chaos.* Generally, Angelou dislikes Hellman's autobiographical work, finding it to be "one-dimensional" or "romantic" or "self-centered" or "elitist." In her view Hellman invented blacks who are "cardboard characters." Further, Hellman "never represented a large group of people."

Angelou's objections to Hellman seem excessive. Perhaps they are reflections of differences in race or class or perhaps in lifestyle: Hellman's

teenage abortion, described in *An Unfinished Woman,* would have given her a different perspective from Angelou's, for whom the theme of teenage motherhood was so crucial. Angelou's objections seem even more emphatic when placed side by side with her affinity for the Chinese American autobiographer Maxine Hong Kingston. Kingston's *Woman Warrior,* which traces the development and ancestry of a young Chinese American woman, has frequently been compared to *I Know Why the Caged Bird Sings*—by Stephanie A. Demetrakopoulous and, in 1991, by Helen M. Buss. Angelou enjoys the parallels with Kingston and even uses the phrase "woman warrior" in *Wouldn't Take Nothing for My Journey Now.*

For most reviewers, Angelou's work must be perceived within an African American feminist tradition. Joanne Braxton, for instance, claims not only that Angelou's literary ancestors are African American women writers but also that her autobiographical impulse "derives essentially from her celebration of the black women who nurtured her." A close study of *All God's Children Need Traveling Shoes* further reveals that her autobiographical roots, while planted in the literary traditions of African American women writers like Linda Brent and Zora Neale Hurston, are further nurtured by the soil of Mother Africa: an Africa first understood through the harrowing experience of the African American slave and then reframed through Angelou's residency in Egypt and Ghana.

In *All God's Children Need Traveling Shoes,* Angelou writes, "Many years earlier I, or rather someone very like me and certainly related to me, had been taken from Africa by force." Angelou's identification with slavery is both personal and formal; the slave narrative is an intuitive structure discernible in each of the five volumes but most prominent in the fifth volume. Set in West Africa, *All God's Children Need Traveling Shoes* echoes—as do all of the volumes—both the structure of traditional African American autobiographies and the structure of the slave narrative.

The slave narrative in its earliest form was the recollection by a former slave of her or his struggles in the journey from Africa to America and, once in America, from bondage to liberation. Many of these narratives were oral, translated into written words through the sponsorship of a white benefactor, although some narratives, written by slaves, celebrate the achievement of literacy as a major theme. (Frederick Douglass' *Narrative,* for example). William L. Andrews, an authority on the antebellum slave narrative, stresses the connection between freedom and literacy: "In the slave narrative the quest is toward freedom from physical bondage and the enlightenment that literacy can offer to the restricted self- and social consciousness of the slave."

Like the slave narrative, Angelou's autobiographies are informed by the motif of the journey and its opportunities for enlightenment. Her quest takes her from ignorance to consciousness, from muteness to articulation, from racial bondage to liberation. The narrator, in the course of her journey, crosses the racially imposed barricades of a southern town to travel to St. Louis, Los Angeles, Mexico, France, Israel, and at last to Africa and the Accra airport. Her journey thus mirrors the movement of the slave narrative, with its recalled journey from Africa to America, its catalog of hardships, and its promised ending in some sort of emancipation. For Maya Angelou the emancipation ensues in part from her continuous efforts as a writer, in part from her redefinition of self as mother and woman, in part from her profound rediscovery of her African heritage.

Through the autobiographical narrative form, Angelou found her own "voice," whereas as an actress or singer she had given voice to other people's words, although often within the oral tradition of the African diaspora, as in her calypso performances described in *Singin' and Swingin' and Gettin' Merry Like Christmas.* In

the 1986 essay, "My Grandson, Home at Last," she mentions reading her grandson the *Brer Rabbit* tales. *Brer Rabbit,* one of several African American variants of a West African trickster tale, is also in some ways a slave narrative, the story of someone trapped, bound, but finally freed through his own ingenuity, his own skill with words (Toni Morrison uses the same image to great effect in *Tar Baby*).

In evoking the slave narrative, Angelou is not alone among her contemporaries; Hazel B. Carby claims that women's slave narratives "haunt the texts" of contemporary black women writers, repeating the themes of flight, servitude, rape, humiliation, poverty, and the separation of mother and child. In *Incidents in the Life of a Slave Girl* (1861), the best known of the slave narratives by women, Linda Brent (Harriet Jacobs) describes the anguish of this separation. Brent's first awareness of being a slave occurs at the death of her mother; much of Brent's quest involves her search for her daughter, Ellen, who was sold as a child to another master. In a section entitled "The Children Sold" Brent writes, "I bit my lips till the blood came to keep from crying out. Were my children with their grandmother, or had the speculator carried them off? The suspense was dreadful." She compares this moment to "the darkest cloud that hung over my life." The grandmother, like Momma Henderson of *I Know Why the Caged Bird Sings,* plays a crucial nurturing role in Brent's story. Her stabilizing function is common to both African American and West African societies, as Mildred A. Hill-Lubin has demonstrated in a 1986 essay on the grandmother.

Many contemporary African American women writers are engaged, like Angelou, in the process of re-envisioning the slave narrative from a mother's point of view. In *Beloved* (1987), a historical novel that owes much to the black autobiographical tradition, Toni Morrison reconstructs the narrative of a woman slave who murdered her baby to save it from white male violence. In her 1989 novel, *The Temple of My Familiar,* Alice Walker's heroine charts the dreadful journey into slavery, recalling ordeals that include the death of her mother and, afterward, the horrendous passage from Africa in a slave ship, where nursing mothers shared their milk with the starving children. Aunt Cuney, a mother figure in Paule Marshall's *Praisesong to the Widow* (1984), retells the narrative of Ibo slaves who crossed from West Africa to the shores of South Carolina. Marshall, Walker, and Morrison, like so many other African American women who have taken the journey, attest to the connection, only sometimes spoken, between their stories and earlier narratives of survival.

As an autobiographer, Angelou cannot insert herself into a fictionalized past. Nonetheless, the problems facing her as an African American woman echo those of the plantation system recreated by writers such as Morrison, Walker, and Marshall. Racial violence, loneliness, cultural isolation, rape, personal humiliation, silence, and separation from loved ones—all these can be found in Angelou's autobiographies. Fortunately, these negative experiences have often found relief through cultural constructs, among them the spiritual, signifying, playacting, the blues, black love, the folktale, farce, conversation, film, quilting, storytelling, and rap.

The theme of the journey, so prominent in the slave narratives, is reiterated in the title of Angelou's 1993 best-seller, *Wouldn't Take Nothing for My Journey Now*. The journey is philosophical rather than narrative, in the form of a series of short meditations resembling the *Analects* of Confucius (551–479 B.C.) but told from a female perspective and punctuated by an occasional poem. In this book Angelou offers advice that ranges from trivial matters like choosing clothing colors to profound issues dealing with death and racism. The book is at its most compelling when it is autobiographical, when it recounts episodes involving Bailey, or

Clyde, or Vivian Baxter, or Annie Henderson. The sketch from *I Know Why the Caged Bird Sings* about how Momma sold chicken to factory workers is lavishly retold; the death of Momma Henderson, so emotionally narrated in *Singin' and Swingin' and Gettin' Merry Like Christmas*, is revived again in a musing on death, through the use of similar words and images.

At times Angelou recollects autobiographical moments that seem to have no direct bearing on the series. In one anecdote she describes being honored at Terry's Pub, a bar for "the black and hip in New York City," after being named the *New York Post*'s Person of the Week. She drinks too many martinis and, looking for a man, foolishly throws herself on a group of African American journalists. She tells them of her many skills in cooking, languages, and lovemaking, embarrassing not only herself but the five men as well. Tactfully escorted home by a friend, she sobers up and begins a meditation which takes her back to her first marriage to a Greek, Tosh Angelos, and to her subsequent unwillingness to form a relationship outside her race. This episode, seemingly detached from the five-volumed narrative, is nonetheless connected to it by way of attitudes, opinions, and specific associations with other self-revelatory embarrassments, for example her public confrontation of her husband Make's mistress in *The Heart of a Woman*. The pervasive autobiographical content helps to steer *Wouldn't Take Nothing for My Journey Now* away from a tendency to sermonize on proper conduct or virtue. Yet the sermonizing itself can be viewed as a reference to the African American tradition of preaching, exemplified by Martin Luther King, who figures so prominently in *The Heart of a Woman*.

The autobiographical perspective informs Angelou's poetry as well as her prose, although usually the poetry is more distanced in its revelation of the author's experience. Priscilla R. Ramsey discusses this distancing in a number of Angelou's love poems and speculates on the parallels between the poetic and autobiographical treatment surrounding her attachment to men. Joanne Braxton comments that most of the poetry "has some autobiographical content, and through much of it Angelou celebrates her dark womanhood."

Much of the autobiographical content, while it relies on the standard, first-person point of view, is veiled through the use of a persona or through an unspecified, presumably female position. In the poem "In Retrospect," for example, a lonely lover recalls the passing of last year's seasons:

Last year changed its seasons
subtly, stripped its sultry winds
for the reds of dying leaves. . . .

A similar perspective is presented in "I Almost Remember," where an unidentified older person recalls the "black / brown hands and / white thin yellowed fingers" of children who had slipped away, neglected.

In other poems, though, Angelou, in an approach comparable to the autobiographical segments of *Wouldn't Take Nothing for My Journey Now,* writes directly about her family: about her lame uncle in "Willie"; about her ancestral ties with her brother in "For Bailey"; about her roots, in "My Arkansas"; about her dauntless mother in "Call Letters: Mrs. V. B."

Of the various African American poets who have preceded her, Paul Laurence Dunbar receives the greatest acknowledgment; Angelou named *I Know Why the Caged Bird Sings* after a phrase in his 1896 poem, "Sympathy." The caged bird, symbolic of the chained slave, frequently reappears in Angelou's poems about racial injustice. Other poets who influenced her are Langston Hughes, Gwendolyn Brooks, and James Weldon Johnson. Angelou's flexible use of ballad form in poems like "The Gamut" or

"Remembering" is reminiscent of Hughes, the master of the "ballad-blues" structure in African American poetry, and of Brooks, who experimented with rhythm, race, and style in "the ballad of chocolate Mabbie" (1944) and other early poems. James Weldon Johnson, who was Annie Henderson's favorite poet, had an impact on Angelou in several of the spiritual poems, such as "Just Like Job" and "Thank You, Lord."

"On the Pulse of Morning" seized the imagination of America: first, because its unveiling was televised amidst the enthusiasm surrounding the Clintons of Arkansas; and second, because the poem offered hope for the dream of social change. Before Angelou, only one other American poet had been invited to read at an inauguration—this was Robert Frost, at the request of President John F. Kennedy in 1961. Written two decades earlier than the ceremony itself, Frost's "The Gift Outright" is politically conservative; its praise of the land moving "westward" pays no heed to the African Americans and Native Americans sacrificed to American expansionism. Angelou's ode, on the contrary, presents a litany of the oppressed: the Sioux, the Apache, the gay, the homeless, the Muslim, and others. It is a long poem—over one hundred lines as opposed to Frost's sixteen—written in a free form. At the inauguration, Angelou's theatrical rendering of "On the Pulse of Morning" was in a sense a culmination of the black oral tradition, returning to the roots of early African American literature in which former slaves like Frederick Douglass stood on podiums in cramped abolitionist meeting halls to articulate their concerns about the brutality of slavery.

There are three dominant images in the poem: the tree, the river, and the rock. The triple image evokes memories of a number of earlier British and American poems, including Walt Whitman's star / lilac / bird triad in "When Lilacs Last in the Dooryard Bloom'd," his elegy for Abraham

Lincoln. The Whitman poem, with its concerns for the president, its freedom of form and spirit, its controlling symbol of the bird, and its three-unit image patterns, may well have influenced "On the Pulse of Morning."

Of Angelou's images, each had appeared in her own earlier works, the river most prominently. In "Slave Coffle," from the 1983 collection *Shaker, Why Don't You Sing?*, the river of escape eludes the fingers of the doomed slave. In *Now Sheba Sings the Song*, a long poem modeled in part on the biblical lushness of Song of Solomon, all three metaphors are present: Sheba sees trees bending to weep for murdered slaves; she identifies with the eternal life of rocks and mountains; and she, as poet, has the power of breath to blow boats across the surface of the Mississippi and up the Nile.

Of the three metaphors that dominate "On the Pulse of Morning," the river is the one that has yielded forth a storehouse of associations for African American poets, both in the oral tradition of spirituals like "Roll, Jordan, Roll" and in the written poetry of James Weldon Johnson, Langston Hughes, Jean Toomer, and others. "On the Pulse of Morning" seems particularly reminiscent of the Hughes 1921 poem, "The Negro Speaks of Rivers," which anticipates Angelou's ode through its broad geographical focus and its celebration of the "ancient, dusky rivers" of the world. Angelou's poem also recalls a lesser- known work by Jean Toomer called "Brown River, Smile." Toomer also makes symbolic use of the river in order to praise other races—including the "great African races" and the "red races"—and, as Angelou would do six decades later, calls for a new day, crying for, in Toomer's words, a "new America / to be spiritualized by each new American." Like Hughes and Toomer before her, Angelou speaks for African Americans in their quest for peace and freedom, speaking through the voice of the sacred river:

Come, clad in peace,
And I will sing the songs
The Creator gave to me when I and the
Tree and the Rock were one.

In her crying of the river, Angelou at the same time cries the songs of her ancestors. In Ghana, with the help of her friends the poet Kwesi Brew and the folk specialist Efua Sutherland, Angelou made contact with African oral tradition and with contemporary African poetry. These connections are most dynamic in the undercurrents of animism (a belief that objects in nature can have souls or spirits) in "On the Pulse of Morning." Many traditional West African religions claim that the elements of nature are part of the spiritual life, and that skulls, trees, masks, and drums are capable of speech and cognition. One finds similar concepts in contemporary African poems: Leopold Senghor's "Prayer to Masks"; David Diop's "Africa, to My Mother"; and Birago Diop's "Vanity" are three examples. The speaking objects in Angelou's poem (the tree, the rock, and the river) underscore this ancient African belief, one that she describes and affirms in *Wouldn't Take Nothing for My Journey Now*: "all things are inhabited by spirits which must be appeased and to which one can appeal. So, for example, when a master drummer prepares to carve a new drum, he approaches the selected tree and speaks to the spirit residing there." Angelou's breadth of references to the African and African American traditions, epitomized by the oral elements of speech making and elocution inherent in both traditions, contribute to the vigor and credibility of her inaugural ode.

"On the Pulse of Morning" is finally an autobiographical poem, the work of a woman whose ability to recall and remember is remarkable. As in so many of her lyrics, the autobiographical voice is unspecified; here the river is speaking, but behind it one hears the poet / woman lamenting for her lost children and urging the survivors to build a new world, to "study war no more." "On the Pulse of Morning" is a poem made possible because of Angelou's accumulated knowledge—her struggles in Arkansas and California, her experiences as a traveler, her achievements in public speaking and acting, and her ability to transform the ideologies of her ancestors on this "bright morning" of hope. She took this same hope with her to Washington when she spoke at the Million Man March.

In *All God's Children Need Traveling Shoes* Angelou writes of her collective past: "Although separated from our languages, our families and customs, we have dared to continue to live. We had crossed the unknowable oceans in chains and had written its mystery into 'Deep River, my home is over Jordan.'" In her autobiographies other modes of transportation both replace and recall the slave ship and the boat over the River Jordan: the segregated train that brings Maya and Bailey from California at the beginning of *I Know Why the Caged Bird Sings;* the plane in *The Heart of a Woman* that flies Maya and Guy across the continent of Africa, from Egypt to Ghana; and the plane that will take her to America at the end of *All God's Children Need Traveling Shoes.* Angelou's narrative voyage, paramount in the autobiographies but evident in her poems and musings as well, opens up a powerful connection with the past for readers who have the freedom to travel with her.

Gather Together in My Name. New York: Random House, 1974.

Singin' and Swingin' and Gettin' Merry Like Christmas. New York: Random House, 1976.

The Heart of a Woman. New York: Random House, 1981.

"Why I Moved Back to the South." *Ebony,* February 1982, pp. 130–134.

All God's Children Need Traveling Shoes. New York: Random House, 1986.

"My Grandson, Home at Last." *Woman's Day,* August 1986, pp. 46–55.

POETRY

Just Give Me a Cool Drink of Water 'fore I Diiie. New York: Random House, 1971.

Oh Pray My Wings Are Gonna Fit Me Well. New York: Random House, 1975.

And Still I Rise. New York: Random House, 1978.

Shaker, Why Don't You Sing? New York: Random House, 1983.

Poems: Maya Angelou. New York: Random House, 1986.

Now Sheba Sings the Song. With artist Tom Feelings. New York: E. P. Dutton, 1987.

I Shall Not Be Moved. New York: Random House, 1990.

Life Doesn't Frighten Me. With artist Jean-Michel Basquiat. New York: Stewart, Tabori & Chang, 1993.

The Complete Collected Poems of Maya Angelou. New York: Random House, 1994.

Phenomenal Woman. 1978. New York: Random House, 1995.

MEMOIR

Wouldn't Take Nothing for My Journey Now. New York: Random House, 1993.

Selected Bibliography

WORKS OF MAYA ANGELOU

AUTOBIOGRAPHIES

I Know Why the Caged Bird Sings. New York: Random House, 1970.

BIOGRAPHICAL AND CRITICAL STUDIES

Andrews, William L. *To Tell a Free Story: The First Century of Afro-American Autobiography, 1760–1865.* Urbana: University of Illinois Press, 1986.

Arensberg, Liliane K. "Death as Metaphor of Self in *I Know Why the Caged Bird Sings.*" *College Language Association Journal,* 20:273–296 (1976).

Blackburn, Regina. "In Search of the Black Female Self: African American Women's Autobiographies and Ethnicity." In *Women's Autobiography.* Edited by Estelle Jelinek. Bloomington: Indiana University Press, 1980. Pp. 133–148.

Bloom, Lynn Z. "Heritages: Dimensions of Mother-Daughter Relationships in Women's Autobiographies." In *The Lost Tradition: Mothers and Daughters in Literature.* Edited by Kathy M. Davidson and E. M. Broner. New York: Ungar, 1980. Pp. 291–303.

Braxton, Joanne M. *Black Women Writing Autobiography: A Tradition Within a Tradition.* Philadelphia: Temple University Press, 1989.

Burgher, Mary. "Images of Self and Race in the Autobiographies of Black Women." In *Sturdy Black Bridges.* Edited by Roseann P. Bell, Bettye J. Parker, and Beverly Guy-Sheftall. Garden City: Doubleday, 1979. Pp. 107–122.

Buss, Helen M. "Reading for the Double Discourse of American Women's Autobiography." *A B: Auto-Biography Studies,* 6, no. 1:95–108 (1991).

Butterfield, Stephen. *Black Autobiography in America.* Amherst: University of Massachusetts Press, 1974.

Cameron, Dee Birch. "A Maya Angelou Bibliography." *Bulletin of Bibliography,* 36, no. 1:50–52 (1979).

Carby, Hazel V. *Reconstructing Womanhood: The Emergence of the Afro-American Woman Novelist.* New York: Oxford University Press, 1987.

Chick, Nancy. "Maya Angelou: A Twentieth Century Scheherazade." Master's thesis, University of Georgia, 1992.

Cudjoe, Selwyn. "Maya Angelou and the Autobiographical Statement." In *Black Women Writers (1950–1980): A Critical Evaluation.* Edited by Mari Evans. Garden City: Doubleday, 1984. Pp. 6–24.

Demetrakopoulous, Stephanie A. "The Metaphysics of Matrilinearism in Women's Autobiography: Studies of Mead's *Blackberry Winter,* Hellman's *Pentimento,* Angelou's *I Know Why the Caged Bird Sings,* and Kingston's *The Woman Warrior.*" In *Women's Autobiography: Essays in Criticism.* Edited by Estelle Jelinek. Bloomington: Indiana University Press, 1980. Pp. 180–205.

Gates, Henry Louis, Jr. *Figures in Black: Words, Signs, and the "Racial" Self.* New York: Oxford University Press, 1987.

Gruesser, John C. "Afro-American Travel Literature and Africanist Discourse." *Black American Literature Forum,* 24, no. 1:5–20 (Spring 1990).

Hill-Lubin, Mildred A. "The Grandmother in African and African-American Literature: A Survivor of the Extended Family." In *Ngambika: Studies of Women in African Literature.* Edited by Carole B. Davies and Anne A. Graves. Trenton: Africa World, 1986. Pp. 257–270.

Kael, Pauline. "A Woman for All Seasons?" In *Critical Essays on Lillian Hellman.* Edited by Mark W. Estrin. Boston: G. K. Hall, 1989. Pp. 252–257.

Kent, George E. "*I Know Why the Caged Bird Sings* and Black Autobiographical Tradition." *Kansas Quarterly,* 7, no. 3:72–78 (1975).

Lupton, Mary Jane. "Singing the Black Mother: Maya Angelou and Autobiographical Continuity." *Black American Literature Forum,* 24, no 2:257–275 (1990).

———. Review Essay of *Order Out of Chaos* by Dolly A. McPherson. *Black American Literature Forum,* 24, no. 3:809–814 (1990).

McPherson, Dolly A. *Order Out of Chaos: The Autobiographical Works of Maya Angelou.* New York: Peter Lang, 1990.

Meyers, Linda Mae Zarpentine. "Maya Angelou and the Multiplicity of Self." Master's thesis, Morgan State University, 1995.

Neubauer, Carol E. "Displacement and Autobiographical Style in Maya Angelou's *The Heart of a Woman.*" *Black American Literature Forum,* 17, no. 3:123–129 (1983).

———. "Maya Angelou: Self and a Song of Freedom in the Southern Tradition." In *Southern Women Writers: The New Generation.* Edited by Tonette Bond Inge. Tuscaloosa: University of Alabama Press, 1990. Pp. 114–142. Reprinted in *Contemporary Literary Criticism,* 77:21–32 (1990).

O'Neale, Sondra. "Reconstruction of the Composite Self: New Images of Black Women in Maya Angelou's Continuing Autobiography." In *Black Women Writers (1950–1980): A Critical Evaluation.* Edited by Mari Evans. Garden City: Doubleday, 1984. Pp. 25–36.

Raynaud, Claudine. "Rites of Coherence: Autobiographical Writings by Hurston, Brooks, Angelou, and Lorde." *Dissertation Abstracts International,* 53, no. 3:812A (September 1992).

Schmidt, Jan Zlotnik. "The Other: A Study of the Persona in Several Contemporary Women's Autobiographies.'' *College English Association Critic*, 42, no. 1:24–31 (1980).

Smith, Sidonie Ann. ''The Song of a Caged Bird: Maya Angelou's Quest after Self-Acceptance.'' *Southern Humanities Review* 7:365–375 (1973).

Stetson, Erlene. ''Studying Slavery: Some Literary and Pedagogical Considerations on the Black Female Slave.'' In *But Some of Us Are Brave.* Edited by Gloria T. Hull, Patricia Bell Scott, and Barbara Smith. Old Westbury and New York: Feminist Press, 1982. Pp. 61–84.

Starling, Marion Wilson. *The Slave Narrative.* Boston: G. K. Hall, 1981.

Weixlmann, Joe. ''African American Autobiography: A Bibliographical Essay.'' *Black American Literature Forum*, 24, no. 2:375–415 (1990).

MAJOR INTERVIEWS

Benson, Carol. ''Out of the Cage and Still Singing.'' *Writers Digest*, January 1975, pp. 18–20.

Chrisman, Robert. ''The *Black Scholar* Interviews Maya Angelou.'' *Black Scholar*, 8, no. 4:44–52 (January/February 1977).

Elliot, Jeffrey M., editor. *Conversations with Maya Angelou.* Jackson: University Press of Mississippi, 1989.

McPherson, Dolly A. ''An Addendum: A Conversation with Maya Angelou.'' In *Order Out of Chaos: The Autobiographical Works of Maya Angelou.* New York: Peter Lang, 1990. Pp. 131–162.

Neubauer, Carol E. ''An Interview with Maya Angelou.'' *Massachusetts Review* 28, no. 2:286–292 (Spring 1987).

Redmond, Eugene B. ''Boldness of Language And Breadth: An Interview with Maya Angelou.'' *Black American Literature Forum*, 22, no. 2:156–157 (Summer 1988).

Tate, Claudia. ''Maya Angelou.'' In *Black Woman Writers at Work*, edited by Claudia Tate. New York: Continuum, 1983. Pp. 1–11.

—MARY JANE LUPTON

Louis Auchincloss

1917–

"IT HAS BEEN said that his childhood is a writer's entire capital" is the epigraph of Louis Auchincloss' short memoir, *A Writer's Capital,* which appeared in 1974. Although Auchincloss (pronounced aw-kin-closs) thinks of himself primarily as a novelist, this gracefully written and well-shaped piece of nonfiction provides an ideal introduction to his fiction. And although he is the very opposite of a confessional writer, his life inspires and sustains all his novels and short stories. Few American writers have obeyed the familiar precept "Write about yourself" more conscientiously, but what is most interesting about Auchincloss is the way he has transformed his own experiences into the raw material of his fiction. His life has given him a way of looking not at himself but at society, at America. That Auchincloss became a writer at all is somewhat surprising, given his background. How it happened that he transcended his familial inheritance—a privileged life in a closely knit family that effectively conveyed the message that the arts were for dilettantes and women and that commercial pursuit was for men—and became a man of letters is the story of *A Writer's Capital.*

Louis Auchincloss' best fiction—*The House of Five Talents* (1960), *Portrait in Brownstone* (1962), and *The Rector of Justin* (1964)—earned for him a well-deserved place in the pantheon of America's best writers, as evidenced by his election to the National Institute of Arts and Letters in 1965. In addition to these three excellent novels, he has written twenty-one others, fourteen collections of short stories, seventeen books of nonfiction, and two books of edited diaries. Even as he approached his eighties, Auchincloss showed no sign of slowing down. He himself concedes that perhaps he has written too much, which accounts, he supposes, for his being underappreciated and sometimes ignored by critics. Even in the 1960s, his best decade as a writer, his name was conspicuously absent from a list of the top twenty post–World War II novelists issued by two hundred of the nation's literary critics.

A good case can be made that it is not his fecundity but his subject matter that accounts for the critical neglect. His books take on a whole society—the upper echelons of the northeastern (mostly New York) Protestant establishment and its decline as a ruling class. Upper-class WASPs—the acronym (for "white Anglo-Saxon Protestants") first appeared in print in 1957—have not lost all power, Auchincloss knows, but they have lost their monopoly on power. Just how monopolistic this power was is aptly expressed by a fictional character in Auchincloss' short story "The Fabbri Tape," in *Narcissa and Other Fables* (1983):

In my youth American society and government were almost entirely in the hands of big business and the legal profession, and both of these were very white and very Protestant. What we now call ethnic groups, Jews, Irish and Italians, had managed to get hold of political organizations in the larger cities, but even there the financial districts—the real centers of power—remained predominantly WASP. I do not mean that there was not plenty of opportunity in New York City for a young lawyer of Italian-American origin, but if he wanted to join the Union Club or the Piping Rock, if he wanted to send his sons to Groton or Andover, if he hoped ever to be president of the American Bar Association or achieve high federal office, it was going to be a lot easier for him if he became Episcopalian and treated his homeland as an exotic memory rather than a present-day inspiration.

Many if not most Americans claim not to believe in the existence of a ruling class, but it existed and still exists, although it is no longer comprised so exclusively of the East Coast establishment. It occupies the command posts of capitalism and government at the "radiant center" of American society, as Thorstein Veblen had located it, in his *Theory of the Leisure Class* (1899). That Americans seem unaware of its power is not surprising since the ruling class spares no pains in promoting the belief that it does not exist and succeeds in this deception because the public wants to believe in an egalitarian myth. Critics are not different from the general public. From 1950, when a reviewer for the *New York Herald Tribune Book Review* belittled Auchincloss' "thin slice of privileged rich in American society," until 1993, when another, in the *New Republic,* criticized the novelist's nonchalance about his own class's standing in the way of rising ethnics, the majority of critics have dismissed Auchincloss' world (his subject matter) as anachronistic, claustrophobic, rigid, and irrelevant. One, Granville Hicks, who reviewed Auchincloss' books over a period of twenty years, admitted it was the author's subject matter—the doings of the well-to-do and the well-bred—that irritated him, but he regularly praised Auchincloss' literary technique in book after book.

Not all critics, however, have felt this way. The most prominent of Auchincloss' defenders was Gore Vidal. In a 1974 essay in the *New York Review of Books,* he made fun of those who did not see that Auchincloss' world was the ruling class of the United States: "Such is the vastness of our society and the remoteness of academics and book-chatterers from actual power that those who should be in this writer's debt have no idea what a useful service he renders us by revealing and, in some ways, by betraying his class." "Betraying his class" is that aspect of Auchincloss many of the critics do not perceive. While his great theme is the loss of WASP authority, he unmistakably shows it was lost by the narrow-mindedness, smugness, and flabbiness of his own class. He subversively sees from within the citadel, as it were, his characters' pretensions, their hypocrisies, and their inability to be true to their own class's values.

Louis Stanton Auchincloss was born in Lawrence, on Long Island's south shore, the site of his parents' weekend house, on September 27, 1917. His parents, four grandparents, and eight great-grandparents were all New Yorkers, though two, the Dixons, lived in Brooklyn, which did not become part of the city until after their time. After meeting Auchincloss at Brooke Astor's in the mid-1960s, First Lady Lady Bird Johnson described him in *A White House Diary* (1970) as "very good company, easy to talk to—polished, very Eastern. I couldn't imagine him living or writing about life west of the Mississippi River." She could have said "Hudson River" and been just as accurate. When an Auchincloss character leaves Manhattan, his destination is most often Newport, Bar Harbor (where the author's own family spent summers), Southampton, or the north shore of Long Island, all upper-middle-class appendages of that great city on the Hudson.

The first Auchincloss in America was Hugh, of Paisley, Scotland, who arrived in 1803 on the ship *Factor.* Hugh Auchincloss and subsequent Auchinclosses prospered in the dry goods business and through marriage, becoming kin to the great colonial and, much later, robber baron families. The colonial Winthrop heritage turns up in the middle names of the author's brother and oldest son and is the family that unifies the nine stories in *The Winthrop Covenant,* Auchincloss' portrayal of the rise and fall of the Puritan ethic in America, which he published in 1976.

The Auchincloss marriage that most engaged the novelist was not the Winthrop alliance, however, but the marriage of his great-grandparents Charles Handy Russell and Caroline Howland, whose daughter Joanna was Auchincloss' grandmother. Charles Handy Russell is the model for the protagonist in his great-grandson's Civil War novel, *Watchfires,* which came out in 1982. Russell's two homes, one in Manhattan at Thirty-seventh Street and Fifth Avenue, which shows up regularly in the diaries of his friends Philip Hone and Charles Templeton Strong, later edited by Louis Auchincloss for *The Hone and Strong Diaries of Old Manhattan* (1989), and the other in Newport, the house Edith Wharton obviously had in mind for Julius Beaufort's house in *The Age of Innocence,* grace the dust jacket of *Watchfires.*

Other Auchinclosses are used in various fictional and nonfictional stories, but since the dominant influence in Louis Auchincloss' development was his mother Priscilla, it is her family's history that stimulated the novelist's imagination far more than the Auchinclosses'. Various reincarnations of the Dixons and Stantons appear in several stories, most notably "The Wagnerians," in *Tales of Manhattan* (1967), a moving account of the writer's great-uncle Edmund Stanton's motives and behavior from 1886 to 1891, when he was general manager of the Metropolitan Opera, and *Portrait in Brownstone,* a re-creation of the sense of life his mother had

conveyed about her Dixon relatives. "When I am told that I have confined my fiction to too small a world," he complained in *A Writer's Capital,* "I find it difficult to comprehend. For it seems to me as if I should never come to the end of the variety of types represented by my relatives alone."

But Auchincloss had far more than a group, however large it was, of familial characters to fictionalize. As he himself told a Soviet audience in the spring of 1991, he grew up in circumstances that offered him a "wider than ordinary perspective of the great public events of the day."

He spent six years at Groton, a small New England Episcopalian boarding school with illustrious alumni that includes a president of the United States, two secretaries of state, a covey of ambassadors, the senior partners of the country's most elite law firms and investment banking houses. In what is certainly one of his three best novels, *The Rector of Justin,* he wrote about the school, exploring the innately American paradox of the "deeply religious [headmaster] who tried valiantly but essentially ineffectually to educate the sons of business men and bankers who wanted their sons to have the outward marks of Christian gentlemen without in any way dulling their competitive energies." In short, Groton was a training ground of the establishment.

At preparatory school and at Yale, which he attended after Groton, he made friends with men who helped to orchestrate the disastrous Vietnam War. Perplexed as to how individuals of such high intelligence and goodwill could have led America into this morass, he wrote *Honorable Men,* which appeared in 1985. He had a front-row seat, he said, to observe the rich get richer in the 1920s and then experience violent reversal of their fortunes in the depression of the 1930s. His own father was a partner in the powerful law firm Davis Polk & Wardwell, which handled all the legal work for J. P. Morgan & Company. Morgan's managing partner, George Whitney, was the brother of Richard Whitney, a president of the New York Stock Exchange who was convicted of embezzlement in 1937, all of which is fictionalized in *The Embezzler,* published in 1966. As a Wall Street lawyer himself, Auchincloss worked within the ruling circle of American capitalism, using it as the setting in story after story in which he scrutinized the moral and ethical limits on the exercise of self-interest (the pursuit of happiness), one of the few American novelists to recognize and deal with this eminently American dilemma. He is ''the only serious writer seriously writing about the American business world—our ruling class, after all,'' said the critic John Leonard in *Forbes.*

Louis Auchincloss was as acutely perceptive in depicting the wives and mothers of the city's civic and business leaders as he was with the men. Critic after critic singles out the believability of his female characters, agreeing that he far outdistances any of his contemporaries in his understanding of women. He credits this special sensitivity to the deep intimacy he established with his mother early in his life. She was a powerful influence on him and his writing in every way. She was a voracious reader who formed literary opinions that were, as he put it in interviews with Vincent Piket, ''pungent, incisive, and always interesting.'' The more than one hundred letters that passed between mother and son during the latter's service on landing craft during World War II attest to the accuracy of his judgment, for the letters were always about the books each was reading. Auchincloss so respected her literary judgment that he submitted each finished manuscript for her inspection before submitting it to Houghton Mifflin, his publisher for half a century. She objected to almost everything, on the grounds that he was betraying allegiance to his own people and begged him to camouflage a resemblance to someone or other she thought was too identifiable. He always refused but kept

showing her subsequent work because she was able to ''put her finger on every soggy spot.''

Priscilla Auchincloss' influence went far beyond literary matters. She taught her son and his three siblings that loyalty to family and to community was self-sustaining. She idealized her own Dixon family and her husband's law partners and the Morgan bankers they represented, revering them as full of financial probity and wisdom. But even as a young boy, Louis discerned a discrepancy between his mother's idealization and the reality he observed, and therein lies the source of the novelist's strong sense of irony, which permeates everything he writes and which accounts for his simultaneous insider-outsider view of the world he grew up in and never left. The difficulty, he wrote in *A Writer's Capital,* was that the family lived so uninterruptedly and so continuously with the people Priscilla Auchincloss admired that the writer could not help but notice how mistaken his mother was in her assessments.

> I observed that often the only interesting thing about some of the families near whom we lived was their wealth. I saw perfectly that their big houses, their shining cars, and their glittering yachts were designed to impress just such onlookers as myself. And I began to see that there was diversion and interest in the rivalries of the social game. When I bubbled over at the family board with snobbish observations and gossip about our wealthy neighbors, Mother and Father were genuinely astounded and depressed.

Despite a sense of irony about and distance from all he observed, Auchincloss did adopt much of his mother's value system, as his fiction makes abundantly clear. He consistently stands for what he deemed valuable in the culture of the past—stoicism, duty, order, all values directed toward maintaining a stable society—during an era that has often tried to discard the past and spurned many of its values as repressive. In describing his father's faith as ''a sturdy reliance on the maintenance of forms to hold up the structure of a thinly civilized world,'' the narrator of Auchincloss' 1995 novel, *The Education of Oscar Fairfax,* embodies what it is about the novelist's worldview that contrasts so startlingly with the contemporary zeitgeist, according to which ''maintenance of forms'' equals elitism. Small wonder the label of irrelevancy is so often attached to Auchincloss' novels. Moreover, the novelist upholds these values in an even, decorous, reserved, and lucid style. In short, Auchincloss is a classicist in a Romantic period. His writing, unlike the often inward-oriented fiction that celebrates the subjective self alienated from the social order, was decidedly out of step with the times.

Auchincloss' first published novel, *The Indifferent Children* (1947), was much like the next five apprenticeship novels: *Sybil* (1951), *A Law for the Lion* (1953), *The Great World and Timothy Colt* (1956), *Venus in Sparta* (1958), and *The Pursuit of the Prodigal* (1959). All six, plus the short story collections *The Injustice Collectors* (1950) and *The Romantic Egoists* (1954), are autobiographical, not in a societal sense, as all his post-1960 books are, but in a psychological sense. Their themes, the successful or frustrated resolution of the worries and motivations of their protagonists, male and female, mirror the author's own attempts at resolution. They are all stories of moneyed individuals going through spiritual and vocational crises that had begun in childhood. All concern individuals trapped either by their families' expectations of what is proper for them to do in life or by their own versions of what the family wants of them. From *A Law for the Lion* on, the books reflect the two and a half years of psychoanalysis the author underwent. Auchincloss' chief crisis was whether to be a writer or a lawyer, which he finally resolved by being both. This compromise led to his four best novels, the next four in fact, which shift from the

psychological to the social. Louis Auchincloss had found himself by staying on home turf and chronicling the WASP as an endangered species. Not until much later in his career did he return to early concerns. ''The Epicurean,'' for example, one of the stories published in *Three Lives* in 1993, is about the self-delusion of a man who thinks he can overcome his stoic heritage and turn himself into a connoisseur of pleasure. He cannot, of course, for he is, like Auchincloss himself, too much a product of his heritage.

Auchincloss had confined the life of privilege to the background in his first eight books, but beginning with his ninth, the background of privilege becomes the theme. In other words, he started using his own social milieu as a source of thematic as well as background material for his fiction, which seemed to liberate him to employ his literary gifts more fully. In *The House of Five Talents,* the first of such novels and the only serious literary rendering of the robber barons as a group, Auchincloss looks squarely at the children, grandchildren, and great-grandchildren of one staggeringly rich magnate, to show how the recipients of that wealth had fared in life. Despite their very public and gaudy consumerism—they dwelt in eclectic chateaux up and down Fifth Avenue, traveled in private railroad cars to their country estates in Lenox, Massachusetts, the Adirondacks, Bar Harbor, Newport, and Asheville, North Carolina, cruised aboard their families' steam yachts in the Mediterranean, and, during the season in New York, danced until daylight with eligible young men and women from families as rich as their own—and despite the insularity money provides, they were not immune to hurt, the novelist reveals, especially the hurt that results from their eventual discovery that in their world the self is worthless when separated from what it owns.

Auchincloss based *The House of Five Talents* on several of New York's nineteenth-century millionaire families, with special attention to the

Vanderbilts. Specifically, he encouraged his wife's maternal grandmother, Florence Adele Sloane Burden Tobin (she was called Adele) with whom he and his wife frequently spent weekends during the first three years of their marriage on her four-hundred-acre Long Island estate, to talk about growing up during the 1890s, the apogee of the gilded age. (After Mrs. Tobin died in 1960, Auchincloss discovered a diary she had kept from 1893 to 1896; he published an annotated version of it, *Maverick in Mauve,* in 1983.) Stimulated by Adele Tobin's ''vivid and colorful sense of the past'' and his own reading about robber baron families (which showed, as Auchincloss put it in *The House of Five Talents,* ''figures . . . kept repeating—the daughter who married a duke, the son who became a crook, the grandson who became a Communist''), Auchincloss shows what five generations of the fictional financier Julius Millinder's descendants did with the hundred million dollars he had accumulated by the time of his death in 1886, and in so doing, the novelist brings a class and an era to life.

Auchincloss tells the story from the point of view of the financier's granddaughter, Augusta (Gussie) Millinder, a person much less perspicacious than her creator. Although the story shifts its focus from one place and family member to another, it is always told through Gussie's eyes. Despite an ever-widening complexity of characters, Auchincloss never loses his control over the large scene nor over his sure sense of the periods, showing the gradual shift that took place between 1886 and 1948, the time covered by the novel, from the lavish and open expenditure of the nouveau riche to the much later inconspicuous consumption of the very wealthy. Because of Gussie's training in art history, she comments frequently on art and architecture, comments that are credible and do not sound out of voice or character, as they sometimes do in the mouths of businessmen in other Auchincloss novels. Her lively descriptions of the houses and gardens,

pictures and clothes of Julius Millinder's twelve living grandchildren, who own estates around the globe, display the author's knowledge and love of the arts and capture the swaggering opulence of the robber baron era.

Gussie Millinder is less interested in how her tycoon grandfather had made his money than in what the money did to his descendants over seven decades. Having money makes Gussie suspicious of outsiders' attitudes toward that money. Afraid that her assured inheritance was her principal attraction, she decided to remain single. Her mother, whose fixed principle ''that every human being was fundamentally motivated by a financial goal and that those who would not recognize this were either fools or hypocrites,'' asks her squeamish daughter, ''What's the good of your father's money but to give you a good position?'' Nonetheless, in early middle age, Gussie resolved to be loved for herself.

''What is yourself?'' a sister-in-law asks. ''We're all bits and pieces of our background, our tastes, our inheritances, even our clothes. It's only natural for people to be curious because you're a Millinder and live in a big house. It's up to you to turn that curiosity into something better!'' ''It was the simplest idea in the world,'' Gussie reflects, ''yet it changed my life.'' Although Gussie is in her middle forties when she makes this ''discovery,'' she does change her life: she becomes the family matriarch and chronicler. Her scrutiny of the second, third (her own), and fourth generations of Millinders—with incidental glimpses at the fifth—form a social document that, despite the personal limitations money had imposed on her, is provocative and accurate. Gussie is right to call her fictional memoir a history not of a family but of a fortune. She sees the Millinder inheritance as the source of the family's prominence and decline. She concludes that Millinder money was more important than the Millinders were.

The founding father had had none of the social

ambitions his children unleashed as soon as he died and that put the Millinder name on the social map. The unequal bequests made to his two sons (Fred's business acumen laid claim to twice the amount settled on Cyrus, Gussie's father) incites a hilarious social rivalry between their wives. Eliza, who is Gussie's mother, and Daisy, Fred's wife, compete in giving lavish dinner parties, in collecting high-priced art, in attracting the best foreign aristocrats as spouses for their daughters, even in designing their Newport houses. Their struggle for precedence, which they see in heroic terms, but which Gussie sees more realistically, gives the novel an exuberance unseen before in Auchincloss' writing. The entire novel is made up of a series of scenes that aptly define characters and the times, but it is above all Gussie's awarenesses, as well as the author's omniscience, that make *The House of Five Talents* a powerful novel. It became the author's first bestseller and prompted his first appearance on the front page of the *New York Times Book Review.*

Auchincloss' next novel, *Portrait in Brownstone,* is a fictional rendering of his mother's Dixon forebears. The Denisons of the novel are, like the real-life Dixons, a close family bound together by a shared sense of duty and privilege. Auchincloss establishes Denison allegiance and affection in a series of scenes and in so doing accurately recreates the bygone Brownstone era of New York City at the turn of the century. But nostalgia for a simpler New York is not the point of the novel.

Above all else, *Portrait in Brownstone* depicts the decline of clan loyalty and traditions and its eventual outcome, the disruption of an ordered society. By alternating points of view, telling Ida's story in the first person and other characters' stories in the third person, Auchincloss allows the protagonist, Ida, to emerge as the strongest, most pragmatic, and most sympathetic character in the book. She marries a cold and calculating man who makes fun of her idealization of family solidarity and who has an affair with one of her cousins. Yet Ida remains true to the duty and discipline she learned as a child, never letting any family member down, not even the alcoholic cousin who tried to steal her husband. What Ida sees, as the others do not, is that what her husband and cousin disparage and cast aside is worthwhile, for even if clan loyalty has been something of an illusion, it is a surer guide to life in changing times than what they have chosen. Her cousin and husband rebel against their milieu's rigid social code, not realizing it is the only discipline to be had in the unsettled time they live in and not to be discarded lightly.

In *Portrait in Brownstone* Auchincloss has depicted a central problem of the modern world: namely, the lack of a moral community, the absence of shared values that give a society a commonality that confers an identity on a collection of competing individuals. Like its predecessor, *Portrait in Brownstone* became a best-seller and was reviewed on the front page of the *New York Times Book Review.* These successes, however, were eclipsed by the triumph of Auchincloss' next and perhaps best-known novel, *The Rector of Justin*, published in 1964.

Auchincloss was in his teens when he started writing about his six most impressionable years, which had been spent at a church-affiliated boarding school. He said he had had an inkling that the boarding school would be his grand theme long before he felt ready to take it on. Even so, Groton had figured in several published short stories and novels beginning as early as his college years, when he wrote the short story ''At the Chelton-Pulver Game'' for the *Yale Literary Magazine,* but not until he was forty-six years old did he write *The Rector of Justin.*

Auchincloss attended Groton in the early 1930s, during the era of the great headmasters—Samuel Drury of St. Paul's, William Greenough Thayer of St. Mark's, Frank Boyden of Deerfield, and Endicott Peabody of Groton. What fascinated the novelist was what he saw as the central problem of all New England Protestant church schools during the days of the great headmasters: namely, the distance between their piety and idealism and the crass materialism of the families whose sons attended the schools and whose fortunes supplied the schools' endowments. This gap between spirituality and secularism inspired the theme of *The Rector of Justin.*

The novel is the fictional biography of the clerical headmaster of Justin Martyr, the Reverend Francis Prescott. His life story is told by six people: the finicky, fastidious old Horace Havistock, Prescott's boyhood friend; malicious, destructive Jules Griscam, a Justin student in the class of 1922 who hates the rector; David Griscam, Jules's father, an alumnus (class of 1893), longtime trustee, and millionaire; Cordelia, the rector's neurotic, rebellious daughter; Charley Strong, football captain, senior prefect of the class of 1911, shrapnel victim of World War I, and Cordelia's lover; and finally, and principally, Brian Aspinwall, fifty years younger than the rector and unlike him in every way except in his strong faith. Of the book's twenty-four chapters, three are from the pen of Horace Havistock; two are David Griscam's notes; two chapters relate Cordelia's story as set forth in a transcript by Brian from memory of two long conversations with Cordelia; one is Charley Strong's manuscript; three are Jules Griscam's memoirs; and thirteen chapters, including the first four and last five, are Brian's journal from the time he meets Francis Prescott and prepares for his first encounter with the boys of Justin Martyr in the fall of 1939 to April 1947, when the rector is four months dead. The journal consists of Brian's notes for his proposed biography of Prescott.

Each narrator speaks in his own voice, from the histrionic, narcissistic, almost hallucinatory style of Charley Strong, a style the antithesis of Auchincloss' own, to the precious, mincing speech of Horace Havistock. The novelist used shifting points of view both to paint a multiple portrait that matches the complexity of Francis Prescott and to examine his influence on his students so that the reader will ask whether the education he provides has a positive or negative effect. The six points of view, moreover, make the personalities and biases of each ''narrator'' convincingly clear.

Auchincloss' method is risky, especially assigning, as he did, the major share of telling Prescott's story to Brian, a minor character at that, and bringing in the main character only ''as seen by.'' Readers' judgments of the rector, not to mention of the novel as a whole, could be and probably are conditioned by their evaluation of Brian. If they dislike Brian, can they accept Brian's high opinion of the rector or what he thinks of Cordelia and Charley, an acceptance that is important thematically? And what if readers get bored by Brian's timidity, vacillation, lack of confidence, and physical weakness? Auchincloss made certain that none of these potential dangers were realized, precisely because readers see Prescott through many eyes. Moreover, the novelist wisely shows that Brian wins the admiration of the book's most hard-nosed character, the millionaire David Griscam, who comes to see why people like and admire the meek and shy Brian. ''You speak straight to the heart,'' he tells the young Justin Martyr master.

The need for Brian is historical. Readers follow his first acquaintance with the rector in 1939 into 1941, the last two years of Prescott's headmastership, and then on into the remaining years of his life; they witness the muted antagonism between the retired headmaster, still living on campus, and the new headmaster; and finally, they experience the climax of this antagonism, which occurs during the diamond jubilee week in the spring of 1946. Although Justin Martyr has never been richer, stronger, more selective in admissions, nor so loyally supported by its alumni,

Prescott suddenly sees his life as a failure, a realization set off by the new headmaster's proposal to liberalize admission policies. The discussion of this proposal among the school's trustees, many of whom object to the opening up of admissions, forces Prescott to admit that "only I . . . ever thought [Justin Martyr] was different. Only I failed to see that snobbishness and materialism were intrinsic in its make-up."

This first section of the novel deals with Brian's "present time." Then Auchincloss backs up and shows his reader the different stages of Prescott's life, which are like period pieces. The Horace Havistock chapters illustrate the novelist's technique. From Havistock, readers learn that the rector's father had died a hero during the Civil War, at Chancellorsville, and that his grief-stricken mother died shortly after. Although an orphan, he had the "best connections," who send him to boarding school in Dublin, New Hampshire, in the 1870s. The man the rector becomes is forming. At school he is self-disciplined, sports-minded, bright, and self-assured in judgments of right and wrong. He believes that one must play by the rules, say what one believes, and stick by one's friends. Similarly, it is all right to be hard, satirical, funny, even bitter, but never cynical. As a sixth former (last year of high school), Frank Prescott had already decided he must someday found a church school "as a source of regeneration" in the corrupt, modern world. Havistock also tells about Prescott's years at Oxford, his first job in finance in New York City, his first serious courtship, his removal to Boston to study for the ministry (although the church means little to him, he is preparing to set up his own church school), and finally his marriage.

The biographical facts, in addition to those provided by other witnesses, together make up a full picture of the growth and development of a multifaceted man who believes that dignity and moral conduct do not come naturally to men but require eternal vigilance and discipline. Francis Prescott "in total" is an odd composite of a charming conversationalist who is highly suspect of the arts, a stern disciplinarian who believes in competitive, contact sports such as football, and a man, not surprisingly, who becomes a headmaster who will "move mountains" for his boys, as long as they will accept his authority. Anyone who questions his dictates is in trouble, however. The rector of Justin Martyr is shown to be a fascinating man—noble yet petty, kind yet sensitive, godlike yet magnificently human, and above all else, a man to whom personal faith in God is everything.

Readers are never meant to question the headmaster's faith, which is solid and very real. What they are meant to see is his naïveté in believing that his boys accept and practice the faith he holds so strongly. Even so, the rector's world is one of tranquility and order, of good, sane, practical, decent, hard-working, productive industriousness, even if, to Prescott's despair, faith in God has lost its hold on the twentieth century.

Auchincloss succeeds magnificently in conveying a rich portrait of this complex man precisely because he so skillfully employs multiple points of view, a skill he claims to have learned in the navy during World War II, when he served as defense counsel in court-martial cases. He represented several obviously guilty sailors whose only chance for acquittal or a lessened sentence was to make a credible statement of mitigation, which they had to deliver themselves. If it looked as if Lieutenant Auchincloss had prepared the statement, it did the sailor no good. His job then was to write and rewrite a statement in each sailor's voice until he got it right, and then to have the sailor memorize and practice delivering it. He became so adept at imitating the sailors' voices that the presiding officer in Auchincloss' last court-martial case congratulated the defendant for his frank plea and censured Auchincloss "as a lazy, good-for-nothing counsel" who had done nothing but plead guilty and leave the job of defense to his poor client.

He must also have learned something about voice from Ruth Draper, the monologist who lived in the same apartment building as his family. He had seen all her monologues on stage and went often to the parties she gave for her nieces and nephews, for whom she always performed. Writing in another's voice is exactly like doing a monologue: writer and performer put on different hats and strut about their stages. Wherever or however Auchincloss learned the technique of manipulating voice, which he also exhibited in the two preceding novels, its effect is riveting in this book. Readers are swept along by *The Rector of Justin*, for the gradual unfolding of the rector's character is fascinating. Moreover, the novel provides yet another penetrating scrutiny of the odd symbiosis of materialism and religion that Alexis de Tocqueville discerned in the American experience a hundred years earlier.

A literary masterpiece, *The Rector of Justin* sold more than two million copies in two years and vied with Saul Bellow's *Herzog* for first place on the *New York Times* best-seller list for almost a year. Although many first-rate critics called it the best book of 1964, the usual number of critics castigated Auchincloss for his subject matter. One, in the *New York Review of Books*, called prep-school life a trivial subject. Virgilia Peterson pointed out on the front page of the *New York Times Book Review* in July 1964 that "like it or not, and justly or not, the preponderance of our leadership in government, the professions, and business comes, still today, out of that social minority which preempts Mr. Auchincloss's field of vision." In fact, Auchincloss had already determined that his next novel should concern that social minority's business interests, specifically by focusing on the arrogance and insularity of the banking and business class that dominated the nation's commerce. Auchincloss' embodiment of this arrogance is Guy Prime of *The Embezzler*.

Wall Street in the 1930s was the battleground between the epic forces of big finance and big government, a struggle that began when the Securities and Exchange Acts of 1933 and 1934 established the Securities and Exchange Commission and brought the securities industry under its control, and ended when Richard Whitney, who served five elected terms as president of the New York Stock Exchange, was sentenced to prison for embezzlement. His nephew Robert Whitney had been in Auchincloss' form at Groton. In fact, Richard Whitney himself was an alumnus of Groton (Groton headmaster and cofounder Endicott Peabody often visited Whitney during his incarceration at Sing Sing prison) and a member of the well-connected Whitney family, all of whom were closely associated with the Auchinclosses. As the novelist later was quoted as saying, Richard Whitney's crime "just *rocked* society." Still, the novelist could not resist using Whitney's crime as plot for *The Embezzler*, despite protests from the Whitneys and the Auchinclosses about resurrecting the case three decades after its close. Auchincloss went ahead anyway, insisting, quite accurately, that his protagonist Guy Prime is not Richard Whitney.

The Embezzler has no central narrative voice but comprises three memoirs: Guy Prime's, his wife's, and a friend's. Taken together they present overlapping and contradictory versions of the man and tantalizingly probe the mystery of human motivation. The novel also gives an accurate picture of the world of finance before World War II, especially of the widespread speculation and wholesale borrowing characteristic of the 1920s and 1930s, before the New Deal tamed Wall Street. But *The Embezzler* does not measure up to the richness of detail nor the all-embracing themes of Auchincloss' three preceding novels. Moreover, Guy Prime is no Francis Prescott, so the unraveling of the vagaries of character does not lead to the larger ethical and moral issues raised by the rector's life.

The book did well—Auchincloss' fourth appearance on the front page of the *New York Times Book Review,* his second Book-of-the-Month Club main selection, his second National Book Award nomination, and his fifth appearance on the best-seller lists, but it was his last big success. Future books had far more modest sales, and for a few years the novelist failed to sell paperback rights. *The Embezzler* was also the last book in which he used the device of multiple narrators, with the exception of *The House of the Prophet,* published in 1980, a novelistic interpretation of the underlying motivation for the columnist Walter Lippmann's aloofness.

At the same time that Auchincloss started exploring historically and culturally New York's ruling class, he began publishing literary essays. His first collection of critical essays came out in 1961, and he has produced a steady stream of critical writings since then, into the 1990s. He has written about French history and literature (Versailles, Richelieu, Proust, Daudet, Bourget, Corneille, Racine, and Saint-Simon), about English writers (primarily Shakespeare and the nineteenth-century novelists), and about the Americans (Henry James, Edith Wharton, whose direct descendant he is said to be, Emily Dickinson, Henry Adams, Theodore Dreiser, nine women novelists, including Willa Cather, Katherine Anne Porter, and Carson McCullers, John P. Marquand, and John O'Hara).

What these essays have in common is their clear thinking and commonsensical judgment. His first principle of good writing, one he takes seriously, is to entertain. "Her tragedy as a writer," he says of George Eliot in *Reflections of a Jacobite* (1961), "is that she never learned the simple lesson that an entertainer must entertain." In the same volume, in defense of Proust and implicitly of himself, he takes the position that since "snobbishness reigns on all levels [of society], why does it matter what level one selects to study?" Eminently pragmatic, he writes in *Motiveless Malignity* in 1969, "*King Lear* strikes so directly into family life that I suspect that

many parents since 1605 have had the old man's dread example in mind while considering settlements on their offspring. As a lawyer I can think of more than a few." There is no theorizing or abstraction about Auchincloss' literary criticism, for he writes for no other and no better purpose than to induce his reader to read whatever writer he has under consideration. Just as reading *A Writer's Capital* is helpful to understanding the wellsprings of Auchincloss' subject matter, so too are the literary essays for providing a valuable gloss on his literary technique.

His literary criticism unmistakably acknowledges the novel as Auchincloss' principal concern. Yet the novelist has written enough short stories to fill fourteen volumes. The seeds of all the novels after the first can be discerned in the stories, which seem to have afforded Auchincloss a way and a place to try out new ideas. The notable exceptions are the legal stories that he confined pretty much to collections such as *Powers of Attorney* (1963) and *The Partners* (1974). Legal matters do show up in the novels from time to time, but other than *The Great World and Timothy Colt* and *Diary of a Yuppie* (1986), only peripherally. The language of the law provided a source of ready reference for the fiction dealing with themes other than the law. Linn Tremain's question to a young associate about the courtship of his niece in *Portrait in Brownstone,* for example, means that "Derrick, as the lawyers put it, was 'on notice.' " In the same novel, a childless marriage is said to be "in default of issue." Legal terms like these, as well as legal situations such as probate and divorce matters, appear from novel to novel, but have no essential connection to the novel's theme.

To understand twentieth-century corporate law in America, a reader would do well to turn to the novels and short stories that deal primarily and thematically with the world of law. These are about lawyers being lawyers and about the inner working of their firms, not about winning or losing big, publicized, dramatic courtroom battles. While the courtroom trial may be theatrical, the essential spirit of the law is not dramatic. After all, the law's purpose is to mediate, often to diffuse, not to incite conflict, which is why the majority of disputes are settled out of court. Most of Auchincloss' stories turn on the management and office politics of firms, the real world of most attorneys. "What goes on within the lawyer's office is . . . packed with drama," Auchincloss said in a speech before a meeting of the American College of Probate Counsel in 1971. "I have always found that this field makes for the quickest writing as the stories seem to write themselves. When I published a group of connected stories about a fictional law firm entitled *Powers of Attorney,* I got dozens of letters from people in firms all over the country asking how in God's name I had known about their Mrs. X or Mr. Y. What they did not realize was human types abound in certain territories." Every large law firm has had the senior partner who, after having served in Washington and having "been bitten by the federal bug," disdains prosaic everyday practice; the corporate men who "looked down on everything outside their department"; the litigator who treats his department as a firm within a firm; the elderly partner terrified that he has not kept up; and the secretary of the deceased founding partner who feels it beneath her dignity to serve anyone else. In dozens of Auchincloss' short stories, plots turn on the mundane and sometimes trivial interactions among these types.

In presenting sketches of Manhattan legal life, a rich area seldom tapped by writers, Auchincloss draws an accurate, sociological picture of the sweeping changes that have made the practice of law today different from practice in 1946, when Auchincloss started work at Sullivan and Cromwell, just as legal practice in mid-century differed from a firm's legal custom when his father began lawyering in 1911. Everything has changed, from moral and ethical standards to the new gargantuan size of firms to how law firms are managed to the coming of women into the profession. When Auchincloss tried to write a one-act play based on an early story, "The Mavericks," for PBS, a simple update from the 1950s to the 1980s proved impossible. "I had to do the whole thing from scratch," he marveled. "I might as well have been writing in the Renaissance. It was incredible how things had changed." Quite predictably, change generated tensions between the old-fashioned general practitioners, who in professing adherence to their firm's traditions romanticized the past, and their young associates, who had experienced nothing other than firms with specialized departments and powerful corporate clients.

Henry Knox, the senior partner of the fictional firm in *The Great World and Timothy Colt* believed and taught his young associates the idealistic notion that lawyers brought order to the business world before the government stepped in. Loosely based on Lansing Reed, a warm and engaging man who had been the leading partner to guide the growth of Davis Polk during the years Louis Auchincloss' father worked there, Knox expresses an outlook that was prevalent in the elite firms, at least until the 1950s.

Robert Service, the fictional yuppie of the 1986 novel *Diary of a Yuppie,* thinks it is hypocritical of men such as Knox to point pridefully to ideals of the past while enjoying the profits of the present. Service believes that men are naturally greedy and selfish and that, as they pursue money and power, anything short of crime is permitted. His law firm is based on the maxim that the law is a game, albeit a game with very strict rules. "You have to stay meticulously within the law; the least misstep, if caught, involves an instant penalty. But there is no particular moral opprobrium in incurring a penalty, any more than there is in being offside in football.'' His firm is necessarily different from the firm Henry Knox strove to build.

"The Double Gap," a marvelous Chekhovian story from the collection *Second Chance,* published in 1970, clearly presents the two opposing attitudes represented by Knox and Service. In the story Albert Ellsworth of Carter & Ellsworth makes it his "policy to keep the spirit of Elihu Cowden Carter alive.'' He makes Carter's "memory and his image the trademark" of the firm, and, if anything, he overdoes it. Each associate gets an Ellsworth-penned biography of Carter, who was slain by a Latin American assassin; Carter's French furniture lines the reception area; a John Singer Sargent portrait of him hangs in a spot no one entering the firm can miss; bronze tablets with his sayings adorn the watercoolers; a glass-topped case with his decorations from foreign governments stands in the library; and his bloodstained vest gilds the main conference room. "You cooly manufactured a religion and a creed to hold your office together," Ellsworth's grandson charges. But Ellsworth believes that a "law firm is something much more than its clients' problems," that lawyers "must be dedicated to something higher than monetary reward," yet he admits to looking the other way when the Great American Fruit Company, a major client, bribed courts in Dutch Honduras, accepting that practice as the only way to do business in Central America, and he has allowed the firm to try a case before a judge who he knew had been fixed. His grandson fails to see why he should join Ellsworth's firm, in which lawyers preach high ethical canons that have "the function, at least in the minds of your generation, of raising the lawyer to a higher moral plane than that of his client" yet practice law as tools of clients.

At the heart of all Auchincloss' legal fiction is the ethical concern that arises from the hardboiled adage of one of the century's ablest corporate attorneys, Elihu Root: "The client never wants to be told he can't do what he wants to do; he wants to be told how to do it, and it is the lawyer's business to tell him how.'' A fictional lawyer is a useful foil for exploring the moral restraints of such an ethic, because a lawyer is paid to be an energetic servant and not a moral auditor of his clients' interests. "If ever you have the good fortune to secure a big company for your client," a partner in Tower, Tilney & Webb, the fictional firm of *Powers of Attorney,* informs a subordinate, "you will learn the word 'unbiased' has no further meaning for you. . . . A good lawyer eats, lives and breathes for his clients." Clitus Tilney wistfully acknowledges the truth of this remark: "I wish we could return to the days . . . before we were captured by the corporations. Before we became simple mouthpieces.'' Both men are suggesting that the successful practitioner keeps his sense of moral outrage within the boundaries of his clients' interests. To do otherwise is not to live in the real world. Several stories indicate that many partners are not cynical opportunists but frustrated idealists who have learned to temper their idealism. The rhetorical question "Well, did you and I make the world?" brings to a pragmatic conclusion two stories— "Power of Suggestion," from *Powers of Attorney,* and "The Senior Partner's Ethics," from *Skinny Island* (1987)—that raise complex moral questions.

In the decade and a half after 1980, large firms got even larger, owing primarily to mergers and acquisitions. At first the most powerful corporate firms refused to handle hostile takeovers, so companies interested in acquiring unfriendly target companies and the target companies themselves turned to firms that did not look on this activity as unseemly. Since takeover practice is extremely lucrative—for the company that is the target of a takeover effort, the struggle is a life-or-death effort in which no expense is spared, and even a friendly merger needs a lawyer experienced in hostile takeovers to look out for and fend off any potential raiding companies—it was soon embraced even by firms at the pinnacle of the legal world. "Could lawyers in the past have done that?" a character from the PBS television play "The Mavericks" asks. Auchincloss answers that "it's perfectly true that when takeovers started, a lot of the big firms looked very much down their noses at that kind of practice, where you sort of crept up on somebody and then pounced." "I guess it's the huggermugger of the thing that sticks in my craw," a fictional lawyer in "The Tender Offer," from the collection *Narcissa and Other Fables,* complains. They all do it today, Auchincloss says. "If they were going to be corporate lawyers, that was the name of the game." A fictional partner from "The Tender Offer" who disdains corporate takeovers reflects the novelist's thinking when he says, "Even the vocabulary gets me down. Terms like 'bear hug' and 'blitzkrieg,' and 'shark repellent'!"

The largest law firms have acquired the characteristics of the corporations they represent. Since the profession of law has become the business of law, the old security of partners, who can now be fired and are often, is gone. In his fiction, Auchincloss takes no side on these matters; he simply reports them. If pressed, however, he says he would side with the older-style lawyers because "these people are much more attractive, amiable, lovable. . . . They're slightly less rapacious and cutthroat." Beeky Ehninger, a "gentlemanly" fifty-six-year-old attorney in *The Partners* is one of those. He brings the story "The Merger – II" and the collection *The Partners* to a close by deciding quixotically to set up a new firm with all the rejects (he calls them "duplicates") who were to have been let go after his firm merged with another. Auchincloss sees Ehninger's act as more generous than practical. Practical or not, the author's sympathy tends to come down on the side of the Beeky Ehningers, but his sympathy is tempered. "After all, look at the game they're in," he told an interviewer.

"If they were really totally idealistic people, would they be in the practice of law at all? Wouldn't they be missionaries of some sort? Or working for legal aid?"

With an economy of style and alertness of eye, but without moralizing, Auchincloss depicts the ethical complexities inherent in a profession whose ethos is so client-centered. Most of the stories are gems of irony, ambivalence, ambiguity, metaphor: all techniques of presenting two or more views of experience simultaneously. How else could he so vividly embody the inherent difficulties of occupying, as lawyers do, a unique position within society, for they are caught between clients' demands and the law, between private and public interests.

Auchincloss owes a literary debt to the law. His own plain, unfussy, precise style of writing dovetails nicely with the needs of the legal world, wherein words and phrases are constantly defined and redefined in relation to specific human conflicts. Though he has never concealed the fact that writing has given him more fulfillment than the practice of law, the law has provided nearly limitless capital and has helped shape his writing. Legal thought encourages precision through the imagining and denying of alternate actions available to the client, as true for the writer as for the lawyer. A much-quoted remark of Samuel Johnson sums up the profitable union of law and literature for Louis Auchincloss: "Lawyers know life practically. A bookish man should have them to converse with. They have what he wants."

The legal stories confirm what most Americans think about lawyers; money is all-important to them. They serve, after all, a society bent on making money. But to no group is money more important than to those who run the museums in New York. As president of the board of the Museum of the City of New York for a quarter of a century, the country's first museum solely dedicated to preserving a city's past, Auchincloss knew the denizens of the city's cultural institutions well. This was a world as rife with ethical perplexities, giant egos, and petty scheming as big-time law. Defending Auchincloss from the charge of old-fashionedness, the writer Tom Wolfe told a public television interviewer recently that, on the contrary, in betraying the whole business of curators' and collectors' motivations and jealousies, Auchincloss showed himself to be contemporary, absolutely of the moment, striking a theme never before struck in serious American fiction.

The novelist wrote several short stories and one full-length novel set in the art world. *The Golden Calves*, published in 1988, is a full-length portrait of a New York museum whose curators and board members are dominated by duplicity, greed, and self-aggrandizement. Set in and around the fictional Museum of North America, very like the Museum of the City of New York in its lack of endowment and resulting financial pressures, the novel characterizes wealthy collectors as people after social recognition. The biblical title, though, alludes to art as a new religion in the sense that people worship artifacts instead of God. In a plot-heavy story, *The Golden Calves* raises questions about the nature of collecting, the role of museums, and what it means when curators and collectors glorify art instead of God. It is a tale of corruption and betrayal, in which the bequest of a rich woman is disregarded by her scheming lawyer, who also heads the museum's board of directors, all of which suggests a real-life case concerning a bequest made to the august Metropolitan Museum of Art that the museum de-accessioned and sold against the donor's written wishes.

Museum boards, top Wall Street law firms and financial institutions, New England preparatory schools, Ivy League colleges, robber barons, and Brownstone New York's upper bourgeoisie comprise the "great world," as Louis Auchincloss has often referred to the ruling class. This is his

life and subject matter. "To have witnessed the disintegration of an economic ruling class . . . from a front row seat," he has said, "is all a novelist could ask." It was, and he made the most of it.

Most critics note how similar Auchincloss' subject matter is to that of Henry James's books of the middle years and Edith Wharton's portrayal of an older New York. Yet their New York had a recognizable power structure: civic, business, and social leaders came from the same families. In recording the breakup of this monolithic power, Auchincloss brings their stories up to date. His subject matter gives a more complete accounting of America, a story after all of money (and its resultant power), or, as Gore Vidal has written, "the real protagonist of America."

Clearly Auchincloss' subject matter is neither insignificant nor irrelevant, as so many critics charge. In fact, Gore Vidal was right on target when he wrote in an essay on Auchincloss, "Real Class," in the *New York Review of Books* in July 1974, that "the world Auchincloss writes about, the domain of Wall Street bankers and lawyers and stockbrokers, is thought to be irrelevant, a faded and fading genteel-gentile enclave when, in actual fact, this little world comprises the altogether too vigorous and self-renewing ruling class of the United States—an oligarchy that is in firm control of the Chase Manhattan Bank, American foreign policy and the decision-making processes of both divisions of the Property Party."

Auchincloss' qualities—polish, wit, sparkle, and candor—are consistently displayed in his fiction and nonfiction. The novelist has transformed the material of his life into narratives that have their own dynamics and causation and counterpoint in a lucid, simple, and elegant style. The self is revealed in the style. His writing manifests a way of thought: his control of words implies a corresponding control of emotions. As Benjamin DeMott has written, Auchincloss never writhes in print. The measured quality of the prose combined with graceful treatment of the sad joys of human lives imparts a serenity and a sense of wistfulness to all he writes, especially a wistful sympathy for idealists who have got to compromise to survive. He has an unsentimental and penetrating view of a world in which no force is exerted without a consequence. Above all else, he is a masterful storyteller.

Granted, a perfunctoriness of treatment has marked much of his later work. His interest in the conception and plan of these books is evident; in fact, plots of some are quite complex. But an impatience to fill them out results in an attenuation, a thinness. Speed affects dialogue too. Many characters sound like Louis Auchincloss, full of literary allusions, witty retorts, and old-fashioned expressions, just as some of the historical characters sound too contemporary. Characters can get compressed treatment, so they seem two-dimensional. Many of the books do not make a lasting impression, so that after reading several, it is difficult to set one apart from the other. Still, his great books are outstanding literarily. Critics do not judge all of Shakespeare's plays by the standards of *King Lear,* and there is no reason to judge all of Auchincloss' work by the measure of *The Rector of Justin.*

Quite naturally Auchincloss wonders how posterity will judge him and his books. Speaking at a writers' conference sponsored by Pepperdine University in Moscow in 1990, he said that although he did not mean to compare himself to Edith Wharton, still, he felt as she did about her critics. He then quoted from a letter Wharton wrote to Mrs. Cadwalader Jones in 1925: ''You will wonder that the priestess of the life of reason should take such things to heart, and I wonder too. I have never minded before, but as my work reaches its close, I feel so sure that it is either nothing or far more than they know. And I wonder a little desolately which.''

Like George Bernard Shaw, Louis Auchincloss is something of a ''Johnny-one-note,'' and

also like the great dramatist, his variations on a theme are endlessly entertaining, witty, and on target. Shaw, of course, has passed the test of time, and so too will Auchincloss. The time will come when he will be looked on as one of the century's most important American literary voices. He has chronicled, after all, the lives, motivations, familial legacies, values, and behavior of that group of immigrants who made America what it is. America did not become a Spanish country or a French country, though it easily could have. America became an Anglo-Saxon country that accommodated Hispanic, French, and just about every other nationality. The most successful of the immigrants who adapted to the country's Anglo-Saxon ways are those whose experience Auchincloss writes about. His theme, then, is as great as America is great, and in some cases his execution of that theme matches its greatness.

When Louis Auchincloss wrote about the education of a good man, an unsentimental and commonsensical man, in his novel *The Education of Oscar Fairfax,* he could have been writing of himself. ''[T]here was . . . [an] entity inside of Oscar, an observer who observed. . . . [T]he semi-Solipsist lurking in my psyche has played a permanent and distracting role in my whole life. People have been my constant preoccupation. It has not always been clear, however, whether they existed only in me or I in them. Existed, that is, in the sense of what I could do *with* them, or *to* them, or perhaps, ultimately *for* them.'' The real-life novelist tells and retells their stories, keeps them alive, and makes them integral to the story of America.

Selected Bibliography

WORKS OF LOUIS AUCHINCLOSS

All the books by Louis Auchincloss were published by Houghton Mifflin, except where otherwise noted.

NOVELS

The Indifferent Children. Englewood Cliffs, N.J.: Prentice-Hall, 1947. Published under the pseudonym Andrew Lee.

Sybil. 1951.

A Law for the Lion. 1953

The Great World and Timothy Colt. 1956.

Venus in Sparta. 1958.

The Pursuit of the Prodigal. 1959.

The House of Five Talents. 1960.

Portrait in Brownstone. 1962.

The Rector of Justin. 1964.

The Embezzler. 1966.

A World of Profit. 1968.

I Come as a Thief. 1972.

The Dark Lady. 1977.

The Country Cousin. 1978.

The House of the Prophet. 1980.

The Cat and the King. 1981.

Watchfires. 1982.

Exit Lady Masham. 1983.

The Book Class. 1984.

Honorable Men. 1985.

Diary of a Yuppie. 1986.

The Golden Calves. 1988.

The Lady of Situations. 1990.

Family Fortunes: Three Collected Novels [reprint of *The House of Five Talents, Portrait in Brownstone,* and *The Rector of Justin*] Salt Lake City: Galahad, 1993.

The Education of Oscar Fairfax. 1995.

SHORT STORY COLLECTIONS

The Injustice Collectors. 1950.

The Romantic Egoists. 1954.

Powers of Attorney. 1963.

Tales of Manhattan. 1967.

Second Chance; Tales of Two Generations. 1970.

The Partners. 1974.

The Winthrop Covenant. 1976.

Narcissa, and Other Fables. 1983.

Skinny Island: More Tales of Manhattan. 1987.

Fellow Passengers: A Novel in Portraits. 1989.

False Gods. 1992.

Three Lives. 1993.

The Collected Stories of Louis Auchincloss. 1994.

Tales of Yesteryear. 1994.

NONFICTION

Reflections of a Jacobite. 1961.

Edith Wharton. University of Minnesota pamphlets on American writers, no. 12. Minneapolis: University of Minnesota Press, 1962.

Ellen Glasgow. University of Minnesota pamphlets on American writers, no. 33. Minneapolis: University of Minnesota Press, 1964.

Pioneers and Caretakers: A Study of Nine Women Novelists. Minneapolis: University of Minnesota Press, 1965.

Motiveless Malignity. 1969.

Henry Adams. University of Minnesota pamphlets on American writers, no. 93. Minneapolis: University of Minnesota Press, 1971.

Edith Wharton: A Woman in Her Time. New York: Viking, 1971.

Richelieu. New York: Viking, 1972.

A Writer's Capital. Minneapolis: University of Minnesota Press, 1974.

Reading Henry James. Minneapolis: University of Minnesota Press, 1975.

Persons of Consequence: Queen Victoria and Her Circle. New York: Random House, 1979.

Life, Law, and Letters: Essays and Sketches. 1979.

Maverick in Mauve: The Diary of a Romantic Age, ed. New York: Doubleday, 1983.

False Dawn: Women in The Age of the Sun King. New York: Anchor/Doubleday, 1984.

The Vanderbilt Era: Profiles of a Gilded Age. New York: Scribners, 1988.

The Hone & Strong Diaries of Old Manhattan, ed. New York: Abbeville, 1989.

J. P. Morgan: The Financier as Collector. New York: Abrams, 1990.

Love without Wings: Some Friendships in Literature and Politics. 1991.

The Style's the Man: Reflections on Proust, Fitzgerald, Wharton, Vidal, and Others. New York: Scribners, 1994.

ARCHIVES AND BIBLIOGRAPHIES

Columbia University, New York. Rare Book and Manuscript Library. Columbia University, James Oliver Brown Collection (his agent) and Curtis Brown Collection (his current agent).

Groton School, Groton, Mass. Archives. Auchincloss, Anne and Gordon. Interivew of Auchincloss for an oral history of Groton, Class of 1935.

Harvard University, Cambridge, Mass. Houghton Mifflin Collection. Contains Houghton, Mifflin's Louis Auchincloss files.

University of Virginia, Charlottesville, Va. Manuscripts Department.

Yale University, New Haven, Conn. Beinecke Library. Holds several of Auchincloss' manuscripts.

Yale University, New Haven, Conn. Sterling Library. Gordon Auchincloss Collection; Walter Lippman Collection; Drama Archives; Class of 1939 papers.

BIOGRAPHICAL AND CRITICAL STUDIES

Adams, Robert. "Saturday Night and Sunday Morning." *New York Review of Books,* July 9, 1964, pp. 14–16.

Bryan, C. D. B. "Under the Auchincloss Shell." *New York Times Magazine,* February 11, 1979, pp. 35, 37, 61, 66.

Bryer, Jackson. *Louis Auchincloss and His Critics: A Bibliographical Record.* Boston: G. K. Hall, 1977.

Dahl, Christopher. *Louis Auchincloss.* New York: Ungar, 1986.

Dolbier, Maurice. "Auchincloss' Best Novel." *New York Herald Tribune,* July 13, 1964, p. 23.

Gelderman, Carol. *Louis Auchincloss: A Writer's Life.* New York: Crown, 1993.

Leonard, John. "What Have American Writers Got against Businessmen?" *Forbes,* May 15, 1977, p. 121.

Peterson, Virgilia. "A Crucible Covered with Ivy." *New York Times Book Review,* July 12, 1964, pp. 1, 20.

Piket, Vincent. *Louis Auchincloss; The Growth of a Novelist.* New York: St. Martin's, 1991.

Rosenberg, Scott. "A Double Life in Perfect Balance." *American Lawyer,* February 1983, pp. 42–44.

Tuttleton, James. "The Image of Lost Elegance and Virtue." *American Literature,* 43:616–632 (1972).

Vidal, Gore. "Real Class." *New York Review of Books,* July 18, 1974, pp. 10–11. Reprinted as "The Great World and Louis Auchincloss," in his *Matters of Fact and Fiction.* New York: Random House, 1977. Reprinted in his *United States: Essays 1952–1992,* New York: Random House, 1993.

Wynn, Judith. "Auchincloss the Ambivalent." *Chicago Tribune Books,* January 1, 1995, p. 1.

INTERVIEWS

Lindin, Patricia. "The Museum That Saved the City." *Town and Country,* September 1987, pp. 230–233.

Newquist, Roy. "Louis Auchincloss." In *Counterpoint.* Edited by Roy Newquist. Chicago: Rand McNally, 1965. Pp. 31–38.

Nichols, Lewis. "Talk with Mr. Auchincloss." *New York Times Book Review,* September 27, 1953, p. 28.

———. "Talk with Louis Auchincloss." *New York Times,* October 21, 1956, p. 56.

Piket, Vincent. "An Interview with Louis Auchincloss." *Dutch Quarterly Review of Anglo-American Letters,* 18:20–37 (1988).

Plimpton, George. "Louis Auchincloss: The Art of Fiction CXXXVIII." *Paris Review,* 132:73–94 (Fall 1994).

Ross, Jean. "Auchincloss, An Interview." *Contemporary Authors,* New Revision Series, vol. 29. Detroit: Gale, 1990. Pp. 26–31.

Smith, Dinitia. "The Old Master and the Yuppie." *New York,* August 18, 1986, pp. 30–34.

—CAROL GELDERMAN

Donald Barthelme

1931–1989

THROUGHOUT MOST OF his life, Donald Barthelme presented to the world a perversely contradictory persona. Whether defining his career or creating a new literary form, he defied categorization. His sense of nonconformity also expressed itself in one of his most persistent themes: satirizing writers. He addressed both his colleagues and his audience from a somewhat detached position, earning membership in the community of Manhattan intelligentsia even as he continued to mock the concerns of that community in his fiction. Paradoxically, it was that very vantage point of disengagement, of wary and wretchedly aloof distrust of the earnest, the solemn, and the institutionally approved, which became a seminal element in determining his success as an institutionally approved writer.

Some readers object to Barthelme's humor as trivializing. In his review of Barthelme's collection of short stories *Great Days* (1979), Denis Donaghue likens Barthelme's fiction to "the blowing of dandelion fluff: an inconsequential but not unpleasant way of passing the time." On the other hand, Anatole Broyard finds Barthelme's short story collection *Unspeakable Practices, Unnatural Acts* (1968) "so funny that most readers will never know how serious [Barthelme] is." Charles Molesworth reads Barthelme's characters—comically distressed by their intractable uncertainties—as translations of

forbiddingly erudite literary theory into accessible literary practice: "For [literary theorist Roland] Barthes, 'neither-norism' is a way of defusing desire, of managing an otherwise unknowable world. It is what Barthelme's characters sometimes descend to, what they are often threatened with, and what the author himself is always confronting." Barthelme's sophisticated but wounded skepticism, mingled incongruously with a tragically bemused whimsy, has proven captivating both to readers of the *New Yorker,* which began publishing Barthelme's work in the early 1960s, and to the graduate students of literature who have since the mid-1980s made writing dissertations on Barthelme's work a burgeoning academic industry.

Barthelme was as difficult to place geographically as he was professionally. While growing up in Texas, he cultivated an urbane and bookish wit more suited to Manhattan. Yet, after escaping the cultural confines of Texas to spend most of his adult life on the east coast, he affected cowboy boots in his strolls about Greenwich Village. He was similarly ambiguous in his views of academia. He never managed to complete his undergraduate work at the University of Houston, where his father was a professor, and later, in his novels and his many short stories, he frequently portrayed traditional male academicians (and all other paternal authority figures) as wistful, would-be fascists disseminating more paranoid rumor than useful knowledge. And yet, even as he insulted and indicted intellectuals of all kinds, he went on to win and value the highest accolades academia had to offer. In 1966, a Guggenheim Fellowship award helped him support his family while he finished work on his first novel, *Snow White* (1967); and in 1972 he was honored with a National Institute of Arts and Letters Award. He went on to become a professor himself, teaching without a degree at three major universities, including his father's own University of Houston.

Barthelme felt strongly about many of the subjects he disparages in his fiction. He was, despite his scathing satires of film critics, an enthusiastic filmgoer. As a boy in Texas, he regularly escaped the afternoon heat in the cool darkness of movie houses. As an undergraduate, he reviewed films for the student newspaper. As a much honored, seasoned writer, he reviewed films for the *New Yorker* in the fall of 1979, taking his position as institutionally approved cinema maven quite seriously even as he continued to lampoon art films, their theorists, and their audiences. He began his career as an editor of museum catalogs, yet he has an art critic in *Snow White* doing nothing loftier than assessing the cultural value of shower curtains; he even casts doubt on the aesthetician's qualifications for making pronouncements on this issue. And yet, his last interviews record his own serious attempts to resolve fundamental aesthetic debates.

Barthelme's combined interests in the visual and literary arts can be traced to his early exposure to literature and art in his parents' home. His parents, Donald Barthelme and Helen Bechtold, met at the University of Pennsylvania, where his father was studying architecture and his mother was an English major. Barthelme was born on April 7, 1931, in Philadelphia. When he was two, his parents moved to Houston, where his father began his own architectural firm and, soon after, began teaching at the University of Houston. High and no-so-high art, in both visual and textual form, were strewn about the house. Collections of Norse mythology mingled with the novels of John Dos Passos and *The Subtreasury of American Humor* on the coffee tables. Architects and their students would come and go through the house, talking of Mies van der Rohe. Barthelme's father had designed the house in imitation of one of Mies van der Rohe's tradition-shattering creations, the Tugendhat house in Czechoslovakia; the strangeness of the Barthelme home in the Texas landscape remained one of Barthelme's defining memories. He also recalled the Texas architects' worries that they were too removed from centers of contemporary architectural developments: he told Jerome Klinkowitz that they came together to ask each other, "What was Mies doing, what was Aalto doing." Such fashion-conscious conversations contributed to the family's status as something of an anomaly in Texas in the 1930s, and Barthelme became rather more anomalous among his teen-aged peers when he began reading James Joyce and T. S. Eliot and imitating them in his work for the high-school newspaper.

Barthelme studied journalism in college, became an editor as well as film reviewer for the college paper, and, after dropping out in his junior year in 1951, was able to continue combining his interests in writing and in the visual arts by reporting on cultural events of all kinds for the *Houston Post*. Even after he was drafted in 1953, he continued polishing his writing and editing skills: the army did not need him out in the field, as a truce was signed the day he arrived in Korea, and he was therefore available to edit the army newspaper, first in Korea and later in Japan. Barthelme had little to say about this period in interviews; as an undercredentialed but nonetheless overeducated youth drafted into a suddenly idle army, Barthelme might have been even more out of place in the army than he was among his fellow Texans. But "Thailand" (in *Sixty Stories*, 1981) presents an interesting conversation between an aging Korean veteran (who did see action in the field) and a callow, supercilious aesthete, unhappily trapped in a hospital clinic waiting room, who responds to the old man's reminiscences of battles and memorable furloughs with rude but unspoken comments:

> It's Rest and Recreation where you zip off to Tokyo and sample the delights of that great city for a week.
>
> I am young, thought the listener, young, young, praise the Lord I am young.
>
> ... It was a golden revel, said the sergeant, if you liked curry and I did and do. Beef curry, chicken curry, the delicate Thai worm curry, all your various fish curries and vegetable curries.... [A]nytime I wanted a vehicle of any type for any purpose all I had to do was call Nick and he'd redline that vehicle and send it over to me with a driver—
>
> I too have a life, thought the listener, but it is motes of dust in the air....
>
> The Chinese pulled all these night attacks, said the sergeant.
>
> The babble of God-given senility, said the listener to his inner ear.
>
> It was terrifying. There'd be these terrifying bugles, you'd sit up in your sleeping bag hearing the bugles which sounded like they were coming from every which way, all around you, everybody grabbing his weapon and running around like a chicken with his head cut off, DivArty would be putting down a barrage you could hear it but God knows what they thought they were firing at, your communications trenches would be full of insane Chinese, flares popping in the sky—
>
> I consign you to history, said his hearer. I close, forever, the book.
>
> Once, they wanted to send me to cooks-and-bakers school, said the sergeant who was wearing a dull-red bathrobe, but I told them no, I couldn't feature myself a cook, that's why I was in heavy weapons. This party at Thailand was the high point of that tour. I never before or since saw thirty-seven washtubs full of curry and I would like to go to that country someday and talk to those people some

more, they were great people.... I was on this plane going from Atlanta to Brooke Medical Center in San Antonio, I had to have some scans, there were all these young troopers on the plane, they were all little girls. Looked to be about sixteen. They all had these OD turtlenecks with Class A uniforms if you can imagine, they were the sloppiest soldiers I ever did see, the all-volunteer Army I suppose I know I shouldn't criticize.

> Go to cooks-and-bakers school, bake there, thought the young man. Bake a bathrobe of bread.
>
> Thirty-seven damn washtubs, said the sergeant. If you can imagine.
>
> *Requiescat in pace.*
>
> They don't really have worm curry, said the sergeant. I just made that up to fool you.

The story leaves off there. During his stint in the army, Barthelme would have met many such tale-telling veterans, but perhaps he was less of a snob than the narrator here. The callow youth in this story should have been warned that he was in the presence of a literary artist, one who makes things up to fool the audience, when the old man's vocabulary and syntax waver between the diction of the dirt farmer and that of the gourmand who appreciates a "golden revel" of "delicate curry." The young man thinks he is trapped in this conversation by circumstances, but he is in fact in the thrall of a master narrator, one who directs the young man's responses with as much authority as a film director marshaling his actors.

Barthelme was often accused of elitism, though his own family spanned a broad range of cultural classes, and he regularly returned to Texas to spend time with them. While he often castigates rednecks in his work, he just as often shows a genuine empathy with characters who, like the tale-telling sergeant, would not display well at a Manhattan brunch. In his later years, Barthelme would wander the streets of Greenwich Village and find at least a slight sense of comaraderie with the street people who wrote intriguingly philosophical graffiti on the walls; "We are all writers," he would note.

After being released from service in 1955, Barthelme returned briefly to his reporter's position, but the next year he left the *Post* to work in the University of Houston's public relations office, where he edited a faculty newsletter and wrote speeches for the college president. The formal banalities required by such work did not escape Barthelme's satire. The narrator of Barthelme's story "See the Moon?" (in *Sixty Stories*) takes a similar position working for a college president who is also a retired admiral:

> "Exemplary," the Placement Officer said. "You seem married, mature, malleable, how would you like to affiliate yourself with us here at the old school? We have a spot for a poppycock man, to write the admiral's speeches. Have you ever done poppycock?"
> I said no but maybe I could fake it.
> "Excellent, excellent," the Placement Officer said. "I see you have grasp. And you can sup at the Faculty Club. And there is a ten-percent discount on tickets for all home games."
> The admiral shook my hand. "You will be a credit to us, George," he said. I wrote poppycock, sometimes cockypap. At four o'clock the faculty hoisted the cocktail flag. We drank daiquiris on each other's sterns.

Barthelme supplemented his public relations job with many additional occupations during this period, such as enrolling in philosophy courses, where he developed a particular interest in phenomenology and existentialism. In 1956, he founded and edited a literary magazine, *Forum,* publishing the work of such writers as Alain Robbe-Grillet, Jean-Paul Sartre, and Leslie Fiedler.

Barthelme's reading during the late 1950s is frequently echoed in his early stories. In the early 1960s he became particularly interested in Henri Bergson's theories of time. The past cannot be outrun, in Bergson's view, because the phenomena of the past remain permanent elements in our subjective experience of the world, so that the past perpetually flows into the future. For Bar-

thelme's characters, who almost always have a desire to erase their past lives and start over with a clean slate, this leakage of the past into the future is a form of phenomenological contamination. In Barthelme's story "Will You Tell Me?" (in *Sixty Stories*), the characters find their present lives disrupted by lingering artifacts that attest to their past guilt or ineptitude and compromise their enjoyment of the present moment. Maturing children, like sapling trees grown to fruition, stand both as phenomena to be dealt with at the present moment and as reminders of the past moments of their conception and raising, disallowing any engagement unencumbered by the reverberations of memory. Memory colors the older characters' view of the younger characters, and thus the past continues to burble into the present, which in turn will seep into the future, and none of the characters, no matter how assiduously globe-trotting they become, can escape their own past experiences. Barthelme alerts the reader to the story's serious intentions by describing one of the characters as having been moved to tears by Bergson's philosophy. But, in a manner typical of his work, Barthelme immediately undercuts any sense of earnest philosophical speculation by putting the moment in a mundane perspective:

> Charles started to cry. He had been reading Bergson. He was surprised by his own weeping, and in a state of surprise, decided to get something to eat. Irene was not at home. There was nothing in the refrigerator. What was he going to do for lunch? Go to the drugstore?

The contrast of great emotion, great intellectual work, and a deflating return to the quotidian demands of the body—the mingling of lofty thought with debased physical necessities— appears again a few pages further on in the same story, when he juxtaposes physical appetites and comforts with an entirely unexpected allusion to the phenomenology of Edmund Husserl:

> Inge stretched her right and left arms luxuriously. You have brought me so much marvelous happi-

ness Paul that although I know you will go away soon to consort once more with Hilda, that all-time all-timer girl, it still pleases me to be here in this good Dansk bed with you. Do you want to talk about phenomenological reduction now? or do you want a muffin?

Hilda, the ''all-time all-timer girl,'' represents Paul's social past flowing into and coloring his (and Inge's) experience of the present sexual encounter. Inge's startling equation of philosophical discussion and eating a muffin—presented as equally viable options at this moment—seems incongruous, but on closer reading is an entirely reasonable remark for someone who has been thinking about Husserl's comments on ''phenomenological reduction.'' On the one hand, Husserl tells us, phenomena cannot be examined until the examiner has suspended belief in a material reality and found a plane, or ''epoch,'' where phenomena exist only as objects of thought or subjective experience, not as objects of sensory verification. On the other hand, Husserl later reconsidered what happens at the level of the ''phenomenological epoch''; in particular, he questioned the isolated status of the examiner of phenomena, the ''transcendental ego.'' This entity, Husserl determined in his last lectures, cannot live up to its name. Rather, the transcendental ego must be ''correlative'' to the world and cannot be independent of material reality. What Inge is offering Paul, then, is not merely a joking choice between incongruities, but a choice involving Husserlian theory drawn from different points in Husserl's career. Shall we be transcendent and discuss phenomenological reduction? Or shall we admit that we are correlates of the material world, that we are elemental, body-bound beings who have very much enjoyed sex in this comfortable bed and would now like to eat a muffin?

Barthelme's characters are no more successful at answering such problematic questions than was Husserl, who ended his career questioning all of his earlier work. Looking back on his own generation of writers from the vantage point of the 1980s, Barthelme told J. D. O'Hara, ''Our Song of Songs is The Uncertainty Principle.'' He is alluding here to the work of the twentieth-century mathematician and logician Kurt Gödel, whose uncertainty principle denied the possibility of defining the parameters of a mathematical system from within that system. Literary theorists seized upon this arcane mathematical problem as analogous to that of the literary artist who would, from within the limits of his fictional work, pronounce upon the limits and potentials of the art of fiction. While literary critics deal with these metafictional conundrums at a theoretical level, Barthelme's characters find analogous problems in their daily lives, where problems of uncertainty compromise their ability to make choices or take action of any kind. They cannot see themselves from outside their own subjective prisons; they lack faith not only in an omniscient God but in their own capacity to know anything whatsoever. Parents try to teach their children, but only perpetuate their own bungling errors, born of limited human epistemological capacities. In the title and subject of *The Dead Father*, Barthelme addresses the contemporary state of knowledge and authority:

> Fathers are teachers of the true and not-true, and no father ever knowingly teaches what is not true. In a cloud of unknowing, then, the father proceeds with his instruction. Tough meat should be hammered well between two stones before it is placed on the fire ... Do not forget to clean your rifle barrel immediately. To find honey, tie a feather or straw to the leg of a bee, throw him into the air, and peer alertly after him as he flies slowly back to the hive. ... Satanic operations should not be conducted without first consulting the Bibliothèque Nationale. When Satan at last appears to you, try not to act surprised. Then get down to hard bargaining. If he likes neither the beads nor the books, offer him a cold beer. Then—
>
> Fathers teach much that is of value. Much that is not.

Barthelme borrows the phrase ''cloud of unknowing'' here from the title of a medieval mystic's treatise instructing the reader on how to meet God. The anonymous author notes that union with the divine cannot be achieved until the seeker forgets the distractions of his past sins, forgetting, if not forgiving, his own unworthiness so that he might approach God from within a cloud of unknowing. Barthelme's characters never achieve this grace. Their "unknowing" is not a chosen condition, but an inescapable one.

This situation drives many of his characters mad. Their madness may take the form of incoherent babbling, mindless and rampant sexual profligacy, or tyrannical abuse of anyone who wanders within their reach. The worst form of madness in Barthelme's fiction is that which involves the deluded certainty that knowledge is in fact possible. Those who claim to know anything are categorized with inquisitors, intellectual sadists, and demented academic despots, like the schoolteacher, Miss R., in "The Indian Uprising" (in *Sixty Stories*) who harangues, rather than teaches, her students: " 'You know nothing,' she said, 'you feel nothing, you are locked in a most savage and terrible ignorance, I despise you, my boy, *mon cher,* my heart. You may attend but you must not attend now, you must attend later, a day or a week or an hour, you are making me ill.' "

Barthelme's concern with the dynamics of authority shapes much of his fiction, and finds its most frequent expression in his meditations on the tensions between the artist and antecedent literary giants, the giants whose works formed the curriculum at the University of Houston when he studied there. His experimental literary techniques, while defying traditional classifications established by earlier authors, have become paradigms of postmodern practice, foundations of a new tradition which paradoxically rejects the concept of tradition. His experiments are almost always combinatorial, yoking seemingly incompatible elements into rigorously edited, brief literary pieces which do not fall within any known category. He seems to have gotten the most pleasure out of combining literary and visual elements, as in his combinations of brief, fragmented texts with collages of old engravings. The illustrations often seem only obliquely related to the written material. Typically, Barthelme discourages any critics who would find some hidden meaning in his visual addenda; for example, he claims in the preface to *Guilty Pleasures* (1974) that the stories in these pastiches are nothing more than "pretexts for the pleasure of cutting up and pasting together pictures, a secret vice gone public." However, most commentators on these pieces have ignored Barthelme's comments and gone on to find in the gap between text and picture both a description of postmodern sensibility, and a space for reader participation in the creative process. Maurice Couturier and Régis Durand see possibilities of contemporary psychological and literary representationalism at work in Barthelme's collages:

> In many of these fictions, we find side by side a highly fragmented text and a seemingly random sequence of extravagant pictures which usually have nothing to do (apparently) with the text. We might return to "Brain Damage" [one of the illustrated stories collected in *City Life* (1970)]; here, in a fiction that precisely deals with, or rather simulates, madness . . . [t]he last picture . . . represents a nun with an open umbrella who is partly concealed by the huge breast of a monumental woman. Though a nun is actually mentioned in the story, there is no echo to this scene anywhere. But then, Barthelme seems to suggest, madness ("brain damage") consists essentially in this inability to find coherence in the world: it cannot be described or analyzed properly; it can only be mimicked or mirrored.
>
> It would be wrong, however, totally to naturalize this fiction in psychiatric terms. As we have already said, Barthelme deliberately tries to do away with rhetoric and challenges us to produce our own interpretations. . . . [W]e cannot enjoy [the pictures] passively but are forced to position our eyes properly. We are caught in the pencilled web and seem unable to disentangle ourselves.

Barthelme juxtaposed artistic genres and caught the public eye beginning with his earliest work in the 1960s. In the following quarter century, Barthelme would be hailed as a formative force propelling successive waves of literary experimentation, praised for his startlingly innovative articulations of the Urban Everyman experience, criticized for dehumanizing the human condition with flat and repetitious characterizations, and denounced as an irresponsible trivializer of desperately serious ethical and political debates. While many authors elicit mixed reviews from their readers, few elicit such wildly and fervently disparate responses as Barthelme did, and very few indeed manage to maintain such a large and diverse audience as Barthelme held throughout most of his career. His frequent contributions to the *New Yorker* consistently enhanced the circulation of that popular publication for two decades, appealing to an audience sufficiently literate to notice and accept Barthelme's arcane literary, philosophical, and historical allusions. While maintaining his popular appeal, however, Barthelme was simultaneously assembling a body of work that has in recent years found an increasing audience among literary historians. Doctoral candidates choosing Barthelme as their dissertation subject generally find in Barthelme's work anticipations, applications, or rejections of the specialized theories of Claude Lévi-Strauss, Jacques Lacan, Jacques Derrida, or Jean Baudrillard. Perhaps most of Barthelme's readers would find the doctoral candidates' interpretations of his work as difficult to understand as the theories they apply; one of Barthelme's many gifts was his ability to engage a wide audience in many different ways.

His first published story, "L'Lapse," which appeared in the *New Yorker* in 1963 and was reprinted in *Guilty Pleasures,* combines the genres of short story and dramatic screenplay. It is also remarkably untraditional in its fragmentary nature, beginning after certain events had already transpired and ending on a point of discomfiting irresolution. The story takes the form of a fragment of a screenplay showing us a rambling conversation between two lovers: Marcello, "a wealthy film critic" and "failed poet," and Anna, "a lengthy, elegant beauty, blond, whose extreme nervousness is exteriorized in thumb-sucking." The conversation begins as a tutorial in writing, in a Manhattan apartment that comes to resemble a film set, with Marcello both tutoring and directing Anna in her lines and actions. Barthelme would continue to use such dialogic exchanges in his later work, where the conversations become increasingly difficult to follow. The voices here are clearly identified, and the conversation is relatively linear and coherent. The story is subtitled "A Scenario for Michelangelo Antonioni"; it soon becomes clear that Anna is trying to compose a review of an Antonioni film and that Marcello is teaching her the fundamentals of clichéd commentary:

MARCELLO: Now go on. It's one of the year's ten best, I suppose?

ANNA: One of the year's ten best. Urgent. Sheer cinematic excitement.

MARCELLO: A magnificent, ironic parable?

ANNA: A magnificent ironic parable. Eerily symbolic in intent and effect. Beautiful to watch. (*Inserts thumb*)

MARCELLO: Say something about style.

ANNA: A deft and skillful style full of pictorial chic?

MARCELLO (*moodily*):   Not bad.

ANNA (*without hope*):   An outstanding film for discriminating moviegoers. Does not merely survive repeated visits, it repays them. Original and remarkable. Intellectual suspense, mystery and excitement. A film to see. A film worth seeing. A film of disturbing beauty. Marvelously realized. (*Turns face away*) Oh, Marcello, it's no good. I can't do it. Last night . . .

MARCELLO (*sharply, annoyed*):   I don't want to talk about last night. Now, what about the director?

ANNA: A sensualist with a camera.

MARCELLO: That's very good. Go on. This is a review in depth.

ANNA: A poet with a camera. A philosopher with a camera. Another damn Italian with a camera.

Anna goes on to admit that she found the film boring, and Marcello's defense of the film (he claims that she had been bored by techniques which were, although neither new nor interesting, nonetheless brilliant) fails to elicit the appropriate response. He gives up the argument and instead directs her to act out one of the most common scenes of 1960s' Italian cinema:

MARCELLO: Anna, I think it's time for your walk.

ANNA: My long, long, aimless walk? Marcello, I don't want to go today.

MARCELLO (*slowly,* con amore):   Anna, you must. It's a convention.

ANNA (*thumb*):   Will there be meaningless incidents?

MARCELLO (*bored again*):   One assumes.

ANNA: A little girl playing with a balloon?

MARCELLO: Undoubtedly.

ANNA: An old man with a terrible lined face reading an Armenian newspaper?

MARCELLO: Wasn't he there yesterday?

ANNA (*despair*):   Of course. Of course.

(*Shot of empty street with man lurking in doorway. Is it Orson Welles? No, unfortunately, it is not Orson Welles. Shot of electricity lurking in wall outlet. Shot of hoarding advertising* Sodom and Gomorrah. *Shot of I beams stacked randomly in field. Shot of empty benches in park. Medium shot of tree branches afflicted with Memling's Rot.*)

Anna's walk does not cheer her. We learn that she is depressed not by her listless response to the film, but because she and Marcello have

proven themselves unchic: unlike the characters in the Italian films that dazzled most American film critics in the early 1960s, Anna and Marcello seem unable to avoid successful—but most unfashionable—communication with each other. In Anna and Marcello's world, all fashionable life imitates Antonioni's cinematic art, or the art of other Italians imitating Antonioni, or other *auteurs* imitating the Italians who are imitating Antonioni. Anna and Marcello carry this fashion—art imitating art—into their own lives. They feel obliged not only to admire Italian films, but to translate that brand of cinematic reality into their own reality, creating a reality which imitates art imitating art. Manhattan becomes in this story an entirely rhetorical, unreal city, where written clichés and cinematic clichés engender infinite copies of the always already clichéd original copy. All currently fashionable artistic gestures, whether visual or verbal, refer here only to other, precedent artistic gestures. But Anna and Marcello find each other's comments entirely too firmly linked to an intelligible, meaningful universe outside the confines of cinematic celluloid:

ANNA: It's so *déclassé*. I can't bear it. (*Reinserts thumb*)

MARCELLO: It's my fault. I have a tendency to make myself clear. I mean . . .

ANNA (*bitterly*):   I *know* what you mean.

. . . .

ANNA: Marcello, *why* do we communicate? Why you and me? Last night, when we *talked* to each other . . . I couldn't bear it. Why can't we be like other people? Why can't we spend our time in mindless eroticism, like everybody else?

MARCELLO (*hangs head*):   I don't know.

ANNA: Last night when we were talking about pure cinema, and I called for a transvaluation of all values, and you said that light was the absence of light—we weren't communicating then, were we? It was just jargon, wasn't it? Just noise?

MARCELLO (*facing the truth*):   No, Anna, I'm afraid we *were* communicating. On a rather low level.

ANNA (*frenzied, all thumbs*):   I want my life to be *really* meaningless. Like in that film. Such boredom! Such emptiness! Such febrile elegance! It was penetratingly different, a magnificent ironic parable, one of the year's ten best! *Marcello!*

MARCELLO: Meaninglessness like that is not for everybody. Not for you and me, *cara.*

The screenplay/story ends with Anna and Marcello's problem unresolved, in the manner of one of Antonioni's films. The story thus imitates another work of art, but it also undermines that imitation by clearly describing, with some comic distortion, a real situation in a real city, subtly critiquing the real inhabitants of Manhattan, who are here tweaked for their unreflecting devotion to current cultural vogue.

Communicating even the most mundane, ordinary sorts of truth becomes, in the aesthetic theories of the twentieth century, as problematic as describing the face of God. In the early years of Barthelme's career, many artists surrendered the attempt to describe nature; the conventional languages of the arts, visual and verbal, began to seem inadequate to convey either reality itself or the artist's experience of that reality. Art seemed capable of describing only other art; the artist's profession seemed limited to alluding in an incestuously intertextual manner to the work of other artists. One of Barthelme's narrators tries to find something to celebrate in this situation. In "Sentence" (in *Forty Stories,* 1987) the narrator tries to show us the inside of his own mind, rattling off a stream of thoughts in one long, unbroken sentence which he offers as a portrait of his own subjective consciousness, the one kind of nature he feels qualified to describe with confidence. He must admit in the end that his sentence is of only limited and temporary meaning to the reader, unlike the more permanent cre-

ations of God himself. He has thus failed as an artist. However, he attempts to valorize that very failure when he concludes that "the sentence itself is a man-made object, not the one we wanted of course, but still a construction of man, a structure to be treasured for its weakness, as opposed to the strength of stones."

A review of Barthelme's stories and novels will show him treasuring the work of other writers, even as he seems to be denying their validity. He quite deliberately and obviously lifts images, quotes, characters, and concepts from his favorite literary works, twists and crops and upends them, and calls the result his own. He baldly announces these pieces as revisions of earlier stories, playing with combinations of genres ranging from folk legend (see "Bluebeard," in *Forty Stories*) to Christian hagiography ("The Temptation of St. Anthony," also in *Forty Stories*), children's literature (see *Snow White;* "The Glass Mountain," in *City Life;* and "The Sandman," reprinted in *Sixty Stories*), and the nineteenth-century novel ("Eugénie Grandet," in *Sixty Stories*). Full appreciation of Barthelme's other stories often depends upon the reader recognizing them as revisions of specific authorial styles or individual works, as when he parodies James Joyce's prose style in "For I'm the Boy" or when he updates T. S. Eliot's *The Waste Land* (1922) in his own story "Will You Tell Me?" (both stories reprinted in *Sixty Stories*). Barthelme's most extended borrowings occur in his novels. He appropriates and revises the basic plot in William Faulkner's *As I Lay Dying* (1930) in his own novel *The Dead Father* (1975), for instance, and rewrites Thomas Malory's fifteenth-century revision (*Le Morte Darthur*) of twelfth-century revisions of fifth-century Arthurian legends in *The King* (1990), in which Arthur and his knights have been temporally dislocated to London during the Blitz. Some of his most startling reworkings form the basis of his shorter works, however, as when he weirdly but effectively combines characters and settings from *The Bobbsey Twins* series of children's books with direct quotes from Ernest Hemingway's "The Short Happy Life of Francis Macomber" (1936) to create an undeniably derivative but nonetheless entirely astonishing effect in the two-page story "Then."

As Barthelme settled into his career as a new kind of chronicler of Manhattan city life, he was surrounded by artists concerned with two problems: the apparent death of representational art, and their own sense of belatedness in the canons of Western literary and visual arts. The 1960s saw a mushrooming of anxiety over these issues. As Barthelme's friend and colleague John Barth would pronounce in his 1967 essay "The Literature of Exhaustion," artists who would accommodate the conventional expectations of the novel reader (or, by extension, the film or museum audience) could, given the enormous body of works that substantiate contemporary conventions, no longer hope to avoid repeating what had already been done. Art in the latter decades of the twentieth century seemed to develop an ironic preoccupation with its own workings.

Art that refers only to other art is ironic in its admission of its own limitations, and it may in that sense be compared to the phenomenon of "self-consuming artifacts," which the literary critic Stanley Fish began writing about in the 1960s. But in "L'Lapse," Barthelme layers his ironies with the suggestion that even fashionable irony can be taken only so far before it collapses upon itself in onanistic self-absorption. (Barthelme once remarked to Lois Gordon that "Irony is like masturbation." Yet, in his most widely read and quoted nonfiction essay, "Not-Knowing," he denounces other critics who use this simile to denounce postmodern fiction.) "L'Lapse" parodies Antonioni, but it also parodies itself. This complex layering might be expected to make the story unpalatable to a popular audience, but Barthelme designed the story to seduce even those readers disinclined to wrestle with such convoluted considerations: the story offers absolution to any moviegoer who ever found an art film boring, and it makes them laugh while being absolved. He continued to combine these techniques in almost all of his future work, writing stories and novels which meditate upon the difficulties of writing stories and novels, and moving his audience to relieved laughter at the absurd consequences of such overly self-obsessed meditations.

Barthelme was at least slightly obsessed not only with problems of postmodern aesthetics, but also with the problematics of the parent-child relationship, a relationship his narrators usually find to be as self-reflexive as the most omphalo-skeptic of aesthetic disquisitions. Barthelme's fathers and sons become mirror reflections of each other, despite all efforts to break the cycle of familial influence. Barthelme usually depicts the anxieties of parental influence as intolerable to all concerned parties. His fictional families feel lucky to have avoided murdering each other. His fathers and mothers are typical of the new generation of parents coming to power in the 1960s, a generation determined to avoid the errors of their predecessors. In the novel *Snow White,* Barthelme parodies those predecessors, the now-supplanted parents who raised their children by the book, consulting texts written by pathologically authoritarian child psychologists. In this drastically revised version of the Snow White fairy tale, the seven dwarves are attending a most unpleasant party (very like the children's party in the disturbing pastiche "Then") in which the festivities are governed and made nightmarish by mysterious but universally known party-behavior rules. The dwarves are attending the party because of a vague but imperative social rule that requires their attendance. In addition to the general strictures applying to all the guests, Paul, one of the dwarves, has subscribed to a monastic rule of silence before attending the party:

Paul came to the party in his robes. He wasn't allowed to eat or drink anything, or say anything. That was the Rule. We went to the howling party sitting primly along the side of the room in a row, the seven of us and Snow White. Our social intercourse for the quarter. We discussed the bat theory of child-raising with the mothers there meanwhile paying attention to a vat of rum under the harpsichord. Edward [another of the dwarves] didn't want to discuss the bat theory of child-raising (delicate memories) so he discussed Harald Bluetooth, a king of Scandinavia during a certain period, the Bluetooth period. But the mothers wanted to talk. "Spare the bat and the child rots," said the mothers. "Rots inside." "But how do you know when to employ it? The magic moment?" "We have a book which tells us such things," the mothers said. "We look it up in the book. On page 331 begins a twelve-page discussion of batting the baby. A well-worn page." We got away from those mothers as fast as we could.

What Barthelme's characters discover, however, is that authoritarianism cannot be avoided. Edward tries to talk about something else, moving from a discussion of parental authoritarianism to a new subject, Harald Bluetooth. But Harald Bluetooth, according to historians of tenth-century Scandinavia, was himself one of those abusive medieval tyrants who, after his own conversion to the Christian religion and its doctrines of mercy and forgiveness, violently forced all the citizens of his country to accept those gentle doctrines. Similarly, Barthelme's fictional parents, trying to avoid the textually authorized violence of earlier schools of parental techniques, find themselves committing another kind of violence in order to enforce the new rules of nonviolence. In *Forty Stories'* "The Baby," an earnestly well-intentioned father has been reading the new child-rearing manuals published in the 1960s, when child-batting was not the technique of choice. But the children in Barthelme's stories are much more powerful than their fathers have been led to expect. He maps his parent-child interactions around comically distressing images

of destruction. The rules detailed in the new manuals are inadequate for meeting with the hostility even toddlers are capable of:

> The first thing the baby did wrong was to tear pages out of her books. So we made a rule that each time she tore a page out of a book she had to stay alone in her room for four hours, behind the closed door. . . . I began to get a little worried. When I added up her indebtedness, in terms of hours, I could see that she wasn't going to get out of her room until 1992, if then. Also, she was looking pretty wan. She hadn't been to the park in weeks. We had more or less of an ethical crisis on our hands.
>
> I solved it by declaring that it was *all right* to tear pages out of books, and moreover, that it was all right to *have torn* pages out of books in the past. That is one of the satisfying things about being a parent—you've got a lot of moves, each one good as gold. The baby and I sit happily on the floor, side by side, tearing pages out of books, and sometimes, just for fun, we go out on the street and smash a windshield together.

There are no rule books available to tell fathers how to avoid imposing rules upon children; books *are* rules, in Barthelme's fiction, whether the books are child-rearing manuals or great Russian novels which defy follow-up efforts by lesser, later authors. In this story, it is the child who teaches the father, and the lesson is that the first thing we must do is destroy all the books.

The conflicts that figure so large in Barthelme's descriptions of family life are sometimes mere skirmishes, and sometimes expressed merely as silent thoughts. In some cases, violence is only potential, visible only in Barthelme's choice of similes or metaphors, as when one of his more beleaguered narrators offers his son a cautionary analogy to be remembered when the son comes to the age of fatherhood himself. Just as the book-mangling father in "The Baby" arrives at a truly radical form of revolution against the traditions of child-rearing, so does the father in "See the Moon?" (in *Sixty Stories*), who advises not a new way of raising children, but a cessation of procreation altogether. When you begin to consider fatherhood, he instructs his son, consider again:

> What you don't understand is, it's like somebody walks up to you and says, I have a battleship I can't use, would you like to have a battleship? And you say, yes yes, I've never had a battleship, I've always wanted one. And he says, it has four sixteen-inch guns forward, and a catapult for launching scout planes. And you say, I've always wanted to launch scout planes. And he says, *it's yours,* and then you have this battleship. And then you have to paint it, because it's rusting, and clean it, because it's dirty, and anchor it somewhere, because the Police Department wants you to get it off the streets. And the crew is crying, and there are silverfish in the chartroom and a funny knocking noise in Fire Control, water rising in the No. 2 hold, and the chaplain can't find the Palestrina tapes for the Sunday service. And you can't get anybody to sit with it. And finally you discover that what you have here is this great, big, pink-and-blue rockabye *battleship.*

The battleship is a bother, a large lump of metal with many attendant obligations. But the possibilities for violence inherent in this currently lumpen battleship are undeniable. Such a battleship/child, cared for in the manner implied above and allowed to reach maturity, might in taking command of its own bridge be quite likely to turn the forward guns back against the volubly inconvenienced father.

Another of Barthelme's fictional fathers is more explicit in describing the rancor motivating the most daily of domestic dramas. In "Critique de la Vie Quotidienne" (in *Sixty Stories*), a father recalls how his child rejected parental fiat by turning his own body into a weapon:

> "If you insist on overburdening the bed," we said, "you must sleep at the bottom, with the feet." "But I don't want to sleep with the feet," the child said. "Sleep with the feet," we said, "they won't hurt you." "The feet kick," the child said, "in the middle of the night." "The feet or the floor," we said. "Take your choice." "Why can't I sleep with

the heads," the child asked, "like everybody else?" "Because you are a child," we said, and the child subsided, whimpering, the final arguments in the case having been presented and the verdict in. But in truth the child was not without recourse; it urinated in the bed, in the vicinity of the feet. "God damn it," I said, inventing this formulation at the instant of need. "What the devil is happening, at the bottom of the bed?" "I couldn't help it," the child said. "It just came out." "I forgot to bring the plastic sheet," Wanda said. "Holy hell," I said. "Is there to be no end to this *family life?*"

> I spoke to the child and the child spoke to me and the merest pleasantry trembled with enough animus to bring down an elephant.

In many of Barthelme's stories, such discordant moments seem to grow naturally and inevitably out of the human condition, a poorly planned situation in which men are doomed to varying degrees of discomfort simply by their participation in the natural cycles of courtship, marriage, and reproduction. One of the dwarves in *Snow White* worries that his own cycle of failure to achieve happiness is a biological, not a personally engineered, fate: "It is almost as if we were designed that way. As if that were part of the cosmic design."

The Dead Father, Barthelme's longest meditation on the problem of cyclically unsuccessful human relationships, lists several varieties of "mad fathers," including one subcategory that consists of those who "have been driven to distraction by the intricacies of living with others." Just as two of Snow White's dwarves conclude that withdrawal is the way to avoid conflict, and just as the father in "See the Moon?" concludes that refusing to procreate would have been his best choice, so the protagonist of *The Dead Father* ends his advice to sons on a nihilistic note. Barthelme's narrator concludes that section of the novel with a proposal for the future improvement of the human condition, but the only improvement he can conceive is a repudiation of everything that makes life worth living. The proposal, imbued with a comic futility recalling Jonathan Swift, perpetuates the same military images that thread through so many of Barthelme's family romances. Sons are not to be battleship commanders in the future, but something both less domineering and less significant:

> Patricide: Patricide is a bad idea, first because it is contrary to law and custom and second because it proves, beyond a doubt, that the father's every fluted accusation against you was correct: you are a thoroughly bad individual, a patricide!—member of a class of persons universally ill-regarded. It is all right to feel this hot emotion, but not to act upon it. And it is not necessary. It is not necessary to slay your father, time will slay him, that is a virtual certainty. Your true task lies elsewhere.
>
> Your true task, as a son, is to reproduce every one of the enormities touched upon in this manual, but in attenuated form. You must become your father, but a paler, weaker version of him. The enormities go with the job, but close study will allow you to perform the job less well than it has previously been done, thus moving toward a golden age of decency, quiet, and calmed fevers. Your contribution will not be a small one, but ''small'' is one of the concepts that you should shoot for. If your father was a captain in Battery D, then content yourself with a corporalship in the same battery. Do not attend the annual reunions. Do not drink beer or sing songs at the reunions. Begin by whispering, in front of a mirror, for thirty minutes a day. Then tie your hands behind your back for thirty minutes a day, or get someone else to do this for you. Then, choose one of your most deeply held beliefs, such as the belief that your honors and awards have something to do with you, and abjure it. Friends will help you abjure it, and can be telephoned if you begin to backslide. You see the pattern, put it into practice. *Fatherhood can be, if not conquered, at least ''turned down'' in this generation*—by the combined efforts of all of us together.

The damaged son speaking here locates the origin of all forms of human achievement—but particularly those in literature and the military—in the testosterone-based aggression and self-aggrandizement typical of the patriarchal figures marching destructively through Barthelme's novels and stories. While traditional male behaviors are condemned in the despairing cri de coeur of this bleak proposal, it should be noted that women have no place whatsoever in this system. Women form an entirely separate set of problems for Barthelme's male protagonists.

Barthelme published many satirical portraits of feminists, and many portraits of cuckolded and emasculated men, men drained of all energy by their interactions with competitive and aggressive women. Paul, the monastic dwarf voluntarily submitting to a rule of silence, has been driven to this extremity by his relationship with Snow White, whom Barthelme has rewritten as a coldly unappealing character. While the original Snow White happily served as housemaid to the dwarves, Barthelme's Snow White is a liberated nymphomaniac who requires seven enslaved dwarves to satisfy her sexual desires and run errands for her. The dwarves' leader, Bill, responds like the dwarf-monk Paul, not merely avoiding Snow White, but avoiding all human contact:

> Bill can't bear to be touched. That is new too. To have anyone touch him is unbearable. Not just Snow White but also Kevin, Edward, Hubert, Henry, Clem or Dan [the other dwarves]. That is a peculiar aspect of Bill, the leader. We speculate that he doesn't want to be involved in human situations any more. A withdrawal.

Feminism always poisons heterosexual relations in Barthelme's work, yet Barthelme is not entirely unsympathetic to Snow White's plight. She finds herself in a transition period where women are technically freed but not welcomed in their new freedom. She hangs her hair out the window (borrowing from another fairy tale), but no one responds to this invitation. ''No one has come to climb up,'' she remarks after a time. ''That says it all. This time is the wrong time for me. I am in the wrong time.''

Twenty years after writing *Snow White*, Barthelme wrote another novel, *Paradise* (1986), in which the sexual situation is reversed. In this novel, it is the male character who is living in the wrong time. Simon, an architect having a midlife crisis, finds himself separated from his wife and living in a Manhattan apartment with three female out-of-towners who cook and clean and sleep with him in between job-hunting forays. The women initially planned to stay only until they established themselves in careers and apartments of their own, but the temporary arrangement becomes informally permanent as time passes. The architect is astonished at his luck, early in the novel: he seems to be realizing every fantasy he ever had while living with his wife in Philadelphia. But his dreams have come true too late. He is too old to satisfy the women sexually and too damaged emotionally to satisfy them on any other level:

> Dore will come in and demand to know where my penis has got to. I don't know, I'll say, it was there yesterday, more or less. You call that *there,* she'll say, scornfully, and I'll say, I am a poor relic, a poor husk, a leftover, a single yellow bean covered with Cling Wrap sailing on a flawed plate through the refrigerator of life. Yes, she'll say, excuses, you promised us Eden, you did, I remember, not anything you said in so many words but by implication, you implied that we would be happy forever together . . . I didn't! I'll say, or scream, I always said that things would turn out badly, consult the records, look at the transcript, you have no right to—

Simon is temporally dislocated in this living arrangement, just as Snow White is in the earlier novel. Women have changed, and he has not changed along with them—he has simply become a more decrepit version of his original self, one burdened with age and its weight of leaking, seeping Bergsonian experience. He is beset with health problems, and he is tortured by a nostalgia so great as to cripple him in his new relationships. He broods upon his preference for outmoded ar-

chitectural techniques, and the following meditation can be read as his comment on changing cultural values and the problems they pose not just for aging architects, but for aging lovers tragically displaced in their own fantasies of sexual freedom: "He himself had settled for being a competent, sometimes inventive architect with a tragic sense of brick. Brick was his favorite material as the fortress was the architectural metaphor that he had, more and more, to resist. To force himself into freshness, he thought about bamboo."

In Barthelme's work after 1975, it becomes increasingly the case that his narrators cannot keep up with changing mores, and their relapses into nostalgic fits of cultural atavism become more frequent. This tendency in content parallels a tendency in the form of Barthelme's work. His interest in experimental narrative structures seems to have peaked near the end of the 1970s, and his novels in the 1980s present the reader with relatively linear, coherent narratives. In his last novel, Barthelme resorts to allegory, the long-outdated brick fortress of the Western literary tradition. *The King,* which was published posthumously, is structured entirely around a single allegorical parallel drawn between the Arthurian Holy Grail and the twentieth century's nuclear bomb. In addition to availing himself of a quite traditional literary technique, Barthelme indulges his characters in a good bit of traditional misogyny and maintains the central fact of the original Arthurian legend—that the fall of Arthurian society was brought about by a woman's outsized sexual appetite.

While Barthelme's female characters are often injurious to their male lovers, and while his fictional children are always hostile to their parents, Barthelme invites his readers to laugh at his perplexed narrators, rather than to despair with them. While some readers take issue with Barthelme's use of female characters, and some insist on using Barthelme's work as a basis for psychoanalytic analyses of the author's pathologies, many readers find Barthelme's candidly unembarrassed characterizations refreshing. His barbed satires are unsparing and universal, and his literary creations include many writers and other artists made laughably ineffectual not so much by their sexual histories as by the grindingly, oppressively general facts of urban life in the twentieth century. In all but his most obscure works, Barthelme speaks in a voice many readers recognize and cherish. After Barthelme's death, from throat cancer, ''The Talk of the Town'' (the *New Yorker,* August 14, 1989) quoted a colleague lamenting Barthelme's passing as a personal loss:

> He always seemed to be writing about my trashiest thoughts and my night fears and my darkest secrets, but he understood them better than I did, and he seemed to find them sweeter and classier than I ever could. For a long time, I felt I was going to be all right as long as he was around and writing. Having him for a friend was the greatest compliment of my life.

Thomas Pynchon agreed with this acute assessment of Barthelme's appeal. Barthelme's most experimental works still manage, with or without coherent plots, to convey a sensibility his readers can understand from their own experience. He conveys thoughts or moods the reader has met alone in the night. In writing his preface to *The Teachings of Don B.* (1992), a posthumous publication of Barthelme's uncollected writings, Pynchon praises Barthelme as one of the rare writers ''who know instinctively how to stash the merchandise, bamboozle the inspectors, and smuggle their nocturnal contraband right on past the checkpoints of daylight 'reality.' ''

The praise Barthelme received from Pynchon and other colleagues should remind us not to assume that Barthelme's parodic treatment of intellectuals in his fiction bespeaks a personal disregard for his fellow artists. Art of all kinds played a prominent role in Barthelme's life, including religious art. His sacrilegious parodies

only confirm his abiding concern with the experience and artistic expression of religious doubts and certitudes. He depicts nuns, priests, and monks as clowns, unreflecting robots, or sinners, and he once remarked that he thought he did his best writing on Sunday, a day of rest for the observant, precisely because he was a lapsed Catholic; despite his disavowals, however, his Catholic education shapes his characters' views of the cosmos throughout his work. One character wonders about the necessity of Christ's being crucified on each individual inhabited planet in the universe. In ''The Photographs'' (in *Guilty Pleasures*), two scientists find proof of the existence of a human soul, en route to Heaven, photographed in flight near the planet Jupiter. In *Forty Stories'* ''Lightning,'' a character interviews people who have been struck by lightning, hoping to find proof of God in their memories of these events. One of the few Barthelme characters whose life is described as enviable is one of the lightning victims, an elderly monk who spends his post-lightning days gardening and listening to radio rock stations on his Walkman:

> Proudly he showed Connors the small device with its delicate earphones. ''A special dispensation. I guess they figured I was near-to-dead, therefore it was all right to bend the Rule a bit. I simply love it. Have you heard the Cars?'' Standing in a beet field with the brown-habited monk Connors felt the depth of the man's happiness and wondered if he himself ought to rethink his attitude toward Christianity. It would not be so bad to spend one's days pulling beets in the warm sun while listening to the Cars and then retire to one's cell at night to read St. Augustine and catch up on Rod Stewart and the B-52s.

The monk's incongruous taste in music makes him another comic character; the theological weight of this passage is further compromised by its resemblance to the urbanely condescending fantasies of bucolic banality that appear so often in ''The Talk of the Town'' column in the *New Yorker,* a column Barthelme frequently contributed to. Nonetheless, when viewed in the context of Barthelme's work as a whole, this passage takes on a certain poignancy, a remembrance of past comforts and simplicities. A lapsed theologian in "January" (in *Forty Stories*) echoes this sentiment: "I can do without certitude. I would have liked to have had faith."

At the end of his career, Barthelme remained silent on the future of literature, admitting that his silence grew from ignorance. He could not see where literature was going next, after the postmodernist rejection of tradition. His own experiments had become traditions in their own right, and he objected to critics who had begun to treat his work as an object of historical research. He feared that, for all his experimentalism, he had in fact become the thing he had been rebelling against: the intellectual father to be diminished into a footnote by the next generation of writers. But the critics writing of Barthelme in recent years have continued praising, not belittling, his work. Attempting to summarize Barthelme's achievements, Lance Olsen writes in "Slumgullions" that Barthelme's oeuvre exemplifies "postmodern fiction that writes new scripts both using and abusing the old in order to represent, as Jean-François Lyotard puts it, a stronger sense of the unpresentable." Barthelme's fiction has been echoed in the works of a new generation of writers in the 1990s. The novelist Oscar Hijuelos, one of Barthelme's former students, remembers him not as one of the oppressive, demented, failed pedagogues Barthelme wrote of so often, but as an inspiring teacher, a "word man" and "lover of language." After his death, his colleagues at the *New Yorker* reviewed Barthelme's work more kindly than Barthelme did himself; in "The Talk of the Town" (August 14, 1989), they found that he had in fact managed to transcend the aesthetic problems he found so dismaying, and that even the most absurdly startling utterances of his apparently "brain-damaged" characters "were set down in a manner that magically carried memories and meanings and overtones, bringing them intact to the page, where they let loose (in the reader) a responding instinctive flood of recognition, irony, and sadness." It would seem, then, that Barthelme had succeeded in communicating with his readers, even as he denied the possibility of such success.

Selected Bibliography

WORKS OF DONALD BARTHELME

NOVELS

Snow White. New York: Atheneum, 1967; New York: Bantam, 1968; London: Jonathan Cape, 1968; London: Panther, 1971.

The Dead Father. New York: Farrar, Straus and Giroux, 1975; New York: Pocket, 1976; London: Routledge & Kegan Paul, 1977; New York: Penguin, 1986.

Paradise. New York: Putnam, 1986; New York: Penguin, 1987.

Sam's Bar: An American Landscape. Illustrations by Seymour Chwast. New York: Doubleday/Dolphin, 1987.

The King. New York: Harper & Row, 1990; London: Secker and Warburg, 1991.

SHORT STORY COLLECTIONS

Come Back, Dr. Caligari. Boston: Little, Brown, 1964; Garden City, New York: Doubleday, 1965; London: Eyre & Spottiswode, 1966.

Unspeakable Practices, Unnatural Acts. New York: Farrar, Straus and Giroux, 1968; New York: Bantam, 1969; London: Jonathan Cape, 1969; New York: Pocket, 1976.

City Life. New York: Farrar, Straus and Giroux, 1970; New York: Bantam, 1971; London: Jonathan Cape, 1971; New York: Pocket, 1976.

Sadness. New York: Farrar, Straus and Giroux, 1972; London: Jonathan Cape, 1973; New York: Bantam, 1974.

Guilty Pleasures. New York: Farrar, Straus and Giroux, 1974; New York: Delta, 1976.

Amateurs. New York: Farrar, Straus and Giroux, 1976; London: Routledge & Kegan Paul, 1977.

Great Days. New York: Farrar, Straus and Giroux, 1979; London: Routledge & Kegan Paul, 1979; New York: Pocket, 1980.

Sixty Stories. New York: Putnam, 1981; New York: Dutton, 1982; London: Secker and Warburg, 1989.

Overnight to Many Distant Cities. New York: Putnam's, 1983; New York: Penguin, 1985.

Forty Stories. New York: Putnam, 1987; New York: Penguin, 1989; London: Secker and Warburg, 1988; London: Futura, 1989.

The Teachings of Don B. New York: Random, 1992.

UNCOLLECTED STORIES

"Man's Face." *New Yorker,* May 30, 1964, p. 29.

"Then." *Mother,* 3:22–23 (November–December 1964). Reprinted in *Review of Contemporary Fiction* 11:34–35 (Summer 1991).

"Philadelphia." *New Yorker,* November 30, 1968, pp. 56–58.

"Newsletter." *New Yorker,* July 11, 1970, p. 23.

"Adventure." *Harper's Bazaar,* December 1970, pp. 92–95.

"The Story Thus Far." *New Yorker,* May 1971, pp. 42–45.

"Natural History." *Harper's,* August 1971, pp. 44–45.

"Three." *Fiction,* 1(1):13 (1972).

"Edwards, Amelia." *New Yorker,* September 9, 1972, pp. 34–36.

"A Man." *New Yorker,* December 30, 1972, pp. 26–27.

"The Inauguration." *Harper's,* January 1973, pp. 86–87.

"The Bed." *Viva,* 1:68–70 (March 1974).

"The Dassaud Prize." *New Yorker,* January 12, 1976, pp. 26–29.

"Momma." *New Yorker,* October 2, 1978, pp. 32–33.

"Kissing the President." *New Yorker,* August 1, 1983, p. 31.

"Affection." *New Yorker,* November 7, 1983, pp. 45–47.

"The Author." *New Yorker,* June 15, 1987, p. 27.

"Tickets." *New Yorker,* March 6, 1989, p. 32.

CHILDREN'S FICTION

The Slightly Irregular Fire Engine; or, The Hithering Thithering Djinn. New York: Farrar, Straus and Giroux, 1971.

LIMITED EDITIONS

Here in the Village. Northridge, Calif.: Lord John Press, 1978. 325 copies, with a frontispiece collage by Barthelme.

The Emerald. Los Angeles: Sylvester & Orphanos, 1980. 330 copies; story reprinted in *Sixty Stories,* 389–417.

Presents. Dallas: Pressworks, 1980. 375 copies, with collages by Barthelme.

Young Oriental Bride. Northridge, Calif.: Lord John Press, 1980. 330 copies.

ESSAYS AND COMMENTARY

Introduction to *Architectural Graphics* [exhibition catalog]. Houston: Contemporary Arts Museum, April 1960.

The Emerging Figure (exhibition catalog). Houston: Contemporary Arts Museum, May–June 1961.

Ways and Means (exhibition catalog). Houston: Contemporary Arts Museum, October–November 1961.

"The Case of the Vanishing Product." *Harper's,* October 1961, pp. 30–32.

"After Joyce." *Location,* 1:13–16 (Summer 1964).

"The Tired Terror of Graham Greene" (review of *The Comedians*). *Holiday,* 39:146, 148–149 (April 1966).

"The Elegance is Under Control" (review of John Kenneth Galbraith's *The Triumph*). *New York Times Book Review,* April 21, 1968, pp. 4–5.

Preface, *she: 3 December 1970 to 16 January 1971* (exhibition catalog). New York: Cordier & Ekstrom, 1970.

Untitled commentary on "Paraguay." In *Writer's Choice.* Edited by Rust Hills. New York: David McKay, 1974. Pp. 25–26.

"Robert Morris." In *Robert Morris: Feb. 10–Mar. 6, 1976* (exhibition catalog). New York: Washburn Gallery, 1976. Pp. 3–4.

"A Symposium on Fiction" (with William H. Gass, Grace Paley, and Walker Percy). *Shenandoah,* 27:3–31. (Winter 1976).

"Current Cinema." *New Yorker,* September 10, 1979, pp. 120–122; September 17, 1979, pp. 132–134; September 24, 1979, pp. 132–133; October 1, 1979, pp. 103–105; October 8, 1979, pp. 164–166; October 15, 1979, pp. 182–184.

"The Most Wonderful Trick" (on John Hawkes). *New York Times Book Review,* November 25, 1984, p. 3.

"Appreciation by Donald Barthelme." In *Robert*

Rauschenberg: Work from Four Series, a Sesquicentennial Exhibition (exhibition catalog). Houston: Contemporary Arts Museum, 1985.

"Not-Knowing." *Georgia Review,* 39:509–522 (Fall 1985).

One + One: Collaborations of Artists and Writers. Written with Janet Landay. Houston: Glassell School of Art, Museum of Fine Art–Houston, 1988.

BIBLIOGRAPHIES

Klinkowitz, Jerome. "Donald Barthelme: A Checklist, 1957–1974." *Critique: Studies in Modern Fiction* 16, no. 3:49–58 (1975).

Klinkowitz, Jerome, Asa B. Pieratt Jr., and Robert Murray Davis. *Donald Barthelme: A Comprehensive Bibliography and Annotated Secondary Checklist.* Hamden, Conn.: Archon, 1977.

McCaffery, Larry. "Donald Barthelme, Robert Coover, William H. Gass: Three Checklists," *Bulletin of Bibliography,* 31:101–106 (July–September 1974).

Weisenburger, Steven. "Donald Barthelme: A Bibliography." *The Review of Contemporary Fiction,* 11:108–113 (Summer 1991).

See also the ample citations in the book-length critical studies listed below by Bruss, Couturier, Gordon, Kuehl, Maltby, Molesworth, Roe, Stengel, Trachtenberg, and Wilde.

AUDIO RECORDINGS

Come Back, Dr. Caligari. Cassette 114. Deland, Fla.: Everett/Edwards, 1970.

Donald Barthelme. BC 2720.01, 2720.02, 2720.03, and 2720.04. North Hollywood, Calif.: Pacifica Radio Archive, 1976. Four-audiocassette set. Barthelme reads selections from *The Dead Father, Snow White, City Life, The Slightly Irregular Fire Engine, Come Back, Dr. Caligari*; he also discusses his own writing and teaching practices.

"Donald Barthelme." *Six Interviews.* Washington, D.C.: Tapes for Readers, 1978. Audiocassette.

New Sounds in American Fiction. Edited and introduced by Gordon Lish. Cummings 51612. Menlo Park, Calif.: New Sounds, 1969. Barthelme reads "The Piano Player."

Selected Shorts: A Celebration of the Short Story. New York: National Public Radio, 1989. Audiocassette no. 2.

BIOGRAPHICAL AND CRITICAL STUDIES

Achilles, Jochen. "Donald Barthelme's Aesthetic of Inversion: Caligari's Come-Back as Caligari's Leave-Taking." *Journal of Narrative Technique,* 12:105–120 (Spring 1982).

Aldridge, John W. "Donald Barthelme and the Doggy Life." *Atlantic,* 222:89–91 (July 1968). Reprinted in Aldridge's collected essays, *The Devil in the Fire: Retrospective Essays on American Literature and Culture.* New York: Harper's Magazine Press, 1972. Pp. 261–266.

Berman, Jaye. "A Quite of Many Colors: Women and Masquerade in Donald Barthelme's Postmodern Parody Novels." In *Feminism, Bakhtin, and the Dialogic.* Edited by Dale M. Bauer and Susan Jaret McKinstry. Albany: State University of New York Press, 1991. Pp. 123–33.

Bocock, Maclin. " 'The Indian Uprising' or Donald Barthelme's Strange Object Covered with Fur." *Fiction International,* 4/5:134–146 (1975).

Bruss, Paul. *Victims: Textual Strategies in Recent American Fiction.* Lewisburg, Penn.: Bucknell University Press, 1981. Pp. 101–166.

Campbell, Ewing. "Dark Matter: Barthelme's Fantastic, Freudian Subtext in 'The Sandman.' " *Studies in Short Fiction,* 27:517–524 (Fall 1990).

Clark, Beverly Lyon. "In Search of Barthelme's Weeping Father." *Philological Quarterly,* 62:419–433 (Fall 1983).

Cowley, Julian. " 'Weeping Map Intense Activity Din': Reading Donald Barthelme." *University of Toronto Quarterly,* 60:292–304 (Winter 1990–1991).

Couturier, Maurice, and Régis Durand. *Donald Barthelme.* London and New York: Methuen, 1982.

Cullum, Charles. " 'An Ecstasy of Admiration for What Is': Contingent Human Values in the Fiction of Donald Barthelme." *Michigan Academician,* 24:333–341 (Winter 1992).

Culler, Jonathan. "Junk and Rubbish: A Semiotic Approach." *Diacritics,* 15:2–13 (Fall 1985).

Dickstein, Morris. "Fiction Hot and Kool: Dilemmas of the Experimental Writer." *TriQuarterly,* 33:257–272 (Spring 1975).

Ditsky, John M. " 'With Ingenuity and Hard Work, Distracted': The Narrative Style of Donald Barthelme." *Style,* 9:388–400 (Summer 1975).

Durand, Régis. "On the Pertinaciousness of the Father, the Son, and the Subject: The Case of Donald Barthelme." In *Critical Angles: European Views of Contemporary American Literature.* Edited by Marc Chénetier. Carbondale: Southern Illinois University Press, 1986. Pp. 153–163.

Evans, Walter. "Comanches and Civilization in Donald Barthelme's 'The Indian Uprising.' " *Arizona Quarterly,* 42:45–52 (Spring 1986).

Flowers, Betty. "Barthelme's *Snow White:* The Reader–Patient Relationship." *Critique: Studies in Modern Fiction,* 16, no. 3:33–43 (1975).

Gass, William H. "The Leading Edge of the Trash Phenomenon." *New York Review of Books,* April 25, 1968, pp. 5–6. Reprinted in his collected essays, *Fiction and the Figures of Life.* New York: Knopf, 1970. Pp. 97–103.

Giles, James R. "The 'Marivaudian Being' Drowns His Children: Dehumanization in Donald Barthelme's 'Robert Kennedy Saved from Drowning' and Joyce Carol Oates' *Wonderland.*" *Southern Humanities Review,* 9:63–75 (Winter 1975).

Gordon, Lois G. *Donald Barthelme.* Boston: Twayne, 1981.

Graff, Gerald. "Babbitt at the Abyss: The Social Context of PostModern American Fiction." *TriQuarterly,* 33:305–337 (Spring 1975).

———. "The Myth of the PostModernist Breakthrough." *TriQuarterly,* 26:383–417 (Winter 1973).

Guerard, Albert J. "Notes on the Rhetoric of AntiRealist Fiction." *TriQuarterly,* 30:3–50 (Spring 1974).

Hendin, Josephine. "Angries: S-M as a Literary Style." *Harper's,* February 1974, pp. 87–93.

Herr, Cheryl. "Fathers, Daughters, Anxiety, and Fiction." In *Discontented Discourses: Feminism/ Textual Intervention/Psychoanalysis.* Edited by Marleen S. Barr and Richard Feldstein. Urbana: University of Illinois Press, 1989. Pp. 173–207.

Johnson, R. E., Jr. " 'Bees Barking in the Night': The End and Beginning of Donald Barthelme's Narrative." *Boundary* 2, no. 5:71–92 (Fall 1976).

Klinkowitz, Jerome. "Donald Barthelme." In *Literary Disruptions/The Making of a Post-Contemporary American Fiction.* Urbana: University of Illinois Press, 1975. Pp. 62–81.

———. "Donald Barthelme's SuperFiction." *Critique: Studies in Modern Fiction,* 16, no. 3:5–18 (1975).

———. *Donald Barthelme: An Exhibition.* Durham: Duke University Press, 1991.

Kreutzer, Eberhard. "City Spectacles as Artistic Acts: Donald Barthelme's 'The Balloon' and 'The Glass Mountain.' " *Anglistik und Englischunterricht,* 13:43–55 (April 1981).

Krupnick, Mark C. "Notes from the Funhouse." *Modern Occasions,* 1:108–112 (Fall 1970).

Kuehl, John. *Alternate Worlds: A Study of Postmodern Antirealistic American Fiction.* New York: New York University Press, 1989. Pp. 97–100, 112–116, 162–164, and passim.

Leitch, Thomas M. "Donald Barthelme and the End of the Road." *Modern Fiction Studies,* 26:129–143 (Spring 1982).

Leland, John. "Remarks Re-marked: What Curios of Signs!" *Boundary* 2, no. 5:795–811 (Spring 1977).

Lilly, Paul, Jr. "Comic Strategies in the Fiction of Barthelme and Kosinski." *Publications of the Missouri Philological Association,* 4:25–32 (1979).

Malmgren, Carl. "Barthes's *S/Z* and Barthelme's 'The Zombies': Cacographic Interruption of a Text." *PTL,* 3:209–221 (1978).

Maloy, Barbara. "Barthelme's *The Dead Father:* Analysis of an Allegory." *Linguistics in Literature* 2, no. 2:43–119 (1977).

Maltby, Paul. *Dissident Postmodernists: Barthelme, Coover, Pynchon.* Philadelphia: University of Pennsylvania Press, 1991.

Martin, Carter. "A Fantastic Pairing: Edward Taylor and Donald Barthelme." In *The Scope of the Fantastic: Theory, Technique, Major Authors.* Edited by Robert A. Collins, Howard D. Pearce, and Eric S. Rabin. Westport, Conn.: Greenwood, 1985. Pp. 183–190.

McCaffery, Larry. *The Metafictional Muse: The Work of Robert Coover, Donald Barthelme, and William Gass.* Pittsburgh: University of Pittsburgh Press, 1982. Pp. 99–150.

McVicker, Jeanette. "Donald Barthelme's *The Dead Father:* 'Girls Talk' and the Displacement of the *Logos.*" *Boundary* 2, no. 16:363–390 (Winter/ Spring 1989).

Molesworth, Charles. *Donald Barthelme's Fiction: The Ironist Saved from Drowning.* Columbia: University of Missouri Press, 1982.

Oates, Joyce Carol. "Whose Side Are You On?" *New York Times Book Review,* June 4, 1972, p. 63.

Olsen, Lance. "Linguistic Pratfalls." In his *Circus of the Mind in Motion: Postmodernism and the Comic Vision.* Detroit: Wayne State University Press, 1990. Pp. 104–114.

———. "Slumgullions, or Some Notes toward Trying to Introduce Donald Barthelme." *Review of Contemporary Fiction,* 11:7–15 (Summer 1991).

———, ed. *The Review of Contemporary Fiction,* 11 (Summer 1991). Special issue containing 9 perspectives on Barthelme's works, Barthelme's "Then," and Weisenburger's bibliography.

Owens, Clarke. "Donald Barthelme's Existential Acts of Art." In *Since Flannery O'Connor: Essays on the Contemporary American Short Story.* Edited by Loren Logsdon and Charles W. Mayer. Macomb, Ill.: Western Illinois University Press, 1987. Pp. 72–82.

Patterson, Richard F., ed. *Critical Essays on Donald Barthelme.* New York: G. K. Hall, 1992.

Philips, K. J. "Ladies' Voices in Donald Barthelme's *The Dead Father* and Gertrude Stein's Dialogues." *International Fiction Review,* 12:34–37 (Winter 1985).

Porush, David. "Technology and Postmodernism: Cybernetic Fiction." *Sub-stance,* 27:92–100 (1980).

Roe, Barbara L. *Donald Barthelme: A Study of the Short Fiction.* Boston: Twayne, 1992.

Rother, James. "Parafiction: The Adjacent Universe of Barth, Barthelme, Pynchon, and Nabokov." *Boundary* 2, no. 5:21–44 (Fall 1976).

Scholes, Robert. "Metafiction." *Iowa Review,* 1:100–115 (Fall 1970).

Springer, Mary Doyle. "Aristotle in Contemporary Literature: Barthelme's 'Views of My Father Weeping.' " In *Narrative Poetics: Innovations, Limits, Challenges.* Edited by James Phelan. Columbus, Ohio: Center for Comparative Studies in Humanities, 1987. Pp. 93–102.

Stengel, Wayne B. *The Shape of Art in the Short Stories of Donald Barthelme.* Baton Rouge: Louisiana State University Press, 1985.

Trachtenberg, Stanley. *Understanding Donald Barthelme.* Columbia: University of South Carolina Press, 1990.

Upton, Lee. "Failed Artists in Donald Barthelme's *Sixty Stories.*" *Critique: Studies in Modern Fiction,* 26:11–17 (Fall 1984).

Warde, William B. "Barthelme's 'The Piano Player': Surreal and Mock Tragic." *Xavier Review,* 1, nos. 1–2:58–64 (1985).

———. "A Collage Approach: Donald Barthelme's Literary Fragments." *Journal of American Culture,* 8, no. 1:51–56 (1985).

Whalen, Tom. "Wonderful Elegance: Barthelme's 'The Party.' " *Critique: Studies in Modern Fiction,* 16, no. 3:45–48 (1975).

Wilde, Alan. *Horizons of Assent: Modernism, Postmodernism, and the Ironic Imagination.* Baltimore: Johns Hopkins University Press, 1981. Pp. 166–188.

———. *Middle Grounds: Studies in Contemporary American Fiction.* Philadelphia: University of Pennsylvania Press, 1987. Pp. 24–42, 161–172.

Zeitlin, Michael. "Father-Murder and Father-Rescue: The Post-Freudian Allegories of Donald Barthelme." *Contemporary Literature,* 34:182–203 (Summer 1993).

INTERVIEWS

Baker, John F. "PW Interviews Donald Barthelme." *Publisher's Weekly,* November 11, 1974, pp. 6–7.

Brans, Jo. "Embracing the World: An Interview with Donald Barthelme." *Southwest Review,* 67:121–137 (Spring 1982).

Klinkowitz, Jerome. "Donald Barthelme." In *The New Fiction: Interviews with Innovative American Writers.* Edited by Joe David Bellamy. Urbana: University of Illinois Press, 1974. Pp. 45–54.

McCaffery, Larry. "An Interview with Donald Barthelme." *Partisan Review,* 49, no. 2:184–193 (1982). Reprinted in *Anything Can Happen: Interviews with Contemporary American Novelists.* Edited by Tom LeClair and Larry McCaffery. Urbana: University of Illinois Press, 1983. Pp. 32–44.

O'Hara, J. D. "Donald Barthelme: The Art of Fiction LXVI." *Paris Review,* 80:181–210 (Summer 1981).

—GWEN CRANE

Robert Bly

1926–

*D*URING THE EIGHTIES and early nineties, because of the attention given to his nonfiction bestseller, *Iron John: A Book about Men,* published in 1990, and because of his TV interviews, videocassette recordings, and the shows that appeared on public television on him—plus the extremely popular conferences and seminars he organized and participated in throughout the world—Robert Bly achieved national and even international recognition. Obviously, Bly became so visible largely because of the media coverage he received. But his fame is also attributable to the numerous popular poetry readings he has given in this country and in other countries for thirty years, as well as to his ever-active political presence (which began with his participation in protests against the Vietnam War) and to his work with the men's movement and, even earlier, with the women's movement. But Bly's increasingly public presence—indeed by the midnineties he seemed to have become almost omnipresent in the media—should not overshadow the poetry he has written. Bly is one of the strongest, most respected, and most imitated poets of the second half of the twentieth century.

Properly seen, Bly's roles as poet, critic, editor, antiwar demonstrator, translator, media spokesman, and self-proclaimed social conscience of contemporary society all represent different parts of his complex, seemingly omnivorous, ever-expanding personality. For Robert Bly is one of those writers who seems to need constantly to reinvent himself. And, indeed, in the course of his long career Bly has gone through a surprisingly large number of conspicuous changes. These include not only the thematic, formal, and stylistic changes evidenced in his writing but transformations in the psyche and the personality of the man himself. Each of these distinct changes is authentic Bly, but each of them is less drastic than any of them might at first seem. In retrospect, they appear to be almost inevitable, even predictable, the shifts that any poet attuned to the world around him might make. For all his seeming shape-shifting, and for all his attempts to orchestrate the literary life around him and provide an ongoing apology for his own work, Bly has been surprisingly consistent throughout his considerably varied activist and literary careers.

Born into the Norwegian Lutheran community of Madison, Minnesota, which he has lived in or near for most of his life, Bly, early on, was made to "feel somehow eternal," somehow "out of" and floating over "the stream of life," as he says in his essay from 1976, "Being a Lutheran Boy-God in Minnesota." Indeed, Bly's background and his early life instilled in him a sense of aloofness that he describes in one of the interviews included in *Talking All Morning*—a collection of interviews, essays, and poems he published in 1980—as almost "an instinct" to be alone.

After high school, Bly spent two years in the navy and then entered St. Olaf College. After one year there, he transferred to Harvard, where he immediately assumed an active role in the literary community. Graduating from Harvard in 1950, Bly moved back to Minnesota; then, in January 1951, he moved to New York City and lived there alone for several years, "longing for 'the depths,' " as he explains in his *Selected Poems,* reading extensively and writing poems. After this period of solitude in New York, Bly moved to Iowa in 1954 and enrolled in the University of Iowa's creative writing program, where his M.A. thesis was a collection of poems entitled "Steps Toward Poverty and Death." In 1955 he married and returned to Minnesota and then, shortly thereafter, traveled to Norway on a Fulbright grant to translate Norwegian poetry. Back again in Minnesota, he founded his literary magazine, *The Fifties* (which changed names with the decades, becoming *The Sixties, The Seventies,* and *The Eighties*). In the late 1950s Bly met James Wright, a fellow poet and immediate friend, with whom he established a strong and lasting relationship that was beneficial to each of them both personally and professionally. Between them, Bly and Wright created and put into practice what came to be known as the deep image poem.

In the essay that prefaces the first section of his *Selected Poems* (published in 1986) Bly comments on his earliest work: "My first poetry seems to me now to keep out a despair that I couldn't quite bring into the house." Therefore, as he later reports in an interview in *Talking All Morning,* even though he had been writing poems "for fifteen or sixteen years," he postponed the publication of his first book of poetry, *Silence in the Snowy Fields,* until 1962. Since this book had such a long gestation period it is not surprising that, for all the seeming simplicity of the individual poems and their arrangement, Bly con-

structed the book with great care. And although it could not have been detected in 1962, it can now be seen that *Silence in the Snowy Fields* anticipated the thematic journey that Bly was to take over his long career. Since the poems in this book were so new and so unique, the critical response to them was immediate—and enthusiastic. *Silence in the Snowy Fields* not only established Bly's presence as a powerful new voice on the poetic scene, it remains perhaps his single most significant, most abiding accomplishment.

In an early version of his essay from 1967, "Looking for Dragon Smoke" (which was reprinted in 1969 in a collection called *Naked Poetry* edited by Stephen Berg and Robert Mezey), Bly writes that "in the true poem . . . form and . . . content . . . have the same swiftness and darkness" and that "both are expressions of a certain rebellious energy rising in the psyche." In the short prose introduction that he composed for the poems from *Silence in the Snowy Fields* that he included in his *Selected Poems,* Bly says that there is a danger in staying "too long in solitude," and "yet at certain moments, particularly moments alone" one can "pass into a deep of the mind." As Bly describes it, it was "in such moments, prepared for by solitude and reading, [that he] wrote a kind of poem [he] had never written before." And, indeed, it was a different kind of poem, one that *was* new.

It is impossible to overestimate the enormous impact that *Silence in the Snowy Fields* had on the literary landscape of contemporary American poetry and on other poets, young and old, worldwide. It set a standard by which much contemporary poetry was judged. Bly's short lyrics, apparently simple and straightforward yet so enigmatically deep and mysterious, ushered in one of the dominant movements of the 1960s, which came to be known as deep image poetry. Wright's book *The Branch Will Not Break* (1963) was also significant in terms of deep image poetry. Deep image poems, as Bly defined them in his essay, "Some Notes on French Poetry," published in 1961, do not exclude the intellect but appeal primarily to ("trust") the unconscious. They "leap" from one image to another, just as the mind does. Perhaps the classic paradigm of Bly's deep image poetry in *Silence in the Snowy Fields* is "Driving toward the Lac Qui Parle River." It contains lines in which water is described as "kneeling in the moonlight" and "lamplight," as falling "on all fours in the grass." With images like these Bly created a kind of poem that Lawrence Kramer in an essay from 1983, "A Sensible Emptiness," characterized as a "poem of immanence . . . written to be a fragment of a lost, privileged presence." Such poems occur throughout Bly's canon and have come to be seen as his most famous fingerprints on the page of contemporary poetry.

One of the dominant metaphors in Bly's canon has to do with "the road," which he frequently calls "the road of inwardness" in works such as *Sleepers Joining Hands*, published in 1973, and *Talking All Morning*. Bly says that he first developed a sense of this "road" during the time he spent in New York City, living and reading in solitude, and that it prepared him for the poems he finally collected in *Silence in the Snowy Fields* and for what was ahead of him both as a man and as a poet. In the opening poem of the last section of this first book Bly writes, "The road goes on ahead, it is all clear." But if what was ahead of him was "all clear" to Bly himself, this was certainly not the case for many of his readers—even for those who were his new admirers.

The readers and critics who had imagined that they had successfully "placed" Bly in relation to contemporary American poetry based on the poems in *Silence in the Snowy Fields* were surprised, even shocked, by Bly's next book, *The Light around the Body*, published in 1967. Although structurally many of the poems in *The*

Light around the Body are similar to those in *Silence in the Snowy Fields*, thematically these two books could not be more different. Unlike the bucolic, post-Romantic deep image poems of *Silence in the Snowy Fields*, which seem to exist almost outside of society, the poems in *The Light around the Body* are fiercely outspoken, angry antiwar poems against American society, politicians in Washington, and the war in Vietnam. These are poems that name names and take stands—just as Bly and others did in political rallies against the war. In 1966 Bly's Sixties Press published a collection he coedited with David Ray, *A Poetry Reading against the Vietnam War*, and that same year Bly, Ray, and others organized American Writers against the Vietnam War. In 1970 Bly edited a second collection, *Forty Poems Touching on Recent American History*. Among contemporary poets Bly was conspicuous at draft card turn-ins, the demonstration at the Pentagon in 1967, and many other marches and poetry readings organized to protest the war in Vietnam.

Almost simultaneously with the publication of *The Light around the Body* Bly published two essays—"On Political Poetry" and "Leaping Up into Political Poetry"—in which he argued that "a poem can be a political act" and lamented the fact that the United States had never produced a poet who had taken "a clear stand" and written "great poetry" that had "serious political meaning." Obviously, Bly was himself attempting to fill this void with poems in *The Light around the Body* like "Asian Peace Offers Rejected without Publication," "At a March against the Vietnam War," and "Driving through Minnesota during the Hanoi Bombings." Many of the poems in *The Light around the Body*, especially those in the third, central section of the book, are specific and insistent in their focus on the Vietnam War and in their criticism of particular individuals. For instance, two lines from "Asian Peace Offers Rejected without Publication" read, "Men like

Rusk are not men: / They are bombs waiting to be loaded in a darkened hangar.'' (When Bly reprinted this poem in his *Selected Poems* he revised and softened the first of these lines so it became, ''Men like Rusk are not men only—.'')

The outspoken, angry poems in *The Light around the Body* are those that will inevitably be most immediately and most clearly remembered; they are the poems that earned the book what may be perhaps the most controversial National Book Award ever awarded. (In their citation the NBA judges, three fellow poets, speaking no doubt for many in the literary community and in the country at large, said, ''If we poets had to choose something that would be for us our Address on the State of the Nation, it would be this book.'') But it is important to note that *The Light around the Body* not only is a diatribe against the Vietnam War but also includes a number of poems reminiscent of the lyrics in *Silence in the Snowy Fields.* There is an apocalyptic tone to some of the most outspoken of the socially conscious and the most blatant antiwar poems. ''Those Being Eaten by America,'' for instance, ends with the line, ''The world will soon break up into small colonies of the saved.'' This line suggests the same sentiment that Bly attempted to communicate when, during his acceptance speech at the NBA ceremony (published in *Tennessee Poetry Journal* in 1969), he called one of the young men up from the audience and, handing him the check he had just been awarded, said, ''I ask you to use this money . . . to counsel other young . . . men not to destroy their spiritual lives by participating in this war.''

''Counting Small-Boned Bodies,'' one of Bly's best-known and most often anthologized poems, is perhaps at once the most vociferous antiwar poem in *The Light around the Body* and Bly's most overt statement of the way in which ''spiritual lives''—as well as physical lives—may be destroyed by war. Alluding to those TV reporters who gave a running count of the day's casualties on the evening news, Bly's speaker in this poem counts corpses over and over again. He attempts to make his job less gruesome, less grotesque, less terrifying—and tries to make the war itself seem less horrible—by imagining ways he might make the bodies ''smaller.'' The final three tercets of this poem show Bly at his best—both as a lyric poet and as an antiwar protester:

If we could only make the bodies smaller,
The size of skulls,
We could make a whole plain white with skulls in
    the moonlight!

If we could only make the bodies smaller,
Maybe we could get
A whole year's kill in front of us on a desk!

If we could only make the bodies smaller,
We could fit
A body into a finger-ring, for a keepsake forever.

In his first two books Bly seemed to present two separate sides of his vision in terms of two rather different kinds of poems; in his third major book, *Sleepers Joining Hands,* he attempted to synthesize the themes and styles of *Silence in the Snowy Fields* and *The Light around the Body.* Furthermore, *Sleepers Joining Hands* is a hybrid book in another way, made up as it is of two parts poetry and, between them, a twenty-page prose essay, ''I Came Out of the Mother Naked.'' In *Talking All Morning* Bly himself (echoing some of the criticism that he received) says that his essay ''is full of mad generalizations.'' Even so, the essay is important for an understanding of much of Bly's work, early and late, including, of course, what he was trying to accomplish in *Sleepers Joining Hands.*

''I Came Out of the Mother Naked'' received an enormous amount of commentary, both positive and negative. The essay contains Bly's most detailed and specific summarizations of some of the basic background information one needs in order to achieve a complete understanding of many of his poems. "I Came Out of the Mother Naked" is an especially important theoretical document. Indeed, as I suggested in 1994, in my book *Robert Bly: The Poet and His Critics*, it is "arguably the single most important essay Bly has written." The primary thesis, as Bly explains, has to do with "some ideas about Great Mother culture." The "Great Mother," according to Bly, is "a union of four 'force fields.' " He traces the significance and influence of the "Great Mother" back to ancient times. But, as is usual with Bly, the essay leaps around among many topics and covers a good deal of ground. The most important issues Bly deals with here include: the significance of archetypes, Freudian and Jungian psychology (Jung, in particular, is an especially important influence on Bly), the dark-light dichotomy of consciousness, and the work on the "new brain" (or "third brain") conducted by neurologists like Paul MacLean. By the end of his essay Bly comes to the conclusion that "after hundreds of years of being motionless, the Great Mother is moving again in the psyche."

"Sleepers Joining Hands," Bly's long title poem, is divided into four parts. It begins as a kind of reverie in which the public and private worlds of the speaker merge to form another, "shadow" reality, neither public nor private, neither fully conscious nor entirely unconscious. By the end of the third section of the poem, the speaker, having passed through a "night sea-journey"—which is clearly a metaphor for the visionary experience central to Bly's thinking in general, as well as in this particular poem— awakens and is ready to "join hands" with the reader, who is described in the final section as "you."

The other long poem in *Sleepers Joining Hands* is "The Teeth Mother Naked at Last." It is Bly's most detailed, most explicit, and most blatant antiwar poem. In his preface to *A Poetry Reading against the Vietnam War* Bly argues that the "really serious evil" of the Vietnam War, "rarely discussed," is the "harm it will do" to America and Americans "inwardly." This notion is clearly a principal theme in "The Teeth Mother Naked at Last." And even though Bly documents the atrocities of the war in graphic terms—

> if one of those children came near that we have set on fire,
>
> . . . .
>
> If one of those children came toward me with both hands
> in the air, fire rising along both elbows

—he also forces everything back on the individual psyche. "If . . ." then, the speaker in the poem says, "I would suddenly go back to my animal brain," within which, Bly suggests, there is the possibility for both political and psychic renewal and for redemption. In "The Teeth Mother Naked at Last," as in many of his other antiwar poems, Bly seems to want to illustrate what he had said in his essay "Leaping Up into Political Poetry," namely, that a "true political poem" is a "political act" that "comes out of the deepest privacy" and attempts to "deepen awareness."

In *Sleepers Joining Hands* Bly summarized his poetic career to date and also laid the groundwork for future work. Donald Hall was quite right, therefore, to suggest in his review of the book in 1973 that *Sleepers Joining Hands* is both "the earliest and latest of Bly's works." With *The Morning Glory* and *This Body Is Made of Camphor and Gopherwood*, his next two major books, published respectively in 1975 and 1977, Bly turned in another, totally different direction—as might by now have been expected. This shift was not simply a matter of changing themes; indeed, in some ways, it constituted a return to the themes of *Silence in the Snowy Fields* and to Bly's earliest source materials. But *The Morning Glory* and *This Body Is Made of Camphor and Gopherwood* did represent a major stylistic change in Bly's work: the poems in these books are in prose. Although it had a long tradition in Europe (especially in France) the prose poem was a relatively new form in America and Bly was largely responsible for introducing it. By using it so frequently and effectively himself, he almost single-handedly managed to make this "genreless genre" into one of the major genres in American poetry during the 1970s.

As is usual with Bly, there were reasons for his making this move. In one of the essays in *Talking All Morning* he argues that prose poems surface in circumstances in which a society—and especially its poetry—has begun to move too close to the "abstract" and so loses sight of itself and its own most appropriate directions or its own best goals. The prose poem, according to Bly, serves as a means whereby poets may adjust or reorient themselves and society. It is easy enough to see how Bly associated these notions with America in the aftermath of the Vietnam War. In my essay from 1977, "Defining the Age," I argued, following Bly's suggestion, that Bly's shift to the prose poem was his attempt to find "a way of maintaining the possibility of poetry in an age about to abandon it." But it is also clear enough that Bly must have been a bit worried about the "abstraction" of his own work after he finished *Sleepers Joining Hands*, which, as I noted in the introduction to my 1992 *Critical Essays on Robert Bly*, is Bly's most "abstract" book. Thus, perhaps for the health of his own poetic career as well as for the health of the nation, Bly turned to the prose poem and cultivated it extensively both in theory and in practice throughout the 1970s. Bly's dual goals, as he suggested in two separate essays, were to help "balance" the "abstract" ("The Prose Poem as an Evolving Form," 1986) and to speak "in a low voice to someone he is sure is listening" ("What the Prose Poem Carries with It," 1977). The "low voice" of Bly's prose poems is a voice speaking in carefully crafted language. And the prose poems certainly have been carefully "listened" to.

Among the many well-known and most often anthologized prose poems in *The Morning Glory* and *This Body Is Made of Camphor and Gopherwood*, one of the finest, most typical, and most memorable is "A Hollow Tree." It begins casually enough with the speaker alone, walking aimlessly during an indeterminate time of year in what is apparently an open field. He comes upon "an old hollow cottonwood stump" and stops to look inside it. What he finds there is surprising, even stunning. Inside the stump, he tells us, it is "early spring" and then, that "its Siamese temple walls are all brown and ancient" and then, that "the walls have been worked on by the intricate ones." The poem ends:

> Inside the hollow walls there is privacy and secrecy, dim light. And yet some creature has died here.
> On the temple floor feathers, gray feathers, many of them with a fluted white tip. Many feathers. In the silence many feathers.

In his essay "The Prose Poem as an Evolving Form," in a passage clearly commenting on "A Hollow Tree," Bly writes, "When the human mind honors a stump . . . by giving it human attention in the right way, something in the soul is released; and often through the stump we receive information we wouldn't have received by thinking or by fantasy." "A Hollow Tree" typifies Bly's usual poetic practice in the middle of his career, and it also serves as a good example of his considerable success with this particular genre. In his prose poems, as Ralph J. Mills Jr. was the first to suggest in an essay—" 'The Body with the Lamp Lit Inside' "—that was published in 1976–1977, Bly quite effectively combines description and vision. As Mills says of "A Hollow Tree," it is often the case with Bly's prose poems that "the feeling of factual accuracy lasts . . . just [long] enough to provide a context for what follows and to lead the reader to the place where vision takes command."

Thus in the prose poems of *The Morning Glory* and *This Body Is Made of Camphor and Gopherwood* Bly successfully worked his way through—and beyond—a potential period of personal and poetic "abstraction" and, in the course of doing so, managed to write some of the finest, most memorable, and most important poems of his career. Bly was now ready both to return briefly to his earliest beginnings and then to go on in quite another new direction.

The brief return to beginnings was with his next collection of poetry, *This Tree Will Be Here for a Thousand Years*. In *Talking All Morning* Bly explains that he had written "snowy fields" poems "without pause, maybe eight or nine a year" since the publication of *Silence in the Snowy Fields*. He published twenty of these "snowy fields" poems under the title *Old Man Rubbing His Eyes* in 1975, then added twenty-four more and published them as *This Tree Will Be Here for a Thousand Years* in 1979. In his essay "The Two Presences," which serves as a preface to the latter book, Bly notes that the poems which follow "form a volume added to *Silence in the Snowy Fields*; the two books make one book." He also suggests that, like the poems in *Silence in the Snowy Fields*, the poems in *This Tree Will Be Here for a Thousand Years* "try to achieve 'two presences' " through theme, syntax, and structure (both books contain forty-four poems). In an additional note on the poems from *Silence in the Snowy Fields* and *This Tree Will Be Here for a Thousand Years* that he included in his *Selected Poems* Bly indicated that he would publish a "third group" of "snowy fields" poems.

This Tree Will Be Here for a Thousand Years is thematically similar to *Silence in the Snowy Fields*. The dominant metaphor in both books is that of a journey, but each book describes this journey differently. Whereas in *Silence in the Snowy Fields* the journey is described chronologically and the persona of the poems moves from a private toward a public "presence," in *This Tree Will Be Here for a Thousand Years* the journey is depicted as cyclical and suggests a return to beginnings. The two books are considerably different in tone: *This Tree Will Be Here for a Thousand Years* is a much more brooding, much darker book than *Silence in the Snowy Fields*. And this "darkening" suggests another significant change in Bly's direction—one immediately visible in the writing Bly produced subsequently—namely, a shift away from what he loosely terms the "mother consciousness" represented in and by the earlier books and toward the "father consciousness" of the later ones. Thus *This Tree Will Be Here for a Thousand Years* marks an extremely important transition in Bly's work.

In "The Two Presences" Bly describes how he understands the poems in *This Tree Will Be Here for a Thousand Years*:

> Each of the poems that follow contains an instant, sometimes twenty seconds long, sometimes longer, when I was aware of two separate energies: my own consciousness, which is insecure, anxious, massive, earthbound, persistent, cunning, hopeful; and a second consciousness which is none of these things. The second consciousness has a melancholy tone, the tear inside the stone, what Lucretius calls "the tears of things", an energy circling downward, felt often in autumn, or moving slowly around apple trees or stars.

He adds, "sometimes I admire the poems that follow for their quality of doubleness ... the presence in them simultaneously of two presences. . . . Sometimes they seem to me too impersonal." The "impersonality" of these poems takes the form of a pervasive sense of loss or absence. But loss and absence, as Bly understands them, are neither necessarily nor inherently negative. Kramer has quite rightly argued that Bly, by "groping forward metonymically" in these poems, celebrates absence and thus achieves what Kramer calls "a sensible emptiness."

This Tree Will Be Here for a Thousand Years received some of the most contradictory and some of the most vehemently negative criticism Bly ever received. The range of responses to the book is dramatized by four conflicting comments on two lines in "Women We Never See Again" (lines which clearly hark back to "A Hollow Tree"):

> Sometimes when you put your hand into a hollow tree
> you touch the dark places between the stars.

Eliot Weinberger, writing in the *Nation* in November 1979, called these lines "a remark" that "might be charming if uttered by a 6-year-old." But in a piece in *Harper's* that appeared a few months later Hayden Carruth defended the lines, saying, "Not many of Bly's readers have done that, I imagine"—put a hand into a hollow tree—"but I ... *have*.... I'm damned if he isn't right." Kramer described Bly's hollow tree in "A Sensible Emptiness" as "a site of sudden epiphany." Howard Nelson in his book *Robert Bly: An Introduction to the Poetry*, published in 1984, cited these same lines as an example of the kind of "intuitive moments" that are "perhaps the principal reward of *This Tree Will Be Here for a Thousand Years*."

In 1992 Bly published a revised edition of *This Tree Will Be Here for a Thousand Years*. Thirty-four of the original forty-four poems were altered, twenty-two of them substantially. This revised version of the book is, essentially, totally different from the book published previously under the same title, but it went almost completely unnoticed by critics. The scope and significance of Bly's revisions can be seen in, for example, "Women We Never See Again." Bly changed his title to "Women We Love Whom We Never See Again" and revised the poem itself considerably. The original single stanza of ten lines became thirteen lines divided into four stanzas;

the last five lines of the original version were largely revised away or replaced by significantly different lines. The two lines that had gotten so much attention in the original version remain, however, exactly the same—as if Bly wanted to send a message to his critics.

Bly's next book, *The Man in the Black Coat Turns*, published in 1981, is a hybrid. The central section, consisting of six prose poems, is buttressed on both sides by poems in verse. Thematically *The Man in the Black Coat Turns* represents another return to beginnings, just as *This Tree Will Be Here for a Thousand Years* did. But unlike *This Tree Will Be Here for a Thousand Years*, which circles back to *Silence in the Snowy Fields*, when *The Man in the Black Coat Turns* circles back to the past, it returns to another, different point of departure, a new beginning that goes back to an emphasis on the masculine rather than on the feminine. Although the three books share themes, a tone, and even a technique, *The Man in the Black Coat Turns* (together with Bly's next book, a companion volume, *Loving a Woman in Two Worlds*) collects much more personal and private poems (especially poems that deal with his father and with his wife) than the ones in *Silence in the Snowy Fields* and *This Tree Will Be Here for a Thousand Years*.

The prose poems in the central section of *The Man in the Black Coat Turns* are crucial to an understanding of what Bly was about not only in this book but at this stage of his career. On the surface these poems seem to be similar to the earlier prose poems in *The Morning Glory* and in *This Body Is Made of Camphor and Gopherwood*, but both in form and theme they are actually quite different. In his remarks on the selection of poems from *The Man in the Black Coat Turns* in his *Selected Poems* Bly indicates that he wanted these particular prose poems to "rise out of some darkness beneath us," to "break water . . . for a moment before [they sink] . . . again'' beneath the surface. In using this metaphor Bly suggests that with *The Man in the Black Coat Turns* he was "fishing'' for something much deeper in the psyche and much closer to his quest for or goal of masculine consciousness. He explains this concept of "fishing'': "In this book I fished in male waters.'' He describes these "waters'' as "containing and nourishing some secret and moving life down below.'' Elaborating upon the metaphor he adds: "I've often made a net of words in order to catch a perception . . . which I knew would be gone a few seconds later.'' But, he asks, "what about a net for the thoughts we have thought for so many years,'' the thoughts that "we wrote in our journal ten years . . . or twenty years before that?'' He asks further, "What sort of form is proper for . . . heavy thought-poems?'' Then he answers his own questions and defines what he intended in *The Man in the Black Coat Turns* by saying that he had attempted to "knit . . . together in sound'' stanzas having the "same number of beats'' in order to "please the old sober and spontaneous ancestor males,'' a kind of mythological, masculine presence.

It is conspicuous that the poems in *The Man in the Black Coat Turns* are poems that have to do with "male consciousness.'' Ten years before this book appeared, in a symposium paper entitled "What's New in American and Canadian Poetry,'' Bly said that he had noticed a "spiritual inflation'' in his life that, he suggested, indicated a new development in his thinking. He described this "inflation'' as a concern with "father consciousness.'' During the next ten years, while he was working on the poems that were to become *The Man in the Black Coat Turns*, Bly frequently talked about men, the men's movement, and "father consciousness'' in interviews and essays. His most important pronouncements on "father consciousness'' can be found in his essay "Being a Lutheran Boy-God in Minnesota''—in which he described his own father as "wearing a large black coat''—and in his analysis of the "Iron John'' story and its relationship to contemporary men and to their questions and concerns in *Iron John: A Book about Men.* In the latter he discusses his conception of the "deep male.'' This concept of the deep male stems from the Grimm brothers' fairy tale "Iron John'' in which Iron John, an ancient "hairy man,'' is discovered "lying on the bottom of a pond . . . covered with hair from head to foot.'' Bly elaborates, "contact with Iron John requires a willingness to descend into the male psyche and accept what's dark down there, including the nourishing dark.'' In *The Rag and Bone Shop of the Heart: Poems for Men* a collection he coedited with James Hillman and Michael Meade in 1992, Bly describes "masculine sadness'' as a "holy thing'' and argues that men become "more alive'' as they age.

Bly wrote the poems in *The Man in the Black Coat Turns* directly out of his experience of male consciousness. Many of his critics and readers reacted to the book strictly on the basis of their own experience. As might be expected, the responses were considerably varied. It certainly seems to be the case that a number of Bly's reviewers took the opportunity to comment on the book as a way of lauding or attacking Bly himself for his increasing popularity and media visibility—as well as for his personal, political, and theoretical positions on life, literature, and male-female psychology. (Some critics later seized upon *Loving a Woman in Two Worlds* for the same purpose.) Brown Miller in her 1983 essay "Searching for Poetry: Real vs. Fake'' called *The Man in the Black Coat Turns* "a clear case of an established poet larded by his own theories and specialities of style, turning them into fetishes.'' Bly, she wrote, was "self-consciously trying to be the poet we expect him to be''; he was writing poems that "fit his theories'' in a futile attempt to "prove them valid.'' These poems, Miller complained, are largely meaningless, even though they have "the façade of Bly's earlier, better work.'' Marjorie

Perloff, writing in the Spring/Summer 1982 issue of *Parnassus,* argued that the autobiographical poems in *The Man in the Black Coat Turns* constituted a "swerve" toward a kind of poem that Bly had previously "always scorned"; these poems, she said, went directly counter to the mainstream of his earlier (and better) poems of "immanent presence." Indeed, Perloff charged, Bly's new book represented a distinct, sentimental falling off from his earlier poetry of "images": here he became "pontifical" in poems that insisted on "mythic correspondences" that remained "murky." Too often Bly was reduced to mere "phrase-making."

On the other hand there were also those who gave *The Man in the Black Coat Turns* quite positive reviews. Paul Stuewe, writing in *Quill & Quire,* called the book a "hauntingly" allusive accomplishment. In *American Book Review* Mark Jarman argued that Bly had "never been more moving." Peter Stitt, in a review for the *New York Times,* said *The Man in the Black Coat Turns* was "crackl[ing] with energy . . . [and] liveliness," that it was "easily [Bly's] richest, most complex book." In fact, the most substantial reviews of the collection were largely favorable. Most of the major critics who reviewed the book saw it—as indeed it proved to be—as a new beginning for Bly. To Howard Nelson it was "an affirmative book." Richard P. Sugg argued in his 1986 book *Robert Bly* that Bly had made a "declaration" with the book and found a "new use" for his poetry as a way of entering "into the stream of nature's energies." Victoria Frenkel Harris in her 1992 book *The Incorporative Consciousness of Robert Bly* described Bly's achievement as tracing the "history of [all] men in a man." I noted in my essay from 1982, "Still the Place Where Creation Does Some Work on Itself," that with *The Man in the Black Coat Turns* Bly had opened "the door of the self" to write some of the most "authentic" poems of his entire career. Bly himself observed in the first of the prose poems in the central section of the book, "Many times in poems I have escaped—from myself. . . . Now more and more I long for what I cannot escape from." In this book Bly clearly faced himself.

Having considered "male consciousness" in *The Man in the Black Coat Turns* Bly next turned (as his title seemed to suggest that he would) to focus on "female consciousness" in *Loving a Woman in Two Worlds,* the collection he published in 1985. His giving attention to "female consciousness" was not really new—even though it seemed new to some of his critics. In essays, in interviews, and in poems like "The Teeth Mother Naked at Last" (originally published as early as 1970), Bly had long been advocating the equality of female and male "consciousnesses." Indeed, as Bly himself observes in the *Selected Poems,* it was as far back as 1973 . . . [that he] began the poems that eventually became *Loving a Woman in Two Worlds.*" In addition, Bly's long interest in the writings of C. G. Jung and Erich Neumann, so clearly evident in his essay "I Came Out of the Mother Naked" and in many of the poems in *Sleepers Joining Hands,* ought also to be remembered in this context. One need only recall several representative passages in Jung's *The Spirit in Man* ("The creative process has a feminine quality, and . . . creative work arises from unconscious depths . . . from the realm of the Mothers") or in Neumann's "On the Moon and Matriarchal Consciousness" ("matriarchal consciousness is not confined to women" but exists in men as part of their "anima-consciousness"—a phenomenon that is "particularly true of creative people" since "the creative is by its inherent nature related to matriarchal consciousness") to realize the significance of these thinkers as continuing sources for Bly's thought and work.

The poems in *Loving a Woman in Two Worlds* describe the course of a relationship, moving through the stages of meeting, courtship, and marriage in general terms. (In 1979 Bly and his first wife, Carol, divorced; in 1980 Bly married Ruth Ray.) One of the earliest poems, "The Whole Moisty Night," suggests the main theme of the book in two succinct lines:

The body meets its wife far out at sea.
Its lamp remains lit the whole moisty night.

Loving a Woman in Two Worlds is primarily made up of love poems; any number of the poems have sexual themes. Many of them are short: almost half of the fifty poems in the book are less than nine lines long, and eleven of them are only four lines each. Some of these short poems are what Bly calls Ramages, a form Bly invented. The Ramage, as Bly defines it (in a letter to the author), is an eight-line poem composed of eighty-five syllables that repeat certain sound patterns to "set the tonal structure of the poem," what Bly calls "the key."

In his introduction to the poems from *Loving a Woman in Two Worlds* in his *Selected Poems* Bly attempts to define the limits that need to be imposed on love poems so as to keep them from going "out of tune"—something which, he acknowledged, can "so easily" occur. Most critics would argue that at least some of the love poems in *Loving a Woman in Two Worlds* have gone "out of tune." When the book first appeared many of Bly's critics, taken by surprise, were probably initially confused by it—and then a bit embarrassed as well. Not knowing what to say about these new poems, many critics generally sympathetic to Bly said nothing at all, while unsympathetic critics assailed them: *Loving a Woman in Two Worlds* has been the most fiercely attacked as well as the least seriously analyzed of Bly's major books. Even Harris, one of Bly's staunchest defenders, claimed that although Bly's "desire to recuperate the fallen status of women" in *Loving a Woman in Two Worlds* is "unques-

tionable," by "valorizing intuition" through his reliance on Jung, Neumann, and others who exhibit allegiance to "remnants" of the very patriarchy Bly was ostensibly denouncing, Bly actually "trivializes" women. He presents "patriarchal portraits" of women; that is, poems in which women remain only "objects," only "the other." Harris does acknowledge, however, that here, for the first time in his poetry, Bly describes "an actual woman."

Although Harris' basic theoretical position is one that not all critics agree with, they have often agreed with her criticisms of specific poems, especially with her assessment of the way those poems treat women. Robert Rehder, for instance, in his essay "Which Way to the Future?"—which is included in my collection, *Critical Essays on Robert Bly* (1992)—said that the woman in "all the poems" in *Loving a Woman in Two Worlds* is an "extremely shadowy figure" who virtually never speaks, has "no behavior," and whose "body is mostly metaphors." But the best summary of the various responses to this book may be found, perhaps, in the words of another poet, Fred Chappell, who said in his review in the *New York Times Book Review* that in *Loving a Woman in Two Worlds* Bly had "broken no promises" even though the book "holds no surprises." For Chappell and others, this book stands as a most important addition to Bly's body of work, work that has "impressively persuaded a generation of poets and readers."

If the *Selected Poems*, which appeared in 1986 only a few months after *Loving a Woman in Two Worlds*, contributed to the lack of attention accorded to its predecessor, it received, surprisingly, considerable attention itself—although not nearly as much attention as many of Bly's individual books received. Inevitably a kind of reader's guide to a poet's career, any collection of selected poems published during the writer's lifetime is bound to be simultaneously definitive and incomplete. Bly's *Selected Poems* failed to follow any of the conventional or established norms for such a book. As I suggested in my essay "Robert Bly," the *Selected Poems* was

> unique in several ways. First, Bly took his title seriously. Considering the number of poems he had published in his career, this rather thin "selection" from his previous work might be thought of as extremely modest. Second, his book contain[s] a large number of heavily revised or, indeed, totally rewritten poems. Third, it contain[s] early, "new" poems—some never before published, others never before collected. Fourth, Bly rearranged the order of the poems from the previously published individual books for the sake of a new thematic unity in the *Selected Poems*—even moving poems originally published in one book to a selection largely devoted to another. Finally, Bly added short explanatory prose prefaces to each of the nine sections of the book, and appended two additional critical essays as "afterthoughts." In short, Bly's *Selected Poems* [is] as unconventional as, in some ways, each of his earlier individual books.

Reactions to a volume of selected poems inevitably differ appreciably from responses to the previously published books from which the poems are chosen. When a poet selects and arranges his poems he summarizes his career and gives his own subtle—or, in Bly's case (especially in terms of the prefatory essays he inserted as introductions to the various sections of his book), not so subtle—suggestions as to how he prefers his past work to be read and, at the same time, he points toward future works; he also attempts to control his current critical standing, as well as the way his reputation will be fixed finally. Thus, any "selected" collection is extremely important. Bly's organization of his *Selected Poems* was obviously strategic.

It is somewhat surprising, therefore, to discover that most of Bly's critics failed to treat this book as definitive or unique—or, even, to treat it at all. There are several ways to account for this paucity of critical attention. The distinctive qualities of the *Selected Poems*, so unlike what the stereotype of Bly would lead one to expect, may have either frightened critics away or may have seemed to demand of them a greater critical commitment than they were willing or able to give. Or, Bly's comments on the various sections of the book may have made it seem self-explanatory and therefore in need of no additional critical commentary. Or, perhaps critics had simply lost interest in Bly. While any or all of these possibilities may explain why the book received so few reviews and so little additional analysis, the most obvious and understandable reason may be that, because Bly was extremely active during this period—as a translator, men's movement spokesperson and conference organizer, media guru, even cult figure—his various roles and his growing popularity compromised or diminished his presence as a poet.

The responses to Bly's "idiosyncratic" book—which, as Askold Melnyczuk argued in the *Partisan Review* in 1988, could be seen as "either a tombstone or a capstone" to Bly's career—were varied. Roger Mitchell called the *Selected Poems* a "disappointment" in his essay "Robert Bly and the Trouble with America," which was also published in 1988. Over the years, Mitchell said, readers "had been lulled into thinking . . . that more had been accomplished" by Bly than was in fact the case. Perhaps the most flamboyant response to the *Selected Poems* was Philip Dacey's characterization of it in his review published in 1986, "Saint Robert." Dacey called Bly an "American Norwegian Lutheran Buddhist pagan Sufi Jungian" saint "impressed by his own unworthiness" who "steadily play[s] a sub-note of agony" and for whom poems are a "kind of religious device." Dacey compared Bly's poetic career to a "spiritual pilgrimage" by a "penitent" who "confesses to a father-(mother-?) confessor," then suggested that Bly was "at once penitent *and* priest, the ailing [one] who would heal himself and others." This clearly was an extreme position. Predictably, most of Bly's critics situated themselves in the safe middle ground. Joyce Peseroff, for example, in "Minnesota Transcendentalist," a review published in 1986, said that the *Selected Poems* was "a mellow ending to a good journey, one that is not over yet."

As has been noted, Bly is an inveterate reviser. Nowhere is this more evident than in the *Selected Poems.* Something of the significance of the changes and revisions Bly made to his earlier poems before he included them in the *Selected Poems* can be seen simply by comparing title changes: "Like the New Moon I Will Live My Life" in *Jumping Out of Bed* became "Early Spring between Madison and Bellingham"; "In the Courtyard of the Isleta Missions" in *The Morning Glory* became "Ants"; "Looking from Inside My Body" and "Falling into Holes in Our Sentences" in *This Body Is Made of Camphor and Gopherwood* became "The Upward Moon and the Downward Moon" and "The Watcher"; "A Third Body" in *Loving a Woman in Two Worlds* became "A Man and a Woman Sit Near Each Other." In addition and more important, many of the poems themselves were rewritten for the *Selected Poems*; indeed, some of them were almost completely transformed. For example, the last two stanzas of "Night of First Snow" in *This Tree Will Be Here for a Thousand Years* read:

> A woman wades out toward the wicker basket,
> floating,
> rocking in darkening reeds.
> The child and the light are half asleep.
> What is human lies in the way the basket is rocking.
>
> Black and white end in the gray color of the sky.
> What is human lies in the three hairs, caught,
> the rabbit left behind
> as he scooted under the granary joist.

In the *Selected Poems* the passage appears as a single, quite different stanza:

> Between boards I see three hairs a rabbit left behind
> As he scooted under the fence.
> A woman walks out toward the wicker basket
> Rocking in darkening reeds.
> The Bride is inside the basket where Moses sleeps.
> What is human lies in the way the basket is rocking.

Bly's next book, published in 1992, *What Have I Ever Lost by Dying?* might be thought of as an addendum to the *Selected Poems*, limited exclusively to the genre of the prose poem. Made up of five titled sections and a short preface in which Bly briefly describes the history behind the book and his own practice of writing prose poems, *What Have I Ever Lost by Dying?* contains twenty-four poems from *The Morning Glory,* the ten *Point Reyes Poems* originally published in 1974, several poems each from *This Tree Will Be Here for a Thousand Years* and *The Man in the Black Coat Turns,* one from *This Body Is Made of Camphor and Gopherwood,* fifteen from the *Selected Poems,* and the ten poems by Bly from *Ten Poems of Francis Ponge Translated by Robert Bly and Ten Poems of Robert Bly Inspired by the Poems of Francis Ponge,* which Bly published in 1990. As he had for the *Selected Poems,* Bly altered the original wording of a number of these poems; in some cases he actually revised poems twice before including them in *What Have I Ever Lost by Dying?*

The poems in this book generally focus on what is seen—and they often end in visions. Typically a poem in this collection begins with reference to an actual place and then quickly moves to a figurative level before it either circles back to the literal subject of the beginning or flies off into a kind of "fantasy." In "Disappointment and Desire," his introduction to *What Have I Ever Lost by Dying?*, Bly explains that when he began writing prose poems he "hoped that a writer could describe an object or a creature without claiming it"; now, he says, he knows that

that is not possible. He adds, "I have learned also to accept the fantasy that often appears toward the end of the poem."

"The Starfish" is a good example of Bly's best work in *What Have I Ever Lost by Dying?* It starts: "It is low tide. Fog. I have climbed down the cliffs from Pierce Ranch to the tide pools." Then the speaker makes a discovery: "In six inches of clear water I notice a purple starfish." The starfish is described: "It is about the size of the bottom of a pail."

> It is a delicate purple, the color of old carbon paper, or an attic dress. . . . One arm is especially active and curves up over its own body as if a dinosaur were looking behind him.
> . . . The starfish is a glacier, going sixty miles a year!

Having picked the starfish up and examined it closely, the speaker puts it back into the water and watches as it "unfolds . . . and slides down into his rock groin, the snaillike feelers waving as if nothing had happened, and nothing has." Nothing has happened—and everything has. The poems in *What Have I Ever Lost by Dying?*, like so many of Bly's earlier poems, often end in epiphanies, which although usually limited to something small are nonetheless significant. Careful observation, subtle detail, and openness to surprise and insight have been at the center of Bly's work from the beginning of his career. The little ceremony in one of these poems finished, the poet turns to investigate something else, to experience another revelation.

In the best of these poems, Bly lets description express the discoveries. And although there are, not surprisingly, some instances in these poems in which Bly lapses into what might be called pure prose, that does not happen often. Generally speaking, Bly's prose poems in this book are superb examples of the kind of discoveries possible, even inevitable if given the proper solitude and "receptivity," to one who watches and waits. In the final poem, "A Chunk of Ame-

thyst," Bly describes the "elegant corridors" of the stone, which "give and take light," turn "four or five faces toward us at once, and four or five meanings enter the mind." Indeed, Bly often seems to be a poet who, as Leslie C. Chang said in her review of this book in 1993, "can meditate a stone into being." In short, the prose poems in *What Have I Ever Lost by Dying?* are an excellent collection of Bly's best work in this genre, and since his poems in prose are some of his finest poems, the book conveniently gathers together some of the strongest work in his entire career.

Bly's next major book, *Meditations on the Insatiable Soul*, published in 1994, is his first collection of totally new poems since *Loving a Woman in Two Worlds*. Intentionally or not, it reads rather like a summary of Bly's entire career. It is a powerful and important book. The poems in the first section are mostly "meditations"; they are similar to the "meditative" poems in *Silence in the Snowy Fields* and in *This Tree Will Be Here for a Thousand Years*. In them Bly pays homage to a number of friends and "teachers," most of them other poets (James Wright, Donald Hall, William Stafford, Wallace Stevens) and to the simple anonymous men and women who live out their lives loving one another and "wronging" each other, without knowing why they do so. In "Men and Women," the first poem in the book, Bly writes:

> Men wrong women, because a woman wants the
>   two things
> Joined, but the man wants sawn boards,
> He wants roads diverging, and jackdaws flying,
> Heaven and earth parted. Women wrong men,
> Because the woman wants doves returning at dusk,
> Clothes folded, and giants sitting down at table.
> One wants an eternal river—which one? And the
>   other wants
> A river that makes its own way to the ocean.

The second section of *Meditations on the Insatiable Soul*, reminiscent of a number of earlier poems about fathers (especially poems in *The Man in the Black Coat Turns*), consists of ten poems specifically about Bly's complicated, often combative relationship with his father. Individually and as a sequence these are some of Bly's most moving poems. They are straightforward, personal, honest, heartfelt: "I do not want / Or need to be shamed / By him any longer." "My arm on the bedrail / Rests there, relaxed, / With new love," he writes in "My Father at Eighty-Five." In "A Dream of the Blacksmith's Room": "I dreamt last night you / Lived near me, not / Dead at all. . . ."

In "The Exhausted Bug," a prose poem clearly written at about the same time as *Meditations on the Insatiable Soul* (and dedicated to his father) but collected in the chapbook Bly published in 1993, *Gratitude to Old Teachers*, he describes "a tiny, hard-shelled" bug that has "exhausted itself" in the "cloisonné dish" on his desk. He says that "clearly the fire of life is flickering out" for the bug. The poem ends with this moving paragraph-stanza:

> The sharp lamplight lit up the dish; it is odd that I did not see him before. I will take him outdoors in the still chill spring air and let him drink the melted snow of late afternoon on this day when I have written of my father stretched out in his coffin.

The third section of *Meditations on the Insatiable Soul* contains the title poem and one other "meditation." These poems are similar to those in *Sleepers Joining Hands* in that they express—although in a much more muted voice—related political and psychological themes; they recall especially the two poems "The Teeth Mother Naked at Last" and "Sleepers Joining Hands." In the *Meditations*, however, specifically in the poem "Anger against Children," "the sleepers sleep," "the rage [has gone] inward at last," and then, too, "the time of grief has come."

In the fourth and final section of *Meditations on the Insatiable Soul* Bly moves away from the personal and back to the mythological and the historical—which, as if he were reminding himself, he says, in "St. George, the Dragon, and the Virgin," is "what we have forgotten." This section includes a sequence of five poems with variations on the title "How David Did Not Care" ("How the Saint" and "Vincentine" and so on "Did Not Care"). These poems repeat the phrase "For not to care is this" and follow it with such definitions as: "To love the orphans / And the fatherless, To dance as we sink / . . . To let the resonating / Box of the body sound" ("How David Did Not Care") and "To love the sunlight, / As it falls on the table, / To leap out of misery" ("How Jonah Did Not Care"). The final poem in the book has a quintessential Bly title, "The Sun Crosses Heaven from West to East Bringing Samson Back to the Womb." The last two lines of this poem read:

> The sun, no longer haunted by sunset and shadows,
> Sinks down in the Eastern ocean and is born.

Thus *Meditations on the Insatiable Soul* ends with a reversal—and the suggestion of yet another new beginning.

Bly, clearly, is a poet who seems to need to reinvent himself regularly—and to revise his poems to keep pace with the emergence of each new thematic shift in his life. If his penchant for constant writing has created problems for critics and has been frustrating to readers over the years, it has also helped to create the sense of excitement and expectation that has surrounded each of Bly's new books. Bly is a poet who resists all the tendencies that critics naturally have to place him firmly within a movement or to identify him with a specific tradition, to pin him down to one primary theme or thesis or to attempt to confine him within the constraints of one critical approach. In short, Robert Bly is a poet who, at the age of seventy, is still alive and active and as exciting as ever to watch and to wait for. One can only guess at what he might do next—and look forward to it.

In *The Soul Is Here for Its Own Joy*, a collection of "Sacred Poems from Many Cultures" Bly edited and published in 1995, he describes Kabir, the medieval Hindu poet he has long been interested in, and often translated, in terms that might be applied to Bly himself. He says that even though some of Kabir's poems "are clearly intended for close disciples," and even though they often "drop . . . suddenly from high, elevated language to the vernacular," they are composed primarily to be "sung to everyone" without any of the "usual distinctions . . . between men and women." Kabir, Bly says, "wants faithfulness over years." That is precisely what Bly wants—and what the majority of his readers have given him.

Selected Bibliography

WORKS OF ROBERT BLY

POETRY

The Lion's Tail and Eyes: Poems Written out of Laziness and Silence. Coauthored with James Wright and William Duffy. Madison, Minn.: The Sixties Press, 1962.

Silence in the Snowy Fields. Middletown, Conn.: Wesleyan University Press, 1962.

The Light around the Body. New York: Harper & Row, 1967.

The Teeth Mother Naked at Last. San Francisco: City Lights Books, 1970.

Jumping Out of Bed. Barre, Mass.: Barre Publishers, 1973.

Sleepers Joining Hands. New York: Harper & Row, 1973.

Point Reyes Poems. Half Moon Bay, Calif.: Mudra, 1974.

The Morning Glory. New York: Harper & Row, 1975.

Old Man Rubbing His Eyes. Greensboro, N.C.: Unicorn Press, 1975.

This Body Is Made of Camphor and Gopherwood. New York: Harper & Row, 1977.

This Tree Will Be Here for a Thousand Years. New York: Harper & Row, 1979; 1992.

The Man in the Black Coat Turns. New York: Dial Press, 1981.

Loving a Woman in Two Worlds. New York: Dial Press, 1985.

Selected Poems. New York: Harper & Row, 1986.

What Have I Ever Lost by Dying? New York: HarperCollins, 1992.

Gratitude to Old Teachers. Brockport, N.Y.: BOA Editions, 1993.

Meditations on the Insatiable Soul. New York: HarperCollins, 1994.

PROSE

The Eight Stages of Translation. Boston: Rowan Tree Press, 1983.

A Little Book on the Human Shadow. Memphis, Tenn.: Raccoon Books, 1986.

The Pillow and the Key: Commentary on the Fairy Tale Iron John. St. Paul, Minn.: Ally Press, 1987.

American Poetry: Wildness and Domesticity. New York: Harper & Row, 1990.

Iron John: A Book about Men. Reading, Mass.: Addison-Wesley, 1990.

Remembering James Wright. St. Paul, Minn.: Ally Press, 1991.

ESSAYS

"Five Decades of Modern American Poetry." *The Fifties,* 1:36–39 (1958).

"Poetry in an Age of Expansion." *Nation,* April 22, 1961, pp. 350–354.

"Some Notes on French Poetry." *The Sixties,* 5:66–70 (Fall 1961).

"Prose vs Poetry." *Choice: A Magazine of Poetry and Photography,* 2:65–80 (1962).

"A Wrong Turning in American Poetry." *Choice,* 3:33–47 (1963).

"The Dead World and the Live World." *The Sixties,* 8:2–7 (Spring 1966).

"Leaping Up into Political Poetry." *London Magazine,* 7:82–87 (Spring 1967).

"On Political Poetry." *Nation,* April 24, 1967, pp. 522–524.

"On Pablo Neruda." *Nation,* March 25, 1968, pp. 414–417.

"Looking for Dragon Smoke." In *Naked Poetry: Recent American Poetry in Open Forms.* Edited by Stephen Berg and Robert Mezey. Indianapolis, Ind.: Bobbs-Merrill, 1969. Pp. 161–164.

"Symposium: What's New in American and Canadian Poetry." *New,* 15:17–20 (April/May 1971).

"American Poetry: On the Way to the Hermetic." *Books Abroad,* 46:17–24 (1972).

"The Three Brains." *The Seventies,* 1:61–69 (1972).

"I Came Out of the Mother Naked." See his *Sleepers Joining Hands.* Pp. 29–50.

"Developing the Underneath." *American Poetry Review,* 2, no. 6:44–45 (November/December 1973).

"The Writer's Sense of Place." *South Dakota Review,* 13:73–75 (Autumn 1975).

"Being a Lutheran Boy-God in Minnesota." In *Growing Up in Minnesota: Ten Writers Remember Their Childhoods.* Edited by Chester G. Anderson. Minneapolis: University of Minnesota Press, 1976. Pp. 205–219.

"What the Prose Poem Carries with It." *American Poetry Review,* 6, no. 3:44–45 (May/June 1977).

"Where Have All the Critics Gone." *Nation,* April 22, 1978, pp. 456–459.

"The Two Presences." See his *This Tree Will Be Here for a Thousand Years.* Pp. 9–11.

"Two Stages of an Artist's Life." *Georgia Review,* 34, no. 1:105–109 (Spring 1980).

"Recognizing the Image as a Form of Intelligence." *Field,* 24:17–27 (Spring 1981).

"In Search of an American Muse." *New York Times Book Review,* January 22, 1984.

"Whitman's Line as a Public Form." See his *Selected Poems.* Pp. 194–198.

"The Prose Poem as an Evolving Form." See his *Selected Poems.* Pp. 199–204.

"Men's Initiation Rites." *Utne Reader,* April/May 1986, pp. 42–49.

"Disappointment and Desire." See his *What Have I Ever Lost by Dying?* P. xv.

BIBLIOGRAPHIES

Davis, William V. In his *Robert Bly: The Poet and His Critics.* Columbia, S.C.: Camden House, 1994.

Harris, Victoria Frenkel. In her *The Incorporative Consciousness of Robert Bly.* Carbondale: Southern Illinois University Press, 1992.

Roberson, William H. *Robert Bly: A Primary and Secondary Bibliography.* Metuchen, N.J.: Scarecrow Press, 1986.

TRANSLATED WORKS

Twenty Poems of Georg Trakl. Translated with James Wright. Madison, Minn.: The Sixties Press, 1961.

Twenty Poems of César Vallejo. Translated with John Knoepfle and James Wright. Madison, Minn.: The Sixties Press, 1962.

Forty Poems: Juan Ramón Jiménez. Madison, Minn.: The Sixties Press, 1967.

Twenty Poems of Pablo Neruda. Translated with James Wright. Madison, Minn.: The Sixties Press, 1967.

I Do Best Alone at Night: Poems by Gunnar Ekelöf. Translated with Christina Paulston. Washington, D.C.: Charioteer Press, 1968.

Twenty Poems of Tomas Tranströmer. Madison, Minn.: The Seventies Press, 1970.

Neruda and Vallejo: Selected Poems. Boston: Beacon Press, 1971.

Lorca and Jiménez: Selected Poems. Boston: Beacon Press, 1973.

Friends, You Drank Some Darkness: Three Swedish Poets. Boston: Beacon Press, 1975.

The Kabir Book: Forty-Four of the Ecstatic Poems of Kabir. Boston: Beacon Press, 1977.

Selected Poems of Rainer Maria Rilke. New York: Harper & Row, 1981.

Times Alone: Selected Poems of Antonio Machado. Middletown, Conn.: Wesleyan University Press, 1983.

Ten Poems of Francis Ponge Translated by Robert Bly and Ten Poems of Robert Bly Inspired by the Poems of Francis Ponge. Riverview, New Brunswick: Owl's Head Press, 1990.

EDITED WORKS

A Poetry Reading against the Vietnam War. Coedited with David Ray. Madison, Minn.: The Sixties Press, 1966.

Forty Poems Touching on Recent American History. Boston: Beacon Press, 1970.

Leaping Poetry: An Idea with Poems and Translations. Boston: Beacon Press, 1975.

News of the Universe: Poems of Twofold Consciousness. San Francisco: Sierra Club Books, 1980.

The Rag and Bone Shop of the Heart: Poems for Men. Coedited with James Hillman and Michael Meade. New York: HarperCollins, 1992.

The Darkness around Us Is Deep: Selected Poems of William Stafford. New York: HarperCollins, 1993.

The Soul Is Here for Its Own Joy: Sacred Poems from Many Cultures. Hopewell, N.J.: Ecco Press, 1995.

BIOGRAPHICAL AND CRITICAL STUDIES

Atkinson, Michael. "Robert Bly's *Sleepers Joining Hands*: Shadow and Self." *Iowa Review,* 7, no. 4:135–153 (Fall 1976).

Baker, Deborah. "Making a Farm: A Literary Biography of Robert Bly." *Poetry East,* 4/5:145–189 (Spring/Summer 1981).

Carruth, Hayden. "Poets on the Fringe." *Harper's,* January 1980, p. 79.

Chang, Leslie C. Review of *What Have I Ever Lost by Dying? Harvard Review,* 3:187–188 (1993).

Chappell, Fred. "Sepia Photographs and Jazz Solos." *New York Times Book Review,* October 13, 1985, p. 15.

Dacey, Philip. "The Reverend Robert E. Bly, Pastor, Church of the Blessed Unity: A Look at 'A Man Writes to a Part of Himself.'" *Pebble,* 18/19/20:1–7 (1979).

———. "Saint Robert." *American Book Review,* 8:13–14 (1986).

Daniels, Stevie, Lyndia LeMole, and Sherman Goldman. "Robert Bly on the Great Mother and the New Father." *East/West Journal,* August 1978, pp. 25–33; September 1978, pp. 42–46.

Davis, William V. "Defining the Age." *Moons and Lion Tailes,* 2, no. 3:85–89 (1977).

———. "'Hair in a Baboon's Ear': The Politics of Robert Bly's Early Poetry." *Carleton Miscellany,* 18, no. 1:74–84 (Winter 1979–1980).

———. "Camphor and Gopherwood: Robert Bly's Recent Poems in Prose." *Modern Poetry Studies,* 11, nos. 1–2:88–102 (1982).

———. "'Still the Place Where Creation Does Some Work on Itself': Robert Bly's Most Recent Work." See *Robert Bly: When Sleepers Awake.* Edited by Joyce Peseroff. Pp. 237–46.

———. *Understanding Robert Bly.* Columbia, S.C.: University of South Carolina Press, 1988.

———, ed. *Critical Essays on Robert Bly.* New York: G. K. Hall, 1992.

———. "Robert Bly." In *Critical Survey of Poetry: English Language Series.* Edited by Frank N. Magill. Pasadena, Calif.: Salem Press, 1992. Pp. 266–275.

———. *Robert Bly: The Poet and His Critics.* Columbia, S.C.: Camden House, 1994.

Dodd, Wayne. "Back to the Snowy Fields." See *Critical Essays on Robert Bly.* Edited by William V. Davis. Pp. 107–113.

Friberg, Ingegard. *Moving Inward: A Study of Robert Bly's Poetry.* Göteborg, Sweden: Acta Universitatis Gothoburgensis, 1977.

Gioia, Dana. "The Successful Career of Robert Bly." *Hudson Review,* 40, no. 2:207–223 (Summer 1987).

Gitzen, Julian. "Floating on Solitude: The Poetry of Robert Bly." *Modern Poetry Studies,* 7, no. 3:231–241 (Winter 1976).

Hall, Donald. "Notes on Robert Bly and *Sleepers Joining Hands.*" *Ohio Review,* 15:89–93 (Fall 1973).

———. "Young Bly." See *Critical Essays on Robert Bly.* Edited by William V. Davis. Pp. 27–29.

Harris, Victoria Frenkel. "Scribe, Inscription, Inscribed: Sexuality in the Poetry of Robert Bly and Adrienne Rich." In *Discontented Discourses: Feminism / Textual Intervention / Psychoanalysis.* Edited by Marleen S. Barr and Richard Feldstein. Urbana, Ill.: University of Illinois Press, 1989. Pp. 117–137.

———. "'Walking Swiftly' with Freedom: Robert Bly's Prose Poems." *American Poetry,* 7, no. 2:13–30 (Winter 1990).

———. *The Incorporative Consciousness of Robert Bly.* Carbondale, Ill.: Southern Illinois University Press, 1992.

Heyen, William. "Inward to the World: The Poetry of Robert Bly." *The Far Point,* 3:42–50 (Fall/Winter 1969).

Howard, Richard. "'Like Those Before, We Move to the Death We Love.'" In his *Alone with America: Essays on the Art of Poetry in the United States since 1950.* New York: Atheneum, 1969. Pp. 38–48.

Jarman, Mark. "The Poetry of Non Sequitur." *American Book Review,* 4, no. 4:13–14 (May/June 1982).

Jones, Richard, and Kate Daniels, eds. *Of Solitude and Silence: Writings on Robert Bly.* Boston: Beacon Press, 1981.

Kalaidjian, Walter. "From Silence to Subversion: Robert Bly's Political Surrealism." *Modern Poetry Studies,* 11, no. 3:289–306 (1983).

Kramer, Lawrence. "A Sensible Emptiness: Robert Bly and the Poetics of Immanence." *Contemporary Literature,* 24, no. 4:449–62 (Winter 1983).

Lacey, Paul A. "The Live World." In his *The Inner War: Forms and Themes in Recent American Poetry.* Philadelphia: Fortress Press, 1972. Pp. 32–56.

Libby, Anthony. "Robert Bly Alive in Darkness." *Iowa Review,* 3:78–89 (Summer 1972).

———. "Fire and Light: Four Poets in the End and Beyond." *Iowa Review,* 4, no. 2:111–26 (Spring 1973).

Matthews, William. "Thinking about Robert Bly." *Tennessee Poetry Journal,* 2:49–57 (Winter 1969).

Melnyczuk, Askold. "Robert Bly." *Partisan Review,* 65, no. 1:167–71 (1988).

Mersmann, James F. "Robert Bly: Watering the Rocks." In his *Out of the Vietnam Vortex: A Study of Poets and Poetry Against the War.* Lawrence, Kans.: University of Kansas Press, 1974. Pp. 113–57.

Miller, Brown. "Searching for Poetry: Real vs. Fake." *San Francisco Review of Books,* July 8, 1983, p. 22.

Mills, Ralph J., Jr. " 'The Body with the Lamp Lit Inside': Robert Bly's New Poems." *Northeast,* 3, no. 2:37–47 (Winter 1976–1977).

———. " 'Of Energy Compacted and Whirling': Robert Bly's Recent Prose Poems." *New Mexico Humanities Review,* 4, no. 2:29–49 (Summer 1981).

Mitchell, Roger. "Robert Bly and the Trouble with American Poetry." *Ohio Review,* 42:86–92 (1988).

Molesworth, Charles. "Thrashing in the Depths: The Poetry of Robert Bly." *Rocky Mountain Review of Language and Literature,* 29, nos. 3–4:95–117 (Autumn 1975).

———. "Domesticating the Sublime: Bly's Latest Poems." *Ohio Review,* 19, no. 3:56–66 (1978).

Moran, Ronald, and George Lensing. "The Emotive Imagination: A New Departure in American Poetry." *Southern Review,* N. s. 3:51–67 (January 1967).

Nelson, Howard. *Robert Bly: An Introduction to the Poetry.* New York: Columbia University Press, 1984.

Perloff, Marjorie. "Soft Touch." *Parnassus,* 10, no. 1:221–230 (Spring/Summer 1982).

Peseroff, Joyce, ed. *Robert Bly: When Sleepers Awake.* Ann Arbor, Mich.: University of Michigan Press, 1984.

———. "Minnesota Transcendentalist." *New York Times Book Review,* May 25, 1986, p. 2.

Rehder, Robert. "Which Way to the Future?" See *Critical Essays on Robert Bly.* Edited by William V. Davis. Pp. 267–282.

Richman, Robert. "The Poetry of Robert Bly." *New Criterion,* 5, no. 4:37–46 (1986).

Smith, Thomas R., ed. *Walking Swiftly: Writings and Images on the Occasion of Robert Bly's 65th Birthday.* St. Paul, Minn.: Ally Press, 1992.

Solotaroff, Ted. "Captain Bly." *Nation,* September 9, 1991, pp. 270–274.

Stitt, Peter. "Dark Volumes." *New York Times Book Review,* February 14, 1982, pp. 15, 37.

———. "The Startling Journeys of Robert Bly." See *Critical Essays on Robert Bly.* Edited by William V. Davis. Pp. 283–291.

Stuewe, Paul. Review of *The Man in the Black Coat Turns. Quill & Quire,* 48:39 (1982).

Sugg, Richard P. "Robert Bly and the Poetics of Evolutionary Psychology." *Journal of Evolutionary Psychology,* 6, nos. 1–2:33–37 (1985).

———. *Robert Bly.* Boston: Twayne, 1986.

Weinberger, Eliot. "Gloves on a Mouse." *Nation,* November 17, 1979, pp. 503–504.

INTERVIEWS

Bly, Robert. *Talking All Morning.* Ann Arbor, Mich.: University of Michigan Press, 1980. A collection of interviews, essays, and poems.

Shakarchi, Joseph. "An Interview with Robert Bly." *Massachusetts Review,* 23, no. 2:226–243 (1982).

Thompson, Keith. "What Men Really Want." *New Age Journal,* 7 (May 1982).

———. "Connecting with the Wild Man inside All Males." *Utne Reader,* November/December 1989, p. 58.

Wagenheim, Jeff. "The Secret Life of Men." *New Age Journal,* October 1990, pp. 40–45, 106–113.

—WILLIAM V. DAVIS

Paul Bowles

1910–

A N INVETERATE TRAVELER, composer, and writer, Paul Bowles is a remarkable figure whose life and work have embodied and responded to the major impulses of the twentieth century. His life itself would be of considerable interest even had he not produced countless musical scores (including several operas), four novels, more than sixty short stories, numerous travel pieces, an unrevealing autobiography, and dozens of translations of stories by local Moroccan storytellers. His autobiography, *Without Stopping,* which was published in 1972, reads like a who's who of twentieth-century arts and letters. Among those whose lives intersected with Bowles's are Aaron Copland, Gertrude Stein, Djuna Barnes, Christopher Isherwood, Kurt Schwitters, Claude McKay, W. H. Auden, Tennessee Williams, William S. Burroughs, Allen Ginsberg, and Patricia Highsmith. During the thirties, forties, and fifties Bowles journeyed—always by ship or overland—relentlessly, almost frantically, to and from New York, into the heart of North Africa's deserts, into the depths of the tropical forests of Latin America, and around the globe to the small island of Taprobane, off the coast of Sri Lanka, an island he finally bought when he learned it was up for sale. These landscapes become backdrops for Bowles's fiction. Bowles wrote in his preface to *A Distant Episode: The Selected Stories* (1988): "It seems a practical procedure to

let the place determine the characters who will inhabit it.''

Bowles's fictional worlds typically feature American travelers in exotic and hostile foreign settings who fall prey to disease, psychological disintegration, or terror. Man is adrift in an endless existential quest to piece together meaning in an increasingly chaotic, barbaric, and horrifying world. Bowles's music, on the other hand, is more cheerful and benign. In his collection of essays *Setting the Tone,* the composer Ned Rorem contrasted Bowles's literary and musical styles, observing that while Bowles's fiction is "dark and cruel, clearly meant to horrify in an impersonal sort of way,'' his music is "nostalgic and witty, evoking the times and places of its conception.'' In both his musical and literary works, Bowles has been most comfortable and consistently successful with shorter forms. And, whether writing music or stories, he shows scrupulous attention to detail, structure, rhythm and counterpoint, and the creation of a mood and tone.

An only child, Paul Frederic Bowles was born in Jamaica, Long Island, on December 30, 1910, to Rena and Claude Bowles. Bowles fondly remembers his mother reading Poe to him in his early years, while he chiefly remembers his father, a dentist, as a strict disciplinarian. One regimen Bowles recalls his father imposing was the practice of "Fletcherization," named for the nutritionist Horace Fletcher, whereby Paul was made to chew each mouthful of food forty times before swallowing it. Bowles also recounts in his autobiography hearing his grandmother tell him that his father had tried to kill him when he was a baby, by leaving him virtually naked in a basket by an open window in the dead of winter. Whether that incident indeed happened or not, Bowles seemed ready and willing to believe it; thus it left a deep impression on his psychic map.

A sense of Bowles's rebellion against his father's authority, and his flight toward art as a refuge, can be felt in "The Frozen Fields," one of just a half dozen or so stories set in the United States, which Bowles wrote en route to Sri Lanka in 1956, not long after his parents had visited him in Tangier. The story features a six-year-old boy named Donald who goes with his parents to spend Christmas on his grandparents' farm in New England. Throughout the story Donald and his father are at odds. In the opening scene his father shouts at him to stop scratching pictures into the ice on the window of the train. At another point his father throws him down roughly in the snow and stuffs snow down his neck. Donald finds considerably more sympathy from a rather flamboyant man named Mr. Gordon—a "friend" of his Uncle Ivor—who lavishes him with Christmas gifts. In a dream Donald has at the story's end, he finds himself running off with a wolf he has befriended.

"The Frozen Fields" is one of Bowles's most autobiographical stories. The fictional farm is doubtlessly drawn from his grandparents' Happy Hollow Farm in Massachusetts, which he often visited as a boy, while Donald is a portrait of Bowles as a young man. The father in the story bears a striking resemblance to Bowles's own father, and Uncle Ivor is clearly based on Paul's Uncle Guy. As in so many other instances in Bowles's fiction, the fragile worlds of children are vulnerable to adult whims and outbursts. Dreams, the creation of art, and travel provide channels for escape.

Bowles began drawing maps and spinning fictions in notebooks when he was quite young. In his early teens he wrote a number of crime stories featuring a character named Volga Merna, "the Snake Woman," who could evade capture with her ability to alter her appearance. Bowles's high school French teacher, who was well versed in modern literature, noticed Bowles's aptitude and nurtured his literary interests. Bowles's literary aspirations were boosted even more when, at the age of seventeen, one of his poems, "Spire Song," was accepted for publication in the twelfth volume of *transition,* a magazine edited in Paris by Eugène Jolas and whose contributors included many major proponents of modernism, such as Djuna Barnes, James Joyce, Paul Éluard, and Gertrude Stein.

In his late teens Bowles enrolled in the University of Virginia, conscious that Edgar Allan Poe had studied there nearly a century earlier. Neither writer, however, completed his course work. Like so many American writers (notably, James Fenimore Cooper, Nathaniel Hawthorne, Henry James, and Edith Wharton), Bowles felt the pull of Europe. In 1929, without telling his parents, he set sail for Europe on the *Rijndam,* taking with him a copy of André Gide's *The Counterfeiters* (1926). His decision would seem to have been prompted by a desire to elude parental and collegiate authority, as well as by his native curiosity and lust for adventure. This first tour, short-lived as it was, whetted Bowles's appetite for travel and more sustained associations with the centers of cultural production.

Back in New York he met the composer and music critic Henry Cowell, who referred him to Aaron Copland for studies in composition. When Copland announced plans to go to Europe, Bowles was quick to follow suit. In Paris he received advice on his life and career from both

Copland and Virgil Thomson, briefly and intermittently studying music composition with the legendary Nadia Boulanger. Bowles was never one to admire the German Romantic composers such as Beethoven; instead he listened keenly to, and learned from, the European moderns—Francis Poulenc, Paul Hindemith, Igor Stravinsky, Darius Milhaud, and Sergey Prokofiev.

While in Paris the young Bowles, impeccably dressed and boyishly charming, found that doors opened quite easily before him. One of those on whom Bowles called was Gertrude Stein, who had set up residence in Paris two decades earlier and lived, with her lover Alice B. Toklas, on rue de Fleurus. Later in his life, Bowles's apartment in Tangier served as a magnet for writers, artists, and the just-plain-curious, much like Stein's home had earlier. Stein, perhaps best known for her modernist ''nonsense'' poetry, her championing of artists such as Pablo Picasso and Henri Matisse, and her *Autobiography of Alice B. Toklas* (1933), rather paternalistically took on the young Bowles, whom she called ''Freddy,'' a name she thought suited him better than ''Paul.''

A free and independent spirit, Stein served not only as an important literary model for Bowles, but proffered bits of advice concerning his career. Her opinion of his poetry (''It's not poetry,'' she remarked upon reading samples he had given her) may have pushed him toward fiction. It was Stein also, according to Bowles, who first urged the young composer (for at that time his primary identity was attached to music, not literature) to go to Morocco. Stein herself had been to Tangier and thought the place perfectly suited to Bowles's temperament. Playfully suggesting a kind of literary colonialism, Stein reputedly said, ''I have France. Ernest [Hemingway] has Spain. That leaves Morocco for you.'' In recounting the anecdote, Bowles consciously linked himself to two of the century's literary giants, solidly establishing his pedigree.

*　　*　　*

With Stein's suggestion propelling him, Bowles set off on a trip in 1931 that included a stop in Tangier. The place immediately captured his imagination. Years later in his autobiography, *Without Stopping,* he recalled his response to the small, quaint port, looking north toward the Iberian peninsula from the Maghreb:

> If I said that Tangier struck me as a dream city, I should mean it in the strict sense. Its topography was rich in prototypal dream scenes: covered streets like corridors with doors opening into rooms on each side, hidden terraces high above the sea, streets consisting only of steps, dark impasses, small squares built on sloping terrain so that they looked like ballet sets designed in false perspective, with alleys leading off in several directions; as well as the classical dream equipment of tunnels, ramparts, ruins, dungeons, and cliffs.

This initial contact was the beginning of Bowles's lifelong romance with Morocco. As was the case with Edgar Allan Poe, architectural features, profoundly Gothic, captured Bowles's attention, serving, perhaps, as an objective manifestation of the writer's psychic landscape. The place stirred something deep in his unconscious, and provided him with a fresh landscape and culture to exploit imaginatively. Just a decade or so before Bowles's discovery of Morocco, another American writer, Edith Wharton, had noted the country's charms during a visit there. ''If one loses one's way,'' she writes in *In Morocco* (1920), ''civilization vanishes as though it were a magic carpet rolled up by a djinn.'' All this fascinated and allured Bowles, who—like other modern romantics of the West, such as Paul Gauguin, Pablo Picasso, Pierre Loti, William Butler Yeats, D. H. Lawrence, and so many others—sought in the primitive some force that might oppose or counteract the dominant modern order, with its massive, inhumane bureaucracies, its authoritarian psychoanalytic programs, its war machines, its unswerving faith in rational thought. In North Africa Bowles found a place where magic, storytelling, *djun* (genies), the power of curse, and a kind of primitive spirit were all alive.

From 1930 to 1933, Bowles traveled considerably, mostly in North Africa, writing music along the way. On his 1931 trip to Berlin, which he found cold and uninspiring, he met Christopher Isherwood and Stephen Spender. Some have suggested that Isherwood named Sally Bowles in his *Berlin Stories* after Paul. During these years of travel Bowles composed a sonata for oboe and clarinet; a sonata for flute and piano; a cantata for soprano, chorus, and harmonium, *Par le Détroit*; and *Scènes d'Anabase,* a chamber work based on a piece by the French poet Saint-John Perse.

Throughout the thirties and the early forties Bowles kept up his nomadic lifestyle, using New York (a city he often expressed disdain for) as his base. In the thirties Bowles found that his cosmopolitanism ran against the grain of an American parochialism and that his formalist aesthetic was at odds with the ideological approaches to art that were then in vogue. Bowles's movements were determined as much by personal finances and opportunity as by design. In 1934, for example, he left New York for Morocco, having convinced a Colonel Williams to take him as his assistant. When resources ran low, he was forced to come home. En route to New York (by ship again) he made stops in Puerto Rico and Venezuela, storing up memories and images of landscapes he was later to use in his fiction.

During this time Bowles did a considerable amount of composing. He wrote the score for Lincoln Kirstein's ballet *Yankee Clipper,* built around a travel motif and featuring various musical styles to evoke various ports of call. He also completed a song cycle, *Memnon,* based on a text by Jean Cocteau, and "Letter to Freddy," setting to music words from a letter Stein had written to him. "Letter to Freddy" was published in a focus on Bowles in the April 1935 issue of *New Music,* a journal associated with Henry

Cowell. In 1936 he collaborated with Orson Welles on a Federal Theater Project production called *Horse Eats Hay,* producing the music for the show. Bowles also tried his hand at film scores, including those for *Bride of Samoa* (1933) and *Venus and Adonis* (1935).

In 1937 Bowles met Jane Auer, whom he married the following year. He was then twenty-seven; she was twenty. The ensuing marriage was, by all accounts, unconventional. Each, while maintaining close ties to the other, developed intimate relationships with friends of their own sex. At the time of their marriage it was actually Jane who was more devoted to her work as a writer. Her first and only completed novel, *Two Serious Ladies*, was published in 1943. Originally she had titled it *Three Serious Ladies*, but Paul, in reviewing the manuscript, advised that one of the ladies—a Señora Córdoba—be dropped.

Characters modeled after the Bowleses can be found in a variety of places in both writers' works. Paul's story "Call at Corazón" gives fictional shape to the Bowleses' honeymoon trip, in 1938, which took them to the Caribbean and Colón, Panama, among other places. The man and woman in the story struggle to balance their individual needs with those demanded by the relationship. In her portrayal of Mr. and Mrs. Copperfield in *Two Serious Ladies*, Jane draws from that same trip, invoking precisely the same themes Paul handles in his story. In Paul's fourth novel, *Up Above the World,* which was published in 1966, Dr. Slade is, like Mr. Copperfield, a somewhat distant, cold, and unsympathetic almost misanthropic character. Port and Kit in Paul's first novel, *The Sheltering Sky,* which came out in 1949, are yet other incarnations of the Bowleses. In a fragment titled "The Iron Table," published in *My Sister's Hand in Mine: The Collected Works of Jane Bowles* (1978), Jane sketches a scene featuring a couple who voice opinions nearly identical to those of Kit and Port in the opening scenes of *The Sheltering Sky:*

"The whole civilization is going to pieces," he said.

Her voice was sorrowful. "I know it." Her answers to his ceaseless complaining about the West's contamination of Moslem culture had become increasingly unpredictable. Today, because she felt that he was in a very irritable mood and in need of an argument, she automatically agreed with him. "It's going to pieces so quickly, too," she said, and her tone was sepulchral.

He looked at her without any light in his blue eyes. "There are places where the culture has remained untouched," he announced as if for the first time. "If we went into the desert you wouldn't have to face all this. Wouldn't you love that?" He was punishing her for her swift agreement with him a moment earlier. He knew she had no desire to go to the desert, and that she believed it was not possible to continue trying to escape from the Industrial Revolution. . . .

"Why do you ask me if I wouldn't love to go into the desert, when you know as well as I do I wouldn't. . . ."

"Well," he said. "You change. Sometimes you say you *would* like to go."

It was true. She did change. Sometimes she would run to him with bright eyes. "Let's go," she would say. "Let's go into the desert." But she never did this if she was sober.

This scene captures, as well as any, the dynamic between Jane and Paul.

Jane's personality and literary style stand in marked contrast to Paul's. She was socially gregarious while he was relatively reserved. Her quirky prose bursts at the seams, flying off unexpectedly in one direction or another. His is remarkably controlled, maintaining an external mask of propriety to balance the disturbing elements below the surface. Tennessee Williams, who knew both of the Bowleses, encouraged Jane's work as a playwright. He welcomed the 1953 New York production of Jane's play *In the Summer House,* for which Paul wrote the music, calling it "not only the most original play I have ever read, I think it is also the oddest and the funniest and one of the most touching. . . . It is one of those very rare plays which

are not tested by the theatre but by which the theatre is tested."

The decade of the forties was an amazingly productive period for Paul Bowles. It was, as well, a transitional period, during which he gradually moved away from composing and focused increasingly on his writing. For a ten-year period stretching from the mid-forties to the mid-fifties, Bowles seemed to keep the two activities in balance, dividing his energies between them.

During this time Bowles's musical output was prodigious. One of Bowles's best-known works, "Music for a Farce," came from another collaboration with Orson Welles, *Too Much Johnson,* in 1938. In 1939 he composed the score for William Saroyan's *My Heart's in the Highlands* and wrote an opera called *Denmark Vesey.* In 1940 he composed incidental music for productions of Saroyan's *Love's Old Sweet Song* and Shakespeare's *Twelfth Night* as well as the score for a Soil Erosion Service film, *Roots in the Soil.* In 1941 he wrote music for Philip Barry's production of *Liberty Jones* and Lillian Hellman's *Watch on the Rhine;* the same year he did music for Kirstein's ballet *Pastorela.* In 1943 the Museum of Modern Art in New York put on a performance of Bowles's opera *The Wind Remains,* the libretto of which was adapted from a play by Federico García Lorca; it was conducted by Leonard Bernstein and choreographed by Merce Cunningham. In 1944 Bowles scored the film *Congo* and *Colloque Sentimental,* a ballet whose sets were designed by the surrealist artist Salvador Dalí. In 1946 Bowles composed his Sonata for Two Pianos, and during 1947 he wrote his Concerto for Pianoforte, Winds, and Percussion.

The purpose of listing these works is to give a sense of the magnitude of Bowles's musical output, which has not been widely appreciated. Especially prodigious was his work in composing scores for the theater, a form that suited his talents. As Virgil Thomson put it, "Paul had a unique gift for the theater. It's something you either have or you don't, and Paul did.'' Altogether Bowles wrote incidental theater music for thirty-three shows, including several plays by Tennessee Williams. Collaboration between the two began with *Glass Menagerie* in 1944, and later Bowles set Williams' lyrics to music in a choral piece called *Blue Mountain Ballads* (1946) and composed scores for Williams' plays *Summer and Smoke* (1948) and *Sweet Bird of Youth* (1959).

During this time, not surprisingly, Bowles counted among his friends and colleagues many of the biggest names in the New York music world: Samuel Barber, Leonard Bernstein, Gian Carlo Menotti, John Cage, Ned Rorem, and Peggy Glanville-Hicks, as well as Virgil Thomson and Aaron Copland. For a short time in the early forties the Bowleses lived at 7 Middagh Street in Brooklyn Heights, sharing the house with W. H. Auden, Benjamin Britten, Peter Pears, and Thomas Mann's son Golo. Gypsy Rose Lee had been a previous tenant, and Carson McCullers and Richard Wright moved in after.

By the mid-forties Bowles had begun to devote more attention to writing, and his efforts paid off. In 1942 he took over the job of music critic for the *New York Herald Tribune* from Thomson. Over the next several years he wrote hundreds of reviews, including spotlights on jazz and folk music as well as classical performances. The rigor and demands of writing quickly for deadlines inculcated the habit and discipline of writing. The form of the review, furthermore, imposes a certain economy of expression, which is found, too, in Bowles's short stories.

In 1945 Bowles took on what he later called ''an undistinguished translation'' of Jean-Paul Sartre's *Huis Clos* (1944), a play better known to English readers by the title Bowles gave it—*No Exit*. His early experimental story ''The Scorpion'' (a kind of anthropological myth) was published by *View* in 1945 as well. The following

year ''The Echo'' appeared in *Harper's Bazaar* and ''A Distant Episode'' appeared in *Partisan Review* in 1947. These early stories display thematic concerns and stylistic characteristics that have become closely associated with Bowles: foreign settings; shock and betrayal; deep, simmering tensions between characters (parents and children) threatening to erupt at any point; rich verbal textures; and economy.

For the setting of ''The Echo,'' written in New York, Bowles draws on his memories of Latin American landscapes. A young American coed named Aileen travels to Colombia to visit her mother, who has built a striking home hanging over a gorge in Jamonocal, not far from Barranquilla. The home itself, precariously perched on the hillside, is a central emblem for the state of human relationships in the story. Hoping for an intimate reunion with her mother, Aileen finds instead that her mother's affections and interests are directed toward another woman, Prue. The friction between the daughter and the mother's companion builds, breaking out at one point in a nasty altercation. In the end, Aileen leaves, failing to meet the expectations of her visit. Throughout the story the landscape takes on an ominous quality, intensifying the sense of potential threat and vulnerability.

''A Distant Episode,'' one of Bowles's best-known stories, inscribes a narrative pattern Bowles was to follow and expand on in *The Sheltering Sky:* a journey farther and farther away from civilization, leading finally to speechlessness, madness, and death. The central character in the story, called only ''Professor,'' returns to Aïn Tadouirt, an imaginary town in the south of Morocco. Although trained as a linguist, the professor is an inept reader of what goes on around him. He is lured into the desert, where he loses his way and is captured by the Reguibat, a fierce tribe. He is beaten and tortured. They cut out his tongue. He apparently loses all memory. Tin can lids are tied to his body, and he is made to perform as a kind of clown. Rousing back to consciousness, he murders a member of the tribe. He is arrested by the French, but escapes, dodging a bullet, and is driven into the desert, where he has little chance of survival.

No one has ever said Bowles is for the fainthearted. Responding to the critic Oliver Evans' comments on "A Distant Episode" in an interview, Bowles said, "Shock is a *sine qua non* to the story. You don't teach a thing like that unless you are able, in some way, to make the reader understand what the situation would be like to *him*. And that involves shock."

Many have speculated that seeing Jane's work did much to rekindle Paul's own writerly ambitions—as well as a desire to be doing exactly what he wanted, rather than responding to and fitting in to others' work. Wish for greater pecuniary reward might also have motivated him. In 1947, after Paul had received an advance from Doubleday to write a novel and while Jane was still in the United States, she wrote to Paul: "Perhaps writing *will* be a means to nomadic life for you, but I hope you won't slowly stop writing music, altogether. I think you will do both." For a while he did, but it became increasingly difficult to maintain his connection with New York, which was necessary to his work as a composer. Furthermore, he soon enjoyed considerable success (and greater financial rewards) from his writing.

Advance in hand, Bowles set sail for Casablanca in 1947. Since that time, with the exception of journeys to Fez, Sri Lanka, and California, he has resided for the most part in Tangier. Bowles has customarily made good use of his times aboard ship, either for writing or composing. On his trip from New York to Casablanca, on board the *Fernscape,* he drafted one of his most powerful and controversial stories, "Pages from Cold Point." The story takes the form of undated diary entries made by Norton, an American university professor who, supported by an

inheritance left him when his wife Hope died, has found refuge on a Caribbean island. In a tone befitting the time just after the bombing of Hiroshima and Nagasaki, Norton proclaims that civilization is doomed. The central drama in the story revolves around three men: Norton, his son Racky, and Norton's older brother Charles, a successful lawyer back in the United States. When Norton hears complaints that Racky has been involved in illicit trade with the men and boys of the community, he is reluctant to confront his son. Racky's manipulation of and flirtation with his father culminate one evening when Norton returns from a walk and finds his son naked in his bed. While nothing happens explicitly, the undercurrents are powerfully suggestive. Like "The Echo," this story examines unsettling dynamics between parent and child that threaten the very basis of familial order.

Bowles began to write his first novel in Fez and continued while traveling on the Iberian peninsula and in North Africa. He established a method of writing by which scenes were reinforced with "details reported from life during the day of writing, regardless of whether the resulting juxtaposition was apposite or not," as Bowles described in *Without Stopping. The Sheltering Sky,* the resulting novel, enjoyed considerable success upon its publication in England and the United States, staying on the best-seller list in the United States for eleven weeks in 1950. Made into a movie by Bernardo Bertolucci in 1990, the novel remains Bowles's best-known and most popular work.

The opening scenes of the novel show an American couple, Port and Kit Moresby, who have gotten off the boat in North Africa, seeking a place as far removed as possible from the effects of World War II. When Kit laments that in modern times "the people of each country get more like the people of every other country," Port agrees and tells her that she will find everything in the Sahara truly different. Their rudderless quest takes them from one oasis to the other—from the coast to Boussif, to Aïn Krofra to El Ga'a to Sbâ—farther and farther into the desert. The metaphysical import of one of the novel's central figures is revealed in a conversation between Kit and Port:

> "The sky here's very strange. I often have the sensation when I look at it that it's a solid thing up there, protecting us from what's behind." . . .
> "But what *is* behind?" Her voice was very small.
> "Nothing, I suppose. Just darkness. Absolute night."

Thus Bowles joins the ranks of modern writers whose work displays a decidedly nihilistic worldview.

From the outset the relationship between the couple, married for more than a decade and childless, is unstable. The restless Port, charged by the excitement of the exotic and the romance of the unknown, wanders off to find pleasure with a native woman. Kit, in response, forms a short-lived liaison with Tunner, their American traveling companion. As much as Kit seems to crave intimacy with Port, he either is unwilling or unable to take on the responsibilities and constraints of love. Anyone at all familiar with the Bowleses will see similarities between Port and Paul, and Kit and Jane.

A surprising feature of the plot is Port's death, which occurs three-quarters of the way through the novel, after he has contracted typhoid. The third book of the novel, "The Sky," traces Kit's journey after her husband's death. Left to fend for herself, she could turn to Tunner, but chooses instead to head off on foot into the desert, severing her ties to the past, perhaps as a means of coping with her grief. There she is picked up by Belqassim and his band of fellow camel drivers and becomes a sexual object, subject to Belqassim's will. Their journey ultimately takes them to a village in the Sudan. In male guise, having lost nearly all memory of her past, Kit remains captive to Belqassim for some time, until her senses are aroused and she finally effects an escape, rebelling against his often violent means of control. "I've got to get out. I've got to get out," she tells herself. After some effort, a completely dissembled Kit does, at the end of the novel, find her way back to civilization.

On the heels of *The Sheltering Sky* came *The Delicate Prey and Other Stories* (1950). With these two books Bowles broke onto the literary scene full force. The collection includes a total of seventeen stories, "The Scorpion," "A Distant Episode," "The Echo," and "Pages from Cold Point" among them. One of the stories that gave Bowles a certain notoriety, and likely provoked Leslie Fiedler to dub the author a "pornographer of terror," was "The Delicate Prey." Told in its bald outlines, the tale, set in North Africa and featuring no Europeans, is utterly gruesome. When a lone member of the Moungari tribe comes upon three traveling Filali leather merchants, they unwittingly trust him. The two older Filala fall into the Moungari's trap and are murdered. The remaining Filala, a boy named Driss, wakes to find himself alone in the presence of the predator. The drug-intranced Moungari overpowers the young boy, cuts off his penis, stuffs it in an incision he makes in the boy's stomach, then takes his pleasure with the boy.

These kinds of bristling scenes, for which Bowles is perhaps best known, are meant to disturb us. A bit sadistically, he likes to see his readers squirm. Horror preys on our unconscious fears and excites our sense of vulnerability. As Bowles would have it, horror reminds us of the malevolent forces lurking in the dark.

Because of their unflinching brutality, the stories set in North Africa tend to overshadow those set elsewhere. Yet, it is worth noting that nearly half of the stories in *The Delicate Prey* are set in Latin America and two ("How Many Midnights'' and ''You Are Not I'') in the United States. In his Latin American stories Bowles again skillfully invokes a sense of place. In addition to ''The Echo,'' ''Pages from Cold Point,'' and ''Call at Corazón,'' which have already been discussed, mention should be made of ''At Paso Rojo,'' ''Pastor Dowe at Tacaté,'' ''Under the Sky,'' and ''Señor Ong and Señor Ha.'' In writing all these stories Bowles relied on memories and knowledge absorbed on his various wanderings through the region in the thirties and forties.

In 1952 Bowles published his second novel, *Let It Come Down.* In the preface to an edition published thirty years later, the writer tells how the novel got its start as he was passing through the Straits of Gibraltar on a Polish freighter late in 1949, en route to Sri Lanka.

> I stood on deck watching the flashes of the lighthouse at Cape Spartel, the northwestern corner of Africa. As we sailed eastward I could distinguish the lights of certain houses on the Old Mountain. Then when we came nearer to Tangier, a thin fog settled over the water, and only the glow of the city's lights was visible, reflecting in the sky. That was when I felt an unreasoning and powerful desire to be in Tangier. Up until that moment it had not even occurred to me to write a book about the international city.

Bowles then retired to his cabin to start work on a scene that takes place on the cliffs he had just passed, which later found its place in the novel. He wrote portions of the novel on the ship to and in Sri Lanka, completing it when he returned to Morocco and took up residence briefly in Xauen, a small village in the Rif.

Let It Come Down, whose title is drawn from Shakespeare's *Macbeth,* is the story of a young American, Nelson Dyar, who comes to Morocco to escape the clutches of his father and the boredom of New York employment and unemployment. Once in Tangier, he gradually becomes enmeshed in a web of entanglements, including a

''friendship'' with a young Moroccan, Thami Beidaoui. The structure and design of this novel are quite different from that of *The Sheltering Sky.* By manipulating point of view and by plotting carefully, Bowles creates interesting juxtapositions between the views of the American expatriate and the local Moroccans with whom he comes in contact. The narratives of Dyar and Thami are gradually woven together more tightly, yet in the end we may wonder whether greater proximity necessarily leads to understanding. In the fourth and last book of the novel, ''Another Kind of Silence,'' Thami and Dyar literally inhabit the same space and time, first escaping Tangier together in a boat, then climbing Djebel Musa, and, finally, like fugitives, taking refuge in a small cabin in the Rif. On their sea voyage Dyar looks at Thami, uncomprehendingly.

> His mind turned to wondering what kind of man it was who sat near him on the floor, saying nothing. He had talked with Thami, sat and drunk with him, but during all the moments they had been in one another's company it never had occurred to him to ask himself what thoughts went on behind those inexpressive features.

The novel's end, consistent with Bowles's aesthetic, is both shocking and morbid. Dyar, possessed by his kif-induced hallucinations, drives a nail into Thami's eardrum. Not so surprisingly, William S. Burroughs has singled out this scene and that of Port's typhoid hallucinations in *The Sheltering Sky* as among his favorite passages in contemporary literature.

In 1955, three years after *Let It Come Down,* Bowles's third novel, *The Spider's House,* was published. The theme of vulnerability is registered in the Koranic verse from which the novel takes its title: ''The likeness of those who choose other patrons than Allah is as the likeness of the spider when she taketh unto herself a house, and lo! the frailest of all houses is the spider's house, if they but knew.'' His longest, most stationary, least popular, and least shocking novel, *The Spider's House* centers on the lives of a young Moroccan boy, Amar, and an American journalist, John Stenham, in the old Moroccan capital Fez during a period of political insurrection and social change. In his preface to the novel, Bowles tells how he had originally set out in 1954 to depict the traditional, almost medieval life of Fez, but found that this way of life was being radically transformed right before his eyes. French rule was crumbling; Moroccan nationalism, promoted by the Istiqlal Party, was on the rise. The novel, then, was shaped to respond to and represent these new forces.

One of the achievements of *The Spider's House* is Bowles's extended development of the young Moroccan, Amar, doubtless one of the most thorough and true fictional portrayals of an Arab by a Western writer. Indeed, the density of the novel's description of Moroccan culture may account for the fact that it has not been as widely known as Bowles's other novels. Two books of the novel, ''The Master of Wisdom'' and ''Sins Are Finished,'' are given over to Amar's story. We see him playing with friends, watching his family, thinking in the solitude of an orchard, and being beaten by his father. His upbringing has been Muslim, and his is a traditionally ordered universe in which Allah is the most powerful and merciful. Yet, even within rigid religious structures, the boy registers doubts as he tries to determine just what his place in the universe is and what his religion means to him. As disturbance comes to Fez, Amar learns that the traditional Aïd el Kebir festival will not be celebrated as it has been in the past. He doesn't understand why. Unwittingly the boy eventually finds himself caught up in the Istiqlal, which assumes he knows more than he does.

Bowles skillfully arranges the convergence of the narratives of Amar and Stenham, both of whom are shown to lack knowledge of the political events swirling around them. Stenham and his American friend Lee ''Polly'' Burroughs take in Amar and develop a kind of friendship during which the differences between East and West, between Christianity and Islam, become a source of tension and discussion. Stenham's whole quest, we learn, is for an oasis of beauty in the modern world; he sees it nearly fulfilled in the traditional form of Moroccan life tilting so precariously toward modernity. Stenham's fear is that the corruption of the West (advertising, technology, cars, canned music, and so on) will spread to Islamic societies, damaging or even destroying the more traditional Moroccan culture. To Stenham, Amar was ''a consolation, a living proof that today's triumph was not yet total; he personified Stenham's infantile hopes that time might still be halted and man set back to his origins.'' During one exchange between Amar and Stenham, the Moroccan bursts out, ''You're a Nazarene, a Christian. That's why you talk that way. If you were a Moslem and said such things, you'd be killed or struck blind here, this minute. Christians have good hearts, but they don't know anything. They think they can change what has been written. They're afraid to die because they don't understand what death is for. And if you're afraid to die, then you don't know what life is for. How can you live?''

Amar and Stenham, to some extent, through their conversations and interactions, transcend cultural boundaries; they both refuse to be taken in by the independence movement, which for both threatens to obliterate a world of clear and solid meaning. While Stenham resembles Bowles in many ways (both have New England heritages, both are writers, and both are former members of the Communist Party, and so on), the character of Amar owes much to Bowles's intimate relationship with the young artist Ahmed Yacoubi, whom he first met in Fez in 1947. His friendship with Yacoubi and creation of the young Amar are paeans to innocence and a pre-rational world. In the novel the relationship between the man and the boy is quite dramatically severed. The last scene shows Amar taking a ride in a car with Stenham and Polly, who are headed toward Meknès. The Americans finally deposit the boy on the edge of town, telling him they can take him no farther. Amar is then seen running after the car, hoping it will stop and take him aboard. This can be seen as a powerful symbol of the dynamic between the United States and the Third World.

Bowles's production during the fifties includes musical works as well. During that decade, he completed, among other pieces, his *Picnic Cantata* (1954), his opera *Yerma* (1958), and scores for Jane's *In the Summer House* (1953), *Edwin Booth* (1958), and *Sweet Bird of Youth* (1959). In 1958 a Rockefeller Foundation grant enabled Bowles to embark on a project taping samples of indigenous Moroccan music. Bowles must have found the project appealing because it brought together his musical interests and his anthropological interest in threatened, primitive cultures. His interest in the repetitive rhythms and seductive flute melodies of Moroccan music is thoroughly consistent with his interest in magic potions, drug trances, and the rituals of self-flagellation among the Jilala and Hamadsha cults. Bowles records this experience in ethnomusicology, which stretched over a two-year period, in a piece called "The Rif, to Music," which was included in his collection of travel essays, *Their Heads Are Green and Their Hands Are Blue: Scenes from the Non-Christian World,* first published in 1963, along with essays based on trips to Istanbul, India, Sri Lanka, and the Sahara and "All Parrots Speak," an essay expressing his passion for parrots.

In his foreword to the volume, Bowles writes, "Each time I go to a place I have not seen before, I hope it will be as different as possible from the places I already know. . . . If people and their manner of living were alike everywhere, there would not be much point in moving from one place to another." The essays in this volume betray the same fascination with the primitive worlds, undisturbed by "progress," that is found in his fiction. "In Tunisia, Algeria, and Morocco," Bowles writes, "there are still people whose lives proceed according to the ancient pattern of concord between God and man, agreement between theory and practice, identity of word and flesh (or however one prefers to conceive and define that pristine state of existence we intuitively feel we once enjoyed and now have lost)." In mourning the passing of the multitude of traditional cultures and the spread of a monolithic, homogeneous modern lifestyle, Bowles blames, as much as the West, local elites and government officials, who often view traditional practices, sometimes based in the supernatural, as a source of embarrassment and backwardness.

Near the end of his autobiography, Bowles closes a chapter dealing with the late fifties, by writing, "I did not know it, but the good years were over." Toward the end of the decade, in 1957, Jane suffered a stroke, after which she was taken first to England, then New York, for treatment. Her health steadily declined until her death in 1973. A product of that trip to London in 1958 is Paul's story "Tapiama." Bowles describes the circumstances surrounding the story's inception:

That autumn, in the course of a London epidemic, I caught Asian flu. During the nine days I spent in bed, I ran a high fever which prompted me to write a story about the effects of an imaginary South American drink, the *cumbiamba*. It was called "Tapiama" and was something of an experiment for me, being the only fever-directed piece I had written. On the tenth day, when the story was finished and typed in duplicate, my thermometer showed ninety-eight and six-tenths. I got up, dressed, and went to Harrod's. A few hours later I was delirious.

The narrative trajectory and thematic content of the story are familiar, calling to mind ''A Distant Episode.'' The scantily developed protagonist is a photographer traveling in an unnamed Latin American country. Plagued by insects and heat, he leaves his hotel room one night. His aimless wanderings take him first to a bar where he is served an imaginary concoction, the *cumbiamba*. Suffering from hallucinations, he leaves the bar and finds his way to a nearby river. He is last seen floating down the river on a small boat.

By the end of the fifties, Bowles had been discovered by a number of figures associated with the American Beat movement, who made pilgrimages to his apartment in Tangier. It must have seemed to these irreverent young rebels that Bowles had been there before them. As Norman Mailer proclaimed in *Advertisements for Myself* (1959), ''Paul Bowles opened the world of Hip. He let in the murder, the drugs, the incest, the death of the Square (Port Moresby), the call of the orgy, the end of civilization.''

William S. Burroughs was the first Beat to come to Tangier, in 1954, where he worked on his drug habit, wrote *Interzone,* and enjoyed the company of young men. Within time, other Beats passed through, among them Allen Ginsberg, Gregory Corso, and Jack Kerouac. It was in Tangier, too, that Burroughs, with Ginsberg's help, put together his novel *Naked Lunch* (1959). Bowles described Burroughs' technique in *Without Stopping*:

> All around the walls he installed wide shelves at a convenient height for writing in a standing position. On these he spread his collection of scrapbooks, crowded with clippings, letters, photographs, passages written in longhand, and postcards, and these formed the material for his writing. He would go from one scrapbook to another, taking a phrase here and a sentence there, which he used either verbatim or after subjecting it to one of his chopping procedures.

Nothing could be further from Bowles's very methodical approach to writing, where each sentence would be perfected before he moved to the next, where one thought led logically, inevitably to the next. But as much as his aesthetics differed from the Beats, they shared a passion for life on the edge.

During the early sixties, while the Beats were coming and going from Tangier, Bowles was working on a handful of stories that were to be published in 1962 by City Lights Books in San Francisco under the title *A Hundred Camels in the Courtyard.* It was Allen Ginsberg who put Bowles in contact with Lawrence Ferlinghetti at City Lights, which had published Ginsberg's *Howl.* Bowles's small book of stories, while written in Morocco, seems almost tailored to the tastes and fashions of the emerging sixties counterculture. Not only do these stories break new ground in representing the effects of cannabis, or kif, they demonstrate experiment in structure as well. In composing three of the stories, Bowles made a list of a number of events and happenings over the past year. He then selected a handful for each story, creating a kind of artificial logic as he wove the incidents together. The fourth story, ''He of the Assembly,'' employs a different principle, one that creates a new, somewhat confusing narrative pattern. The story is composed of seven paragraphs, each told from a distinct point of view.

In 1962, Bowles also wrote his fine story ''The Time of Friendship,'' the title used for a collection of his short stories published in 1967. Here Bowles returns to themes found in one of his earliest stories, ''Tea on the Mountain,'' and *The Spider's House.* In ''The Time of Friendship'' a Swiss schoolteacher named Fräulein Windling, who has regularly gone to the Sahara to escape the cold rationality of her homeland, strikes up a friendship with a boy named Slimane. As much as the two are fascinated with one another, their friendship cannot withstand the multitude of cultural differences separating them. On her last visit to the Sahara, she finds that historical forces—tensions between the locals and the French colonial regime—have disrupted the friendship. In the end, similar to the ending of *The Spider's House,* the Swiss woman leaves the boy behind, but not without having left a deep impression and arousing his curiosity and desire for the West.

Bowles's fourth and final novel, *Up Above the World,* published in 1966, is often set apart from his other novels, partly because it is the only novel set in Latin America. Bowles himself said in *Without Stopping* that he began writing the novel as a "purely pleasurable pastime" and suggested it was conceived of as a "thriller." These remarks may have had some bearing on its critical reception. At first glance the novel does seem to be uncharacteristic. Yet, while it *is* different, *Up Above the World* is quintessential Bowles, containing the usual ingredients of Bowles's fiction: an exotic landscape, a somewhat estranged married couple, a journey away from consciousness and civilization, the intervention of terror, and a preoccupation with the question of to what extent man controls his destiny.

Dr. and Mrs. Slade, on their "anniversary expedition," are traveling aboard a ship sailing along the coast of Latin America when Mrs. Slade befriends a disheveled middle-aged woman named Mrs. Rainmantle. At a certain port of call, where Mrs. Rainmantle is expecting to rendezvous with her son, the hotel in which the Slades and Mrs. Rainmantle are staying burns down; the Slades have already checked out but Mrs. Rainmantle is killed. Dr. Slade later reads of the death in the newspaper and chooses not to share the news with his wife.

In a seemingly unrelated set of events, Dr. Slade meets a young man named Grover Soto (Grove for short), who takes the Slades to his impressive home above the city, where he enacts a carefully plotted scheme whereby the Slades are separately taken off into the countryside to a hacienda, held hostage, and subjected to drugs

and taped sound effects, which produce disorientation and vivid hallucinations. The Slades do not survive the ordeal.

Up Above the World is marked by a prevailing sense of suspense, which is achieved by means of a fast pace, the constant presence of foreboding and terror, a tight and efficient structure, and short chapters. In a letter to Alice B. Toklas, Bowles once remarked that his earlier stories could be thought of as mysteries, which is true of this novel as well. We, like the Slades, can only speculate as to what is going on and why. It is some time before we learn that Grove, Mrs. Rainmantle's son, is responsible for setting the fire that killed his mother. His pursuit of the Slades is based on the erroneous assumption that they know something about the murder. Grove plots his mother's murder and pursues the Slades with the same precision and deftness Bowles consistently brings to his own craft.

Bowles continued to travel in the sixties, though his pace slowed somewhat. In 1966 he went to Thailand, to research a book about Bangkok. Though he never wrote that book, he uses Thailand as the setting for a very fine story, "You Have Left Your Lotus Pods on the Bus," written in 1971 and published in the collection of stories *Things Gone and Things Still Here,* which came out in 1977. The amusing events recounted in the story center around misunderstandings and misreadings of cultures. At one point a Thai man speculates ridiculously about why Western men wear ties and the meaning of their various lengths and styles. At another point Americans find the rantings of a man at the back of a bus incomprehensible. It turns out he is helping the driver negotiate the obstacle-cluttered roads.

Following a short stint teaching at San Fernando State University, an arrangement worked out by his friend Oliver Evans, whom he met and traveled with in Thailand, Bowles made no trips to the United States for over twenty-five years. His wife's steady deterioration was among the factors conspiring against a carefree nomadism. In the sixties Jane began to make trips to a sanatorium in Málaga, Spain, for treatment. She died in Málaga on May 3, 1973.

Understandably, Bowles's production waned somewhat in the late sixties and early seventies. Two years before Jane's death Bowles finished his autobiography, *Without Stopping*, a chore he found laborious. During this period, perhaps in part to fill a void, he devoted more of his time to the transcription of local Maghrebi stories. Actually Bowles had begun to transcribe oral stories much earlier, first with Ahmed Yacoubi and then with Larbi Layachi (Driss ben Hamed Charhadi). Layachi's *A Life Full of Holes*, published in 1964, is a simply told, often witty account of the (likely autobiographical) experiences of a young Moroccan man's youth, including encounters with Europeans. "A good storyteller keeps the thread of his narrative almost equally taut at all points," Bowles notes in his introduction. This quality, which he appreciated in Layachi's very natural spinning of a story, was a quality Bowles himself sought in his own work. In the introduction Bowles tells how Layachi, the illiterate storyteller, was first amazed at the very notion of a book and the possibility of publishing one's stories, which he termed "lies." One senses here, as with his relationship with Yacoubi, Bowles's profound sympathy for a childlike naïveté, for a prepsychoanalytic worldview. Here was life before the Fall, before the constraining rigors of rationalism had set in.

The same dynamics have operated in Bowles's relationship with Mohammed Mrabet, a collaborative friendship that has lasted nearly three decades. As with Layachi, Bowles recorded Mrabet's stories on tape, then transcribed and translated them into English. The first of Mrabet's stories, *Love with a Few Hairs*, published in 1967, like *A Life Full of Holes*, relates various episodes in the life of a young Moroccan, including, again, interactions with Westerners. Altogether Bowles and Mrabet produced nearly a dozen books between 1967 and 1986. During those years, Mrabet was a constant companion of Bowles.

Because they are oral storytellers, Layachi and Mrabet are not known to Arabic readers. Such is not the case, however, with Mohamed Choukri, a well-known Moroccan writer whose book *For Bread Alone* Bowles translated from French (not the original Arabic). Bowles has also translated a small collection of works in French by Isabelle Eberhardt, titled *The Oblivion Seekers*, published by City Lights in 1975. In the life of this adventuresome Swiss woman—who at the turn of the last century traveled (often disguised as a man) in the Sahara, wrote, and became absorbed with the Arabic language and Sufi mysticism—Bowles must have seen something of himself. Bowles has also translated from Spanish collections of stories by the Guatemalan writer Rodrigo Rey Rosa, yet another literary pilgrim who made his way to Bowles's apartment in Tangier. Bowles's work in translation, particularly his translations of Moroccan storytellers, has affected his own prose style. The stories he wrote in the seventies and eighties are more simply told and have more of an oral quality; sentences are generally shorter and first-person narration is used with greater frequency.

During the early eighties Bowles stayed put in Tangier, teaching in a summer program sponsored by New York's School of Visual Arts. The publication of *Collected Stories, 1939–1976* in 1980 has kept Bowles's work in circulation and solidified his reputation. In his introduction to the volume, Gore Vidal claims that Bowles's short stories "are among the best ever written by an American." While Bowles has written no novel since 1964, he has continued to write stories, perhaps because that form requires less sustained concentration. As he wrote in a letter to his parents in the early sixties, while working on *Up Above the World:*

With a novel the work is a good deal more than just consecrating so many hours of the day to sitting at a desk writing words;—it is living in the midst of the artificial world one is creating, and letting no detail of everyday life enter sufficiently into one's mind to become more real than or take precedence over what one is inventing. That is, living in the atmosphere of the novel has to become and stay more real than living in one's own life.

In the eighties Bowles published two more volumes of new stories, *Midnight Mass* (1981) and *Unwelcome Words* (1988), and a marvelous little book called *Points in Time* (1982), which defies generic classification. *Points in Time* contains a dozen or so historical anecdotes, lyrically rendered, most of which involve cultural clashes between the Muslim, Christian, and Jewish worldviews, many ending in violence. In one story, for example, a crew of Moroccan sailors become pirates and seize a Spanish ship:

Then we shouted: *allah akbar!* and went onto the ship.
    Only three of our men were lost. We finished off all the Spaniards, took what we could into the boats, and went back to the port.
    Now that we had seen their blood, we felt better.

In the end we are told, "It is pleasing to the Most High that the riches of the infidels should be returned to Islam."

The stories in *Midnight Mass* and *Unwelcome Words,* besides being simpler on a narrative level, depict a more settled existence, reflecting Bowles's more sedentary life at this stage. Many of the stories feature expatriates in postcolonial Tangier dealing with local help, problems concerning property, and an ever-growing city beset by problems afflicting all modern cities— pollution, overcrowding, traffic, violent crime, and the overtaking of vernacular forms by modernist architecture. A nostalgic mood permeates many of the stories, especially those in *Unwelcome Words* that feature an older narrator. Lamentably, the world has become more crowded and more ugly, and Tangier has vastly changed since Bowles first visited the city in 1931. Rather than traveling in hopes of seeing something new and exciting, the writer waits in Tangier, to see what washes up.

The title story of *Midnight Mass* tells of a Westerner who comes back to Tangier eight years after his mother's death to try to reclaim the family house. He finds the place inhabited by local Moroccans and is unable to get it back. In "Madame and Ahmad" a Moroccan gardener uses his cleverness to preserve his relationship with his wealthy Western employer. Duncan March in "The Eye" may have become a "victim of a slow poisoning by native employees," while Monsieur Ducros in "Rumor and a Ladder" devises an ingenious way to circumvent currency laws and get money out of Morocco. In "In the Red Room," which Shannon Ravenal included in *The Best American Short Stories of the Eighties,* Bowles unravels the mystery of why a young Singhalese man named Justu Gonzag treats a certain red room as though it were a personal shrine.

The longest and most significant story in *Midnight Mass* is "Here to Learn," which tells the story of Malika, a young Moroccan woman, and her journey from her home to the West, through Spain, Paris, Switzerland, and eventually Los Angeles, escorted by a string of men. The last of the men, Tex, she marries. When he dies unexpectedly, Malika is left free and independent, with a considerable fortune. The last scenes show her returning to Morocco to visit her mother, only to discover she is too late to see her mother alive. While much of Bowles's early fiction portrayed Westerners' first encounters with North Africa, this story reverses the process. We see things filtered through Malika's consciousness. Bowles's extended exile in Morocco likely helped him to construct Malika sympathetically. He also had had firsthand experience watching Moroccans such as Ahmed Yacoubi, Larbi Layachi, and Mohammed Mrabet encountering the West for the first time.

In *Unwelcome Words* Bowles shows that he has continued to experiment with form. Three of the seven stories ("Massachusetts 1932," "New York 1965," and "Tangier 1975") are dramatic monologues. In others he returns to a longtime fascination with the gruesome and the perverse. In "Julian Vreden" a young man poisons his parents. In "Hugh Harper" we are introduced to a man whose gastronomical habits include "a taste for human blood." The host in "Dinner at Sir Nigel's" entertains his guests with a Marquis de Sade–like performance in which he wields a whip before a group of black women.

Bowles uses his own persona as the writer of the six letters that make up "Unwelcome Words." Here the writer complains about the declining quality of postal service, the horridness of nineteenth-century Romantic music, and the poor quality of Moroccan hashish these days. "You ask me for news about me: my daily life, what I think about, my opinions on external events," Bowles writes to his correspondent, and goes on to depict a postcolonial scene where resentment and greed flourish and foreigners are often preyed upon. As for his own life? *"Ma vie est posthume,"* he writes in one letter.

These last stories can be read alongside *Days: Tangier Journal, 1987–1989*, which the author describes as "a record of daily life in today's Tangier." The tone in these journal entries is resigned and detached, as he comments on his role in Bertolucci's film of *The Sheltering Sky;* a lavish party thrown by Malcolm Forbes; visits from Buffie Johnson, Patricia Highsmith, and Phillip Ramey; battling TV crews, translators, and biographers; the comings and goings of Mrabet and Bowles's driver, Abdelouahaid Boulaich; Bowles's hernia operation; changes in life during the holy month of Ramadan; and the behavior of spiders in his apartment. Bowles's seemingly objective observations of a spider, on one occasion, oddly mirror his own condition. "It looks smaller and feebler than before," he writes. "If it's a different individual, what has happened to the original, and why does this one hang exactly in the place where that one hung?"

While Bowles's work tapered off noticeably in the eighties and early nineties, as his own health deteriorated, a few works have appeared since the publication of *Unwelcome Words*. One is a fine story, "In Absentia" (1987), which like "Unwelcome Words" takes an epistolary form. The unnamed letter writer again, in a letter to his correspondent, Pamela Loeffler, wistfully remembers an age gone by, one in which correspondence was valued:

> I see you understand the pleasure that can be got from writing letters. In other centuries this was taken for granted. Not any longer. Only a few people carry on true correspondences. No time, the rest tell you. Quicker to telephone. Like saying a photograph is more satisfying than a painting. There wasn't all that much time for writing letters in the past, either, but time was found, as it generally can be for whatever gives pleasure.

Bowles finds his values all the more under seige by the advancing forces of technology at the end of the twentieth century.

"Too Far from Home," the novella from which Daniel Halpern takes the title of his *Selected Writings of Paul Bowles* (1993), is a welcome addition to the Bowles oeuvre. Once more Bowles brilliantly evokes a sense of place, this time a village along the Niger River. Anita, an American who is visiting her brother Tom, a painter who is there on a Guggenheim grant, chronicles her impressions of the place in letters to friends back home. "This is certainly the antithesis of New York and of any place you can think of in the U.S.A.," she writes to one friend. She finds the food, the heat, and the natives more difficult to handle than does her brother, whom she finds unsympathetic. The story pivots on a disturbing racial incident involving two American tourists who nearly run down Sekou, a close African friend of Tom, while he is with Anita in the local market. "You've gone too far from home, my friends, and you're going to have trouble,'' Anita warns the bikers. Indeed, she is right, something does happen to them. Dream, desire, guilt, repression, and racism mingle to produce a sinister and haunting effect.

A writer's place within the canon of literature is determined by our assessment of the quality and depth of the writer's work and the degree to which it speaks to our own concerns. Assessments of that sort, we have learned, are ever in process; thus literary reputations fluctuate over time. Paul Bowles has often been thought to be a fringe figure, writing against, or at least outside of, the mainstream tradition. As with Poe, critics have often not known quite how to fit Bowles into the history of American literature. This difficulty, as Gore Vidal has suggested, might be in part due to the writer's expatriate status. It may also be that Bowles's fiction has been unpalatable to traditional moralists.

During the late eighties and early nineties, Bowles has received an increasing amount of serious critical attention, securing his reputation. Two biographies—Christopher Sawyer-Lauçanno's *An Invisible Spectator* (1989) and Gena Dagel Caponi's *Paul Bowles: Romantic Savage* (1994)—have been published, and more are likely to come. Michelle Green's gossipy account of the modern expatriate experience in Tangier, *The Dream at the End of the World: Paul Bowles and the Literary Renegades in Tangier* (1991), likewise has helped keep the Bowles legend alive. At the same time, Bertolucci's film version of *The Sheltering Sky* has drawn attention to the writer. Millicent Dillon's *The Portable Paul and Jane Bowles* (1994) and Daniel Halpern's *Too Far from Home: Selected Writings of Paul Bowles* have kept his work in circulation, while Jeffrey Miller's *In Touch: The Letters of Paul Bowles* provides another resource for scholars and an intriguing entry into the writer's life. In September 1995, Bowles returned to New York for the first time in twenty-six years,

to be on hand for a festival of his music performed by the Eos Ensemble under the direction of Jonathan Sheffer. The considerable interest in this highly publicized event confirms Bowles's stature and place in American arts and letters.

Toward the end of the series of letters that make up the story ''Unwelcome Words,'' the letter writer (Bowles) remarks that his correspondent seems not to be appreciating his letters. They are doing his correspondent no good. ''There's obviously nothing I can do from here to help you,'' he writes. Then, later, he pleads with his correspondent to acknowledge his good intentions. ''I hope you'll remember (you won't) that I made this small and futile attempt to help you remain human.'' This plea might well be taken as Bowles's literary apologia. His fictions, as much as they may make us bristle with horror, remind us of our humanity.

Selected Bibliography

WORKS OF PAUL BOWLES

COLLECTIONS OF STORIES
The Delicate Prey and Other Stories. New York: Random House, 1950; Ecco, 1972.
A Little Stone. London: Lehmann, 1950.
The Hours After Noon. London: Heinemann, 1959.
A Hundred Camels in the Courtyard. San Francisco: City Lights, 1962.
The Time of Friendship. New York: Holt, Rinehart & Winston, 1967.
Pages from Cold Point and Other Stories. London: Peter Owen, 1968.
Three Tales. New York: Hallman, 1975.
Things Gone and Things Still Here. Santa Barbara, Calif.: Black Sparrow, 1977.
Midnight Mass. Santa Barbara, Calif.: Black Sparrow, 1981; London: Peter Owen, 1985.
Call at Corazón and Other Stories. London: Peter Owen, 1988.

Unwelcome Words: Seven Stories. Bolinas, Calif.: Tombouctou, 1988.

A Thousand Days for Mokhtar. London: Peter Owen, 1989.

UNCOLLECTED STORIES PUBLISHED IN PERIODICALS

"Bluey," *View,* 3:81–82 (October 1943).

"In Absentia," *Antaeus,* 58:7–26 (Spring 1987).

NOVELS

The Sheltering Sky. London: Lehmann, 1949; New York: New Directions, 1949; Ecco, 1978; London: Peter Owen, 1981. New York: Vintage, 1990.

Let It Come Down. London: Lehmann, 1952; New York: Random House, 1952; Santa Barbara, Calif.: Black Sparrow, 1980; London: Peter Owen, 1984.

The Spider's House. New York: Random House, 1955; London: Macdonald, 1957; Santa Barbara, Calif.: Black Sparrow, 1982.

Up Above the World. New York: Simon & Schuster, 1966; London: Peter Owen, 1967; New York: Ecco, 1982; London: Peter Owen, 1982.

"A Novel Fragment." *Library Chronicle of the University of Texas at Austin,* 30:67–71 (1985).

POETRY

Next to Nothing: Collected Poems, 1926–1977. Santa Barbara, Calif.: Black Sparrow, 1981.

NONFICTION PROSE

Yallah. New York: McDowell, Obolensky, 1957.

"The Challenge to Identity." *Nation,* April 26, 1958, p. 360.

"The Ball at Sidi Hosni." *Kulchur,* 2:8 (1960).

Their Heads Are Green. London: Peter Owen, 1963; New York: Random House, 1963; Ecco, 1984 (published as *Their Heads Are Green and Their Hands Are Blue: Scenes from the Non-Christian World*).

Without Stopping: An Autobiography. New York: Putnam, 1972; London: Peter Owen, 1972; New York: Ecco, 1985.

Points in Time. London: Peter Owen, 1982; New York: Ecco, 1984.

Two Years Beside the Strait: Tangier Journal, 1987–1989. London: Peter Owen, 1989; New York: Ecco, 1991 (published as *Days: Tangier Journal, 1987–1989*).

Morocco. Text by Paul Bowles; photographs by Barry Brukoff. New York: Abrams, 1993.

Paul Bowles Photographs: How Could I Send a Picture into the Desert? Edited by Susan Bischoff in collaboration with the Swiss Foundation for Photography. New York: Scalo, 1994.

TRANSLATIONS

Frison-Roche, Roger. *The Lost Trail of the Sahara.* New York: Prentice-Hall, 1951.

Sartre, Jean-Paul. *No Exit.* New York: French, 1958.

Layachi, Larbi (Driss ben Hamed Charhadi). *A Life Full of Holes.* New York: Grove, 1964; London: Weidenfeld and Nicolson, 1964.

Mrabet, Mohammed. *Love with a Few Hairs.* London: Peter Owen 1967; New York: Braziller, 1968; San Francisco: City Lights, 1986.

Mrabet, Mohammed. *The Lemon.* London: Peter Owen, 1969; New York: McGraw-Hill, 1972; San Francisco: City Lights, 1986.

Mrabet, Mohammed. *M'Hashish.* San Francisco: City Lights, 1969; London: Peter Owen, 1988.

Choukri, Mohamed (Muhammad Shukri). *For Bread Alone.* London: Peter Owen, 1974; San Francisco: City Lights, 1987.

Mrabet, Mohammed. *The Boy Who Set the Fire & Other Stories.* Santa Barbara, Calif.: Black Sparrow, 1974; San Francisco: City Lights, 1988.

Choukri, Mohamed (Muhammad Shukri). *Jean Genet in Tangier.* New York: Ecco, 1974.

Mrabet, Mohammed. *Hadidan Aharam.* Santa Barbara, Calif.: Black Sparrow, 1975.

Eberhardt, Isabelle. *The Oblivion Seekers.* San Francisco: City Lights, 1975; London: Peter Owen, 1987.

Mrabet, Mohammed. *Look and Move On.* Santa Barbara, Calif.: Black Sparrow, 1976; London: Peter Owen, 1989.

Mrabet, Mohammed. *Harmless Poisons, Blameless Sins.* Santa Barbara, Calif.: Black Sparrow, 1976.

Mrabet, Mohammed. *The Big Mirror.* Santa Barbara, Calif.: Black Sparrow, 1977.

Choukri, Mohamed (Muhammad Shukri). *Tennessee Williams in Tangier.* Santa Barbara, Calif.: Cadmus, 1979.

Boulaich, Abdeslam, et al. *Five Eyes: Stories.* Santa Barbara, Calif.: Black Sparrow, 1979.

Mrabet, Mohammed. *The Beach Cafe & The Voice.* Santa Barbara, Calif.: Black Sparrow, 1980.

Rey Rosa, Rodrigo. *The Path Doubles Back.* New York: Red Ozier, 1982.

Mrabet, Mohammed. *The Chest.* Bolinas, Calif.: Tombouctou, 1983.

Rey Rosa, Rodrigo. *The Beggar's Knife.* San Francisco: City Lights, 1985.

Jean Ferry, et al. *She Woke Me Up So I Killed Her.* San Francisco: Cadmus, 1985.

Mrabet, Mohammed. *Marriage with Papers.* Bolinas, Calif.: Tombouctou, 1986.

Mrabet, Mohammed. *Chocolate Creams and Dollars.* New York: Inanout, 1992.

Rey Rosa, Rodrigo. *Dust on Her Tongue.* London: Peter Owen, 1989; San Francisco: City Lights, 1992.

COLLECTED WORKS

Collected Stories, 1939–1976. Santa Barbara, Calif.: Black Sparrow, 1979.

A Distant Episode: The Selected Stories. New York: Ecco, 1988.

Too Far from Home: Selected Writings of Paul Bowles. Edited by Daniel Halpern. New York: Ecco, 1993.

The Portable Paul and Jane Bowles. Edited by Millicent Dillon. New York: Penguin, 1994.

COLLECTED LETTERS

In Touch: The Letters of Paul Bowles. Edited by Jeffrey Miller. New York: Farrar, Straus and Giroux, 1994.

ARCHIVES AND BIBLIOGRAPHIES

Alderman Library, University of Virginia.

Harry Ransom Humanities Research Center, University of Texas, Austin.

McLeod, Cecil R. *Paul Bowles: A Checklist, 1929–1969.* Flint, Mich.: Apple Tree, 1970.

Miller, Jeffrey. *Paul Bowles: A Descriptive Bibliography.* Santa Barbara, Calif.: Black Sparrow, 1986.

Rare Book and Manuscript Library, Butler Library, Columbia University.

Special Collections, University of Delaware Library, University of Delaware.

BIOGRAPHICAL AND CRITICAL STUDIES

BOOKS

Bertens, Johannes Willem. *The Fiction of Paul Bowles: The Soul Is the Weariest Part of the Body.* Amsterdam: *Costerus,* 21 (1979).

Briatte, Robert. *Paul Bowles, 2117 Tanger Socco.* Paris: Plon, 1989.

Caponi, Gena Dagel. *Paul Bowles: Romantic Savage.* Carbondale: Southern Illinois University Press, 1994.

Green, Michelle. *The Dream at the End of the World: Paul Bowles and the Literary Renegades in Tangier.* New York: HarperCollins, 1991.

Hibbard, Allen. *Paul Bowles: A Study of the Short Fiction.* New York: Twayne, 1993.

Patteson, Richard F. *A World Outside: The Fiction of Paul Bowles.* Austin: University of Texas Press, 1987.

Pounds, Wayne. *Paul Bowles: The Inner Geography.* New York: Peter Lang, 1985.

Pulsifer, Gary, ed. *Paul Bowles by His Friends.* London: Peter Owen, 1992.

Rochat, Joyce Hamilton. "The Naturalistic-Existential Rapprochement in Albert Camus' *L'Etranger* and Paul Bowles' *Let It Come Down*: A Comparative Study in Absurdism." Ph.D. dissertation, Michigan State University, 1971.

Sawyer-Lauçanno, Christopher. *An Invisible Spectator: A Biography of Paul Bowles.* New York: Weidenfeld and Nicolson, 1989.

Stewart, Lawrence D. *Paul Bowles: The Illumination of North Africa.* Carbondale and Edwardsville: Southern Illinois University Press, 1974.

Swan, Caludia, ed. *Paul Bowles Music.* New York: Eos Music, 1995.

ARTICLES

Craft, Robert. "Pipe Dreams." *New York Review of Books,* November 23, 1989, pp. 6ff.

Dagel, Gena. "A Nomad in New York: Paul Bowles, 1933–48." *American Music,* Fall 1989, pp. 278–314.

Ditsky, John. "*The Time of Friendship:* The Short Fiction of Paul Bowles." *Twentieth Century Literature,* 34, nos. 3–4:373–387 (1986).

Eisinger, Chester E. "Paul Bowles and the Passionate Pursuit of Disengagement." In *Fiction of the Forties.* Chicago: University of Chicago Press, 1963.

Evans, Oliver. "Paul Bowles and the 'Natural' Man." *Critique,* 1, no. 3:43–59 (1959).

Fiedler, Leslie A. "Style and Anti-Style in the Short Story." *Kenyon Review,* Winter 1951, pp. 155–172.

Field, Edward. "Tea at Paul Bowles's." *Raritan,* 12:92–111 (Winter 1993).

Friedman, Ellen G. "Variations on Mystery-Thriller: Paul Bowles' *Up Above the World.*" *Armchair Detective,* 19:279–284 (Summer 1986).

Al Ghalith, Asad. "Paul Bowles's Portrayal of Islam in His Moroccan Short Stories." *International Fiction Review,* 19, no. 2:103–108 (1992).

Hamovitch, Mitzi Berger. "Release from Torment: The Fragmented Double in *Let It Come Down.*" *Twentieth Century Literature,* 32:440–450 (Fall/Winter 1986).

Hassan, Ihab. "The Pilgrim as Prey: A Note on Paul Bowles." *Western Review,* 19:23–36 (1954).

Hibbard, Allen. "Expatriation and Narration in Two Works by Paul Bowles." *West Virginia Philological Papers,* 32:61–71 (1986).

Howard, Maureen. "Other Voices." Review of *A Time of Friendship. Partisan Review,* Winter 1968, pp. 141–152.

Jackson, Charles. "On the Seamier Side." Review of *The Delicate Prey. New York Times Book Review,* December 3, 1950, p. 6.

Lehan, Richard. "Existentialism in Recent American Fiction: The Demonic Quest." *Texas Studies in Literature and Language,* Summer 1959, pp. 181–202.

Lerner, Bennett. "Paul Bowles: Lost and Found." In *Perspectives on Music: Essays on Collections at the HRC.* Edited by Dave Oliphant and Thomas Zigal. Austin, Tex.: HRC, 1985. P. 149.

Lesser, Wendy. "*Collected Stories*: Paul Bowles." *American Book Review,* 2:24 (May 1980). Reprinted in *Review of Contemporary Fiction,* 2, no. 3:32–41 (1982).

Maier, John. "Morocco in the Fiction of Paul Bowles." In *The Atlantic Connection: 200 Years of Moroccan-American Relations, 1786–1986.* Edited by Mohammed El Mansour. Rabat: Edino, 1990. Pp. 245–258.

———. "Two Moroccan Storytellers in Paul Bowles's *Five Eyes.*" *Postmodern Culture,* 1, no. 3 (1991).

Malin, Irving. "Drastic Points." *Review of Contemporary Fiction,* 2, no. 3:30–32 (1982).

———. "*The Time of Friendship,* by Paul Bowles." *Studies in Short Fiction,* 4, no. 3:311–313 (1968).

McAuliffe, Jody. "The Church of the Desert: Reflections on *The Sheltering Sky.*" *South Atlantic Quarterly,* 91:419–426 (Spring 1992).

McInerney, Jay. "Paul Bowles in Exile." *Vanity Fair,* September 1985, pp. 68ff.

Moss, Marilyn. "The Child in the Text: Autobiography, Fiction, and the Aesthetics of Deception in *Without Stopping.*" *Twentieth Century Literature,* 32:314–333 (Fall/Winter 1986).

Mottram, Eric. "Paul Bowles: Staticity and Terror." *Review of Contemporary Fiction,* 3, no. 2:6–30 (1982).

Oates, Joyce Carol. "Bleak Craft." Review of *Collected Stories. New York Times Book Review,* September 30, 1979, p. 9. Reprinted in Oates's collection of essays *The Profane Art,* under the title "Before God Was Love." New York: Dutton, 1983. Pp. 128–131.

Olson, Steven E. "Alien Terrain: Paul Bowles's Filial Landscapes." *Twentieth Century Literature,* 34, nos. 3–4:334–349 (1986).

Patteson, Richard F. "Paul Bowles: Two Unfinished Projects." *Library Chronicle of the University of Texas at Austin,* 30:57–65 (1985).

———. "Paul Bowles/Mohammed Mrabet: Translation, Transformation, and Transcultural Discourse." *Journal of Narrative Technique,* 22:180–190 (Fall 1992).

Pounds, Wayne. "Paul Bowles and *The Delicate Prey*: The Psychology of Predation." *Revue Belge de Philologie et d'Histoire,* 59, no. 3:620–633 (1981).

Rainwater, Catherine. " 'Sinister Overtones,' 'Terrible Phrases': Poe's Influence on the Writings of Paul Bowles." *Essays in Literature,* 2:253–266 (Fall 1984).

Rorem, Ned. "Paul Bowles." In *Setting the Tone.* New York: Limelight, 1984. P. 355. (Originally published in *New Republic,* April 22, 1972, p. 24.

Rountree, Mary Martin. "Paul Bowles: Translations from the Moghrebi." *Twentieth Century Literature,* 34, nos. 3–4:388–401 (1986).

St. Louis, Ralph. "The Affirming Silence: Paul Bowles's 'Pastor Dowe at Tacaté.' " *Studies in Short Fiction,* 24:381–386 (Fall 1987).

Solotaroff, Theodore. "The Desert Within." Review of *The Time of Friendship. New Republic,* September 2, 1967, 29. Reprinted in his *The Red Hot Vacuum.* New York: Atheneum, 1970. Pp. 254–260.

Stewart, Lawrence. "Paul Bowles and 'The Frozen

Fields' of Vision.'' *Review of Contemporary Fiction,* 2, no. 3:64–71 (1982).

Williams, Marcellette, G. '' 'Tea in the Sahara': The Function of Time in the Work of Paul Bowles.'' *Twentieth Century Literature* 32:408–423 (Fall/Winter 1986).

Williams, Tennessee. ''The Human Psyche—Alone.'' Review of *The Delicate Prey. Saturday Review of Literature,* December 23, 1950, pp. 19–20.

INTERVIEWS

Bailey, Jeffrey. Interview with Paul Bowles. *Paris Review,* 81:62–98 (1981).

Bowles, Paul. *Conversations with Paul Bowles.* Edited by Gena Dagel Caponi. Jackson: University Press of Mississippi, 1993.

Breit, Harvey. ''Talk with Paul Bowles.'' *New York Times Book Review,* March 9, 1952, p. 19.

Elghandor, Abdelhak. ''Atavism and Civilization: An Interview with Paul Bowles.'' *Ariel,* 25:7–30 (April 1994).

Evans, Oliver. ''An Interview with Paul Bowles.'' *Mediterranean Review,* 1:3–15 (Winter 1971).

Halpern, Daniel. Interview with Paul Bowles. *Tri-Quarterly,* 33:159–177 (Spring 1975).

Pina-Rosales, Gerardo. ''En Tanger con Paul Bowles: Entrevista.'' *Nuez: Revista de Arte y Literatura,* 2:5–6, 8–9 (1990).

Rogers, Michael. ''Conversation in Morocco.'' *Rolling Stone,* May 23, 1974, pp. 48–54.

''Stories of Violence.'' Interview. *Newsweek* (International), August 4, 1986, p. 48.

—ALLEN HIBBARD

Ray Bradbury

1920–

Since Ray Bradbury regards his fictions as masks or metaphors for his life, there is merit in presenting a brief account of his life and career before proceeding to matters of literary criticism and interpretation. Ray Douglas Bradbury was born in Waukegan, Illinois, on August 22, 1920, son of Leonard Spaulding Bradbury, an electrical lineman, and Ester Moberg Bradbury, a native of Sweden. Waukegan was later idealized by Bradbury as Green Town, Illinois, in *Dandelion Wine* (1957), a novel of childhood reveries. Bradbury's childhood is extremely important to him as a constant source of intense sensations, feelings, and images that generate stories. His early interest in horror fiction was sparked by his seeing the film *The Hunchback of Notre Dame* at age three (Bradbury claims to have a photographic memory). When he was six, an aunt read him the Oz books of L. Frank Baum, which were to have a great effect on the way he later wrote fantasy. Critics such as Brian Attebery have discussed Bradbury's relationship to the Oz books and the American fantasy tradition. Bradbury's year-old sister, Elizabeth, died of pneumonia in 1927, leaving him with mixed feelings of sorrow and guilt, some of which probably emerged in ''The Lake'' (1944), which he considers to be his first story of literary value. In 1928 he was sick with whooping cough and missed three months of school. During his convalescence, his mother read to him from the works of Edgar Allan Poe. This experience is probably the source of the reading and reverie scenes in his utopian novel *Fahrenheit 451* (1953).

Bradbury was thoroughly immersed in the popular culture of his day. By 1928 he had discovered science fiction in Hugo Gernsback's pulp magazine *Amazing Stories*. It was also around this time that he began to collect the comic strip adventures of Buck Rogers (in 1969 he wrote an introduction to *The Collected Works of Buck Rogers in the 25th Century*) and read the Martian tales of Edgar Rice Burroughs, to which he wrote his own sequel. Between the ages of ten and eleven, traveling circuses and carnivals began to exert a major influence on his imagination. He met Blackstone the Magician and Mr. Electrico, who was later fictionalized in *Something Wicked This Way Comes* (1962).

In 1934 the Bradbury family moved permanently to Los Angeles, after a short stay (1932–1933) in Tucson, Arizona. In Tucson, Ray talked his way into a job with radio station KGAR, reading the comic pages to children each Saturday. The job lasted four months. Bradbury entered Los Angeles High School in September 1935 with the ambition of becoming a writer. He took courses in poetry and short story writing and discovered the work of Thomas Wolfe, to whom he later paid tribute in the short story

"Forever and the Earth" (in *Long after Midnight*). In 1937 Bradbury became a member of the Los Angeles chapter of the Science Fiction League. Through this organization he met many writers and artists involved in early science fiction fandom such as Robert Heinlein and Henry Kuttner. He published his first story in the club magazine in 1938, the year he graduated from high school—the end of his formal education.

From 1939 to 1942 Bradbury peddled newspapers on Los Angeles street corners while he launched his own mimeographed fan magazine, *Futuria Fantasia*. During this time he was also absorbed in reading Hemingway and Steinbeck, who were strong stylistic influences. In 1941 he made his first professional sale, "Pendulum," a collaboration with Henry Hasse, to *Super Science Stories* (not one of the leading science fiction magazines). Thereafter he began to alternate science fiction with horror and detective fiction, publishing his stories in *Weird Tales* and *Detective Tales*. Eye trouble kept Bradbury out of World War II, but these years of creative struggle have been fictionalized in his novel *Death Is a Lonely Business* (1985), set in a decaying Venice, California, in 1949.

In 1945, Bradbury went to Mexico to collect masks for the Los Angeles County Museum. On the trip he visited the mummies in the catacombs at Guanajuato, an experience that terrified him. Several of his fictions have a Mexican locale and are filled with Mexican folkways, especially "The Next in Line," a horror story (1947), and *The Halloween Tree* (1972), a juvenile novel. The next several years brought change and recognition. On September 27, 1947, Bradbury married Marguerite McClure, a U.C.L.A. graduate. (They have four children.) Arkham House published his first collection of horror and macabre stories, *Dark Carnival* (1947), and several of his stories in a mainstream vein were selected for the O. Henry Award *Prize Stories* (1947, 1948) and *Best American Short Stories* (1948).

These were early signs that Bradbury was leaving the pulps behind. He began to publish stories in *The Saturday Evening Post, Collier's, McCall's,* and *Esquire.* However, it was with the publication of *The Martian Chronicles* in 1950 that he received his first important critical acclaim. The book received a rave review from Christopher Isherwood, and suddenly Bradbury was taken seriously by intellectuals as an important writer with significant themes. For a while he was tempted by the lure of Hollywood. He began writing for movies in 1952, with a film treatment called "The Meteor," which became the first 3-D science fiction film under the title *It Came from Outer Space.* In 1953 he went to Ireland to work with the director John Huston, writing the screenplay for *Moby Dick.* Bradbury fictionalized his Hollywood experiences in the novel *A Graveyard for Lunatics* (1990) and his ambivalent relationship with Huston—as well as the Irish national character—in *Green Shadows, White Whale* (1992).

There is no doubt that Bradbury did much to lend intellectual respectability to science fiction in the 1950s with such books as *The Martian Chronicles* and his utopian novel, *Fahrenheit 451,* in addition to his many short story collections, notably *The Illustrated Man* (1951) and *The Golden Apples of the Sun* (1953). However, Bradbury is by no means an intellectual. As a matter of fact, he tends to identify intellectualism and rationality with pessimism and the inability to affirm life. Nonetheless, he does possess a coherent aesthetic of fantasy to which other fantasy writers have paid tribute (notably Stephen King in his *Danse Macabre*), and he has written important critical articles on science fiction. Though he has never received a major science fiction award—neither Hugo nor Nebula—he has won others, including representation in the Science Fiction Hall of Fame (chosen by the members of the Science Fiction Writers of America). In 1954 he received an award from the National

Institute of Arts and Letters for his contribution to American literature. He conceptualized films for the U.S. Pavilion at the New York World's Fair in 1964 and, more recently, for Disney's EPCOT Center. In 1984 Bradbury received the Jules Verne Award and the Valentine Davies Award from the Writers Guild of America for his cinema work. Since 1985 he has adapted his stories for a half-hour show on cable television, *The Ray Bradbury Theatre*. In 1989, he received the Grand Master Award from the Science Fiction Writers of America, in recognition of his style and his role in broadening the appeal of science fiction.

Despite the fact that his most important work was produced in the 1950s, Bradbury was in the 1960s and 1970s still an enormously popular writer. Indeed, the Apollo 15 crew in 1971 named a section of the moon Dandelion Crater in honor of his work. None of his major works has ever gone out of print, and they are often reissued in hardcover. In fact, he is the only American author to have his stories institutionalized in a weekly television program. But only in the 1980s did his work begin to receive the serious critical appreciation it deserves. It is important to note that although Bradbury's output has been primarily that of a short story writer, he has shaped his stories on occasion into larger, unified narrative structures. Considered formally, his fiction ranges from collections of stories such as *The Golden Apples of the Sun* to novels such as *Death Is a Lonely Business*. Between these two poles lie such works as *The Martian Chronicles*, which, although lacking a central character, does have a consistent theme (the invasion and colonization of the planet Mars by Earth) and a recurring landscape. *The Martian Chronicles* is a completed short story cycle, for which certain stories—originally published in pulp science fiction magazines such as *Planet Stories*—were selected, grouped, edited, revised, and interconnected. *The Illustrated Man* (1951) is closer to a typical collection because it employs only the framing device of the Illustrated Man, whose body bears the illustrations of the eighteen stories. This is the only unifying element in an otherwise disparate collection of stories. Bradbury's later collections, such as *Dinosaur Tales* (1983) and *A Memory of Murder* (1984), are united only by subject matter or by genre (such as mystery stories). And *Green Shadows, White Whale* reworks twelve of Bradbury's previously published Irish stories into a novel, adding new material in the form of a narrative of his visit to Ireland.

Genre, and Bradbury's use—or misuse—of it, is the key issue in understanding his work. Although Bradbury is the one writer in America who is most often called upon to represent to the general public the genre of science fiction, more often than not he is solemnly drummed out of the science fiction corps by purists who do not like the simultaneous presence of science and reverie in his writings. He has even been accused by ''hard'' science fiction writers, such as Stanislaw Lem, of giving up the programmatic rationalism of science in favor of irrationalism, of degrading the genre. His intellect, so this argument goes, fails to match his stylistic know-how and his artistic talent. Certainly Bradbury's themes can be viewed as ''old-fashioned'' in an ethical and philosophical sense. For instance, he often writes with evident nostalgia about childhood in the small towns of the American Midwest, even when these small towns are fantastically transported to Mars. But it is no accident that one of his most famous stories (''Mars Is Heaven!,'' now included in *The Martian Chronicles* as ''The Third Expedition'') is one in which this very nostalgia for the past is put in confrontation with rational and scientific modes of explanation. However, reason does not offer a satisfying explanation for what happens at the end of the story—the Martians continue with their illusions after the Earth invasion has been defeated. In other words, Bradbury is quite aware of the generic rules and expectations belonging to science fiction, but intentionally transgresses them to produce certain uncanny effects. He also can be highly ironic about his own themes, especially about childhood (consider ''The Playground,'' in which childhood is literally hell). It is perhaps best to think of Bradbury as primarily a fantasist and a writer of moral fables, bearing in mind that his evident concern for the effects of technology on society and the individual, expressed in such works as *Fahrenheit 451*, have earned him a rightful place in science fiction as well.

Bradbury has made few overtly theoretical statements about fantasy, but from introductions, poems, and prefaces that he has written, it is evident that he subscribes to the aesthetic of fantasy (first identified by Stephen King), which is based on an oscillation between two opposing artistic impulses: an illusion-forming or Apollonian mode that preserves cultural myths, and a Dionysian mode that destroys them when they become rigid or are no longer useful for life. The intensification and enjoyment of life in this world is the goal of all of Bradbury's fantasy, and he accomplishes this by wearing—and subsequently discarding—as many fictional masks or identities (that is, his characters) as possible in the context of a novel or short story. Like Nietzsche, who coined the terms ''Apollonian'' and ''Dionysian,'' Bradbury has resisted anything that would devalue existence in this world. But like the French surrealists who welcomed him as a kindred spirit (see the French critics Michel Carrouges and Michel Deutsch), he would transform—or, rather, penetrate—reality by the use of unconscious and dream materials that a too programmatic rationalism would repress.

In 1968 Bradbury wrote ''Death Warmed Over''—an unproduced television fantasy about Halloween—in which he summarized his views on the nature of fantasy. In this scenario Bradbury and the Phantom of the Opera sit in an otherwise empty theater and comment on all the famous horror and fantasy films of the past as autumn leaves are blown from the street and into a projector where they are cast as images across ''the velvet abyss'' onto a ghostly screen. This fantasy/theatrical set gives Bradbury a framework within which to vent his spleen about what he takes to be the literalness of the modern horror film, which seems to spare the viewers nothing in its search for the true and terrible image (later reiterated in the controversies surrounding the ''splatterpunk'' horror movement, for which the literalness, not the suggestion, of horror is paramount). For Bradbury, fantasy must have a system of symbolic meanings, and he offers many convincing reasons why the detour through the metaphorical realm of appearances is a necessary part of the historical genesis of fantasy—which includes, in his view, myths, folktales, religions, and personal myths (such as his own Green Town, Illinois) as well as modern fantasy. I will quote at length from this scenario to give the reader a sense of the developing argument and its highly metaphorical style, skipping over, for the moment, the obvious element of staging and theatricality in the text itself. Bradbury asks several rhetorical questions about the origins of myth and religion:

> What were we doing? Naming the unnamable. Why? Because man by his very nature must describe. The names change from generation to generation, but the need to name goes on. We were picturing the unpicturable. For, consider, does death have a size, shape, color, breadth, width? No, it is ''deep'' beyond infinity and ''far'' beyond eternity. It is forever encapsulated in the skull we carry, a symbol to itself, behind our masking face.
>
> Our religions, our tribal as well as personal myths, tried to find symbols then for the vacuum, the void, the elevator shaft down which we must all journey and no stops evermore again. We had to know. We had to lie, and accept the lie of labels and names, even while we knew we lied, for we had work to do, cities to build, children to rear, much to love and know. Thus we gave gifts of

names to ward off the night some little while, to give us time to think on other things. . . .

What are we saying here? Let me recapitulate. The basic facts of man's life upon earth are these: You will love. You will not be loved. People will treat you well. People will treat you badly. You will grow old. You will die. We *know* this.

You cannot tell a man that death and age are after him again and again all his lifetime without freezing his mind ahead of the reality. He must be told these truths by indirection. You must not hit him with lightning. You must polarize the lightning through transformers, which are the arts, then tell him to grab hold of the one-cent Electrocute Yourself for a Penny Machine. His hair may stand up, his heart beat swiftly as he juices his veins. But the truth, thus fed, will make him free. . . .

A new generation will scramble the sick bones of this one. And the health and strength of that generation will be built on the ability to fantasize. To fantasize is to remain sane. . . .

To these [intellectuals, psychologists] I say: Give us back our small fears to help us cure the large. We cannot destroy the large death, the one that takes us all. We need a tiny one to be crushed in our hand to give us confidence. The complete and utter truth, completely known, is madness. Do not kick us off the cliff and send us screaming down to that. For God's sake, give us our morsel of poisoned popcorn to munch in the cinema dark.

Critics familiar with the general text of contemporary philosophical literary criticism have pointed out the Nietzschean rhetoric of these passages, and indeed Bradbury has paid tribute elsewhere to this philosopher in a poem that could well stand as his *ars poetica* ("We Have Our Arts So We Won't Die of Truth," in *The Complete Poems*). Nor would it be difficult to see, in an examination of the full text, how Bradbury's argument, presented thematically here, is in form self-deconstructing. For one narrative voice—the thematic one presented in the passage above—tells the "truth" about fantasy while another voice, Bradbury the stage manager of a television scenario, asserts that literal truth is deadly and therefore must be framed as an illusion.

There are many affinities of thought between what Bradbury said about fantasy and what Nietzsche said of tragic art. However the issue of Nietzsche's early pessimism and its relationship to his later "healthful" writings is understood, all readers of *The Birth of Tragedy* know by means of what ruse the destructiveness of unmediated truth is avoided: instead of being directly experienced, it is represented. The artistic vision exalts power, heals the will, and gives strength to look upon the horrible and the absurd. Horror is transformed into the sublime and the absurd is rendered comic. Bradbury's poison popcorn and the Electrocute Yourself for a Penny Machine are examples of the latter. Mankind is rescued by the essential theatricality of art. Furthermore, Nietzsche in a striking metaphor asserts that the light of the Apollonian world of the dream can be compared to the mirror image of a well-known optical phenomenon: being blinded by the sun. Similarly, Bradbury suggests that the terror and horror of existence have to be "polarized" and filtered by the arts. Only this can make life livable.

What is more, in a beautifully resonant metaphor that is very much his own, Bradbury asserts that man forever encapsulates the natural symbol of the unpicturable abyss in his own skull, a "symbol to itself," thereby indicating the nonmimetic character of fantastic art. Bradbury's text is both an intellectual inquiry into the origins of fantastic art and a work of art itself. And the artist, one senses, is expected to wear many convincing masks—these are the signs of his vitality. Otherwise the dream is bypassed to capture and kill with facts, or things that appear as facts (Bradbury is careful to add the qualification; perhaps there are no such things as facts, for Dionysian insight reveals the illusory nature of all "reality"). As with Nietzsche, in Bradbury's aesthetic there is a fundamental discordance between art and truth. Faces are masks that hide the truth, and one senses that those faces—however grotesque and frightening they may become—are worth more than the truth.

Perhaps the most significant affinity between the two writers is that Bradbury in a very Nietzschean manner diagnoses the sickness and health of our present civilization, predicting that the next generation will scramble the sick bones of this one. Reading allegorically, one might say that for Bradbury literal truth is death. The way to restore literary health to worn-out conventions is not to be more literal, but to create metaphors of metaphors, new interpretations. Without the ability to fantasize in the name of life, culture loses the healthy natural power of its creativity. Nietzsche would say that new myths have to be born continually out of the Dionysian womb. Myths—and metaphors—provide the ability to name the abyss. Only a culture ringed and defined by myths is a complete and unified culture. Bradbury's use of the myth of the American frontier in his Martian stories is one major instance of this sort of rejuvenation of old myths, and critics such as David Mogen have studied this aspect of Bradbury's work extensively.

Bradbury's fantastic worlds are not marred by an anemic otherworldliness that is sometimes to be found in writers of modern fantasy. On the contrary, even when his stories offer an escape to other worlds, these other worlds exist primarily as intensifications of the life of this world. For instance, *The Martian Chronicles,* which purports to be a history of the invasion and colonization of Mars, transforms historiography itself into a form of dreaming, into fantastic art. It alternates a Dionysian critique of all life-destroying modes of emplotting history—the Christian myth of redemption, the bourgeois doctrine of progress—with a defense of historiography in the poetic or metaphorical mode, restaging the American myth of the rejuvenating wilderness in the process. Furthermore, the invasion of Mars as Bradbury imagines it is an occasion to

invent and restage ingenious thematic figures of the will to life—the noble Martians, the artist, the superior man, who each affirm the life of this world—in enchanting and sometimes terrifying stories that interplay memory and forgetfulness, music and masks. Bradbury as historian is a master of metaphorical identifications. In the end the reader becomes the Martian, but along the way experiences a kaleidoscopic transformation of objects and events that occupy the historical field. Bradbury as fantastic historian transforms familiar things into the unfamiliar (and vice versa), transgressing the generic rules of science fiction, inviting the reader to experience the uncanny and the marvelous. For instance, in "The Third Expedition" ("Mars Is Heaven!"), the Earthmen seem to be at home on Mars, but actually this is an illusion created by the Martians to deceive and destroy them. The story is very uncanny in its effect. What seems to be most familiar—one's family—turns out to be the most strange and alien. Critics such as Jorg Hienger have pointed out the play of the familiar and the strange in this famous story, noting that the German word *unheimlich* (uncanny is one of its meanings) means literally "un-home-like." The result is that the overly historical modern consciousness, which has lost all feeling for the strangeness and astonishment of life, is overcome. *The Martian Chronicles* offers a homeopathic cure—a return to history in the metaphorical mode.

Much of what the reader knows about Martian civilization at its height comes from Spender, the archaeologist of "And the Moon Be Still as Bright," a story that provides much insight into the value system of *The Martian Chronicles*. According to Spender, the Martians "discovered the secret of life among animals," which do not question life. The Martians knew how to blend art into their living instead of keeping it separate, as on Earth. Spender gains his insights into Martian culture from reading a book of Martian philosophy, which is said to be at least ten thousand years old. Apparently the Martians went through crises in their development as a culture, but in creating an artistic culture they escaped nihilism by knowing when to stop questioning and by not allowing the theoretical side of consciousness to dominate and rigidify their conceptions of the world.

This is no doubt what Spender implies when he says that humans had become too much human on Mars as well (the phrase itself is reminiscent of Nietzsche's phrase ''all-too-human''). And how else, incidentally, can the decline of the Martians, who by the time of the second expedition have a good deal of their population locked away in asylums, be explained? Sheer will to life is not a sufficient explanation. At the height of their civilization, however, the Martians were able to veil the painful knowledge of the absurdity of life with artistic illusions, which allowed them to ''forget'' the destructive questioning of rationalism. The surviving Martian art contains many images of animals. They knew when to stop (that is, before the point of absolute nihilism) and therefore were only apparently naive. According to Spender, life does not and cannot justify itself; it has no need to do so. Only humans feel a need to justify their existence because only humans, of all the animals, are conscious of the historical nature of their being and of their modernity at the same time. Nietzsche's way out of this all-too human paradox was to argue that only art can justify life to humans. Bradbury is saying that humans need a fantastic art with a life-preserving purpose, one in which all ugliness and discord are transmuted into an aesthetic game that the will, in its utter exuberance, plays with itself.

Spender says the Martians did not try to provide an answer or solution to the supreme question but, rather, tried to show how—in a time of conflict—this question might have arisen in the first place. Once this is made clear, it no longer seems important to solve the problem on its own terms. To the Martians, a philosophical problem is a question not to be answered but to be overcome. Thus, the question of the meaning of life becomes ''senseless'' in a new way—they have the answer before the question ever arises, once the society regains stability. This can only be what Spender means when he says that the Martians ''blended'' science, religion, and art. Surely he does not mean the Martians discovered the meaning of life in some transcendental symbol of God (and what god but Dionysus could be represented by such ''pagan'' animal images?). Of course this whole passage is meant to be taken as a diagnosis of the cultural situation on Earth, in which religion denies art, science denies religion, and philosophy denies science, so that modern humanity is hurled further and further into the depths of an ironic consciousness, deprived of faith in its own reason, imagination, and will, and is finally driven to despair of life itself.

Bradbury's next attempt at cultural criticism, *Fahrenheit 451,* is a utopian novel. As such, it alternates a critique of mass culture and technology—the negative effects of enlightenment and progress—with blissful reveries of Earth that restore the utopian imagination. Because of this alternation the novel may seem to be politically dualistic. But clearly, Bradbury stands with those who believe in rational enlightenment and the critique of prejudices, and wants to expose the distortions of communication brought about by hidden violence and domination. That is why his hero, Montag the Fireman, rediscovers the meaning of the books he is burning. Yet in his reading Montag also romantically affirms the authority of tradition and myth. On the one hand the novel is a critique of mass culture represented by the ''utopian'' status quo, which is seen as oppressive with its constant stimulation of pseudoneeds for the narcissistic personality (the main target is advertising, which is subjected to a vitriolic critique). Mass culture culminates in the reduction of all higher values to a "paste pudding norm," as Fire Chief Beatty, the defender of the status quo, himself succinctly puts it. But on the other hand Bradbury is aware of the paradox that although the process of enlightenment brought about by science and technology is necessary, the critical dissolution of dogmas produces not liberation but indifference. The process is not emancipatory but nihilistic. Myths are also necessary for a healthy culture. The book takes the form of a three-part "diagnosis" of the cultural disease known as nihilism. The first part shows Montag becoming sick; the second part deals with a search for an antidote—the "naive" value of imaginative and pleasurable reading—and the third with a revaluation of values, as Montag understands the true value of books: preserving the utopian ideal.

Fahrenheit 451 is thus much more than a "febrile protest against book burning," as one critic called it, or even censorship. It embodies cultural criticism in the aesthetic form of the utopian novel. Fire Chief Beatty is certainly the most interesting character in the novel because of what he tells us about the American culture industry and because he is an ironic portrait of the utopian "Old Wise Man." His is a nihilism that does not recognize itself (indeed, his very name suggests the circus animal trainer Clyde Beatty). Before Montag can begin to read in earnest, Fire Chief Beatty arrives to ask him when he will be well again. He gives Montag what he hopes will be an antidote for his sickness: a lesson in firemen's history. Ironically, that history itself is an incisive indictment of the American culture industry. It describes the many forms of distorted communication taking place in the American culture industry, from outright censorship of forbidden books to official state ideology with its leveling of all values to the unconscious and barbaric repetition of the same. Like a machine rotating in one spot, Beatty's rhetoric gives the impression

of life and vitality, but it actually has none. It is scarcely more than a montage of superstructural effects that tells little about the basic economic conditions that led up to the present "utopia." Beatty idolizes fire, the power of the state to reduce everything to an ashy sameness, and death. Fire to him is an antibiotic, an agent of stability and sanitation, for it seemingly destroys the upsurge of threatening new values. Although constantly changing and producing a fascinating world of phenomena, fire is an eternal value to him because it destroys differences. As an advocate of mass culture, he believes that members of society must all be the same. Repetition of the same will, in turn, produce the greatest happiness for the greatest number of people. Beatty understands Montag's attraction to books but claims that he himself overcame it. But significantly—and despite his apparent air of beatitude—he almost pleads with Montag not to allow "the torrent of melancholy and drear philosophy" to drown his happy world.

What Beatty fears most, we infer, is our present cultural situation with its conflict of interpretations. He only wants people to be crammed full of positivist facts that do not change, even though he ridicules the scientific explanation of fire in terms of friction and molecules as "gobbledygook." Facts must be worn as emblems on every fireman's arm, like the fact that book paper catches fire and burns at 451 degrees Fahrenheit. His entire history of modernity is negative and defensive because he cannot affirm differences that are a result of the will to power playing itself out in history or in art. Beatty is a nihilist with no real way of overcoming nihilism. He thinks that the sight of such a bleak and useless existence as humanity has discovered in this century and the last has made him feel only bestial and lonely. Beatty knows that humanity has lost dignity in its own eyes to an incredible extent in trying to measure the universe. And as for books,

"Well, Montag, take my word for it, I've had to read a few in my time, to know what I was about, and the books say *nothing!* Nothing you can teach or believe. They're about nonexistent people, figments of imagination, if they're fiction. And if they're nonfiction, it's worse, one professor calling another an idiot, one philosopher screaming down another's gullet. All of them running about, putting out the stars and extinguishing the sun. You come away lost."

Beatty is obsessed with the pessimistic "truth" about life—philosophy claims to know the eternal truth, but in fact there are only interpretations that have power for a while—yet he cannot see the value of literary fictions recognized as such. Beatty's philosophical position, which Nietzsche would surely have understood in all its implications as a form of nihilism, amounts to an absurd evaluation: because of their pessimism, philosophers put out fires (stars and suns) instead of igniting them, as the good, optimistic firemen must do. Beatty is happy with ideology but cannot tolerate fictions. The novel ends not in negation but by affirming differences. The eternal recurrence of the utopian ideal rises, like the phoenix, from the flames of humanity's self-destructive nihilism as the book people, after the destruction of nuclear war, literally become the books they have memorized.

Dandelion Wine does not embody cultural criticism. It is, rather, a nostalgic novel of reveries that manages to balance the narrative development of its twelve-year-old protagonist, Douglas Spaulding, with a permanent core of childhood. Three times the novel puts before us (June, July, and August 1928) daydreamlike scenes of wine-making that combine and synthesize the scattered elements of the poetic universe: earth, air, fire, and water. Wine, its production, and its drinking is Bradbury's symbol of a restored oneness with the principle of life. Although the nightmare is given its due in the story of Lavinia Nebbs and the Lonely One, as well as in the ravine that runs through the town (representing the abyss), and although Douglas has to undergo the pain of individuation and loss, Bradbury ultimately rejects tragic representation.

Douglas' sense of being and plenitude—which he discovers early in the novel while gathering fox grapes—cannot continue forever without interruption. John Huff, "the only living god in the whole of Green Town," leaves him to go to Milwaukee; Colonel Freeleigh, a kind of embodied "time machine," dies of old age, as does Douglas' great-grandmother; and the Lonely One murders several women in the town. In writing about these events in the back of his notepad, Douglas interprets these facts as leading inevitably to the conclusion that he, too, must die. In late August he becomes sick from the heat, which separates him from his bodily self. But Mr. Jonas, the junkman, cures him with a dose of reverie, a reverie of cool, stimulating air. Douglas is told to drink with his nose while Mr. Jonas reads the labels and small print on a bottle: "GREEN DUSK FOR DREAMING BRAND PURE NORTHERN AIR." It is the healthy and bracing imaginary climate of cold air and white Arctic heights contained in this word-reverie that convinces Douglas to affirm his life again. Of course, the bottle does not contain any such substance in reality; it is only Douglas' saving capacity to dream that has been brought to life. But it saves him nonetheless.

On the book's last page, Douglas dreams of dandelion wine, understanding now its true value as a life-sustaining fiction:

> And if he should forget [the summer past], the dandelion wine stood in the cellar, numbered huge for each and every day. He would go there often, stare straight into the sun until he could stare no more, then close his eyes and consider the burned spots, the fleeting scars left dancing on his warm eyelids; arranging, rearranging each fire and reflection until the pattern was clear. . . .
> So thinking, he slept.
> And, sleeping, put an end to Summer, 1928.

After the Dionysian dancing of the spots behind the eyelids, Douglas goes to sleep, putting an end to the illusions of summer. But they can be recovered; such things are possible in the shelter of reverie, in the cellars of being. In Nietzsche's *Birth of Tragedy*, the myths of tragic representation are described as bright images that healing nature projects before us after a glance into the dark abyss. At the beginning of the novel, Douglas wonders how to make sense of the interchange he senses going on between civilization, the town, and "the softly blowing abyss," where a "million deaths and rebirths" happen every hour. Through the security provided by reverie, Douglas has learned the Dionysian wisdom of the abyss in a manageable way. In fact, Douglas feels so secure that he imagines deliberately staring into the sun to provoke and later master the "fleeting scars" of becoming.

If tragic myth is an Apollonian illusion composed of "luminous spots to cure eyes damaged by a gruesome night" (Nietzsche's words), then reveries create representations that may cure us after we have stared directly into the sun, which actively interprets and loves the Earth, as can be seen in Montag's water reverie in *Fahrenheit 451*. Reverie may double the self; it may even bring it to the limits of consciousness, as it does here, but in Bradbury's aesthetics of fantasy, tragic pessimism and representation have been reversed for the affirmation of life. To read *Dandelion Wine* is to discover a beneficial elixir of words that attracts happy images, allowing us to reimagine the archetypal pattern of our own childhood. And indeed young Douglas' life is saved by this Dionysian wine. As befits the aesthetics of fantasy as Bradbury understands it, the self in reverie is not brought to the point of annihilation without the promise of rebirth.

Like *Fahrenheit 451*, *Something Wicked This Way Comes* (1962) also effects a revaluation, this time of our conventional notions of bad conscience and good and evil, through the destruction of a supernatural carnival that invades a small town in October. The carnival seems to be an allegory of psychoanalysis, which feeds off human desire created by lack. Mr. Halloway begins the story as an aging man desiring his lost youth. He learns to see himself not as a stable person who is either good or evil but as a succession of arrivals and departures (the titles, incidentally, of two of the book's parts). Having gained this radical perspective on identity, Halloway realizes that the only thing possible to do is to push the ridiculous masquerade of the carnival to its limits, toward a revaluation of values. Making use of the unsuspected Dionysian power of laughter, Halloway bursts the carnival apart at its seams, shattering the mirror maze and its anguish of petty narcissism. Eventually he slays the Dust Witch with a bullet on which he has marked his smile. Halloway has to teach his son Will the value of laughter for life. Then he and Will bring Jim Nightshade, captured by the evil father, Mr. Dark, back to life with mirth, harmonica playing, and mimic dancing. Halloway also kills Mr. Dark, who has transformed himself into a boy, with a loving, fatherly embrace. He literally kills with kindness, and before he dies, Mr. Dark accuses him of being "evil."

The laughter that is born from slaying the Dust Witch is not just a physiological response to tickling. In Nietzschean terms it represents the power of interpretation. To laugh at evil requires discipline and strength, an entire method that understands evil's byways and techniques and that actively appropriates them. As Nietzsche put it in *Thus Spoke Zarathustra*: "Not by wrath does one kill, but by laughter. Come, let us kill the spirit of gravity!" In Nietzsche's late philosophy, laughter is an antidote for afflictions produced by the spirit of gravity that makes life a burden. So in Bradbury, too, when the Dust Witch comes to read Halloway's pain and regret and to make him part of the carnival, he laughs, prompted by her tickling. Actually he does more than laugh. He laughs hysterically, he guffaws, he chokes and hollers with mirth.

Mr. Dark's illustrations disperse and melt away, leaving the freaks with no place in which to recognize themselves. This dispersal of the carnival machine—which on the allegorical level seems to represent Bradbury's struggle with psychoanalysis—is in itself a rather frightening affair, for it seems almost as if nothing in humans—not even their bodies—is sufficiently stable to serve as a basis for self-recognition or for understanding others. We will never know who the freaks were, even though they are liberated into intensities and differences, for they disappear in all directions like shadows. Miss Foley (the boys' teacher) and the others captured from Green Town leave with them.

The carnival of interiority is finished, though it may return again under different masks. The haters and despisers of life will always be around, Mr. Halloway seems to imply: "The fight's just begun." But laughter will be available as a principle that affirms life, as a balm that makes light of one's wounds. Always a dualist in fantasy, Bradbury here shows the worlds of the Apollonian and the Dionysian affected by a transvaluation of values. It now seems entirely appropriate for the Dionysian "father" to kill his Apollonian "son," who represents the poisoned ruses and formal disguises of psychoanalysis. By making his fantasy responsive to the situation of the fantastic after Freud—and to the whole tragic nature of interiority (repression, guilt, anguish) that Freud's work represents in our literary culture—Bradbury has written a new chapter in the history of laughter. With this book he also gave his readers fair warning. Henceforth, those who read Bradbury without laughing, without laughing often, and at times doubling up with laughter, might as well not be reading him. Indeed, laughter is the only thing pronounced holy by this wildly rhetorical book that builds a fantastic roller coaster across the abyss.

In his later works, such as *Death Is a Lonely Business*, parody and humor again operate to undermine morbid interiority. Bradbury's first novel in twenty-three years is a sort of carnivalized detective story that is also an oblique projection of his own creative processes. In it death is both the nightmare that stalks the young Bradbury and the alter ego that he must reject. The hero, an autobiographical stand-in for Bradbury as a young man, is a penniless and love-starved writer living in fog-bound, dilapidated Venice, California, in the late 1940s, producing his early fantasy classics (such as, "The Fog Horn") for *Dime Detective* and *Weird Tales*. It seems that death is stalking and killing the "Lonelies"—eccentrics living their lives on the edge of despair or in the past—and the plot of the book is involved with finding out who death's agent and friend in the community really is, before it can kill the hero.

Death turns out to be a pretentious, reclusive little fellow named A. L. Shrank, whose name and library (stocked with "pessimists" such as Spengler, Schopenhauer, Freud, and "dread Nietzsche") suggest his significance. Shrank is a shrink—that is, a psychoanalyst, or "meadow doctor to lost creatures," as he calls himself. For Bradbury—who is both author and character here—he represents the whole threat of overintellectualism in our literary culture. Bradbury jokingly refers to him as "Sigmund Freud's Munchkin son," but his fears of psychoanalytic culture are not so easily dismissed. Bradbury is fascinated, yet afraid to talk to Shrank, who seems to know everything about him, because of the dire knowledge of literary melancholy he possesses. Listening at Shrank's door, he wonders:

In there, between precipice shelves of dusty books, did I hear Sigmund Freud whispering a penis is only a penis, but a good cigar is a smoke? Hamlet dying and taking everyone along? Virginia Woolf, like drowned Ophelia, stretched out to dry on that couch, telling her sad tale? Tarot cards being shuffled? Heads being felt like cantaloupes? Pens scratching?

The hero eventually defeats A. L. Shrank, as much by affirming his life as by physical struggle, for he believes fervently that he is not going to end up as a Lonely, but instead is going to write "damned fine books and be loved." *Death Is a Lonely Business* can be understood as autobiographical detective fantasy exploring the modernist theme of the death of the author. But Bradbury's involvement with autobiographical fiction raises many interesting issues about the relationship of life and art. In particular, how is it possible to read such a doubled act of autobiography/fiction? Is death literal or a metaphor? Or in some uncanny way both? For what Bradbury discovers is that Death himself is a Lonely who has been murdering people. To survive as an author, the narrator, Bradbury, must endow his own creative dreams with life by writing about Death's murders, thereby avoiding becoming a Lonely himself. In the end Bradbury reveals the hidden pun or twist in his title: Death is not only a business concerning Lonelies but also the business of a Lonely. Yet Bradbury acknowledges that Death is what gives creative inspiration to his work. True to his aesthetic of fantasy, Death can never be confronted directly, but only through the mask of metaphor, in this case A. L. Shrank.

As previously mentioned, literal truth for Bradbury is death. This much is made very clear by *The Halloween Tree* (1972), Bradbury's children's novel. Despite the surface simplicity, *The Halloween Tree* embodies many of his ideas about fantastic art. Because it takes place on Halloween, Bradbury's favorite holiday, the delight and intoxicating joy he obviously takes in this ultimately pagan celebration are communicated to the reader in no uncertain terms. The play of masking and unmasking in particular, which is at the heart of all Bradbury's fantasy, is nowhere more successfully employed than here to make the world itself seem a fable. As the philosopher of Halloween, Death removes the ancient mask he has worn under the reign of single truth (all human history, morality, and religion having been reduced to the fear of him in "Death Warmed Over!") to put on the plurality of masks demanded by Dionysian enchantment and carnivalization.

The plot has a doubly interwoven structure, taking the form of a quest for the origins of Halloween and the search for a boy named Pipkin— "an assemblage of speeds, smells, textures; a cross section of all the boys who ever ran, fell, got up, and ran again"—who disappears mysteriously at the beginning of Halloween night. Pipkin's worshipful gang of friends is led by Tom Skelton, who is the center of orientation in the novel and whose responses the reader therefore strives to emulate. The gang is led on this quest by Death himself, masked under the wonderfully sonorous name of Carapace Clavicle Moundshroud. After tearing apart the old and many-layered circus posters that decorate the side of a barn, in a scene carefully constructed to suggest or mime the ritual *sparagmos* (the sacrifice of animals by dismemberment) associated with the god Dionysus, the boys, together with Moundshroud, construct a kite of destructions out of the fragmented pictures of animals. Hanging onto this kite as a stabilizing tail, they fly backward in time and space to ancient Egypt, where they witness the rituals devoted to the death and rebirth of the god Osiris, then spy on similar celebrations going on in Greece and Rome with the help of a giant telescope mounted on top of a pyramid, then onward to the Celtic festival of Samhain (according to folklorists, the actual origin of Halloween). During the Middle Ages, they magically re-create the symbolic Christian art imprisoning the terror of chaos on the frozen facade of Notre Dame, and last they visit contemporary

Mexico, where the sugary festivities for the Day of the Dead are in progress.

At each of these historical stages, the boys encounter Pipkin, who is elusively masked in various forms—as a dead Egyptian prince recently mummified, as a gargoyle on Notre Dame—and at each stage the significance of their costumes is explained by Moundshroud. In Mexico, Death makes a bargain with them. He will let Pipkin (who is actually in the hospital with appendicitis) live if they will each agree to forfeit a year from the end of their lives. The boys unselfishly agree to this risk, and Moundshroud returns them home, where a restored Pipkin is waiting for them. The ostensible moral to be drawn seems to be that common cause, the sharing of love and risks together, gives significance to life even in the face of death.

Only in the last few pages of this novel do the representational and the philosophical levels (or showing and telling) begin to be at variance with one another. Before returning the boys home to the ordinary world, Moundshroud shows them the function and structure of the House of Haunts. This structure is Bradbury's house of fantastic fiction. But precisely because it is a structure, however lively its description may be—and techniques of exaggeration are nowhere more in evidence than in the rhetoric evoking this vast cemetery of a house and its creaking gothic machinery—one doubts its ability to contain Dionysian experience. Moundshroud commands the boys to slide down a gigantic banister to the respective historical levels where they think their individual disguises and masks belong, telling them that the celebrations they have witnessed are in essence all the same. But can the reader's experience of dispersal in time and space, and such a play of masking and unmasking as has in part been indicated here, be contained within such a framework? Moundshroud suggests that it is all one, that all the celebrations are the same. In one sense this is clearly the Nietzschean per-

spective that the truth is always the same, always horrible and will-negating. The House of Haunts is a workable metaphor of the need for many fantastic representations. But it is a static metaphor that can never contain the reader's temporal experience of the Dionysian, which is best expressed by ecstatic poetry, perhaps the very verse Death speaks in tearing himself apart, to the boys' unbounded delight:

> O autumn winds that bake and burn
> And all the world to darkness turn,
> Now storm and seize and make of me
> A swarm of leaves from Autumn's Tree!

What Bradbury fears most as a writer (and this may be true of every imaginative writer, even those who celebrate their own authorial death or disappearance into the work of art) is not so much literal death as creative death, the death of the imagination. The ramifications of this theme—literal death versus the death of the imagination—are explored in one of Bradbury's longest stories, which he also shaped into a play, "Pillar of Fire." Originally published in 1948, "Pillar of Fire," in both its story and its stage versions, is the closest Bradbury has ever come to tragic representation. According to Bradbury, it was a rehearsal for *Fahrenheit 451*. Certainly both these stories develop a politics of the fantastic capable of responding to the increasing censorship of fantasy in America during the 1950s. (As an example of this censorship, L. Frank Baum's *The Wonderful Wizard of Oz*—one of the books Bradbury most loved—was removed from children's libraries across the country because of its alleged harmful effects on science education. In fact, Bradbury places the Emerald City on Mars in another of his politically based fantasies from this period, "The Exiles" [collected in *The Illustrated Man*]. But Baum is understandably absent from the darker horrors of "Pillar of Fire.")

The plot is fantastic in construction, designed so that readers hesitate between a supernatural and a scientific explanation of the uncanny events that happen when William Lantry rises from his grave in the year 2349. Is Lantry really one of the walking dead, or is he an extraordinary case of suspended animation? It seems clear from the outset that he is a zombie, and this is confirmed at the end. Appropriately, the story is set in Salem—prime Puritan territory—where the last graveyard had been preserved as a tourist attraction by the government, as a reminder of a barbaric custom. But now this graveyard (as well as alien tombs on Mars; the story evokes Bradbury's Martian stories) is scheduled for destruction. The state seeks thereby to make absolute its control over the world of darkness, death, and decay, and over all writers whose imaginations are attracted to it. We learn from Lantry's visit to a library that the Great Burning of 2265 destroyed all the "unclean" writings of the past: Edgar Allan Poe, H. P. Lovecraft, and Ambrose Bierce, among others. Lantry realizes with a shock that if he is destroyed, all memory of such literature will be destroyed as well, because he is the last person—or, rather, the last *dead* person—to remember them.

The society into which Lantry is reborn could be described as an extreme Apollonian culture, as is evident from the symbolism it employs. It worships the sun of rationality, emblazoned everywhere on public buildings. The dead of this society are burned in a centralized rite, in Incinerators that are warm, cozy temples where soothing music plays and the fear of death is abolished through ceremonies that deify fire. As Lantry watches the operation of the Salem Incinerator, the golden coffins of the dead covered with sun symbols slowly roll in. After a brief ceremony they are cast into a flue. On the altar are written the words "We that are born of the sun return to the sun," a fantastic reversal of the words normally spoken at Christian burials.

It is these gigantic Incinerators as myths of an Apollonian culture that Lantry wants to explode. Because deviant behavior is not expected, he manages to infiltrate the Salem Incinerator and to destroy it, killing hundreds of people in the surrounding towns. He hopes thereby to effect a revolution, to "manufacture friends" by creating more walking dead. But in this rational world the dead remain dead. Because while living they never imagined that the dead might walk, they cannot be resurrected by Lantry's magical procedures. He draws symbols of long-dead sorcerers on the floor of the makeshift morgue next to the bodies and chants his own magic formulas, to no avail. Eventually, he is picked up by the authorities and is interrogated by a man named McClure, who is the twenty-fourth century's version of a psychoanalyst and something of a detective as well. McClure tries to analyze Lantry's mortified behavior, his paleness and lack of breath, as a self-induced psychosis, but is slowly unnerved when he finds that Lantry is the real thing, one of the walking dead. Lantry is a logical impossibility to a mind such as McClure's. After a brief struggle in which Lantry tries to murder McClure, he is subdued and condemned to a second death by the state, a death that is the death of every fantastic writer in history, because only Lantry remembers them. If this were a Christian fantasy in the mode of J. R. R. Tolkien or C. S. Lewis, the evident compassion of McClure for his victim would have resulted in his conversion to the imagination at the end, thereby saving it. But Bradbury really wants his readers to feel the shock of seeing the imagination die forever, and on this level of response, the story is quite effective. The second death, the death of the imagination, becomes more terrible than the physical death.

Bradbury's later fiction explores the link between his aesthetic of fantasy and film. *A Graveyard for Lunatics* is about the madness of film. Bradbury treats the Hollywood studio production system—in which the creative screenwriter was often just an anonymous cog in a gigantic machine—as a madhouse. Everyone from the producer to the director to the actors manifests some form of insanity, from paranoia to schizophrenia, and from obsessional neurosis to perversions (the novel includes one catatonic character locked away in an asylum, the wife of the studio head). Bradbury refers to his adolescent self as "the Crazy," one who was utterly mad about film. A young writer with a successful book to his credit, he now works inside the film factory, "a victim of my own romance and infatuated madness over films that controlled life when it ran out of control beyond the Spanish wrought-iron gates [outside the studio]."

Once again, the threat is creative death, for screenwriters are not remembered. The novel opens on Halloween, 1954, a few years after the end of *Death Is a Lonely Business*. Bradbury and his friend Roy Holdstrom (a character based on Bradbury's real-life friend, special effects wizard Ray Harryhausen) have been hired by Maximus Films to "write, build, and birth the most incredibly hideous animal in Hollywood history." This apotheosis of the monster film has the working title "The Beast." Such a creature first has to be imagined, however. Bradbury can approach such a scarifying vision only through the writer's art, through metaphor. Holdstrom, on the other hand, can work from real-life models. His art is made to be seen. Although Bradbury is mad about film, film itself has difficulty using metaphor. One of the primary effects of cinema illusion is that what is seen on the screen is often taken to be literally and really there, and not a metaphor for something else. Early in the book Bradbury argues with the studio head, Manny Leiber, that "the scare comes from night shadows, things unseen." Leiber rejects this aesthetic of suggestion for the crude notion that "people want to see what scares them." Bradbury is forced, at least initially, to write his screenplay around an absent center, leaving room for the monster.

Once again Bradbury uses the conventions of detective fiction in order to fictionalize his creative anxieties during this early period of his career, and to resolve aesthetic problems. The plot of this novel is convoluted, but it is finally revealed that the whole thing is a practical joke played by Stanislau Groc, a cosmetologist employed by the studio. Described by Bradbury as a man hardly larger than one of the midget actors who played Munchkins in *The Wizard of Oz*, he is a pessimist and a clear parallel with A. L. Shrank. Groc wants to reveal to the world—possibly his motive is blackmail—that J. C. Arbuthnot, once head of Maximus Films but thought to have died in a car accident, still lives, though nearly insane and horribly mutilated. Groc contrives to have Bradbury and Holdstrom hired by the studio to do a monster picture and arranges for them to see the disfigured Arbuthnot in a restaurant. Arbuthnot then becomes the living model for Holdstrom's Beast, but the studio (Manny Leiber) is embarrassed to the point of destroying his work and fires him, not knowing that he has prepared three minutes of test film. Finding out just why the studio is acting so strangely in regard to Holdstrom's art—which after all is designed to show the monster in all its horrid detail—involves us and Bradbury in mystery, seeming madness, and the aesthetics of fantastic representation.

Near the end we are told that "The Beast" was an "impossible film" all along (270). Holdstrom's three minutes showed that it was possible at least to put such a creature on film, *but only as a mask*. In viewing the fragmentary footage, Bradbury is at first overcome with terror—uncannily, the Beast seems to be looking directly at him—but then realizes that it is Holdstrom himself *pretending* to be the Beast, wearing makeup. The reader must remember here that even before it was filmed, the model clay head was already described as "the finest work he had ever done . . . [and that Holdstrom was] a dreamer alone behind his terrible, awful, most dreadfully appalling mask.'' Bradbury thus contains the horrific filmic effect of ''The Beast''—his gaze at the viewer—by revealing it as a fantastic illusion, a mask beneath a mask.

Moby Dick was something of an impossible film for Bradbury. Aside from its humorous Irish material (previously published as short stories), *Green Shadows, White Whale* details Bradbury's visit to Ireland to confront two beasts, the director John Huston and Melville's white whale. Imagining an incredible future for himself as a screenwriter for a genius director, he soon learns that Huston is a very difficult man to work for, even for someone bent on destroying him. Bradbury records several attempts by Huston to humiliate him and his creative efforts, a game that Bradbury never really understands (though he alludes to homoerotic reasons). Eventually Bradbury wins out over the womanizing Huston by writing a story about Huston being destroyed by a banshee, instead of the required screenplay pages. His victory over the whale—how to capture the literary force of Melville's novel on film—not surprisingly comes when, struggling through his last days in Ireland, he finds a central metaphor holding the entire screenplay together: ''What nailed it fast was hammering the Spanish gold ounce to the mast. If I hadn't fastened on that for starters, the other metaphors . . . might not have surfaced to swim in the bleached shadow of the Whale.'' This central metaphor acts as a ''solar presence'' in the screenplay, a center of meaning that controls all of the various tropes Bradbury was able eventually to glean from Melville's pages.

Ray Bradbury is a writer who made his personal obsessions with popular culture and film into immensely successful stories. By the fifth decade of his career, he produced a significant body of writing that uses the conventions of pulp genre fiction—fantasy, science fiction, and detective fiction—in order to embody cultural criticism and to investigate the role such fictions must play in our technological society. Bradbury's crucial role in broadening the audience for science fiction cannot be disputed. His move to detective fiction in the 1980s, however, disappointed some of his fans. Historically, detective fiction combined with science fiction has mostly been the preserve of rationalists such as Isaac Asimov. But Bradbury's use of the genre—which depends more on the carnivalization of the Ross Macdonald school of hard-boiled American detective fiction than on classical models—needs to be viewed in the broader context of his aesthetic. Bradbury's aesthetic demands that the terrible truths of life be transformed into art, often with the aid of humor. In whatever genre this is expressed, his imaginative world is one in which ''true'' art can never be decadent or pessimistic. This is why Bradbury resists psychoanalysis, which has become the dominant model of our literary culture. In some of his more polemical essays, he may even appear to be anti-intellectual. But a close reading of his major works—and there is a growing body of criticism about them—reveals that his ''message'' has always been the laughingly enthusiastic affirmation of life in this world.

Selected Bibliography

WORKS OF RAY BRADBURY

FICTION
Dark Carnival. Sauk City, Wis.: Arkham House, 1947.
The Martian Chronicles. Garden City, N.Y.: Doubleday, 1950.
The Illustrated Man. Garden City, N.Y.: Doubleday, 1951.

Fahrenheit 451. Garden City, N.Y.: Ballantine, 1953.

The Golden Apples of the Sun. Garden City, N.Y.: Doubleday, 1953.

The October Country. Garden City, N.Y.: Ballantine, 1955.

Switch on the Night. Garden City, N.Y.: Pantheon, 1955.

Dandelion Wine. Garden City, N.Y.: Doubleday, 1957.

A Medicine for Melancholy. Garden City, N.Y.: Doubleday, 1959.

R is for Rocket. Garden City, N.Y.: Doubleday, 1962.

Something Wicked This Way Comes. New York: Simon and Schuster, 1962.

The Machineries of Joy. New York: Simon and Schuster, 1964.

S is for Space. Garden City, N.Y.: Doubleday, 1966.

I Sing the Body Electric! New York: Knopf, 1969.

The Halloween Tree. New York: Knopf, 1972.

Long after Midnight. New York: Knopf, 1976.

The Stories of Ray Bradbury. New York: Knopf, 1980.

Dinosaur Tales. New York: Bantam, 1983.

A Memory of Murder. New York: Dell, 1984.

Death Is a Lonely Business. New York: Knopf, 1985.

The Toynbee Convector. New York: Knopf, 1988.

A Graveyard for Lunatics. New York: Knopf, 1990.

Green Shadows, White Whale. New York: Knopf, 1992.

POETRY

When Elephants Last in the Dooryard Bloomed: Celebrations for Almost Any Day of the Year. New York: Knopf, 1973.

Where Robot Mice and Robot Men Run Round in Robot Towns: New Poems, Both Light and Dark. New York: Knopf, 1977.

The Haunted Computer and the Android Pope. New York: Knopf, 1981.

The Complete Poems of Ray Bradbury. New York: Ballantine, 1982.

DRAMA

The Anthem Sprinters and Other Antics. New York: Dial Press, 1963.

The Wonderful Ice Cream Suit and Other Plays. New York: Bantam, 1972.

Pillar of Fire and Other Plays for Today, Tomorrow, and Beyond Tomorrow. New York: Bantam, 1975.

ESSAYS

"Death Warmed Over." *Playboy*, January 1968, pp. 101–102, 252–253.

Zen and the Art of Writing, and the Joy of Writing. Santa Barbara, Calif.: Capra Press, 1973.

Yestermorrow: Obvious Answers to Impossible Futures. Santa Barbara, Calif.: Capra Press, 1991.

MANUSCRIPT PAPERS

There is a collection of Bradbury's manuscripts at the University Library, University of California at Los Angeles.

A large and accessible collection of manuscripts and other items is at the Popular Culture Center, Bowling Green State University.

BIOGRAPHICAL AND CRITICAL STUDIES

Attebery, Brian. *The Fantasy Tradition in American Literature: From Irving to LeGuin.* Bloomington: Indiana University Press, 1980.

Carrouges, Michel. "Ray Bradbury, les martiens, et nous." *Monde-Nouveau paru*, 79:56–63 (May 1954).

Deutsch, Michel. "Ray Bradbury et la poésie du futur." *Critique*, 22:604–611 (July 1957).

Disch, Thomas M. "Tops in Brand-Name Recognition." *New York Times Book Review*, October 26, 1980, pp. 14, 32–33.

Dobzynski, Charles. "Ray Bradbury, fabuliste de notre temps." *Europe*, no. 139–140:76–87 (July-August 1957).

Eller, Jon R. "The Stories of Ray Bradbury: An Annotated Finding List (1938–1991)." *Bulletin of Bibliography*, 49, no. 1:27–51 (March 1992).

Guffey, George R. "The Unconscious, Fantasy and Science Fiction: Transformations in Bradbury's *The Martian Chronicles* and Lem's *Solaris*." In *Bridges to Fantasy*. Edited by George E. Slusser, Eric S. Rabkin, and Robert Scholes. Carbondale: Southern Illinois University Press, 1982. Pp. 142–159.

Hienger, Jorg. "The Uncanny and Science Fiction." Translated by Elsa Schieder. *Science-Fiction Studies*, 6, no. 2:144–152 (July 1979).

Huntington, John. "Utopian and Anti-Utopian Logic: H. G. Wells and His Successors." *Science-Fiction Studies*, 27, no. 2:122–146 (July 1982).

Indick, Ben P. *Ray Bradbury, Dramatist.* 2d ed. Essays on Fantastic Literature, no. 3. San Bernardino, Calif.: Borgo Press, 1992. Revised edition of *The Drama of Ray Bradbury*.

Ingram, Forrest L. *Representative Short Story Cycles of the Twentieth Century, Studies in a Literary Genre*. The Hague: Mouton, 1971.

Isherwood, Christopher. "Review of *The Martian Chronicles*." *Tomorrow*, October 1950, pp. 56–58.

Johnson, Wayne L. *Ray Bradbury*. New York: Ungar, 1980.

Kagle, Stephen E. "Homage to Melville: Ray Bradbury and the Nineteenth Century Romance." In *The Celebration of the Fantastic*. Edited by Donald E. Morse, Marshall B. Tymn, and Csilla Bertha. Westport, Conn.: Greenwood, 1992. Pp. 279–289.

King, Stephen. *Danse Macabre*. New York: Everest House, 1981.

Lem, Stanislaw. "The Time-Travel Story and Related Matter of SF Structuring." *Science-Fiction Studies*, l, no. 3:143–154 (Spring 1974).

Mogen, David. *Ray Bradbury*. Boston: Twayne, 1986.

Moskowitz, Sam. "Ray Bradbury." In his *Seekers of Tomorrow: Makers of Modern Science Fiction*. New York: Ballantine, 1967. Pp. 351–370.

Nolan, William F. "Ray Bradbury: Prose Poet in the Age of Silence." *Magazine of Fantasy and Science Fiction*, 24:7–22 (May 1963).

———. *The Bradbury Companion*. Detroit: Gale Research, 1975.

Olander, Joseph D., and Martin Harry Greenberg, eds. *Ray Bradbury*. New York: Taplinger, 1980.

Sisario, Peter. "A Study of the Allusions in Bradbury's *Fahrenheit 451*." *English Journal*, 59:201–206 (February 1970).

Slusser, George Edgar. *The Bradbury Chronicles*. The Milford Series, Popular Writers of Today, vol. 4. San Bernadino, Calif.: Borgo Press, 1977.

Sullivan, Anita T. "Ray Bradbury and Fantasy." *English Journal*, 61:1309–1314 (December 1972).

Touponce, William F. "The Existential Fabulous: A Reading of Ray Bradbury's 'The Golden Apples of the Sun.' " In *Other Worlds: Fantasy and Science Fiction Since 1939*. Edited by John Teunissen. Winnipeg: MOSAIC, 1980. Pp. 203–218.

———. *Ray Bradbury and the Poetics of Reverie: Fantasy, Science-Fiction, and the Reader*. Studies in Speculative Fiction no. 2. Edited by Robert Scholes. Ann Arbor, Mich.: UMI Research Press, 1984.

———. "Some Aspects of Surrealism in the Work of Ray Bradbury." *Extrapolation*, 25, no. 3:228–238 (Fall 1984).

———. "Laughter and Freedom in Ray Bradbury's *Something Wicked This Way Comes*." *Children's Literature Association Quarterly*, 13, no. 1:17–21 (Spring 1988).

———. *Ray Bradbury*. Starmont Reader's Guide no. 31. Mercer Island, Wash.: Starmont House, 1989.

Valis, Noël M. "*The Martian Chronicles* and Jorge Luis Borges." *Extrapolation*, 20, no. 1:50–59 (Spring 1979).

—WILLIAM F. TOUPONCE

Raymond Chandler

1888–1959

*T*HAT WE HAVE a dominant American-based tradition of "hard-boiled" detective fiction, as opposed to the classic English tradition of brilliant amateur sleuths deciphering clues in country manor houses, is due in large part to Raymond Chandler. That the detective story has, at its best, become a vehicle for character analysis, social commentary, exploration of stylistic possibilities, and experiments with point of view is due in large part to Raymond Chandler. That theoretical critics such as Roland Barthes, F. R. Jameson, and Geoffrey Hartman have taken a serious professional interest in detective fiction is due in large part to Raymond Chandler. That all this should be so is ironic because Raymond Chandler always felt a greater affinity with English life and culture than with American; it is ironic because he came to professional writing late in life, settling on crime fiction as a relatively quick and easy way to make money after alcoholism and the Great Depression had ended his career as an oil executive; and it is ironic because, despite his eventual desire to create art rather than formulaic detective stories, he hated abstract, intellectual discussions of literature, which made him intensely uneasy. In other words, little in the outward events of Raymond Chandler's first forty-four years would lead one to predict the accomplishments of the next twenty-seven, or their lasting influence.

*   *   *

Chandler was born in Chicago on July 23, 1888, to an Irish mother and a Pennsylvania Quaker father whose own ancestors had come from Ireland in the seventeenth and eighteenth centuries. His father, Maurice, was an alcoholic, as Chandler would become. Possibly some of Chandler's self-loathing in later years resulted from his following the pattern of a man he despised as "an utter swine." Raymond never again saw his father after his parents divorced when he was seven. He and his mother, Florence, then moved to England, where they lived in Upper Norwood, a suburb south of London, with her sister Ethel and, in Chandler's words, his "stupid and arrogant grandmother." Natasha Spender, Chandler's close friend at the end of his life, recounts in *The World of Raymond Chandler* (1978) that the mother and son "were made to feel like disgraced poor relations." At an early age Chandler assumed the role of his mother's protector by absorbing the humiliations and "moralizing condescension" meted out by his female relatives.

In 1900 the household moved to Dulwich, a fashionable suburb in South London, so that Raymond could attend Dulwich College, a well-known public (i.e., private) school. There he studied classical and modern subjects with schoolmasters who instilled a respect for clear prose as well as the Christian and classical virtues. The defiantly old-fashioned morality of Philip Marlowe, Chandler's greatest creation, has its roots in Dulwich, as Chandler later acknowledged in claiming that his classical education gave him a surprisingly good "basis for writing novels in a hard-boiled vernacular." The approach to writing he learned at Dulwich also had a lasting influence. Instructors would require the boys to translate Latin passages into English and then, at a later date, to translate their English back into Latin. Chandler followed the same method in teaching himself the craft of detective fiction, first reducing stories by Dashiell Hammett and others he admired to a skeletal plot outline and then rewriting them in his own style.

Chandler graduated from Dulwich with vague ambitions of being a writer, but his family decided on a career in the civil service instead. After a period of study in France and Germany, he returned to London in 1907, became a naturalized British subject, and took the six-day civil service examination. Out of six hundred candidates he placed third overall, first in the classics. He gained a record-keeping job in the Naval Stores Branch but resigned after six months to pursue his writing, much to the dismay of his family.

After a poor stint as a reporter for the *Daily Express,* Chandler joined the staff of the liberal *Westminster Gazette.* His writings there show a dualism that characterizes his novels. Between 1908 and 1912 he published twenty-seven sentimental, idealistic, yearningly romantic—and not especially good—poems with such titles as "The Unknown Love," "The Perfect Knight," and "Time Shall Not Die"; he also published a series of satirical sketches.

By 1912, Chandler was frustrated with his lack of genuine literary accomplishment, despondent over a failed love, and upset by the suicide of a friend whom he considered a greater talent. He borrowed five hundred pounds from his uncle

and sailed for America. The trip changed the course of his life. On board he met Warren and Alma Lloyd, he a Yale Ph.D. in philosophy and she a sculptor. Chandler accepted their invitation to visit them in Los Angeles, where they owned a family oil business. Warren helped Chandler get a bookkeeping job at the Los Angeles Creamery and brought him into the lively intellectual circle centered around Friday night gatherings at the Lloyds'. Among the regular guests were Julian Pascal, a distinguished composer and pianist, and his wife Cissy, who was to become Chandler's wife despite being eighteen years his senior.

Shortly after the United States entered World War I, Chandler enlisted in the Canadian Army because, as he later explained it, "it was still natural for me to prefer a British uniform." In June 1918, a German artillery attack killed every man in his unit except him. Aside from one brief sketch recounting the horror of a soldier "alone in a universe of incredibly brutal noise," he never directly treated the experience in his writing and rarely spoke of the war. Only years later, in *The Long Goodbye* (1953), did he touch upon it tangentially in the war-ravaged figure of Terry Lennox.

When the war ended, Chandler was thirty and rootless. He drifted down the West Coast from Vancouver, where he had been discharged, eventually returning to Los Angeles and renewing his friendships there. He also fell in love with Cissy Pascal, a vibrant and cultivated woman who looked much younger than her forty-eight years. After her divorce from Julian in 1920, she lived with or near Chandler until they married in 1924, following the death of Chandler's mother, whom Chandler had been caring for and who had strongly opposed the relationship.

By this time, Warren Lloyd had helped Chandler become an auditor in the Dabney Oil Syndicate, where Lloyd's brother was a partner. In the early 1920s about one-fifth of the world's crude oil came from the Los Angeles area. Boom times, hard work, aptitude, and a series of fortunate circumstances propelled Chandler to a vice-presidency and a thousand-dollar-a-month salary well before the end of the decade. Gradually, though, his life started to unravel. His rapid rise occasioned jealousy, and his tough, autocratic business style bred enemies. Cissy, approaching sixty, was frequently ill and now obviously much older than her husband, who began appearing alone at public functions and having office affairs. With the onset of the Depression, Chandler developed a terrible drinking problem, eventually disappearing on binges for weeks at a time. He frequently threatened suicide and attempted it at least once. In 1932 he was fired. He found himself at forty-four a broken man—an alcoholic with no job, no prospects, little money, and an aging, sickly wife. At this miserable juncture, having little left to lose, he decided to do what he had always wanted to do: write.

Chandler started with poems and fictional sketches. The one surviving example of these initial attempts is ''Beer in the Sergeant Major's Hat, or The Sun Also Sneezes,'' an affectionate parody of Hemingway. Such self-indulgent fun, however, would not pay the rent. Chandler knew that he had to find a more serviceable vehicle. Even while desperate, he disdained writing for such slick magazines as *Cosmopolitan* and the *Saturday Evening Post* because of ''their fundamental dishonesty in the matter of character and motivation.'' But he was drawn to pulp fiction when he realized that ''I might be able to write this stuff and get paid while I was learning.''

He chose *Black Mask,* one of the best pulp magazines, as his outlet. Under the editorship of Joseph T. ''Cap'' Shaw, it favored stories that, compared with the industry standard, emphasized character development over intricate mechanical plotting, analysis of human behavior over analysis of carefully embedded clues. Among its regular contributors were Erle Stanley Gardner and Dashiell Hammett, who became Chandler's major influence.

In particular, Chandler valued Hammett for blazing a trail away from the detective-story-as-tale-of-ratiocination derived from Edgar Allan Poe. Hammett's stories were less concerned with demonstrating the exercise of deductive powers than with exploring a human response to living in a corrupt, dangerous modern world. As Chandler wrote in 1944, in ''The Simple Art of Murder,'' Hammett ''took murder out of the Venetian vase and dropped it in the alley.'' He put the language of the alley in the mouths and minds of his characters. He used detail and observation to reveal mood and character. Most of all, he wrote stories one would want to read even if the last chapter were missing.

And yet Chandler felt that he could exceed Hammett as a stylist, that he could make language resonate in a way Hammett could not, that he could say things Hammett ''did not know how to say, or feel the need of saying.'' His ambition was to write serious fiction using the detective-story format, ''to exceed the limits of a formula without destroying it.'' His method, adapted from Dulwich, was to prepare a detailed synopsis of a story he admired and then rewrite it in his own words.

Soon he began to develop plots that were his own, albeit somewhat formulaic. He continued in his method of writing and rewriting each story, as he would throughout his career, often starting all over again if he was unsatisfied with any part of it. After spending five months rewriting ''Blackmailers Don't Shoot,'' he submitted it to *Black Mask.* Shaw paid him $180, one cent a word, and Chandler's first story was published in December 1933. Although it is not merely the ''pure pastiche'' and ''goddamn pose'' Chandler later called it, neither is it the piece of polished perfection that *Black Mask* deemed it. The story is interesting, though, not only for introducing characteristic elements but also for showing how far Chandler progressed by the publication of *The Big Sleep* in 1939.

''Blackmailers'' is a rather confused jumble of double and triple crossings among a set of Hollywood types. The rising star's career is threatened by her earlier romance with the racketeer, a plot device that recurs in *The Little Sister* (1949). If blackmailers don't shoot, everyone else does. As is typical of the early fiction, violence and gunplay take the place of the detailed descriptions and characterization of the novels. The detective Mallory is a rudimentary Marlowe— tough, honest, independent, persistent, and smart enough to see farther into the mystery than he was supposed to. His repartee, though, lacks something of Marlowe's wit: ''Do that again and I'll put a slug in your guts, copper. So help me, I will.'' Nor is there any of the startling poetry with which Marlowe conveys his inner world. The third-person limited point of view does not allow us to see into anyone's mind, much less the detective's, and the characters seem like flat cutouts set artificially moving on collision courses, hardly the recognizably human figures of the novels who are driven by complex and antithetical needs.

An important trait of Chandler's narratives is already apparent, though: a degree of irresolution in a genre in which the convention is to tie up every loose end, to fit every piece of the puzzle into place. It is never fully clear who did what or why. Mallory does not even know whether he will return home to Chicago or stick around Hollywood. Chandler kept him in Hollywood, where he developed quickly into one of the most original and significant creations in detective fiction.

Four years and a dozen stories intervene between ''Blackmailers Don't Shoot'' and ''Red Wind,'' which appeared in the January 1938 issue of *Dime Detective Magazine*. Philip Marlowe is now Chandler's first-person narrator, a dimensional man with a gift for observation and a need for reflection, a poetic streak and a self-deflating humor, a romantic idealism and a cynical pessimism about the world and human nature. Most of all, he has a penchant for stepping into trouble almost accidentally, and then deliberately stepping in further. Part of his motivation is curiosity, part is knight errantry. As in the novels, his impulse to shield the lady in distress causes him to risk physical danger and also professional suicide by incurring the enmity of the law. The main plot device, a scheme to steal jewelry in order to sell it back to the owner, figures in *Farewell, My Lovely* (1940), and the necklace that symbolizes a tragic once-in-a-lifetime love is central to the mystery of *The Long Goodbye*. And of course blackmail is the spring, as in most of Chandler.

Despite his rapid development and regular publication, the years of pulp fiction were hard ones for Chandler. Even in the best of them, he never earned more than a tenth of his salary as an oil executive. He and Cissy moved constantly from one furnished apartment to another. The compulsive rootlessness at least gave him first-hand knowledge of a wide variety of locations in and around Los Angeles. He was, however, starting to find the short fiction artistically as well as financially unrewarding. Chandler had used the stories to learn and practice his craft—to experiment with tone, subject matter, narrative construction, point of view, and characterization, especially of his detective. But the magazine format's demand for constant action forced him to downplay his real strengths, extended dialogue and vivid description, and to stress his acknowledged weakness, plotting. He was ready to paint more freely, and on a larger canvas.

Chandler began writing *The Big Sleep* in the spring of 1938 by ''cannibalizing'' earlier stories, especially ''Killer in the Rain'' and ''The Curtain.'' By stitching together existing materials, he could spend less time on plot construction and more on building links between different scenes through development of character and setting. He found the method so congenial that he employed it for several of the later novels, though never again with such ease. *The Big Sleep* was completed in three months. Published in 1939, it sold extremely well for a first novel and relieved Chandler's financial distress. It also established Chandler as an important writer, not merely of detective stories but of fiction. The dimensions that the pulp format could not accommodate are evident from the opening of chapter one. Philip Marlowe arrives at the Sternwood mansion sporting a powder-blue suit with matching accessories and a cockiness tinged with wry self-mockery: "I was neat, clean, shaved and sober, and I didn't care who knew it."

Marlowe then describes the setting, observing and interpreting details in such a way as to foreshadow the action, establish a pattern of imagery and symbolic reference, and comment ironically on his own character and situation:

> Over the entrance doors, which would have let in a troop of Indian elephants, there was a broad stained-glass panel showing a knight in dark armor rescuing a lady who was tied to a tree and didn't have any clothes on but some very long and convenient hair. The knight had pushed the vizor of his helmet back to be sociable, and he was fiddling with the knots on the ropes that tied the lady to the tree and not getting anywhere. I stood there and thought that if I lived in the house, I would sooner or later have to climb up there and help him. He didn't seem to be really trying.

The bound lady proves to be Carmen Sternwood, although as befits the modern debasement of the paradigm her hair is cut short and a pornographer is using naked photos of her for blackmail.

The knight is fumbling and ineffectual, even comically anachronistic, but Marlowe recognizes that he will probably find himself in the role. This early he reveals his salient trait: he is torn between a romantic idealism—manifested in a chivalric code of honor, service, and self-sacrifice—and a cynical, world-weary pessimism about human nature, societal corruption, and the efficacy of individual action. Later in the story, fending off the naked Carmen, he looks down at the chessboard on which he is playing a game against himself and thinks, "The move with the knight was wrong. Knights had no meaning in this game." But he keeps trying to play it.

Most of Marlowe's complexities spring from this dualism, none more so than the remarkable range of voices and styles in which he speaks, observes, and reflects. At times he sounds like Hemingway, a writer Chandler admired and Marlowe had read: "I braked the car against the curb and switched the headlights off and sat with my hands on the wheel." In the next sentence he sounds more like Fitzgerald: "Under the thinning fog the surf curled and creamed, almost without sound, like a thought trying to form itself on the edge of consciousness."

One might say that Chandler had not yet digested his models very thoroughly or settled on his own voice, except that the voices persist throughout his fiction and correspond to fundamental divisions in Marlowe's nature, divisions that make him a complex, absorbing character and a very unusual private eye: "At seven-twenty a single flash of hard white light shot out of Geiger's house like a wave of summer lightning. As the darkness folded back on it and ate it up a thin tinkling scream echoed out and lost itself among the rain-drenched trees." The passage begins as if by Joe Friday and ends as if by John Keats. The precise notation of the time of the event is typical of a detective, but the movement into poetic descriptions of sensory impressions is not.

Raymond Chandler is a stylist attentive to nuance, figurative language, symbolic imagery, and poetic tropes; his great achievement is to create a detective who is himself just such a stylist. Marlowe clearly enjoys exploiting the possibilities for verbal play that his role as narrator affords. He specializes in startling similes: the rapidly failing General Sternwood "spoke again, slowly, using his strength as carefully as an out-of-work showgirl uses her last good pair of stockings." Outside the Sternwood mansion "the sunshine was as empty as a headwaiter's smile." Although not likely to be mistaken for a metaphysical poet, Marlowe has a predilection for what Samuel Johnson called "heterogeneous ideas . . . yoked by violence together."

In his more poetic moods, Marlowe also has a penchant for synesthesia, or the description of one sensory experience in terms of another sense, as in "thick silence folded down." When given to irony or self-mockery, Marlowe employs a vast repertoire of techniques ranging from comically inflated descriptions to terse, surprising zeugmas in which a word bears the same grammatical relation to two or more sentence elements but with a very different meaning in each case. For example, in tailing a car through traffic, Marlowe is forced "to make a left turn and a lot of enemies"; later he goes to bed "full of whiskey and frustration." He is certainly not above using a pun to undercut a serious mood. Before the echo of the thin, tinkling scream lost itself among the rain-drenched trees, Marlowe was out of the car and running to the pornographer Geiger's house. Inside he found Carmen drugged and naked before a large camera and Geiger shot dead. Geiger's murderer had fled with the plateholder containing the photographic images of Carmen. Says Marlowe, "I didn't like this development."

That such effects are Marlowe's and not just Chandler's is shown by Marlowe's self-consciousness about them. On first hearing Mona Mars's "smooth silvery voice" he thinks, "It had a tiny tinkle in it, like bells in a doll's house. I thought that was silly as soon as I thought of it." The description of Mona's voice, which does nothing to forward the action but characterizes her, is exactly the dimension Chandler wanted to gain in moving from the short story to the novel. But if his main purpose was to characterize Mona, he could have omitted or replaced a simile he found wanting; his only reason for keeping it and including Marlowe's commentary is to characterize Marlowe as a man with the ability, and the need, to craft the story he tells. When questioned by General Sternwood, Marlowe reluctantly divulges, "I'm thirty-three years old, went to college once and can still speak English if there's any demand for it. There isn't much in my trade." Hence the laconic outer self. But the inner self demands it, as evidenced by Marlowe's very telling of the tales.

Nor will Marlowe's inner self let him leave apparent problems and injustices alone, even if he endangers himself or exceeds the scope of his job in pursuing them. The General hires Marlowe only to investigate what are presented as his daughter Carmen's gambling debts. Suspecting that these may be initial attempts at blackmail, Marlowe presses further, ultimately uncovering the connection between Carmen and Geiger. Geiger's murder draws Marlowe in further to the world of racketeer Eddie Mars, who seems to have some illicit hold on Vivian Regan, Sternwood's first daughter. Vivian had been married to a bootlegger, Rusty Regan, who disappeared without word some months before Marlowe is retained by the General—disappeared with the wife of Eddie Mars, so the rumor goes and the police apparently believe. The General, who had come to love Rusty as a son, was particularly hurt by his abrupt departure.

In due course, Geiger's homosexual roommate kills the man who he thinks killed Geiger and who did steal the photographic plates. Marlowe recovers the photos, concealing a murder and suppressing evidence for a time so that Carmen is not mentioned in the police reports and the General is thus spared knowledge of her activities. Marlowe has done his job, above and beyond the call of duty, and has $500 coming. "The smart thing for me to do was to take another drink and forget the whole mess. That being the obviously smart thing to do, I called Eddie Mars'' and pursued the matter of Rusty Regan without permission from the General. Several killings later, it turns out that the psychotic Carmen had murdered Rusty for rejecting her sexual advances, just as she had tried to shoot the temptation-proof Marlowe. Vivian was forced to enlist the aid of Eddie Mars in the cover-up, and he has been, in her words, bleeding her white. The phrase is not just a cliché. On his first visit to the Sternwood mansion, Marlowe registered something in the color scheme of Vivian's room: ''The white made the ivory look dirty and the ivory made the white look bled out.'' Such use of symbolic detail is the mark of Chandler's distinction, and one of his self-conscious narrator's few satisfactions. Another is that the General will die without ever knowing the truth.

But these are lonely satisfactions. Marlowe's inner self has no company—no fellow professional to share his understandings with, no woman to share his life or even his bed. His rigid code of fidelity to his employer has made him deny the dangerous but alluring Vivian. Mona Mars, whose naive faith in her husband powerfully attracted him, disappears after helping him escape Eddie's hit man. Marlowe never sees her again. The novel ends with a feeling of unfulfillment, of irresolution, that is unusual for the detective story. We do not know whether Vivian will have Carmen committed to an institution or how Marlowe will deal with Eddie Mars. And Marlowe himself seems far less assured than the self-confident, nattily attired detective who came ''calling on four million dollars'' just a few days earlier. The irony in his voice is not from wisecracks but from brooding over what it means to be ''sleeping the big sleep.'' He has solved the case, but as a result he has pulled himself, and us, deeper into the intractable mystery of human evil.

In February 1939 Chandler wrote to Alfred A. Knopf that ''*The Big Sleep* is very unequally written. There are scenes that are all right, but there are other scenes still much too pulpy. . . . To acquire delicacy without losing power, that's the problem.'' Throughout the year Chandler attempted to master the problem while working simultaneously on two books drawn from earlier stories. For one he cannibalized ''Try the Girl'' and ''Mandarin's Jade''; after several entire rewrites and title changes, *Farewell, My Lovely,* was published in 1940. At first less commercially successful than *The Big Sleep,* it received highly favorable reviews and is still considered one of Chandler's best; Chandler himself called it his own favorite, although he had not then written *The Long Goodbye.*

The novel begins with Philip Marlowe in a bad neighborhood, having failed to locate a runaway husband. He observes an enormous, gaudily dressed white man enter a black-run gambling hotel. Moments later someone sails across the sidewalk and lands in the gutter. Marlowe crosses the street and stands before the double doors thinking, ''It wasn't any of my business. So I pushed them open and looked in,'' thus precipitating the chain of events that constitutes the story. The giant, Moose Malloy, has just been released from prison after serving time for robbery and is returning to the site of a club where his girlfriend Velma Valento used to sing. Velma may still have the stolen money, but Moose is searching out of love, not greed. Marlowe witnesses Moose kill the manager, who tried to eject him before he found what he was after. Since the man was black, the police don't care much about the murder. They would, however, like to track down Moose and Velma. To earn himself a little goodwill, Marlowe agrees to help the police look for Velma. His search takes him to Jessie Florian, the alcoholic widow of the owner of the club where Velma sang. After getting her drunk, he takes potential evidence to give to the police and then, disgusted with himself, withdraws from the case. So he thinks.

A Lindsay Marriott calls to offer him a job—accompanying Marriott while he buys back a jade necklace that was stolen from an unnamed lady. They drive to a remote canyon, where Marlowe is struck from behind and knocked out. Anne Riordan arrives on the scene; she had seen the headlights and, like Marlowe, couldn't resist investigating. Marriott has been murdered and his money for the necklace stolen. Left behind, though, is his cigarette case containing marijuana cigarettes. By the time Marlowe is functioning the next day, Anne has traced the theft report on the necklace to Helen Grayle and arranged for a meeting. Marlowe cuts open one of the reefers and finds the card of ''Jules Amthor, Psychic Consultant.'' Warned off the case by Lieutenant Randall, he instead calls Amthor and arranges to see him about Marriott. On a hunch, he checks the title on Jesse Florian's property and finds that it is held by Marriott. Marlowe visits the Grayle mansion, where Helen Grayle outdrinks and nearly seduces him, interrupted only by the awkward appearance of her aged husband.

Marlowe now becomes entangled in a series of bizarre misadventures that suggest a broad conspiracy against him. Finally, while Moose is hiding in Marlowe's apartment, Marlowe confronts Helen with his suspicions: she is Velma; she set up Moose after the robbery; and she killed Marriott because he knew her secret. The business with the necklace was just a ruse; Marriott thought he was leading Marlowe into an ambush. Velma had been willing to pay Marriott a little blackmail, given her husband's tremendous wealth, but when Marlowe began nosing around Jesse Florian's she decided to sever the connection with her past. Moose emerges, still smitten and apparently willing to forgive. Velma fatally shoots him and then flees. Three months later she is captured in Baltimore, where she is working as a club singer, by a cop who recognizes her from the old days. She kills the policeman and then herself.

Again, deliberately, the ending is untidy. Marlowe and the reader look for a satisfactory explanation that links all of the different characters and subplots, but there isn't one. The linking principle appears to be not conspiracy but rather coincidence operating within a milieu of corruption. We don't learn exactly how various characters, such as Amthor and Marriott, are connected to one another. We don't know what finally happens between Marlowe and Anne, last seen making her play for him. We don't know what motivated Velma to shoot herself rather than return for a trial she would probably have won, given her husband's money, Moose's violent history, and the lack of evidence connecting her to Marriott's murder. Marlowe speculates that she may have decided to ''give a break to the only man who had ever really given her one. . . . An old man who had loved not wisely, but too well.'' Randall replies sharply, ''That's just sentimental.'' Marlowe agrees that he is probably wrong, and so this story too ends with the unanswerable mystery overshadowing the solution of the crime. Closure, as Roland Barthes observes of modern fiction, is ''simultaneously set up and disappointed.''

And again, this sense of unfulfillment describes Marlowe's life. He is without friendship. Lieutenant Randall is a tough, shrewd, principled cop whom Marlowe comes to respect, yet when Marlowe tries to compare their indefatigable but futile efforts to those of a stubborn pink bug in Randall's office, ''He didn't know what I was talking about.'' No doubt he missed the allusion to *Othello* too. Marlowe is also without love. Anne, who is clearly offering it to him, is bright, lively, curious, and attractive, yet Marlowe reflexively distances himself from her while shielding her from trouble. He is the chivalric knight seeking the unholy Grayle, and his code seems to include chastity as well as integrity and the pursuit of justice: the ''nice little girl,'' as he calls Anne, is not to be violated, and he will not let himself be violated by the woman without virtue, although she might tempt him.

Another possibility has occasionally been suggested: Marlowe's, and Chandler's, repressed homsexuality. Both at various times voice their aversion to homosexuals, but of course aversion can be the mind's own disguise for what it does not want to acknowledge. Natasha Spender has said that she and others who knew about Chandler's life assumed that such might be the case. Chandler, however, had numerous heterosexual affairs, despite doting on Cissy, and is never known to have been with a man. The homosexuals in his fiction appear as stereotypes whom Marlowe generally disdains. But despite his expressed attitudes, Marlowe is often oddly unguarded in his appreciation of male beauty—of Carol Lundgren, Geiger's lover in *The Big Sleep,* of Jules Amthor, of Lindsay Marriott, and of others. Much has been made especially of his first encounter with Red, a man he meets by chance on the Bay City waterfront and feels suddenly drawn to: "His voice was soft, dreamy, so delicate for a big man that it was startling. . . . I looked at him again. He had the eyes you never see, that you only read about. Violet eyes. Almost purple. Eyes like a girl, a lovely girl. His skin was as soft as silk. Lightly reddened, but it would never tan." Much has also been made of the vehement disgust that Marlowe occasionally shows toward female sexuality, as when he "savagely" tears his bed to pieces after expelling the seductive Carmen from it.

The matter of Chandler's or Marlowe's sexuality cannot be definitively settled. Like his author, the detective remains a complex and lonely man, often divided from others by being divided within himself and isolated by a fear of intimacy masked as self-reliance. When Red asks Marlowe whether he might need help finding Moose, Marlowe replies: "I need a company of marines. But either I do it alone or I don't do it. So long."

Marlowe also reveals a deep ambivalence about wealth. On the one hand, he is as responsive to fine furnishings as he is to the charms of the women or men he cannot let himself have. In particular, he often describes interiors with a sensitive and well-informed eye. He does so partly because he is a trained observer who records and analyzes details for their significance; he also does so simply because his aesthetic side responds to beauty. On the other hand, Marlowe regards the trappings of wealth with cynicism and suspicion, knowing that they are a facade behind which to hide evil. Chandler pronounced that he and Marlowe "despise" the upper classes "because they are phoney." Marlowe takes a grim Puritanical pride in the shabbiness of his office and apartment, which he touts as emblems of his honesty. Of course his office is in Hollywood, a latter-day Vanity Fair that delivers a world of sumptuous, seductive illusions. This same Hollywood began to take an interest in Marlowe: in 1941 RKO bought the film rights to *Farewell, My Lovely.* Chandler sold them for only $2,000.

The early 1940s were difficult years for Chandler. Cissy's health was bad and money a constant worry. Distracted from his work by the war, he was attempting to finish *The Lady in the Lake,* the novel he had been writing along with *Farewell, My Lovely.* When frustrated, he would turn to one of several short stories and yet another novel. This one, not drawn from earlier material, was completed first and published in 1942 as *The High Window.* Its theme, a strong person's selfish manipulation of the weak, is reminiscent of Nathaniel Hawthorne and Henry James, one of Chandler's idols. Again, the rich are the source of evil. So keen is Chandler's resentment that the book has a shrill tone and melodramatic edginess. Chandler attempts to leaven this tone with humorous scenes and, of course, Marlowe's wisecracks, but the novel has an uneasy feel to it, and Chandler was not especially happy with the result. It had, he wrote to his publisher, Blanche Knopf, "no action, no likable characters, no nothing. The detective does nothing."

Chandler exaggerates the faults. Marlowe is kept busy and does ultimately expose a number of wicked schemes, but many critics have complained that the book seems misanthropic in its absence of admirable or even decent specimens of humanity. The most sympathetic of a very unsympathetic lot is Merle Davis, Mrs. Murdock's neurotic, guilt-ridden, and emotionally abused secretary who becomes this novel's lady in distress. *The High Window* is really two stories that are somewhat awkwardly woven together: the story of how Mrs. Murdock psychologically bullies Merle into believing herself responsible for the death of Mrs. Murdock's first husband, Horace Bright, some eight years earlier, and the story of a scheme to counterfeit an antique gold coin, the Brasher Doubloon, stolen from the collection of Mrs. Murdock's deceased second husband. The connection between the two stories is Louis Vannier, who planned the counterfeit scheme and who is also blackmailing Mrs. Murdock with some very improbable evidence of her guilt in the death of Horace Bright, a photograph he happened to be shooting from across the street exactly as she pushed her husband out of a high window. Just as implausible are Mrs. Murdock's ability to convince Merle that she had pushed Mr. Bright because he was threatening her sexually, or even Mrs. Murdock's reason for doing so, given Vannier's evidence.

Naturally, Marlowe knows nothing of all this when he is first summoned to the Murdock house. Mrs. Murdock suspects that her unsuitable daughter-in-law, a nightclub singer named Linda Conquest, has stolen the coin from her late husband's collection. She wants Marlowe to find Linda, get the coin back, and make her agree to an uncontested divorce—all without police, publicity, or the knowledge of her son Leslie. Marlowe is, if anything, flintier than ever. He insists on hav-

ing it known that he will do things his way and according to his rules. When the formidable Mrs. Murdock insists that the matter "be handled with delicacy," he replies, "If you hire me, you'll get all the delicacy I have. If I don't have enough delicacy [to frame Linda if necessary], maybe you'd better not hire me."

MRS. MURDOCK: "You don't like me very well, do you?"
MARLOWE: "Does anybody?"

Once more, Marlowe's curiosity and persistence compel him to delve further than he was hired, or desired, to go. He thus becomes the catalyst who precipitates actions based on hatreds, fears, and greeds that had been hanging in delicate, uneasy suspension for years.

As in earlier cases, many of Marlowe's breakthroughs come not from methodical ratiocination in the manner of Poe's Dupin or Conan Doyle's Holmes but from flashes of insight, hunches based on what makes sense in human terms. The same instinct that led him (in *Farewell, My Lovely*) to equate Helen and Velma or to sense (in *The Big Sleep*) that a spurned Carmen had killed Rusty Regan operates again here, along with a keen eye for interiors: feeling that the painting of a man in doublet and hose leaning out of a high window does not fit the decor of Vannier's room, Marlowe inspects the backing and finds the photograph that connects the threads of the case.

Marlowe sends Merle Davis back to her parents, freeing her from Mrs. Murdock's tower but not her spell: the girl cannot absorb the evidence of Mrs. Murdock's guilt or her own innocence. Satisfaction, a sense of closure, still eludes Marlowe. He feels as though "I had written a poem and it was very good and I had lost it and would never remember it again." He sees the moonlight "cold and clear, like the justice we dream of but don't find." And again, he seems alone in his search. He makes a heartfelt attempt to explain his code to Lieutenant Breeze, who shrugs it off as a rationalization for bending the law. The novel ends with Marlowe alone, playing out a chess game by the grandmaster José Raúl Capablanca. "Beautiful cold remorseless chess, almost creepy in its silent implacability." This degree of closure achieved, Marlowe looks at himself in the mirror: " 'You and Capablanca,' I said."

The Lady in the Lake, published the next year, 1943, cannibalizes Chandler's earlier short stories "The Lady in the Lake" (1939), "Bay City Blues" (1938), and "No Crime in the Mountains" (1941). Chandler had been working on it intermittently since 1939 while he and Cissy moved about from Los Angeles and Santa Monica to Riverside and Big Bear Lake. Similarly, the story bounces back and forth between the environs of Los Angeles and Bay City (Santa Monica) and the fictional mountain retreat of Little Fawn Lake. Chandler made the interweaving narrative lines so tangled and complicated that critics have suspected him of parodying the genre's demand for intricate plots and its reliance on coincidence. It is Chandler's story of mistaken identity, an elaborate bit of legerdemain and misdirection that keeps everyone, including Marlowe, looking the wrong way until the end. The novel begins, as usual, with Marlowe's being hired to handle a fairly routine matter. Businessman Derace Kingsley last saw his wife Crystal a month ago at their mountain cabin. Soon after he received a telegram saying that she was going to Mexico to get a divorce and marry playboy Chris Lavery. Given their troubled relationship, Kingsley is willing to let the matter go until he bumps into Lavery, who denies any knowledge of it.

The inner Marlowe feels himself aging, an empty life passing him by, but the outer Marlowe is still the same man who in his younger days was fired by the district attorney's office for insubordination. He is deliberately abrasive, as if trying to establish his own toughness and independence. "I don't like your manner," says Kingsley after a Marlovian wisecrack. "That's all right," Marlowe replies, "I'm not selling it." Kingsley retains him, and Marlowe immediately becomes enmeshed in a larger and more dangerous web than anyone suspected. In the critic William Stowe's phrase, Marlowe's brand of detection is more akin to hermeneutics than to semiotics: rather than decode signs to explicate a set and preexisting reality, he alters events by the very act of investigating them and creates more questions by his questioning.

Not that he is happy in his role as catalyst: every line of inquiry produces a new death. On discovering Lavery's body, he thinks "murder-a-day Marlowe. . . . They have the meat wagon following him around to follow up on the business he finds." Lavery, it turns out, had found the body of the wife of his neighbor, Dr. Almore, a drug-dispensing physician who had treated Crystal for alcoholism. The death was ruled a suicide, but a cover-up involving Bay City cop Lieutenant Degarmo is rumored. Dr. Almore's nurse, Mildred Haviland, has also disappeared.

At Little Fawn Lake, Marlowe interrogates the caretaker, Bill Chess, whose wife Muriel ran away the same night that Crystal vanished. They see something in the lake that proves to be the decomposed body of a woman. A distraught Chess identifies it as Muriel's. Many twists and reversals later, it turns out to be Crystal's. She was murdered by Mildred Haviland, who had been having an affair with Almore and had murdered his wife. She then fled to Riverside leaving Almore and her husband, Lieutenant Degarmo, to manage the cover-up. There, as Muriel, she met and married Chess, leaving him when she could make Crystal's death appear to be her own. She happened to encounter Lavery on the way, whom she knew slightly from his visits to Crystal at the lake, and seduced him into accompanying her to El Paso, where she sent the telegram to Kingsley. Ultimately, the distraught Degarmo murders her.

Marlowe unravels this tangled skein at the end of the novel in a manner that parodies, or at least patterns itself on, the disclosure scene in the classic detective story. With the chief suspects and the local constable in attendance, he delivers a fifteen-hundred-word step-by-step account of how it all happened, even employing such stock phrases as ''That disposes of motive, and we come to means and opportunity.'' Parody seems likely since Marlowe has already mocked several developments in the case as crime-novel clichés. Moreover, Chandler complained to his publisher that American audiences did not recognize the burlesque in his work. One would like to think that the interlocking farfetched coincidences here are offered in this spirit. The motivation for much of the important action, though, also seems strained and implausible, and the ending is oddly abrupt. The previous novels close with some kind of summary meditation by Marlowe. This one stops with Degarmo—whom Marlowe and the sheriff have strangely allowed to escape—being shot by wartime sentries as he drives away. Marlowe sees them reach into the car and lift something out: ''Something that had been a man.'' The end.

Just as Marlowe felt himself becoming older and more spent, less equal to the task, so Chandler was prone to despondency during the writing of *The Lady in the Lake.* Depressed by the war, he volunteered for officer training in the Canadian Army but was rejected because of his age. Cissy turned seventy in 1940. And although Chandler the man was hardly gregarious, Chandler the writer was as isolated in his profession as Marlowe the detective was in his. Chandler did not publish another piece of fiction for six years. Hollywood, the setting for his stories, became the setting for his life. Having already sold the film rights to *Farewell, My Lovely* (released as *Murder, My Sweet*) and *The High Window* (released as *Time to*

Kill), he was asked in 1943 to collaborate with Billy Wilder on a script for James M. Cain's *Double Indemnity.* Wilder found him ''one of the greatest creative minds'' he had worked with, but also ''kind of acid, sour, grouchy,'' always suspicious of being patronized. Chandler called the experience ''agonizing.'' Still, the movie was a great success, earning an Oscar nomination for the screenplay and establishing Chandler as a screenwriter in demand.

Somewhat like Marlowe, Chandler continued to be acerbic toward industry people in high places but open and helpful to the powerless, especially young writers. He began to drink again and to have affairs. He loved Cissy, but she was seventy-three and he was surrounded by young women. His working relationships with directors, producers, and studio heads continued to be difficult. While working on an original screenplay for *The Blue Dahlia* in 1945, he took offense at the offer of a bonus to finish the script on time, regarding it as both a bribe and a sign of doubt about him. He became so distraught that he could not work unless drunk. The studio had to arrange for secretaries and doctors to attend him and for two limousines to stand ready at all times to run household errands or deliver finished copy. The screenplay was completed, but it was not Chandler's best, and he was upset at alterations made during the filming. Although pleased with Howard Hawks's *The Big Sleep* (1946), starring Humphrey Bogart and Lauren Bacall, with a screenplay by William Faulkner and Leigh Brackett, he was very unhappy with Robert Montgomery's filming of *The Lady in the Lake* (1947), on which he collaborated.

Soon afterward, the Chandlers moved to La Jolla, where Chandler hoped to finish a new novel, *The Little Sister,* which was finally published in 1949. He stopped to write a screenplay, tentatively titled *Playback,* that dispensed with both Marlowe and the Los Angeles setting. Neither he nor the studio was satisfied with the product, and it was dropped. But as Chandler wrote to his London publisher, he was becoming bored with Marlowe, who was "getting self-conscious, trying to live up to his reputation among the quasi-intellectuals." Chandler frequently complained about the work in progress, writing, for example, to the *New York Herald-Tribune* reviewer James Sandoe, "It's the only book of mine I have actively disliked. It was written in a bad mood and I think that comes through." Reviews of the book were mixed, depending on how the reviewer responded to its cynical, misanthropic tone.

Despite being overly complicated and melodramatic, *The Little Sister* has the typical Chandler strengths of sharp dialogue and skillful use of language. It also marks Chandler's only artistic attempt to address the phenomenon of Hollywood. The film industry would seem to be a natural subject for him, with its ready-made themes of richly fabricated illusion masking a grim reality, of underhanded power struggles and manipulations, of personal excess leading to scandal and blackmail. Curiously, despite his experience as an insider, Chandler made little use of it. Marlowe had occasionally commented that cops or gangsters or nightclub owners were patterning themselves after B-movie figures. Once Linda Conquest (in *The High Window*) shot back, "And what about the wise-cracking snooper with the last year's gags and the come hither smile?" But only in *The Little Sister* does Chandler more fully explore the meaning of the film industry, which becomes the backdrop for the action, the basis for thematic treatments, the source of key characters, and the frame of reference by which the characters define and interpret one another.

The story opens with a bitter-sounding Marlowe putting off a potential client with insults and complaints about his depression. When she tells him he talks too much, he replies, "Lonely men always talk too much." The client is Orfa-

may Quest, whose name lends credence to Chandler's claim that he was "spoofing more and more" to counter his boredom with the detective-story format. Marlowe, who complains, "I don't want to work. I don't want anything," finally takes the case because "I was just plain bored with doing nothing." Orfamay has come from Kansas seeking her brother Orrin, who has stopped writing home. In attempting to find him, Marlowe steps into a plot to blackmail rising film star Mavis Weld over her romantic attachment to a midwestern racketeer come to Hollywood under a new identity. His investigation provokes a string of murders, by gun or ice pick, stemming from greed, fear, and sexual jealousy. Aside from being overly complicated, the plot relies on a number of extremely implausible coincidences and finally begins to undermine itself when characters' later actions subvert the rationales for their earlier ones.

Of interest, though, are Chandler's dark humor and grisly absurdity, bordering on surrealism. Marlowe finds a key piece of evidence inside the toupee of a dead man with the ice pick still protruding; he then puts the hairpiece "carefully back on the dead egg-bald head" of "Dr. Hambleton, retired (and how) optometrist," who is sporting "the new style in neckwear." Such are the light-hearted moments. Also of interest is Marlowe when serious, Chandler's portrait of a strong man standing frightened before an abyss of depression as he senses his inner reserves draining away after years of futile striving: "I felt as if I had spent my life knocking at doors in cheap hotels that nobody bothered to open." Alone, he has to keep interrupting his embittered litany to reign himself back—"Hold it, Marlowe, you're not human tonight." Finally he asks, "Why would I be?" He has no answer. Nor does he find any by solving the interlocking crimes: "Sometimes when I'm low I try to reason it out. But it gets too complicated." A displaced Puritan looking for truth behind the visible signs, he is overmatched by a world consisting of vanity and illusion, where even death seems strangely haphazard and baseless, arising from nothing more substantial than the aped conventions of B-movies.

Two chapters in *The Little Sister* suggest that Chandler was chafing under the limitations of the genre. Neither has anything to do with advancing the story. Chapter 13 consists of Marlowe's ruminations on the Hollywood movie culture. Chapter 30 is Marlowe's fantastic encounter with an elfin cop who says his sole function at the police station is to "establish a mood." This he does at night so that he can spend his days playing Mozart and Bach. He can also handle guns and cards with preternatural dexterity. Marlowe looks away when another cop enters the room and turns back to find him gone.

Chandler wrote in letters and notebooks of his desire to create a work of fantasy. He never accomplished that goal, but he had a more attainable one—what he described in a 1949 letter as "a novel of character and atmosphere with an overtone of violence of fear." He interrupted this project for what proved to be his final attempt at screenwriting, an adaptation of Patricia Highsmith's *Strangers on a Train*. Chandler and the director Alfred Hitchcock were constantly at odds over how best to tell the story, and finally the script had to be rewritten by Czenzi Ormonde. Sulking over the film's success, Chandler declared his break from a medium that typically requires "no contribution from the audience but a mouthful of popcorn."

Cissy's health deteriorated during these years, and Chandler, now approaching sixty-five, suffered frequently from bronchitis, chronic sore throats, and skin allergies so severe that he required morphine to endure them. He forged ahead with the writing, though, and finished *The Long Goodbye* in July 1953. It is his most ambitious work, an attempt to examine the charac-

ters and the society in which they live; to confront the difficult and sometimes contradictory aspects of his own personality; to explore the possibilities for morally significant action; and especially to consider the nature of friendship and love. "I don't care whether the mystery was fairly obvious," he wrote in May 1952, "but I cared about the people, about this strange corrupt world we live in, and how any man who tries to be honest looks in the end either sentimental or plain foolish."

Again, Marlowe is the prime example. He initiates the adventure by helping a drunken man after the woman with him drives off in disgust. The man turns out to be Terry Lennox, a physically and emotionally scarred British war veteran with whom Marlowe forms an unprecedented bond. The woman is Sylvia, his ex-wife and daughter of the ultra-rich newspaper magnate Harlan Potter. To Marlowe's disgust, Terry remarries Sylvia and allows himself to become a "kept poodle." Disapproval drives Terry away until he appears one morning at Marlowe's, distraught and carrying a gun. He asks Marlowe to take him to the Tijuana airport and Marlowe agrees, despite the obvious advantages of remaining uninvolved. Saying good-bye, Terry hints that he has killed Sylvia. In spite of persistent and at times brutal interrogation by the police, Marlowe will not compromise his friend, whom he does not believe capable of the violent murder even after seeing what purports to be a confession Terry wrote before shooting himself in a Mexican hotel.

Marlowe suspects that Potter is behind a frame-up and begins to investigate, his only client being allegiance to his friend's memory. Around this time Marlowe is enlisted by Eileen Wade to find her husband Roger, a writer of historical romances who has disappeared after inexplicable episodes of alcoholism and threatened violence. Marlowe succeeds but senses that Eileen has another agenda. He becomes uncharacteristically involved in their personal lives, learning that Eileen had lost the man she loved in the war and discovering that Roger had been having an affair with Sylvia Lennox. Roger is killed by a gunshot to the head. The police rule it suicide, but the circumstances are suspicious.

Marlowe ultimately determines that Terry Lennox was Eileen's lost love and first husband. She found him again, accidentally, after he had become a drunken idler married to Sylvia. That more than Sylvia's affair with Roger drove Eileen to murder. Terry let himself be blamed to protect her and to atone for Sylvia's unhappiness, and Harlan Potter assisted to avoid scandalous publicity. Roger tried to live with the secret but was beginning to break; Eileen killed him when Marlowe began peering into the cracks. Exposed, she takes an overdose of Demerol. The official finding is accidental death. Marlowe, inviting the wrath of all the powerful forces intent on maintaining the public fiction, leaks a copy of Eileen's suicide note to the press, clearing Terry's name.

At the end of the novel, Terry reappears, almost unrecognizable after plastic surgery, and explains how he faked his death. Marlowe feels used. Recognizing that Terry's easy acquiescence to a self-indulgent, amoral life contributed to Sylvia's death and that his complicity in the cover-up led to Roger's and Eileen's, Marlowe is forced to choose between his moral code and his companion. In an especially poignant closing scene, Marlowe rejects Terry's attempt to restore their friendship.

The Long Goodbye is Chandler's most autobiographical novel, containing what many have recognized as three different self-portraits. Terry Lennox in this scheme is the lost, alienated, self-pitying side of Chandler—always the outsider—who could never again see life steadily and see it whole after the trauma of war. Roger Wade is the middle-aged writer, grappling with alcoholism and self-disgust, who feels a mixture of defensiveness and contempt for the genre that brought

him success. And Marlowe is the hybrid cynic-romantic, the lonely idealist whose unbending standard isolates him. Though not without sympathy, it is this Chandler that prevails and passes judgment on the others.

Marlowe is again the most complex and interesting character, whether as a self-portrait or in his own right. He is again the man who will show dogged devotion for a few dollars a day but cannot be bought at any price, and he spends much of the novel refusing money that he doesn't feel he has earned on his own terms. He is again a man with strong physical desires and a strong aversion to the physical. Sitting poolside, he "carnally" watches a girl with "a luscious figure." But actually he is drawn by the ethereal elements of the scene and repulsed by the carnal. As she dives, "spray came high enough to catch the sun and make rainbows that were almost as pretty as the girl." Out of the pool, she "wobbled her bottom" over to a man who pats her thigh. "She opened her mouth like a firebucket and laughed. That terminated my interest in her."

Marlowe's squeamish recoil from vulgarity is immediately juxtaposed with the arrival of "a dream" whose "hair was the pale gold of a fairy princess" and whose "exquisitely pure" smile excites a four-hundred-word disquisition on different types of blondes. Marlowe concludes, "The dream across the way was none of these, not even of that kind of world. She was unclassifiable." She is Eileen Wade, and it takes Marlowe most of the novel to realize what underlies his romantic vision. In their one approach to a sexual encounter, Marlowe reacts with a mixture of erotic passion and startled aversion. "Saved" by circumstance, he deliberately drinks himself unconscious.

Chandler has previously used romantic paradigms to structure his fiction or characterize Marlowe. In *The Long Goodbye* he explores the darker side of romanticism. The self-destructive Roger wishes "to cease upon the midnight with no pain,'' then contemptuously assumes that the allusion to Keats will be lost on Marlowe. It isn't. Alluding to the same stanza in ''Ode to a Nightingale,'' Marlowe recognizes in Eileen the morbid romanticism of one who kills because she is ''in love with death.'' She had idealized her wartime love with Terry into an absolute that could bear no worldly stain. In her note she writes, ''He should have died young in the snow of Norway, my lover that I gave to death. . . . The tragedy of life . . . is not that beautiful things die young, but that they grow old and mean. It will not happen to me.''

Despite what he learns of Eileen, Marlowe follows her example—twice. He too rejects the Terry who returns to him tainted; and like Eileen, he is hurt more by the loss of the past than by the loss of a future. Near the end of the novel Marlowe has an intense one-night love affair with Linda Loring, Sylvia's sister. She represents the future, offering marriage in place of ''the loneliness of a pretty empty kind of life.'' In delivering her to Marlowe, Linda's chauffeur questions him about the meaning of key lines from T. S. Eliot's ''Love Song of J. Alfred Prufrock,'' the poem of a frightened, lonely, aging man's failure to reach out. Marlowe made better use of Keats: he dismisses the insights of ''Prufrock'' and rejects Linda's offer, saying he's ''spoiled by independence.'' In reality, he fears the dwindling of their passion into stale indifference. Like Eileen, he would rather have it die young. After sending Linda away, he ''pulled the bed to pieces and remade it,'' just as he had done after rejecting Carmen Sternwood (in *The Big Sleep*) years earlier. ''To say goodbye is to die a little,'' he tells himself. He is choosing a little of the romantic death that Eileen took in full measure.

Cissy Chandler died on December 12, 1954. Her husband, then sixty-six, was devastated. Through their difficulties, he had adored her and relied on her to give his life meaning. Two months after her death he attempted suicide and had to be hospitalized. Before his own death five years later, he would be hospitalized several more times for suicidal depression or alcoholism. In April 1955 he traveled back to London, where he was sustained by Natasha and Stephen Spender and a circle of their friends who formed a ''shuttle service'' to watch him through the worst times. According to Natasha, when Chandler was not threatening suicide ''his fantasy seemed entirely to be used in acting out romantic Don Quixote illusions'' of shielding his protectors from imaginary dangers.

For more than two years after Cissy's death, Chandler was unable to produce any sustained writing. But with the help and encouragement of Helga Greene, who became his literary agent, he reworked *Playback* into a novel that reinstated Marlowe and southern California—this time ''Esmeralda'' (La Jolla) rather than Los Angeles. Published in 1958, it is Chandler's last and least-regarded novel, an anomaly in many ways. For one, it is a mystery without a murder, or, given the rather confused plotline, something of a muddle without a murder. Marlowe is hired by attorney Clyde Umney to trail a young woman and report on her whereabouts. He completes his assignment but becomes curious about her plight; naturally, he pursues the matter.

Marlowe's chivalric code of duty and aversion to money bring matters to a comic pass when he and the woman, Betty Mayfield, argue about the terms of his employment. She wants to pay him $5,000 to go away and leave her alone. He holds out for $500 so that he can protect her as his client. He tells the exasperated Betty, ''It isn't money I want. It's some sort of understanding of what the hell I'm doing and why.'' In the end, he refuses any money from anyone. When Clark Brandon, a racketeer trying to go legitimate, asks how much he owes for Marlowe's services, Marlowe replies, ''Nothing. I just want to know what happened.'' Chandler's own distrust of money is also intact. The prosperous facade of Esmeralda's Grand Street hides the squalor of Polton's Lane, "the back yard of elegance," immediately behind. In one of the book's most powerful scenes, Marlowe must go there to find the junkie night attendant for the parking lot of Brandon's luxury hotel. The man has hanged himself in the privy.

The attitudes toward sex have relaxed, however. Chandler had previously said that he wanted his detective to be a catalyst, not a Casanova, and Marlowe typically imposed rigid restrictions on himself. Here he has affairs with both his client, Betty, and Umney's secretary, Helen Vermilyea. Still, he remains the "ferocious romantic" Chandler described himself as being. Marlowe does not want to make love to Helen in the bed he shared with Linda: "I had a dream here once, a year and a half ago. There's still a shred of it left. I'd like it to stay in charge." Something of Eileen Wade (in *The Long Goodbye*) survives in Marlowe and Helen, who also views love in absolute terms: "I'll never see you again and I don't want to. It would have to be forever or not at all." Ironically, their uncompromising romanticism commits them to a life alone.

Or so it would seem. Marlowe returns to the emptiness of his rented house and thinks, "Alcohol was no cure for this. Nothing was any cure but the hard inner heart that asked for nothing from anyone." Then, through what Vladimir Nabokov dubbed "*deus ex telephonica,*" Marlowe is suddenly saved. Linda calls from Paris and begs him to marry her. He accepts, so long as *he* can pay for the plane ticket. When he hangs up, "the empty room . . . was no longer empty. . . . The air was full of music." This ending has been criticized for being tacked on and overly sentimental. Certainly it represents the wish fulfillment of the man who confessed to Helga Greene while working on the book, "the older I get, the more desperately I long for the presence of someone I love, to hold her and touch her . . . nothing else is any good at all." He told *Newsweek* (July 21, 1958), "I thought it was time Marlowe was given something worth having. . . . You see, there's a lot of him in me, his

loneliness." Chandler began another novel, with Marlowe married to Linda and chafing under their lifestyle in Palm Springs. *The Poodle Springs Story,* later completed by Robert B. Parker and published as *Poodle Springs,* was to be structured as "a running fight interspersed with amorous interludes," but the years of depression and alcoholic abuse overtook Chandler before he could finish it. He died in La Jolla on March 26, 1959.

Two weeks later, an abridged version of "The Pencil" appeared in the *London Daily Mail* as "Marlowe Takes on the Syndicate." It contains much that is characteristic of Chandler and Marlowe. At the end, several key points remain unresolved and the fates of several characters, including Marlowe and Anne Riordan, are left open. He is beginning to long for the kind of life he could have with her, but his code is still an impediment: "I'm too shop-soiled for a girl like you." When last seen, they aren't making plans for the future but rather puzzling over the unexplained elements of the case. "What I like about you," Anne says, "is that when you don't know an answer you make one up." What a temptation for an uncompromising, compulsively scrupulous detective, and what a useful expedient for a mystery writer with higher aspirations than plotsmithing.

Marlowe and Chandler were both impatient with the limits of the genre they lived in. While hiding from hit men who are seeking to "pencil him out," Marlowe buys a crime story and tries to read himself to sleep. Bad move. "The paperback scared me so badly that I put two guns under my pillow. . . . Then I asked myself why I was reading this drivel when I could have been memorizing *The Brothers Karamazov.*" No doubt Chandler would rather have been writing something along those lines. He fell short of his grandest ambitions, but he triumphed in his dream of exceeding the limits of the detective formula without destroying it. Instead he transformed it, preparing the way for successors such as Robert B. Parker and Ross Macdonald. He created a character who stands firmly in the tradition of American loner heroes such as Leatherstocking, Ishmael, Huck Finn, and Nick Adams—a character who, as Chandler observed in his notebook, represents the "American mind; a heavy portion of rugged idealism, a dash of good hard vulgarity, a strong overtone of strident wit, an equally strong undertone of pure sentimentalism, an ocean of slang, and an utterly unexpected range of sensitivity."

Thus equipped, Philip Marlowe became a remarkably acute instrument for viewing and recording a complex, disturbing world in transition. Through his eyes and voice, Raymond Chandler delivered matchless portraits of Los Angeles at a critical juncture in American history, registering as only a cynical romantic could the loss of an old order and the uncertain beginnings of a new one. The assessment of W. H. Auden stands: Chandler's works "should be read and judged not as escape literature, but as works of art."

Selected Bibliography

WORKS OF RAYMOND CHANDLER

NOVELS

The Big Sleep. New York: Knopf, 1939; London: Hamish Hamilton, 1939.

Farewell, My Lovely. New York: Knopf, 1940; London: Hamish Hamilton, 1940.

The High Window. New York: Knopf, 1942; London: Hamish Hamilton, 1943.

The Lady in the Lake. New York: Knopf, 1943; London: Hamish Hamilton, 1944.

The Little Sister. Boston: Houghton Mifflin, 1949; London: Hamish Hamilton, 1949.

The Long Goodbye. London: Hamish Hamilton, 1953. Boston: Houghton Mifflin, 1954.

Playback. Boston: Houghton Mifflin, 1958; London: Hamish Hamilton, 1958.

SHORT STORIES

"Blackmailers Don't Shoot." *Black Mask,* December 1933.

"Smart-Aleck Kill." *Black Mask,* July 1934.

"Finger Man." *Black Mask,* October 1934.

"Killer in the Rain." *Black Mask,* January 1935.

"Nevada Gas." *Black Mask,* June 1935.

"Spanish Blood." *Black Mask,* November 1935.

"Guns at Cyrano's." *Black Mask,* January 1936.

"The Man Who Liked Dogs." *Black Mask,* March 1936.

"Noon Street Nemesis" (republished as "Pick-up on Noon Street"). *Detective Fiction Weekly,* May 30, 1936.

"Goldfish." *Black Mask,* June 1936.

"The Curtain." *Black Mask,* September 1936.

"Try the Girl." *Black Mask,* January 1937.

"Mandarin's Jade." *Dime Detective Magazine,* November 1937.

"Red Wind." *Dime Detective Magazine,* January 1938.

"The King in Yellow." *Dime Detective Magazine,* March 1938.

"Bay City Blues." *Dime Detective Magazine,* June 1938.

"The Lady in the Lake." *Dime Detective Magazine,* January 1939.

"Pearls Are a Nuisance." *Dime Detective Magazine,* April 1939.

"Trouble Is My Business." *Dime Detective Magazine,* August 1939.

"I'll Be Waiting." *Saturday Evening Post,* October 14, 1939.

"The Bronze Door." *Unknown,* November 1939.

"No Crime in the Mountains." *Detective Story,* September 1941.

"Professor Bingo's Snuff." *Park East,* June–August 1951; *Go,* June–July 1951.

"Marlowe Takes on the Syndicate." *London Daily Mail,* April 6–10, 1959; also published as "Wrong Pidgeon." *Manhunt,* February 1961. Reprinted as "The Pencil."

ESSAYS

"The Simple Art of Murder." *Atlantic Monthly,* December 1944.

"Writers in Hollywood." *Atlantic Monthly,* November 1945.

"Critical Notes." *Screen Writer,* July 1947.

"Oscar Night in Hollywood." *Atlantic Monthly,* March 1948.

"The Simple Art of Murder." *Saturday Review of Literature,* April 15, 1950. Revised version of the December 1944 *Atlantic Monthly* article.

"Ten Per Cent of Your Life." *Atlantic Monthly,* February 1952.

CORRESPONDENCE AND OTHER WORKS

The Blue Dahlia. Carbondale: Southern Illinois University Press, 1976. Reprint of Chandler's 1945 screenplay.

Chandler before Marlowe: Raymond Chandler's Early Prose and Poetry, 1908–1912. Edited by Matthew J. Bruccoli, introduction by Jacques Barzun. Columbia: University of South Carolina Press, 1973.

The Notebooks of Raymond Chandler and English Summer: A Gothic Romance. Edited by Frank MacShane. New York: Ecco, 1976.

Raymond Chandler on Writing. Boston: Houghton Mifflin, 1962.

Raymond Chandler Speaking. Edited by Dorothy Gardiner and Katherine Sorley Walker. Boston: Houghton Mifflin, 1962 [1977]. Contains excerpts from Chandler's letters and the surviving fragment of *The Poodle Springs Story.*

Selected Letters of Raymond Chandler. Edited by Frank MacShane. New York: Columbia University Press, 1981.

COLLECTED EDITIONS

The Simple Art of Murder. Boston: Houghton Mifflin, 1950. Contains selected stories and the essay "The Simple Art of Murder."

Killer in the Rain. Edited by Philip Durham. Boston: Houghton Mifflin, 1964. Contains selected short stories.

The Midnight Raymond Chandler. Edited by Joan Kahn. Boston: Houghton Mifflin, 1971. Contains *The Little Sister, The Long Goodbye,* and selected short works.

Raymond Chandler: Stories and Early Novels. Edited by Frank MacShane. New York: Library of America, 1995. Contains early magazine fiction, *The Big Sleep, Farewell, My Lovely,* and *The High Window.*

Raymond Chandler: Later Novels and Other Writings. Edited by Frank MacShane. New York: Library of America, 1995. Contains *The Lady in the Lake, The Little Sister, The Long Goodbye, Playback,* the screenplay for *Double Indemnity,* and selected essays and letters.

ARCHIVES AND BIBLIOGRAPHIES

Department of Special Collections, Research Library, University of California at Los Angeles. Contains manuscripts, notebooks, translations, memorabilia, and Chandleriana.

Bruccoli, Matthew J. *Raymond Chandler: A Checklist.* Kent, Ohio: Kent State University Press, 1968.

———. *Raymond Chandler: A Descriptive Bibliography.* Pittsburgh: University of Pittsburgh Press, 1979.

BIOGRAPHICAL AND CRITICAL STUDIES

Beekman, E. M. "Raymond Chandler and an American Genre." *Massachusetts Review* (Winter 1973): 149–73.

Durham, Philip. *Down These Mean Streets a Man Must Go: Raymond Chandler's Knight.* Chapel Hill: University of North Carolina Press, 1963.

Gross, Miriam, ed. *The World of Raymond Chandler.* New York: A & W, 1978.

Jameson, Fredric. "On Raymond Chandler." *Southern Review,* 6:624–650 (1970).

MacShane, Frank. *The Life of Raymond Chandler.* New York: Dutton, 1976.

Merling, William H. *Raymond Chandler.* Boston: Twayne, 1986.

Newlin, Keith. *Hardboiled Burlesque: Raymond Chandler's Comic Style.* New York: Brownstone, 1984.

Pendo, Stephen. *Raymond Chandler on Screen: His Novels into Film.* Metuchen, N.J.: Scarecrow, 1976.

Pollock, Wilson. "Man with a Toy Gun." *New Republic,* May 7, 1962, pp. 21–22.

Porter, J. C. "End of the Trail: The American West of Dashiell Hammett and Raymond Chandler." *Western Historical Quarterly* (October 1975):411–24.

Reck, T. S. "Raymond Chandler's Los Angeles." *Nation,* December 20, 1975, pp. 661–663.

Ruhm, Herbert. "Raymond Chandler: From Bloomsbury to the Jungle—and Beyond." In

Tough Guy Writers of the Thirties. Edited by David Madden. Carbondale: Southern Illinois University Press, 1968.

Speir, Jerry. *Raymond Chandler.* New York: Ungar, 1981.

Thorpe, Edward. *Chandlertown: The Los Angeles of Philip Marlowe.* New York: St. Martin's, 1983.

Wolfe, Peter. *Something More Than Night: The Case of Raymond Chandler.* Bowling Green, Ohio: Bowling Green State University Press, 1985.

SELECTED WORKS OF GENERAL RELEVANCE.

Auden, W. H. "The Guilty Vicarage." *Harper's,* May 1948.

Barzun, Jacques, and Wendell Hertig Taylor. *A Cat-alogue of Crime.* New York: Harper & Row, 1971.

Hartman, Geoffrey H. "Literature High and Low: The Case of the Mystery Story." In *The Fate of Reading and Other Essays.* Chicago: University of Chicago Press, 1975.

Macdonald, Ross. *On Crime Writing.* Santa Barbara, Calif.: Capra, 1973.

Most, Glenn W., and William W. Stowe, eds. *The Poetics of Murder: Detective Fiction and Literary Theory.* San Diego: Harcourt Brace Jovanovich, 1983.

Poirier, Richard. *A World Elsewhere: The Place of Style in American Literature.* New York: Oxford University Press, 1966.

Symons, Julian. *Bloody Murder: From the Detective Story to the Crime Novel: A History.* London: Penguin, 1972.

—PETER L. COOPER

Robert Creeley

1926—

*I*N CHARLES OLSON's essay "Projective Verse," there appears what is perhaps the latter half of the twentieth century's single most influential statement on poetics: "Form is never more than an extension of content." The sentence was contained in a letter from Robert Creeley, a man sixteen years Olson's junior. Forty and twenty-four years old when the decade began, the two were the oldest and youngest of a new generation of poets. At the time, neither had been widely published, and both were diligently, perhaps obsessively (their correspondence runs to nine volumes) searching out an appropriate response to the values of the New Criticism, which discussed poetry as a play of formal ambiguities without reference to the author's intent. They countered with a poetics of response to the poet's immediate experience unqualified by externally imposed meters and linear rhetoric. In short, their theory salvaged a radical intentionality and returned it to intelligent discourse.

Although it has been argued, rightfully, that English metrical history and linear rhetoric are parts of most poets' immediate experience, the poetry that looks to or can be traced to Olson's "Projective Verse" certainly feels different on reading and looks different on the page. What happened was that the field of what could be considered appropriate compositional devices opened out into the immediacy of the writer's perception, personality, or drive, and both reader and writer had to deal with the horror or weirdness or sublimity of the poet's personality, or, often enough, its apparent boredom. Those are all part of what is meant by "content" in Olson's essay. As well as acting as an alternative guide to the constellation of images and ideas as presented and stated in a poem, the "content" enters and creates the play of sound, almost magnetizing the syllables to the patterns and tensions of the writer's mind in the act of composition. One of the most interesting ways, then, to approach Robert Creeley's work is through an exploration of diverse aspects of "content" and how they interplay with the form, the artifact of the poem, thus allowing us to retrace his nomadic trek through the terrain of silence and articulation.

When reading Creeley's early work, such as *The Charm* (1969), a collection of singly published poems and thin chapbooks from early in his career; *For Love* (1962); and the first section of *Words* (1967), one feels oneself sliding over fractured aural surfaces, skating swiftly over cracks in the ice, where the ice is a unit of continuous sound. This journey often gives the impression of a breakneck run through a series of jarring halts and glides, which, when the dissections of sound come quickly, leaves one with an overriding sense of a nervous, aggressive tentativeness. A line takes us through what are quite remarkable moving constellations of sound and delay. The sounds, taken in isolation, display a sensuous perfection and classic grace that are continually halted and broken. Creeley maintains that "the truncated line, or the short, seemingly broken line [he] was using in [his] first poems, comes from the somewhat broken emotions that were involved in them" (quoted in Arthur Ford's *Robert Creeley*). Although Creeley was probably specifically referring to the breakup of a marriage, those emotions likely have deeper roots in the poet's "content," and this aural dialectic of the flawless and hesitant can be read as a redramatization of conflicts that arose early in the poet's life. In "The Ball Game" (from *For Love*), he says:

> Early in life the line is straight
> made straight
> against the grain.
> .   .   .   .   .   .
>   take me at the age of 13
> and for some reason there, no matter the particular
> reason.

Here the "line" can be read as the poetic line as well as the vector or trajectory of one's psychological development. The two senses of *line* merge—note that the line is "against the grain"—and mirror the inextricability of psyche and artifact as well as forcing a reading of the poem beyond its surface incipiency.

Robert Creeley was born on May 21, 1926, in West Acton, Massachusetts. His father, a successful doctor and hospital administrator in Arlington, died when the poet was almost six, leaving him to grow up as the only male member of his immediate family, a situation Creeley once described to Tom Clark as being "like growing up in the forest attended by wolves" (*Robert Creeley and the Genius of the American Common Place*). The picture of his mother that arises from the many interviews and poems that treat of her is, however, more ambivalent. He has described her to Clark as his "one conduit to reality." Although he tries to remain objective, even tender, one often notes a condescension in his treatment of this "one conduit." He often uses the words "unsophisticated" and "diffident" to describe her, and one is left with the sense that she, more out of hopelessness than concern for the development of her son as a decisive man, would often present him with decisions to be made and then tell him the choice was his. Creeley relates a story to Clark in which his uncle unfairly subjected him to neglect, shunning him and even turning many family members against him through some supposed fault of Creeley's. The uncle even called Creeley's mother to complain. As he relates it in the Clark interview, his mother said, "Well, Bob, what do you think? Whatever you decide. . . . Do you want to apologize?" Creeley refused, saying that none of the accusations were true, and she responded, "Well, o.k. . . . It's up to you if you don't want to apologize." Creeley, in his late teens, saw his mother quite clearly refusing to support him, not knowing what to do, and leaving the young man to understand the situation and his feelings about it on his own while still, one would guess, implying that an apology was in order. The "conduit" here seems to be one of tacit moral judgment, and the boy can neither defend himself against it nor engage in clear dialogue with it.

In fairness to his mother, and as Creeley points out, his father's death left her with both an estate and debts too big for her to handle competently. The drop in income from $30,000 to $2,700 per year left his mother drained and the young Creeley baffled at the loss of ease and indulgence as well as the loss of his father's decisiveness and loquaciousness. "All I had left, I suppose resentfully, were the echoes of what he'd provided. And too often those proved useless," he told Clark. The episodes he related to Clark nearly all tell of his mother's fiscal or emotional incompetence masked by stoicism and / or tacit negative judgment of him. That the young man *felt* the implied judgment is made evident in a poem from *Memory Gardens* (1986), "Mother's Things."

I wanted approval, . . .

such size of her still
calls out to me
with that silently
expressive will.

One can imagine that in his first mature work as a poet the "silently expressive will" called out even louder than in this work, published when Creeley was sixty, and it could almost be taken as given that the baffled need for approval from one so baffled and silent herself was a deeply inward drive that is expressed in the poet's "content." Something was missing.

In one of Creeley's first published poems, "Poem for D. H. Lawrence," collected in *The Charm,* he writes:

Always the self returns to
self-consciousness, seeing
the figure drawn by the window
by its own hand, standing
alone and unwanted by others

Here, in an image repeated throughout the poem, we are first given the pane of glass, the window that transparently separates the self and is a figure of the disjunction more and more present in Creeley's poems as he matures. This poem follows closely on "Return," his first published poem, which was written when Creeley was nineteen on his return to Harvard from India and Burma, where he was an ambulance driver in World War II. The image of quiet doors in "Return" has already turned in "Poem for D. H. Lawrence" into a brittle window of frustration that he looks through into a world from which he is obviously alienated. The push of syllables, the straining of ideas toward coherence, seem drawn

on the threshold of completion that is always deferred against that glass of "silently / expressive will" he must have stood before, inarticulate throughout his youth, yearning to please. It seems a poem less of return than of its frustration.

His response, it seems, to such frustration (or to the existential alienation fashionable at the time) has been a prissy perfectionism. He said in his preface to *The Charm* that he is "very didactic and very involved with 'with doing it right.' " This claim is echoed in the poet's habits of obsessively emptying ashtrays or picking lint off the carpet, habits one would hardly expect from a cursory reading of his early work. Take, for example, "Still Life Or," from *The Charm*:

mobiles:
          that the wind can catch at,
against itself,
                    a leaf or a contrivance of wires,
in the stairwell,
to be looked at from below.

We have arranged the form of a formula here,
have taken the heart out
                              & the wind
is vague emotion.

To count on these aspirants
these contenders for the to-be-looked-at part
of these actions
                    these most helpful movements
needs
a strong & constant wind.
                    That will not rise above the speed
which we have calculated,
                    that the leaf
remain
          that the wires
be not too much shaken.

On first glance the poem feels slanted, at times dejectedly off-center, almost as though the lines themselves were figured by the mobile, a collection of tenuously hanging, haphazard fragments, or jiggling in a shaken constellation. There is the reappearance throughout the work of dejection, as in the lines "have taken the heart out" and "vague emotion." It is there that one sees a diffidence akin to that with which he describes his mother, in his faithless projection of a wind that would make the mobile move wildly—of course, not too wildly—and in the last stanza. Here hope, contention, recognition, and being able "to count on" are nearly dismissed, or else counted on to be insufficient. Descriptors in this stanza pile up like discarded scraps that could be used as material of construction, but in their near interchangeability, they lose any possibility of being integral parts of a coherence, and the rejection of repeated words and images becomes as much a part of the act of composition as construction. Rejection is part of the visibility of "content" that creates the form of the poem—leaves held together by wires. Interestingly, one does not make a mobile of leaves, so in this case the act of construction is done largely through substitution, the image floats free of any proposed idea or description, as though by naming leaves as a material of construction—the "to-be-looked-at part"—they are placed in the realm of the hypothetical or at the very least extremely ephemeral, and the more displaced the work becomes from the concrete, the messier it all looks. Of course, leaves also fall.

It cannot be overlooked that to *aspire* is not only to hope and work toward a better condition, but to breathe; the word contains breath and wind as its etymological root. Wind and rising are both contained in one of the descriptors of the hypothetical mobile in the second stanza. And, of course, it is wind that would move those pieces, should they come to exist. Form and external mover become confused and are allowed to remain confused, as any honest practitioner of projective verse would well allow them. Psychologically, reality and desire are often confused. Fortunately, Creeley does not try to rescue poetry from psyche.

Where we see the fussiness, the perfectionism, is in the odd and baffled balance the poem maintains. There is the obvious search for the perfect wind somewhere between the one "above the speed / which we have calculated" and the one that "is vague emotion," "against itself." There is the poise of these three winds and the swift, strong run of the individual lines themselves, elegant and simple in isolated phrasal construction. And there is the obvious use of such words as "calculated," "formula," and "contrivance" to describe the mobile itself, all of them referring to the clean and mathematically precise. Here one sees the maintenance of control and the dejection it offers, the frustration of completion. Note how flimsy the mobile is and how tenuous the control over it (which is ultimately successful), in that the poem works like its subject, a hung collection of lovely surfaces moving as a whole unsatisfactorily, off-center and out of step across the dissecting slices of its silences found in its syncopations and caesuras.

Creeley's preface to *For Love* begins, "Wherever it is one stumbles (to get to wherever) at least some way will exist, so to speak, as and when a man takes this or that step—for which, god bless him. Insofar as these poems are such places, always they were ones stumbled into." The quote suggests that composition stumbles from content into form. And Creeley's stumbling is still involved with that encounter with the silently judgmental mother incapable of clear and certain response. He says further, almost defining the tension, "How much I should like to please! It is a constant concern. That is, however, hopeful and pompous, and not altogether true. I write poems because it pleases me, very much." Early in the volume, this same feeling of wanting to please is extended into his friendships, in this case a literary friendship with the German editor and poet Rainer Gerhardt. In "For Rainer Gerhardt," Creeley writes:

friendship, the wandering & inexhaustible wish to
be of use, somehow
to be helpful

when it isn't simple,—wish
otherwise, convulsed, and leading
nowhere I can go.

The directionless lurching that results from an
ill-understood intent to please echoes the constant and cringing examination of every move's
appropriateness or every line's unassailability evident in Creeley's halts and hesitations. He makes
perfectionism his defense, and each act breaks
off too soon in some abyss of nervous and rather
too close evaluation. Act and response have too
short a separation, so short that the act is interrupted, truncated, by its own reflection, in a short-
circuit loop. Completion would mean satisfaction
or self-approval, so it must be deferred while
awaiting response, a difficult place for writers,
who of course have no immediate audience.
Completion must be delayed or interrupted with
alternatives, and the poems move in a series of
flawless fits and delays, here in a syntactic unit
that short-circuits itself.

In more extreme examples, the poems sometimes begin with tight, almost opaque proposi-
tions of ideas whose halting attempts at
development dissolve in their own repeated
sounds. This motion is figured in "The Death of
Venus," from *For Love*. In the poem's opening
dream sequence a woman's body, the object of
desire, transforms into a porpoise "rising lucid
from the mist," an animal that is sleek and lovely
yet incapable of either erotically appropriate or
satisfactorily human response. From there,

The sound of waves killed speech
but there were gestures—

of my own, it was to call her closer,
of hers, . . .

Not only does the poet say that "the sound of
waves killed speech," but the syntax itself is

interrupted and twisted toward the end of the
passage. The possibility of a transfer of meaning
or a statement of desire is lost within, "killed"
by the ocean spray of syllable and pure music.
The poem ends with the porpoise filling "her
lungs with water" (a very unporpoise-like thing
to do) and sinking to the clear bottom of the sea,
where the object of sexual desire or meaning or
completion sits unattainable and dead—and, one
imagines, lovely.

A perhaps more telling example, one that is in
easier parallel with Creeley's life as he lived it
during the composition of these books, is "The
Disappointment" (from *For Love*):

Had you the eyes of a goat,
they would be almond, half-green, half-

yellow, an almond
shape to them, Were you

less as you are, cat-like, a brush
head, sad, sad, un-

goatlike.

One notices the immediate juxtaposition of two
subjunctives and their disappointed completion.
They are proposed and immediately deferred, but
what is most telling is how the descriptive spec-
ificity of the first four lines—saying what is in
effect absent, though desired—becomes gradually less grounded in either the possible or the
synecdochical. What form, after all, is suggested
by that which he claims would be "cat-like, a
brush/head"? In any case, cats have eyes much
like the goat's described here. By this point at-
tribution of the repeated "sad" is really in question. What is sad? Is it the speaker, the one
spoken to, or the whole mess of dissatisfaction?
The poem starts us out with the expectation of a
simple rhetorical move from proposition to actuality, but no actuality is ever stated. One expects
the formula "if a, then b," but what we get is

"if a, if b . . . ," a formula that produces the poetics of a delay, of deferred satisfaction so complete it becomes suspension.

This kind of suspension was also characteristic of Creeley's life during this time. He attended Harvard from 1943 to 1947 with the interruption of a short stint in the field service. At Harvard he spent more time listening to jazz than attending classes and dropped out during his senior year, narrowly avoiding receiving a degree. During his last year he married Ann McKinnon. After dropping out, he and his wife tried subsistence farming in New Hampshire. Their first child, a son named David, was born in 1948. The farm was started with funds from his wife's trust fund, and when they proved insufficient to cover its expense and to support another son (Tom, born in 1950) and the small magazine Creeley founded, the couple moved to France in 1951. The failed magazine was taken over by Cid Corman, a poet and editor, and renamed *Origin.* It became the first voice for Creeley, Olson, and many other poets eventually associated with the Black Mountain, or projective verse, movement.

Creeley and his wife moved to Mallorca, an island off the coast of Spain, in 1952, the year their daughter Charlotte was born. They lived there intermittently for several years, during which Creeley established Divers Press and published the first edition of *The Black Mountain Review,* a magazine of work from Black Mountain College's students and faculty. He taught at Black Mountain College (an experimental school founded in North Carolina in the 1930s) from 1954–1956 under Charles Olson's rectorship, even though he had no university degree. During this time the family maintained their home in Mallorca. In 1955, they made what was supposed to be·a permanent move to Black Mountain College, but were divorced that same year. Creeley went off to visit San Francisco, encountered the emerging Beat movement, and left Black Moun-

tain permanently to go to Albuquerque in 1956. He also met Bobbie Louise Hawkins, whom he married in 1957, the year their first daughter, Sarah, was born.

While living in Albuquerque, Creeley taught at a private boys' school after Olson granted him a B.A. in 1956 from Black Mountain College. The degree was granted on the basis that he had taught the courses he would have taken to complete the program he started at Harvard. In 1959 he and his wife and their two daughters (another daughter, Katherine, was born in 1959) moved to Guatemala, where he worked as a tutor on a coffee plantation. He received an M.A. from the University of New Mexico in 1960 and taught there before moving to the University of British Columbia in Vancouver in 1962, the year of *For Love*'s publication. During the period from 1945 to 1959 he wrote most of the poems published in *The Charm* as well as some of those published in *For Love.*

Through his mid-twenties and into his late thirties, Creeley stumbled—much like his ideal poem—around Europe, the United States, and Guatemala, fathering five children and marrying two women. As we've seen already, in Creeley the ideal stumbler lives in a state of tension with the barely submerged perfectionist. The experimental, disjunctive master of sound—poetry's version of the jazz musician Thelonious Monk—is in conflict with the young man eager to please, to be of use. As he says in "The Immoral Proposition" (*For Love*), he is

. . . The unsure

egoist [who] is not
good for himself.

This comment comes from a man who cannot accept satiety, completion, in either his art (witness the broken lines and suspended development) or his career. We have also seen in "The Death of Venus" that this attitude is echoed in an ambivalent feeling toward women or perhaps toward eroticism itself. Many direct statements of sexual desire in his early work are either filled with longing or tinged with the obscene or violent, and the one other commonly stated desire is for quiet, perhaps most tellingly in "A Song" (*For Love*):

> I had wanted a quiet testament
> and I had wanted, among other things,
> a song.
>   That was to be
> of a like monotony.
>   (A grace
> Simply. Very very quiet.

It is natural that one so tense might want exactly that, but what rescues this poem from stating the obvious is the ambivalence of the desire for quiet, both "a grace" and "a like monotony." Quiet and repose are somehow, like women, both desired and unacceptable, leading this poem to read like a noble sublimation of repression couched as grace. Creeley has said, in an interview with Clark, that he loved the Baptist hymns he grew up with, and they are certainly sublimated repression masking as grace, though perhaps a grace of a different sort.

In the latter part of *For Love,* Creeley clearly equates acceptance by women with salvation, release from pain. The last poem of the book, "For Love," which is dedicated to Bobbie Louise Hawkins, contains the lines:

> Today, what is it that
> is finally so helpless,
>
> different, despairs of its own
> statement, wants to
> turn away, endlessly

The speaker asks to be allowed to

> . . . stumble into
> not the confession but
> the obsession I begin with
> now. For you

This "you" is said to be or to have (both meanings are possible) "some time beyond place" in which she has been vagabond, constantly turning away from places within wide space. The "time beyond space" is another variation on the quiet doorways (one of which is said to be his) of "Return," the poem he wrote at nineteen after his return from World War II. It is a place of comfort and belonging and is best and most clearly identified with women in "The Door" (from *For Love*).

Late in "The Door," Creeley says quite clearly that "she will be the door in the wall / to the garden in sunlight." "She" is also variously called "you," "You," and "the Lady," echoing the courtly love tradition of medieval Europe. In that tradition, the undeserving sinful man writes poems in which the infinite compassion and intercessionary powers of the Blessed Mother figure the earthly woman's assent to love, as though this love, of such a pure order that by its nature it paradoxically frustrates desire, were an act or aspect of theological grace. Creeley does not go quite that far, but earlier in the poem the sunlit garden is inhabited by "the Graces in long Victorian dresses, / of which my grandmother had spoken." This image leads us back through the quiet door of "Return" to the "grace" of "A Song." The Graces, sublimated by their new vestiture, are "young" and "obtainable" and lost in his grandmother's rumors of a time famous for its sexual repression. In the mention of his grandmother's dress the hint of incest is unavoidable, as is the association with the monotony written of in "A Song." His "Lady," admittedly, is not one of the doubly anachronistic Graces in their classical and Victorian guises, but rather a liminal conductor toward them, as Beatrice conducted Dante toward the Virgin's presence. Creeley says, "and you follow after them also / in the service of God and Truth."

It should be noted how much the music of this poem echoes Kenneth Rexroth's free translations of Dante. Rexroth, a leader of the San Francisco Renaissance, or Beat movement, a movement toward poetic freedom as important as Black Mountain, was terribly and unjustifiably jealous of Creeley when Creeley was in San Francisco, suspecting him of seducing his lover. Perhaps Creeley mimics Rexroth's voice as some unconscious atonement for the guilt he may on some level have accepted. This section of the book is dated 1956–1958, when Creeley was in San Francisco and between wives, in the early days of his courtship with Bobbie Louise Hawkins. When one remembers his situation and that his uncle had also made unjustified and damaging accusations against him, it is easy to empathize with his need to identify with men like the knights errant, those men eternally and ideally pure-hearted. Creeley had also just broken off professional relations with Olson—yet another of the many broken relationships with older men that began with the death of his father. With his life in a complete mess—he was drinking so heavily that his friend, the Beat writer Jack Kerouac, of all people, used to lead him out of bars in fear for his life— Creeley wrote in lines of unbroken elegance, steadily, throughout "The Door," perhaps as a defense against what must have seemed like immanent annihilation.

It is interesting to note that the poet speaks in lines that within themselves alternate between utterly elegant strength and abject pleading, a comic voice skilled in verse, part the silent film comedian Charlie Chaplin, part the Delta blues singer Robert Johnson, part the troubadour Bernart de Ventadorn.

> Inside You would also be tall,
> more tall, more beautiful,
> Come toward me from the wall, I want to be with
>   You.

> So I screamed to You,
> who hears as the wind, and changes
> . . . .

> Running to the door, I ran down
> as a clock runs down. Walked backwards,
> stumbled, sat down
> hard on the floor near the wall.
> . . . .
> My knees were iron, I rusted in worship, of You.

> For that one sings, one
> writes the spring poem, one goes on walking.
> The Lady has always moved to the next town

It should be noted that the lines are no longer twisted, but have been smoothed out, have attained a formal rectitude in a time of loss and betrayal that was absent in times more ostensibly happy for Creeley.

Creeley's sense of what it is to be a man was probably shaped early in his short relationship with his father, which ended in what the five-year-old saw as an abandonment the father was helpless to prevent. He well remembered his father being taken to an ambulance in the snow. He never saw him again. From early on, Creeley's sense of men as attractively powerful and his ability to trust, rely on, and identify with that power was called traumatically into question. His sense must have been that men provide for and then abandon others despite their best efforts not to. Power is both ineffective and futile; it is, in effect, absent in that neither commitment nor betrayal are really chosen.

An incident that could illustrate this point occurred when Creeley was four. He and his father were driving in the family car when coal from a coal chute somehow struck the windshield by accident. A piece of glass lodged in Creeley's left eye, causing deterioration of sight to the point of near total blindness. What understanding Creeley could have had of the irony of his father's position as a physician and hospital administrator powerless to help his son is impossible to say, of course, but given the resentment he felt at his death and his family's concomitant loss of comfort, one imagines that an inarticulate and baffled resentment must have existed on some level. What his father could do nothing about, his mother was forced to deal with as the damaged eye grew larger, causing young Creeley headaches and threatening sight in the other eye. One day, as she often did, his mother took him to the hospital where she occasionally worked as a nurse. But on this occasion, rather than waiting in the car, Creeley was brought inside and checked in. His mother explained that his left eye was to be removed. Creeley, in an interview with Clark, says, "So when she said now this doctor is going to take your eye out I remembered feeling betrayed for being tricked in this curious way; so I certainly didn't like it. I must have held it against her emotionally for some time for putting me in this situation." One has to ask what can be done against such silent will, as displayed by Creeley's mother, perhaps rather frightened of expressing itself. The cruelty of cowardice and silence is not usually so obvious.

One reaction was simply to become verbal. Creeley was thought of during his childhood as a very quiet child and regarded suspiciously. His father, however, had been loquacious, as were most of his male relatives, the accusatory uncle in particular. Clark has said that Creeley has "associated verbalness with maleness." Creeley assents. He goes on to say, "When I was then in the company of my peer group—at the boys' school in New Hampshire, Holderness, I quickly did acquire the nickname 'Senator,' since truly I *was* always talking. I never shut up." In that statement one can feel what a release it must have been for Creeley to be out from under a suspicious eye and simply let himself go, which he probably did quite argumentatively, given the nickname. Although he "didn't know how to deal with [his uncle's] maleness," he quickly learned the same style of being a man in age-appropriate company. He found that one can gain one's place, temporarily, by verbal assertion, or at least by uninterruptible talk.

Creeley's often anthologized "I Know a Man" (in *For Love*) makes this point clear and offers further understanding of what verbalness meant to him:

As I sd to my
friend, because I am
always talking,—John, I

sd, which was not his
name, the darkness sur-
rounds us, what

can we do against
it, or else, shall we &
why not, buy a goddamn big car,

drive, he sd, for
christ's sake, look
out where yr going.

If one recalls his lines on being helpful from "For Rainer Gerhardt"—"when it isn't simple, —wish / otherwise, convulsed, and leading / nowhere I can go"—the desperation out of which it was written becomes clear. Here the lines are syncopated like abrupt halts between a rapid lift and sharp delay, like fugitive and interrupted bullets shot against nothing. The lines come as if from a trapped and terribly frightened animal that "the darkness surrounds" in his urgent need to flee, to go anywhere other than where he is. The poem is ostensibly a recounting of an event; an obsessive voice narrates about a character who talks obsessively like flitting layers of ghosts. As the speaker drives through the fifth line, out of composition and into narration, he seems to be terrified of reentering the character who had to speak those lines, rapidly bouncing from his narrative distance into identification and, possibly, self-quotation. As he successfully enters the character, the first line he is allowed to speak without interruption is "the darkness sur- / rounds us," as though reidentification with the trapped and terrified allows him to propose the solution "buy a goddamn big car." At this point the fussy perfectionism of many poems has been abandoned—perhaps beyond it there is only darkness, but at least it is acknowledged.

The abandonment of fussiness achieves formal concreteness in his choosing to publish the last stanza with neither quotation marks to identify speakers nor periods to indicate where each speaker stops speaking. It is open to question who says "drive" and who says "for / christ's sake, look / out where yr going." To ascribe either to the narrator is grammatically possible, and this ambiguity raises several possible interpretations. John, "which was not his / name," might be a projected foil to the speaker. Alternatively, if he says "drive," thereby approving their buying "a goddamn big car," he might be his straight man. That Creeley gives way to the impulse to break out is articulated clearly, but much of the old voice remains. Essentially the same kind of interruption—a form of truncation—takes place here as in the more suffocated poems, especially if John is seen as a second self with whom he conducts an interior dialogue, a male counterego from whom he can get a response. The speaker still needs an "other" to give him approval. At any rate *someone* is told to "look / out where yr going," one of the three disembodied voices speaking here who are in and of the surrounding dark.

The act of self-abandonment is still impossible in the reemergence of the cautious voice. It remains unclear whether or not they ever buy a car. Notice the inflammatory bravado of "goddamn big," the studied cool of "& / why not." Most teenage boys know this scene very well and know how unlikely it is that one would ever just buy a car and drive. The lines can be read as adolescent toughness and desperation that stays in the realm of talk, in this case probably within a dissociating self. Only commas mark the pauses in speech, which is significant in that there is no time during this dialogue when the two stop long enough to buy a car. On first reading, it is possible, if one

has sufficiently entered the space of the poem, not to hear the word "buy" and to ride the impression that the two are standing beside a hot-looking car with the keys left in the ignition. How else could they so rapidly go from wondering what to do to being in the car and watching where they are going without ever pausing in their talk? One certainly can't believe they went through the process of buying a car without suspending the need for verisimilitude. This uncertainty beautifully underscores the surreality of the scene, suspending dialogue in a darkness that must be devoid of objects, a dark hell, the incipiency of heavy-metal adolescence. The scene is impossible to situate, a literal nowhere, and one cannot drive out of nowhere.

This lingering adolescent misery is explored more clearly, though perhaps not as directly, in many other poems of this period, particularly in "The Crow" (*For Love*). In the last two lines Creeley says, "Sickness is the hatred of a repentance / knowing there is nothing he wants." In a clear statement of the futility of desire, the poet sums up his reaction to a Puritan upbringing—a mass of tangled feelings, such as hate, repentance, sickness, and denial, all of which center around the crow whose murder by the speaker initiates in him a series of emotional absences. Puritanism, with its emphasis on denial, is of course relevant to an understanding of a poem about repentance. Repentance is the expected counter to desire and satisfaction. That Creeley attended a Baptist church with his family and became associated with such movements as the Beats, who were ostensibly anything but repressed, strongly suggests that he would reject repentance. It is the crow who wants nothing (maybe only now that it is dead); thus, more than is the case with other images, it pays to see the crow as representing a part of Creeley himself, the one who represses. Many people with the same history would also like to kill it.

There is a famous photograph of Creeley in

which he is pictured with a hooded smile leaning over a carved crow. He paratactically relates himself to the bird, and parataxis—the juxtaposing of similar objects or ideas so that their striking similarities can be noticed without the use of a connective—was certainly a common device used by the Black Mountain group of poets. On the surface Creeley looks diffident, inviting, mild, and the smile seems to toy with the viewers and draw them toward him, over and across the crow. But in Creeley's face there is a certain menace; it is a face that does not trust and will at least become defensive if any attempt at intimacy is made.

"The Crow" is much more complex, or at least ambivalent, than this reading makes it out to be. It contains the understanding that hatred of old repentance does not represent freedom from it, an understanding many other young poets of the time entirely missed. First of all, hatred is equated quite clearly with sickness. Moreover, the poem begins with the crow hating the speaker "because [he] will not feed him," or, we are meant to understand, continue believing in the value of guilt. The relationship of the two is dependent from the beginning on hate, so the crow is killed as the speaker tries to free himself from self-disgust. The crow's death also frees the speaker to leave, as though his affection or responsibility for the crow had in some way trapped him. He has to leave behind this mocking black cawing thing, but as in "I Know a Man," it is unclear where exactly he wants to go. He at least seems to be free of guilt over abandoning the crow, which was an object of derision to begin with—"there is nothing I laugh at"—however dependent on the crow he was. There might be nothing left to abandon or ridicule, but his dependence on the crow comes through clearly in his saying that the result of the crow's death was more dis-ease.

Far from being the only image of violence in Creeley's work, "The Crow" is only the clearest example of self-directed rage. Often this rage took the form, at least in his poems, of imagined violence against others. Toward the beginning of "From Pico & the Women: A Life" (from *The Charm*), he says,

> . . . Disuse, good father,

> these things have rusted and
> we know a man who speaks more
> freely . . .

in the desire to *"by speech / utter him."* The identity of "him" is unclear, since Creeley had just been speaking of loving rather than knowing God, but speech, uninhibited speech, is already a substitute for frustrated knowledge. The poem continues:

> He will be sleeping somewhere
> else, little rabbit, in the long
> grass, in the hole of his own

> making. He will be sleeping and
> it will be our fear that lies
> so . . .
> . . . .
> . . . It is our lion of fire, our
> triumphant animal, with his own

> victories, our hearts' conquesting
> beast, little rabbit, that will
> not bite you nor otherwise harm.

The need to repress the violence inherent in any act done out of frustration and fear is clearly present, feared, and repressed as soon as the possibility is articulated. "But," as Creeley says in the same volume, in "The Bird, the Bird, the Bird":

> . . . how otherwise to oblige the
> demon, who it is, there

> implacable, but content.

His explorations of violence were, to say the least, brave in their articulation of desires at which most of us cringe. In "The Pedigree" (from *The Charm*), he begins,

> Or if I will not rape
> my own daughter
>   "What will I do?"

He goes on to say that in any "occasion" there is an element

> . . . so
> necessary, we do not
>   "witless"
> perform it.

It is as though he conceives of the necessary as that which needs to be repressed, perhaps overly polarizing the libido and the superego in a reversal of the Puritan stance that enacts the same overpolarization.

Often, as this poem might suggest, the same eye was turned on women. In "An Obscene Poem" (from *The Charm*), after describing his wife crouched in a bikini behind some "jagged encumbrance," he describes her as

> . . . a dull movement
> on the sands
>
> and lightly at low tide
> on the rocks
> bland, undulant

In "Alba," from the same volume, he describes a woman in a short series of complimentary images followed by a qualification:

> Your tits are rosy in the dawn
> albeit the smallness of them.
> Your lips are red and bright with love
> albeit I lie upon them.
>
> And hence the grossness of the act

It is significant that the qualifier for the image of the lips is that they are involved in a sexual act with him, as though beauty is less desired in satisfaction. The poem goes on only to say that the sex act "reinstitutes the virgin ground," but that statement seems like a rationalized withdrawal from the poem's direction.

The women are described in these poems in much the same way he describes the wind in "Still Life Or" and, more tellingly, in the way he describes his emotional state in "Helas" (*The Charm*). In "Helas" he says, "The day is the indefinite," "will not take them to hand," "the head / revolves, turns in the wind but lacks / its delight," "which are vague," and "no edge from the wind." Against the vagueness and the revolving head he proposes "an axe-edge / take[n] to its stone" with "(nothing else but / to bite home!" It is an image of striking against the vague, with an axe or with bitterness. Much as in most adolescent music since the advent of heavy metal, the response to boredom is violence, and inasmuch as boredom is the result of repression, we see the necessary element—that "which is so necessary we do not perform it"—proposed in "The Pedigree." Creeley's famous statement of this violence as a response to repression is from "The Warning" (*For Love*):

> For love—I would
> split open your head and put
> a candle in
> behind the eyes.

It is as though to wake these unresponsive women up he has to break forcefully into their dullness and light them up. Love is wanted, certainly, but when it is frustrated, a violent response flares up throughout his early work, marked extensively with a passive-aggressive dull flame.

In 1964 Creeley was writing the last few poems of the first section of *Words,* among them, "One Way," "Some Afternoon," and "Anger." They represent the culmination of Creeley's exploration of violence and anger in his marital relationships and are perhaps what brought him to the place in the volume where his writing seems to bifurcate and bring the opposites— desire for the pleasures of place, object, and woman and his sublimation and rejection of them in the formal excellence of his poems—that were formerly held in tension into a flipping thesis and antithesis. In these three poems it seems that anger settles momentarily around images of clutter and disorder, which are results of, or represent slanted personifications of, the woman. In "One Way," the man

> . . . raises
> his hand to
> not strike her, as
>
> again his hand
> is raised, she has
> gone.

The woman leaves the room; he is left in

> All the locked time, all the letting go
>
> down into it, as a
> locked room, come to.

This isolation results in a "center shifted," and the character stares blankly at the unchanged "disorder" and "accumulations" about him in the room. Here a deferred act of violence and one of abandonment bring an awareness of mess, neglect, and the piles of detritus that mark lost time, which we know this poet hates. The mess appears as the rubble of a bleak and bombed-out wreck of a man, but it is within this ruin that a "center shifted" is noted. In "Anger" this same situation is described, this time moving the subject who accumulates from "they" to "he" in two lines, as though what she left behind becomes unbearably his, and he is stained by it. Almost any thing, any physical object, becomes plain mess in these three poems.

In "Some Afternoon," Creeley writes, using the first person,

> I see
>
> myself and family,
> and friends, and

> animals attached,
> the house, the road
>
> all go forward
> in a huge
> flash, shaken
> with that act,
>
> . . . . . .
> Nothing left
> after the initial
> blast . . . .

This volume has an epigraph by the poet William Carlos Williams: "There is, in short, / a counter stress / born of the sexual shock." And the poems now deal with shock—they literalize shock—in a world that has become too much, as though anger had blasted out the sensual world of things, and there is nothing more joyless. In "Some Afternoon," Creeley seems also to incorporate the old disjunctiveness he had been working out in formal play now as an emotional horror:

> the tangible faces
> smile, breaking
> into tangible pieces.

Things are not only a mess, but also, with the inclusion of personal loves as objects of rubble, a way of experiencing the pain of disintegration and dehumanization. In "Anger" he writes:

> He is angry. His
> face grows—as if
> a moon rose
>
> of black light,
> convulsively darkening.

The main character becomes that moon:

> . . . an open
> hole of horror, of
>
> nothing as if not
> enough there is
> nothing. A pit—
>
> . . . .

        a hole

    for anger and
    fills it
    with himself.

Creeley later called this image "a kind of perverse well of shit—a deep hole," which he goes on to relate to a time in childhood when, wearing a "classic sailor's suit," he fell into a cesspool.

While still in this extremity of anger, the only way that the speakers in these poems seem to be able to crawl out of the shit is by creating an intolerable other to destroy. The poem ends with a short section containing the bald statement:

    All you say you want
    to do to yourself you do
    to someone else as yourself.

Since we need to be brought closer to such emotion until we quit repressing it, "Anger" contains lines more sickening than self-pitying at times. Statements of detachment within the same sentence become lines where distances between narrator and narrated, character and character and—before we are aware—poet and reader are obliterated in a sadomasochism difficult to stomach if we are courageous enough to feel it.

    You were not involved,

    even if your head was cut off,
    or each finger

    twisted
    from its shape until it broke,

    and you screamed too
    with the other, in pleasure.

Perhaps the act of writing becomes here a sadomasochistic act calling for the reader's identification with that much misery and violence.

Robert Creeley's later interviews and poems portray him as a good man, a gentle man. Re-member that the hand was raised *not* to strike. And it is pertinent to ask what response such a person could make when finding himself in a sadomasochistic position he could hardly find tenable. A hint of what this response might be comes from the ambivalent treatment given physical objects that are not part of the poet's complex of domestic associations. This response strikes one as odd at first, but is borne out in critical writings from two and three years later as well as in the second section of *Words.* In "Anger" the opening section treats of a truck that passes during a silent and sullenly uncomfortable domestic scene. Creeley characterizes the house as "descriptive," and then a truck passes by, shining its headlights into the room:

    . . . all
    familiar impact

    as it passed
    so close. He
    hated it.

In the volume's title poem, "Words," which begins as an attempt at reconciliation, he simply presents

    . . . the twisted
    place I
    cannot speak,

    .   .   .   .
    . . . a tongue
    rotten with what

    it tastes— . . . .

It is in this revulsion at sense and objects, or in self-pitying despair over the loss of joy in them, that the poet initiates a rejection of place and image, on the one hand, and, sometimes, an over-reliance on their quiet, on the other. Meaning is terrible, or even disgusting, and objects are accumulations that leave a bitter residue or hated for the fact that they are there to be related to at all. Content and form split and become uneasy partners in a marriage attempting reconciliation. In this poem, words are echoes of that distant and traumatic time of anger, they are

. . . a
clear, fine
ash [which] sifts,
like dust,

from nowhere.

In his critical writings one can chart Creeley's beginning ambivalence, both in practice and in theory, about the meaning of projective verse, or field composition. The sense of projection, that is, objects invested with "content" or "psychic charge"—as in, for example, "The Gift" and many early works—becomes complicated and overshadowed by another sense of the projective. This new sense disassociates itself from the constellating of objects. Thus the syllable, which Olson called the "king and pin of versification" in "Projective Verse," starts to float free of the object, becomes more self-referential, as poetry as a whole certainly did in the Language poetry school of the 1970s, which views language as an opaque object in a constant flux of self-referential play. This idea of sound also lifts out of the old sense of organic breath as the determiner of rhythm and pulse. It is submerged by the kind of flattening of sound that occurs throughout Creeley's middle period, from the second section of *Words* through *Later* (1979).

In Creeley's "Introduction to *The New Writing in the USA*" (in *The Collected Essays of Robert Creeley*), he reacts to critical statements typical of academics of the day about the poets of the 1940s confronting rule and objective measures, imposed forms, and so on with the assertion "Confronting such *rule,* men were driven back upon the particulars of their own experi-

ence, the literal *things* of an immediate environment." Creeley then goes on to quote what he says is one of the earliest cogent reactions to that state of poetry, made by William Carlos Williams: "Therefore each speech having its own character the poetry it engenders will be peculiar to that speech also in its own intrinsic form. . . . When a man makes a poem, makes it, mind you, he takes words as he finds them." This passage Creeley chose to provide the historical context for his own poetry and theory is one that speaks of words as an "intense expression of his perceptions and ardors"—objects are not mentioned by Williams at all. Williams' quote leaves one with a sense of words shot full and vibrating, nearly dissolving with the intensity of desire, but the objects of desire are absent. According to Creeley, in the same essay, the "most active definition" of the type of poetry described by Williams is a poem of John Wieners, a poet often associated with projective verse:

At last. I come to the last defense.

My poems contain no
wilde beestes, no
lady of the lake . . .
. . . .
Only the score of a man's
struggle . . . .

The struggle, in Creeley's excerpt of Wieners, is given only in raw metaphors:

. . . love
and its twisted faces,
my hands claw out at.

They could hardly be considered concrete particulars in the sense of Ezra Pound's image from *The Cantos* "an ant's forefoot up-held me" or the subject of Olson's poem "Piper's Rocks," a group of rocks off the coast of Massachusetts. Most of Creeley's poems could have been written anywhere within a broad geographic zone.

Significantly, Creeley lived during most of the time up through his writing of "Introduction to *The New Writing in the USA*" in New Mexico, Guatemala, Mallorca, San Francisco, and Mexico, but one has to read his autobiography to know that. Most of his poems from the last two sections of *For Love* are more occupied with the images from pre-Elizabethan song, such as flowers and the lady, and with cars than with the concrete particulars of place.

But those images are there, and they stay there in Creeley's more recent work. He never quite took sides in the rift in American poetry that split poets into the opaque style of Language poetry and a naively descriptive voice that produced lines that read like "My grandmother washes dishes as the cat purrs" ad infinitum in the 1970s. Toward the end of "Introduction to *The New Writing in the USA,*" Creeley speaks of writing, his and others, in terms of its "distance from the usual habit of *description*—by which I mean that practice that wants to 'accompany' the *real* but which assumes itself as 'objectively' outside that context in some way." According to Creeley, most descriptive voices assume a transparency of language that makes the self's participation in the act of description unnecessary. He is speaking of how the subject must enter the writing and jar it from its close proximity to the objects and events it describes. The self cannot be erased, in this theory, which is the margin of distance that separates Creeley from the Language poets. He says that this idea is clarified by Edward Dorn, who wrote about Olson's poetry, "the Place [Gloucester, Mass.] is brought forward fully in form conceived entirely by the activation of a man who is under its spell."

Creeley follows with the statement "To tell the story, is all one can do." In an earlier essay, on Louis Zukofsky ("Louis Zukofsky: *All: The Collected Short Poems, 1923–1958*" in *The Collected Essays of Robert Creeley*), Creeley discusses a line from the poet's "A," often quoted

by writers calling into question the Language poets' work. The passage reads, "Who had better sing and tell stories / Before all will be abstracted." According to Creeley this quote calls for a poetry of the formal play of words without necessary reference to outside objects. "It is a sense that proposes poetry to be evidence as to its own activity, apart from any other sense of description or of a convenience to some elsewhere considered reality of things." Creeley is using the acts of song and story as antithetical to "description" and "reality." Zukofsky's lines themselves, however, seem to ask for the preservation of a referential language. Stories refer to external, or at least imagined, chains of events. One way of reading Creeley's misinterpretation of Zukofsky is as a result of his loss of faith in the sensory world described in the sequence of poems about anger in *Words*. But Creeley's move away from description initiated poetry as a play of language that could be considered valuable or necessary beyond its capacity to refer and/or provide coherence.

The break with reference and narrative in Creeley's theory of the period works out, or at least parallels, formal characteristics of his poetry already discussed—the disjunctive, interrupted, and hesitant play of sounds. He quotes Warren Tallman on the subject of fiction in "Introduction to *The New Writing in the USA*": "The narrative line has tended to weaken, merge with, and be dominated by the sum of variations." Tallman draws a parallel to "jazz when the melody merges with the improvisations and the improvisations dominate." Creeley compares this notion with Olson's and Ernest Fenollosa's idea that the sentence itself is not a complete thought, "since such completion is impossible." The frustration of completion by this time serves not only to drive the formal play of sound but also to break narrative into "variation," digression, and backward pulls against linearity and even eventually to break phones and graphs from meaning.

Creeley's notion of an autonomous language is an attempt to theorize about his psychological "content," which was a bifurcation of the tensions that had earlier driven his poems. The poems of *Words* often appear on one or the other side of the split so that those that *are* imagistic crystallize the content to the point of containment and isolation, while others drift nearly completely free of context and reference.

Two poems from late in *Words* serve to illustrate the extremes. "A Piece" reads in its entirety:

> One and
> one, two,
> three.

"The Farm" reads:

> Tips of celery,
> clouds of
>
> grass—one
> day I'll go away.

In the first example, which Creeley says was "one of the poems most irritating to reviewers," we encounter a poem acting as a verbal construct freed of any "code of significance," as Cynthia Edelberg puts it in *Robert Creeley's Poetry: A Critical Introduction.* Creeley, she says, was "experimenting with what the linguist Roman Jakobson called the 'supposed orphanhood' " of the poetic line. Jakobson's orphanhood of the line refers to words and syntactic units set free of the authority of a poem's unifying structure. These orphan lines tend to float in strange and seemingly dislocated relation to the rest of the poem's verbal texture, developing, he says, a "network of variously compelling affinities." What these affinities are is hard to paraphrase, but they seem, in practice, to involve composing

poems in sound fields, where words float into webs of aural and rhythmic play divorced from context or producing strange and dissonant fields of meaning. "The Farm" gives us a picture of quiet, the words less referential than visually suggestive and unencumbered by their relationship to any meaning. The statement at the end only clinches the elegiac feeling of the first two and a half lines. But the first spring appearance of the celery tips is held in ironic relation to the speaker's sense that he will leave, separated from a field of new growth. The sense of irony occurs between the dissonant senses of separation and incipient burgeoning much as the imagination's eye stutters in the stanza break between clouds and grass.

It is also in the time between hearing a word and then imagining what it refers to (visualized and made audible in the break between stanzas) that emotion and statement are found in this last book written during the end of Creeley's several years of stable residence in New Mexico during the 1960s. The statements in these poems are as delicately poised as those in Creeley's other work, bringing bald statement a measure of grace in its isolation, repetition, and attention. One example is "Was":

> The face
> was
> beautiful.
>
> She was
> a pleasure.
> She
>
> tried
> to please.

The separation of poetic voices continued largely through 1979, reaching its most important stage in the volumes *Pieces* (1969), *A Day Book* (1972), and *Hello* (1978). Creeley spent much of this time teaching at the State University of New York in Buffalo while living in Bolinas, California, and London and taking trips around the world giving readings of his work. Many of these poems are episodic, journalistic entries and jottings that capture fleeting impressions, sights, and emotions as well as create many more poems like ''A Piece.'' During the time he was writing fragile and delicate poems of orphan lines, Creeley's marriage to Bobbie Louise Hawkins dissolved (in 1976), his fame and recognition as a poet grew among academics, and his poems became sweeter as they grew more fragmented. This phase drew to a close, and a new one began when, during a reading tour of Australia and Southeast Asia, he met his third wife, Penelope Highton. His poems have gradually gathered into the quiet cohesiveness, gentleness, and nostalgia that characterizes his work through the 1990s.

In *Later* there appears the often anthologized ''Prayer to Hermes.'' It marks, appropriately, a crossroads in the poet's life—the change from early to late middle age. Written when he was between the ages of fifty and fifty-three, this transition would seem appropriate, but it probably also had something to do with settling into a stable marriage and a less disjunctive poetics. The poem begins:

> Hermes, god
> of crossed sticks,
> crossed existence,

which could well figure a crossing and reuniting of the voices and concerns that had been floating free of each other for the past thirteen years. He also says:

> I see the ways
>
> of knowing, of
> securing, life grow
> ridiculous . . . .

His old track seems to have worn out, or else the track that confused dispersal with reconciliation

(by breaking writing into fragments as a way to defer confronting pain) has finally scattered to the four winds. The poem ends with a statement that the speaker will find solace in openness, that is, making oneself known demands a cohesiveness and dependence on the referential nature of word and narrative.

Creeley's old anger and the disjunctiveness and dispersal of voice evident in his earlier work never entirely left him, but in its more obvious expressions it is mitigated, even mocked. ''Self-Portrait,'' from *Mirrors* (1983), begins ''He wants to be / a brutal old man'' and continues more graphically with superbly crafted lines in the same vein. However, the first two stanzas soften the opening statement by placing it in the realm of the desired and not yet real, as though Creeley does not really have the energy for the kind of hate he claims to want. The poem ends ''. . . And / he loves, but hates equally.'' That may be true, but it is difficult to find poetic statements of hate equalling those of love in Creeley's from *Later* to the mid-1990s. The desire is suspect.

''Self-Portrait'' is followed in *Mirrors* by ''Mother's Voice,'' in which he identifies with his mother's distancing and negative voice, a voice that denies, as she did, rather than striking out, as though he has lost the battle with her. Then comes ''Bresson's Movies,'' which describes Creeley's changing identifications with characters in the movies of the director Robert Bresson. He says that in his youth he identified with a young man's distance from the girl he loved, but now he identifies with an

> aging Lancelot . . .
> .   .   .   .
>
> dazed, bleeding, both he
> and his horse are,
> trying to get back to
> the castle . . . .

This reference to the bleeding knight—one remembers ''The Door''—seems to most powerfully figure the sense of the poet in his later work. Having been in a battle in which he was injured— one guesses he lost—the knight tries to go home, return to his old protections and domesticity with a renewed sense of and need for his home and origin. This movement parallels that in his poetry, where he turns away from the experimental and daring to the simple and reminiscent.

This movement back seems to have started in the volume *Hello* with "So There," dedicated to his third wife, Penelope. The two were not yet married, and the poem was probably written while he was in New Zealand on his reading tour. It speaks of Penelope's rising from bed to look out the window one morning. That simple act is said to give him "a sudden deep, sad / longing, to want / / to stay." This yearning to stay pervades descriptions of past times spent sitting quietly with friends over wine and chicken and the description of another simple meal with Penelope, which he says is "like home." These images are suspended in a quiet and gentleness one reads with relief. This quiet is placed in contrast to his need to continue wearily traveling, as though the world could offer no rest. His sadness is provoked by her looking out the window to the wide sea, which like his "heart's pulled in" as to her breath. Here there is in love a simultaneity of rest and displacement, but the displacement longs for rest. That much is finally, though momentarily, unambivalent.

Creeley, in his association of himself with Odysseus (although he is an Odysseus without an oar to plant), sees his Penelope as the wife of Odysseus, who was the center and resting place set against war and journeying. The name Odysseus stems from the Greek for "wrath," and it may be that identification that Creeley wishes to transcend. In "If I Had My Way," from *Later,*

blurs of discontent would fade,

and there be
old time meadows
with brown and white cows.

This is

     ... the place
     we live in
     day by day, to learn
     love ....

He seems to say here that his greatest desire is to enter the space of a nostalgic past, as though love were the reintegration of the past. It may be. "If I Had My Way" is followed by "Prayer to Hermes," but this nostalgia and love, rather than simply old age, has been powerfully specified as the state to which he is crossing. Love is perhaps identified with surrender, and although Creeley may be ambivalent about surrender to the point of repressing it, it suffuses his poetry with a real sense of calm, and with his ambivalence creates a new tension behind his poems. Perhaps he accepts surrender only if Lancelot bleeds.

Creeley's three volumes *Memory Gardens, Windows* (1988), and *It* (1989), mark yet another phase of his career, one in which he wrote his most satisfying work. In these poems he pushes beyond his early halting, uncertain voice, the fragmentation of his middle period, and the near transparent nostalgia of his work of the early 1980s. The "content" gains a certainty that drives the syllables and syntactic force of the poems forward in a powerful and contained thrust and regains the syncopated beat and interest of his early work without being confused and stymied by it. In "Fathers," from *Memory Gardens,* the short stanzas that had divided his poems are abandoned, and Creeley writes in a sustained voice that pulses through his ambivalence, fear, love, and recovery to an incantatory power unmatched in any of his earlier work:

     in winter then, a ground
     of battered snow crusted
     at the edges under
     it all, there under
     my fathers their

faded women, friends,
the family all echoed,
names trees more tangible
physical place more tangible
the air of this place the road
going past to Watertown
or down to my mother's
grave, my father's grave . . .

It is here that Creeley seems at once to bury and recover his family and their names, allowing himself and them to rest in his native ground. It is also here that he finds the male voice he had been searching for for so long. The poem ends:

. . . his [father's] acerbic
edge cuts the hands to
hold him, hold on, wants
the ground, *wants* this frozen ground.

Remember, in this context, early poems such as "Helas," where he cried out for a hard edge to strike against dullness, and his many poems equating roaring desire and speech with his father. The end of "Fathers" is an amazing embodiment of the voice Creeley has long needed. The haziness he descried in "Still Life Or" is gone, as is the ambivalence of description in the anger sequence from *Words*. He writes in a voice that so clearly "*wants* this frozen ground." He is Lancelot returning home, bleeding in his identification with the "ground / of battered snow," the trees and places "more tangible" than any personal history or psychology. Speaker and that which is spoken of seem nearly fused in a transcendence living on as voice in its own embodiment of print and air and mind, still hung with the ambivalence of living that makes it matter.

As poems such as "Fathers" make evident, Creeley, although he never abandoned older forms of expression, continues to experiment, using new voices as he learns to trust and engage in a fuller emotional life and in further formal variation. Unlike many artists who reach a stride and remain with it, often becoming stale, he seems to diversify, and his work gains in interest with his deepening experience. Rather than becoming old, his voice and command of language mature. In *Windows* and *It* a direct and forceful philosophical statement runs so hard at the heels of its own energy that it seems to spin off into run-on sentences that each breed statements in midarticulation like a superfetating flower that blooms out of another flower rather than its own stem. In "Shadow" (from *It*), he says:

There is a shadow
to intention a place
it comes through and
is itself each stasis
of its mindedness ex-
plicit walled into
semblance it is a
seemingly living place
it wants it fades it
comes and goes it puts
a yellow flower in a pot
in a circle and looks.

In a new voice Creeley forces the language's curve of syntactic energy into constellations of the nominative. It certainly does not halt and backtrack on itself; rather it fuses the things of the world into tight groupings of objects held together more by their own magnetic attraction and the power of Creeley's voice than any apparatus of conventional grammar. Although this voice is evident everywhere, particularly in "Calendar," a collection of twelve small poems about the months of the year, and "Helsinki Window," it is most clearly visible in this section of "If" (all from *Windows*), which is at once comic, lovely, and poignant:

light on facing building up to
faint wash blue up on feet ache
now old toes wornout joints make
the wings of an angel so I'd fly.

Selected Bibliography

WORKS OF ROBERT CREELEY

POETRY

Le Fou. Columbus, Ohio: Golden Goose Press, 1952.

The Immoral Proposition. Illustrated by René Laubies. Karlsruhe-Durlach, Germany: J. Williams, 1953.

The Kind of Act Of. Palma de Mallorca: Divers Press, 1953.

All That Is Lovely in Men. Illustrated by Dan Rice. Asheville, N.C.: J. Williams, 1955.

A Form of Women: Poems. New York: Jargon/Corinth, 1959.

For Love: Poems, 1950–1960. New York: Scribners, 1962.

Words. New York: Scribners, 1967.

The Finger. Illustrated by Bobbie Creeley. Los Angeles, Calif.: Black Sparrow Press, 1968.

The Charm: Early and Uncollected Poems. San Francisco: Four Seasons Foundation, 1969.

Pieces. New York: Scribners, 1969.

1 2 3 4 5 6 7 8 9 0. Illustrated by Arthur Okamura. Berkeley, Calif.: Shambala, 1971.

St. Martin's. Illustrated by Bobbie Creeley. Los Angeles, Calif.: Black Sparrow Press, 1971.

A Day Book. New York: Scribners, 1972.

His Idea. With photographs by Elsa Dorfman. Toronto: Coach House Press, 1973.

Thirty Things. Illustrated by Bobbie Creeley. Los Angeles, Calif.: Black Sparrow Press, 1974.

Backwards. Knotting, England: Sceptre, 1975.

Away. Santa Barbara, Calif.: Black Sparrow Press, 1976.

Hello. New York: New Directions, 1978.

Later. New York: New Directions, 1979.

The Collected Poems of Robert Creeley, 1945–1975. Berkeley: University of California Press, 1982.

Echoes. West Branch, Iowa: Toothpaste Press, 1982.

Mirrors. New York: New Directions, 1983.

Memory Gardens. New York: New Directions, 1986.

Windows. New York: New Directions, 1988.

It: Francesco Clemente / 64 Pastels, Robert Creeley / 12 Poems. Zurich: Edition Gallery Bruno Bischofberger, 1989.

Selected Poems. Berkeley: University of California Press, 1991.

NOVEL

The Island. New York: Scribners, 1963.

SHORT STORIES

The Gold Diggers. Palma de Mallorca: Divers Press, 1954.

The Gold Diggers and Other Stories. New York: Scribners, 1965.

Mabel: A Story and Other Prose. London: Marion Boyars, 1976.

ESSAYS

A Quick Graph: Collected Notes and Essays. Edited by Donald Allen. San Francisco: Four Seasons Foundation, 1970.

Presences: A Text for Marisol. With 61 photographs of the sculptures of Marisol. New York: Scribners, 1976.

Was That a Real Poem and Other Essays. Edited by Donald Allen. Bolinas, Calif.: Four Seasons Foundation, 1979.

The Collected Essays of Robert Creeley. Berkeley: University of California Press, 1989.

RADIO PLAY

Listen. Illustrated by Bobbie Creeley. Santa Barbara, Calif.: Black Sparrow, 1972.

AUTOBIOGRAPHY

Autobiography. New York: Hanuman, 1991.

CORRESPONDENCE

Charles Olson and Robert Creeley: The Complete Correspondence. Edited by George Butterick. 9 vols. Santa Barbara, Calif.: Black Sparrow Press, 1980–1989.

Irving Layton and Robert Creeley: The Complete Correspondence, 1953–1978. Edited by Ekbert Faas and Sabrina Reed. Montreal and Kingston: McGill-Queen's University Press, 1989.

COLLECTED WORKS

A Sense of Measure. London: Calder & Boyars, 1972.

The Collected Prose of Robert Creeley. London and New York: Marion Boyars, 1984. Berkeley: University of California Press, 1987.

BIBLIOGRAPHIES

Murray, Timothy, and Stephen Boardway. "A Year-by-Year Bibliography of Robert Creeley." In *Robert Creeley: The Poet's Workshop*. Edited by Carroll Terrell. Orono: National Poetry Foundation, University of Maine, 1984.

Novik, Mary. *Robert Creeley: An Inventory, 1945–1970*. Kent, Ohio: Kent State University Press, 1973.

Prestianni, Vincent. "Robert Creeley: An Analytic Bibliography of Bibliographies." *Sagetrieb*, 10, no. 1–2:209–213 (1991).

BIOGRAPHICAL AND CRITICAL STUDIES

Allen, Donald, ed. *The New American Poetry: 1945–1960*. New York: Grove Press, 1960.

Allen, Donald, and Warren Tallman, eds. *The Poetics of the New American Poetry*. New York: Grove Press, 1973.

Altieri, Charles. "The Unsure Egoist: Robert Creeley and the Theme of Nothingness." *Contemporary Literature*, 13:162–185 (1972).

Bacon, Terry. "Closure in Robert Creeley's Poetry." *Modern Poetry Studies*, 8:227–247 (1977).

Cameron, Allen. " 'Love Comes Quietly': The Poetry of Robert Creeley." *Chicago Review*, 19, no. 2:92–103 (1967).

Clark, Tom. *Robert Creeley and the Genius of the American Common Place*. New York: New Directions, 1993.

Conniff, Brian. *The Lyric and Modern Poetry: Olson, Creeley, Bunting*. New York: Peter Lang, 1988.

Duberman, Martin. *Black Mountain: An Exploration in Community*. New York: Norton, 1993.

Edelberg, Cynthia Dubin. *Robert Creeley's Poetry: A Critical Introduction*. Albuquerque: University of New Mexico Press, 1978.

Ford, Arthur. *Robert Creeley*. Boston: Twayne, 1978.

Fox, Willard. *Robert Creeley, Edward Dorn, and Robert Duncan: A Reference Guide*. Boston: G. K. Hall, 1988.

Fredman, Stephen. *Poet's Prose: The Crisis in American. Verse*. Cambridge: Cambridge University Press, 1983.

Hammond, John. "Solipsism and the Sexual Imagination in Robert Creeley's Fiction." *Critique: Studies in Modern Fiction*, 16, no. 3:59–69 (1975).

Hatlen, Bruce, ed. *Special Issue: Robert Creeley*. *Sagetrieb*, 1, no. 3:15–200 (1982). Includes, in addition to the Sheppard interview listed below, Michael McClure, "These Decades Are Echoes" (15–18), Harald Mesch, "Robert Creeley's Epistemological Path" (57–85), Charles Bernstein, "Hearing 'Here': Robert Creeley's Poetics of Duration" (87–95), Jerry McGuire, "No Boundaries: Robert Creeley As Post-Modern Man" (97–118), George Butterick, "Robert Creeley and the Tradition" (119–134), Albert Cook, "The Construct of Image" (135–139), Cynthia Dubin Edelberg, "Creeley's Orphan Lines: The Rhythmic Character of the Sequences" (143–162), Jed Rasula, "Placing Pieces" (163–169), Michael Heller, "A Note on Words: To Break with Insistence" (171–174), Linda Wagner, " 'Oh, Pioneers!': One Sense of Creeley's 'Place' " (175–181), Timothy Murray, "The Robert Creeley Collection at Washington University, St. Louis, Missouri" (191–200).

Keller, Lynn. "Lessons from William Carlos Williams: Robert Creeley's Early Poetry." *Modern Language Quarterly*, 43:369–394 (December 1982).

Oberg, Arthur. *Modern American Lyric: Lowell, Berryman, Creeley, and Plath*. New Brunswick, N.J.: Rutgers University Press, 1978.

Olson, Charles. "Projective Verse." In his *Selected Writings*. Edited by Robert Creeley. New York: New Directions, 1966.

Paul, Sherman. *The Lost America of Love: Rereading Robert Creeley, Edward Dorn, and Robert Duncan*. Baton Rouge: Louisiana State University Press, 1981.

Scalapino, Leslie. " 'Thinking Serially' in *For Love, Words*, and *Pieces*." *Talisman*, 8:42–48 (Spring 1992).

Sheffler, Ronald. *The Development of Robert Creeley's Poetry*. Amherst: University of Massachusetts Press, 1971.

Smith, Leverett. "Robert Creeley: 'A So-Called Larger View.' " *Sagetrieb*, 7, no. 2:53–68 (1988).

Spanos, William, ed. *Robert Creeley: A Gathering*. *Boundary 2*, 6, nos. 3–7 (1978). Includes, in addition to the Spanos interview listed below, George Butterick, "Creeley and Olson: The Beginning" (129–134), Michael Rumaker, "Robert Creeley at Black Mountain" (137–170), Paul Mariani, " 'Fire

of a Very Real Order': Creeley and Williams''
(173–190), William Sylvester, "Robert Creeley's
Poetics: I Know That I Hear You" (193–210),
Robert Kern, "Composition as Recognition: Robert Creeley and Postmodern Poetics" (211–230),
Robert Duncan, "After *For Love*" (233–239),
Kenneth Cox, "Address and Posture in the Early
Poetry of Robert Creeley" (241–246), Samuel
Moon, "The Springs of Action: A Psychological
Portrait of Robert Creeley (Part I: The Whip)"
(247–262), Cynthia Dubin Edelberg, "Robert
Creeley's *Words:* The Comedy of the Intellect"
(265–291), Robert Duncan, "A Reading of *Thirty
Things*" (293–299), Linda Wagner, "Robert Creeley's Late Poems: Contexts" (301–308), John Vernon, "The City of Its Occasion: Robert Creeley"
(309–327), Peter Quartermain, "Robert Creeley:
What Counts" (329–334), Paul Diehl, "The Literal Activity of Robert Creeley" (335–346),
William Navero, "Robert Creeley: Close. In the
Mind. Some Times. Some What" (347–352), Albert Cook, "Reflections on Creeley" (353–362),
Robert von Hallberg, "Robert Creeley and the Pleasures of System" (365–379), Sherman Paul, "Rereading Creeley" (381–418), Robert Grenier, "A
Packet for Robert Creeley" (421–441), Allen Ginsberg, "On Creeley's Ear Mind" (443–444), Edward Dorn, "Of Robert Creeley" (447–448), Tom
Clark, " 'Desperate Perhaps, and Even Foolish— /
—But God Knows Useful': Creeley and the Experience of Space" (453–456), Duncan McNaughton,
"Bullshitting about Creeley" (457–459), Warren
Tallman, "Haw: A Dream for Robert Creeley"
(461–464), Nathaniel Mackey, "*The Gold Diggers:* Projective Prose" (469–487), Marjorie Perloff, "Four Times Five: Robert Creeley's *The
Island*" (491–507), Charles Altieri, "Placing Creeley's Recent Work: A Poetics of Conjecture"
(513–539), Michael Davidson, "The Presence of
the Present: Morality and the Problem of Value in
Robert Creeley's Recent Prose" (545–564).

Terrell, Carroll, ed. *Robert Creeley: The Poet's Workshop.* Orono: National Poetry Foundation, University of Maine, 1984.

Wilson, John, ed. *Robert Creeley's Life and Work: A Sense of Increment.* Ann Arbor: University of Michigan Press, 1988.

INTERVIEWS

Allen, Donald, ed. *Contexts of Poetry: Interviews, 1961–1971.* Bolinas, Calif.: Four Seasons Foundation, 1973.

Bacon, Terry. "How He Knows How to Stop: Creeley on Closure." *American Poetry Review,* 5, no. 6:5–7 (1976).

"Craft Interview with Robert Creeley." *New York Quarterly,* 13:18–47 (1973).

Creeley, Robert. *Tales out of School: Selected Interviews.* Ann Arbor: University of Michigan Press, 1993.

Creeley, Robert, and Susan Howe. "Four-Part Harmony: Robert Creeley and Susan Howe Talk It Out." *Village Voice Literary Supplement,* 124:21–22 (April 1994).

Elliot, David. "An Interview with Robert Creeley." *Sagetrieb,* 10:45–65 (1991).

Faas, Ekbert. Interview. In *Towards a New American Poetics: Essays and Interviews.* Santa Barbara, Calif.: Black Sparrow Press, 1978.

Milner, Philip. "Interview with Robert Creeley." *Antigonish Review,* 26:36–47 (1976).

Sheppard, Robert. "Stories: Being an Information. An Interview." *Sagetrieb,* 1:35–56 (1982).

Spanos, William. "Talking with Robert Creeley." *Boundary 2,* 6, nos. 3–7:13–74 (1978).

—BILL PIPER

Countee Cullen

1903–1946

"*I* KNOW, IN any case, that the most crucial time in my own development,'' wrote James Baldwin in *Notes of a Native Son* (1955),

> came when I was forced to recognize that I was a kind of bastard of the West . . . I brought to Shakespeare, Bach, Rembrandt, to the stones of Paris, to the cathedral at Chartres, and to the Empire State Building, a special attitude. These were not really my creations, they did not contain my history . . . I was an interloper; this was not my heritage. At the same time I had no other heritage which I could possibly hope to use—I had certainly been unfitted for the jungle or the tribe. I would have to appropriate these white centuries, I would have to make them mine.

It is fitting that Countee Cullen's former student should so compellingly describe Cullen's own situation. As adopted sons of fundamentalist ministers, former students at DeWitt Clinton High School, former editors of the school's literary magazine, homosexuals, and renowned black literary men attracted to Europe and European cultures, Baldwin and Cullen had a great deal in common. As African American artists, they were equally sensitive to being surrounded by the symbols and ideas of an alien, even hostile, culture that they had no hand in building but could not abandon. Baldwin's repeated use of the word ''heritage'' may bring to mind the title of what is

arguably Cullen's most famous poem, in which he grapples with the idea of being a product of the dominant religion of the West—Christianity:

> Quaint, outlandish heathen gods
> Black men fashion out of rods,
> Clay, and brittle bits of stone,
> In a likeness like their own,
> My conversion came high-priced;
> I belong to Jesus Christ,
> Preacher of humility;
> Heathen gods are naught to me.

Unlike Baldwin, who considered himself as having only one viable heritage, Cullen underwent a ''conversion'' at no small cost. Moreover, in wishing that he might have a god more immediately in his own image, Cullen expresses a divided perspective:

> Father, Son, and Holy Ghost,
> So I make an idle boast;
> Jesus of the twice-turned cheek,
> Lamb of God, although I speak
> With my mouth thus, in my heart
> Do I play a double part.
> Ever at Thy glowing altar
> Must my heart grow sick and falter,
> Wishing He I served were black,
> Thinking then it would not lack
> Precedent of pain to guide it,
> Let who would or might deride it;
> . . . .
> Lord, I fashion dark gods, too.

Cullen's mention of "play[ing] a double part" echoes the famous quotation from W. E. B. Du Bois's *The Souls of Black Folk,* the African American intellectual book most admired by blacks since its publication in 1903: "One ever feels his twoness,—an American, a Negro; two souls, two thoughts, two unreconciled strivings; two warring ideals in one dark body . . . The history of the American Negro is the history of this strife." Cullen, however, suggests something like playacting, a kind of deception, as the narrator pretends an allegiance to something for which he does not honestly have feelings. But the narrator also seems to wonder whether he can actually possess the African-ness that he feels is locked within his soul and his imagination. For Cullen, the history of African American intellectuals (and the narrator of the poem is clearly an intellectual or artistic figure) is the history of a certain type of identity strife that can only be ended through an act of the imagination, through the imaging of a romanticized Africa, through an act of sheer will that will not bring them back to the past but only help them to understand the complexity of their present and their presence in the Western world. "Heritage" is a poem, in effect, about what it costs a black person to be Western and Christian.

The matter of the African-ness (or folk essence) of the black American was much the concern of many of the literary figures of the Harlem Renaissance, the first significant and self-conscious flowering of African American literature and, more important, literary aspiration and ambition. This renaissance took place during the extraordinary period of the 1920s, which saw the urbanization and modernization of African American life and culture. Central to the Harlem Renaissance are several writers whose works are now essential to the American literary canon. Poet, novelist, translator, and journalist Langston Hughes; novelist, anthropologist, and playwright Zora Neale Hurston; and novelist, anthologist,

historian, poet, and elder statesman James Weldon Johnson come to mind immediately as major figures associated with the era. Jamaican novelist and poet Claude McKay stands, perhaps, only slightly below Hughes, Hurston, and Johnson. Jean Toomer published in 1923 what is doubtlessly the era's most distinguished novel, *Cane.* There were others—such as novelists Wallace Thurman, Nella Larsen, and Jessie Fauset, and poet Georgia Douglas Johnson—who at various times in the 1920s were touted as rising talents.

But in 1925, Countee Cullen, at the age of twenty-two, was the most celebrated and probably the most famous black writer in America. Headlines such as "Countee Cullen, Young Negro Poet Aids Understanding of His Race," " 'Black Pan' Sings Again," "A Young Poet of Death and African Beauty," "Harvard Negro Poet Wins Another Prize," and "A Negro Shropshire Lad" were common both in the black and white press. The 1924 publication of his poem "The Shroud of Color" in H. L. Mencken's *American Mercury* was the talk of the intellectual and artistic black community. Few books by a black writer were more eagerly anticipated by the white and black public than Cullen's first collection of poems, *Color,* in 1925. Few writers had won as many literary prizes at such a young age as Cullen. He was, indeed, a boy wonder, an Ariel, as black literary critic J. Saunders Reddings called him. In the early and mid-1920s, Cullen embodied many of the hopes, aspirations, and maturing expressive possibilities of his people. It was once a commonplace for all educated black people to have memorized lines from Countee Cullen's work or even whole works themselves. They knew passages such as this one from "Heritage":

What is Africa to me:
Copper sun or scarlet sea,
Jungle star or jungle track,
Strong bronzed men, or regal black
Women from whose loins I sprang
When the birds of Eden sang?

One three centuries removed
From the scenes his fathers loved,
Spicy grove, cinnamon tree,
What is Africa to me?

Or this closing couplet from "Yet Do I Marvel":

Yet do I marvel at this curious thing:
To make a poet black, and bid him sing!

Or "Incident":

Once riding in old Baltimore,
Heart-filled, head-filled with glee,
I saw a Baltimorean
Keep looking straight at me.

Now I was eight and very small,
And he was no whit bigger,
And so I smiled, but he poked out
His tongue, and called me, "Nigger."

I saw the whole of Baltimore
From May until December;
Of all the things that happened there
That's all that I remember.

As the late African American literary critic Darwin Turner pointed out, Countee Cullen was "poet laureate of the Harlem Renaissance . . . the most popular Afro-American writer since Paul Laurence Dunbar." It has thus always remained a question: why was Cullen unable to maintain his promising start? Why did his career falter? What happened to this extraordinarily gifted young man? Part of the problem with understanding Cullen's reputation may be that he became in the cultural eye a mere schoolhouse poet, a writer who is regarded not in a holistic manner as a living artist but as a remote figure in a mist—like Henry Wadsworth Longfellow, Sidney Lanier, William Cullen Bryant, or even A. E. Housman (a major influence on Cullen)—whom one knows through a few overly familiar works disembodied from a corpus. It is difficult for many readers today to understand Cullen as a working poet and even more difficult to understand the shape and nature of his literary ambition. An additional burden for the reader is Cullen's penchant for strict metrical forms such as the ballad, the Spenserian stanza, and the Shakespearean and Petrarchan sonnets, forms that occasionally seem inadequate to his thematic needs. His lack of innovation in the use of these forms make certain poems seem either too facile, a bit strained, or wooden. This burden has been particularly detrimental to his reputation as black poetry became more associated with black folk, oral, and musical expression; with free verse; and with performance art.

Yet there are two important reasons to revisit Cullen's career. First, he deserves greater critical favor as a poet than has been bestowed upon him for he did, indeed, produce some first-rank work. Second, an accounting for his intense popularity during the Harlem Renaissance would reveal much about both African American letters and the place of the black writer in America.

"There is not much to say about these earlier years of Cullen," wrote James Weldon Johnson about the younger poet in his *Book of American Negro Poetry* (1922), "unless he himself should say it." Cullen never chose to write about this time in his life, at least not directly. (French critic Jean Wagner sees this silence as indicative of an inferiority complex concerning his origins.) Perhaps Countee Cullen has never been fully understood as a poet or a writer because he has never been understood fully as a man. There is, and always has been, a quality of unknown that surrounds Cullen, a quality that is not better symbolized than by the official, but varied, accounts of his height. His passports of both 1934 and 1938 give his height as five feet, three inches; his selective service registrant card of 1942 lists him as five feet and ten inches; and his war ration book number 3, issued when Cullen was forty years old, gives his height as five feet, seven inches. He was either very short or about the stature of the average man—a striking difference.

Although we know that Cullen was born on May 30, 1903, we still do not know where. In James W. Tuttleton's extremely useful essay "Countee Cullen at 'The Heights,' " which provides a detailed account of Cullen's undergraduate years at New York University, we learn that Cullen's college transcript of 1922, for which he himself provided the information, lists his place of birth as Louisville, Kentucky. However, at one point in Cullen's self-invention, during the most intense phase of his public career, he wanted to be associated with New York City, perhaps as some sort of Mecca. In his *Caroling Dusk: An Anthology of Verse by Negro Poets* (1927), Cullen wrote in the biographical headnote to his selection of his own poetry that he was born in New York City. This anthology appeared three years after the publication of "The Shroud of Color" in the *American Mercury,* two years after the critically and commercially successful publication of his first book of poems, *Color,* and two years after having won first prize in the Witter Bynner Poetry contest, *Poetry* magazine's John Reed Memorial Prize for "Threnody for a Brown Girl," the Amy Spingarn Award of *The Crisis* magazine for "Two Moods of Love," second prize in *Opportunity* magazine's first poetry contest for "To One Who Said Me Nay," election to Phi Beta Kappa, and second prize in the poetry contest of *Palms* for "Wisdom Cometh with the Years." Cullen was to state publicly for the rest of his life that New York City was his place of birth; it is listed as such in his 1928 French identity card, in James Weldon Johnson's headnote about Cullen in the 1931 edition of *The Book of American Negro Poetry,* and in his 1934 and 1938 passports. Around the time of Cullen's death, stories began to circulate that he was born in Baltimore. But there is little evidence for this except, one supposes, the famous Cullen poem "Incident," which uses Baltimore as a setting, and the fact that Cullen's foster father grew up in Baltimore.

And what are we to make of Cullen's assertion in *Caroling Dusk* that he was "reared in the conservative atmosphere of a Methodist parsonage"? The implication here is that his adoptive parents, the Reverend Dr. Frederick A. and Carolyn Belle (Mitchell) Cullen of the Salem Methodist Episcopal Church in Harlem, were, in fact, his real parents. But according to scholars Cullen was not adopted until either 1914 or 1918, when he was already either eleven or fifteen years old. (There are no records to confirm either date.) Complicating matters is the claim by Harold Jackman, Cullen's closest friend, that the adoption of Cullen was never made official. As of 1995, we do not know where Countee Cullen was born; we do not know who his natural parents were; and we do not know exactly when he was adopted or when he started living with the Reverend and Mrs. Cullen. We do know that he went by the name of Countee L. Porter until he entered high school and began publishing poetry. He then became Countee P. Cullen. By 1925, he was simply Countee Cullen.

Ample evidence exists that Cullen enjoyed a close relationship with his foster parents, who may well have inspired his intense Christian consciousness. He was, by all accounts, a dutiful son, loving and devoted. The Shakespearean sonnet "Tribute (To My Mother)," which appeared in *The Black Christ and Other Poems* (1929) and was written while Cullen was in France on a Guggenheim fellowship in 1928 and 1929, suggests the influence of his mother's morality:

Because man is not virtuous in himself,
Not kind, nor given to sweet charities,
Save goaded by the little kindling elf
Of some dear face it pleasures him to please;
Some men who else were humbled to the dust,
Have marveled that the chastening hand should
     stay,
And never dreamed they held their lives in trust
To one the victor loved a world away.

Carolyn Cullen was, for many years, a leading soprano in her husband's church choir. Cullen, who loved music and who apparently loved his mother's singing, heard her every week for many years. Also, he probably heard some of the choir rehearsals and his mother singing around the house. She was an able pianist as well. Cullen always saw his poetry as singing, as music, and we might say that his mother exercised some influence over him in his becoming a poet, providing at least significant inspiration.

But it was apparently with his foster father that the poet enjoyed his closest relationship. Cullen wrote three poems for his father during the course of his career: "Dad" first appeared in *The Magpie* in 1922; "Fruit of the Flower" (which also contains stanzas about his mother) was first published in *Harper's* in 1924 and included in *Color*; and "Lines for My Father" appeared in *Copper Sun*, Cullen's second collection of poetry (1927). Dr. Cullen certainly deserved admiration for his accomplishments. Born and reared in dire poverty, he attended the State Normal School in Baltimore and completed college and theological studies at Morgan State College in Baltimore. He was called to the ministry and became a Methodist pastor. He was later granted an honorary degree from Gammon Theological Seminary in Atlanta, Georgia. He arrived in New York City in 1902 after having spent two years pastoring small churches in the Baltimore area. He was assigned to the Salem Methodist Episcopal Church, then a storefront mission. By the mid-1920s, the church could boast a membership of over twenty-five hundred members; a large educational program that included subjects such as French, Latin, typewriting, shorthand, and math; five large choirs and a full orchestra; and a highly competitive youth athletic club that included a particularly notable amateur boxing program of which Dr. Cullen seemed quite proud. (The great Sugar Ray Robinson learned how to box during the Depression at Dr. Cullen's church.) Countee Cullen's father was active in the National Association for the Advancement of Colored People

(NAACP) all his life and served for many years as president of the Harlem branch.

As an orphan, Cullen probably felt as much gratitude as respect for his foster father. Yet there must have been some tension between the two men; the father was a strict fundamentalist, whereas Cullen experienced intellectual doubts and often expressed a kind of ongoing quarrel with Christianity in many of his poems. In terms of behavior, Cullen, even as an adult, would keep secret from his father his occasional episodes of wild carousing, of drinking, dancing, and gambling. According to Jean Wagner, Cullen's father was homosexual or had homosexual tendencies and some pronounced homosexual mannerisms. (He and his wife never had children of their own.) What sort of tension or shame this may have been for Cullen is unclear. It is difficult to say whether the father's homosexuality influenced the son's. It is equally difficult to say whether the father's apparent homosexuality was a source of tension for the father himself or the son in seeing these tendencies in himself and not wishing to be a hypocrite, simply because fundamentalist Christians vehemently condemn homosexuality.

If excelling in school is a way for a child, particularly an orphan, to win a parent's favor, then surely Cullen played the role of an overachiever to his best advantage. On February 4, 1918, he enrolled in DeWitt Clinton High School, a highly regarded boys' school that was almost exclusively white. (Considering the racial composition of the student body, it is ironic that it was while Cullen was at DeWitt Clinton that he made the most important and enduring friendship of his life, with a handsome West Indian boy named Harold Jackman—to whom he would eventually dedicate a number of his works and give his handwritten copy of *The Ballad of the Brown Girl* as a Christmas gift in 1923, with whom he would travel to Europe several times in the 1930s, and to whom he would leave a good portion of his papers when he died.) Cullen was an active student, serving as vice president of the senior class, associate editor of the 1921 *Magpie* (the school's literary magazine), and editor of the *Clinton News*. He also won the Douglas Fairbanks Oratorical Contest and the Magpie Cup. It was in high school that Cullen received significant recognition as a poet by winning first prize in a citywide poetry contest sponsored by the Empire Federation of Women's Clubs. His winning entry was titled ''I Have a Rendezvous with Life.'' This acclaim had many people talking about Cullen as having a future as a major poet. One may argue that it was this initial success by Cullen and not the September 1923 publication of Jean Toomer's *Cane* that really kicked off the Harlem Renaissance; for if anyone was being groomed, being intellectually and culturally conditioned and bred to be a major black crossover literary figure in the culturally elite form of literature, lyric poetry, it was this thin, shy black boy.

Cullen forged his style as a poet at New York University, which he attended on a New York State Regents Scholarship from 1922 to 1925. As James W. Tuttleton informs us, he took ''courses in introductory English, French, Latin (always with *cum laude* grades), math, physics, geology, philosophy, Greek, [and] physical science'' while writing most of the poems for which he would become famous when they appeared in *Color* and *Copper Sun*. Cullen took most of his English courses with Hyder E. Rollins, who wrote several treatises on the ballad during Cullen's stay at NYU. He also fell in love with Keats at this time, a love that would lead him to become a leading Keats scholar. That Rollins was a big influence on Cullen's development, as Tuttleton argues, can scarcely be gainsaid: Cullen wrote his undergraduate thesis on Edna St. Vincent Millay for him and asked him to write in support of his (successful) 1928 application for a Guggenheim Fellowship. ''Is it any wonder,

then,'' writes Tuttleton, ''that Cullen's first three volumes, *Color* (1925), *Copper Sun* (1927), and *The Ballad of the Brown Girl* (1927), are full of ballad settings, characters, and stylistic features?'' It is also no wonder that the first two books show the strong influences of Keats and Millay. Many of the poems Cullen wrote as an undergraduate appeared in the university literary magazine, *The Arch,* including three major poems: ''Spirit Birth,'' which became ''The Shroud of Color,'' ''The Ballad of the Brown Girl,'' and ''Heritage.'' Cullen generally was very highly regarded and apparently well-liked by other undergraduates. When *Color* was published in Cullen's senior year, he was heartily congratulated by both faculty and students, including a handwritten note of appreciation from the chancellor.

Cullen went to Harvard after graduating Phi Beta Kappa from NYU. It seemed the proper place to bring one phase of his education to an end. He received his master of arts from Harvard in 1926 and, in December of that year, began to write a column titled ''The Dark Tower'' for *Opportunity,* the magazine the National Urban League had started just a few years earlier.

Cullen stamped the 1920s as much as anyone else did, although he had neither the personality nor the vision to be a leader of either a political movement or a literary school. The title of his column, ''The Dark Tower,'' became the name of the literary salon that A'Lelia Walker, daughter of Madame C. J. Walker and heiress of the Walker ''beauty culture'' fortune, started in 1928 in her fashionable townhouse at 108 West 136th Street in Harlem. It was the place for the black intelligentsia and slumming whites who sought something exotic; on the walls one could read Cullen's poetry and the poetry of Langston Hughes. In the era of black nationalist Marcus Garvey, Cullen, in his poem ''Heritage,'' posed the central question, *''What is Africa to me?''* (Cullen himself was fascinated by Garvey, and surely the popularization of the imaginative quest for a homeland and an African essence was partly the result of Cullen transferring his personal state of orphanhood and adoption to the race as a whole.) And in his "Yet Do I Marvel" he produced, according to James Weldon Johnson in *Black Manhattan* (1930), "the two most poignant lines in American literature": "Yet do I marvel at this curious thing: / To make a poet black, and bid him sing!"

Countee Cullen expressed his credo, in part, when he spoke with Margaret Sperry in 1924:

> If I am going to be a poet at all, I am going to be POET and not NEGRO POET. That is what has hindered the development of artists among us. Their one note has been the concern with their race. That is all very well, none of us can get away from it. I cannot at times. You will see it in my verse. The consciousness of this is too poignant at times. I cannot escape it. But what I mean is this: I shall not write of negro subjects for the purpose of propaganda. That is not what a poet is concerned with. Of course, when the emotion rising out of the fact that I am a negro is strong, I express it. But that is another matter.

Cullen further elaborates his credo in his *Caroling Dusk:*

> I have called this collection an anthology of verse by Negro poets rather than an anthology of Negro verse, since this latter designation would be more confusing than accurate. Negro poetry, it seems to me, in the sense that we speak of Russian, French, or Chinese poetry, must emanate from some country other than this in some language other than our own. Moreover, the attempt to corral the outbursts of the ebony muse into some definite mold to which all poetry by Negroes will conform seems altogether futile and aside from the facts. This country's Negro writers may here and there turn some singular facet toward the literary sun, but in the main, since theirs is also the heritage of the English language, their work will not present any serious aberration from the poetic tendencies of their times. The conservatives, the middlers, and the arch heretics will be found among them as among the white poets; and to say that the pulse beat of their verse shows generally such a fever, or

the symptoms of such an ague, will prove on closer examination merely the moment's exaggeration of a physician anxious to establish a new literary ailment. As heretical as it may sound, there is the probability that Negro poets, dependent as they are on the English language, may have more to gain from the rich background of English and American poetry than from any nebulous atavistic yearnings toward an African inheritance. Some of the poets herein represented will eventually find inclusion in any discriminatingly ordered anthology of American verse, and there will be no reason for giving such selections the needless distinction of a separate section marked Negro verse.

The totality of Cullen's position was criticized by Langston Hughes in his famous essay "The Negro Artist and the Racial Mountain," published in the *Nation* on June 23, 1926. Hughes, indeed, espoused a position directly opposed to Cullen's as he fashioned a more openly social and political poetry based on jazz and blues motives and black vernacular. Deeply influenced by Walt Whitman and Carl Sandberg, Hughes concerned himself with the Negro's creative formulation of an American nationalism. Hughes's approach became far more influential in African American poetry than did Cullen's more generalist approach (witness the work of the Black Arts Movement poets Amiri Baraka, Ted Joans, Sterling Brown, and Robert Hayden or Rap musicians). Both Hughes and Cullen would agree that black poets should be allowed to be whatever they wish and write whatever they choose. It was on the question of literary heritage that the two men differed.

Oddly, despite Cullen's insistence on being free from a racial burden or racial expectation as a poet, a significant portion of his poetry deals with racial themes. Indeed, the poems for which he is most remembered are arguably his most explicitly racial works. Moreover, his reworking of historical material, such as *The Ballad of the Brown Girl* and *The Medea,* was often to make a nonracial work blatantly (and sometimes, as in the case of *The Ballad of the Brown Girl,* mistakenly) racial. Yet his assimilationist position and high status worked against a just appreciation of his merits. He was the exemplar of the New Negro artist (the original name for the Harlem Renaissance was the New Negro Movement, and probably the most crucial publication of the era was Alain Locke's 1925 anthology, *The New Negro: An Interpretation*)—the black poet who had mastered white forms and was, indeed, a literary figure respected by whites. This was of great importance to the black audience of the Harlem Renaissance, indicating a preoccupation with bourgeois respectability and an aspiration that African American cultural inventions would find their fullest expressions in some sort of blend with white literary forms and traditions. Cullen's reputation has never recovered from the charge of inauthenticity that subsequent generations have directed at such preoccupations and aspirations.

Countee Cullen established his credentials as the Renaissance's leading man of letters in three ways. He certified his poetic knowledge and abilities by going to and graduating from white schools (DeWitt Clinton High, New York University, and Harvard). This meant that he had legitimate training, something virtually no black poet had had before. (Dunbar, the race's greatest poet before the Harlem Renaissance, had only finished high school.) Next, he put together an anthology, which was an assertion of authority about a black literary canon and a black poetic tradition. Finally, and most important, he became a rigorous critic. The preface to his anthology was simply one of a long line of critical pronouncements. Other examples include his ''Dark Tower'' columns, which ran fairly regularly through 1927 and 1928.

Cullen solidified his position as a leading social light of the Harlem Renaissance by marrying the daughter of W. E. B. Du Bois, Nina Yolande, on April 9, 1928, in his foster father's church.

The wedding of the leading literary figure of the New Negro Movement to the only child of the leading old-guard black intellectual was the biggest social event of the era. The entire world of the Talented Tenth, the black bourgeois elite for whom Cullen represented so much, was there; it was a showcase of the New Negro.

The publication of *The Black Christ and Other Poems* in 1929, however, was the last fruit of Countee Cullen's career in the limelight. In the thirties, Cullen was to experience life differently, no longer the black literary wonder boy. His marriage ended in 1930: Cullen's homosexuality, a clash of decidedly different temperaments and interests, and Yolande's sexual interest in a leading jazz musician, all contributed to the marriage's swift end. Cullen's novel, *One Way to Heaven,* was not reviewed by either *The Crisis* or *Opportunity.* It was a critical failure. By the end of the decade, he was attacked by the black literary establishment, which had once so staunchly supported him, on the very tenets of his own critical creed; his play written with Arna Bontemps, *St. Louis Woman,* was thought to be degrading to blacks. His literary output decreased from 1930 to the end of his life in 1946. Many have speculated on Cullen's reduced output. Some reasons may have been writer's block, lack of inspiration, or sheer laziness, but one reason must have been that after 1929, when Cullen's Guggenheim Fellowship ended, his public school teaching cut into the time he had to write. Perhaps he no longer wanted a career as a writer or no longer so fervently desired a career as a lyric poet.

A serious evaluation of Cullen's major poetry must recognize two related themes: race and Christianity. His ''chief problem has been that of reconciling a Christian upbringing with a pagan inclination,'' to use his own words; this dilemma became his pose. Poems such as ''Heritage,'' ''The Black Christ,'' ''The Shroud of Color,'' ''The Litany of the Dark People,'' and ''Pagan Prayer'' are the product of a writer who cannot reconcile his blackness, which he refers to as his paganism, and his Christianity. What Cullen finds attractive as a writer is the basic ambiguity that exists in the meaning of his being a black Christian. That ambiguity results from the historical link between the blacks' political freedom and God's religious salvation, a kind of uneasy meshing of the sacred and secular. These poems also reflect Cullen's concern with the identification of the Negro's humanity in terms of tragic suffering. His greatest religious poems—"The Litany of the Dark People," "The Shroud of Color," "The Black Christ"—describe what it means to be entrapped by the myth of victimization.

Cullen's ideological stance is anything but simple and straightforward. In "Heritage," for example, he uses the phrase "So I lie" five times. It seems there is a great deal of lying going on in the poem, not only lying as in the sense of reposing but also lying in the sense of dishonesty and duplicity. (Several other works evince a preoccupation with the theme of deception. This may reflect his own duplicity about his homosexuality.) Some readers have criticized "Heritage" for not offering more realistic images of Africa, decrying Cullen's ignorance—the "cinnamon tree" is not native to Africa, for instance, and lines such as the following provide hackneyed images that make Africa seem a Garden of Eden out of Jean-Jacques Rousseau:

> Cooper sun or scarlet sea,
> Jungle star or jungle track,
> Strong bronzed men, or regal black
> Women from whose loins I sprang
> . . . .
> ... the song
> Sung by wild barbaric birds
> Goading massive jungle herds,
> Juggernauts of flesh that pass
> Trampling tall defiant grass

These images of Africa may thus be seen as one way in which the narrator is lying. What indeed is Africa supposed to mean? Is the poem about the inability of the African American mind to conjure up a usable Africa (and, thus, a usable past)? The poem deals with the black narrator's own Trinity—Body ("the dark blood dammed within"—the word "dammed" of course is a pun), Mind ("Africa? A book one thumbs / Listlessly, till slumber comes"), and Heart / spirit ("Lord, forgive me if my need / Sometimes shapes a human creed")—which has been thoroughly "civilized" or acculturated, trapped in an impotence of language and reflection derived from European influences.

In typical Romantic terms, Cullen is not simply concerned with the perfectibility of the black Christian; he also focuses on the perfectibility of the black Christian's God. His most profound long poem, "The Black Christ," investigates contradictions in the Christ figure. As Jean Wagner writes:

> This contradiction within the Christ symbol enables us to penetrate more deeply, down to the level at which Cullen's racial consciousness and his conscience are closely intertwined. While meditating on the factors that oppose the two hostile races, he once more came upon the same irreconcilable elements that also divided the individual against himself and against God.

"The Black Christ" is the only Cullen poem that is centrally concerned with conversion. In fact, the poem is about the politicization of conversion, for in the poem Cullen wishes to reverse the tradition of liberal Christian redemption. Evil is removed from the providential history of the self and deposited into the providential history of mankind. What the atheistic narrator of the poem demands is recognition from God that blacks do indeed exist in his sight. The recognition comes in the form of a miracle—the resurrection of his lynched brother, Jim. And it is this resurrection that makes Jim the black Christ, not simply the fact that he is lynched. Indeed, in reworking the entire Christ idea, Cullen totally politicized or made the political significance of Christ for a black believer completely *explicit and intelligible.*

Jim, a militant, handsome black boy, kills a white man who insults him and his white girlfriend while they are enjoying the coming of spring. The unnatural behavior of the white man is suggested by his threatening to harm spring:

> His vile and puny fingers churned
> Our world about that sang and burned
> A while as never world before.
> He had unlatched an icy door,
> And let the winter in once more.
> To kill a man is a woeful thing,
> But he who lays a hand on spring
> Clutches the first bird by its throat
> And throttles it in the midst of a note;
> Whose breath upon the leaf-proud tree
> Turns all that wealth to penury.

Cullen combines here the standard Romantic/ poetic conceit—spring (nature) and sex—with the American politics of race. Note how Jim the rebel kills the white man not for any violent acts on his part, but merely for his speech:

> I had gone on unheeding but
> He struck me down, he called her slut,
> And black man's mistress, bawdy whore,
> And such like names, and many more,—
>
> . . . .
> ... My right
> I knew could not outweigh his might
> Who had the law for satellite—
> Only I turned to look at her,
> The early spring's first worshiper,
> (Spring, what have you to answer for?)
> The blood had fled from either cheek
> And from her lips; she could not speak,
> But she could only stand and stare
> And let her pain stab through the air.
> I think a blow to heart or head
> Had hurt her less than what he said.
> A blow can be so quick and kind,
> But words will feast upon the mind

> And gnaw the heart down to a shred,
> And leave you living, yet leave you dead.

First, this is an absolute reversal of Christ, for it was Christ himself who died for his speech, his claims of being the Messiah and being able to forgive sins. Here, the Christ figure does not die for his speech but rather kills because he has been victimized by the speech of his oppressor—defined, trapped, and degraded by it. Second, Jim represents the defiance, self-assertion, and confidence of the "New" Negro in a way that is the opposite of Cullen himself. Cullen represents thought; Jim, as a counterstatement, represents action. Thus, "The Black Christ" is not simply a case of making a sacrificial black lamb into a Christ figure but rather a reinvention of the myth of disobedience to authority, which is the cornerstone of Christian theology, so that disobedience is understood as the assertion of political and moral right. The poem's presentation of disobedience to the white man's authority goes counter to the prevailing social myth of blacks and Christianity; namely, that the religion made them passive and, indeed, obedient. Certainly, that element is represented in the poem by Jim's and the narrator's mother, but it is not ultimately what the poem suggests being a black Christian means.

Whatever merit "The Black Christ" as a poem possesses, however, was not sufficient to propel Cullen forward as a black literary figure. For some, "The Black Christ"—with its faulty rhymes, clumsy diction, and unsure measures— was the worst poem Cullen ever wrote. It surely indicated for many a lack of growth. Cullen, in 1929, with five books published, did not seem to be getting better.

After he returned from a nearly two-year stay in France from 1928 to 1929, partly financed by his fellowship, Cullen finished his novel, *One Way to Heaven,* by October 1931. He received his teacher's certificate from the New York Board of Education in December 1931, which certified him to teach French in junior high school. He started teaching in the New York schools as a substitute teacher in 1932. Throughout the early thirties, he received offers of professorships from black colleges and universities, which he refused because he was reluctant to leave New York. Cullen received his official appointment to the New York public schools on December 3, 1934. In 1935, *The Medea and Some Poems* was published, making Cullen the first black American writer to do a major Greek drama translation in prose. He wrote the choruses as lyric poems, which, through a commission from the actor John Houseman, were set to music by Virgil Thomson in 1935 for women's choir and percussion. In thinking about the shape of Cullen's career, it is easy to see why he would translate *The Medea*; it simply authenticated his own traditionalist and classical taste and credentials. Interestingly, he was attracted to this drama for much the same reason he was attracted to *The Ballad of the Brown Girl*: once again, his creative racial misreading made him think of *The Medea* in racial terms, involving a woman of color betrayed.

He married for a second time in 1940. The union with the sister of a good friend, Ida Roberson, proved to be much more successful than his first, more celebrated marriage. He wrote two children's books with ''Christopher Cat'' his own house pet, entitled *The Lost Zoo: (A Rhyme for the Young, But Not Too Young)* (1940) and *My Lives and How I Lost Them* (1942), the first in verse, the second in prose. While many thought the writing of children's books showed that Cullen was losing his powers, Langston Hughes, who wrote a number of children's books himself, thought that Cullen seemed reengaged in the forties and that the children's books showed Cullen to have revived his poetic interests and abilities. These books did not, however, serve to revive Cullen's career as an important writer.

In 1945, Cullen began to compile the poems that were to make up *On These I Stand: An Anthology of the Best Poems of Countee Cullen* (1947) as his health was deteriorating. What this meant in how Cullen viewed the shape of his career and his future as a writer is unclear. Poets periodically publish volumes of selected poems as a way of reassessing, recontextualizing, and revising their work. It may also have been a way for him to clear the decks if he was about to enter a new phase of work. Song-lyric writing, the drama, and children's literature interested him, and he may have been able to sustain and even revitalize his career had he continued to write in these genres. Moreover, despite the fact that his health was bad, he certainly did not think he was going to die soon. During his last months, he was more concerned about his father's health than his own. Countee Cullen died of high blood pressure and uremic poisoning on January 9, 1946, at the age of forty-two.

Selected Bibliography

WORKS OF COUNTEE CULLEN

POETRY

Color. New York: Harper & Brothers, 1925.
The Ballad of the Brown Girl: An Old Ballad Retold. New York: Harper & Brothers, 1927.
Copper Sun. New York: Harper & Brothers, 1927.
The Black Christ and Other Poems. New York: Harper & Brothers, 1929.
The Medea and Some Poems. New York: Harper & Brothers, 1935.

PROSE

One Way to Heaven. New York: Harper & Brothers, 1932.

CHILDREN'S BOOKS

The Lost Zoo (A Rhyme for the Young, But Not Too Young). New York: Harper & Brothers, 1940.

My Lives and How I Lost Them. New York: Harper & Brothers, 1942.

DRAMA

(with Arna Bontemps) *St. Louis Woman.* In *Black Theatre.* Edited by Lindsay Patterson. New York: Dodd, Mead, 1971. First performed in New York at the Martin Beck Theatre, March 30, 1946.

ANTHOLOGIES

On These I Stand: An Anthology of the Best Poems of Countee Cullen. New York: Harper & Brothers, 1947.

My Soul's High Song: The Collected Writings of Countee Cullen, Voice of the Harlem Renaissance. Edited by Gerald Early. New York: Anchor, 1991.

EDITION

Caroling Dusk: An Anthology of Verse by Negro Poets. Edited by and with contributions from Cullen. New York: Harper & Brothers, 1927.

PAPERS

Manuscripts and letters are to be found at Atlanta University; at the University of California, Berkeley; in the James Weldon Johnson collection at the Beinecke Rare Book and Manuscript Library, Yale University; in the Countee Cullen Papers, Amistad Research Center, Tulane University; and in the Schomburg Collection at the New York Public Library.

BIBLIOGRAPHY

Perry, Margaret. *A Bio-Bibliography of Countée P. Cullen.* Westport, Conn.: Greenwood, 1971.

BIOGRAPHICAL AND CRITICAL STUDIES

Baker, Houston A. *Afro-American Poetics: Revisions of Harlem and the Black Aesthetic.* Madison: University of Wisconsin Press, 1988.

———. *Modernism and the Harlem Renaissance.* Chicago: University of Chicago Press, 1987.

Ferguson, Blanche E. *Countee Cullen and the Negro Renaissance.* New York: Dodd, Mead, 1966.

Huggins, Nathan I. *Harlem Renaissance.* New York: Oxford University Press, 1971.

Lewis, David L. *When Harlem Was in Vogue.* New York: Knopf, 1981.

Perry, Margaret. *Silence to the Drums: A Survey of the Literature of the Harlem Renaissance.* Westport, Conn.: Greenwood, 1976.

Redmond, Eugene B. *Drumvoices: The Mission of Afro-American Poetry: A Critical History.* Garden City, New York: Anchor, 1976.

Shucard, Alan R. *Countee Cullen.* Boston: Twayne, 1984.

Turner, Darwin T. *In a Minor Chord: Three Afro-American Writers and Their Search for Identity.* Carbondale: Southern Illinois University Press, 1971.

Tuttleton, James W. "Countee Cullen at 'The Heights.'" In *The Harlem Renaissance: Revaluations.* Edited by Amritjit Singh, William S. Shiver, and Stanley Brodwin. New York: Garland, 1989.

Wagner, Jean. *Black Poets of the United States: From Paul Laurence Dunbar to Langston Hughes.* Trans. by Kenneth Douglas. Urbana: University of Illinois Press, 1973.

INTERVIEW

Sperry, Margaret. "Countee P. Cullen, Negro Boy Poet, Tells His Story." *Brooklyn Daily Eagle,* February 10, 1924.

—GERALD EARLY

James Dickey

1923–

JAMES DICKEY IS a poet and novelist whose narrative and lyrical powers plunge readers into a passionate exploration of experience. It is this power of engaging the reader that has established Dickey as one of the most significant writers in post–World War II American letters. Key to the complex intelligence in his art is the Dickey Self, the central point of view that serves as an "informing principle" for what is experienced within the poem or novel. Yet it is primarily the Dickey Self that has polarized critical and popular reactions to his works. N. Michael Niflis states in his essay "A Special Kind of Fantasy: James Dickey on the Razor's Edge" that "Dickey is our greatest American poet. And I bar none—not Roethke . . . not Jeffers, not Stevens. Dickey gives us experiences we have never seen before in poetry." The Dickey Self has been characterized by his supporters as the Energized Man, the robust male figure whose enthusiastic risk-taking is his vehicle for overcoming the inconsequentialities of ordinary life. Ernest Suarez in *James Dickey and the Politics of Canon* defines this figure as the "savage ideal" that depends upon "the relationship between romanticism and hedonism." In contrast, Michael Mesic states in his discussion in *American Poetry since 1960*:

I cannot accept as valid a view of life based on a sad coupling of the assumptions of the entrepre-

neur, competitive athlete, dominant male, and glory seeker—the hero in contrived heroic situations. . . . Dickey never audibly questions the values of the cult of masculinity: physical strength and health, unswerving determination, and above all success. . . . He does worry often and hard about his ability to *pass the test*, even when no test, at the moment, presents itself.

These strongly contrasting views of Dickey's work indicate the intense emotional response his poetry and fiction evoke from readers—a response the writer relishes.

To achieve this end, Dickey constantly pursues new voices, new approaches, and new themes within his own artistic framework, but no matter what genre he selects, the Dickey Self dominates. His major subjects and themes emanate from the Self's connection with the Other—a person, animal, or inanimate object outside the Self. As H. L. Weatherby asserts in an early important discussion, "The Way of Exchange in James Dickey's Poetry," when the Self is able to connect with the Other, an exchange of identities occurs between the two, producing new, heightened perspectives. In "Approaching Prayer" (in *Helmets*) for example, a bow hunter encounters a wild boar and, as Weatherby describes, the hunter "sees himself shooting the boar through the eyes of the boar being shot"—a deeply spiritual and emotional exchange that suggests a oneness with the heart of nature, with God. When such exchanges fail, as they do increasingly with each successive volume, Dickey dramatizes the impact of those failures.

In a career that, in the mid-1990s, has spanned nearly forty years, Dickey has produced work in many genres—including nearly twenty volumes of poetry, three novels, two screenplays, three collections of essays, two children's books, one journal, and one collection of interviews. His 1966 National Book Award for *Buckdancer's Choice*, the popular and critical success of the 1970 novel *Deliverance* and of its 1972 movie version (for which Dickey wrote the screenplay and in which he played the part of Sheriff Bullard), and his reading of his poem "The Strength of Fields" at President Jimmy Carter's inaugural celebration in 1977 marked Dickey's height of recognition as one of America's foremost writers.

James Lafayette Dickey, the second son of Eugene Dickey, a lawyer, and of Maibelle Swift Dickey, was born on February 2, 1923, in Buckhead, Georgia, an affluent suburb of Atlanta where he spent his childhood. A high school football and track star, he entered Clemson A&M (now Clemson University) in 1942 and was a tailback on the freshman football squad. At the end of his first semester, he volunteered for active duty in the U.S. Army Air Corps. From 1943 to 1945 he participated in approximately one hundred missions as a member of the 418th Night Fighter Squadron in the South Pacific.

After the war, Dickey enrolled at Vanderbilt University, a change in schools that reflected his shift in interests. At Vanderbilt he majored in English and philosophy and minored in astronomy. On November 4, 1948, he married Maxine Syerson; they had two sons, Christopher and Kevin. In 1949 Dickey earned a B.A. in English, magna cum laude, and in 1950 an M.A. His thesis at Vanderbilt was titled "Symbol and Image in the Shorter Poems of Herman Melville." Dickey began his teaching career at Rice Institute (now University) in September 1950. In December of that year, he was recalled to active military duty with the advent of the Korean conflict and served in the air force training command. He returned to Rice in 1952, after completing this second tour of duty, and began making notes for a novel that thirty-five years later he would publish as *Alnilam* (1987).

A 1954 *Sewanee Review* fellowship allowed Dickey to travel to Europe and, for the first time in his life, to concentrate wholly on writing poetry. He returned to the United States a year later and, with the help of Andrew Lytle, obtained a teaching position at the University of Florida. He resigned this appointment in the spring of 1956, following a dispute concerning his reading of his poem "The Father's Body" to a local women's group. Dickey immediately went to New York to begin a successful career as an advertising copywriter and, later, an executive for the McCann-Erickson agency. For the next three years he traveled from one agency to another, then returned to Atlanta in 1960. At one point in his career, before leaving advertising permanently in 1961, he wrote the Coca-Cola advertisements for the nationally televised Eddie Fisher program.

In 1958 Dickey was awarded the Civic and Arts Foundation Prize by the Union League Club of Chicago for poems published in *Poetry: A Magazine of Verse*, and in 1959 he won the Longview Foundation Award and the Vachel Lindsay Prize. In 1960 a collection of his poetry, *Into the Stone and Other Poems*, was published—with work by Paris Leary and Jon Swan —in *Poets of Today VII*. A Guggenheim fellowship allowed Dickey to spend 1961–1962 in Positano, Italy, where he composed *Drowning with Others* (1962) and, he recalled in a January 1992 *South Carolina Review* essay, experienced the genesis of his novel *Deliverance* (1970).

The whole of my novel *Deliverance* came from an image that appeared to me when I was half asleep in full sunlight after a picnic in Italy, where I was living at the time. . . . The image was that of a man standing at the top of a cliff: that, and no more. The picture was powerful and urgent, but I had no clue as to any meaning, if there was or could be one: one discovered, one assigned.

Upon returning to the United States in 1962, Dickey spent the next seven years as poet-in-residence at such schools as Reed College, San Fernando Valley State College (now California State University at Northridge), and the University of Wisconsin at Madison. His recognition as a poet was enhanced in 1966, when he received the National Book Award, the Poetry Society of America's Melville Cane Award, and a National Institute of Arts and Letters Award.

During the tumultuous 1960s and 1970s—the decades of the civil rights movement and the Vietnam war—Dickey's popular and critical recognition was accompanied by occasionally vitriolic attacks. Such critics as Robert Bly assumed that because he was an ardent southerner, he automatically opposed the civil rights movement, and that because he had served in two wars, he favored U.S. involvement in Vietnam. These unwarranted assumptions, provoked by the political activism of the time, caused Dickey some degree of distress and sparked lively debate with Bly, whose Sixties Press had published Dickey's first collection of criticism, *The Suspect in Poetry* (1964).

From 1966 to 1968 Dickey served as consultant in poetry in English for the Library of Congress. In the fall of 1969 he was appointed first Carolina Professor of English and poet-in-residence at the University of South Carolina at Columbia, where he has lived, taught, and written ever since. Following the death of Maxine Dickey in 1976, Dickey married Deborah Dodson; they have a daughter, Bronwen. On May 18, 1988, he was inducted into the American Acad-

emy of Arts and Letters, and in 1989 he was selected as one of the judges of the Yale Series of Younger Poets, a further indication of his influence on American writers.

Early in his career Dickey was known primarily as a narrative poet, one whose treatment of such activities as combat, bow hunting, camping, football, and guitar playing provided a fresh departure from the academic and the "confessional" modes of his contemporaries. In his first three collections he seeks to make each line a memorable statement, often relying on a three-beat anapestic rhythm for emphasis. In his fourth collection, *Buckdancer's Choice*, Dickey expands and "opens" the poetic line on the page, in an attempt to avoid subject matter and structure that appear artificial, and to capture authentic speech rhythms and diction. In later collections he experiments with trying to represent how the human mind works by grouping images in short blocks of words on the page. Dickey comments on the "open" quality he desires in poetry in "James Dickey on Yeats: An Interview," collected in *The Voiced Connections of James Dickey*: "Yeats speaks in a letter to Dorothy Wellesley of the good poem having a conclusion like the click of a closed box. I don't want to do that myself . . . I want the poem to open out. I don't want it to be final at all." Dickey comments further, in "The Poet Turns on Himself" (in *Babel to Byzantium*), that the open poem "would have none of the neatness of most of those poems we call 'works of art' but would have the capacity to involve the reader in it, in all its imperfections and impurities, rather than offering him a (supposedly) perfected and perfect work for contemplation, judgment, and evaluation." Dickey's approach permits an inward, psychological exploration of his protagonists, and in his later poetry shifts his focus from story to a concern with language, from narrative to a heightened expression of lyricism.

Known as an adherent of spontaneity and enthusiasm in life, advocating passion and imagination over rationality, Dickey is, nonetheless, a careful orchestrator of each volume of his poetry, organizing it around a controlling motif or theme. The 1960 collection *Into the Stone* focuses on his encounters with death within his family and his initial examination of his role as a survivor of World War II. *Drowning with Others*, which appeared two years later, concentrates on Dickey's attempts to gain a balance between the living and the dead as he increasingly perceives that he is suspended between these two worlds. *Helmets* (1964) dramatizes his various devices to guard against death, devices that help him experience life more fully. In *Buckdancer's Choice* (1965) Dickey's embracing of life allows him to explore the moral ambiguities, the choiceless choices, embodied in his southern heritage, his wartime involvement, and his familial roles. *Falling*, which first appeared in *Poems 1957–1967* (1967), centrally treats rising and/or falling actions, expanding their significance to encompass the themes of reincarnation and transformation.

In *The Eye-Beaters, Blood, Victory, Madness, Buckhead and Mercy* (1970), Dickey's voice and vision darken as he contemplates the aging process, addressing two halves of his Self, his youth and his middle adulthood; as the potential for his own death increases, he confronts the conflict between transience and permanence. In *The Zodiac* (1976) Dickey employs the drunken, perhaps insane persona of Henrik Marsman, a Dutch poet–sailor who died in World War II, to examine the artistic imagination in ascendance over the mathematical, rational mind. The desperate tone of *The Zodiac* is countered in 1979 with *The Strength of Fields*, a quietly contemplative volume that suggests a growing personal calm within the writer. *Puella* (1982) illustrates Dickey's interest in perspectives different from his own as he dramatizes the female psyche of Deborah, his second wife, "male-imagined," and as he experiments with compressed poetic phrases

derived from Gerard Manley Hopkins. *The Eagle's Mile* (1990), which like *Puella* employs an increasingly lyrical, "magical" diction, dramatizes the protagonist's relationship with earth, sea, and air, his heroic but ultimately doomed struggles to escape earth and death. Thus, each of these collections marks a stage in Dickey's definition of himself as poet and man.

Dickey explores a rich variety of subjects and themes in his poetry. Yet clearly the experience and topic that dominates his imagination and memory, his life and career, is his participation in combat during World War II. War provides a framework for his vision of life and his fulfillment of it: his drive to make experience meaningful and consequential; his ongoing relationship with the living and the dead; his turning to nature, rather than man, as his aesthetic model; his belief in love and in family; and finally his insistence on the Self as a qualified certainty in an uncertain world. The war also serves as a specific subject and a larger metaphor for the individual's struggle to survive, if not triumph over, death. Permeating his poetry, the war directly serves as the subject of two of his three novels and colors the third.

In his first collection of poetry, *Into the Stone*, Dickey uses the vehicle of his imagination to transform unspeakable deaths into transcendent expressions of the connections between life, death, and art. "The Performance," one of Dickey's best-known poems, involves three main actors caught in the deadly drama of war: Donald Armstrong, a captured American pilot who defies his own death by performing gymnastic tricks before being beheaded; the Japanese soldier whose task is to behead Armstrong but breaks down "in a blaze of tears" before completing his grisly job; and the poet–speaker who unifies the entire experience through his imaginative re-creation of Armstrong's last moments. The narrator characterizes Armstrong as "kingly," brave, and dignified, granting that his friend died heroically while anguishing at his own unexplainable survival.

Dickey's relationship with his older brother, Eugene, offers a similar internal dilemma dramatized in "The String." Dickey explains in *Self-Interviews*:

> I *did* have an older brother, Eugene, who died before I was born, and I *did* gather by implication and hints of family relatives that my mother, an invalid with angina pectoris, would not have dared to have another child if Gene had lived. I was the child who was born as a result of this situation. And I always felt a sense of guilt that my birth depended on my brother's death.

In "The String," the speaker establishes a balance between his own living son and the memory of his dead brother. He teaches his son the string tricks with which his dead brother entertained himself while dying. The structures the protagonist devises are a delicate but determined link between the living and the dead, between the narrator and his dead brother. The speaker envisions his brother as having woven a celestial "city" to which he has ascended. Yet Eugene, who "thought like a spider," has also entrapped his brother in death's "maze," for the narrator–poet had been conceived "Out of grief . . . To replace the incredible child." Dickey's allegiance to the dead consequently carries a sense of honoring their memory and of being entrapped by them.

One means of countering the pain the living speaker feels is through love. The title poem "Into the Stone" illustrates Dickey's view that a woman's love offers hope for a renewal into a wholly intense life. Yet, significantly, lovers are addressed in terms of the dead. The speaker asserts that "Like the dead, I have newly arisen" and travels to a woman to whom he has given his "heart all the way into moonlight." The promise of love defeats death: "No thing that shall die as

I step / May fall, or not sing of rebirth," for "The dead have their chance in my body." That love is couched in imagery of death indicates the pervasive hold of death on the poet's imagination.

Dickey often portrays the dead as existing in an underworld reminiscent of Greek mythology's Hades, which is bounded by the River Styx. The dead travel to and from this underworld by rivers or underground streams, providing a symbolic dimension to water imagery that complements the conventional Christian associations that Dickey sometimes develops. The dead souls are humanized, ascending from their subterranean dwelling or descending from a heavenly location to involve themselves in the lives and imaginations of Dickey's speakers. His protagonists feel pitted against the dead but also try to connect with them to gain insight into death and knowledge about living fully.

In *Drowning with Others*, Dickey's vision and voice gain real complexity as his sense of being caught between the dead and the living increases. His speaker is both attracted to and repelled by the dead; he is vulnerable to and apprehensive about their hold on him, and searches for ways to protect himself from their influence. In "Armor" he puts on a metal suit but finds that the physical shield does not guard him emotionally from the dead; in "The Tree House at Night," he feels his dead brother drawing him higher and closer to heaven, and he is torn between the angel and a living brother, one above and one with him on earth.

Dickey's concern for preserving and protecting life extends beyond himself to others. In the significantly titled poem "The Lifeguard," Dickey's speaker is a young man who has failed in his duty to protect a "village of children," for one boy has drowned. The speaker repeatedly dives in search of the drowned boy, spurred on by "the change in the children's faces / At my defeat." While beneath the water, he calls out and believes that he hears the dead child answer. The two cry out to each other until both rise and break the surface of the water. In moonlight—the source of poetic vision and, in this case, mad despair—and in the light given off by the grave, the lifeguard pulls the boy to ''the heart of a distant forest.'' He hopes to bring him back to life but resigns himself at last that he has failed, and instead holds in his ''arms a child / Of water, water, water.''

Dickey's inability to check death's advances on himself or others drives him to seek an even more complex means of comprehending death and the dead. Especially in his third collection, *Helmets*, Dickey concentrates on the use of head and body adornments to guard his speaker from threatening forces. Yet these devices are not simply protective. Whenever he puts on various head or body coverings—masks, clothes, gamecock spurs, hollow animal heads—the speaker gains an altered point of view. He adopts the perspective—the vision, the thoughts, and the feelings—of the previous inhabiter of the covering and thus gains a degree of communication with the dead. When he puts on the helmet of a dead soldier, for example, in ''Drinking from a Helmet,'' the protagonist acquires the last thoughts of that dead soldier.

''Drinking from a Helmet'' is organized into four major divisions. The first section presents the seventeen-year-old speaker's premonition of his own death. A fierce battle rages around him, and not wishing to endanger himself by removing his own helmet, the young soldier grabs a dead comrade's helmet to drink from. The second section of the poem portrays what happens when the speaker drinks water from the borrowed helmet. As he swallows the water, his vision is suddenly distorted by whirling, surrealistic images: ''Grass pouring down from the sun'' and ''Bright circles . . . inward and outward'' that cause him to realize he is ''trembling forward through something / Just born of me.'' What is ''born'' within him foreshadows the next stage

of his experience, his crossing over the ordinary boundary between the living and the dead.

In the poem's third section, the speaker assumes a new character. Upon fitting the borrowed helmet on his head, he gains the dead soldier's last thoughts: 'The dead cannot rise up, / But their last thought hovers somewhere / For whoever finds it.'' This dead young soldier's last thought is a poignant, lyrical vision of two brothers bicycling through California redwoods. In the final section the tranquil vision provides the speaker with a meaningful contrast to the horror of the battlefield. However, the realization of what the dead feel and think provides only a momentary peace, for all too soon the speaker returns to the brutal reality of the battlefield.

Helmets is filled with poems in which figures assume protective devices to acquire knowledge of the dead and the living. When they are not protected by helmets, they suffer painful physical or spiritual damage. In ''The Scarred Girl,'' for example, a young woman must live her life seeing how others respond to her severely disfigured face, the result of an accident in which she was hurled head-first through a car windshield. To compensate for her outward appearance, she has developed an inner beauty, yet people she encounters are initially repulsed by her. Without a literal or metaphorical helmet, she becomes one of the damaged, wounded people who suffer a lifelong agony in body and spirit. She is eventually cut off as well from those who could provide comfort, completing her sense of spiritual isolation.

Buckdancer's Choice, Dickey's National Book Award–winning collection and the first volume in his self-described ''central motion,'' both expands themes of his earlier books and gives them a deeper psychological and moral focus. Dickey now experiments with his innovative ''open'' lines on the page to convey these forces at work within and upon his protagonists. ''The Firebombing,'' one of the monuments of World War

II literature, concerns the speaker's attempts to envision what happened after he bombed Japanese cities and people. As an American flier, his primary task was to accomplish bombing sorties with as much technical skill as possible. From high above his target he adopted an "honored aesthetic evil, / The greatest sense of power in one's life." Twenty years later, however, as he roams through his own home, the ordinary details of his household remind him of what he destroyed in the homes of his enemy. His anguish results from the realization that although "All families lie together," he has been responsible for those who have been "burned alive." Moreover, since he was far removed from the actual scenes of destruction, he must imaginatively visualize rather than simply remember such scenes, comparable to his task in "The Performance." Yet whereas in "The Performance" the imagination creates a glorious portrait of courage, grace, and compassion, in "The Firebombing" it devises indelible scenes of destruction: "With this in the dark of the mind, / Death will not be what it should."

The speaker's central conflict concerns the nature and degree of his moral responsibility. On the one hand, he has simply fulfilled his duty as an American pilot in wartime; on the other, he has participated in the destruction of "families" undeniably like his own. However, rather than simplifying his moral dilemma through choosing either one or the other of these stances—a simplification that would, at least, provide personal resolution for him—he remains forever suspended, not knowing whether he is to absolve or to damn himself: "Absolution? Sentence? No matter; / The thing itself is in that." Dickey's refusal to reduce these moral complexities to one clear position contributed to the attacks on him for his refusal to adopt a single clear position on the Vietnam conflict.

Dickey's honesty in addressing difficult moral quandaries reappears in his treatment of American social issues, particularly those involving racial relationships in the South. "Slave Quarters," like "The Firebombing," frankly addresses a moral impasse, though here it balances a rich, passionate heritage against a horrendous system of domination. The poem focuses on the sexual relationship between a white male slave owner and his black female slave; beyond the impediments of race and class, they mate with genuine passion, though their connection is that of master and slave, aggressor and victim. After mating, the slaveholder feels no sense of obligation to or concern for the woman he has slept with or for the child they have created.

The speaker in "Slave Quarters" is a contemporary white male southerner who fuses the past and the present through his imagination. He is fully aware that master-slave relationships were reprehensible because unequal and manipulative, yet he also cannot deny his admiration for the social and cultural system that depended upon such relationships. The plantation owner had cultivated a wilderness into a thriving region, bringing order and sophistication to the new world. In his essay "Notes on the Decline of Outrage," Dickey states that every white southerner must come to terms with the region's past:

> Not for a moment does he entertain the notion that these prejudices are just, fitting, or reasonable. But neither can he deny that they belong to him by inheritance, as they belong to other Southerners. Yet this does not mean that they cannot be seen for what they are, that they cannot be appraised and understood.

By exploring and acknowledging the ambiguities of his world, Dickey expands even further his investigation of those subjects "which in memory are most persistent and obsessive," as he states in his essay "The Poet Turns on Himself."

In *Falling*, which appears as the final section of *Poems 1957–1967*, Dickey presents a motif of rising to and falling from great heights: "Reincarnation,'' in which a deskbound office worker is reborn as a seabird that soars above the oceans; ''Bread,'' in which a World War II flying crew is shot down from the sky; ''Falling,'' in which a flight attendant plummets to her death from an airplane; ''The Leap,'' in which Jane MacNaughton jumps to her death; ''Dark Ones,'' in which people go home and ''fall / Down'' in their ''souls to pray for light / To fail''; and ''Power and Light,'' in which a man climbs telephone poles by day and descends into the darkness of his basement by night. Perhaps the most extensive use of this imagery occurs in ''May Day Sermon to the Women of Gilmer County, Georgia, by a Woman Preacher Leaving the Baptist Church,'' in which the speaker preaches about a fall from grace that, in turn, allows for a rise into a fuller life. This rising and falling motif dramatizes a major Dickey theme of reincarnation and transformation of his protagonists.

''For the Last Wolverine'' illustrates the volume's rising and falling imagery through a drama of nature's life-and-death cycle. Imagining a snowbound, sub-Arctic setting, the speaker cries out for nature's last wolverine to climb a dying spruce tree and then to mate with the last bald eagle. The speaker hopes that from the union of these two fierce creatures a mythical offspring will be born. This beast will rise in ''holy war'' against those—road builders, fur trappers, and railroad crews—who are responsible for imposing man's destruction on the wilderness. The hoped-for rise in the power of nature over mankind is to be accomplished from nature's own version of a Christlike savior. All three of the figures—the wolverine, the tree, and the eagle—are the last of their fallen species, but through the narrator's imagination they rise again in splendor to defeat threatening forces. The speaker ends with a prayerful plea to let such creatures die but ''not die / Out.''

Whereas in the collections concluding with *Falling* Dickey gradually expands his range of personae, developing speakers that are not always identifiable with the poet himself, in his 1970 volume, *The Eye-Beaters, Blood, Victory, Madness, Buckhead and Mercy*, he presents a central figure who closely reflects his own character and concerns. An often introspective, at times dark collection, *The Eye-Beaters* provides a speaker who looks back at his life to ascertain what it has been and has become. The principal figure examines the aging process, as in ''Two Poems of Going Home,'' or experiences physical illness, as in ''Diabetes'' and ''The Cancer Match,'' or encounters mysterious fears, as in ''Knock.'' He often addresses the two halves of the Self, the remembered and imaginatively recreated younger Self and older Self that he has become.

''Two Poems of Going Home''—''Living There'' and ''Looking for the Buckhead Boys'' —best illustrate how the speaker confronts change and loss in his life. In ''Living There'' the protagonist identifies himself as ''The Keeper,'' a fitting title because he maintains and feels caught by two households for which he bears a deep responsibility: the childhood home that ''lives only / In my head,'' and the home of his adulthood, in which he is both a husband and a father of sons. Yet as he ponders the death of his own father—''the fixer the wagon-master''—and his childhood home, now gone, he is engulfed in the notion of life's transience. Realizing that his present family and house will also soon be gone, he agonizes over his powerlessness to halt time's effects on his family:

Why does the Keeper go blind
With sunset? The mad, weeping Keeper who can't keep
A God-damned thing who knows he can't keep everything
Or anything alive: none of his rooms, his people
His past, his youth, himself,
But cannot let them die?''

Although he realizes that he and the present home will be the material of his son's memories, he feels deeply his inability to withstand the losses caused by the passage of time.

A similar theme governs the companion poem, "Looking for the Buckhead Boys," in which, longing to find a connection with his youth, the narrator returns to his hometown. Yet as the first lines suggest—"Some of the time, going home, I go / Blind and can't find it"—he realizes the difficulty of his task. The speaker's blindness illustrates his momentary inability to connect his memory's view of his home with the town's present circumstances. As he revisits his hometown, the protagonist notes that the town's businesses and other sites that served as signposts of his adolescence have changed or been torn down. He learns from Mr. Hamby, the hardware merchant who supplies the speaker with information about those in "the Book of the Dead"—"the 1939 / North Fulton High School Annual"—that many of the Buckhead Boys have met with only limited success, if not absolute failure. Yet the speaker persists in trying to find one person from his class, for if he can connect with one person, "even one / I'm home."

The one Buckhead Boy who remains in the town, Charlie Gates, has been symbolically half-blinded by "lime in his eye from the goal line." Meeting Charlie, a Gulf gasoline station attendant, the speaker feels exhilarated, but instead of openly declaring his feelings, he simply thinks, "Charlie, Charlie, we have won away from / We have won at home / In the last minute." The narrator must phrase his affection for Charlie in "code"; in emotionally laden understatement, he can ask only that his friend "Fill 'er up. Fill 'er up, Charlie." In so doing, the narrator realizes that he cannot fully connect with or resurrect his past, his youth; rather, all he can offer is hidden warmth and a recognition that the past is irretrievable, which, in turn, make his own past more complex and poignant.

"Living There" and "Looking for the Buckhead Boys" dramatize the theme of emotional isolation that appears throughout this volume in ailing, middle-aged, anguished protagonists, figures who embody "Variations on Estrangement," the subtitle of "Turning Away." They are figures who have a deep awareness of the passage of time, of change, and of subsequent personal loss.

Ironically, this darkening of theme appeared during the 1970s, the decade of Dickey's greatest productivity and visibility. His creative output and his apparent taste for public attention—both for himself and for poets and poetry in general—drew substantial comment, both positive and negative. Given his risk-taking character, it is perhaps not surprising that during this decade Dickey began to abandon the forms that had won him success and instead embraced new, experimental techniques in an ongoing effort to revitalize and redefine his poetic voice.

Early in his career, Dickey asserted that he was trying to win back for poetry the narrative power lost to the novel. Yet as early as *The Eye-Beaters*, in such long poems as "Pine," he was beginning to experiment with what he called "associational imagery," imagery that draws on emotional or psychological relationships rather than logical ones. Throughout his career Dickey has forced himself as a poet to undergo change, to remake himself, to discover new voices and new techniques. Almost certainly the success he achieved in the late 1960s and early 1970s compelled him to deemphasize narrative and to focus instead on innovations in character, language, and form, thereby creating a narrative-lyrical hybrid.

The Zodiac, Dickey's long 1976 poem, is the first extended expression of his developing hybrid. In *The Zodiac*, Dickey again returns to a World War II subject, basing his volume on a work of the same title by Dutch poet Henrik Marsman, who was killed in a 1940 North Atlantic torpedo attack. The poem's twelve-part division initially suggests but does not develop a correspondence to the twelve signs of the zodiac; instead, the work emerges as a complex dramatic monologue in which narrative thrust is subsumed by the thoughts and experiences of the protagonist, the figure of Marsman himself as rendered by Dickey.

Marsman serves as the primary voice throughout the poem, yet his role as a speaker is fused with that of a second speaker, an omniscient "I" who is engaged with and reacts to Marsman's struggles with the universe, time, and history in part 1—a section that constitutes nearly half of the work. Parts 2 through 7 concentrate on Marsman's belief that mathematics and philosophy cannot reveal the secrets of the universe. In parts 8 through 11 Marsman examines his own life, using memory, dreams, and fantasy as his sources of comprehension; and in part 12 he finds a degree of acceptance of his circumstances.

Through the persona of Marsman, Dickey dramatizes the visionary poet's attempt to grasp—by means of imagination rather than intellect—the mysteries of God's creative powers. Three main characters emerge in the poem: God, creator of the universe; Pythagoras, the embodiment of human reason; and Marsman, the personification of the visionary poet. Through what Marsman calls the philosopher's "insane mathematics," Pythagoras ascribes a numerical value to virtually all elements of the natural world but particularly to the celestial objects—sun, moon, and stars; he thus explains man's history and being, as well as God's special art, the music of the spheres.

Though admirable and inventive, Pythagoras' quantified explanations of the human and the divine represent an ineffective antithesis to Marsman's belief that the visionary poet comes closer to comprehending the universe and God because he depends on the imagination rather than on reason. Marsman turns to remembered events, nightmarish dreams, and alcohol-induced fantasies to transcend reality and attain the visionary.

Through agonized long nights of the soul, he struggles to understand his personal history, believing that if he can comprehend his own history, mankind can understand its history. Although he fails to discern fully the meaning of his own life, Marsman does realize that one's personal history and mankind's history—and time and the universe—are determined not by mathematical quantities but by human feelings, the emotions that give mankind a sense of being fully alive.

In the poem's final part, Marsman's tone shifts from grief over his struggles to a quiet acceptance. He has tried to comprehend the mysteries of God's creation but realizes that these secrets will remain partially hidden; thus, he prepares for a different exploration. He desires to have his soul put into "a solar boat" in which it will sail quietly toward light and "the morning / Land that sleeps." Although Marsman's course steers him directly toward his own death, his final stance carries the suggestion that death is in some degree defeated through art, that the artist and his work retain a measure of immortality achieved "through a reliance on art" rather than on the intellect.

Written at about the same time as *The Zodiac*, Dickey's inaugural poem "The Strength of Fields" (the title poem of his 1979 collection) surprises through its calm, almost ceremonial tone. "The Strength of Fields" portrays a man, the president-elect, who must confront weighty responsibilities and difficult decisions, yet who approaches these burdens with a sense of optimism. As a southerner, the speaker feels a close kinship to the land and to nature in general. He walks his farmland at night, searching for the "Dear Lord of all the fields" as a means of granting him inner strength to face forthcoming duties. The source of his strength, "the source / Of the power" that can sustain him as he prepares to assume the heavy duties of office, has been his physical and spiritual ties to the land. He appeals to the heavens, to the dead beneath the ground, and to nature itself—sources of Dickey's poetic vision as well—and his entreaty is answered with the hallmark of southern society: "More kindness." Such an answer suggests that the speaker has attained harmony with his surroundings and with himself, which gives the poem and the collection in which it appears a serenity unusual for Dickey.

If *The Zodiac* reveals Dickey abandoning pure narrative for imagistically charged dramatic monologue, his major collection of the 1980s, *Puella* (1982), shows him experimenting with language to create Hopkins-like lyricism unlike anything he had achieved before. *Puella* focuses on coming-of-age experiences of Deborah, Dickey's second wife, as "male-imagined" by the speaker. Dickey declares in "The Poet Turns on Himself" (in *Babel to Byzantium*) that a character's evolution is traced through a "fusion of inner and outer states, of dream, fantasy, and illusion where everything partakes of the protagonist's mental processes and creates a single impression." Thus, Deborah is dramatized through her developing physical, psychological, and imaginative awareness of her own Self. She burns a childhood doll, and as she watches the fires consume the symbol of her childhood, she announces, "I am leaving," and begins her journey into womanhood. As she travels among strangers, she asks if she is their child and discovers that she is not a child of ordinary people but instead a person created from inner lightning, her own "root-system of fire." This internal fire often seeks artistic expression through her unique sound while playing the piano or her presence while dressing in her wedding costume of her ancestors. The volume's thematic conclusion appears in the penultimate poem, "The Surround," subtitled "Imagining Herself as the Environment, / She Speaks to James Wright at Sundown." Deborah's speech to the recently dead lyrical poet becomes a touching prayer for him as he journeys from life to death. As day dissolves into night, sunlight turns into moonlight, the poet is transformed into his own private "surround" while Deborah embodies "the Environment," an emblem of her own life's wholeness.

The motif in *Puella* of the living and the dead being transformed by and through nature to a new form of existence appears again as a dominant theme in Dickey's 1990 collection, *The Eagle's Mile*. So, too, does the association of the central figure with the ancient elements of life (fire, air, water, and earth); however, in *The Eagle's Mile* Dickey establishes an ascending hierarchy of these elements—earth, sea, air, fire—as vehicles for his speaker's transformation.

Many poems in *The Eagle's Mile* rely on the motif of circularity, of the "sweeping" motion of flying through the air, of sailing on the ocean, of walking along a beach. The physical, literal levels move effortlessly into almost transcendent images of the eternal cycle of the living reconnecting with the dead. The speaker's experiences range from meditations at a grave site, to the drama of a daughter's birth, to the "monotonous awe" of a snowstorm, to the internal monologue of a man watching eagles circle high above the earth.

The earth is the solid place on which the speaker wanders alone. Earth is also frequently associated with death, as in "Tomb Stone," in which the speaker, while visiting a loved one's grave, perceives that "deep enough / In death, the earth becomes / Absolute earth." In contrast, the living stand above the dead as a "vertical body / That breathes the rectangular solitude / Risen over" the dead. Though able to connect with the dead by breathing the air of this "solitude," the protagonist understands that this relationship will disappear as he leaves the grave site. In "Gila Bend," the speaker revisits the aerial gunnery range he flew over more than forty years before, as a World War II trainee. Now, as he walks across the fierce, hot earth, each step causes a physical torment, as if he were being branded by the sand. His agony evokes emotional distress as the speaker recalls those who trained here when "no man could get / To his feet, even to rise face-out / Full-force from the grave." In the context of death, the "Absolute earth" is akin to hell, in which one is trapped forever.

Whereas the earth is fixed, the sea is mobile. In "Expanses," the landbound speaker walks along the beach, gazing upon the "chopped soft road" of water, which inspires in him a "Joy like short grass." Yet, he proclaims, one should not "confuse the sea / With any kind of heart: never to mix blood with something / As free as foam." Instead, the sea can grant only a degree of "trouble-free" release from the earth or provide a setting for a greater release; in "Moon Flock," for example, while looking "Straight out over the night sea," the speaker attempts to overcome the frustration of his condition by straining "to grow wings," desiring to "leap / Leap till he's nearly forever / Overhead: overhead floating" in air.

Dickey asserts that air is "greater than sea" and the fixed, solid earth. The struggle to achieve liberating flight, to rise above earth and death, is the central theme of this volume. The speaker in "Eagles" comes to know the "circular truth / Of the void" as he watches an eagle circling high above him. He realizes, too, that the larger the bird, the greater its capability to be buoyed up by the air, free and wild, which "makes of air a thing that would be liberty / Enough for any world but this one." Air is consistently associated with escape, with liberating release, from the earth's hold on its creatures or from death's entrapment.

The Eagle's Mile portrays a speaker who refuses to look away from the void but struggles to transcend the limitations of his earthbound life—and its final outcome, the grave—by searching for means of liberation and escape through the sea but, most important, through the air. His frustration leads to a kind of joy that reflects his celebration at being a full participant in the natural drama. The unexpressed counter to that joy, however, is the realization that he cannot fly, that he is earthbound, and that ultimately he will become "Absolute earth."

Dickey's novels demonstrate clear connections with his poetry, exploring similar subjects and themes. *Deliverance* (1970), *Alnilam* (1987), and *To the White Sea* (1993) either literally dramatize events of World War II or metaphorically evoke combat experiences. *Deliverance* is a fast-paced, compelling study of contemporary suburban men placed in physically dangerous and morally primitive circumstances. *Alnilam*, in contrast, is a brooding, nearly static philosophical exploration of an individual's quest to rise beyond restrictions to a meaningful life. *To the White Sea* focuses on the brutal character of the individual and, by extension, society when war reduces life to primitive requirements for survival.

In *Deliverance*, four Atlanta men, while on a weekend canoeing-camping trip in the mountainous region of north Georgia, are accosted by two mountain men who sodomize one of them and threaten to do the same to the protagonist. Before the mountain men can complete their assault, a third suburbanite kills one of the attackers by shooting him through the back with a hunting arrow; the other attacker flees into the woods. Thus, the weekend excursion turns into a savage kill-or-be-killed trial.

Each of the four suburbanites—Bobby Trippe, Drew Ballinger, Lewis Medlock, and the protagonist, Ed Gentry—represents an alternative mode of response to the danger they face from the savage mountain men. Bobby Trippe, who suffers sexual humiliation, urges his friends to flee. Drew Ballinger, who later dies, pleads for reason and recourse to courts of justice. Lewis Medlock advocates meeting violence with violence in man-to-man combat; however, he is rendered ineffectual when he suffers a disabling injury. Thus, Ed Gentry must assume the leadership role in securing the survival of himself and his friends. Gentry's eventual triumph over the menace of the mountain men combines elements of the proposed solutions offered by the other three and, as a consequence, proves the most successful, appropriate resolution to their dilemma: he flees in order to fight later; he turns to courts of justice, albeit the justice of nature rather than of civilization; and he engages in brutal hand-to-hand combat.

The central focus of the novel is Gentry's transformation from a "get-through-the-day-man" who is "mainly interested in sliding" to a figure who gains control over himself and his life. Even his name, Gentry, suggests a dilettante's relationship to the land. Before he travels to the north Georgia setting on the weekend excursion, Gentry has refined his work, his relationships, and his life to a level of inconsequential ease: "I was a mechanic of the graphic arts, and when I could get the problem to appear mechanical to me, and not the result of inspiration, I could do something with it. . . . And that, as far as art was concerned, was it." His life requires little effort, makes few demands.

With Lewis Medlock's training, Gentry has prepared himself for the difficult physical ordeal in the mountains; with guidance from nature, Gentry gains a spiritual strength for violent confrontations to come. He undergoes a physical and spiritual baptism into nature when he steps into the waist-deep river and feels the water swirling around the creative-sexual parts. "It [the river] felt profound, its motion built into it by the composition of the earth for hundreds of miles upstream and down, and by thousands of years. The standing there was so good, so fresh and various and continuous, so vital and uncaring around my genitals, that I hated to leave it."

Yet Gentry's connection with nature is most fully revealed through his climb up a cliff to hunt the surviving mountain man, who may or may not be stalking the surviving suburbanites. Before he begins his ascent, Gentry again steps into the river "to get a renewed feel of all the elements present." Attaining the summit, he reduces hunting the man to a mechanical problem, forming a predator–prey relationship: "I'll . . . look for him like I'm some kind of an animal. . . . quiet and deadly. I could be a snake." He thinks as the mountain man thinks—"our minds fuse"—and adopts the predatory "indifference" necessary to kill the man. He anticipates where his prey will emerge from the woods and climbs a tree with his bow and arrows. When the mountain man fulfills his intended role, Gentry shoots him. His shot is unerring, but he falls from the tree as he shoots, wounding himself in the side with his remaining arrow. To make certain he has killed the man, Gentry tracks his bloody trail by getting down on his hands and knees and smelling it as if he were an animal. At this point, Gentry's transformation into one of nature's creatures is complete, as he thinks and acts like a predator in order to survive.

When he finds the body of the man he has shot, Gentry cannot identify him positively as the one who intended to sodomize him. Nor can he be certain, later in the novel, that the man is the deputy sheriff's missing brother-in-law. Neither can he or the others in his group be confident, when they find Drew's body, that he had been killed by a rifle shot. The concern about right and wrong remains, but Dickey purposely leaves these questions unanswered. *Deliverance* is not a simple tale of violation and revenge; rather, it is a story of men who must learn to live with uncertainty about their own guilt or innocence after encountering a deadly, irrational force. Like the speaker in "The Firebombing," the survivors of this deadly encounter cannot know whether they have earned forgiveness or sentence.

Significantly, however, Ed Gentry achieves deliverance from an inconsequential slider's life into a life of purpose; he has been transformed by the knowledge that he can encounter and triumph in a life-threatening circumstance. He therefore returns to Atlanta and civilization a changed man, rejuvenated into a more passionate participation in life.

Dickey's second novel, *Alnilam*, is set primarily at a training base for Army Air Corps recruits in Peckover, North Carolina, during the early stages of World War II. The novel's title refers to the middle star in the three-star belt of the constellation Orion, thereby establishing a thematic-symbolic motif of centrality: Alnilam "has to be a moving center. . . . The central star. . . . The moving center. . . . It carries you with it, and yet it's always the center. You follow. Everything follows, and holds together," a cadet explains to the protagonist, Frank Cahill. Though centrality is a major concern of the novel, its two primary characters, Frank and Joel Cahill, father and son, are initially figures outside of the social mainstream.

Frank Cahill is portrayed as a man estranged from personal and social commitments, a man who functions as a detached observer in the fortresslike Atlanta amusement park he has constructed. Because of his mechanical approach to marriage, his wife left him while she was pregnant with their only child, Joel. Frank consequently has never seen or known his son, and because diabetes has blinded him, he knows that he will never literally see his son, though he undertakes a search for the young man. Yet once Frank is blind, his character, like Oedipus, evolves: he sees with an inner vision that gives him insight into people and events because, despite his blindness, he depends on more sensory than intellectual comprehension. At points in the novel Dickey represents Frank's blind inner vision in bold type on the left side of the page, and renders the seeing characters' words and actions and the major events in the novel in normal type on the right side of the page. This innovative technique is intended to give the novel a visual impact similar to that produced by Dickey's "opening out" of poetry on the printed page.

As Frank's search begins, Joel Cahill is presumed dead, killed in a fiery training accident. To learn about his son, Frank, accompanied by his wolflike guide dog Zack, travels to the air base where Joel was taking his flight training. There, Frank questions a variety of people about the details of his son's character and the crash that may have killed him. He discovers that his son has created an organization of fellow cadets whose purpose in part has been to rebel against the military bureaucracy. This cult, called Alnilam, has developed in response to Joel's charismatic, messianic leadership. Joel has been a gifted pilot and a mystic whose theories about flying and about the element of air are recorded in his notebook, along with passages from Percy Bysshe Shelley, the archetypal Romantic rebel. These notebook entries operate as near-divine scripture for his followers. Their philosophy merges the mathematics of navigation with poetic meditations on the body and the air. Alnilam is intended to elevate its members above the ordinary, into a condition of "precision mysticism"—"Navigation was really a form of poetry. So was mathematics in general"—that leads believers to become "weightless, in the Second Body, the Old Brain, but still [to] control the ground under our feet."

The cadets focus on the Alnilam Project, an event in which the student pilots plan to crash their airplanes on the tarmac and create chaos on the Sunday of their graduation from basic training. The ensuing disorder on their base will, they predict, set off similar disruptions at other bases across the country and provoke a nationwide revolution within the military. The Alnilam cadets assert that the training they are currently undergoing is mere preparation for the real war that will take place after the world war. They envision a destruction of the "system slave," the embodiment of those limited, mechanical people whose lives are controlled by regulations and institutions and who, in turn, inflict limitations on others. The Alnilam cadets will triumph over these limited people to create a "world of nihilism and music," the energized life of the imaginative, Byronic man.

Though their philosophy is murky, Frank Cahill is impressed by the youthful zeal of the cadets. The members of the group revel in their athletic prowess, the esprit de corps of male bonding, and the significance of their rebellion against military strictures. His admiration for his son and the other cadets drives Frank to experience his son's activities at the base: taking the controls of an airplane; dining and sleeping with his son's lover; chafing, as did his son, against the restrictions imposed on him by regulations-bound military personnel; and participating in the Alnilam cadets' athletic games, discussions, and fights. The knowledge that he gains about Joel leads Frank to admire the boy's messianic power over others but also to realize that such a power carries destructive features. He determines that "there was a side of his boy that he would not have liked," as he perceives that Joel's secret cult formulates an intellectual-mystic system that actually suppresses the individual by enforcing a group identity. Ironically, the cadets are as blind in their adherence to their system as the mechanical military "system slave" they rebel against.

At Boyd McLendon's Peckover Hotel, Frank enters into a different community of men, those who are associated with the air base but who are apart from the cadets' cult. Within this setting, Frank participates in important discussions with McLendon, Captain Lennox Whitehall, and Captain Claude Faulstick. Together, McLendon, Whitehall, Faulstick, and Frank form "a special group" in which each man acknowledges the unique achievements of the others; they are thus unlike the Alnilam cadets, who subordinate the individual to the group.

Captain Whitehall is an authentic war hero who saved the lives of his crew members during a horrifying mission in the South Pacific.

Through his intellectual skills, he was able to navigate the airplane to safety, a rescue that created an emotional bond among his crew. Since Whitehall was driven as much by his concern for his comrades as by his sense of duty and his navigational skills, he represents a harmonious merger of the mind and the heart. His example and his comments about this experience constitute the thematic lesson that the Alnilam cadets have yet to learn but that Frank grasps.

At the beginning of the novel, Frank is imprisoned in the confines of an amusement park that he has designed to avoid involvement with other people. As he undertakes the search for his son, he also embarks on a journey of discovery regarding himself and his relationship to the world. At the Peckover Hotel, Frank achieves a balance between the detachment of his early life and the destructive solidarity of the Alnilam group. Within the community of men at McLendon's Peckover Hotel, he experiences a renewal to life merging the heart and the mind, the individual and society. In the process he gains his own center point, his personal Alnilam.

Throughout his war poetry Dickey poses for himself a personal and artistic challenge to envision what he has not been able to experience firsthand. Particularly in "The Firebombing" Dickey's speaker laments that what haunts him long after the war is that he did not see with his own eyes the nature and extent of the destruction he inflicted on the Japanese homeowners he bombed:

> Think of this   think of this. . . . It is this detachment,
> The honored aesthetic evil,
> The greatest sense of power in one's life,
> That must be shed in bars, or by whatever
> Means. . . . All this, and I am still hungry,
> Still twenty years overweight, still unable
> To get down there or see
> What really happened.

To come to terms with what "really happened," Dickey literally places his protagonist in

To the White Sea on the ground in the midst of ''All-American fire'' in order to imagine and to dramatize the horrific destruction American bombing inflicted on the Japanese. Dickey's narrator, Sergeant Muldrow, records a detailed, first-person reaction to the living through such an apocalypse. A B-29 tail gunner and veteran of many bombing sorties, he is the lone survivor when his plane is shot down over Tokyo. Alone in his enemy's country, Muldrow is armed only with a map of Japan, a .45 pistol, an emergency kit, and his prewar skills learned while growing up in Alaska. To escape the bombing, his enemies, and the war, Muldrow begins a journey from Tokyo to Hokkaido, the northernmost island of Japan.

To accomplish this journey, Muldrow uses the hunting and survival knowledge learned from observing the predator-prey relationship in the wild Alaskan Brooks Range. He employs the techniques of making himself ''invisible'' to the Japanese, adapting camouflage lessons particularly of the lynx and the rabbit. Like Ed Gentry in *Deliverance*, he suspends civilization's mores in order to survive, and reveals himself to be a deadly predator. At the core of his character is an act of violence that took place before he entered the war—the murder of a female graduate student with whom he had an affair while both were living in Alaska. This act emphasizes that, unlike Gentry, Muldrow is not forced into the predator role simply by the dangerous situation in which he finds himself. Instead, his war is with others who invade his personal territory and threaten his seclusive world; it is a war that predates his war with the Japanese. His real combat relates to his struggle for survival against human entanglements, his achievement of the brutal, amoral consciousness of the wild animal.

Muldrow's first site of safety is in the literal and metaphorical bowels of Tokyo, a large sewer pipe where he is submerged in his enemy's offal. This site, repulsive and degrading, empha-sizes the unheroic character of war with which Dickey counters romanticized versions. Muldrow emerges from excrement to escape on a journey northward to the white land and eventually a white sea that represents, he believes, a purer life, a complete escape from the war.

Throughout his journey, whenever he feels threatened by his enemies or whenever he needs to acquire material for his safety or comfort, Muldrow kills. Initially his killings are understandable and justifiable requirements for his escape. Gradually the reader realizes that Muldrow is acting upon his own unique sense of justice. Having witnessed the beheading of an American pilot by Japanese captors, for example, Muldrow later beheads a Japanese peasant woman, placing her severed head in a water-wheel retrieving bucket as an emblem of his retribution. Yet he chooses not to kill three others who do not threaten his well-being, including two small children who discover him while he steals rice from their storage cave.

After making good his escape to the north, Muldrow nearly freezes to death in the winter cold. He is rescued, however, by primitive tribesmen in the northernmost part of Japan. After capturing a bear cub, the villagers amuse themselves by torturing it before its intended sacrifice the next day. Although Muldrow does not express outrage at the tribe's behavior, Dickey's indictment of primitive man's barbarism is expressed in Muldrow's response. In the middle of the night, Muldrow wakens, knifes to death a tribesman guarding the cub, stuffs the dead man's body into the cage, and frees the cub while he makes his own escape. Muldrow's act of retribution indicates his version of a moral balance.

Muldrow's journey ends with his death, yet Dickey purposely makes his death ambiguous, appearing as both a triumphant transcendence and a failed evasion of hostile forces. His death occurs when he is surrounded and then shot to death by Japanese soldiers. Yet Muldrow does escape metaphorically. He kills the old man in whose cabin he stayed, then plasters swan feathers onto his own body with the old man's blood. Then his spirit flies away at the moment his body is riddled with bullets from the soldiers. He thus embodies one of Dickey's persistent themes of transformation through reincarnation. Muldrow flies upward, toward heaven, into a new life. The whiteness of the winter land, the white swan feathers, and the white sea to which he had hoped to escape are reminiscent of Melville's use of whiteness that masks man's comprehension of nature's and, in turn, God's mysteries. Muldrow's voice, like Ishmael's, returns to tell his story, though now as pure spirit from the heaven of animals.

Muldrow's journey is both a literal and a metaphorical journey through man's social evolution, moving from a modern, industrialized society to agrarian communities to a primitive tribe of hunter-gatherers. At the heart of the civilized, the agrarian, and the primitive societies is a deliberate brutality toward man and animal. In one sense, Muldrow's mad savagery serves as a synecdoche for social man in these three stages of communal man. Muldrow's killings are brutal, yet his character pales in comparison to the worldwide slaughter that occurs throughout the war. His journey from civilization toward the white sea corresponds to a psychological retracing of his current circumstances back to his early years in the Alaskan Brooks Range, where he first learned and lived according to the laws of man and animal in their primitive state.

Dickey's three novels interconnect with his poetry, creating in the process an extended multigenre, multivoiced ''variations of one song,'' as he declares in ''Buckdancer's Choice.'' Throughout his career, Dickey's guiding principle has been to create new voices and new forms in each successive volume of poetry and fiction. As a consequence, he remains as vi-

tal and lively and controversial as when he first began his writing career. In the 1990s, Dickey was at work on his fourth novel, which would be based on his service in the South Pacific during World War II, the compelling subject that continue to haunt him fifty years later.

Selected Bibliography

WORKS OF JAMES DICKEY

POETRY

Into the Stone and Other Poems. In *Poets of Today VII.* Edited by John Hall Wheelock. New York: Scribners, 1960.

Drowning with Others. Middletown, Conn.: Wesleyan University Press, 1962.

Helmets: Poems. Middletown, Conn.: Wesleyan University Press, 1964.

Two Poems of the Air. Portland, Ore.: Centicore Press, 1964.

Buckdancer's Choice. Middletown, Conn.: Wesleyan University Press, 1965.

Poems 1957–1967. Middletown, Conn.: Wesleyan University Press, 1967.

The Eye-Beaters, Blood, Victory, Madness, Buckhead and Mercy. Garden City, N.Y.: Doubleday, 1970.

Exchanges. Bloomfield Hills, Mich.: Bruccoli Clark, 1971.

Yevtushenko, Yevgeny. *Stolen Apples.* Includes twelve poems adapted by Dickey. Garden City, N.Y.: Doubleday, 1971.

The Zodiac. Garden City, N.Y.: Doubleday, 1976.

In Pursuit of the Grey Soul. Columbia, S.C.: Bruccoli Clark, 1978.

The Strength of Fields. Garden City, N.Y.: Doubleday, 1979.

The Early Motion. Middletown, Conn.: Wesleyan University Press, 1981.

Falling, May Day Sermon, and Other Poems. Middletown, Conn.: Wesleyan University Press, 1981.

Puella. Garden City, N.Y.: Doubleday, 1982.

The Central Motion: Poems, 1968–1979. Middletown, Conn.: Wesleyan University Press, 1983.

False Youth: Four Seasons. Dallas: Pressworks, 1983.

The Eagle's Mile. Hanover, N.H.: Wesleyan University Press/University Press of New England, 1990.

The Whole Motion: Collected Poems, 1945–1992. Hanover, N.H.: Wesleyan University Press/University Press of New England, 1992.

FICTION

Deliverance. Boston: Houghton Mifflin, 1970.

Alnilam. Garden City, N.Y.: Doubleday, 1987.

Wayfarer: A Voice from the Southern Mountains. Birmingham, Ala.: Oxmoor House, 1988.

To the White Sea. Boston: Houghton Mifflin, 1993.

NONFICTION

The Suspect in Poetry. Madison, Minn.: Sixties Press, 1964.

Spinning the Crystal Ball. Washington, D.C.: Library of Congress, 1967.

Babel to Byzantium: Poets and Poetry Now. New York: Farrar, Straus and Giroux, 1968.

Metaphor as Pure Adventure. Washington, D.C.: Library of Congress, 1968.

"Lightnings or Visuals." *South Atlantic Review*, 57:1–14 (January 1992).

Sorties. Garden City, N.Y.: Doubleday, 1971.

Jericho: The South Beheld. Birmingham, Ala.: Oxmoor House, 1974.

God's Images: The Bible, a New Vision. Birmingham, Ala.: Oxmoor House, 1977.

The Water-Bug's Mittens: Ezra Pound: What We Can Use. Bloomfield Hills, Mich.: Bruccoli Clark, 1980.

The Starry Place Between the Antlers: Why I Live in South Carolina. Bloomfield Hills, Mich. and Columbia, S.C.: Bruccoli Clark, 1981.

Night Hurdling: Poems, Essays, Conversations, Commencements, and Afterwords. Columbia, S.C.: Bruccoli Clark, 1983.

Southern Light. Birmingham, Ala.: Oxmoor House, 1991.

CHILDREN'S BOOKS

Tucky the Hunter. New York: Crown, 1978.

Bronwen, the Traw, and the Shape-Shifter. San Diego: Harcourt Brace Jovanovich; Columbia, S.C.: Bruccoli Clark, 1986.

MANUSCRIPT PAPERS

Special Collections, Emory University Libraries, Atlanta, Georgia. Manuscripts, letters, and substantial amounts of other materials. Also Washington University Libraries, St. Louis, and Library of Congress, Washington, D.C. Manuscripts.

BIBLIOGRAPHIES

Bruccoli, Matthew J., and Judith S. Baughman. *James Dickey: A Descriptive Bibliography*. Pittsburgh: University of Pittsburgh Press, 1990.

"Continuing Bibliography." *James Dickey Newsletter,* 1 (Fall 1984—).

Elledge, Jim. *James Dickey: A Bibliography: 1947–1974*. Metuchen, N.J.: Scarecrow Press, 1979.

———. "James Dickey: A Supplementary Bibliography, 1975–1980: Part I." *Bulletin of Bibliography*, 38:92–100, 104 (April–June 1981).

———. "James Dickey: A Supplementary Bibliography, 1975–1980: Part II." *Bulletin of Bibliography*, 38:150–155 (July–September 1981).

BIOGRAPHICAL AND CRITICAL STUDIES

Alexander, George L. "A Psychoanalytic Observation of the Scopophilic Imagery in James Dickey's *Deliverance*." *James Dickey Newsletter*, 11:2–11 (Fall 1994).

Bartlett, Lee, and Hugh Witemeyer. "Ezra Pound and James Dickey: A Correspondence and a Kinship." *Paideuma*, 11:290–312 (Fall 1982).

Baughman, Ronald. *Understanding James Dickey*. Columbia: University of South Carolina Press, 1985.

———. "James Dickey." In *Dictionary of Literary Biography Documentary Series*, vol. 7: Modern American Poets. Edited by Karen L. Rood. Detroit, New York, Fort Lauderdale, London: Bruccoli Clark LaymanGale, 1989. Pp. 3–126. Contains previously unpublished material from Dickey's private papers.

———. "James Dickey's *Alnilam*: Toward a True Center Point." *South Carolina Review*, 26:173–179 (Spring 1994).

Bennett, Ross. " 'The Firebombing': A Reappraisal." *American Literature*, 52:430–448 (November 1980).

Berry, David C. "Harmony with the Dead: James Dickey's Descent into the Underworld." *Southern Quarterly,* 12:233–244 (April 1974).

Bloom, Harold. "James Dickey: From 'The Other' through *The Early Motion.*" *Southern Review,* 21:63–78 (Winter 1985).

Bloom, Harold, ed. *James Dickey: Modern Critical Views.* New York: Chelsea House, 1987.

Bly, Robert ("Crunk"). "The Collapse of James Dickey." *Sixties,* 9:70–79 (Spring 1967).

Bowers, Neal. *James Dickey: The Poet as Pitchman.* Columbia: University of Missouri Press, 1985.

Calhoun, Richard J., ed. *James Dickey: The Expansive Imagination: A Collection of Critical Essays.* Deland, Fla.: Everett/Edwards, 1973.

Calhoun, Richard J., and Robert W. Hill. *James Dickey.* Boston: Twayne, 1983.

Davison, Peter. "The Difficulties of Being Major: The Poetry of Robert Lowell and James Dickey." *Atlantic Monthly,* 220:116–121 (October 1967).

Greiner, Donald J. "The Harmony of Bestiality in James Dickey's *Deliverance.*" *South Carolina Review,* 5:43–49 (December 1972).

Guillory, Daniel L. "Water Magic in the Poetry of James Dickey." *English Language Notes,* 8:131–137 (December 1970).

Italia, Paul G. "Love and Lust in James Dickey's *Deliverance.*" *Modern Fiction Studies,* 21:203–213 (Summer 1975).

Kirschten, Robert. *James Dickey and the Gentle Ecstasy of Earth: A Reading of the Poems.* Baton Rouge: Louisiana State University Press, 1988.

Kirschten, Robert, ed. *Critical Essays on James Dickey.* New York: G. K. Hall, 1994.

Kostelanetz, Richard. "Flyswatter and Gadfly." *Shenandoah,* 16:92–95 (Spring 1965).

Laurence, Patricia. "James Dickey's *Puella* in Flight." *South Carolina Review,* 26:61–71 (Spring 1994).

Libby, Anthony. "Fire and Light: Four Poets to the End and Beyond." *Iowa Review,* 4:111–126 (Spring 1973).

Lieberman, Laurence. *The Achievement of James Dickey: A Comprehensive Selection of His Poems with a Critical Introduction.* Glenview, Ill.: Scott, Foresman, 1968.

———. "Erotic Pantheism in James Dickey's 'Madness.' " *South Carolina Review,* 26:72–86 (Spring 1994).

Mesic, Michael. "A Note on James Dickey." In *American Poetry since 1960.* Edited by Robert B. Shaw. Cheadle, U.K.: Carcanet, 1973. Pp. 145–153.

Mills, Ralph J. "The Poetry of James Dickey." *Tri-Quarterly,* no. 11:231–242 (Winter 1968).

Niflis, N. Michael. "A Special Kind of Fantasy: James Dickey on the Razor's Edge." *Southwest Review,* 57:311–317 (Autumn 1972).

Oates, Joyce Carol. "Out of Stone, into Flesh: The Imagination of James Dickey." *Modern Poetry Studies,* 5:97–144 (Autumn 1974).

O'Neill, Paul. "The Unlikeliest Poet." *Life,* 61:68–70, 72–74, 77–79 (July 22, 1966).

Pair, Joyce M. " 'The Peace of the Pure Predator': Dickey's Energized Man in *To the White Sea.*" *James Dickey Newsletter,* 10:15–27 (Spring 1994).

Rubin, Louis D., Jr. "Understanding 'The Buckhead Boys.' " *South Carolina Review,* 26:196–197 (Spring 1994).

Smith, Dave. "The Strength of James Dickey." *Poetry,* 137:349–358 (March 1981).

———. "James Dickey's Motions." *South Carolina Review,* 26:41–60 (Spring 1994).

Strange, William C. "To Dream, to Remember: James Dickey's *Buckdancer's Choice.*" *Northwest Review,* 7:33–42 (Fall–Winter 1965–1966).

Suarez, Ernest. *James Dickey and the Politics of Canon: Assessing the Savage Ideal.* Columbia: University of Missouri Press, 1993.

———. " 'Roll God, Roll': Muldrow's Primitive Creed." *James Dickey Newsletter,* 10:3–14 (Spring 1994).

Taylor, Henry. "Going for Broke: A Strategy in James Dickey's Poetry." *South Carolina Review,* 26:27–39 (Spring 1994).

Van Ness, Gordon. *Outbelieving Existence: The Measured Motion of James Dickey.* Columbia, S.C.: Camden House, 1992.

Weatherby, H. L. "The Way of Exchange in James Dickey's Poetry." *Sewanee Review,* 74:669–680 (Summer 1966).

Weigl, Bruce, and T. R. Hummer, eds. *The Imagination as Glory: The Poetry of James Dickey.* Urbana: University of Illinois Press, 1984.

INTERVIEWS

Self-Interviews. Edited by Barbara Reiss and James Reiss. Garden City, N.Y.: Doubleday, 1970.

The Voiced Connections of James Dickey: Interviews and Conversations. Edited by Ronald Baughman. Columbia: University of South Carolina Press, 1989.

Greiner, Donald J. " 'The Iron of English': An Interview with James Dickey." *South Carolina Review*, 26:9–20 (Spring 1994).

SCREENPLAYS

Deliverance. Warner Brothers, 1972. Carbondale: Southern Illinois University Press, 1982.

Call of the Wild. Produced by Charles Fries, 1976.

VIDEOS

Writer's Workshop. Produced by University of South Carolina and the South Carolina ETV Network, 1992. Includes interview with Dickey.

The Sacred Words: The Elements of Poetry. In series *Literary Visions*. Produced by Maryland Public Television, 1992. Part II is an interview with Dickey.

James Dickey at 70: A Tribute. Produced by Department of Media Arts, University of South Carolina, 1993.

—RONALD BAUGHMAN

Joan Didion

1934–

"THE EXTENT TO which certain places dominate the California imagination is apprehended, even by Californians, only dimly," Joan Didion wrote in 1982, in "Girl of the Golden West," an essay that explores Patricia Hearst's kidnapping and her criminal exploits as a member of the Symbionese Liberation Army as a not entirely unexpected series of events at "land's end." Collected in her most recent work, *After Henry* (1992), in the section "California," this composition revisits most of Didion's signature concerns in her thirty-year career as essayist, novelist, and screenwriter: the relative fatalism in a place of natural disasters—earthquakes, floods, landslides, fires—and psychological alienation, entropy, and anomie at the continent's western edge, the distractions and hazards of wealth and fame, the perceptual void at the center of experience, and the struggle to define California.

A native of the Golden State, Didion stakes a personal claim to its imagination—"Deriving not only from the landscape but from the claiming of it, from the romance of emigration, the radical abandonment of established attachments, this imagination remains obdurately symbolic, tending to locate lessons in what the rest of the country perceives only as scenery"—and its importance in understanding Patty Hearst's role in her family's California narrative. For Didion, Patty Hearst represents an extension of the California

ascendancy of the family: Hearst's great-grandfather, who "had arrived in California by foot in 1850 . . . with few graces and no prospects," and who, at the time of his death in 1891, left his widow, Phoebe Apperson Hearst, "a fortune taken from the ground"; her great-grandmother, who "financed her only child [William Randolph Hearst] in the publishing empire he wanted, underwrote a surprising amount of the campus where her great-granddaughter would be enrolled at the time she was kidnapped." Such "lessons" in "scenery" form the aesthetic and perceptual core of Joan Didion's California, the id of America.

It is difficult to imagine Didion's West without the East as an oppositional force. A California native, Didion suffers the regional insecurities of those with ambitions defined by the Eastern publishing establishment. As the westward trek had weathered her ancestors, the journey "back East" tested her literary stamina and achievement without softening her Western perspective. Even a seasonal occasional piece for the *Saturday Evening Post,* "The Big Rock Candy Figgy Pudding Pitfall" (1966), evokes the pioneering spirit Didion imagines in her daily endeavors: "The heart of it is that although I am frail, lazy and unsuited to do anything except what I am paid to do, which is sit by myself and type with one finger, I like to imagine myself a 'can-do' kind of woman, capable of patching the corral fence, pickling enough peaches to feed the hands all winter, and then winning a trip to Minneapolis in the Pillsbury Bake-Off.'' In the late 1980s, a return ''back East'' (she notes with amusement, in *After Henry,* that ''Californians of my daughter's generation speak of going 'out' to New York, a meaningful shift in the perception of one's place in the world'') to New York City after an absence of twenty-five years, signaled a return to her earliest transcontinental perspective as well as to her original readership.

In 1981, the bibliographer Donna Olendorf claimed that Didion's audience had grown from ''a small-but-dedicated group of New York literati to college campuses across the land.'' Such a critique limits Didion's readership to those who are college-educated and have the bicoastal, middle-class sensibilities necessary to ''read'' California and New York as ''texts.'' Readers of *Slouching towards Bethlehem* must respond simultaneously to the ''wagon-train morality'' of the ''Donner-Reed Party, starving in the Sierra snows'' (in ''On Morality'') and to the chic worlds of Spago, Esalen, I. Magnin, and the Plaza. In the same book (in ''Notes from a Native Daughter'') she indulges those who ''share in the pervasive delusion that California is only five hours from New York by air'' even as she insists that ''California is somewhere else,'' a world of geopolitical remove that will become her main topic.

Geopolitical otherness sustains Didion as topic and stance. California with its ''regional spaciness'' expands hemispherically to include Miami, El Salvador, and the fictional South American state of Boca Grande of *A Book of Common Prayer,* in which Didion's authorial presence is generalized into that of the alien observer: *la norteamericana.* Didion recalled in a 1979 *New York Times* interview with Michiko Kakutani: ''A lot of the stories I was brought up on had to do with extreme actions—leaving ev-

erything behind, crossing the trackless wastes, and in those stories the people who stayed behind and had their settled ways—those people were not the people who got the prize. The prize was California.''

Joan Didion was born 5 December 1934 in Sacramento, the daughter of Frank Reese Didion and Eduene Jerrett Didion. A fifth generation ''Daughter of the Golden West'' on her mother's side as well as a direct descendant of a member of the original Donner-Reed party, Didion draws upon the stark Central Valley settings of her childhood as well as its unsettled history to lend context to the extreme circumstances of her characters. She notes in *Slouching towards Bethlehem* (''Notes from a Native Daughter''), ''I come from California, come from a family, or a congeries of families, that has always been in the Sacramento Valley.'' For non-Californians she provides the following explanation: ''It is characteristic of Californians to speak grandly of the past as if it had simultaneously begun, *tabula rasa,* and reached a happy ending on the day the wagons started west.'' Religious ''in a certain way,'' Didion drifted from the Episcopalianism of her childhood because, as she told Sara Davidson, she ''hated the stories . . . though like[d] the words of the Episcopal service [which she would] say . . . over and over in [her] mind.''

Her father, an Army Air Corps officer in World War II (and a draft board officer in Sacramento during the Vietnam War), was stationed at military bases in Colorado and Detroit. This early moving from base to base increased her sense of outsiderhood even as it confirmed her commitment to Sacramento as the one true home and enlarged her sense of ''the West'' as identical with California. Didion recalled in ''Making Up Stories'' that her father's travels offer a means of charting the world and marking history: ''When Detroit is mentioned I think reflexively of my father. I have never before yesterday been in Detroit but my father was stationed there, the last year of World War II. When he came home to California from Detroit he brought me three handkerchiefs of a very heavy silk twill.'' Such mementos become talismans throughout Didion's work as she brings relics from far afield home to California, home to her faded pink bedroom in her parents' home, where she finishes all of her manuscripts.

In February 1953 Didion entered the University of California at Berkeley, an institution that assumed a somewhat haunting and lyrical presence in her writings. In the fall of 1954 she took Mark Schorer's English 106A, a fiction workshop that she recalls in ''Telling Stories'' (in the collection *Telling Stories*) as ''a kind of sacramental experience, an initiation into the grave world of real writers . . . an occasion of acute excitement and dread.'' Reading and stylistically imitating Ernest Hemingway, Henry James, Joseph Conrad, and F. Scott Fitzgerald informed her first attempts at critically evaluated writing. Upon graduation in 1956, she won *Vogue*'s Prix de Paris for her essay on the California architect William Wilson Wurster and went ''away'' (as her grandmother might have put it) to New York City. In *Slouching towards Bethlehem* (''Notes of a Native Daughter'') Didion later recalled, ''What happened in New York and Washington and abroad seemed to impinge not at all upon the Sacramento mind.''

At *Vogue*, working with the editor Allene Talmey, Didion learned to find the right adverbs and ''shock verbs'' as she was put to work writing and rewriting captions, distilling the essence of furniture, fashions, and personalities into a prose style that would never again relax into superfluity. Writing ''merchandising copy'' and ''promotion copy'' was characterized by concision and verve; a sample recalled in ''Telling Stories'' was typical: ''Opposite, above: All through the house, colour, verve, improvised treasures in happy but anomalous coexistence. Here, a Frank Stella, an Art Nouveau stained-glass panel, a Roy Lichtenstein. Not shown: A table covered with brilliant oilcloth, a Mexican find at fifteen cents a yard.'' In the tedium of assigned scripts, words became ''tools, toys, weapons to be deployed strategically on a page.''

By 1963, Didion had advanced to feature editor at *Vogue* and had long been a contributing book and film reviewer for *National Review* and *Mademoiselle*. Even in these early writings, the startling rapprochement between fashion and social critique characterizes every effort. A 1964 *Vogue* column, ''Silver—To Have and to Hurl,'' hints at what would become a Didion trademark: her ability to render in sinister tones the most decorous and commonplace subjects:

> A woman we know admitted a night fear so specific and so plausible (no knife murders here, no arsonists with nylon stockings flattening their noses) that it seemed to verge upon the absurd: she was occasionally obsessed, away from home, by the conviction that someone was, at that moment, stealing certain teaspoons which had belonged to her great-grandmother.

By 1958, Didion's journalism had attracted the attention of John Gregory Dunne, a Princeton-educated editor at *Time*, who became an early confidant and congenial editor. Years of professional camaraderie led to their sharing an apartment in 1963 (the year of her Bread Loaf Fellowship in fiction) and joint editing of her first book, the novel *Run River*. On 30 January 1964, they were married. Three months later, despairing of the Manhattan scene, they moved to Los Angeles. As Didion remembers in *Slouching towards Bethlehem* (''Goodbye to All That''): ''One morning in April (we had been married in January) [my husband] called and told me that he wanted to get out of New York for a while, that he would take a six-month leave of absence, that we would go somewhere.'' For the next twenty-five years, Didion dwelled ''somewhere'' in Los Angeles County.

Whether in Hollywood, Trancas (north of Malibu), or Brentwood Park, Didion established a surprising domesticity despite the pressure-filled schedules of screenwriting and producing regular columns for *Saturday Evening Post* (alternating the "Points West" column with Dunne), *Vogue*, and *National Review*. In 1966 she and Dunne adopted an infant girl, naming her Quintana Roo, and she met Henry Robbins, the agent who became the guardian and guide of her career until his death in 1979.

The demands of personal success coupled with the chaos of the late 1960s brought unexpected trauma and dislocation to the Didion–Dunne household. In the summer of 1968, suffering writer's block unrelieved by endless and directionless driving, Dunne moved to an apartment just off the Strip in Las Vegas, where he lived for a year and a half among gamblers and prostitutes. That same summer, Didion was admitted to a clinic in Santa Monica. The psychiatric report that introduces her 1979 collection of essays, *The White Album*, allows her to conclude:

> The tests mentioned . . . were administered privately, in the outpatient psychiatric clinic at St. John's Hospital in Santa Monica, in the summer of 1968, shortly after I suffered the "attack of vertigo and nausea" mentioned in the first sentence and shortly before I was named a *Los Angeles Times* "Woman of the Year." By way of comment I offer only that an attack of vertigo and nausea does not now seem to me an inappropriate response to the summer of 1968.

In the 1970s Didion firmly secured her reputation as a stylist grounded in Manhattan and Los Angeles: she wrote screenplays with her husband (*Panic in Needle Park* [1971]; *Play It as It Lays* [1972]; *A Star Is Born* [1976]), contributed essays to the *New York Times Book Review* and the *New York Review of Books*, alternated with Dunne writing "The Coast" column for *Esquire*, and completed a quintessential Hollywood novel (*Play It as It Lays* [1970]) and another collection of California essays (*The White Album*). Even that hemispheric tour de force, *A Book of Common Prayer* (1977), seemed a projection of the nation's coastal sensibilities.

By the late 1970s, Didion was acclaimed as one of the country's leading prose writers, one of the "New Journalists" of the mid-1960s (others were Norman Mailer, Tom Wolfe, Truman Capote, Gore Vidal) who invented a range of experimental fictional and nonfictional styles to critique the country's commodity culture. She became an essential commentator on cosmopolitan lifestyles and the global consequences of those lives. As *A Book of Common Prayer* insists, Americans (or, in the particular case of Charlotte Douglas, Californians) who remain "immaculate of history, innocent of politics" fall prey to the complexities of global intrigue and social disintegrations. Increasingly, Didion's travels drew her beyond the familiar social pastiche into what she defined for Sara Davidson as "a deceptive surface that appeared to be one thing and turned color as soon as you looked through it." Sweltering Tarmac, trade winds, and broken communiqués enlarged Didion's world of reference: beyond the hemispheric concerns of her Western vision to include the Pacific intrigues of American cold war policy, a world where even an airport coffee shop may serve as locus classicus for drifting democracies and lost protagonists. Joint ventures with Dunne during this period included alternating columns for *New West* magazine and writing the screenplay for Dunne's *True Confessions* (1981).

In 1982 Didion's visit to El Salvador resulted in three essays for the *New York Review of Books* that were subsequently published as *Salvador* (1983). Hemispheric and Pacific travels and journalistic inquiries throughout the decade inform her novel *Democracy* (1984). A brief residence in Miami inspired Didion to revisit the recent history of American policy in Cuba as it relates to local politics and global intrigue, including the assassination of President Kennedy. Published serially in the *New York Review of Books,* these essays were collected as *Miami* in 1987, marking closure to Didion's geopolitical expansion. After twenty-five years in California, Didion and Dunne returned to Manhattan in 1988.

Occasional essays for the *New York Review of Books* and the *New Yorker,* offering backward glances at the Los Angeles of earthquakes, riots, fires, and rattlesnakes, form Didion's 1992 collection, *After Henry.* Bereft of her native state and her longtime editor, she continues to measure her life in Western cadences. She notes "This will have been only the second fire season over twenty-five years during which I did not have a house somewhere in Los Angeles County" ("Fire Season," in *After Henry*).

Summing up the narrative strategy of her first novel, *Run River* (1963), Didion records her nostalgia for California in her *Paris Review* interview with Linda Kuehl: "I think I really put the novel in Sacramento because I was homesick. I wanted to remember the weather and the rivers." One means of evoking her lost landscape was to anchor the tale in the generational disputes and mores of a California family. Walter Knight, scion of the family that owns the Valley property, becomes a veritable text of California history, a laissez-faire world in which neighbors left each other alone. Though peripheral to the main line of the plot, Knight's autumnal patriarchy informs every scene, representing the founding settler ideal.

Didion told Kuehl that she wished the novel "to be very complicated chronologically, to somehow have the past and present operating simultaneously," but abandoned that device when she discovered that she "wasn't accomplished enough to do that with any clarity." Settling for a linearity of present time, flashback, and present time, *Run River* begins and ends with a murder, suggesting Didion's structural and atmospheric debt to film noir.

Lily Knight McClellan, the protagonist, is thirty-six years old when the novel opens with Everett McClellan's murder of her lover, Ryder Channing. The tensions between the worldviews of these competitors reflect the collapse of Walter Knight's governing California vision. The story, though tentatively constructed out of the twenty-year McClellan marriage, develops more interestingly into a series of intersecting tableaux in which the settler culture of "old" California is systematically displaced by the postwar rise of education and money.

Suicides, murders, abortions, and betrayals—the stock romantic devices of *Run River*—encourage a return to the land, to the simpler world of Walter Knight. Settlement becomes a form of death, as sketched in Lily's memory summoned by the death of her father. Visiting the family graveyard and locating the oldest grave—*"Matthew Broderick Knight, January 2, 1847, until December 6, 1848"*—Lily recalls that child who survived the journey, and died "instead in a room in Sacramento that first winter, while his father, Lily's great-great-grandfather, was building the first house on the ranch." Although *Run River* develops what by now is the familiar Didion interest in disaffected female protagonists, it also demonstrates her commitment to alternating narratives from a man's perspective. She discussed her enthusiasm for Everett McClellan and interest in writing from this angle with Linda Kuehl: "Everett McClellan. I don't remember those parts as being any harder than the other parts. A lot of people thought Everett was 'shadowy,' though. He's the most distinct person in the book to me. I loved him. I loved Lily and Martha but I loved Everett more."

Though Didion recalls her first work being greeted with "deafening disinterest," *Run River* was widely, though cautiously, reviewed. A survey of reviews suggests a decidedly mixed and uncertain response; the harshest reviews reveal an indifference or hostility by the reviewers to

Didion's Western ethos, a disappointment that such a finely wrought style should be wasted on, as the *New Yorker* put it, "human leftovers." Reviewers on both coasts expressed boredom with characters so afflicted by ennui. Considerations in the United Kingdom proved more favorable, but equally deaf to Didion's intentions; "Lily of the Valley" motifs dominated most reviews, with little sense of the relationship Didion insists upon between her characters and the land. Didion's narratorial uncertainty or experimentation was frequently noted as a distraction.

Though the novel has received less academic attention than Didion's later works, several essayists have found it a parable of California's lost pastoral splendor. For many, *Run River* serves as a continuation of the American pastoral, a return to the restorative qualities of the land; for others, it depicts the generational rupture of post–World War II America in which the Edenic landscape succumbs to industrial greed. The most ambitious claims for the work come from Thomas Mallon, who sees Lily as the first of Didion's women to trouble over their relationship to history.

Slouching towards Bethlehem (1968), a collection of nonfiction published from 1961 to 1967 in *American Scholar, California Monthly, New York Times Magazine,* and *Saturday Evening Post,* draws its energy—and title—from one of the last pieces written, for the *Post,* "Hippies: Slouching towards Bethlehem." In "A Preface" Didion notes that the essay, "which derived from some time spent in the Haight-Ashbury district of San Francisco, was . . . both the most imperative of all . . . to write and the only one that made me despondent after it was printed. It was the first time I had dealt directly and flatly with the evidence of atomization, the proof that things fall apart." Most of the essays were written during the mid-1960s for the *Post.* Offering a spirited defense of her work for the *Post,* the magazine

that published much of F. Scott Fitzgerald's Hollywood fiction, Didion declared, "The *Post* is extremely receptive to what the writer wants to do, pays enough for him to be able to do it right, and is meticulous about not changing copy." Her most quoted, though not necessarily most memorable, prefatory comment comes in her self-aware summary: "My only advantage as a reporter is that I am so physically small, so temperamentally unobtrusive, and so neurotically inarticulate that people tend to forget that my presence runs counter to their best interests. And it always does. That is one last thing to remember: *writers are always selling somebody out.*"

The essays defy chronological organization and rely instead upon three broad, thematic constructions: "Life Styles in the Golden Land," "Personals," and "Seven Places of the Mind." Although they share with Didion's novels the sense of being "cautionary tales"—stories you don't wish to happen to you—they enact as well the grander ambition of what Alfred Kazin has called Didion's role as "professional moralist." Individually and collectively, these essays explore the tensions in a California that in "Notes of a Native Daughter" she characterizes as "a place in which a boom mentality and a sense of Chekhovian loss meet in uneasy suspension; in which the mind is troubled by some buried but ineradicable suspicion that things had better work here, because here, beneath that immense bleached sky, is where we run out of continent."

This California is peopled by the icons (John Wayne, Joan Baez) and by the unknown and infamous (Lucille Miller of "Some Dreamers of the Golden Dream," "Comrade Laski, C.P.U.S.A. [M.L.]," the Las Vegas couples of "Marrying Absurd" and Deadeye, Steve, Debbie, and the other abandoned children of "Slouching towards Bethlehem"), the forgotten famous (Howard Hughes of "7000 Romaine, Los Angeles 38"), but ultimately is controlled by the rectitude and exactitude of its Native

Daughter author. Recalling for Susan Stamberg the circumstances of these assignments, Didion insisted that though she considered herself a "moralist" with "a strong West Coast ethic," she nonetheless simply wished to "tell the story" without "mak[ing] a judgment on it." The varied California landscapes evoke for Didion a perpetual sense of loss; the world of *Run River* has succumbed to that of endless development. She notes elegiacally in "Notes of a Native Daughter": "It is hard to *find* California now, unsettling to wonder how much of it was merely imagined or improvised; melancholy to realize how much of anyone's memory is no true memory at all but only the traces of someone else's memory, stories handed down on the family network."

Curiously, though California dominates the entire collection, reviews located its primary strengths in its cultural critique of societal collapse. Few, if any, lingered upon Didion's "native" perspective or the broader concerns of the collection, preferring to dwell upon "hippies" and "lost children." The dated terms of the reviewers' language—"making the scene," "flower children," "telling it like it is"—contrast sharply with the enduring vitality of the essays. For many reviewers, Didion seemed simultaneously "new breed" and the heir to H. L. Mencken. Editors at *Esquire* and *National Review,* long familiar with her work, declared the style and insights of *Slouching towards Bethlehem* brilliant.

Scholars assess Didion's contributions to the New Journalism as well as her ongoing definition of things Western, things Californian. Style and message intertwine in most interpretations of her radical grammar of journalism, suggesting that, for Didion, style is a form of argument.

When Michiko Kakutani reported that by the late 1960s, friends and neighbors referred to Didion as the "Kafka of Brentwood Park," John Gregory Dunne countered, "Joan's really a rather cheerful person who drives a bright yellow Corvette. . . . In person, she doesn't have a dark view of life. She just doesn't expect a lot from it or from people." And so, in spite of the surface similarities between protagonist and author—physical and emotional fragility, yellow Corvette, reddish hair, tendency to migraines—Maria Wyeth remains Didion's alter ego. Didion explained in her *Paris Review* interview:

> There was a certain tendency to read *Play It as It Lays* as an autobiographical novel, I suppose because I lived out here and looked skinny in photographs and nobody knew anything else about me. Actually the only thing Maria and I have in common is an occasional inflection, which I picked up from her—not vice versa—when I was writing the book. I like Maria a lot.

The acclaim that followed *Slouching towards Bethlehem* grew into best-seller status with *Play It as It Lays,* a National Book Award nominee. Suffused with the neurotic tensions inspired by her nonfiction prose, *Play It as It Lays* unsettled even her editor, Henry Robbins, who told Kakutani: "It was a brilliant book but cold, almost icy. A devastating book. When I finished it, I wanted to call her up and ask her if she was all right. I *did* see it as the experience of despair." In "Why I Write," Didion recalled the wish "to write a novel so elliptical and fast that it would be over before you noticed it, a novel so fast that it would hardly exist on the page at all."

Maria Wyeth, "pronounced Mar-*eye*-ah, to get it straight at the outset"—born in Reno, raised in the lost town of Silver Wells, Nevada (a place of "three hundred acres of mesquite and some houses and a Flying A and a zinc mine and a Tonopah & Tidewater RR siding and a trinket shop . . . a midget golf course and a reptile museum and a restaurant with some slots and two crap tables")—dominates the narrative of her social and psychological collapse. Three introductory sketches, disclosures of Maria—from Maria's own first-person perspective (age thirty-one, institutionalized for a collapse into anomie), in Helene's (Maria's confidante) first-person recollections, and in Carter's (Maria's estranged director-husband) first-person, terse, and dismissive recall—in which Didion details the "facts" and perceptions of her protagonist, establish the narratorial strategy of *Play It as It Lays.* Didion explains the novel's narratorial drift in her *Paris Review* interview:

> I wanted to make it all first person but I wasn't good enough. . . . So I began playing with a close third person, just to get something down. By a "close third" I mean not an omniscient third but a third very close to the mind of the character. Suddenly one night I realized that I had some first person and some third person and that I was going to have to go with both, or just not write a book at all.

The eighty-four "scenes" that follow, depict Maria's progressive alienation and collapse into nothingness.

The scene is Hollywood, the set a series of industry locations, simultaneously evoking the tawdriness and glamour of a life at the margins of the entertainment world. Influenced by her father's gambling wisdom (" 'Don't let them bluff you back there because you're holding all the aces' "), Maria falls repeated victim to the vicissitudes and emptiness of her privileged circumstances even as she attempts to redirect her life. Neither her father nor her estranged director-husband, Carter Lang, succeeds in eliciting other than reactive responses from Maria, who, bereft of maternal society (her mother died in a desert car crash, and the "coyotes tore her up before anybody found her," and her four-year-old daughter, Kate, is locked up in a place where "they put electrodes on her head and needles in her spine and try to figure out what went wrong"), can only hope to break free from the paternalism of her environment.

Maria's most celebrated and purposeful act of self-definition is driving the freeways with their "precariously imposed momentum." The articulation of freeway interchanges provides an alternative structure for Maria's drift:

> She drove the San Diego to the Harbor, the Harbor up to the Hollywood, the Hollywood to the Golden State, the Santa Monica, the Santa Ana, the Pasadena, the Ventura. She drove it as a riverman runs a river, every day more attuned to its currents, its deceptions, and just as a riverman feels the pull of the rapids in the lull between sleeping and waking, so Maria lay at night in the still of Beverly Hills and saw the great signs soar overhead at seventy miles an hour, *Normandie ¼ Vermont ¾ Harbor Fwy 1.*

The freeway turns alternately purposeful and lethal, like the rivers of *Run River*—and is equally threatening to Didion, who took the occasion of her *Paris Review* interview to correct impressions of her:

> Actually I don't drive on the freeway. I'm afraid to. I freeze at the top of the entrance, at the instant when you have to let go and join it. Occasionally I *do* get on the freeway—usually because I'm shamed into it—and it's such an extraordinary experience that it sticks in my mind.

By the time of *The White Album,* Didion defined "the freeway experience" as "the only secular communion Los Angeles has."

Though spare and edgy, this world continues to chart the degradation and despair of Didion's earlier novel. Marriages end in divorce, pregnancies in abortion, friendships in suicide, and childhood in institutions. Forever at war with "*as it was,*" Maria nonetheless succumbs repeatedly to the terms of her world contrived in the pages of *Daily Variety* and the *Hollywood Reporter.*

The best-selling Farrar, Straus, and Giroux edition was widely and favorably reviewed. Early assessments display more than regional tensions in reception; they reveal feminist tensions as well. While mainstream male reviewers, East and West, spoke of despair in the desert or social disintegration in California (continuing themes from *Slouching towards Bethlehem*), *Atlantic*'s Phoebe Adams and Gloria Steinem quarreled over whether it was the story of "a self-centered pseudo-actress with a crack in her head" or a "housewife [who] came to cope." "Cold," "careless," and "bleak" described for many reviewers Didion's mental landscape as well as that of her protagonist. Maria's emptiness was often read as a symptom of California's bankrupt hedonism. By far the most disturbing and perceptive review came from Didion's mentor, novelist Mark Schorer, who noted the inherent crisis when "one chooses nullity as one's subject matter" and pronounced Didion's "brilliant manipulation of a staccato style and the brief, cinematic scene, so perfectly appropriate to her Hollywood milieu. . . . [and] Maria . . . this unwilling barometer of pain who chooses to hang there in the freezing desert climate of Who Cares?" a success.

Scholars have been drawn to the nihilism and feminism of the work as well as to the ways Didion's metaphoric style compensates for the impoverishment within her protagonists' lives. Others, invoking F. Scott Fitzgerald and Nathanael West, see *Play It as It Lays* as yet another apocalyptic Hollywood novel. Few critics think beyond the obvious tags of "impoverished," "empty," "atomized," and "doomed" to consider either the source or the significance of Didion's wasteland. Only Cynthia Griffin Wolff, in response to Katherine Henderson's tentative argument that Didion toys with the secularization of American religious heritage, offers a sophisticated and ambitious critical response, asserting that Didion's "ruthless memory . . . recalls all of the most poignant dreams of the American experiment. . . . compels us to seek a definition for the chaos of our society."

The shimmering picture that triggered Didion's next project was the Panama airport at dawn. As she recalled in "Why I Write," "I was in this airport only once, on a plane to Bogotá that stopped for an hour to refuel, but the way it looked that morning remained superimposed on everything I saw until the day I finished *A Book of Common Prayer*." In 1973 Didion and Dunne traveled to Cartagena, Colombia, to represent the United States at a film festival. Suffering from paratyphoid, Didion spent the entire trip sequestered in her hotel room (she recalls "invoking the name 'Jack Valenti' a lot, as if its reiteration could make [her] well"). Though failing generators and tropical storms kept her in the dark and unable to read, they inspired consideration of the relative situations of the Americas. Didion later told Sara Davidson: "In North America, social tensions that arise tend to be undercut and co-opted quite soon, but in Latin America there does not seem to be any political machinery for delaying the revolution. Everything is thrown into bold relief. There is a collapsing of time." The title recalls her family's Episcopalianism as well as her early *Vogue* essay " 'Take No for an Answer,' " in which she says, in the last paragraph, "One finally loses all sense of one's own wants and needs, comes to exist only in the approval of others. Something seems to have been mislaid, and it is futile to look in the drawer with the birth certificate, the passport, and the Book of Common Prayer inscribed by the Bishop." Such idle speculations and contemplations become Didion's third novel, which she characterized for the *Paris Review* as one of "dense texture" with "a lot of plot and an awful lot of places and weather." Comparing the genesis of *A Book of Common Prayer* with that of Fitzgerald's *The Last Tycoon*, Didion notes in "Making Up Stories":

I saw a novel as an object discovered. . . . a mystery. . . . The novel I was working on that spring in Berkeley had begun in 1971 as a book about a woman who was traveling through Mississippi and Louisiana with her ex-husband, who was dying. The novel was to take place entirely in motel rooms off interstate highways.

This "novel without event . . . told in the flat third person" became her novel of "a Central American republic named Boca Grande and . . . involved bombings, a hijacking, a revolution and a number of other theatrical . . . events."

As if to stylistically enact the hemispheric ruptures contemplated on that trip to Cartagena, Didion places the story of forty-year-old Charlotte Douglas—native of Hollister, California (epicenter of the San Andreas earthquake fault), "a married resident of San Francisco . . . five-feet-five inches tall . . . red hair . . . brown eyes . . . NORTE-AMERICANA . . . TURISTA"—in the hands of her "witness," Grace Strasser-Mendana. Grace, a Denver native trained in anthropology ("studied under Kroeber at California and worked with Lévi-Strauss at São Paulo"), now in late middle age and dying of pancreatic cancer, "lost faith" in her academic specialty and method, retired, married a Boca Grande planter, and became a biochemist. Her temperamental and geopolitical remove from Charlotte's circumstances make her narrative oblique, for she can share but few details about the "place where Charlotte died and [she] live[s]." She anxiously legitimizes her voice, claiming that it doesn't matter who she is, because she is a narrator without motive. More troubling, perhaps, is the technical problem of an absent narrator; as Didion explained to *Saturday Review*'s Digby Diehl: "The narrator was not present during most of the events she's telling you about. And her only source is a woman incapable of seeing the truth."

Pressed to outline her narrative at the outset, Grace explains "what happened" to Charlotte: "she left one man, she left a second man, she traveled again with the first; she let him die alone. She lost one child to 'history' and another to 'complications' . . . she imagined herself capable of shedding that baggage and came to Boca Grande, a tourist. *Una turista.*" This would seem to confirm Charlotte's status as "Westerner"; as

Didion notes in "Thinking about Western Thinking":

> It is "different" to be Western, and to pretend that this is no longer or never was so is to ignore the narrative force of the story Westerners learn early: the story that the wilderness was and is redemptive, and that a radical break with civilization and its discontents is distinctly an option.

Charlotte, "immaculate of history, innocent of politics," invests the characteristic Didion protagonist role with an enlarged sense of history and troubled circumstance. Caught within the uncertain emotional web of entanglements with her first husband, erstwhile professor Warren Bogart, her second husband, activist attorney Leonard Douglas, and her daughter, Marin, Charlotte attempts to encounter, even as she disengages, her place in history. Charlotte, a victim of a turbulent decade, demonstrates abandon and vulnerability in the face of the most extreme circumstances. Her daughter, Marin, recalls Patty Hearst's projection of the innocence and contempt of the good life gone wrong:

> Soft Marin. Who at eighteen had been observed with her four best friends detonating a crude pipe bomb in the lobby of the Transamerica Building at 6:30 A.M., hijacking a P.S.A. L-1011 at San Francisco Airport and landing it at Wendover, Utah, where they burned it in time for the story to interrupt the network news and disappeared.

Charlotte's hegira to Boca Grande, a hemispheric retreat, contextualizes her disaffections while exposing her to mortal danger. Involuntarily, Charlotte Douglas, like her daughter, finds that her individual flight from American responsibilities is read by family and foreigners alike as representative of her country's duplicity and ignorance. As Grace's final narration suggests, Charlotte could never shrug off her identity: "I flew back from New Orleans, and Charlotte Douglas's body was found, where it had been thrown, on the lawn of the American Embassy. Since all Embassy personnel had abandoned the building the point was lost on them. Although not on me.''

Early reviews reflected an increased impatience with Didion's trademark style and themes; more than one review mockingly renamed the novel ''Pray It as It Lays'' (*Washington Post, Cleveland Press*), and others expressed boredom with her ennui: ''Slouching towards Babel'' (*Village Voice*), ''Overimagining'' (*Chicago Tribune*), ''No Second Coming'' (*New York Times*), '' 'Common Prayer' Is Far Cry from Pulpit'' (*Boston Herald American*). Joyce Carol Oates provided the most insightful and speculative critique of Didion's narrative strategy in the *New York Times Book Review:* ''The device of the uninvolved narrator is a tricky one, since a number of private details must be presented as if they were within the range of the narrator's experience. But it is a measure of Didion's skill as a novelist that one never questions Mrs. Strasser-Mendana's near omniscience in recalling Charlotte's story.'' Christopher Lehmann-Haupt countered Oates's critique, insisting that Didion ''asks too much of Charlotte, and overburdened as she is by the pitiless cruelty of the narrator's vision, she collapses under the strain.'' Few reviewers were more extravagant with praise and condemnation than Margot Hentoff in the *Village Voice*. Declaring Didion as essayist ''one of our very best writers,'' Hentoff notes, ''She has the capacity, I think, to be the Chekhov of our time, but her novels do not come alive because they are insufficiently distanced from her own anxiety—too relentlessly ironic in tone, too emotionally controlled, as if the form itself were the bars of a cell.''

Academic criticism has concentrated upon the feminist implications of narratorial style and hemispheric historical complications. Some saw buried within the conventions of the romance Didion's attempt to rescript the genre from a feminist perspective. Others saw it as a continuation of her preoccupation with the nullity at the center of existence. Judith Kegan Gardiner develops a broader thesis of paradigmatic shift in which Didion reveals a gender-defined sense of private and public morality.

''Self-absorption is general, as is self-doubt,'' Didion writes in ''Letter from 'Manhattan,' '' her 1979 *New York Review of Books* essay-review of Woody Allen's *Manhattan, Interiors,* and *Annie Hall.* Responding to Allen's angst-ridden world, she identifies a new class in ''the large coastal cities of the United States,'' a ''subworld of people [who are] rigid with apprehension that they will die wearing the wrong sneaker, naming the wrong symphony, preferring *Madame Bovary.*'' What Didion fashions as a harsh critique of Allen's ''ultimate consumer report'' audience seems a projection of the readership of *The White Album.*

This collection of essays, the majority published from 1968 to 1979 in *Esquire,* the *Saturday Evening Post, Life* (or, as Didion notes on the copyright page: ''more specifically, the 'old' *Saturday Evening Post* and the 'old' *Life*''), sustains an associative chain of events recalled in ''Making Up Stories'': from Berkeley's Faculty Club ''the night Saigon fell in 1975'' to ''the murders in Beverly Hills of Sharon Tate Polanski, Jay Sebring, Voitek Frykowski, Steven Parent, and Abigail Folger.''

The collection's spiritual anchorage is the unnamed, white-jacketed 1968 Beatles album that Charles Manson claimed inspired his attempt at ''helter-skelter.'' The recording, popularly known as *The White Album,* saturates Didion's reading of the abrupt end of the decade, achieving reiterative status as the title of the volume, of the first section, and of that section's sole essay. ''The White Album'' essay overwhelms the subsequent occasional pieces—gathered under the suggestive headings ''California Republic,''

"Women," "Sojourns," and "On the Morning after the Sixties"—forcing a retrospective reading of the decade through the lens of the Manson murders. Didion explained to Michiko Kakutani: "*The White Album* is more tentative. I don't have as many answers as I did when I wrote *Slouching.*"

"The White Album" cinematically deliberates on the failure of narrative line to impose historical continuity upon the late 1960s. The "shifting phantasmagoria which is our actual experience" becomes the property of a series of fifteen "flash cuts" between the chaos of her psychological landscape and that of her country. The times, "this period began around 1966 and continued until 1971," cause her "to doubt the premises of all the stories [she] had ever told [her]self" and, by extension, to doubt the country's narratives as well. Personally, the essay charts a time of public success and nervous collapse; historically, it explores the social disjunctions of "images [which] did not fit into any narrative [she] knew." From her " 'senseless-killing' neighborhood" in Hollywood, Didion reflects upon the murders of silent-film star Ramon Navarro and the deaths of Jim Morrison and Janice Joplin; from her freeway perspective, listening to the car radio, she deliberates upon the life and times of Black Panther leaders Huey P. Newton and Eldridge Cleaver (discovering that she has much in common with her fellow author Cleaver), and the political disturbances at San Francisco State College; from a doctor's office, she contemplates her own central nervous system disorder, which "had a name, the kind of name usually associated with telethons, but the name meant nothing and the neurologists did not like to use it," and which seemed to mimic the unnameable disorder of the times.

Inexorably, the essay advances on that summer of "rumors," "stories"—"unmentionable," the "unimaginable"—in Los Angeles in 1969, when "the Sixties ended abruptly . . . ended at the exact moment when word of the murders on Cielo Drive traveled like brushfire through the community." Echoing the Yeatsian imagery of *Slouching towards Bethlehem*, Didion recalls "a time when the dogs barked every night and the moon was always full. On August 9, 1969, I . . . remember all of the day's misinformation very clearly, and I also remember this, and I wish I did not: *I remember that no one was surprised.*" Subsequent visits to Linda Kasabian, Manson cult member in protective custody at Sybil Brand Institute for Women, offer little in the way of narrative continuity for this author in search of a story; they offer instead a deeper, literary submersion into a deadly, societal malaise: "Each of the half-dozen doors that locked behind us as we entered Sybil Brand was a little death, and I would emerge after the interview like Persephone from the underworld, euphoric, elated. Once home I would have two drinks and make myself a hamburger and eat it ravenously."

Of the remaining essays on California and its ways, none continues to trouble readers as persistently as "The Women's Movement." Originally published in the *New York Times Book Review,* this 1972 denunciation of "the 'idea' of the women's movement" reflects Didion's impatience with political collectivism, class interposition (Didion notes in "Thinking about Western Thinking": "I see in myself that peculiarly deluded Western egalitarianism which insists, literally, that we all begin life equal") and historical naïveté. She proclaims the movement to be a product of superstition and boredom; its followers to be in need of romance, not revolution. Discontent with particular men has led to the abandonment of biological destiny. This cumulative, passive estrangement informs the closing "On the Morning after the Sixties," in which Didion recalls that earlier generation of her own education at the University of California, "the last generation to identify with adults," a "silent" generation wary of "the exhilaration of social action'' because it ''seemed to many of us just one more way of escaping the personal, of masking for a while that dread of the meaningless which was man's fate.''

Reviews were divided between those which saw *The White Album* as representative of the national social collapse and those which saw the essays as simply an extension of Didion's psychopathology. Few critics avoided labeling the work ''pessimistic,'' ''wounded,'' or ''neurotic'' even as they praised its style. Wariness characterized Martha Duffy's *New York Review of Books* essay, ''Pictures from an Expedition,'' in which Didion, ''the colorist of panic and depression,'' becomes ''hard'' and guilty of ''callousness, notably in a harangue called 'The Women's Movement.' ''

Scholarly response struggled with the definitional distinctions between New Journalism and personal testimony, hoping to create a working critical vocabulary. The randomness and contingency of the volume, its approximations of verifiable realities, begged for new generic distinctions. And although most critics moved beyond Katherine Henderson's naive observation that Didion ''never writes simply news stories,'' few found terminology sufficient to its definitional demands. Mark Muggli's inventive ''parafictions'' offered no more than Norman Mailer's ''history as novel, novel as history'' tag to his *Armies of the Night.*

''History is context,'' Didion writes in ''Shooters, Inc.'' (in *After Henry*), an essay detailing the ''sideshows abroad'' that presidents cling to when running for reelection. Such hemispheric sideshows, like those developed for *A Book of Common Prayer,* sustain Didion's reports from El Salvador. Drawn from notebooks kept during a two-week visit to the war zone made by Didion and Dunne in 1982, the essays were originally published in the *New York Review of Books.* After two collections of essays

and three novels, Didion was tired of asking questions about California; she was ready to apply the lessons of *Heart of Darkness* to the banality of international politics. For if, as Conrad tells us, ''All Europe contributed to the making of Kurtz'' (the epigraph to *Salvador*), then perhaps all Norteamérica contributed to the making of *Salvador.*

Salvador begins evocatively, as if opening into another one of Didion's fictive landscapes: ''The three-year-old El Salvador International Airport is glassy and white and splendidly isolated . . . the visionary invention of a tourist industry in yet another republic where the leading natural cause of death is gastrointestinal infection.'' The essay drifts into descriptive meditations upon this land where ''Terror is the given of the place.'' She pans cinematically over a landscape where body dumps intersect ''the land of the provisionally living.'' United States Embassy dispatches (''Chronology of Events Related to Salvadoran Situation''), press releases, interviews, and notebooks form the source texts for these essays. Ever the ''demented *gringa*'' (sharing with Charlotte Douglas a *norteamericana*'s obsession with clean water), Didion fights her natural inclination to stray into the ironies of decor:

> This was a shopping center that embodied the future for which El Salvador was presumably being saved, and I wrote it down dutifully, this being the kind of ''color'' I knew how to interpret, the kind of inductive irony, the detail that was supposed to illuminate the story. As I wrote it down I realized that I was no longer much interested in this kind of irony.

Touring with reporters from *Newsweek* and the *Washington Post,* Dunne and Didion become part of an international press corps covering the ''disappeared.'' She notes: ''*Desaparecer,* or 'disappear,' is in Spanish both an intransitive and a transitive verb, and this flexibility has been adopted by those speaking English in El Salvador, as in *John Sullivan was disappeared from the Sheraton; the government disappeared the students.*''

Violence to the language is emblematic of the social destruction surrounding her: "Language as it is now used in El Salvador is the language of advertising, of persuasion, the product being one or another of the *soluciones* crafted in Washington or Panama or Mexico, which is part of the place's pervasive obscenity. This language is shared by Salvadorans and Americans, as if a linguistic deal had been cut." Hoping to find *la verdad,* Didion discovers that she "had stumbled into a code, that . . . *la verdad* as it was used on the bumper stickers favored that spring and summer by ARENA people." The absurdity and estrangement of circumstance grows as she receives, thirdhand, a message from her editor in New York, asking for an interview on the women's movement: "This was not a scenario that played, and I realized then that El Salvador was as inconceivable to Jay Cocks in the high keep of the Time-Life Building in New York as this message was to me in El Salvador."

Carolyn Forché, a sporadic resident of El Salvador who while there translated the works of Claribel Alegría, in an expressive and understanding review for the *Chicago Tribune Book World* saw the essay as "alternately detached and compassionate . . . a sidelong reflection on the limits of the now-old new journalism; a tourist guide manqué; a surrealist docu-drama; a withering indictment of American foreign policy; and a poetic exploration in fear." Reviewers in *Newsweek,* the *Los Angeles Times Book Review,* and *The Listener* found Didion's style, grounded in a neurasthenic and privileged persona, intrusive and inappropriate to her subject. Critics concluded that her powers of observation failed to compensate for her lack of political sophistication and intellectual depth.

Salvador drew agitated comment in a range of political journals by writers fascinated or in-

censed by Didion's trespass into their field. In *Dissent,* for example, Juan Corradi appreciated the unbearable literariness of Didion's exploration, applauding her "lean and splendid book" that "pierces the ideological fictions and takes us to the outer and almost unbearable limits of what we call 'politics,' 'society,' and 'culture'—to the point where those rational notions turn into terror, obscenity, and hallucination." In *New Republic,* Michael Massing dismissed the Didion genre of "the snap book . . . produced by big-name authors who parachute into a country, take a quick look around, then write an entire book about their experience."

Scholars have concentrated on the act of witnessing and the critique of policy inherent in the essay. Feminist critics have noted the diminutive scale and intimacy of the work. Lynne T. Hanley (in *Massachusetts Review*) locates Didion's genius in depicting "a war being waged by identifiable men: husbands, fathers, brothers, lovers, the men sitting at the next table at the Escalón Sheraton." With the increasingly political nature of academic criticism, Didion's apolitical prose frequently has come under attack. Authorial silence or remove does little, in the minds of some scholars, to excuse her stylized deafness to the "apocalypse" of El Salvador.

Travels in El Salvador conditioned Didion to listen critically and move beyond what she described in "Girl of the Golden West" (in *After Henry*) as "the California ear" of one (in that case Patty Hearst) "raised on a history that placed not much emphasis on *why.*" Recalling a broader historical sweep of American foreign policy, inspired by Henry Adams' *Democracy* (1880) as well as by her own *A Book of Common Prayer,* Didion's *Democracy* considers the narrative implications of lost historical perspective—for novelists and for Americans.

In *Democracy* Didion's westering vision extends to American embassies, commissaries, and wardrooms of political and military installations in the Pacific. It is a postwar "cautionary tale" inspired by the faltering assumptions of United States foreign policy, particularly in Vietnam. Didion shuttles ahistorically "around 1952, 1953" and the "spring of 1975," weaving a narrative that leads to the fall of Saigon. The narrative involves the private life and loves of Inez Christian Victor, a woman caught in the socially contrived web of the men of the Christian and Victor families. For these men—her husband, Senator Harry Victor, member of the Alliance for Democratic Institutions, who sees the business of "democracy" as business; the global entrepreneur and Inez's first love, Jack Lovett, "less interested in laser mirrors than in M-16s, AK-47s, FN-FALS, the everyday implements of short-view power," invested with the walk and talk of John Wayne; her uncle, Dwight Christian, knowledgeable and dreamy when the subjects are "Dhahran, Dubai, cost-efficient technology for Aramco"—Inez served as an accessory, one who came "to view most occasions as photo opportunities." When asked the cost of her public life among famous men, Inez responds, "Memory, mainly." This ironic interplay between history and memory informs more than Inez's story; it summons a parallel plot, that of Didion the author.

Metafictional in the extreme, *Democracy* draws together the stylistic strains of Didion's journalism and novels, redefining the parameters of the nonfiction novel. Didion intrudes as boldly as Melville: "Call me the author. *Let the reader be introduced to Joan Didion, upon whose character and doings much will depend of whatever interest these pages may have, as she sits at her writing table in her own room in her own house on Welbeck Street.*" She grounds her authorial narration in an actuality—the spring of 1975, when she "happened to be teaching at Berkeley"—as well as in a fictional construct—"lecturing on the same short-term basis on which Harry Victor had lectured there between the 1972

campaign and the final funding of the Alliance for Democratic Institutions." Narratorial shifts between her autobiographical essays and her novel in progress defeats any easy generic categorization of the work.

A national best-seller, the Simon & Schuster hardcover was followed in the summer of 1985 by a Pocket Books edition. Widely and animatedly reviewed, *Democracy* returned readers and reviewers to the quarrelsome discussions of postmodern fiction. Many reviews anguished over generic categorization, unhappy with any of the received designations—from New Journalism to fiction. What Mary McCarthy's front-page *New York Times Book Review* essay questioned— "What is a live fact—Joan Didion—doing in a work of fiction?"—Christopher Lehmann-Haupt's daily *New York Times* review dismissed, accounting for Didion's authorial intrusion as "the illusion that journalism instead of fiction is going on in the pages of *Democracy*." John Lownsbrough, enlarging the North American reading for the *Toronto Globe and Mail,* was less taken by Didion's authorial presence and more intrigued by the foreign policy implications of her tale, which seemed to him "the flotsam and jetsam of a Manifest Destiny no longer so manifest."

Apart from the politics of Didion's tale, reviewers located the "steamy," "tropical," "exotique" settings not in Didion's travels but in her reading of Somerset Maugham. Essay-reviewers had the leisure to examine such complex issues as *Democracy*'s place in the national rhetoric and the evolution of "higher journalism." In a particularly peevish essay in *American Spectator,* longtime admirer Thomas Mallon withdrew his support, accusing Didion of "lifting everything from her earlier novels" and "expect[ing] us to care about a story she apparently ceased to."

Scholarly essays reflect an increasing sophistication as critics indulge their interests in post-Vietnam complexities, national narratives, and narratological theory. In the most extravagant of these politically inspired, thesis-determined essays, Alan Nadel, searching for evidence of America's "failed cultural narratives," uses *Democracy* as a means of exploring what he insists is the novel's prior narrative, George Kennan's cold war policy of containment, and its exposure of "the personal and national cost of propagating America's colonialist narrative."

The search for *la verdad* that sustains *Salvador* complicates Didion's later fiction and essays. For Didion, her reportage of the 1980s assumes the significance of testimony; her role, that of witness. Differing from the occasional "flash cut" essays of *The White Album, Miami,* originally written for the *New York Review of Books,* encourages a broader reading of race, real estate, and exile in Miami.

With "Havana vanities come to dust in Miami," Didion announces the political and personal trajectories of these essays. Recent assassinations, drug cartels, guerrilla incursions, and local politics coalesce in this attempt to locate the lost narrative of hemispheric history. Foreign policy from Eisenhower to Reagan revolves around the issues of refugees and freedom fighters as Cuba bifurcates into the political realities of Didion's research: Miami and Havana. The revolution subsumes even Miami real estate as "guerrilla discounts" are offered to exiles. Miami race relations may be seen through the lens of the model Cuban exile, a figure constructed to meet the needs of local, state, and federal government interests. South Florida shares a "distant agenda" dictated by the Central Intelligence Agency and Washington, but only the Reagan White House appreciates the "full script" of hemispheric policies. Whatever the particularities of the individual essays, the "continuing opera still called . . . *el exilio,*" the Cuban exile, provides the subtextual narrative.

The best-selling Simon & Schuster edition was followed by a Pocket Books paperback in 1988. Reviews generously appreciated the broader political implications of the essays. *Miami* was perhaps Didion's most widely reviewed work, receiving discerning praise in the usual journals as well as *Cosmopolitan* and *Vogue.* Style and reportage account for the expected success; flirtation with various assassination theories and drug conspiracies accounts for the broader popular appeal.

Essay reviews explored the implications of Didion's essays, associating the surreal quality of *Miami* with nightmarish implications of American foreign policy. Many reviewers noted more than a disjunction between style and content; they complained about a persistent nativism, troubling in essays that claim to assess such streaks in others.

Scholarly attention to *Miami* has been minimal. Sandra K. Hinchman contributed a tentative though appreciative essay to Sharon Felton's *The Critical Response to Joan Didion,* noting Didion's sense of Miami as the "basis for community."

In 1988, Didion returned to New York City, *Slouching towards Bethlehem*'s "Seven Places of Mind," which she then saw as "an infinitely romantic notion, the mysterious nexus of all love and money and power, the shining and perishable dream itself." She reflects in the *New Yorker* and the *New York Review of Books* upon the perishability of private and public dreams.

The death of Didion's longtime editor, Henry Robbins, in July 1979 occasioned this autumnal and self-effacing collection. Didion reflects upon her beginnings—"In the summer of 1966 . . . living in a borrowed house in Brentwood"—and the progression of her career, so dependent upon this lost, enabling presence. She moves as a sporadic, marginal presence in these essays, abandoning these scenes of late-twentieth-century America to an unexpectedly uninvolved voice.

The collection depends upon Didion's repeated redefinitions of the country's obsession with "sentimental education." Whether considering the kidnapping of Patricia Hearst by the Symbionese Liberation Army or the Central Park "wilding" rape case, she is drawn to the ways in which American media appeal to the soft, romantic emotions of their consumers.

After the opening homage to Robbins, "After Henry," the collection is organized around Didion's familiar geopolitical clusters: "Washington," "California," and "New York." Though recognizably Didion, the essays lack the brittle, participatory edge that so characterized her earlier work. Research and noted collaborative sources displace the authorial first person, replacing it with a more objective, reportorial "I."

The "Washington" essays—"In the Realm of the Fisher King" (Peggy Noonan and the sculpting of the Reagan White House), "Insider Baseball" (1988 Bush-Dukakis presidential campaigns), "Shooters Inc." (the political and media imperative for "dramatic events" against which to make policy statements)—collectively and individually voice the familiar Didion ambivalence and mistrust of politics. As she noted decades before, in her interview with Michiko Kakutani, "I never had faith that the answers to human problems lay in anything that could be called political. I thought the answers, if there were answers, lay someplace in man's soul." In addition, the essays critique the unseemly participation of the media in the corruption of national discourse and destiny.

The "California" essays—in particular, "Girl of the Golden West" (life and times of Patricia Hearst), "Pacific Distances" (extended meditation on the randomness of her Pacific journeys from Berkeley to the residential wastelands of Oahu), "Los Angeles Days" (interlocking reflections upon earthquakes, real estate, writers, and the movie industry in Los Angeles), "Down at City Hall" (Tom Bradley and the West Side

politics of Los Angeles)—reflect Didion's residential remove and perspective; she notes in "Los Angeles Days": "What is striking about Los Angeles after a period away is how well it works."

"New York" consists of the collection's celebrated "Sentimental Journeys," the *New York Review of Books* essay about the rape of a woman jogger in Central Park. Didion assumes that the ways race, class, and sex intersect in this case reveal the hidden dynamic of New York's current urban crisis. The particularities of the case not only reflect those of New Yorkers polled by the *Times* who complained "about their loss of flexibility, about their panic, their desolation, their anger, and their sense of impending doom," but also seem to Didion to be part of the attendant corruption when a city or country imposes "a sentimental, or false, narrative on the disparate and often random experience."

Reviews expressed either relief over Didion's progressive objectification of voice and stance or dismay that she continued to aspire to topics within her stylistic range but beyond her intellectual ken. Though genuinely appreciative of her "wonderfully fierce high style," even veteran reviewer John Lownsbrough wearied of Didion's depleted "sentimentalization of herself." Politically conservative reviewers like Christopher Caldwell gave the collection modest praise, less for its style or scope and more for its moral certitude. Scholars have yet to assess *After Henry,* though Laura Julier attempts an early stylistic reading in "Actual Experience, Preferred Narratives." Her suggestive reading of Didion's "imposition of narrative on experience" should prompt future consideration of the narrative of witness in all of her essays.

The larger task of exploring the relationship between Didion's fiction and her essays has yet to be attempted, but may well define the future direction of serious criticism of her work. Caught between the "unerring journalistic eye and ear" that Mark Schorer found so fetching in *Play It as It Lays* and the social and political issues that increasingly dominate her world, Didion produces a stylistically and thematically conflicted body of work in which aesthetic wrestles with temperament. Her writing, though drawn to the particulars of politics, sustains a temperamental aversion to political solutions. What she confided to Michiko Kakutani in 1979 remains true: ''I never had any faith that the answers to human problems lay in anything that could be called political. I thought the answers, if there were answers, lay someplace in man's soul.''

Selected Bibliography

WORKS OF JOAN DIDION

NOVELS

Run River. New York: Ivan Obolensky, 1963; New York: Bantam Books, 1964; New York: Pocket Books, 1978.

Play It as It Lays. New York: Farrar, Straus, and Giroux, 1970; New York: Bantam Books, 1971; New York: Pocket Books, 1978.

A Book of Common Prayer. New York: Simon & Schuster, 1977; New York: Pocket Books, 1978.

Democracy. New York: Simon & Schuster, 1984; New York: Pocket Books, 1985.

NONFICTION

Slouching towards Bethlehem. New York: Farrar, Straus, and Giroux, 1968; New York: Dell, 1969; New York: Pocket Books, 1981.

Telling Stories. Berkeley: Friends of the Bancroft Library, University of California, 1978.

The White Album. New York: Simon & Schuster, 1979; New York: Pocket Books, 1979.

Salvador. New York: Simon & Schuster, 1983; New York: Pocket Books, 1983.

Miami. New York: Simon & Schuster, 1987; New York: Pocket Books, 1988.

After Henry. New York: Simon & Schuster, 1992.

SCREENPLAYS

Didion, Joan, and John Gregory Dunne. *Panic in Needle Park.* Directed by Jerry Schatzberg. Twentieth Century Fox, 1971.

————. *Play It as It Lays.* Directed by Frank Perry. Universal Studios, 1972.

————. *A Star Is Born.* Directed by Frank Pierson. Warner Brothers, 1976.

PERIODICAL ARTICLES

''Berkeley's Giant: The University of California.'' *Mademoiselle,* January 1960, pp. 88–90, 103, 105–107.

''San Francisco Job Hunt.'' *Mademoiselle,* September 1960, pp. 128–129, 168–170.

''New York: The Great Reprieve.'' *Mademoiselle,* February 1961, pp. 102–103, 147–148, 150.

''Jealousy: Is It a Curable Illness?'' *Vogue,* June 1, 1961, pp. 96–97.

''Take No for an Answer.'' *Vogue,* October 1, 1961, pp. 132–133.

''When It Was Magic Time in Jersey.'' *Vogue,* September 15, 1962, pp. 33–35.

''Washington, D.C.: Anything Can Happen Here.'' *Mademoiselle,* November 1962, pp. 132–135, 157–159, 162–163.

''Silver—to Have and to Hurl.'' *Vogue,* April 1, 1964, p. 60.

''Coming Home.'' *Saturday Evening Post,* July 11, 1964, pp. 50–55.

''The Big Rock Candy Figgy Pudding Pitfall.'' *Saturday Evening Post,* December 3, 1966, p. 22.

''In Praise of Unhung Wreaths and Love.'' *Life,* December 19, 1969, p. 2B.

''The Coast: Thinking about Western Thinking.'' *Esquire,* February 1976, pp. 10, 14.

''The Coast: Where *Tonight Show* Guests Go to Rest.'' *Esquire,* October 1976, pp. 25–26, 30.

''Letter from 'Manhattan.' Review of *Manhattan, Interiors,* and *Annie Hall.*'' *New York Review of Books,* August 16, 1979, pp. 18–19.

''Making Up Stories.'' In *The Writer's Craft: Hopwood Lectures, 1965–1981.* Edited by Robert A. Martin. Ann Arbor: University of Michigan Press, 1982. Pp. 231–244.

''An Annotation.'' In *Some Women.* By Robert Mapplethorp. Boston: Little, Brown, 1989.

''Eye on the Prize.'' *New York Review of Books,* September 24, 1992, pp. 57–66.

MANUSCRIPT PAPERS

The Joan Didion–John Gregory Dunne papers (notes, manuscripts, uncorrected galley proofs) are at the Bancroft Library, University of California, Berkeley.

BIBLIOGRAPHIES

Fairbanks, Carol. *Women in Literature: Criticism of the Seventies.* Metuchen, N.J.: Scarecrow Press, 1976. Pp. 55–56.

Henderson, Katherine Usher. "A Bibliography of Writings by Joan Didion." In *American Women Writing Fiction: Memory, Identity, Family, Space.* Edited by Mickey Pearlman. Lexington: University Press of Kentucky, 1989. Pp. 86–89.

Jacobs, Fred Rue. *Joan Didion—Bibliography.* Keene, Calif.: Loop Press, 1977.

Olendorf, Donna. "Joan Didion: A Checklist, 1955–1980." *Bulletin of Bibliography* 32, no. 1:32–44 (1981).

BIOGRAPHICAL MATERIAL

Aronson, Harvey. "Joyce, Joan, and Lois: Woman's Need vs. Writer's Ego." *Cosmopolitan,* January 1971, pp. 102–103, 115–117.

Berges, Marshall. "Home Q and A: Joan Didion and John Gregory Dunne." *Los Angeles Times,* November 28, 1976, Home sec., pp. 48–50, 54, 57.

Braudy, Susan. "Day in the Life of Joan Didion." *Ms.,* February 1977, pp. 65–68, 108–109.

Friedman, Ellen G., ed. *Joan Didion: Essays and Conversations.* Princeton: Ontario Review Press, 1984.

Kakutani, Michiko. "Joan Didion: Staking out California." *New York Times Magazine,* June 10, 1979, pp. 34, 36, 38, 40, 44, 46, 48, 50. Repr. in Friedman, 29–40.

Kazin, Alfred. "Joan Didion: Portrait of a Professional." *Harper's,* December 1971, pp. 112–114, 116, 118, 120–122.

CRITICISM

Adams, Phoebe. "Short Reviews." *Atlantic Monthly,* 226:151 (October 1970).

Amis, Martin. "Joan Didion's Style." In his *The Moronic Inferno and Other Visits to America.* New York: Viking, 1987. Pp. 160–169.

Amster, Betsy. Review of *Democracy. Ms.,* July 1984, pp. 32–33.

Anderson, Chris. "The Cat in the Shimmer." In *Style as Argument.* Edited by Chris Anderson. Carbondale: Southern Illinois University Press, 1987. Pp. 133–174.

Bailey, Peter. "M.S. as Metaphor." *Delta English Studies,* 20:57–71 (February 1985).

Bingham, June. "Hippies on Haight." *The Progressive,* August 1968, pp. 47–48.

Brady, Jennifer H. "Points West, Then and Now: The Fiction of Joan Didion." *Contemporary Literature,* 20, no. 4:452–470 (1979). Repr. in Friedman, pp. 43–59.

Caldwell, Christopher. Review of *After Henry. American Spectator,* 25:62–64 (September 1992).

Carton, Evan. "Joan Didion's Dreampolitics of the Self." *Western Humanities Review,* 40:307–328 (Winter 1986).

Chabot, C. Barry. "Joan Didion's *Play It as It Lays* and the Vacuity of the Here and Now." *Critique,* 21:53–60 (April 1980). Repr. in Friedman, pp. 117–123.

Chase, Chris. "Uncommon Joan Didion." *Chicago Tribune Magazine,* April 3, 1977, pp. 50–61.

Ching, Stuart. " 'A Hard Story to Tell': The Vietnam War in Joan Didion's *Democracy.*" In *Fourteen Landing Zones: Approaches to Vietnam War Literature.* Edited by Philip K. Jason. Iowa City: University of Iowa Press, 1992.

Coale, Samuel Chase. "Didion's Disorder: An American Romancer's Art." *Critique,* 25, no. 1: 160–170 (1984).

Cohen, Jeffrey C. "Metaphor for the Future." *National Review,* November 20, 1987, pp. 54, 56–58.

Corradi, Juan. "A Culture of Fear." *Dissent,* 30:387–389 (Summer 1983).

Crow, Charles. "Home and Transcendence in Los Angeles Fiction." In *Los Angeles in Fiction.* Edited by David Fine. Albuquerque: University of New Mexico Press, 1984. Pp. 189–205.

Duffy, Martha. "Survivor's Report." *Time,* August 10, 1970, pp. 67–68.

———. "An Irate Accent." *Time,* March 20, 1972, pp. 98–99.

———. "Pictures from an Expedition." *New York Review of Books,* August 16, 1979, pp. 43–44.

Eder, George Jackson. "The Little World of Joan Didion." *National Review,* July 8, 1983, pp. 829–830.

Edwards, Thomas R. "An American Education." *New York Review of Books,* May 10, 1984, pp. 23–24.

Epstein, Joseph. "The Sunshine Girls: Renata Adler and Joan Didion." *Commentary* 77: 62–67 (June 1984).

Felton, Sharon. "Joan Didion: A Writer of Scope and Substance." *Hollins Critic,* 26:1–11 (October 1989).

———, ed. *The Critical Response to Joan Didion.* Westport, Conn.: Greenwood Press, 1994.

Flower, Dean. "Fiction Chronicle." *Hudson Review,* 30:311–312 (Summer 1977).

Forché, Carolyn. Review of *Salvador. Chicago Tribune Book World,* March 13, 1983, p. 1.

Forster, Imogen. "Constructing Central America." *Red Letters,* 16:48–55 (Spring–Summer 1984).

Foust, Ronald. "Family Romance and the Image of Woman's Fate in *Play It as It Lays.*" *Journal of Evolutionary Psychology,* 5:43–54 (March 1984).

Friedman, Ellen G. "The Didion Sensibility: An Analysis." In Friedman, pp. 81–90.

———, ed. *Joan Didion: Essays and Conversations.* Princeton: Ontario Review Press, 1984.

Frus, Phyllis. *The Politics and Poetics of Journalistic Narrative: The Timely and the Timeless.* New York: Cambridge University Press, 1994.

Gardner, John. "Moral Fiction." *Saturday Review,* April 1, 1978, pp. 29–30, 32–33.

Gardiner, Judith Kegan. "Evil, Apocalypse, and Feminist Fiction." *Frontiers,* 7, no. 2:74–80 (1983).

Garis, Leslie. "Didion and Dunne: The Rewards of a Literary Marriage." *New York Times Magazine,* February 8, 1987, pp. 18–26, 28, 29.

Geherin, David J. "Nothingness and Beyond: Joan Didion's *Play It as It Lays.*" *Critique,* 16, no. 1:64–78 (1974). Repr. in Friedman, pp. 105–116.

Gelfant, Blanche. *Women Writing in America: Voices in Collage.* Hanover, N.H.: University Press of New England, 1984. Pp. 41–42.

Goffman, Carolyn. "Beyond Reportage in Salvador." *Connecticut Review,* 13:15–22 (Fall 1991).

Goodheart, Lynne Howard. "Joan Didion's *Play It as It Lays*: Alienation and Games of Chance." *San Jose Studies,* 3:64–68 (1977).

Gornick, Vivian. "Toward a Definition of the Female Sensibility." *Village Voice,* May 31, 1973, p. 32.

Gregory, Charles, and William Dorman. "The Children of James Agee." *Journal of Popular Culture* 9:996–1002 (Spring 1976).

Grumbach, Doris. "Pray It as It Lays." *Washington Post Book World,* March 27, 1977, pp. E1, E3.

Hanley, Lynne. "To El Salvador." *Massachusetts Review,* 24, no. 1:13–29 (1983).

———. *Writing War: Fiction, Gender, and Memory.* Amherst: University of Massachusetts Press, 1991.

Harrison, Barbara Grizzuti. "Joan Didion: The Courage of Her Afflictions." *Nation,* September 29, 1979, pp. 277–286.

Heilker, Paul. "The Struggle for Articulation and Didion's Construction of the Reader's Self-Respect in *Slouching towards Bethlehem.*" *CEA Critic* 54:26–36 (Spring/Summer 1992).

Hellman, John. *Fables of Fact: The New Journalism as New Fiction.* Urbana: University of Illinois Press, 1981.

Henderson, Katherine Usher. *Joan Didion.* New York: Frederick Ungar, 1981.

———. "*Run River:* Edenic Vision and Wasteland Nightmare." In Friedman, pp. 91–104.

———. "The Bond between Narrator and Heroine in *Democracy.*" In *American Women Writing Fiction: Memory, Identity, Family, Space.* Edited by Mickey Pearlman. Lexington: University Press of Kentucky, 1989. Pp. 68–93.

Hentoff, Margot. "Slouching towards Babel." *Village Voice,* February 28, 1977, pp. 63–64.

Hertzberg, Hendrik. "California with a New York Edge." *New York Times Book Review,* May 17, 1992, p. 3.

Hiatt, Mary P. "The Sexology of Style." *Language and Style,* 9:98–107 (Spring 1976).

Hinchman, Sandra K. "Making Sense and Making Stories: Problems of Cognition and Narration in Joan Didion's *Play It as It Lays.*" *Centennial Review,* 29, no. 4:457–473 (1985).

Hitchens, Christopher. "The Lovett Latitudes." *Times Literary Supplement,* September 14, 1984, p. 1018.

Hollowell, John. "Against Interpretation: Narrative Strategy in *A Book of Common Prayer.*" In Friedman, pp. 164–176.

Johnson, Diane. "Hard Hit Women." *New York Review of Books,* April 28, 1977, pp. 6–8.

———. "Should Novels Have a Message? Joan Didion, Bertha Harris, and Erica Jong." In her *Terrorists and Novelists.* New York: Knopf, 1982. Pp. 24–33.

Johnson, Hillary. "Eloquent Survivor of the '60s." *Christian Science Monitor,* July 9, 1979, p. B5.

Johnson, Michael L. *The New Journalism.* Lawrence: University Press of Kansas, 1971. Pp. 96–100.

Jones, D. A. N. "Divided Selves." *New York Review of Books,* October 22, 1970, pp. 38–42.

Julier, Laura. "Actual Experience, Preferred Narratives: Didion's *After Henry.*" In Felton, pp. 248–258.

Kasindorf, Martin. "New Directions for the First Family of Angst." *Saturday Review,* April 1982, pp. 14–18.

Kauffmann, Stanley. "Views from the West." *New Republic,* August 4–11, 1979, pp. 30–31.

Kiley, Frederick. "Beyond Words: Narrative Art in Joan Didion's *Salvador.*" In Friedman, pp. 181–188.

Kingston, Maxine Hong. *California Monthly,* April–May 1977, p. 9.

Klinghoffer, David. "News She Can Use." *National Review,* June 22, 1992, pp. 53–54.

Kolodny, Annette. "Some Notes on Defining a 'Feminist Literary Criticism.'" *Critical Inquiry,* 2:75–92 (Autumn 1975).

Lahr, John. "Entrepreneurs of Anxiety." *Horizon,* January 1981, pp. 36, 38–39.

Lardner, Susan. "Facing Facts." *New Yorker,* June 20, 1977, pp. 117–118.

Lehmann-Haupt, Christopher. "No Second Coming." *New York Times,* March 21, 1977, p. 25.

———. Review of *Democracy. New York Times,* April 6, 1984, p. 32.

Lemann, Nicholas. "Mirage of *Miami.*" *New Republic,* November 23, 1987, pp. 37–42.

Logan, William. "Joan Didion: Overimagining." *Chicago Tribune Book World,* March 20, 1977, p. 1.

Loris, Michelle C. *Innocence, Loss, and Recovery in the Art of Joan Didion.* New York: Peter Lang, 1989.

Lounsberry, Barbara. *The Art of Fact: Contemporary Artists of Nonfiction.* Westport, Conn.: Greenwood Press, 1990.

Lownsbrough, John. "Our Lady of the Walking Wounded." *Macleans,* July 9, 1979, p. 43.

———. "Didion Moves East but Remains at Home in the Essay." *Toronto Globe and Mail,* August 22, 1992, p. C5.

McCarthy, Mary. "Love and Death in the Pacific." *New York Times Book Review,* April 22, 1984, pp. 1, 18–19.

Malin, Irving. "The Album of Anxiety." In Friedman, pp. 177–180.

Mallon, Thomas. "The Limits of History in the Novels of Joan Didion." *Critique,* 21:43–52 (April 1980). Repr. in Friedman, pp. 60–67.

———. Review of *Democracy. American Spectator,* August 1984, pp. 43–44.

Massing, Michael. "Big Writers and Little Countries: Snap Books." *New Republic,* May 4, 1987, pp. 21, 24–25.

Mosley, Merritt. "Joan Didion's Symbolic Landscapes." *South Carolina Review,* 21:55–64 (Spring 1989).

Muggli, Mark. "The Poetics of Joan Didion's Journalism." *American Literature,* 59:402–421 (October 1987).

———. "Joan Didion and the Problem of Journalistic Travel Writing." In *Temperamental Journeys: Essays on the Modern Literature of Travel.* Edited by Michael Kowalewski. Athens: University of Georgia Press, 1992.

Nadel, Alan. "Failed Cultural Narratives: America in the Postwar Era and the Story of *Democracy.*" *boundary 2* 19:95–120 (Spring 1992).

Oates, Joyce Carol. "A Taut Novel of Disorder." *New York Times Book Review,* April 3, 1977, pp. 1, 34–35. Repr. in Friedman, pp. 138–141.

Orowan, Florella. "Didion on Democracy—Or the Lack of It." *Christian Science Monitor,* May 16, 1984, p. 19.

Porterfield, Nolan. "The Desolation Game." *North American Review,* 256:70–72 (Winter 1971).

Randisi, Jennifer L. "The Journey Nowhere: Didion's *Run River.*" *Markham Review,* 11:41–43 (Spring 1982).

Raphael, Frederick. "Grace under Pressure." *Saturday Review,* March 5, 1977, pp. 23–25.

Romano, John. "Joan Didion and Her Characters." *Commentary,* July 1977, pp. 61–63. Repr. in Friedman, pp. 142–146.

Russell, George. "Mooning over Miami." *Commentary,* January 1988, pp. 69–72.

Schorer, Mark. "Novels and Nothingness." *American Scholar,* 40:169, 170, 172, 174 (Winter 1970/1971).

Schow, H. Wayne. "*Out of Africa, The White Album,* and the Possibility of Tragic Affirmation." *English Studies,* 67:35–50 (February 1986).

Segal, Lore. "Maria Knew What 'Nothing' Means: *Play It as It Lays. New York Times Book Review,* August 9, 1970, pp. 6, 18.

Sheed, Wilfrid. "An Expert Witness to Pain." *Life,* July 31, 1970, p. 13.

Simard, Rodney. "The Dissociation of Self in Joan Didion's *Play It as It Lays.*" In *Narcissism and the Text.* Edited by Lynne Layton and Barbara Ann Schapiro. New York: New York University Press, 1986. Pp. 273–289.

Simon, John. "De Tenuissimis Clamavi." *National Review,* October 12, 1979, pp. 1311–1312.

Spurr, David. "Colonialist Journalism: Stanley to Didion." *Raritan,* 5:35–50 (Fall 1985).

Stein, Benjamin. "Dinner in the Rain Forest." *National Review,* June 10, 1977, p. 678.

Steinem, Gloria. "Didion Novel of How a Housewife Came to Cope." *Los Angeles Times,* July 5, 1970, Books sec., pp. 1, 9.

Stimpson, Catherine R. "The Case of Ms. Joan Didion." *Ms.,* January 1973, pp. 36–41.

Stineback, David C. "On the Limits of Fiction." *Midwest Quarterly,* 14:339–348 (Summer 1973).

Stout, Janis P. *Strategies of Reticence: Silence and Meaning in the Works of Jane Austen, Willa Cather, Katherine Anne Porter, and Joan Didion.* Charlottesville: University Press of Virginia, 1990.

Strandberg, Victor. "Passion and Delusion in *A Book of Common Prayer.*" *Modern Fiction Studies,* 27, no. 2:225–242 (1981). Repr. in Friedman, pp. 147–163.

Tager, Michael. "The Political Visions of Joan Didion's *Democracy. Critique,* 31:173–184 (Spring 1990).

Toher, Martha Dimes. "Bearing Witness: Explorations in Central America." *New Orleans Review,* 18:42–51 (Summer 1991).

Towers, Robert. "The Decline and Fall of the 60's." *New York Times Book Review,* June 17, 1979, pp. 1, 30.

Tyler, Anne. "Affairs of State." *New Republic,* April 9, 1984, pp. 35–36.

Tynan, Kathleen. "Why They Live Here." *New York Times Book Review,* November 18, 1979, p. 11, 42–43.

Wakefield, Dan. "Places, People, and Personalities: *Slouching towards Bethlehem.*" *New York Times Book Review,* July 21, 1968, p. 8.

Wilcox, Leonard. "Narrative Technique and the Theme of Historical Continuity in the Novels of Joan Didion." In Friedman, pp. 68–80.

Will, George F. "Didion's Fluent in 'Caring.' " Column distributed by *Washington Post* Writers Group, week of May 20, 1984.

Wilson, James Q. "In California." *Commentary,* September 1979, pp. 79–80, 94–96.

Winchell, Mark Royden. *Joan Didion.* 2nd ed. Boston: Twayne, 1989.

Wolfe, Tom, and E. W. Johnson, eds. *The New Journalism.* New York: Harper & Row, 1973.

Wolff, Cynthia Griffin. "*Play It as It Lays* and the New American Heroine." *Contemporary Literature,* 24:480–495 (Winter 1983). Repr. in Friedman, pp. 124–137.

INTERVIEWS

Bandler, Michael. "Portrait of an Author Reading." *Chicago Tribune Book World,* July 1, 1979, pp. 1, 8.

Daley, Maureen. "P.W. Interviews: Joan Didion." *Publishers Weekly,* October 9, 1972, pp. 26–27.

Davidson, Sara. "A Visit with Joan Didion." *New York Times Book Review,* April 3, 1977, pp. 1, 35–38. Repr. in Friedman, 13–21.

Diehl, Digby. "A Myth of Fragility Concealing a Tough Core." *Saturday Review,* March 5, 1977, p. 24.

Kuehl, Linda L. "Art of Fiction." *Paris Review,* 20:143–163 (Fall 1978).

Stamberg, Susan. "Cautionary Tales." April 4, 1977 *National Public Radio* interview. Repr. in Friedman, pp. 22–28.

—*C.K. DORESKI*

E. L. Doctorow

1931–

A PASSIONATE BRAVURA THAT mixes a cleverly engaging narrative with a historical and ethical scrutiny of American character and sensibility marks the writing of E. L. Doctorow. His writing, often luxuriant and dazzling, also features a casual easygoing strain. A wide critical and popular audience has affirmed his stature at the forefront of contemporary literature. Taken as a whole, his works stake out an American vision that is weird, idiosyncratic, often unsettling, but at the same time resplendently colorful, consummately human.

Edgar Laurence Doctorow (named after Edgar Allan Poe) was born in the Bronx in 1931, during the depression that looms so important throughout his oeuvre; both his parents were the children of Russian Jewish immigrants. He graduated from Kenyon College in 1952, where he studied with John Crowe Ransom and majored in philosophy, and then attended Columbia University graduate school for a year. Drafted in 1953, he served in the army in Germany for two years. In 1954, he married Helen Setzer, a writer he met at Columbia whose pen name is Henslee. In their 1990 book, *E. L. Doctorow,* Carol C. Harter and James R. Thompson quote Doctorow as saying, "My life is very quiet, dull bourgeois. A wife and three terrific children. We have a close family life. Sometimes I teach. I tend not to get in fights in bars. I don't go hunting for big game in Africa. I don't box. I love tennis."

Doctorow was a reader for film and television production companies and then worked at New American Library from 1959 to 1964, rising to the position of senior editor. He was employed by Dial Press during the period 1964–1969, eventually becoming vice president. In an interview in 1980 Doctorow told Larry McCaffery, "It was a great life, publishing good books in big printings—and, in those days—selling them for pocket change. You could feel good about the way you made your living." During the academic year 1969–1970, Doctorow held the position of writer-in-residence at the University of California at Irvine; he subsequently accepted similar posts at Sarah Lawrence, Princeton, the University of Utah, and the Yale School of Drama; New York University gave him an endowed chair. He won a Guggenheim Fellowship in 1972; the National Book Critics Circle Award for *Ragtime* in 1976; the National Book Award for *World's Fair* in 1986; and the PEN/Faulkner Award for Fiction as well as the National Book Critics Circle Award for *Billy Bathgate* in 1990. He lives in New Rochelle, New York, in the house on which the one that appears in *Ragtime* is based.

* * *

Doctorow's first novel, *Welcome to Hard Times* (1960) recounts the fortunes of a group of pioneering settlers at a turn-of-the-century Dakota Territory outpost. The novel offers, at least in part, a standard historical/mythical account of the frontier. The pioneers struggle to advance themselves by working the land, sacrificing the comforts of civilization for the challenge of self-reliance. Surviving by their wits and their determined effort, they implant the American spirit of commerce and civilization in the rugged northwest landscape. The enterprise is successful in these terms: the settlers dig wells, which lure businesses, saloons, and prostitutes, and they develop a prosperous service economy to support the nearby gold mines.

But this commercial success is overshadowed by a more sinister failure. The novel opens with a brutal attack on the town by a Bad Man (known at first only as such and, even after he is identified, still ominously depersonalized as, simply, the Bad Man) who rapes, murders, and burns down the town. He wreaks terrifying chaos, apparently without motive, gutting the town and leaving its few surviving inhabitants in shock. Even as the townspeople pull themselves up against the odds of nature and the difficulties of motivating themselves to rebuild what was destroyed, fear of the Bad Man's return incessantly haunts Blue, who is the mayor and narrator, and Molly, a prostitute whom the Bad Man brutalized nearly to death. Others, such as Zar, a Russian entrepreneur and pimp, and Ezra Maple, a general storekeeper, try to repress the sense of omnipotent power and fate that Molly associates with the Bad Man. They tend to their businesses as if hard work could overcome the Bad Man's threat. Blue tries to convince himself that the Bad Man will not return and rampage, that he cannot wipe out a town that has achieved such commercial prosperity as Hard Times has in the year since the devastation.

But Molly's prescience is, in fact, accurate.

Doctorow infuses the novel—as even the narrator subconsciously perceives—with the idea that the Bad Man's danger and evil are constant forces lurking in the landscape. At the end of the novel, the mines run out of gold, dooming Hard Times to the immediate and total economic collapse that had previously created so many other ghost towns (such as the neighboring ones from which Blue and Zar pilfered the lumber they used to build the businesses in Hard Times). Just as the news about the gold mines reaches Hard Times, the Bad Man returns in an incarnation that is as real and physical as was his first, but which also serves as a metaphor for the inevitable forces of chaos that Doctorow sees plaguing the American pioneer enterprise.

The novel is not just about this particular town's history but, by implication, about the pioneering development of the entire country. For instance, one of Blue's functions as town leader is to collect signatures on a petition for statehood. Near the end of the novel he is proud that, as business boomed in Hard Times, he had collected perhaps half-a-hundred names—so the town is literally and institutionally implicated in this country's expansion. America's foundations were developed amid absolute barbarity, Doctorow suggests, and the forces of society, order, and commerce are pathetically powerless against this evil. The historical perspective—the fact that Doctorow writes generations after the continent has been settled—would seem to indicate that the forces of order eventually won. But the ominous tone that pervades the novel suggests that while Americans may *think* we have triumphed over primitive barbarism, the Bad Man is still out there, lurking behind the facades of order.

Doctorow will repeat this theme, this moralistic prophecy, in his later novels. He probes an underlying core of evil—an event (such as the dubious execution of the Isaacsons in *The Book of Daniel*) or an ethos (such as inhuman capitalist exploitation in *The Waterworks*). Later generations attempt to smooth over the evil, creating a facade of propriety and distancing themselves from their tainted origins; or, as in *Billy Bathgate* and *Loon Lake,* the very person who is enmeshed in evil manages to obfuscate it later in his life and pose as an upstanding American citizen. But Doctorow will not let sleeping dogs lie: he relentlessly exposes the depravities of the past and implicitly juxtaposes them against our comfortable but self-delusory perspective in the present. He unsettles our complacency by demonstrating how the sins of the past not only haunt, but determine the present. He insists that all the social and moral structures that Americans celebrate so sanctimoniously today are, in fact, predicated upon—and still intricately intertwined with—the sordid realities of Hobbesian barbarity (in *Welcome to Hard Times*); greedy mobster bullying (in *Billy Bathgate*); manipulative political hysteria and scapegoating (in *The Book of Daniel*).

Welcome to Hard Times is a compelling and depressing study of how such evil manifests itself in the frontier landscape and especially of how it affects innocent, hardworking people. Subtly, though, Doctorow raises the question of whether the settlers in his novel really are innocent or are themselves somehow implicated in the evil that the Bad Man exemplifies simply because, by coming west, they have tried to raise themselves to a level that may be overweeningly ambitious. Molly, for example, had had a perfectly adequate job in New York, as a maid for a wealthy family, before she set out for the west. She sells her body in the Dakota Territory because she finds this preferable to working-class subservience. Doctorow lauds the entrepreneurial spirit of adventure and control of one's own destiny in this account of American settlers. But at the same time he questions whether his characters would all be better off living safer lives, even if they were lives of quiet desperation, rather than gambling on the wealth of the virgin frontier. By the end of the novel, the whole pioneer adventure seems like a crapshoot in which the odds are impossible. Doctorow suggests that the pioneers delude themselves if they imagine they can conquer the territory's obstacles: the omnipotent land that cares nothing for those who live on it; the vast distances that all but sunder any connection to the rest of the world; the deadening and psychologically tormenting winters that force settlers into hibernation for months; the mines that teasingly offer easy wealth but withhold their riches with the fierce grasp of a miser.

When the Bad Man first comes to town, the few inhabitants consider defending themselves, but eventually they only watch passively as his violence unfurls. A conviction of inherent cowardice, thus, can never be effaced even as the town rebuilds itself and manifests the outward signs of civilization and order. Molly, especially, reminds Blue and the others that they failed once and are doomed to fail again in their attempt to stave off the Bad Man's threat. (Blue has lamely attempted to form an ersatz family, taking Molly as a kind of wife and adopting a young boy, Jimmy, who was left orphaned during the Bad Man's opening rampage. But throughout the novel this "family" wholly fails to achieve any degree of closeness or mutual support.) Indeed, given a chance to redeem himself the second time around, Blue again proves to be impotent despite his having a plan of action. Around this central fact of failure, Doctorow weaves his novel; he plays social manners and values against the primordial reality of raw power, which seems fated to vanquish civilization.

The novel is presented in the form of three "ledgers": the Mayor's accounts of the town's history. The ledgers ostensibly record only such facts as who owns what and who is looking for work at the mines, but they actually constitute a vivid imaginative document of the pioneer sensibility: the settlers' ambitions and fantasies and the various frustrations that beset their hopes.

The written document holds significant sway: as scribe, the mayor has ultimate power in this fledgling town. But paradoxically, the writer is powerless to defend the town, to do anything more than chronicle its subservience to the forces of fate, of evil. In her essay, "History as Fate in E. L. Doctorow's Tale of a Western Town," Marilyn Arnold points out that "The more Blue writes the story of Hard Times, the more he feels the weight of the past and the hopeless inescapability of fate. . . . We sense his distending agony as he tries to sort out what has happened."

Writing is Doctorow's paradigm for staking claims on the American imaginative mythos—settling, peopling, storying the land. And this writing, like the literal act of settlement described in *Welcome to Hard Times,* is similarly damned. The writing enacts the same pattern as the town's history: the ledgers offer an eloquent and fascinating account of vintage American adventure, but they peter out along with the town at the end of the novel. Stylistically, Doctorow presents a confusingly fuzzy ineffability, evoking a loss of narrative control, to describe the Bad Man's return. The evil that was so strikingly graphic and clear, at the beginning, becomes elusive and vague by the end. The mayor writes the last lines of his history as his own life blood drains out of him.

Doctorow's most forthright and literal historical study is *The Book of Daniel* (1971), a thinly disguised examination of Julius and Ethel Rosenberg's execution for treason amid Sen. Joseph McCarthy's witch hunts. Doctorow transforms the Rosenbergs' actual story, but in fairly small ways; for example, Paul and Rochelle Isaacson, as Doctorow calls them, are given a son, Daniel, and a daughter, Susan, in place of the two sons that the Rosenbergs had; the betrayer is a family friend, the dentist Selig Mindish, rather than, as in real life, Ethel's brother, David Greenglass, and Mindish lacks the connections Greenglass had to military research.

It is surprising that Doctorow bothers to depart from the basic facts of the Rosenberg case at all, since the basis of his whole story is so obviously recognizable. His provocative exploration of fact and fiction (as well as the indeterminate gray area in between) is in the vein of the nonfiction novel, as epitomized by Truman Capote's *In Cold Blood* (1966). Like that novel, *The Book of Daniel* uses the terrifying destruction of a family as a springboard to explore the ramifications of failed American dreams.

But while Capote meticulously establishes the accuracy of his reportorial credentials, Doctorow writes in a flippantly freewheeling voice, sometimes without concern for historical and factual accuracy. Though many of his novels seem to be based on historical events, settings, and sensibilities, he has frequently downplayed the role of factual research in his fiction. "I don't like documentary fiction," he told Herbert Mitgang in a 1989 interview for the *New York Times.* "There is a transforming thing that happens to some of the facts you learn. When I reach that point, that's where the book starts. Where mythology and history converge, that's where I begin my novels."

While Doctorow is writing about real history—the shame of American demagoguery or xenophobic prejudice—the truth is mediated by his own fictive vision; he does not mind blurring the boundaries between fact and fiction. In an essay called "False Documents," which is collected in *Jack London, Hemingway, and the Constitution* (1993), Doctorow writes, "there is no fiction or nonfiction as we commonly understand the distinction: There is only narrative." He suggests that "the nonfictive premise of a discoverable factual world" is a construct we embrace to flatter ourselves that we live in a rational, just, epistemologically comprehensible society. But actually, Doctorow argues, factual truth eludes nonfictional analysis and narrative—especially in cases that inflame a hysterical national passion, as the Rosenberg trial did—so he suggests that we might as well read novels for our social, political, historical, and moral education. "Doctorow is more concerned with imaginative truth than with historical accuracy," writes Paul Levine in "The Conspiracy of History: E. L. Doctorow's *The Book of Daniel.*" "That is, he is concerned with what *truly* happened rather than with what *really* happened."

Doctorow's fictionalization of the Rosenberg case presents an imaginative interpretation of what the ordeal of the treason trial might have seemed like to the ordinary people involved in it, people like Paul and Rochelle Isaacson and, most of all, like Daniel—a boy who had his family ripped apart by the cold war, by the American government, in a way that a twelve-year-old simply cannot understand. And finally, the meaning of the Rosenberg episode seems to elude not only Daniel but Doctorow as well. The story fades out at the end, in the manner of many of Doctorow's novels. It defies resolution or closure: instead, America is represented as still trying to grapple with the legacy of this episode, fairly ineptly, more than a decade later. (Doctorow frames Daniel's turbulent experience in the 1950s within scenes of the protests and countercultural upheavals of the late 1960s.) As desperately important as closure would be to Daniel, Doctorow seems to judge it inappropriate: his curse—and ours—is to continue living with the inconclusive aftermath of the trials and the execution. In the postmodern mode that was becoming fashionable when *The Book of Daniel* was written, the novel offers a variety of conclusions (the last section is called "Three Endings"), none of which is satisfying in any conventional way. Also in the postmodern style, the narrative voice (as in several of Doctorow's later works) is weirdly erratic, disarmingly unplaceable: not impenetrable, but unusual and distracting enough to remind readers continually that we are in the control of the idiosyncratic author and had better hang on tight. This first-person narrative voice is largely but not wholly Daniel's; his consciousness and perceptions sometimes fluctuate into a third-person voice. Occasionally, too, other characters (Paul, Rochelle) take over the first-person narration without any explicit indication that they are doing so. The voice is close to the action at hand—intimate, incisive—but is also in some ways incapable of fully comprehending immediate events. It is cocky; writerly; impatient; irreverent; intrusive; elusive; confusing; too prominent—characteristics that generally typify the first-person voice throughout Doctorow's works. As with the biblical book of Daniel, the reader is asked to envision or extrapolate, from an odd voice, the weighty and vatic tenor of a mysterious dreamer/prophet.

Doctorow's contribution to this famous story is his psychoemotional analysis of characters in pain. As he does throughout his oeuvre, Doctorow represents this pain as deriving from the ethical depravity he sees pervading American culture. "I find no clues either to their guilt or innocence," Daniel thinks. "Perhaps they are neither guilty nor innocent." Doctorow's subject is not the justice or injustice of the Isaacsons' trial per se; rather, he explores the general barbarity that Daniel and Susan experience, first-hand, as sacrificial victims for all of American society. Daniel believes the nightmare of having one's parents dragged off to jail by FBI agents could have happened to any of thousands of children in identical families and homes. Susan is spared the painful soul-searching that torments her brother: she simply goes crazy from the experience. At the opening of the novel Susan is in a mental hospital. Most of the time she seems detached from reality; she dies at the end, leaving Daniel to deal with the ramifications. But in one of the few moments when Susan is able to engage in prophecy, she intones the novel's mantra: "They're still fucking us."

Daniel and Doctorow take this mantra as their perversely revelatory insight. The execution was not an extraordinary event: it was simply a more publicized variant on the continual cruelty that Doctorow sees throughout history. Interspersed in his narrative, and seeming to be non sequiturs, are brief and graphic images of various forms of barbarity: knouting in tsarist Russia, burning at the stake in Joan of Arc's Europe and the Jim Crow South, drawing and quartering in medieval England, and so forth. Doctorow treats the Isaacsons' execution (described in intensely disturbing detail) as one more example of the barbaric torture of low-status individuals by a corrupt and powerful political establishment. An institution that kills people like the Isaacsons hates and fears anyone who poses a threat to its authority; it tortures and executes its victims to provide an example that will intimidate others who may be contemplating disobedience.

The treason trial exposes patterns of barbarous behavior (Doctorow is always fascinated by historical patterns) and an iceberg underneath: the barbaric sensibility as it has been institutionalized. Daniel and Susan suffer the effects of this sensibility long after the execution. Doctorow details the layers of bitterness, paranoia, and alienation that accrue when the children stay first with relatives who reject them, then at a shelter that represents another sort of institutional barbarism; when they are exploited for publicity by their parents' supporters; when Daniel is unable to finish his doctoral dissertation because he is obsessed with the incomprehensibility of his own history; when 1960s student radical movements try to use Daniel and Susan (and even more exploitatively, the money accumulated in their trust fund) in a way that reenacts how they have been used, abused, by so many other people for so long. The novel is a study in sadomasochism: Daniel and Susan are tormented with cruelty and coldness, dehumanized and oppressed, again and again: "They're still fucking us." In the introduction to his collected essays, *Jack London,* Doctorow describes the dysfunctional pain that typified the period he represents in *The Book of Daniel:* "though the enemy to be contained was the Soviet Union, the creative animus of our warring mind was un-

leashed, to an astonishing degree, upon ourselves." Daniel's misfortune must be extended, Doctorow suggests, to include and implicate all of America. Throughout his novels Doctorow invokes a sense of collective responsibility for the pain that alights on a victim such as Daniel.

Most important to Doctorow, the fact that America allows the cold war and the Isaacsons' execution to occur is related to the fact that America permits itself to get involved in the Vietnam War, a war directed by political leaders who repeat an enduring pattern of committing atrocities against humanity. Doctorow suggests that the Vietnam War (and concomitant anticommunist fervor) emerges out of the sloppiness of American intellectual, political, and legal practices as evidenced by the Isaacson trial. Daniel, who had the misfortune to be at the center of the trial and also the war, symbolically connects the shame of both fiascos.

Ragtime (1975) is the most resplendent of all Doctorow's period pieces. It flourishes with evocative and convincing portraits of the atmosphere, architecture, and zeitgeist of turn-of-the-century New York—though at the expense of the kind of detailed character study that marks Doctorow's other novels. The consciously stylized artifice of *Ragtime,* so richly laden with all the trappings of the era, verges on parody in the mode of technology, progressive ideology, and racial consciousness in early-twentieth-century America, but the characters lack the engaging complexity of Daniel Isaacson or characters in Doctorow's later novels, *Billy Bathgate* (1989) and *The Waterworks* (1994). *Welcome to Hard Times* and *Loon Lake* (1980) feature stylized milieus similar to the one represented in *Ragtime,* but those other novels offer, in addition, a more intimately personal narrative, while in *Ragtime* Doctorow embraces the purely sociocultural realm.

In *Ragtime* Doctorow paints a fantasia composed of continual, weird, unlikely interactions. What if a line could be drawn connecting Sigmund Freud, Harry Houdini, Henry Ford, Emma Goldman, Admiral Peary, J. P. Morgan, Stanford White, Booker T. Washington, and others, among a cast of hundreds? Such improbable connections surround the turmoil of an upper-class family (who are nameless—referred to only as Mother, Father, Younger Brother) that serves as a magnet for these forces, a barometer of the exciting yet dangerous volatility of the first years of the twentieth century. A sense of volatility is expressed in the novel by the fact that the family's business is in fireworks and explosives manufacturing (Doctorow's symbolism in *Ragtime* is rather heavy-handed). With a Dickensian sense of construction and coincidence and a Joycean energy of circulation, Doctorow makes the age's most flamboyant characters pass through the family's lives. Packed with an almost incredible amount of historical and fictional material— adventures, passions, legerdemain, explosions, explorations of frontiers—the novel is an extravaganza, a phantasmagoria.

Doctorow treats the enormously popular ragtime music as a metaphor for the dazzling complexity of turn-of-the-century American society; it provides a unifying theme that encompasses the novel's eclectic, disparate elements. When the family hears Scott Joplin's ''The Maple Leaf''—''a most robust composision, a vigorous music that roused the senses and never stood still a moment—the boy perceived it as light touching various places in space, accumulating in intricate patterns until the entire room was made to glow with its own being.''

The unity suggested by ragtime music, though, endures only ephemerally. At the end of the novel, Doctorow notes that the vogue for ragtime music has passed, but the country is left to deal with the ramifications of its extravagance (though the characters mostly manage to sublimate unpalatable realities amid the plush spectaculars that the age offers). Houdini's amazing feats and Morgan's incomprehensible wealth are the most obvious examples of the American spectacle, and Doctorow finds chinks even here: Houdini is depressed, psychologically resentful of the crowds that clamor for his feats but do not appreciate him as a person; Morgan is simply deranged in his conception of what his wealth entitles him to. (In *The Waterworks* Doctorow also expresses disdain for what he sees as the perversion of noblesse oblige by the supposed patriarchs of American society.)

The dangers that simmer in the America of *Ragtime*—the hypocrisies, the abuse of power, the refusal to acknowledge a just order of relations among people—culminate in World War I, which is just beginning as the novel ends. As he does often in his fiction, Doctorow exploits the audience's historical sense to create dramatic irony; we know, for example, as none of the characters do, that the seemingly infinite bounty that intoxicates America during this period is destined to be deflated by the Great War and then even more devastatingly exhausted by the Depression. While in *Ragtime* Doctorow celebrates the sumptuous achievements amassed by modern New York and a brilliant American empire, he simultaneously offers glimpses into the underside of all this wonder: the horror of immigrants' lives, the shame of child labor, the humiliating disenfranchisement of black Americans, and all the hypocrisy on which the American spectacular is predicated. Doctorow's Freud offers his verdict on a visit to New York:

> The entire population seemed to him over-powered, brash and rude. The vulgar wholesale appropriation of European art and architecture regardless of period or country he found appalling. He had seen in our careless commingling of great wealth and great poverty the chaos of an entropic European civilization. He sat in his quiet cozy study in Vienna, glad to be back. He said to Ernest Jones, America is a mistake, a gigantic mistake.

Each of Doctorow's novels, according to Paul Levine, ''addresses itself in some significant way to Freud's judgment that America was a 'gigantic mistake.' '' That is, Levine continues, Doctorow ''describ[es] the gap in American life between its ideals and its reality.''

Somewhat mitigating its vision of America as a place of vastly excessive wealth, racist hatred, and tormenting poverty, *Ragtime* also depicts a degree of charity in this society: a wealthy woman devotes herself to nurturing a poor Jewish waif from the Lower East Side; Mother takes in a poor black woman and the baby she tried to bury alive at birth and attempts to steady both their lives. But, as happens when Blue attempts to show compassion for Molly and Jimmy in *Welcome to Hard Times,* the forces of greed, violence, and a general American insecurity undermine each attempt to be charitable. No character in *Ragtime* is finally able to go beyond his or her individual needs and embrace the common good. When Doctorow explores the sensibilities of Ford and Morgan—the two characters who are most successful when judged by America's usual standards—he finds them scornful of their fellow citizens and intent on divorcing themselves in every way from the masses.

Large institutional patterns of oppressive dehumanization destroy any small personal inclinations the characters may have to act morally or charitably. The novel ends with a scene of colossal failure: the New York police execute a black man, a ragtime pianist named Coalhouse Walker, who is the father of the baby that Mother had saved. Walker had threatened to bomb J. P. Morgan's personal temple of wealth in retribution for the humiliation he suffered at the hands of some white racists who defaced his car by slashing the roof and leaving a pile of human feces on the seat. Walker's story (an adaptation of Heinrich von Kleist's nineteenth-century German novella, *Michael Kohlhaas*) begins only midway through the novel but emerges as the most forceful of all the interwoven and competing narratives; the episodes of tragic blundering that infuse the novel concentrate in Walker's spectacular defeat. At the novel's end, it seems America has spun wildly out of control—at the very beginning of the century that seemed so full of promise. Thus Doctorow foretells the dangers lurking amid our shows of progress and civilization.

Loon Lake—like the other two novels Doctorow would write during the 1980s, *World's Fair* (1985) and *Billy Bathgate*—is set in the 1930s and features a young protagonist trying to flourish despite the decade's daunting and dreary conditions. He tries to survive the oppressive banality characteristic of society during the Depression by seeking some secret vein of colorful and imaginative potential. Doctorow's political essays make it clear that his taking an interest in the Depression during the Reagan era is not accidental: he describes the 1980s as a period when a massive underclass was brutally victimized by a greedy stratum of wealthy people, resulting in a vastly widening gap between rich and poor, powerful and powerless. With his usual attention to historical parallels and repetitions, Doctorow clearly realized that there were strong echoes of the 1930s in the 1980s. In a 1989 commencement address collected in *Jack London,* Doctorow depicts Reagan's America in these terms: ''we now have hundreds of thousands, perhaps millions, of our citizens lying around in the streets of our cities, sleeping in doorways, begging with Styrofoam cups. We didn't have a class of permanent beggars in this country, in the United States of America, fifteen or twenty years ago.'' In ''The Character of Presidents,'' which is also in *Jack London,* Doctorow indicts Reagan for abandoning the government's commitment to Americans in need: ''[Reagan's] heartfelt pieties and simplistic reductions of thought, his misquotations and exaggerations, his mawkish appeals to rugged self-reliance, spearheaded a devastating assault on the remedial legislation that had been enacted from the New Deal to the Great Society.''

Doctorow depicts money as an all-encompassing symbol of power, status, survival. Especially in a story set in the 1930s, when prosperity was so scarce, it makes sense that Doctorow should focus on wealth—the perfect vehicle for the irony that infuses all moral literature. A few people have so much money, while so many, who are so desperate, have so little. Money enchants Doctorow: not only the literal thrill of what cold hard cash can buy but also what it symbolizes; that is, freedom and sensual allure. Doctorow's narrative is at the same time enamored of wealth and scornful of the moral alienation and psychological despair that seem destined to accompany it. Though the Depression is a potent backdrop to the historical and social forces portrayed in the story, it is explicitly almost absent (as is the case in Doctorow's other two novels about the 1930s). But the multimillionaire autobody maker F. W. Bennett occupies an unusual, detached, highlighted position in the story by virtue of the fact that he has a great deal of money and spends it oddly, at a time when most people in the country are impoverished. Bennett's Adirondack retreat, the sumptuous estate called Loon Lake, provides an ironic counterpoint to the conditions of the industrial American heartland that Joe must negotiate.

Joe, from Paterson, New Jersey, is called Joe Paterson throughout the novel. (Doctorow reveals Joe's actual surname only on the novel's last page), taking his name from his place of origin in the American landscape rather than from his own family lineage. The novel tells of a young man's quest for adventure, passion, and identity as he rambles through the landscape of the fabulously rich and the struggling factory hands. He sucks up experience as he observes and interacts with not only the millionaire, F. W.

Bennett, but also a poet; a sexy kept woman; mobsters; servants; union organizers and infiltrators; and carnival performers. Throughout his travels Joe defines himself against these types. The bulk of the novel portrays this young man's adventures, but its moral resonance is sharpest, perhaps, in the last pages, where Doctorow gives us an account of Joe's subsequent life history. After serving an opportunistic apprenticeship with a wealthy sociopath, an industrial spy, and an array of gangsters, Joe goes on to attend an excellent liberal arts college, graduate cum laude (voted most likely to succeed by his classmates), and serve with distinction in World War II. He works his way smoothly up the classic American ladder of success into the highest echelons of respectable society, serving, by the 1970s, as deputy assistant director of the CIA, ambassador, and on the boards of directors of various corporations. His story is that of a fantasy American everyman.

Doctorow affirms the idea that the 1930s were, as W. H. Auden put it in "September 1, 1939," a "low dishonest decade," one that profoundly corrupted America. His writing depicts the period as epitomized not by the New Deal spirit of optimism and perseverance (as some have characterized that decade). Instead, Doctorow displays a sensibility that evokes the works of John Steinbeck, seeing the 1930s as pervasively corrupt and base. The period reflected the hardships that plagued masses of Americans, hardships that were exacerbated by an ignominious few who sought opportunistically to turn the misfortunes of others to their own profit. In the 1940s, the war offered us a chance to redeem ourselves, to behave heroically in a clear-cut contest between good and evil. Had there only been some challenge of similar clarity during the 1930s, Doctorow's reader may infer, perhaps Americans would not have become so mired in the venality of that era. In any case, if war heroes such as Joe were able to acquire a veneer of respectability, it must have been only a sham given the torpidity of the 1930s in which they came of age. While America's midcentury captains of industry may seem to have had all the trappings of genteel respectability, Doctorow's exposé of the formative depravity of the American soul shows a rotten strain underneath. "There's a certain ethos abroad in the land today," Doctorow said in his interview with Herbert Mitgang, "in which there's no strict demarcation between evil and good. The most surprising people have been caught in dubious activities in the last 10 years—all the way up to the level of our national life. . . . There are perfectly reasonable and proper individuals whose business it is to pollute the atmosphere and to make atomic weapons and to keep secrets from the public." Doctorow's fiction consistently works to undermine the surface of propriety and to demand recognition of how dangerous a seemingly upstanding citizen can be.

Like Doctorow's other novels, *Loon Lake* offers a panorama of vintage Americana that is both affirmative of our national mythic clichés and subversively darkened with the taint of the grotesque. Doctorow celebrates the highway to California and the railroad nomads who traverse the continent, trying to pull themselves up by their bootstraps; the factory production line that builds a strong nation; the natural splendor of Loon Lake's pristine and bountiful wildlife. (Loon Lake seems to figure as an American Eden.) But intermixed with this, belying the glib myths, are a cavalcade of hoboes, carnival freaks, prostitutes and molls, criminals, the impoverished, the unhappy, the duped, the desperate working classes. The American landscape, as spectacular as it is, bears a deep strain of evil. One character, a poet called Warren Penfield, desperately but ineffectually tries to redeem his country through his art. But he proves to be, at his core crudely banal, a hypocrite: "He knew the real evil was his own . . . He was excited by any kind of violence, a parent hitting a child a

man hitting a woman." Gratuitous cruelty infects Doctorow's Americans; for instance, Joe describes in morbid detail the gang rape and brutal death of Fanny, the carnival's fat lady, orchestrated by the carney manager as the culmination of his freak show and defended by the manager's wife: "Of course they never live long, such creatures—the heart won't beat for them . . . All summer Sim Hearn watches—he watches and then he sees the signs—she doesn't take breath as she should—from the bed she cannot lift herself . . . The people know Hearn—he gives something special at end of summer, a grand finale." The casual brutality that suffuses *Loon Lake* makes conventional American ideals seem pathetically flimsy. As he does in his earlier novels, Doctorow presents hypocrisy and brutality as simply inherent and pervasive in the landscape.

Out of this miasma, characters and plots emerge slowly and fuzzily. The narrative voices and tenor fluctuate erratically, sometimes obfuscating more than elucidating the story: Doctorow makes it difficult for his reader to apprehend the details and the logic of the world he represents in *Loon Lake,* perhaps to give the reader an experience that mimics the confusing uncertainties he sees as characteristic of this era. The narrative shifts between first and third person, and between the consciousness of Joe, Penfield, and Bennett. It also jumps around from one point in time to another, with little indication of exactly when shifts and transitions of time, plot, and voice occur or where they will lead. Like several of Doctorow's novels, *Loon Lake* ends in a vague haze, coyly trailing off into imprecision. The plot is never neatly resolved. Perhaps Doctorow means to represent the troubling inconclusiveness afflicting the 1930s. Or perhaps Douglas Fowler is right when he writes in his book, *Understanding E. L. Doctorow* (1992), "Doctorow seems to get tired of the novel nine-tenths of the way through and concludes his tale with a jarring mixture of exasperation, ad hoc invention, and fatigue."

The narrative voice in *Loon Lake* bears affinities to the voice in other Doctorow novels, though it is more intrusive and more difficult here. It runs on, often difficult to read and decipher, though in a way that suggests a studied pose. The languid casualness of the narrator rcalls the style of some other contemporary novelists, such as Kurt Vonnegut, Donald Barthelme, and Tom Robbins, with their fun, loose, unfettered, antiliterary, ''improper'' voices. To Larry McCaffery, Doctorow himself described what he created in *Loon Lake* as ''a discontinuous narrative, with deferred resolutions,'' featuring ''multiple voices that turn out to be the work of one narrator''—a narrator, then, who is a sort of ventriloquist. (Ventriloquism is explicitly invoked in *World's Fair;* it characterizes the technique of several of Doctorow's novels.) The elusive, casual style of *Loon Lake* is not Doctorow's forte, however, as he seems to realize himself: all his other works, before and after *Loon Lake,* are more conventional novels—not rigidly conservative, but certainly less experimental. Douglas Fowler quotes Anthony Burgess' review of *Loon Lake:* it ''displayed 'the admirable faults of the overreacher,' '' Burgess writes. ''[I]f Doctorow had not quite brought off his effort, he had indeed made 'a very honorable attempt at expanding the resources of the genre.' ''

World's Fair is like *The Book of Daniel* without the treason trial. In the same vivid Bronx setting, Doctorow explores the perceptions of a young boy to whom nothing very exceptional happens. The principal characters, a nine-year-old boy named Edgar and his parents, seem to be based on Doctorow and *his* parents, Rose and David; essential details of the characters' lives match details from the author's own. (Like Doctorow's father, for example, the fictional father owns a music store.) In combination with *The Book of Daniel* and *Billy Bathgate, World's Fair* establishes Doctorow as the muse of the Bronx. ''The whole point about the Bronx,'' he told Stephanie Mansfield in a 1989 interview for the

Washington Post, ''is that it was, in a sense, nowhere. It was endless miles of anonymous middle-class neighborhoods that had great vitality, of course, but always struck me as being not quite central to the world. There was always the lack of character—that in itself generated a lot of feverish activity on the part of children, to create an imaginary place for themselves, and a surprising number of writers and artists and filmmakers have come out of there.''

The Bronx literary landscape Doctorow renders does not quite rival Joyce's Dublin, but the comparison is not inappropriate. The Bronx novels, especially *World's Fair,* conjure up a streetscape of the immediate neighborhood—the Grand Concourse, Claremont Park, Morris Avenue, 173d Street—where the writer first became aware of the intrigues taking place in his surroundings, intrigues he meticulously reworks in his fiction. The earlier *Book of Daniel* and the later *Billy Bathgate* are linked with *World's Fair,* loosely forming a Bronx trilogy, by virtue of numerous scenes from the other two books that appear in *World's Fair.* These scenes, vignettes of minimal importance to any of the plots, signal to Doctorow's readers that these novels are inspired by his own powerful, formative, and enduring memories of growing up in the Bronx. The recurring episodes are as trivial as a runaway senile grandmother, a technique for cleaning up a child's vomit (by spilling sawdust over it), the smell of Pechter breads emanating from the nearby factory—and as traumatic as the danger posed by the roughs who frequent gangster Dutch Schultz's beer barns or the memory of a pedestrian carrying grocery bags who is suddenly struck and killed by a car, her blood mixing with the milk from the bottles she was carrying.

Set in the late 1930s, *World's Fair* culminates with the actual World's Fair at the end of the decade. Drawing on a quietly charming compendium of images and memories from his own childhood, Doctorow offers a portrait of a young boy who is clearly (the author realizes in retrospect) already gathering the material from which the adult will create. So the rather plotless narrative is a subtle Künstlerroman: the fictional Edgar is a writer-in-training, winning honorable mention in an essay contest sponsored by the World's Fair on the subject of "the Typical American Boy." Doctorow also depicts Edgar attempting to learn ventriloquism, practicing to project his own voice as if it were coming from someplace else, which is obviously a metaphor for what any novelist does. The convincingly detailed precision of Doctorow's prose highlights the intense seriousness a nine-year-old projects onto a world he is just beginning to figure out. Edgar contemplates, for instance, how his father's Manhattan business operates (and eventually fails); why his parents are unhappy together; why his mother dislikes his friend Meg's unmarried mother, Norma; what feelings of budding sexuality he and Meg share and how these feelings affect their close friendship; what his older brother attempts to escape. In a compelling "collaboration" between the older writer and the younger self he revisits, Doctorow imbues the boy with a cautious intelligence that allows him to probe and experience these issues without succumbing to the possible disappointments that his fragile world might well hold.

Though the fair occupies only a few chapters at the end of the novel, the title generates an anticipation in the reader that parallels Edgar's craving to attend. He is as eager as any young boy to visit the spectacular fair but is afraid to pester his parents about going because he knows times are difficult for them, both financially and emotionally. Finally, though, he gets to visit the fair twice: first with Meg, when Norma invites him to accompany them; then with his family. Norma works in the fair's Amusement Zone where, Edgar discovers, she wrestles in a tank of water with Oscar the Amorous Octopus. As the night wears on, Oscar becomes increasingly lewd, removing Norma's bathing suit entirely.

The visit is, at least in part, a triumphant ad-

venture for Edgar: he takes on the exciting, sleek allure of the World of Tomorrow, the Plaza of Light, the Consolidated Edison diorama of New York City, the technology on display at the RCA exhibit, and the architectural marvels of the Trylon and Perisphere that were the actual fair's stunning visual symbols. All these portend a future life of carefree progress and orderly prosperity, so they feed the rich fantasies of this boy—who is currently stuck in a Bronx muddle. Edgar taps into the fair's vision as a promise that he will have something better than a working-class life in economically depressed America. But the fair also stimulates Edgar's fears; he cannot ignore the fair's seedier aspects. Norma's nudity, for example, not only excites but also disturbs him.

When he returns with his family for his second visit, Edgar notes that the fair "wasn't as clean-looking or as shiny" as when he had first visited it. "I could see everywhere signs of decay. Perhaps this was just in my mind; I knew that in only a month the World's Fair would close forever. But the officials who ran the exhibits seemed less attentive to the visitors, their uniforms not quite crisp." Again, Doctorow depicts Edgar as having the same volatile mixture of emotions he experienced when he came to the fair with Meg and Norma: Edgar is excited by the dazzling display and, especially, by being the knowing guide to the fairground. He is proud that he has brought his family to experience the vision of the fair and opened their eyes to the glories of the future. As his prize for winning the Typical American Boy competition, Edgar gets this all-expenses-paid day at the fair, which enables him to provide his family with what they could not otherwise have afforded. Sensing that his family is drifting apart, crumbling under hostile tensions, Edgar hopes that simply bringing them together in the setting of the fair may somehow inspire them to forge ahead, reconciled, with a renewed sense of optimism.

But diminishing this hope is the peeling paint,

reminding Edgar that even an idealized vision of the future suffers the ravages of present reality; the fair is just a show and cannot finally deliver all the seductive fantasies it offers. Edgar's father, skeptical of the shining utopia the fair seems to promise and aware that the real world cannot be easily transformed into such perfection, taints its innocence for Edgar. Riding with his family through the General Motors Futurama exhibit, Edgar is fascinated by ''the whole splendid panoply of highways and horizons before us, all lit up and alive with motion, an intricate marvel of miniaturization.'' But afterwards his father deconstructs the experience: '' 'It is a wonderful vision, all those highways and all those radio-driven cars. Of course, highways are built with public money,' he said after a moment. 'When the time comes, General Motors isn't going to build the highways, the federal government is. With money from us taxpayers.' He smiled. 'So General Motors is telling us what they expect from us: we must build them the highways so they can sell us the cars.' ''

The father's attitude expresses the cynical, conspiracy-theory vision of capitalist hegemony that pervades Doctorow's novels. Young Edgar is not yet infected by this vision, but Doctorow shows how he first becomes aware of the devious way American society really operates behind a facade of harmonious progress and commonweal. In other ways, too, *World's Fair* represents a foreboding spirit that Doctorow identifies as being latent even in his youth: a spirit that is not as destructive as the ominous atmosphere which besets such characters as Daniel Isaacson, Coalhouse Walker, and Martin Pemberton, but certainly the germ of that atmosphere.

> You learned the world through its dark signs and also from its evil devices, such as slingshots . . . and scumbags. I found a slingshot one day that was beautifully made. Someone had taken great pains with it. . . . I immediately placed a small round stone in the pouch and let fly. It didn't go very far. I tried again, this time pulling back on the

rubber as hard as I could with my right hand and holding my left arm stiff, my hand clenching the frame handle. The stone went like a bullet, pinged a car door, leaving a dent, and then bounced off the carriage of a child sitting in the sun next to my house.

> The mother was furious. She went up the steps of my house and rang the doorbell. But even before my mother came to the door I had dumped the slingshot in the ash can. It was powerful magic, it had some animating force of its own, well beyond the strength in my child's arms. . . .

> But the scumbag, ah the scumbag, here was an item so loathsome, so evil, that the very word itself was too terrible to pronounce. There was a seemingly endless depth of dark meaning attached to this word, with intimations of filth, and degradation, touching on such dark secrets as the young prince of life that I was would live in eternal heavenly sunlight not to know. In order to learn what a scumbag specifically and precisely was, beyond the foul malevolence of the sound of the word, you had to acquire knowledge of sick and menacing excitements to a degree that would inflict permanent damage to your soul. Yet of course I did learn, finally, one summer at the great raucous beach of crashing waves and sand-caked bodies known as Rockaway.

Thoughts like these, and fear for the family dog darting into traffic, his parents' arguments, and a dangerous burst appendix, make up the fabric of Doctorow's relatively tame darkness in this novel. He gives the reader a sense, though, of how the smaller terrors of childhood mesh with the larger ones of adulthood. When Edgar tells his brother about a chalk scrawl he finds on the garage, he tells us, ''I hadn't expected their complete attention. . . . Donald stepped up and raised his arm, and used the sleeves of his sweater as an eraser. The other boys were equally solemn. They took the whole thing seriously. 'It's bad,' Donald told me. 'Whenever you see one of these, make sure to erase it. Use your shoe sole, spit on it, rub it with dirt, do anything. It's a swastika.' ''

In *Billy Bathgate,* Doctorow revisits the essence of the Bad Man who appears in his first novel. This time, however, the bad man is not an outsider who rides into town and disrupts a social enterprise. Instead, he takes the form of the 1930s Bronx mobster Dutch Schultz, who is the central focus of the novel, a perversely heroic character who is situated in a world that lacks even a pretense of law and order. Dutch's casually brutal murders, his sociopathic amorality, are identical to the Bad Man's. But here, through the first-person narrative voice of Billy (an admiring fifteen-year-old who finesses his way into Dutch's gang), Doctorow examines what is going on in the minds of the aggressors rather than the victims: why the gangsters act as they do; what their codes and values are; what they are questing for.

In *Welcome to Hard Times,* Doctorow interweaves a profound strain of evil with the clichés of the American mythic frontier; in *Billy Bathgate* he does the same with the clichés of the immigrant melting pot. As Doctorow portrays them, Dutch's gangsters epitomize the fantasies of all the poor, hardworking Irish, Italians, Jews (and others) who adulate the criminals, vicariously following their daring exploits in daily newspaper installments. The Depression, though never mentioned explicitly, is responsible for elevating murderers to heroes because all moral means to achieve upward mobility have proven futile. Dutch's prosperity is diametrically antithetical to the Depression, which connotes the failure of the American dream in the same way that the western ghost towns and dried-up mines do in *Welcome to Hard Times.* Dutch exemplifies one extreme of the ironic Depression dialectic between good and evil, success and failure, wealth and poverty, very much as F. W. Bennett does in *Loon Lake;* Dutch revels in wealth while the rest of America scrimps. He and the other glamorous, natty mobsters commandeer entire floors of hotels when they travel; the city's most elegant nightclubs are dormant without them, but spring to life as soon as one of the gangsters enters. Billy awes everyone who sees him when

he returns to his Bronx neighborhood, merely because he has associated himself with the criminals.

Doctorow torpedoes vintage American values. Billy's family, which represents the centerpiece of the American mythos, is meaningless. Billy does not know who his father is, and his mother is in the process of going insane throughout the novel. Billy spent part of his youth in an orphanage because his parents were unable to care for him. Doctorow does not disclose Billy's real last name: Bathgate (after his Bronx neighborhood) is his mob moniker. Like Joe Paterson in *Loon Lake,* Billy derives his last name not from his biological parents but from his place in the American landscape; he is the progeny of American culture as a whole. In choosing the name, he tells us, "I was baptizing myself into the gang because then I had an extra name too to use when I felt like it . . . insofar as names went they could be like license plates you could switch on cars, not welded into their construction but only tagged on for the temporary purposes of identification." (When Doctorow "tagged on" the name of Billy Bathgate to this novel's protagonist, he was recycling it from a short work he had written two decades earlier, "The Songs of Billy Bathgate," about the artistic development of a 1960s folk-rock singer.) Billy's real parents and lineage are pathetically irrelevant to him, but among the mobsters, Billy cultivates a close sense of family. They are role models for him, teaching him how to behave and how to survive. They support him and even, Doctorow suggests, love him as no one else in his world can. Dutch is like a father to Billy, and Dutch's moll behaves like a mother, though she also acts as Billy's governess and his lover—certainly they make a weird sort of family. Doctorow does not present this group as a desirable version of the American family but simply as all Billy has available to him.

As in *Welcome to Hard Times,* Doctorow frames his story with a gripping, vivid description of real, murderous evil. He assures his reader that, whatever depravities are perverted into delusory fantasies in the middle of the story, the alpha and omega are undisguisable brutality. *Billy Bathgate* begins with an excruciating account of how Dutch executes his once-trusted henchman, Bo Weinberg. Doctorow luxuriates in the details of how Schultz plants his associate's feet in cement and torments Bo as they wait for the cement to dry before he throws Bo into the Atlantic Ocean. Near the end of the novel, Doctorow presents the Mafia's massacre of Dutch's entire gang. Outside of this frame, though, in the last few pages of the novel, Billy tells what happens to him in later life. The summer he spent with Dutch was like an internship; he goes on, inspired by the cunning and enterprise he learned from the gangsters (and abetted by the fortune he cannily recovered after everyone else had been killed), to whip himself into shape. He performs well in school, attends an Ivy League university, becomes "patriotically employed overseas" during World War II, and finally acquires the vague but apparently impressive condition of having "a certain renown." The device and the details are essentially identical to the coda at the end of *Loon Lake* that sums up Joe Paterson's successful and respectable future. Both novels, the reader learns at the end, have portrayed formative experiences in the lives of characters who embody all-American success; Joe and Billy offer no apologies for their youthful excesses, only a genteel discretion. As Christopher D. Morris suggests in *Models of Misrepresentation: On the Fiction of E. L. Doctorow* (1991), Billy's astute manipulation of the narrative may well mask his own extensive culpability; perhaps he has even betrayed Dutch at the end of the novel to secure his treasure. "Hints do not amount to a case, however," Morris observes, "and Billy is careful never to let his narrative definitively implicate himself." What the young hero learns in this novel is not how to behave nobly but, rather, how to get away with whatever indiscretions one commits.

Doctorow's ultimate point is that greed and brutality are engrained in our culture. Murder lies just below the surface of our polite manners; we are fascinated by it, and it is the logical extension of all that we admire in the American character and the American quest. Doctorow does not excuse or glamorize his villains' murderous rage: the reader is, and is meant to be, repelled by the characters' crass, selfish disregard for human dignity. But at the same time Doctorow is fascinated by the force such characters exert and by the contrast they offer to the rest of society, which must passively endure them when they go on the rampage. The American ethos honors those who set their own courses and act; Doctorow believes that Dutch and his mob are the men who embody this ethos par excellence, while the rest of us are patsies waiting to be picked off by them.

Doctorow's *The Waterworks* exhibits the same kind of cynicism about American history that infuses all his writing. Here again Doctorow expresses the idea that America's grandeur has been built on a patently corrupt foundation. This corruption (of which Boss Tweed is the most prominent, though certainly not the only, exemplar) must have been evident to almost any person thinking critically at the time, Doctorow suggests. What remains a significant and haunting fact for the present is that we cannot escape our origins. Throughout his oeuvre Doctorow denies us the right to plead, as an excuse, that we are not complicit because we were not alive when some corrupt act occurred. He shows the Hobbesian underside of the national psyche in the 1870s in *The Waterworks;* in the 1900s in *Ragtime;* in the 1930s in *Billy Bathgate* and *Loon Lake;* in the 1950s and 1960s in *The Book of Daniel;* in the late twentieth century in his play *Drinks before Dinner* (1978); in the future in his science fiction novel, *Big as Life* (1966). The thrust of all of Doctorow's writing is that our failings have flourished—and will continue to flourish—in every generation. In *The Waterworks,* as the wealthy victimize the masses, the consequences of capitalist depravity infest the entire island of Manhattan:

> As a people we practiced excess. Excess in everything—pleasure, gaudy display, endless toil, and death. Vagrant children slept in the alleys. Ragpicking was a profession. A conspicuously self-satisfied class of new wealth and weak intellect was all aglitter in a setting of mass misery. Out on the edges of town, along the North River or in Washington Heights or on the East River islands, behind stone walls and high hedges, were our institutions of charity, our orphanages, insane asylums, schools for the deaf and dumb, and mission homes for magdalens. They made a sort of Ringstrasse for our venerable civilization.

The Civil War and the Gilded Age that followed it made many New Yorkers rich men, and as in *Ragtime, Loon Lake,* and *Billy Bathgate,* Doctorow describes how one must barter one's soul to accumulate wealth and then hold onto it. He is at his most vatic and incisive when he catalogs the toll that the wealthy take on the masses. A perversely Whitmanesque profusion of details surrounds the youngest victims who litter the postwar urban landscape of New York City:

> All of them had lost their family names, these vagrant Flower Marys, the Jacks and Billys and Rosies. They sold paper or day-old flowers, they went around town with the organ-grinders to play the monkey's part, or indentured themselves to the peddlers of oysters or sweet potatoes. They begged—swarming on any warm night in the streets and alleys of the bawdy districts. They knew the curtain times of the theatres and when the opera let out. . . . They did the menial work of shops and at day's end made their beds on the shop floors. They ran the errands of the underworld, and carried slops, and toted empty beer pails to the saloons, and hauled them back full to the rooms of their keepers, who might pay them with a coin or a kick as whim dictated. More than one brothel specialized in them. They often turned up in hospital wards and church hospices so stunned by the abuses to which they'd

been subjected that they couldn't speak sensibly but could only cower in their rags and gaze upon the kindest nurses or ministrants of charity with abject fear.

The Waterworks is as richly convincing as all of Doctorow's historical novels. The surefooted accuracy of Doctorow's sense of the culture and language of the period combines with a sense of compelling immediacy to produce the feeling that it really is the 1870s as we read this novel. But in a few places the novel's narrator, a newspaper editor named McIlvaine, announces that he is writing not for his own time but for some much later and supposedly more advanced American generation—of course, for ourselves in the 1990s. For example, he says, "You may think you are living in modern time, here and now, but that is the illusion of every age. We did not conduct ourselves as if we were preparatory to your time." In his essay "The Nineteenth New York," which appears in *Jack London,* Doctorow writes about how much of the city of the past persists today:

> The astonishing thing in this city celebrated for tearing itself down and beginning again every generation or so is how much of the nineteenth [century] is still visible. . . . On nights of fog you see it best. Look south, over lower Manhattan: A heavy fog works its way down through the architectural strata. First the World Trade Center disappears, then the fifty- and sixty-story office buildings of glass, then the early-twentieth-century stone Woolworth building . . . story by story the skyline blacks out, modernity deconstructs, and all that is left is the nineteenth-century city. . . . You can walk down Greene Street, in the fine mist, past the iron fronts, and know that this is the city that Melville saw.
>
> The nineteenth is quietly with us in all sorts of fogs and dreams. Perhaps it is, after all, a ghost city that stands to contemporary New York as some panoramic negative print. . . . It is a companion city of the other side, some moral hologram generated from an unknown but intense radiation of historical energy and randomly come to imprint on our dreaming brains.

The past will speak to the present, Doctorow believes, if the present will only listen and hunt out the hidden facts, as his characters do in *The Waterworks*. The moral of Doctorow's seedy world of capitalist amorality, civic corruption, overweening cravings to transcend mortality, and intellectual/scientific depravity is addressed to our own time. In fact, McIlvaine is writing *only* for us: he never can manage to get the story he investigates into the newspapers. It would be an amazing scoop if he could ever compose it in journalistic terms, he knows, but he cannot get it adequately documented, cannot get his publisher to support his exposé, cannot tell the story in a way that would make sense to his readership—so it has to be written for the distant future.

The story is a thriller, a mystery. A brilliant and deranged medical researcher, Dr. Sartorius, convinces some of the city's richest men to disinherit their families and stage their own deaths. They bequeath their fortunes to him in exchange for eternal life; Sartorius keeps the old men alive by scavenging the body fluids and organs of young children. Policemen, politicians, and businessmen all profit from their collusion in the conspiracy. One of the rich men is Augustus Pemberton. The disappearance of his son, Martin, who is a freelance writer for McIlvaine, puts McIlvaine and a policeman, Captaine Donne, on the trail; together they uncover the hidden scheme. Doctorow's other wealthy villains—J. P. Morgan in *Ragtime,* F. W. Bennett in *Loon Lake,* and Dutch Schultz in *Billy Bathgate*—are all avatars of Augustus Pemberton. He is a force of danger and evil: a slave trader, a war profiteer, a ruthless business mogul. Doctorow is fascinated and sickened by the way Pemberton selfishly and wantonly spends his riches when so many people are in need. Yet Augustus is a flat and banal character, despite the fact that he holds so much power. Doctorow subverts his character in the narrative: Pemberton is finally only a type—of the sour, petulant, loveless, hypocrite. Doctorow does not invest him

with the emotional qualities, the humanity, that he bestows on McIlvaine, Martin, or Captain Donne, whose role it is to discover and expose how Augustus Pemberton is a danger to society. In the obituary for Pemberton that gets printed in McIlvaine's newspaper it says that Pemberton's peers respected "the example of his life as a fulfillment of the American ideal." The task Doctorow poses for his readers in *The Waterworks* is to elucidate exactly what this American ideal really is and how we position ourselves with respect to it—or how we might reposition ourselves, once we have been enlightened by reading the novel.

The children whose bodies are plundered to sustain the old men are hidden in an orphanage; they are concealed there after being kidnapped or bought or in some other way snatched from the crowds of suffering, poor New Yorkers. Doctorow thus dramatizes a type of social victimization that is a moral focus in all his novels: the way that the rich prey on the poor ("Dr. Sartorius extracted the blood . . . the bone marrow . . . the glandular matter . . . of children . . . to continue the lives of these elderly, fatally ill men . . ."). When McIlvaine accompanies a police raid on the orphanage and first realizes the scope of the crime, he is so outraged by what his city and his society have become that he fantasizes that the city might be ripped off the face of the earth, given back to nature: "Ever since that day I have dreamt sometimes . . . I, a street rat in my soul, dream even now . . . that if it were possible to lift this littered, paved Manhattan from the earth . . . and all its torn and dripping pipes and conduits and tunnels and tracks and cables—all of it, like a scab from new skin underneath—how seedlings would spout, and freshets bubble up, and brush and grasses would grow over the rolling hills . . . entanglements of vines, and fields of wild blueberry and blackberry." Doctorow warns that only a near-annihilation (like the biblical flood) can redeem American society.

* * *

While Doctorow's literary fame derives from the novels discussed above, he has filled out his career with a range of other enterprises, including forays into other kinds of writing. He has become a prominent voice on public and moral issues, addressing a broad intellectual audience. He has served as director of the Authors Guild and PEN, organizations that he has used to publicize issues that affect writers all over the world. Doctorow, for example, protested PEN's inviting then-Secretary of State George Shultz to address its 1985 congress because he felt that Shultz had failed to protect intellectual communities in such countries as Nicaragua, Chile, Turkey, and South Africa. On another occasion, Doctorow assembled a group of writers to denounce the Iranian government's death threats against Salman Rushdie. Doctorow has been an energetic advocate for reading (a dwindling activity); in 1994, he began plans to launch a cable television channel, Booknet, devoted to programs promoting literature and literacy.

His science fiction novel, *Big as Life,* is a decidedly minor work. "Unquestionably, it's the worst I've done," Doctorow said in his interview with Larry McCaffery. The novel depicts the appearance of two colossal giants from a time-space continuum parallel to our own world in New York harbor who become helpless in our world. While New Yorkers puzzle over the giants, the government seizes upon the occasion to impose an authoritarian military regime. Doctorow also wrote the text for *American Anthem* (1982), a collection of photographs by J. C. Suares.

Lives of the Poets (1984) presents some examples of Doctorow's prose in shorter doses, six short stories and a novella. These works offer essentially open-ended studies of mood and atmosphere. They seem like finger-exercises; one of them, "The Water Works," is in fact a brief sketch that appears almost verbatim in the novel of that title published a decade later. The story is interesting insofar as it gives us an insight into what may be the germ of *The Waterworks,* but—

like many of the pieces in *Lives of the Poets*—it is not fully satisfying on its own terms: this story, like the others in the collection, lacks the intricate breadth of vision that Doctorow's longer fiction features. (Just as Doctorow adapted and developed "The Water Works" in the novel, he integrated two uncollected stories, "Ragtime" and "The Pyramid Club," into *Ragtime.*)

The story "Lives of the Poets" is about artists and writers—people who seem to be very much like Doctorow and his circle, on a dark binge. The lives of the narrator and his fellow artists, as portrayed in a rambling narrative, are messy, somewhat degraded, banal; that is, not at all what one would idealize as poetic. "Between the artist and simple dereliction," the narrator says, "there is a very thin line, I know that." Doctorow punctures whatever delusions readers may have about the poet as a desirable model of human behavior. The voice in this story is vintage Doctorow: freewheeling, loose, unpretentious, engaging, unapologetically self-indulgent. It surveys a range of gripes about modern life and modern art, along with such other haphazard offerings as the lifestyles and atmosphere of New York City, affairs, muggings, how men feel about their penis size, and so forth.

Doctorow has made a single attempt at playwriting, *Drinks before Dinner,* which was directed by Mike Nichols and produced by Joseph Papp at the Public Theater in New York City. (Doctorow's interest in the theater dates to his college days, when he acted in a number of student plays and wrote one. In college, his literary ambition was to be a playwright; he later studied acting and directing at Columbia.) *Drinks before Dinner* is in some way a companion piece to *Lives of the Poets:* it features the same harshly self-incriminating high-society cynicism. The central character's name is Edgar, signaling, as in *World's Fair,* that there is a strong autobiographical element in the play. As in *Lives of the Poets,* Doctorow seems obsessed with the tawdry condition of the elegant New York life that surrounds the contemporary cutting-edge intellect, the would-be prophet plodding through the detritus of contemporary civilization. Where the novella is loose and sloppy, though, the play is crisply taut, with a surreal, stylized diction that Doctorow defends in a lengthy introduction. The style of *Drinks before Dinner,* he says, constitutes his contribution to a theater of ideas. It is written in "a language frankly rhetorical and sometimes incantatory" by "a playwright who prefers a hundred words to one gesture"; it is "a text that neglects the ordinary benefits of characterization and the interaction of ordinarily characterized persons." Doctorow rejected theatrical conventions and wrote the play in an experimental style because, he explains, the typical American "theatrical mode has been so exhausted by television and film." He adds, "I'm astounded it is still thought by playwrights to be useful and interesting."

Drinks before Dinner comes across as a collection of engaging set pieces, or meditations, free-floating non sequiturs, on, for example, the sociological implications of American car culture. The play is philosophical about our times, in a contemporary tenor of familiar dinner party dialogue that vacillates between profundity and quotidian banality. The play anatomizes the dissipation of the so-called crème de la crème. If I may risk doing some psychoanalysis, it seems like a writer's midlife crisis projected, in the form of drama, onto an entire community. In the play, Edgar, an upper-class professional man, invited with his wife to his friends' apartment for dinner, shows up with a gun. He is inconsolable despite the supposedly marvelous fruits of modern culture. Edgar, we learn, had bought the gun a few days earlier, for reasons unclear even to himself, and had been carrying it ever since. At his friends' home, he holds a room of people— people who are pretty much like himself— hostage. During the evening, he tries, with limited success (though cleverly and wryly) to express and ameliorate his dissatisfaction with the state of modern culture and the possibly impending end of the world. He ends the cocktail hour during which the play is set by preparing to sit down with his friends for dinner. He has left the world pretty much the way it was before cocktails but exposed as tawdry, cowardly, hypocritical, impotent.

Doctorow has written a number of essays for such periodicals as *Harper's,* the *New York Times Book Review,* the *Nation,* and *Playboy.* Fourteen of these essays are collected in *Jack London;* in these essays Doctorow makes the same broad-sweeping appraisals of American moral, cultural, political, and intellectual practices as he does in his novels. The essays show that his moralism is grounded in real-world concerns and awareness; they reveal a serious and intelligent political perspective based on a wholehearted liberal humanism. Doctorow sees himself and his literary colleagues, as Shelley has it, as "the unacknowledged legislators of the world." "Writers and politicians mirror each other," Doctorow said in the speech he made when accepting the 1990 PEN/Faulkner Award. "Both [writers and politicians] live in the knowledge that reality is amenable to any construction placed upon it. Writers legislate the spirit world, the secret meanings of places and things, as well as the human secrets. And politicians legislate our outer circumstances." But "politicians have no lifetime office as we have. They rise and fall and their works die and, as it turns out, the truth is more likely to inhere in literature."

Throughout his essays, Doctorow fights for the proper acknowledgment of the writer's political-ethical role. He himself offers a sharp perspective on political matters ranging from constitutional theory and philosophy to the Republicans. He conveys what he believes to be the artist's higher sense of social and moral insight than the short-sighted politician's. One of the essays in *Jack London,* "The Beliefs of Writers," is a major aesthetic statement which makes clear that Doctorow's literary concerns are large, global, moral;

here, with his usual compelling and committed incisiveness, he challenges the contemporary writer to improve the world. "False Documents," another influential essay, "ranges widely over such various questions as a text's credibility, the role of the artist in ancient and modern times, the place of fiction in Western and non-Western societies, and the use of techniques of fiction in the social sciences," writes Christopher Morris. "The essay distinguishes between the power of freedom and the power of the regime, between fiction writers in Western and non-Western countries, between fiction and nonfiction, but during the course of the essay, these distinctions break down, leaving Doctorow with the residual proposition, 'there is only narrative.' "

Doctorow's critical studies of Hemingway, London, Dreiser, Orwell, and Thoreau demonstrate his facility in dealing insightfully with important literary forefathers; they also confirm the sense one gets from his novels that his perspective is basically limited to the imaginative and cultural world of men and that he is not aware of how the literary canon has expanded. The images of women in his novels—molls, prostitutes, frigid women, cloying mothers, insane drifters, seductresses, and other loose sex objects—reveal a seeming inability to bestow upon women characters the kind of fascinating complexity, anguish, emotional energy, or passion with which Doctorow typically endows his male characters. "It is not hard to find female characters in Doctorow's fiction who seem, at least on the level of theme, to be symbolic of the wisdom, the insight, the valuable mystery that the male characters should approach," writes Marshall Bruce Gentry in his 1993 piece on Doctorow and Philip Roth, "Ventriloquists' Conversations." But these women, he continues, are ultimately diminished: "Perhaps Doctorow's notion that character is a function of community is the source of a narrowness in his works. At the end of several of them, if not earlier, we discover that all the voices we have heard are

from a single source—a male narrator. . . . As the contributions of female perspectives are reduced to the conclusive goal of creating a man, we are left feeling that Doctorow's women are typically silenced, controlled, nearly dead."

Several of Doctorow's novels have been filmed—none perfectly, but often engagingly. They feature a range of stars, such as James Cagney, Mandy Patinkin, Howard E. Rollins Jr., Mary Steenburgen, and Norman Mailer in Milos Forman's 1981 version of *Ragtime;* Patinkin and Amanda Plummer in Sidney Lumet's 1983 *Daniel,* for which Doctorow wrote the screenplay; Dustin Hoffman and Bruce Willis in Robert Benton's 1991 *Billy Bathgate.* These films have garnered at least some serious attention by aficionados of both film and fiction; still, all were criticized, to some extent, for being unable to portray comprehensibly the narrative fluctuations and multilevelled plotting of the novels. Doctorow himself called Burt Kennedy's 1967 film of *Welcome to Hard Times,* starring Henry Fonda, the second-worst movie ever made.

In the scene in *World's Fair* in which young Edgar beholds the chalk swastika, Doctorow anticipates the horror of the Holocaust that lay just beyond the novel's present time, as well as a strain of incipient evil in American culture that would spring from such intimations of malevolence. Edgar suffers a few other indications of the danger that the future holds, as when a group of older boys mug him and taunt him with anti-Semitic slurs. The muggers recognize Edgar as a Jew, though he denies being Jewish. This telling episode offers an opportunity to consider the role played by Jewish-American culture in Doctorow's works. *World's Fair* is Doctorow's most Jewish novel in atmosphere, suggesting that, while his Bronx youth was obviously heavily influenced by his ethnicity, he shed some of this influence as he grew up; perhaps the character Edgar's denial that he is Jewish foreshadows the way Doctorow will distance himself from Jewish culture.

Whether Judaism is emphasized, as in *World's Fair,* or more understated, as in many of the other novels, it connotes a strange and somewhat archaic force. The fictional Edgar does not warmly embrace his Jewish heritage. It strongly affects the lives and rhythms of his world (as it does Daniel Isaacson's and Billy Bathgate's), but it also seems to embarrass Edgar and hinder his access to the "ideal" American life epitomized by the fair's World of Tomorrow—a culture that is devoid of ethnicity or difference. Recalling his immigrant grandmother Edgar thinks, "She spoke mostly in the other language, the one I didn't understand. . . . Grandma's room I regarded as a dark den of primitive rites and practices." Watching her lighting the Sabbath candles, he observes, "The sight of my own grandma performing what was, after all, only a ritual blessing seemed to me something else— her enacted submission to the errant and malign forces of life." At another point Edgar remembers "bearded men in black hats and black winter coats who came begging at the door with coin boxes and letters of credentials from yeshivas," and he describes them in terms that suggest derogatory stereotypes: "These itinerant peddlers, beggars and entrepreneurs were often unwholesome-looking or shabby and dirty and had dull blackened eyes from which all light had departed." In *Ragtime,* similarly, the character of Tateh, an immigrant who lives on the Lower East Side, is an unpalatable caricature who portrays the hypocritical self-righteousness and opportunism of extremist Jewish orthodoxy. Tateh sustains his heritage and values (scornfully insulating himself from what he sees as the depravities of the gentile world) for a time while he is impoverished. But eventually he sells out spectacularly, abandoning both his piety and his culture to pose as a European aristocrat, as soon as he finds the opportunity to

make a great deal of money churning out pap in Hollywood.

Anti-Semitism forces upon Edgar at least some awareness of the need to affirm his Jewish identity in order to survive, to be connected to a community that is his own, despite his misgivings. He resolves his identity conflict publicly (if not internally); as he writes in his World's Fair essay, "If [the typical American boy] is Jewish he should say so. If he is anything he should say what it is when challenged." Edgar thus at least partly atones for denying his Judaism to the muggers. Still, he bristles when he sees the winning entry printed in the newspaper; it is an essay that conveys the blandest American platitudes: " 'The typical American boy should possess the same qualities as those of the early American pioneers. He should be handy, dependable, courageous, and loyal to his beliefs.' " Though Edgar never explicitly says so, he seems to believe that he won only honorable mention as a penalty for being Jewish, that the top prize was reserved for an ethnically unmarked American boy.

When Doctorow presents the Isaacsons as scapegoats in *The Book of Daniel,* he associates their fate with the historical pattern that has afflicted Jews for millennia: being forced to carry the burden of blame for social problems in the dominant culture. The anti-Semitic aspects of the Isaacsons' case are not extensively detailed, but Doctorow describes Daniel's biblical namesake in terms that apply equally to the modern young man: During the empires that succeeded Alexander the Great, "It is a bad time for Daniel and his coreligionists, for they are second-class citizens, in a distinctly hostile environment." The prophet Daniel's task was to interpret the confusing dreams, visions, and apparitions of his society's leaders; Daniel Isaacson, too, is cast in the position of having to make sense of the mess that the American political establishment has wreaked. When the biblical prophet tries to placate a gentile regime, the strain is heavy: "Daniel survives three reigns but at considerable personal cost. Toward the end his insights become more diffuse, apocalyptic, hysterical." These words also apply to the latter-day Daniel, who stumbles through the mess of the 1960s, trying to comprehend what America has become. In only one other place Doctorow discusses the ramifications of the Isaacsons' religion: communicating by letter with his wife in prison, Paul writes, "My darling have you noticed how many of the characters in this capitalist drama are Jewish? The defendants, the defense lawyer, the prosecution, the major prosecution witness, the judge. We are putting on this little passion play for our Christian masters. In the concentration camps the Nazis made guards of certain Jews."

In *Billy Bathgate,* the mobster Dutch Schultz and his closest henchmen are Jewish, demonstrating once again Doctorow's willingness to present the very worst villains in society as Jews. Born Arthur Flegenheimer, Dutch converts to Catholicism both to strengthen his alliance with the Mafia and out of envy for the religious order and faith that he perceives Catholics experience. He likes the fact that Catholics pray in unison— " 'I never liked the old men davening in the synagogue, rocking swaying back and forth, everyone mumbling to himself at his own speed, the head going up and down the shoulders rocking, I like a little dignity.' " He sees no contradiction in belonging to more than one religion; referring to a local church he says, "I get a good feeling every time I walk in [a local church], I don't understand Latin, but I don't understand Hebrew neither, so why not both, is there a law against both? Christ was both, for christsake, what's the big deal?" The real irony is not Dutch's choice of Catholicism over Judaism but the fact that he displays any sense of spirituality at all. In fact, Dutch's observations on Judaism are arguably the most forthright theological contemplations that appear anywhere in Doctorow's

work; certainly that indicates something about what Doctorow believes to be the significance of such considerations. Religion is for Dutch, and perhaps for Doctorow as well, a relatively empty signifer.

Several of Doctorow's novels contain no significant references to Jewish Americans. Still, in his essay "Radical Jewish Humanism: The Vision of E. L. Doctorow," John Clayton argues that Jewish cultural and aesthetic sensibility pervade Doctorow's entire corpus. He cites various sensibilities that reflect Jewish themes, such as "an agonized but futile compassion," the experience of suffering for others, and "often seem[ing] to embrace suffering for its own sake"; the characters Blue, Daniel Isaacson, Warren Penfield, and Martin Pemberton illustrate Clayton's point. Jewish literature often expresses "a critical detachment from ordinary institutions and culturally held truths," Clayton writes. Consider, in this light, the fact that Doctorow debunks the frontier myth in *Welcome to Hard Times;* shows hostility to postwar American smugness and anti-Communist patriotism in *The Book of Daniel;* and treats American glory with subversive skepticism in *Ragtime* (and, indeed, in all his novels). Clayton also cites "an attitude of moral seriousness" in art as typical of the Jewish literary tradition; such seriousness also pervades all Doctorow's writing.

In the final analysis, perhaps, the impact of Doctorow's Judaism upon his aesthetic perspective is as polymorphous and nebulous as the effect of his Bronx upbringing, his American cultural background, his political beliefs, his literary and intellectual attitudes, his vatic public persona. All these certainly represent formative influences that figure heavily in Doctorow's writing; but all are subordinated to the iconoclastic and volatile voice that emanates vividly from each novel, a voice resplendent in its integrity and bound to the external world but finally flourishing in a self-sufficient realm of fiction.

Selected Bibliography

WORKS OF E. L. DOCTOROW

NOVELS

Welcome to Hard Times. New York: Simon & Schuster, 1960.
Big as Life. New York: Simon & Schuster, 1966.
The Book of Daniel. New York: Random House, 1971.
Ragtime. New York: Random House, 1975.
Loon Lake. New York: Random House, 1980.
World's Fair. New York: Random House, 1985.
Billy Bathgate. New York: Random House, 1989.
The Waterworks. New York: Random House, 1994.

PLAY

Drinks before Dinner. New York: Random House, 1978.

COLLECTED ESSAYS

Jack London, Hemingway, and the Constitution: Selected Essays, 1977–1992. New York: Random House, 1993.

COLLECTED STORIES

Lives of the Poets: A Novella and Six Stories. New York: Random House, 1994.

UNCOLLECTED SHORT STORIES

''The Pyramid Club.'' *American Review,* 21:256–70 (October 1974).
''Ragtime.'' *American Review,* 20:1–20 (April 1974).
''The Songs of Billy Bathgate.'' *New American Review,* 2:54–69 (1968).

MISCELLANEOUS

American Anthem. Photographs by J. C. Suares. Text by E. L. Doctorow. New York: Stewart, Tabori & Chang, 1982.

BIBLIOGRAPHY

Tokarczyk, Michelle M. *E. L. Doctorow: An Annotated Bibliography.* New York: Garland, 1988.

CRITICAL STUDIES

Arnold, Marilyn. ''History as Fate in E. L. Doctorow's Tale of a Western Town.'' In *E. L. Doctorow: Essays and Conversations,* 207–16. *See* Trenner.
Clayton, John. ''Radical Jewish Humanism: The Vision of E. L. Doctorow.'' In *E. L. Doctorow: Essays and Conversations,* 109–19. *See* Trenner.
Fowler, Douglas. *Understanding E. L. Doctorow.* Columbia, S.C.: University of South Carolina Press, 1992.
Friedl, Herwig, and Dieter Schulz, eds. *E. L. Doctorow: A Democracy of Perception.* Essen: Die Blau Eule, 1988.
Gentry, Marshall Bruce. ''Ventriloquists' Conversations: The Struggle for Gender Dialogue in E. L. Doctorow and Philip Roth.'' *Contemporary Literature,* 34:512–37 (Fall 1993).
Harpham, Geoffrey Galt. ''E. L. Doctorow and the Technology of Narrative.'' *PMLA,* 100:81–95 (January 1985).
Harter, Carol C., and James R. Thompson. *E. L. Doctorow.* Boston: Twayne, 1990.
Levine, Paul. ''The Conspiracy of History: E. L. Doctorow's *The Book of Daniel.*'' In *E. L. Doctorow: Essays and Conversations,* 182–95. *See* Trenner.
Lorsch, Susan E. ''Doctorow's *The Book of Daniel* as *Künstlerroman*: The Politics of Art.'' *Papers on Language and Literature,* 18:384–97 (Winter 1982).
Morris, Christopher D. *Models of Misrepresentation: On the Fiction of E. L. Doctorow.* Jackson, Miss.: University Press of Mississippi, 1991.
Nadel, Alan. ''Hero and Other in Doctorow's *Loon Lake.*'' *College Literature,* 14:136–45 (Spring 1987).
Shelton, Frank W. ''E. L. Doctorow's *Welcome to Hard Times*: The Western and the American Dream.'' *Midwest Quarterly,* 25:7–17 (Autumn 1983).
Trenner, Richard, ed. *E. L. Doctorow: Essays and Conversations.* Princeton, N.J.: Ontario Review Press, 1983.

INTERVIEWS

Mansfield, Stephanie. ''The Liberation of E. L. Doctorow.'' *Washington Post,* February 28, 1989.

McCaffery, Larry. ''A Spirit of Transgression.'' In *E. L. Doctorow: Essays and Conversations,* 31–47. Edited by Richard Trenner.

Mitgang, Herbert. ''Doctorow's People: Old Souls, New Bodies.'' *New York Times,* March 9, 1989.

Trueheart, Charles. ''E. L. Doctorow, PEN in Hand.'' *Washington Post,* May 14, 1990.

—*RANDY MALAMUD*

Rita Dove

1952—

*I*N AN ERA of splintered factions and increasingly local, specialized poetries, Rita Dove has had great success in inspiring something near to a critical consensus on her work. A poet whose name emerged only in the 1980s, Dove pleases both the technicians and the politicians among contemporary readers, and although her poetry is not avant-garde, its occasional surrealism and sound play might interest even the experimental margin of the present poetry scene. As a consequence of this broad appeal and of the quality and complexity of her work, Dove has been recognized as one of the foremost poets of her generation.

However, Rita Dove's style, as polished, straightforward, or experimental as it can be, is not her chief achievement. Instead, readers attend with interest to her intelligent treatment of two related subjects, identity and home. Dove's writing is preoccupied with homecoming: she approaches, defines, and scrutinizes ideas of home repeatedly, while equally concerned with the impossibility of arriving there. Dove has most often been described in terms of that impossibility; her writing often charts a sense of displacement. As an African American woman with Cherokee and Blackfoot ancestors, as a poet and professor in an often anti-intellectual culture, as a "serious traveler" and student of the unfamiliar, Dove's perspective is that of an outsider in more than one

sense. The speakers of her poems are rarely comfortable in their surroundings, and tend to regard scenes of home with a distant and dispassionate eye. The poem "In the Old Neighborhood," for example, which begins her *Selected Poems* (1993), travels backward to view her childhood home newly as a shifting and surreal location:

> Let me go back to the white rock
> on the black lawn, the number
> stenciled in negative light.
> Let me return to the shadow
> of a house moored in the moonlight,
> gables pitched bright above
> the extinguished grass,
>
> and stalk the hushed perimeter,
> roses closed around their scent,
> azaleas dissembling behind the garage
> and the bugeyed pansies
> leaning over, inquisitive,
> in their picketed beds.

Even ordinary backyard flowers become estranged voyeurs as the suburban homestead, a site so associated in the United States with stability and comfortable familiarity, is seen skeptically, from the outside, at night. The fact that this image suggests a photographic negative perhaps emphasizes race as an alienating factor: Dove is black, whereas the stereotypical inhabitant of that American photograph is not.

On the other hand, many of Dove's works of poetry, fiction, and drama manifest her persistent interest in exploring what home might mean. She often dips into her personal history to write about her hometown of Akron (as in her novel *Through the Ivory Gate* [1992]), the middle-class suburbs and mores she knows so well, her own family (most famously in *Thomas and Beulah*, which won the Pulitzer Prize in 1987), and the ordinary details of girlhood, motherhood, and life as a teacher and writer. Her work records both her ''serious travel''—which she defines for Mohamed Taleb-Khyar (1991) as ''trying to understand a place and not just passing through, taking pictures''—and her many homecomings.

Dove's formal choices reflect a similar tension between a striving for accessibility and a deep attraction to what she feels is the essential foreignness of poetry. Appointed poet laureate of the United States in 1993 and again in 1994, Dove declared that her mission was to demystify poetry for the American public, to make it less intimidating to skeptical potential readers. Her own poetry, especially *Thomas and Beulah*, can be characterized as aspiring toward what Marianne Moore in ''England'' dryly calls ''plain American which cats and dogs can read''; her syntax is unambiguous, and her characters are recognizable and sympathetically drawn. She certainly owes at least part of her popularity to this accessibility.

Within a perfectly user-friendly poem, however, Dove is very capable of exercising contradictory impulses. Her comments about her own writing process illumine her opposite drive toward indeterminacy. As she writes poetry, she says, ''I try not to know what I'm doing,'' often composing in the eeriness of the very early morning; to interviewers like Judith Kitchen and Stan Sanvel Rubin she can cite intuition as her ordering principle, and her desire to remain unpredictable to her readers. Even the most ordinary realities of her poems can swerve into magic, as ''seal men'' appear in a bathroom in ''Adolescence II''; Dove has a knack for identifying the bizarre embedded in the familiar. She accuses herself further of a cryptic economy of language; some of her stranger images do refuse to unravel and be perfectly coherent.

Dove apparently feels that this tautness can be a weakness of her poetry. She told William Walsh (1994): ''I also fear making the poem snap shut so tightly that the click of the final line drowns out the poem's subtleties.'' In fact, Dove frequently avoids closure in her poetry and fiction, preferring to end even an entire novel on a moment of lyrical, rather than narrative, intensity. She ends the violent and tragic poem ''The Event,'' upon whose meaning the entire story of *Thomas and Beulah* hinges, on a peaceful, highly inconclusive detail: the river water ''gently shirr[s],'' smoothing over the terrible scene of Lem's death. While her writing itself, then, is usually perfect in its clarity, Dove prefers to leave the ultimate meanings of her works open, for her readers as well as herself, as if too much conclusion could break the trance of reading.

Dove's refusal to succumb to the familiar is deeply interwoven with her insistence on individual vision and identity. As she established herself as a poet in the late 1970s and early 1980s, she drew clear lines between her own project and the kind of writing that she felt was expected of her; with each book she tries to branch off in an untried direction, working in a new line length or from a different psychological perspective. Similarly, Dove rejects what she feels is a too-rigid separation between genres in American letters, preferring to identify herself as a writer rather than simply as a poet, although it is in that genre that she is known best. To date she has tried her hand at short fiction, the novel, and drama as well as at lyric poems and poem sequences. Dove is an experimenter who yet manages to place and keep herself squarely within the American literary mainstream.

*   *   *

Rita Frances Dove was born in Akron, Ohio, on August 28, 1952. Her mother was Elvira Elizabeth Hord. Her father, Ray Dove, worked as an elevator operator at the Goodyear Tire and Rubber Company until he was finally hired as that company's first black chemist. The one child in a family of ten children sent to college, Dove's father had returned from Italy after World War II and received a master's degree in chemistry, graduating at the top of his class. Dove was therefore raised in, as she calls it in her interview with Taleb-Khyar, "a fairly traditional upwardly mobile Black family—upwardly mobile in the second generation." Her parents expected her to achieve a high level of professional success, and strove to put her in the position to do so.

Dove describes her childhood self as shy and bookish; her introduction to the *Selected Poems* recounts her voracious reading of everything from Langston Hughes to Shakespeare to science fiction—her earliest surviving manuscript is "a novel called *Chaos*, which was about robots taking over the earth," written from third or fourth grade spelling lists. Mostly, however, the young Dove discarded her stories and plays, unaware that she could choose writing as a serious passion, much less as a potential occupation. This changed when an eleventh-grade English teacher, Margaret Oechsner, took Dove to meet John Ciardi at a book-signing; suddenly the teenager made the connection between her own productions and "literature," and began to write out of that new awareness.

Equally important in Dove's life at this time was music. Her parents made a wide range of music available to their four children (Dove was the second), and Dove did not abandon this interest as she pursued her education; she still plays the cello as well as the bass viol and the rarer viola da gamba. At Miami University, Dove studied German language and literature but concentrated on English, telling her family that she was

majoring in pre-law while she became increasingly committed to the work she was doing in creative writing workshops. Finally Dove decided, she told Walsh, that

> I would try to become a writer while I was still young and could afford to be poor. I went home for Thanksgiving and told my parents that I was going to be a poet. To their credit, they didn't flinch. My father simply said, "Well, I don't understand poetry, so don't be upset if I don't read it."

In Dove's novel, *Through the Ivory Gate*, which centers on a young woman artist returning to Akron after college, the protagonist's parents are somewhat closer to appalled that their daughter rejects the stable, respectable professions toward which her entire upbringing was to have steered her.

Elected to Phi Beta Kappa and graduating summa cum laude, Dove received her B.A. from Miami University (Ohio) in 1973. Dove would go on to earn an M.F.A. in 1977 from the University of Iowa, where she was a teaching/writing fellow in the Writers' Workshop, but before that she spent an important year as a Fulbright scholar studying modern European literature at the University of Tübingen in Germany. Dove explained to Taleb-Khyar how powerfully she was influenced by her immersion there in the German language:

> In German the verbs often come at the end of a sentence, so in an argument you can sustain your energy until the very end and then throw in the verb that will suddenly make the sentence coalesce. At one point, that might have had an effect on my writing—I began to try to do that in English.

As exciting as her encounters with that language and culture often were, however, in many ways Dove found that first stay in Germany disturbing. In particular, as a black woman in a small German town, Dove was often startled and offended to be the object of blatant stares, pointed fingers, and rude questions. In fact, Dove claimed to Taleb-Khyar that she has never become accustomed to this behavior: ''Once I told a group of children that I was actually a witch and their eyes would dry up like corn flakes when they went to sleep that night; that was a terrible thing to do, but I was so fed up with being on constant display.'' Further, her experiences in Germany made the United States seem like a foreign country, an unreal place impossibly isolated from the rest of the world. This study abroad was one of the many times Dove deliberately embarked on an unexpected path or attempted ''serious travel'': choosing a challenging and marginalizing career, sojourning in an environment that could be hostile but was at the least profoundly foreign, she seems to have thrived on jarring experiences of difference.

The first major document of these experiences —subsequent to two chapbooks, *Ten Poems* (1977) and *The Only Dark Spot in the Sky* (1980) —is the collection of poetry *The Yellow House on the Corner* (1980). Her first full-length collection is based on her master's thesis at Iowa, and carefully positions the young poet in a critical relationship to recent movements in African American poetry. Dove self-consciously writes in the wake of the black arts movement, a flowering of black poetry in the late 1960s and early 1970s associated with black nationalism and promoted by poets such as Amiri Baraka (LeRoi Jones) and Haki Madhubuti (Don L. Lee). She discusses this movement at some length in a history of African American poetry written with Marilyn Nelson Waniek, referring to writing associated with the new black aesthetic as ''the poetics of rage.'' In this piece, ''A Black Rainbow: Modern Afro-American Poetry,'' Dove and Waniek reserve strongest praise for those contemporary poets who emphasize a ''central humanity'' over racial difference; they comment about Gwendolyn Brooks, for example, that ''her career took a sud-

den turn in the Sixties and fell under the detrimental influence of younger, more militant poets,'' and assert about the adherents of the black arts movement that ''this new Black poet, however, turns out to be as manipulated as his accommodating predecessor, fashioned in the forge of the times but a pawn of the reigning literary politics. . . . It was time now to move forward, to explore deeper.''

In her first volume, Dove most clearly distinguishes herself from the African American poetry of the immediate past in ''Upon Meeting Don L. Lee, in a Dream.'' In this encounter, her powerful predecessor is depicted as impotent and weeping, his hair falling out in clumps, his fists helplessly clenched. Dove verbally ''cut[s] him off'' to insist on his present irrelevancy: ''Those years are gone— / What is there now?'' Arnold Rampersad notes Dove's ''eagerness, perhaps even an anxiety, to transcend—if not actually to repudiate—black cultural nationalism in the name of a more inclusive sensibility. . . . Dove must be acutely aware of herself as a poetic reformer.'' Her poetic meeting with Lee depicts this violent repudiation; the black women singers in this dream, whether they are muses or a new generation of poets, leave the fallen precursor behind.

Rampersad goes on to note that the dream context has something of a neutralizing effect on the encounter. After all, no one is responsible for the content of her dreams; the delight that this poem takes in stripping Lee of his potency and its highly sexual violence are mitigated by the poem's apparent fidelity to images generated by the subconscious. The dream context is a recurring one not always made explicit in *The Yellow House on the Corner*. Many poems throughout the book are infused with the surreality of dreams; Dove's poetics of intuition derives some of its power from them, as well as from an angle of vision that combines the freshness of a child's perception with the influence of magic realism. ''Five Elephants'' and ''Adolescence II,'' for example, depict impossible or nonsensical scenes with eerie clarity; these poems are emotionally highly charged while maintaining an intense reserve about their ultimate referents.

This reserve also marks Dove's distance from the confessional zeal that dominates the work of so many of her contemporaries. Her poems are often monologues by characters distinct from herself, as in "Belinda's Petition" and "Someone's Blood," from the book's third section (its least successful), about slavery; when she speaks more personally, her voice can be defamiliarized by these forays into the subconscious as well as by her traveler's distance from domestic or ordinary settings. Her stay in Germany, for instance, and her interest in that culture result in poems like "The Bird Frau" and "The Son." Dove closes the book with "Ö," a poem in which "One word of Swedish has changed the whole neighborhood." In this poem, the yellow house on the corner, permanently dislodged from stable centrality by its encounter with an alien language and the new knowledge associated with that language, "[takes] off over the marshland."

Finally, Dove's first volume introduces her completely unreserved and abiding interest in writing frankly about sexuality. If clearing ground for the next generation of African American poets is part of her poetic project, so is articulating black female sexuality, long mystified and exoticized by literature, from a subject position. The three "Adolescence" poems as well as "A Suite for Augustus" depict the transition from girlhood to a fully sexualized womanhood with none of the anguish of other explorers of this territory, such as Anne Sexton: the speaker in "Suite" tells us how "Then tapwater rinsed orange through my underwear" matter-of-factly, menstruation thus becoming a marker of personal history as plainly recounted as John F. Kennedy's assassination. In *The Yellow House on the Corner*, sexuality is less a site of conflict or confusion than one of fascination, strangeness, and

even magic. Dove is keenly critical, nonetheless, of fairy-tale romance and its distortions of female sexuality. The speaker of "Beauty and the Beast" (Beauty herself) warns her "sisters" to eschew mercy and let their beastly suitors die before they marry blindly. Dove maintains this forthright attitude through her most recent poetry, in which she approaches motherhood with similar straightforwardness.

In an interview with Helen Vendler, Dove describes the differences between her first and second books in terms of the shift in titles. *The Yellow House on the Corner* is, as she puts it, a title "on the edge of domesticity," whereas *Museum* provides "the wide angle, the zoom back," in order to ask the question, "How do you retain culture and make it available to another generation; what gets chosen and what doesn't?" *Museum* is in some ways a more public book than its predecessor—its first section, for example, is archaeological in its approach, beginning with a fossil in "The Fish in the Stone"—but it continues to intermingle public with private history. One of its most powerful sequences, indeed, centers on Dove's own father.

Dove discusses this book in some detail, especially its closing poem, "Parsley," in a 1985 interview with Kitchen and Rubin. Her overall project centers, as does much of her other work, on the issue of memory:

> I suppose what I was trying to do in *Museum* was to deal with certain artifacts that we have in life, not the ordinary artifacts, the ones that you'd expect to find in a museum, but anything that becomes frozen by memory, or by circumstance or by history. . . . The other thing was to get the underside of the story, not to tell the big historical events, but in fact to talk about things which no one will remember but which are just as important in shaping our concept of ourselves and the world we live in.

Again, having begun this book while in Europe, Dove approaches these subjects from a clinical distance that often resembles Marianne Moore's zoological perspective; her range of reference is characteristically wide, from prehistory to the last section, "Primer for the Nuclear Age," from ancient China to her own backyard. This volume contains a page of notes at the end, to contextualize some of the more obscure historical references.

The telescope in the third section, "My Father's Telescope," signals both this distant, at times nearly scientific, viewpoint and the potential for that gap between the writer and the story she tells to collapse. The relationship Dove depicts in this sequence between herself and her father is richly complex: the father nurtures his daughter with miraculous food in "Grape Sherbet," terrifies and initiates her in "Centipede" and "Roses," becomes an inaccessible object of longing to her in "A Father out Walking on the Lawn." "Anti-Father" epitomizes this tension between confessional and cooler public voices; stargazing, it claims that the stars

> draw
>
> closer together
> with years.
>
> And houses
> shrivel, un-lost,
>
> and porches sag;
> neighbors phone
>
> to report cracks
> in the cellar floor,
>
> roots of the willow
> coming up. Stars
>
> speak to a child.
> The past
>
> is silent. . . .
> Just between
>
> me and you,
> woman to man,
>
> outer space is
> inconceivably
>
> intimate.

"Anti-Father" finds intimacy in the most paradoxical places: between isolated neighbors joined by phone wires, and among impossibly distant stars. This poem is also a good example of Dove's interest, in this volume, in working with a shorter line, in creating what she has called a "slim silhouette"; in this case the abbreviated lines that evoke William Carlos Williams and the use of white space mimic the patterns of stars in a mostly empty night sky.

Museum also develops Dove's compulsion, in her poems, to tell stories lyrically. Both "Parsley" and "Agosta the Winged Man and Rasha the Black Dove" experiment with narrative. "Parsley" is a poem Dove often includes in readings; it revolves around a massacre she recounts in the "Notes": "On October 2, 1957, Rafael Trujillo (1891–1961), dictator of the Dominican Republic, ordered 20,000 blacks killed because they could not pronounce the letter 'r' in *perejil,* the Spanish word for parsley." The first section, a villanelle, is from the perspective of the Haitians, circling around the images of cane fields and the general's parrot. The second section, loosely based on the obsessive sestina, tells the story from Trujillo's perspective, interweaving his decision-making process with his memories of his mother. "Parsley" is a culmination, then, of the different kinds of history that concern Dove; it also closes with a meditation on the historical and personal power of language, even of a single sound (here the rolled "r"), repeating the way *The Yellow House on the Corner* closes with that reverberating, transformative "ö."

Of "Agosta the Winged Man and Rasha the Black Dove," Dove remarks to Walsh:

> For the first time I was able to approach narrative in a way that did not merely tell a story from beginning to end as in most of the slave narratives in my first book. . . . The bare bones of Agosta and Rasha's stories come at you in a starburst fashion; little bits of information pop up here and there.

The poem refers to a portrait of two sideshow entertainers painted by Christian Schad in Berlin in 1929; the painting is the cover of *Museum*. The poem looks over Schad's shoulder, following his thoughts as he waits for his subjects to arrive, and considers how he might pose them. Agosta's rib cage is deformed into "crests and fins," whereas Rasha's "only freakishness (in the Berlin of 1929) was that she was black," as Vendler points out in "Rita Dove: Identity Markers." They gaze back at the painter, as Dove says, "merciless," determined to be subjects and not objects of a titillated stare. Dove always encodes her last name somewhere into each volume of poetry, and here, the similarity between her own name and "Rasha the Black Dove" emphasizes her identification with that character, whose portrait even bears a passing resemblance to Dove, gazing calmly at us from the cover.

Museum opens with "Dusting," a poem which later was incorporated into Dove's third and most famous book of poetry, *Thomas and Beulah*. The latter, which won Dove the Pulitzer Prize in 1987, is based (although not explicitly) on the lives of Dove's maternal grandparents; it is dedicated to the poet's mother and takes place in their hometown. Dove takes no overt role in the telling of these stories, although she may be present in the third person as one of the granddaughters on Thomas' lap in "Roast Possum." Nonetheless, her third volume functions to counter or at least modify the dispassion of her previous work in its accessible, sympathetic, highly novelistic focus on two parallel lives; Dove herself claims (to Taleb-Khyar) to be somewhat "suspicious" of the book's popularity because, as she puts it, "It may be the easiest of my books to understand, especially for someone who isn't a regular reader of contemporary poetry."

Thomas and Beulah divides neatly into halves, chronicling the life of each figure in the order given by the title. As John Shoptaw notes, "the lives of Thomas and Beulah rarely intersect: There are few common events in their stories and no Faulknerian climax in which their worlds collide." Only the chronology at the end of the work finally integrates the two existences; Thomas and Beulah occasionally include each other in their reflections, but even the major events they share, including the Great Depression and the births of their four daughters, mean different things to each. This is a tragedy in the sense that Thomas and Beulah, each netted in his or her own losses, never find any solace in union.

Thomas' section, "Mandolin," begins with an experience of grief that profoundly alters the rest of his life. In "The Event," Thomas and his friend Lem, from whom he has been inseparable, set out from Tennessee on a riverboat. Their Mississippi idyll, as apparently poor but untroubled as raft life in *The Adventures of Huckleberry Finn*, is destroyed early by a dare: Lem dives off the rail toward an illusory island and disappears forever under the wheel.

> Lem stripped, spoke easy: *Them's chestnuts,*
> *I believe.* Dove
>
> quick as a gasp. Thomas, dry
> on deck, saw the green crown shake
> as the island slipped
>
> under, dissolved
> in the thickening stream.
> At his feet
>
> the stinking circle of rags,
> the half-shell mandolin.
> Where the wheel turned the water
>
> gently shirred.

This is, importantly, the poem in this volume in which Dove leaves her signature: her name becomes the moment, hanging at the cliff edge of the sixth stanza, when hope shifts to hopelessness, the very "event" that informs this first sequence. Crucially, the dive happens before Thomas meets Beulah; he is defined by an experience prior and exterior to their relationship.

Certainly Thomas continues to revisit that brief moment of union, and to seek forgiveness for his part in destroying it. Piercing his ears in "Variation on Pain" becomes an act of violent penance; he searches for understanding from a grandson in "Roast Possum" and aches with sympathy for his son-in-law in "Variation on Gaining a Son." In "Courtship" Thomas finds himself, as if by accident, wooing Beulah in her family's shiplike parlor; that image and the title echo Thomas' prelapsarian existence on the riverboat, but Thomas never finds a second love with Beulah. He dies alone in the final poem of the section, "Thomas at the Wheel," in which he "drowns" toward Lem at the wheel of his car, unable to reach his medicine in the glove compartment.

The image of the mandolin in the first section is a touchstone, paralleled by the canary in Beulah's story, "Canary in Bloom." The mandolin becomes the symbol of Thomas' secret life of mourning, a life Beulah seeks to bury as she coaxes its player into the choir, or rejects as she wishes for a pianola and a bottle of perfume rather than a mandolin and a bright yellow scarf in "Courtship, Diligence." Thomas, likewise, resents Beulah's canary, "usurper / of his wife's affections," as he resents the dominance in his life of women: he lists his four children by gender in "Compendium" as a monotony of failures, "Girl girl / girl girl." The canary, to Thomas, is an interloper whose small sweet songs cannot rival his remembered music.

To Beulah, the canary stands in place of romantic dreams of which she has had even less taste than Thomas. Beulah's fantasies consist of a Paris she never reaches, or the magical name "Maurice" she attributes to a half-remembered boy at the fair in her childhood in "Dusting." "Weathering Out" shows Beulah disappearing from herself in pregnancy, although the poem ends on a green note, clover persisting between cobblestones; the labors of children and housework do drown out Beulah and her hopes almost entirely, or narrow them down to a mere wish for a room to think in, until her visions literally fade away with glaucoma at the end of the sequence. Beulah, like Thomas, never seems to look for the satisfaction of her longing in her spouse, although her affection for him is enduring. Late in the section, during Thomas' "Recovery" from a stroke, she thinks, "He was lovely then, a pigeon / whose pulse could be seen when the moment / was perfectly still." Here we get a glimpse of what Beulah's loss has been: Thomas was no domestic bird and never really fit into his wife's fantasies, but her nostalgia offers an unrealized possibility, a belated recognition of Thomas' loveliness.

In her early work, Dove writes more powerfully of fathers than mothers; Thomas is ultimately a more compelling character than Beulah, just as the section "My Father's Telescope" goes unmatched by a parallel exploration of the poet's relationship with her mother in *Museum*. In *Grace Notes* (1989), this changes. Dove, with her husband, Fred Viebahn, a German writer she married March 23, 1979, has a daughter, Aviva; her fourth and fifth books of poetry concern themselves more overtly with Dove's own motherhood and daughterhood. In *Grace Notes*, she also allows experience to infiltrate her poetry from her career in academics, first at Arizona State University (whose faculty she joined in 1981 as the only black professor in the seventy-member English department) and at the University of Virginia (where she moved in 1989 and where she became Commonwealth Professor of English in 1993). *Grace Notes* is in these ways Dove's most personal volume of poetry, perhaps because within it, she told Walsh, she tries "to get back to the lyric—more and more relentlessly lyric poems," countering by the authority of her own intimate voice the occluded narrator of her family epic, *Thomas and Beulah*.

Dove explained to Helen Vendler, as she was working on her fourth collection, how *Thomas and Beulah* led her to write more immediately about her own maternity:

> I realized I was in fact feeding some of my own experiences as a young mother into Beulah and I was feeling incredibly uncomfortable about it until I realized that I was harboring an unspoken notion that poems about children and mothers are mushy and you just don't write those things.

Characteristically, sensing a self-imposed limit on her writing, Dove deliberately began work articulating this facet of herself in a collaborative project with a woman photographer at Arizona State University. The central section of *Grace Notes*, in fact, succeeds in depicting mother and child in a non-"mushy" or unsentimental way. Breast-feeding is the subject of "Pastoral"; "Genetic Expedition" observes the apparent racial difference between Dove and her blonde daughter, Dove comparing her own breasts to "the spiked fruits / dangling from natives in the *National Geographic* / my father forbade us to read," in a possible allusion to another poem about identity, gender, and race, Elizabeth Bishop's "In the Waiting Room." In "After Reading *Mickey in the Night Kitchen* for the Third Time before Bed," Dove is quintessentially the late-twentieth-century mother, giving her daughter the now-standard lesson about how to respond to inappropriate touching, and simultaneously receiving a lesson on what divides and unites mother and daughter:

> My daughter spreads her legs
> to find her vagina:
> hairless, this mistaken
> bit of nomenclature
> is what a stranger cannot touch
> without her yelling. She demands

> to see mine and momentarily
> we're a lopsided star
> among the spilled toys,
> my prodigious scallops
> exposed to her neat cameo.

> And yet the same glazed
> tunnel, layered sequences.
> She is three; that makes this
> innocent. *We're pink!*
> she shrieks, and bounds off.

In preparation for violence, mother and daughter form a star, a protected space, exposing to each other what defines them and what they define as vulnerable. Color, knowledge, and sheer scale make the star lopsided, but what the daughter observes is an inner sameness, the link of sex overriding the differences of race and age. Dove concludes the poem by punning on the children's book she alludes to in the poem's title: "we're in the pink / and the pink's in us." She concurs with her daughter's conclusion, emphasizing each one's healthiness, safety, even perfection, as well as exclaiming over the soundness of their connection.

Grace Notes is full of darker poems in which secrets are not named, but it keeps returning to affirm the strength or state of grace found in that mother-daughter relationship: the young woman's golden self-possession in "Summit Beach, 1921," for example, is grace, as is her descendant's defiant readiness in "Crab-Boil." Dove told Vendler that "with *Grace Notes* I had several things in mind: every possible meaning of grace, and of notes, and of grace notes." A grace note is ornamental, not essential to the melody; Dove's lyric returns to its fragmentary solitude after *Thomas and Beulah*, taking its leave from a sustained sequence. The collection features an emphasis on musical imagery as well as a profusion of verbal notes: a letter from mother to daughter whose gaps Dove only barely sketches in "Poem in Which I Refuse Contemplation," scribblings between teacher and student in

"Arrow," notes for study in "Flashcards," mental notes or even poems themselves as notes to a lost parent (possibly Dove's father) in "Your Death" and "The Wake." The emphasis is on partial communication: distances nearly overwhelm these written efforts, but the efforts stand as testaments of Dove's commitment to exchange and expression. Grace as beauty, blessedness, and mercy unites the incomplete pieces, but unobtrusively, momentarily.

The strain of maintaining grace shows in a distinctive feature of the verse itself. Metaphors and similes are often put in the foreground in this volume, nearly to the point of awkwardness, as in "Turning Thirty, I Contemplate Students Bicycling Home." Here the very title marks a forcedness in the act of interpreting that milestone birthday. The pathetic fallacy thunders in and images verge on cliché ("Evening rustles / her skirts of sulky / organza"). In *Grace Notes*, Dove occasionally violates the naturalness of her lyric voice and deliberately undercuts its expected effect of a minor epiphany. In "Ars Poetica" she works similarly, wishing her poem to be a ghost town, in which she is penciled in as a hawk, "a traveling x-marks-the-spot." Even in her most personal collection of poetry to date, Dove insists on "traveling," not wishing to be pinned down into stable identity with that powerful lyric "I." Impermanently marked in pencil, not reliably the truth-confessing speaker of her own poems, Dove persistently refuses to be an easy poet to understand.

Finally, there is in *Grace Notes* the same tension between travel and home that began her poetic career. Despite her ambition to be a traveling "x," shifty and secretive, Dove poetically returns to her Akron childhood; the first section of the book concerns family and reminiscence. It is opened by a quote from Toni Morrison, to whom Dove elsewhere refers as a "personal savior": "All water has a perfect memory and is forever trying to get back to where it was." Before

Dove's great success as a Pulitzer Prize winner and poet laureate, Arnold Rampersad predicted that "she may yet gain her greatest strength by returning to some place closer to her old neighborhood. . . . she may yet as a poet redefine for all of us what 'home' means." Dove's 1993 *Selected Poems*, bringing together her first three volumes in a new publication by a larger press, reminds us how her "perfect memory," her ability to see the world in an uncanny way as a child does, keeps sending her back to that question of home; it is unclear whether she would ever wish to "settle" it.

Dove's *Mother Love* (1995) addresses the darker side of the mother–daughter relationship by recasting the story of Demeter and Persephone. In her introduction, Dove writes that the Greek seasonal myth represents "a modern dilemma as well—there comes a point when a mother can no longer protect her child, when the daughter must go her own way into womanhood." Dove meets this separation from both directions. As Demeter, she is "blown apart by loss," obsessed with her kidnapped child beyond consolation; Dove invokes the photographs of missing children on milk cartons to modernize Demeter's trauma. In "Persephone in Hell," that child is a young woman in Paris, unmindful of her mother's anxiety, who drinks chartreuse with Hades at a chic party. Her fall into the earth is a seduction, not a rape as in her mother's nightmares. Persephone, like the speakers of so many of Dove's earlier poems, is the traveling daughter who can never really return home.

The most poignant moment of mother–daughter contact occurs in the fourth and middle section of *Mother Love*. In "The Bistro Styx," Demeter takes her daughter out to dinner. Persephone, acclimated to Hades–Paris, has grown thin and taken up with a painter. Demeter disapproves of her "aristocratic mole," dressed all in gray, and asks silently, "Are you content to conduct your life / as a cliché and, what's worse, / an anachronism, the brooding artist's demimonde?'' She watches her daughter eat ravenously, Persephone partaking of the fruit that will bind her forever to this underworld, also the forbidden fruit that initiates Eve's sexual awakening and turns her out of the garden:

> Nothing seemed to fill
>
> her up: She swallowed, sliced into a pear,
> speared each tear-shaped lavaliere
> and popped the dripping mess into her pretty
>   mouth.
> Nowhere the bright tufted fields, weighted
>
> vines and sun poured down out of the south.
> ''But are you happy?'' Fearing, I whispered it
> quickly. ''What? You know, Mother''—
>
> she bit into the starry rose of a fig—
> ''one really should try the fruit here.''
> *I've lost her*, I thought, and called for the bill.

The book itself ends with the speaker and her husband traveling in Sicily, driving the racetrack that has been built around the lake where Persephone disappeared; they endlessly circle this still, dark site of that mother–daughter rift but are unable to reach it, as Persephone and Demeter keep missing each other. This image also signals seasonal and generational cycles: images of pregnancy in the second half of the book indicate that Persephone is poised to repeat history.

The formal motif of *Mother Love* is the sonnet; as Gwendolyn Brooks does in her sequence ''the children of the poor,'' Dove converts this form associated with romantic love into a forum for maternal passion. For Brooks, the sonnet represents both the sweetness and the uncertainty of the mother–child relationship; Dove echoes this when she writes in her introduction:

> I like how the sonnet comforts even while its prim borders (but what a pretty fence!) are stultifying; one is constantly bumping up against Order. The Demeter/Persephone cycle of betrayal and regeneration is ideally suited for this form since all

three—mother–goddess, daughter–consort and poet—are struggling to sing in their chains.

Dove's very language here—''(but what a pretty fence!)'' picketed by parentheses—continues to domesticate this form.

Never at home anywhere, however, Dove creates poems that are not truly sonnets, even if they participate in the spirit of the form. Her poems are fourteen lines long, but line length and rhyme are erratic. Further, she interweaves two sonnets in the title poem, strings several in succession in ''Persephone in Hell,'' and ends the book with a densely cyclical poem in eleven sonnetlike sections: there are violations within violations. For Dove this formal deviance has two sides; it ''represents a world gone awry,'' yet is simultaneously ''a talisman against disintegration.'' The sonnet, like the Demeter myth, helps to unify and order the volume more than any of Dove's collections since *Thomas and Beulah*. However, as the quintessential love poem transgressed, the dominant form of *Mother Love* emphasizes the damaged unity of mother and daughter, their disharmony. Dove's future poetry may well continue to zero in on the ''perfect ellipse'' of black water at the center of this book; the relationship she depicts is certainly far from resolution.

Rita Dove's two published works of fiction, the collection *Fifth Sunday* (1985) and the novel *Through the Ivory Gate* (1992), spring from the same autobiographical sources as much of the poetry, sometimes reworking the same material in different contexts. Dove's talent with character blossoms more largely within them, but otherwise the continuities between the two bodies of work are more striking: Dove is concerned with identity and its racial and sexual components, the meanings of family and home, and the transition from girlhood to sexual maturity; she has the same tendency in her fiction as in her poetry to end inconclusively, avoiding as a great peril that last line that "snaps shut too tightly."

Dove herself emphasizes the continuity between her fiction and poetry rather than their dissimilarities. In an interview with William Walsh, she cites successful practitioners of both genres, such as Canadians Margaret Atwood and Michael Ondaatje, and insists,

> I am a writer. I am neither a poet who has tasted the financial fruits of fiction and abandoned poetry, nor am I a poet who has toyed with fiction and decided to 'come back to the fold,' whatever that means. I'd like the genres to embrace each other, rather than be exclusive.

In addition, Dove is conscious of her place within an African American storytelling tradition, and emphasizes that her literary efforts began in short fiction; it is not surprising that she should return to that form. Dove is certainly best known as a poet, and her strongest work to date is in that genre, but she does not intend to limit herself to the "relentlessly lyric" scope of *Grace Notes* anytime soon.

Fifth Sunday is a collection of eight stories, two of which later were incorporated into *Through the Ivory Gate*. Dove experiments in these pieces with different modes of narration: she uses both first and third person, bases one story on journal entries, and in "Damon and Vandalia" tells a story about the attraction between a gay British man who grew up in Japan and a black midwestern woman in alternating first-person narration. Despite this stylistic diversity, however, there is a unity to the kinds of characters Dove portrays and the situations in which they find themselves. Most of the protagonists are women, as in the lead and title story, "Fifth Sunday." The church of Dove's childhood gave over the service, excepting the sermon, on the rare fifth Sunday of the month to the youth of the congregation. In using this title for the book, Dove wishes to bring forward "the idea of being

in control only occasionally, and in strict accordance with the social rules," as she told Kitchen and Rubin: her characters are in conflict with these rules to varying degrees.

"Fifth Sunday" looks over the shoulder of a very proper teenage girl, on such a Sunday, in her small-town church. Valerie, menstruating and more than ready for her first kiss from the minister's son, fiercely desires to manipulate how others see her, but she is "in control only occasionally." She faints in the overheated church, and a woman whom Valerie never identifies suggests that the swooning young woman, who won't even sing in the choir lest she be called "fast," might be pregnant. The story ends with Valerie's unresolved rage, throwing the focus away from the external events of the narrative toward the inner tension between sexuality (connected to her desire to sing) and her cherished public identity as a good girl.

The most successful story in *Fifth Sunday* takes place worlds away from a midwestern small town but grapples with the same questions of identity and expression. "The Spray Paint King" comprises journal entries written by a teenage German boy in a detention home for youthful offenders, for eventual consumption by Dr. Severin, the psychiatrist in charge of his case. The unnamed protagonist describes himself as a "quadroon"; in her interview with Kitchen and Rubin, Dove calls him a "brown baby" growing up in Cologne, the result of a World War II encounter between an African American soldier and a German woman, and emphasizes that it was "this friction between individual artistic protest and social regulations that prompted that story." The protagonist is incarcerated for having spray-painted black art on white walls all over the city, provoking rave reviews from art critics:

> *The young artist's style is reminiscent of Picasso in austerity of line, of Matisse in fantasy and social comment. The bitterness, however, the relentless*

scrutiny of what we so vainly call civilization, the hopelessness which pervades his work, without coquetterie nor call for pathos—these qualities are all his own. He is, so to speak, his generation's appointed messenger.

The young artist, although he enjoys these commentaries enough to cite them, produces his own analysis of his graffiti, precociously anticipating Dr. Severin's interpretation of his work as a defiant assertion of blackness: "I put the stain back on the wall."

The "stain" the narrator wants to reestablish on the whitewashed town is both a mark of black presence in the omnipresent whiteness of Cologne and a sign of that city's guilt. Specifically, he condemns by his painting his father's contribution to the accidental deaths of five men in the building of Severin Bridge. More generally, he means to remind the townspeople that their city is built on the backs of innocent people—in this case, five hapless construction workers literally become part of the town's foundation while the drive to production continues relentlessly. Overlaying and magnifying his father's betrayal is the guilty absence of his grandfather, the American who left his own mark in Germany and then refused responsibility for his creation. The protagonist of "The Spray Paint King" is abandoned to negotiate his black and white, American and German heritage according to his own methods, and his graffiti become explosive but profoundly positive self-assertions.

The main character in *Through the Ivory Gate*, Dove's first full-length novel, is Virginia King, an African American woman not long out of college in Madison, Wisconsin, where she studied drama and mime. She is not unlike "The Spray Paint King," although her own family secrets are different: she, too, keeps an ambivalent distance from her family and community while attempting to carve out a place for herself. The book's action takes place a year or two after Nixon's resignation, when Virginia is an artist-in-residence in her hometown of Akron for the month of October, teaching puppetry to fourth-grade children. The homecoming, told in a linear fashion, is an occasion for flashbacks to her childhood and along the way solves the mysterious crisis that drove the Kings to Arizona during her own fourth-grade year. Meanwhile, Virginia struggles for self-definition and copes with the series of romantic disappointments of her adolescence and adult life.

We are given Virginia's conflicts with her mother, Belle, and her maternal grandmother and namesake, Virginia Evans, in pieces. The book begins with Virginia's childhood contest with these mothers over dolls. Virginia adores a pale-skinned, red-haired doll:

> Then there was Penelope, Penelope with the long red hair and plump good looks of Brenda Starr, Penelope of the creamy skin and dimpling cheeks.... As many as five hairstyles a day— Penelope the Model, Penelope the God-Fearing Nurse, Penelope the Prize-Winning Journalist ... Penelope Had a Man and He Loved Her So.

The doll's streaming red hair represents freedom and possibility for Virginia. Dove reverses a similar scene in Toni Morrison's *The Bluest Eye*, in which that narrator deplores the gift of a fair baby doll, to the outrage of her parents; Virginia, paradoxically, frustrates her mother and grandmother by repudiating an "ugly" black baby doll with painted-on hair, preferring either a brightly dressed Sambo or a white doll to whom she bears no resemblance. Dove pays tribute to Morrison while marking their generational difference and insisting that, however illogically, a black girl can find identification with a white doll empowering.

Like Dove, Virginia plays the cello, although she does not pursue music as her primary artistic outlet, claiming not to have the will to practice sufficiently. Nevertheless, more than puppetry, the cello seems to be an outlet for passionate self-expression; Virginia's mastery of a series of Bach suites parallels her emotional growth. Further, she calls her instrument a substitute mother: "No wonder she'd chosen this monstrosity, this womanly shape she could wrap herself around after her mother had retreated into unexplained grief and intransigent resentment." Virginia's relationship with the cello shapes the novel, but it is a displaced one, a result of her mother's apparent failure to nurture her daughter sufficiently. In *Through the Ivory Gate*, Dove begins to write from the position of a daughter about her mother in a sustained way, anticipating *Mother Love*.

Keeping her music private, Virginia finds a more public artistic role in staging a puppet show with her racially mixed class. During production of the student-written love story including fairy godparents and a talking football, Virginia is wooed by Terry, the divorced father of one of the children. The novel chronicles Virginia's disappointments in dating African American men; persistently, and finally with Terry, Virginia finds herself too educated for the men to whom she is attracted. Her music, her German, her interest in mime set her apart from her race—none of her passions are the prescribed ones. Her thoughts circle obsessively back to Clayton, a hopeless college romance with the one black man with whom she felt a full sympathetic understanding, who leaves Virginia for a man.

Consistently, Virginia refuses to be black according to anyone else's definition; her maverick tastes echo Dove's own eclecticism in *The Yellow House on the Corner*. She eventually moves away from Terry, deciding that she will not marry a man merely because he is eligible and black, thus beginning to take charge of her choices and to understand her past. The novel ends inconclusively but lyrically, at Halloween:

> There were devils and fairies, butterflies and cheetahs, Casper the Friendly Ghost and the Tin Man and princesses and bionic Six Million Dollar men.

They came from all directions and proceeded from porch to porch. Every now and then an astronaut or a Frankenstein would stop to execute his own rapturous little jig, while from the sidelines the grownups watched and waited.

This passage combines many of the story's threads: the empowerment Virginia and her students find through masks, disguising themselves and sampling different identities, is interwoven with the related joy young Virginia found in her red-haired doll. Virginia is at a turning point, and Dove does not map out what is on the other side of the gate, but does emphasize the enormity of possibility her literary double is facing.

Dove told Helen Vendler she wrote *Through the Ivory Gate* "mainly because it's a story I've wanted to tell; it wouldn't leave me alone. But another part of me—the dutiful daughter or something—was always told that if you don't understand something you should study it." Her first novel, like her poetry, does not give over whatever Dove learned easily; in fact, the economy which worries Dove in relation to her poetry is more of a problem in this extended work of fiction. Virginia's key relationships with her grandmother and her mother are frustratingly underdeveloped. Also, the plot of repressed memory in operation here is already a commonplace in contemporary fiction, and Dove is not the best practitioner of it. Still, as always, she writes compellingly of the story's father figure, of Virginia's sexuality, of her struggle for identity intertwined with an ambivalent homecoming: this first novel is a central piece of Dove's expanding canon.

Dove has made excursions into a drama, her third major genre. Although she said, in her interview with William Walsh, that "I don't think I'll ever be a true playwright because to do that I would have to learn the theater scene and work at establishing contacts"—an enterprise the post-Pulitzer and poet laureate writer does not have time to undertake—she does intend to continue practicing this genre. Her two plays published to date are a one-act titled *The Siberian Village* (1991) and a verse play, *The Darker Face of the Earth* (1994).

The Siberian Village engages in a debate that recurs in Dove's writing over the intersections of language and race, challenging the idea that race defines the language one may employ. Robert, the focal character and an ex-convict recently released from eleven years of incarceration, accuses his black female psychiatrist of "shrink talk": to his mind, she has too much to say, and too large and refined a vocabulary with which to make her point. He demands, "Where'd you leave your nigger talk? Back in the maze with the white rats?" Robert later runs into the same trouble with his old friend, intimidating Eddie with his prison-acquired literacy.

Robert is not a sympathetic character at the opening of the drama because of his hostility toward and attempt to silence Dr. Swanson; the final scene of the play goes some way toward illuminating his state of mind. Robert overlays reality with scenes from *The Siberian Village*, a novel bequeathed to him by a cellmate. In scene four the cliché of realist drama, the living room of Robert's new apartment, falls into abrupt darkness; then Robert and the other characters begin to act out the fictional scenes. Robert becomes Sergei Petrovich, the son of a railroad worker in the remote village of Kibirsk, near the Arctic Circle and on the edge of a swamp. Sergei is "born of a Tartar peasant girl, built like a bull": he is well adapted to this life of brutal winters and reeking, mosquito-filled summers. Eddie and Dr. Swanson double as Alexi and Galina, a couple newly arrived at the camp, their crime unknown except for Alexi's frustrated explanation that "I opened my mouth."

Again, speech and language come to the forefront as the central issue. Galina does not speak except repeatedly to utter one sound, "Shh," as if to reproach her too-open husband. Sergei

attributes her near-silence to "the trauma of exile," and is so fascinated by it that he impregnates Galina with "a small blue bull" of a son that kills her in childbirth:

> But I loved Galina's word; I ached to hear her say it. I pushed it out, I eased it out, I sucked it from her tongue. She was not ungrateful. *(pause)* While you shriveled in righteous anger, she grew plump and brown as a bug, only you didn't notice! She honed her living down to a word and lived like an animal in that word. With the word growing in her.

Galina's silence is the opposite of Dr. Swanson's verbosity, yet both are self-willed exiles, Galina choosing to leave her homeland with her husband and enter this frigid, wordless space, Dr. Swanson voluntarily abandoning what Robert assumes is her homeland, her natural "black" language.

Robert clearly prefers this female character silent; her one "word" is barely even that, and death finalizes the gradual quieting of the play's one female voice. The play also consummates the sexual tensions not only between Robert and Swanson but also between Robert and Eddie: Alexi rests in Sergei's arms as Sergei, the survivor, sings the other man a lullaby. Intimacy is interwoven with treachery—it is intimated, further, that both Robert and his deceased cellmate had been imprisoned for murdering their unfaithful lovers. *The Siberian Village* circles warily around these betrayals, interwoven as they are with the power of language, and resulting always in the loss of home forever.

Dove continues this exploration of language, sex, and power in *The Darker Face of the Earth*. A play one reviewer describes as in "blank verse," it is actually written in prosaic, unrhymed lines of varying length; its verse form is nearly unobtrusive enough to be nonexistent. Dove retells the Oedipus story in the context of a South Carolina plantation: the identity confusion that moves the action of the classical tragedy is here a result of miscegenation, two white owners having children by their slaves. Race, class, education, and free/slave status become hopelessly mixed through the corrupting environment of the American slave economy.

The owners of the plantation in question, doubles for Jocasta and her husband, are Amalia and Louis Jennings. Frustrated by Louis' frequent visits to the slave cabins, Amalia defiantly conducts a relationship with one of the slaves and produces a son. She agrees to sell the offspring of the affair, pretending her baby was white and died in childbirth, while her enraged husband and the attending doctor devise a way to kill the child indirectly, placing the newborn in a basket with a pair of spurs for the doctor's long ride back to town. Augustus, of course, does not die, but falls into relatively fortunate circumstances: he is taken up by an English sea captain who treats him well, educates him, and promises to set Augustus free in his will. The estate's executor betrays the will to sell the valuable slave, and Augustus subsequently becomes notorious for his acts of rebellion. Amalia, proud of her heritage as the daughter of a slave breaker, full of bitter confidence from years of running the estate in Louis' effective absence, decides to purchase Augustus, against the advice of her overseer.

Augustus fascinates Amalia, who does not know his real identity, and, following the plot of the original tragedy, he enters into an affair with her and accidentally kills his slave father, Hector, before he learns the full story. He becomes involved with a group of slaves and free blacks that is planning a revolt, and is eventually ordered to kill Louis and Amalia. In this last visit to the great house his history is revealed to both Augustus and Amalia; he is found dithering by the other revolutionaries, and both are killed.

Dove brilliantly resets this familiar story in a circumstance in which lineage did get impossibly mixed, children commonly separated from parents, power sharply divided. The parallels she finds for the individual characters, too, are apt

and suggestive. The slaves become the chorus, site of comment, judgment, and song; Tiresias is transformed into Scylla, a manipulative conjure woman. Scylla is, in fact, depicted as another enslaver, whose superstitions govern the other slaves until Augustus ridicules their fears; she is not a sympathetic character, but her predictions about Augustus are always reliable:

> Your Augustus is a pretty clever nigger—
> been lots of places and knows
> the meanings of words and things like that.
> But something's foul in his blood.
> He may 'pear to be a budding flower,
> but there's a worm
> eating away at the root.
> What's festering inside him
> nothing this side of the living
> can heal. And when a body's
> hurting that bad, a person lose sight of
> what's good or evil. They do anything
> to get relief—anything.

What's festering inside Augustus is hate, as Phebe, who supports Augustus and is more loyal to him than to the revolt, points out. The system of slavery here is a substitute for fate or preordained forces: its peculiar pressures distort people, even or especially compellingly intelligent characters like Amalia and Augustus, beyond recognition or healing. There is no real freedom possible, Dove seems to assert, within this system.

The Darker Face of the Earth attributes power to language not in the way *The Siberian Village* does so much as in the way Frederick Douglass does: education, the ability to read and write, cast Augustus' fate in making him aware enough of the world and his personal worth that slavery becomes intolerable to him. Interestingly, Dove makes the choice to ''mostly standardize'' the slave dialect within the play, ''in order to facilitate reading of the script.'' This decision does bring the play closer to classicism in its language, and probably does make it more accessible to readers, although probably not significantly so:

educated readers have managed well with American literature in various southern vernaculars, from *The Adventures of Huckleberry Finn* to the stories of Charles Chesnutt, Zora Neale Hurston, and William Faulkner. In any case, this choice reflects Dove's insistence on the universal in all her work: her literary interests and attempts consistently cross national, racial, and generic boundaries.

Rita Dove does not belong to any movement or literary circle. To repeat what she has made so clear, she separated herself from the black arts movement at the very beginning of her career, although race informs a great deal of her writing, whether it is about antebellum South Carolina or her daughter. (Vendler, in "Rita Dove: Identity Markers," celebrates Dove for making "this important discovery—that blackness need not be one's central subject, but equally need not be omitted," perhaps missing the point that blackness is inseparably implicated in Dove's self-positioning as an outsider looking homeward.) Dove disavows the influence of magical realism in her poetry, countering William Walsh's question on this subject by exclaiming, "all I can think is: isn't reality magic?" She is neither new formalist nor avant-garde in her style, although she is capable of play in either field; even her literary Americanness is complicated by her strong German ties and her tendency to eye the United States with an outsider's skepticism.

One borough of contemporary American writing in which she is often at home might be a women's literary tradition. Dove herself stresses her early attraction to the work of Toni Morrison; some of her works also seem to allude to the poems of Marianne Moore ("Fish in a Stone") and Elizabeth Bishop ("Genetic Expedition"); Gwendolyn Brooks is an obvious precursor with her vivid depictions of life in her own hometown, as well as the economy of her language and the technical expertise that characterize the first half of Brooks's career; Dove begins "In the Old Neighborhood" with a quote from the feminist poet Adrienne Rich's "Shooting Script."

These are diverse references, and Dove does refer, probably as often, to male writers and artists whose works have captured her imagination. Yet Dove's angle of vision is solidly feminist. She draws clear lines here, too, declaring herself to Taleb-Khyar as "politically . . . a feminist," but separating politics from her literary efforts: "when I walk into my room to write, I don't think of myself in political terms. . . . I would find it a breach of my integrity as a writer to create a character for didactic or propaganda purposes." Whatever intentions in this case divide art from politics, much of the work Dove produces invites feminist interpretation. She depicts women's lives with authority and insight, often articulating women's sexuality and motherhood from a subject position; she is fascinated by the relationship between language, gender, and identity; she reworks domestic space in her poetry with a decidedly critical eye; she writes movingly of women's artistic, intellectual, and personal ambitions. Even her insistence on completely free range as an artist, unhindered by anyone's ideas of what or how it might be appropriate for her to write, can be understood as a feminist stance.

Further, the economy and personal reserve of her poetic style strongly recall preconfessional American poets like Emily Dickinson, Marianne Moore, and H.D. Each of these writers mimicked feminine modesty in order to enter masculine turf, rejecting a sentimental mode then associated with women's poetry; their strategy was initially self-protective but became vastly influential, taken up by mainstream modernism as the new aesthetic of the twentieth century. Dove is much more forward than these poets, more empowered, more public in her mission, yet her approach to the lyric resonates with this tradition. In fact, it advances it, adapting a great lyric mode to contemporary concerns.

Selected Bibliography

WORKS OF RITA DOVE

POETRY

The Yellow House on the Corner. Pittsburgh: Carnegie-Mellon University Press, 1980.

Museum. Pittsburgh: Carnegie-Mellon University Press, 1983.

Thomas and Beulah. Pittsburgh: Carnegie-Mellon University Press, 1986.

Grace Notes. New York: Norton, 1989.

Selected Poems. New York: Pantheon, 1993.

Mother Love. New York: Norton, 1995.

PROSE

Fifth Sunday. Lexington: University of Kentucky/ Callaloo, 1985.

"A Black Rainbow: Modern Afro-American Poetry." Written with Marilyn Nelson Waniek. In *Poetry After Modernism*. Edited by Robert McDowell. Brownsville, Ore.: Story Line Press, 1991. Pp. 217–275.

Through the Ivory Gate. New York: Pantheon, 1992.

DRAMA

"The Siberian Village." *Callaloo*, 14:396–418 (Spring 1991).

The Darker Face of the Earth: A Verse Play. Brownsville, Ore.: Story Line, 1994.

BIOGRAPHICAL AND CRITICAL STUDIES

Georgoudaki, Ekaterini. *Race, Gender, and Class Perspectives in the Works of Maya Angelou, Gwendolyn Brooks, Rita Dove, Nikki Giovanni, and Audre Lorde*. Thessaloniki: Aristotle University of Thessaloniki, 1991.

———. "Rita Dove: Crossing Boundaries." *Callaloo*, 14:419–433 (Spring 1991).

McDowell, Robert. "The Assembling Vision of Rita Dove." In *Conversant Essays: Contemporary Poets on Poetry*. Edited by James McCorkle. Detroit: Wayne State University Press, 1990. Pp. 294–302.

Rampersad, Arnold. "The Poems of Rita Dove." *Callaloo*, 9:52–60 (Winter 1986).

Shoptaw, John. "Segregated Lives: Rita Dove's *Thomas and Beulah*." In *Reading Black, Reading Feminist: A Critical Anthology*. Edited by Henry Louis Gates Jr. New York: Meridian, 1990. Pp. 374–381.

Vendler, Helen. "Rita Dove: Identity Markers." *Callaloo*, 17:381–398 (1994).

INTERVIEWS

Kitchen, Judith, and Stan Sanvel Rubin. " 'The Underside of the Story': A Conversation with Rita Dove." In *The Post-Confessionals: Conversations with American Poets of the Eighties*. Edited by Earl G. Ingersoll, Judith Kitchen, and Stan Sanvel Rubin. Rutherford, N.J.: Fairleigh Dickinson University Press, 1989. Pp. 151–166.

Taleb-Khyar, Mohamed B. "An Interview with Maryse Condé and Rita Dove." *Callaloo*, 14:347–366 (Spring 1991).

Vendler, Helen. "An Interview with Rita Dove." In *Reading Black, Reading Feminist: A Critical Anthology*. Edited by Henry Louis Gates Jr. New York: Meridian, 1990. Pp. 481–491.

Walsh, William. "Isn't Reality Magic? An Interview with Rita Dove." *Kenyon Review*, 16:142–154 (Summer 1994).

—LESLEY WHEELER

Louise Erdrich

1954–

*L*OUISE ERDRICH FEELS compelled to tell the stories of Native Americans; she gives witness to the endurance of Chippewa people. The sheer chance of being a survivor herself, considering the millions who were here in the beginning and the very, very few who survived into the 1920s, drives her storytelling. As we listen to the many storytellers in Erdrich's North Dakota cycle of novels that have come to us since the publication of *Love Medicine* (1984), we try to reconcile the tangled polyphony of speakers. She interconnects the lives of Chippewa families—Kashpaws, Pillagers, Lazarres, Lamartines, Morrisseys, Tooses, and Nanapushes—and their immigrant-descendant, off-reservation neighbors—Adares, Jameses, and Kozkas.

The story of the families begins with *Tracks* (1988), which covers the years 1912 to 1924; continues with *Love Medicine* (1984), which extends the story from 1934 to 1984; and brings the details of the Chippewa families up to what we presume to be the present time in *The Bingo Palace* (1994). This last novel in the originally proposed quartet has no dates designated for the chapters, as her three previous novels do. Approximating the span of *Love Medicine, The Beet Queen* (1988) chronicles the lives of mixed bloods and whites in the town of Argus during the years 1932 to 1972. Although she has no particular recommendation for the reader concerning the order in which to read the four novels, the story lines begin in *Tracks,* which, she declared in an interview with Nancy Feyl Chavkin and Allan Chavkin, "was the first manuscript I finished, the form of all else, still a tangle."

One of her four novels, *Love Medicine,* was revised and expanded in 1993 to clarify events and relationships, in the process making more defined links to *Tracks* and the later *The Bingo Palace,* which, Erdrich declares, "just intervened, proposed itself, took over." Together, these three narratives move events forward over three generations, beginning with Nanapush, survivor of the consumption epidemic of 1912, and ending with Lipsha Morrissey, his descendant through Nanapush's named granddaughter Lulu Lamartine, leaning into the future, an unknown path opening before him. In *Love Medicine,* there is also an indication of a fourth generation with Howard Kashpaw, son of Lynette and King. Thus, instead of the promised quartet of novels, there is actually a trilogy plus a fourth book, *The Beet Queen.* However, Erdrich says she does not know "when these books will begin and end," thus leaving the story lines open for continuance. She also has published two volumes of poetry, *Jacklight* (1984) and *Baptism of Desire* (1989).

Numerous short stories have become chapters in the novels, there have been occasional essays, and the first full-length work of nonfiction, *The*

Blue Jay's Dance: A Birth Year, appeared in 1995. With her husband, Michael Dorris, a collaborator in all her work, Erdrich wrote *Crown of Columbus* (1991) and *Route Two* (1991). Earlier, Erdrich and Dorris had published several short stories under the name Milou North.

When asked the themes of her last narrative, *The Bingo Palace,* Erdrich responded by noting what she considers the usual: "anxiety, money, chance, obsessed love, age, small griefs, failed friendship, self-denial, repressed sexual ardor." To a great extent, all her novels deal with these irritations of life. However, the deeper underlying issues of origin, place, connections to others, adaptability, and vision are the ones that continue to impress themselves on the reader's consciousness. They provoke a desire to interpret events in the lives of tribal people and become involved in their meaning. Like the oral storyteller's audience, readers become cocreators of the text, invited to that role by the many voices, each telling his or her own version of the story. One of the major themes in Erdrich's fiction concerns personal identity within family and tribal structures. Memory, language, trickster energy, and humor contribute to survival of her characters, who testify to the continuance of Chippewa people. To convey the realities of shifting and dwindling communities within and outside tribal culture, Erdrich invents narrative strategies that involve narrators and readers in interpretive dialogue, resulting in new understandings of the effects of the loss of community among both Indians and whites. Slim chances of survival and fragile threads of human endurance continue to amaze the reader of Erdrich's fiction.

Louise Erdrich declares Chippewa, French, Scottish, and German ancestry. An enrolled member of the Turtle Mountain Band, she connects to the people and the place of her beginnings: the Turtle Mountain Reservation, which is located in north-central North Dakota near the Canadian border. This reservation becomes the epicenter of the three novels that chronicle Chippewa family sagas, and it also figures, to a lesser extent, in *The Beet Queen.* Born on June 7, 1954, in Little Falls, Minnesota, Erdrich grew up in a family of nine—mother, Rita Joanne Gourneau, father, Ralph Louis Erdrich, and seven children—in Wahpeton, North Dakota, in a house that belonged to the government. Her parents were employees of the Bureau of Indian Affairs at the Wahpeton Indian School, where her grandfather had been educated. Erdrich's mother and grandparents, Patrick and Mary Gourneau, are from the Turtle Mountain Reservation. The Turtle Mountains cover about four hundred square miles on both sides of the border between the United States and Canada. The land that is not hilly is covered with water. There are at least thirty lakes of various sizes on the thirty-four thousand acres of reservation land, and many marshes. It is, therefore, not surprising that sloughs figure importantly in the terrain of Erdrich's novels. Water imagery predominates in *Love Medicine.*

Although she has never lived on the reservation, Erdrich has visited there often, and she has chosen to identify with her Chippewa origin. She uses the term "Chippewa" to refer to her people; however, the original woodland people were known as Anishinaabeg. In the nineteenth century these tribal people were often referred to as Ojibwa or Ojibway. Gerald Vizenor points out that the designations "Chippewa" and "Ojibwa" are colonial names for the original people.

Erdrich is also a member of the white community by blood and education. In 1972 she was one of the first female students admitted to Dartmouth College, which was then developing its Native American Program. Her husband, Michael Dorris, was a faculty member there and later became the founder and director of the Native American Studies Program. Erdrich graduated from Dartmouth in 1976 with a degree in English and creative writing, and obtained a master's degree in creative writing from Johns Hopkins University in 1979. She and Dorris were married on October 10, 1981.

Erdrich notes the dual citizenship of the individual who lives in the Anglo culture and at the same time remains connected to Indian identity. In an interview with Joseph Bruchac, she commented on the quest for background that is so much a part of her experience: "One of the characteristics of being a mixed-blood is searching. You look back and say, 'Who am I from?' You must question. You must make certain choices. You're able to. And it's a blessing and a curse. All of our searches involve trying to discover where we are from." Erdrich brings her mixed background into her characters' lives, creating the most significant narratives from the basic need to know who and where they came from.

In *Love Medicine,* the heart of the family sagas, understanding one's origin becomes problematic. Lipsha Morrissey has been told his mother tried to drown him in the slough, and his efforts to deal with the uncertainty of his beginnings obscure his ability to find a place for himself in life. Marie Kashpaw, who has raised Lipsha and whom he calls Grandma, says she saved him from his mother's attempts to drown him, but she doesn't identify Lipsha's mother. It remains for his other grandmother, Lulu Lamartine, to reveal that Lipsha is the son of June Kashpaw and Lulu's son, Gerry Nanapush, and to soothe Lipsha's worry about his mother's intent: "June was just real upset about the whole thing. Your Grandma Kashpaw took you on because the truth is she had a fond spot for June, just like she's got one for you." When Lipsha asks Lulu if his mother tried to drown him, she tries to divert his attention to the important information about his parentage. Lulu attributes Lipsha's oddness to his confusion about where he came from: "You never knew who you were. That's one reason why I told you. I thought it was a knowl-

edge that could make or break you." Knowing who you are and where you come from persists as a major theme in Erdrich's novels.

In *The Bingo Palace,* Lipsha tries to hold on to the belief that he was given to Grandma Kashpaw by "a mother who was beautiful but too wild to have raised a boy on her own." But Marie's daughter Zelda, who was brought up with June, makes sure Lipsha knows all the terrible details, how she saw June "slinging a little bundle into the slough." She describes how she made three or four dives before she finally located the gunnysack and her subsequent discovery that it contained Lipsha: "I opened that sack once I was out of the woods. I cried when I saw it was a baby! When you saw me you blinked your eyes wide and then you smiled." Worse than anything else, Lipsha can't dismiss Zelda's account as inventive. The hurt of his mother's action haunts him. Despite the whisky that Zelda has consumed at the bar where he works, Lipsha suspects that Zelda's version of his past is not embroidered, and he fights to forgive June. Lipsha persists in unraveling his family's secrets to satisfy himself and to prove his identity for the bureaucracy. He needs to obtain a band card, "proof-positive self-identification, a complicated thing in Indian Country." Lipsha observes that the dominant culture's bureaucratic requirements work against Indian self-actualization. Lipsha only knows his identity through his grandmothers, Marie and Lulu. Without government acceptance of his identity, his enrollment, and consequently his entitlements, elude him. The security of knowing a mother's love eludes him, too. His romantic pursuit of Shawnee Ray Toose in *The Bingo Palace* is in part a search for a mother. Without a full and clear understanding of origin, Erdrich's characters seem condemned to search; and in that sense, wholeness eludes Lipsha, as it does so many of the characters in her work.

One character who does know where he came

from is Nanapush, who shares the storytelling with Pauline Puyat in *Tracks*. He presents his legacy in his father's words: " 'Nanapush. That's what you'll be called. Because it's got to do with trickery and living in the bush. Because it's got to do with something a girl can't resist. The first Nanapush stole fire. You will steal hearts.' " For white readers, his name takes on mythic proportions in its identification with Prometheus, the fire stealer from Greek mythology. For Indian readers, and especially for the Chippewa audience, the reference to trickery signifies that Nanapush is a descendant of Naanabozho, who, Gerald Vizenor tells us (in *Interior Landscapes*, "Measuring My Blood"), was "the first tribal trickster on the earth. He was comic, a part of the natural world, a spiritual balance in a comic drama, and so he must continue in his stories." Encoded in Nanapush's name is his identity as energy source and stabilizing agent in the lives he touches. He passes his name on to Fleur's child, Lulu, in the ritual of baptism, and in doing so, he ensures the continuance of his own name and adds more ambiguity to Lulu's paternal origin. The uncertainty of the gang rape that Pauline reported when she came back from Argus and the equal uncertainty of Eli as father of Fleur's child fade with the emergence of the name Nanapush. There is no doubt that Fleur was raped, according to Pauline's report, but the account is clouded by Pauline's unreliability as a witness.

In *Tracks*, Fleur, who has survived the consumption epidemic with Nanapush, knows her origin, but according to Nanapush, she and her cousin Moses, the only remaining Pillagers, have suffered the loss of family to the point where it is not clear whether they are in the land of the living or "the other place, boundless, where the dead sit talking, see too much, and regard the living as fools." Fleur's understanding of her origin is obscured by the spirits of her dead family: "She was too young and had no stories or depth of life to rely upon. All she had was raw power, and the names of the dead that filled her. . . . Ogimaakwe, Boss Woman, his wife. Asasaweminikwesens, Chokecherry Girl. Bineshii, Small Bird, also known as Josette. And the last, the boy Ombaashi, He Is Lifted By Wind." The names of dead relatives alone cannot sustain Fleur; yet, like Nanapush, Fleur is a survivor. She is linked to him because he saved her from death by starvation when her family died from the illness called consumption, the dreaded tuberculosis, as deadly as the smallpox that preceded it. The historical reality of the tremendous loss of Indian lives by epidemics takes on human proportions in *Tracks*.

Like Nanapush, Fleur is linked to the traditional tribal ways, but she turns her knowledge into an occult power that Nanapush considers dangerous. She identifies with the animal and spirit world and the land around Lake Matchimanito, but when her power is threatened, she retreats further into the region surrounding the lake where, Nanapush tells Eli Kashpaw, "The leaves speak a cold language that overfills your brain. You want to lie down. You want to never get up." Nanapush connects Fleur to the wildness and witchery of Lake Matchimanito. Fleur's power enchants Eli, who begs Nanapush for sexual knowledge so that he can be a pleasing lover to Fleur. Fleur's sexuality, unrepressed and lavish as the vegetation surrounding the lake, is reported to be linked to Misshepeshu, the water monster, the devil who wants strong and daring young girls.

Tracks' second narrator, Pauline Puyat, denied her origin by asking her father to send her to Argus, where she hoped to erase her identity as a mixed blood: "I wanted to be like my mother, who showed her half-white. I wanted to be like my grandfather, pure Canadian." Wanting to learn the lacemaking trade from the nuns, Pauline begs her father to send her to his sister Regina, whose husband works in a butcher shop,

Kozka's Meats. Instead of learning "to thread the bobbins and spools," she sweeps the floors of the butcher shop and cares for Regina's son Russell as she watches Fleur, who also has come to Argus and has been hired at the butcher shop. Fleur's strength and power to attract men provoke Pauline's understanding of her own thin body and impoverished sexuality. Pauline's repressed sexuality stands in contrast to Fleur's extravagant supply.

Pauline's identity is compromised by her disconnection from her people, but even her rejection of her identity as a mixed blood is somewhat ambiguous, for she learns that her family moved away from the reservation while she worked in Argus. There is an implication that she has been left behind, a castaway, and so she becomes an apprentice to Bernadette Morrissey, helping prepare bodies of the dead, "death's bony whore." In a delusion, Pauline hears Christ asking her to bring more souls, and she responds in a frenzy of zeal. She gives up her baby, conceived in the raw union with Napoleon Morrissey, Bernadette's brother, and enters the convent: "I have no family, . . . I am alone and have no land. Where else would I go but to the nuns?" Pauline will become a handmaiden of God, having strangled the devil with rosary beads: "Eventually, it took on the physical form of Napoleon Morrissey." In a final act of defilement, Pauline desecrates herself physically and spiritually, allowing the blame for Napoleon's death to be assigned to Fleur.

In *Love Medicine,* Marie Lazarre, bastard child of Pauline, rejects her origin, too, but she is able to choose another option besides the church. In this case, sheer ambition counts enough to override the evil she came from and the evil of the convent. Marie confronts the crazed nun, Sister Leopolda, who is actually her own mother. (Sister Leopolda is the name Pauline took when she entered the convent.) Brought up by the Lazares, Marie despises her foster mother, who is a drunk,

and her foster father. She selects Nector Kashpaw as her route to identity, although he considers her "a skinny white girl from a family so low you cannot even think they are in the same class as Kashpaws." Marie's will and her humanity link her to the family she creates with Nector as well as to Lucille, her sister in the foster family of Lazares, whom she rejects. Her feeling for Lucille influences Marie to take Lucille's daughter June into her own family and to raise her as one of her own children; later she takes June's son Lipsha when June rejects him. Marie is strongly identified as a mother-woman by her actions within the family, and she is strongly connected to other females of the tribe. In the expanded version of *Love Medicine,* Marie is coached through the difficult birth of her last child by Rushes Bear (Margaret Kashpaw) and Fleur Pillager. Marie's use of the old Cree language to express her need to be taken by labor contractions (*babaumawaebigowin*) as a boat would be borne by waves identifies her as a traditional Indian woman.

Origin becomes a source of sadness for Lyman Lamartine, one of Lulu's nine offspring by different fathers. He is ambivalent about knowing that he is the son of Nector Kashpaw. "I don't really want to know," he tells Lulu. Part of Lyman's identity went with his brother Henry Jr., a severely traumatized Vietnam veteran, when he drove their red Oldsmobile convertible into the Red River and drowned.

In her revision of *Love Medicine,* Erdrich makes clear the importance of the relationship between origin and identity, particularly with regard to Lyman. The addition of the chapter "The Tomahawk Factory" provides important insights into Lyman's character, especially the inheriting of Nector's business sense, and it also paves the way for Lyman's role as developer of gaming enterprises in *The Bingo Palace.* Lyman's origin and his connection to the tribe are trivialized in his discovery of identity through a U.S. Department of the Treasury 1099 form, which jolts him out of his alcohol- and drug-induced stupor into existence. Filing his income tax return brings him his identity: "I was becoming legitimate, rising from the heap." Heightening the irony of becoming a person by filling out a form is Lyman's discovery that his box number had been mistakenly typed on a form that belonged to someone else. Lyman quickly joins the bureaucracy of the Bureau of Indian Affairs, and in this role must deal with his mother, Lulu, and Marie as they battle over authority and territory in the souvenir factory. In an outburst of anger, Marie identifies Nector as Lyman's father before the assembled workers, prompting bedlam on the assembly line; insults and beads fly through the air, and eventually Anishinabe Enterprises is destroyed. The additional chapter "Lyman's Luck" paves the way for Lyman's future, based on greed and luck —a gambling casino—in *The Bingo Palace*. Still, Lyman hurts when he remembers that Nector had never acknowledged him as a son. When Lyman thinks about it, there is nagging irritation in Lipsha's being given Nector's ceremonial pipe. Eventually Lyman makes a commodity of the sacred piece by buying it from Lipsha.

Albertine Johnson's knowledge of her origin comes through the uncommitted motherhood of her mother, Zelda, and through photos of her soldier father displayed in her mother's house: "All I knew of him was pictures, blond, bleak, and doomed to wander, perhaps as much by Mama's rage at her downfall as by the uniform." Her name is a feminine version of Albert, a link to her mother's "repressed history," for Albertine bears the name of Xavier Albert Toose, the boyfriend Zelda resisted but never relinquished. Albertine's father is dismissed as a mistake by Zelda: "Never marry a Swedish is my rule." In *The Bingo Palace*, Albertine seeks her identity in a ceremony conducted, ironically, by Xavier Toose. She takes the traditional name of Four Soul, a woman "sunk deep in the scattered records of the Pil-

lagers, into the slim and strange substance of the times and names." Albertine must search for an origin from the listing of names of those Chippewa who "in that first decade when people, squeezed westward, starving, came to the reservation to receive rations and then allotted land." Four Soul is the ancestor of Fleur; Albertine's traditional naming connects the lines of Kashpaws and Pillagers in a new tangle. With this naming, Erdrich resurrects the anguish of Chippewa people pushed out of their original land in the forced migration of the tribe.

In *The Beet Queen*, Mary Adare disconnects from her origin by willing herself to forget the loss of her mother, Adelaide, and her brothers: "I'd lost trust in the past. They were part of a fading pattern that was beyond understanding, and brought me no comfort." The mother's abandonment of her family causes Mary to develop an oddness that she recognizes in herself: "I said things too suddenly. I was pigheaded, bitter, moody, and had fits of unreasonable anger." Mary understands that her mother's flight from the Minneapolis Fairgrounds, the loss of her baby brother to a stranger, and the separation from Karl when the boxcar stops in Argus had affected her, creating a compulsion to clutch people to her, particularly Celestine James and her daughter, Dot Adare. Mary is condemned by her past to be a misfit.

Wallace Pfef, Celestine's neighbor, who helps to deliver Dot, connects his origin to a vegetable, the "raw white beet," that grew in the great Ruhr Valley from which his people came. The restlessness of the immigrant resonates in Wallace Pfef's family: "In America, we moved often, complaining that something was not quite right." Pfef finally settles down in Argus to belong to the "Chamber of Commerce, Sugar Beet Promoters, Optimists, Knights of Columbus, park board, and other organizations too numerous to mention." Wallace substitutes fraternal groups for family connections, and, for public consumption, he substitutes a picture of a woman bought at a Minnesota farm auction for a relationship with another human being. The picture serves to satisfy the curiosity of Argus residents who might wonder about his lack of interest in women. Wallace's identity as a homosexual would have placed him on the fringe of midwestern society in the 1930s; his identity as agriculture promoter would place him in the solid center. Sexually repressed, Wallace channels his energy into helping to parent Dot, another outlet to compensate for Karl Adare's sexual rejection of him. The fields of beets lead to the agribusiness of sugar refineries, and the North Dakota landscape of flowering beets fills Wallace Pfef's vision of the prairie.

For Erdrich the prairie with its vast space of land and sky is a homeplace that is imaged in her writing. The endless North Dakota fields of corn, wheat, soybeans, and flax viewed from her childhood home in Wahpeton are always in her mind's eye, directing her attention to the space above, as she noted in "Where I Ought to Be": "I often see this edge of town—the sky and its towering and shifting formations of clouds, that beautiful lighted emptiness—when I am writing."

Ten years later, in her home in the hills of New Hampshire, Erdrich's intense longing for the space of sky had not lessened. She wrote in *The Blue Jay's Dance:* "I want the clean line, the simple line, the clouds marching over it in feathered masses. I suffer from horizon sickness." The great nostalgia for open space, which she considers "both romantically German and pragmatically Ojibwa," informs Erdrich's writing. In the years between 1985, the date of her observation about the longing for place, and *The Blue Jay's Dance* in 1995, there has been no lessening of her identification with the Great Plains as home. Adapting to New England has meant substituting trees for sky; she says she has grown accustomed to the roaring of "thousands and millions of leaves brushing and touching one another," making do with a new landscape, finding a new way to be at home, far from the open space of North Dakota.

Space in Erdrich's novels can be liberating or threatening, and sometimes both at once. In *Love Medicine,* the vast space of the prairie means death for June Kashpaw. She moves across open fields, headed for home after the empty encounter with the mud engineer, Andy. Turning away from the dull orange glow of the oil town of Williston, North Dakota, June keeps going although, as her niece Albertine Johnson says later, "the heaviness in the air, the smell in the clouds," would have told her that a snowstorm was coming. June's death from exposure to cold on the prairie could represent a deliberate decision to end a life that was marked early on by abuse. Lucille Lazarre, in her alcoholic stupor, inflicts physical abuse, and her boyfriend, Leonard, rapes June.

The ambiguity surrounding June's decision to head for home in a snowstorm despite having a bus ticket, which remains throughout *Love Medicine,* suddenly comes clear in the chapter "June's Luck" in *The Bingo Palace.* The impossibility of escaping from the past erupts in June's flight into a space where she can escape from pain that rang everywhere:

> Then she was so small she was just a burning dot, a flung star moving, speeding through the blackness, the air, faster and faster and with no letup until she finally escaped into a part of her mind, where she made one promise before she went out. *Nobody ever hold me again.*

June's entire life turns on that promise. She cannot be held, as her husband, Gordie, knows, nor can she hold anyone else, as her son Lipsha struggles to understand. Lipsha learns that we hurt others as we have been hurt, that his mother's attempts to drown him represent a circular pattern: "I know that she did the same that was done to her—a young girl left out to live on the woods and survive on pine sap and leaves and buried roots.'' The reader, knowing the truth of June's past—that she was raped by her mother's boyfriend—can fill in the space of Lipsha's incomplete understanding. The reasons for June's inability to connect to others are fully understood by the reader but only partially understood by Lipsha.

In *Love Medicine,* June's turning toward home suggests flight from the oppression that has followed her unrelentingly, but it also allows for the possibility of renewal. The Easter season and the egg imagery contribute to the understanding of her transformation. Though she perishes in the cold of a prairie storm that left more snow than it had in forty years, ''June walked over it like water and came home.'' In a transcendence of body, June's spirit comes home to the reservation.

In another flight into space, Adelaide Adare in *The Beet Queen* turns away from her family, scattering her children—Mary, Karl, and a new baby, whom she had refused to name—in all directions. Wandering into the Orphans' Picnic, having had to leave their home when the man who supported them died in a grain-loading accident, the family comes to the grandstand where the Great Omar offers rides to those who want to take a chance, and Adelaide chooses to be one of them. Mary, who has been left to care for her brothers, cannot watch the plane's maneuvers but is alerted to catastrophe by the ever decreasing sound of the plane's engine: ''By the time I dared look into the sky, The Great Omar was flying steadily away from the fairgrounds with my mother.'' In an image reminiscent of June's self-reducing to a burning dot, the orphaned children's pain is represented by the airplane as a white dot, blending into the pale blue sky and vanishing. In retribution, Mary constructs a scene in which Omar, with fuel supply dwindling, must lighten the load of his plane and pushes Adelaide overboard to save himself. In Mary's fantasy,

Adelaide falls through the awful cold, but Mary is unrelenting: ''I had no love for her. That is why, by morning, I allowed her to hit the earth.''

In another leap through space, Karl Adare jumps from the boxcar after his encounter with Giles St. Ambrose and is released into a life of passive helplessness. Rescued by Fleur and nursed back to health, he is brought to the reservation and then to the convent, where the nuns take charge of him; they send him to Minneapolis, to the orphanage on the grounds of which he had been left by his mother. Karl's flight brings him back full circle. He is sent to the seminary, but his days as a priest are marked by rendezvous with ''thin hard hoboes who had slept in the bushes.'' Karl is a bisexual, and his relationship with Celestine James produces Dot, but he can never accept the role of father. Ungrounded so many times in his life, Karl is perpetually traveling in his car, living the life of a salesman always on the road.

In *The Bingo Palace,* Redford, Shawnee Ray Toose's son, experiences the sky threatening him with a frightening premonition of disaster. It comes in the form of a ''large thing made of metal with many barbed hooks, points, and drag chains on it, something like Grandma Zelda's potato peeler, only a giant one that rolled out of the sky, scraping clouds down with it and jabbing or crushing everyone that lay in its path on the ground.'' Left by his mother with his aunts, Mary Fred and Tammy Toose, Redford had been shocked awake by the terrible dream, which is translated into reality by the arrival of Zelda with a tribal police officer and a social worker, with papers to take Redford from his mother's sisters. Mary Fred delivers a blow with a butterfly buckle to Officer Pukwan's chin; in turn, she is knocked out by the butt of Pukwan's gun as she leaps into the air, then falls as if she had been running into the earth.

Flight to doom is countered by a flight that heightens self-knowledge in Dot Adare's ascent into the sky over the Argus fairgrounds. Her flight into space in the crop duster's plane begins as an impulsive escape from the smothering attention of would-be parents and her election as queen of the Beet Festival, contrived by Wallace Pfef. Outraged by his engineering her crowning as the queen of Argus' Beet Queen Festival, Dot soars into space in the crop duster's plane, where she becomes sick from the motion and shock of the dizzying distance from earth, and begs to be returned to land. When the pilot lands, Dot is surprised to find that no one has remained to find out what has become of her except her mother, Celestine, whom she sees as if for the first time: "Her skin is rough. Her whole face seems magnetized, like ore. Her deep brown eyes are circled with dark skin, but full of eagerness. In her eyes I see the force of her love." In returning to her mother, who waits for her on the ground, Dot sees the constancy of her mother's love amid the wreckage of her turbulent adolescence.

Despite tragic occurrences, Erdrich's novels are not tragedies. Somewhere between the edge of tragic events and annihilation there is a thin margin of survival where comedy erupts. In an interview with Bill Moyers, Erdrich notes that the one universal thing about Native Americans, tribe to tribe, may be survival humor. She explains that Indians have developed a humor that allows them to live with the most difficult events in their lives: "You have to be able to poke fun at people who are dominating your life and your family." In the underseam of life, sometimes reduced to a narrow space of existence, Indians must poke fun at themselves, too: "If we took ourselves too seriously in any way, I feel we would be overwhelmed." Twisting and turning on the borderline between two cultures, Indians choose humor as a way to endure.

In *Love Medicine,* the humor of language and situation that is rooted in human vanity seems to overflow in Nector Kashpaw, son of Margaret, husband of Marie, and lover of Lulu. Signed up for a movie right out of school in Flandreau, the Indian boarding school where he first met Lulu, he is to play the part of an Indian who falls off a horse and dies. His experience reinforces the popular conception of Indians initiated by General Custer and generally adopted by whites: the only good Indian is a dead Indian. Although he ultimately rejects that role, Nector says the offers keep coming to him. He is selected to model for a rich old woman who persuades him to forget his dignity: "I was paid by this woman a round two hundred dollars for standing stock still in a diaper." The resulting painting, *The Plunge of the Brave,* hanging in the State Capitol in Bismarck, officially expresses the dominant culture's view of Indians. It shows Nector "jumping off a cliff, naked of course, down into a rocky river. Certain death." Either way, movies or painting, Nector represents dead Indians. The painting becomes a kind of symbol for Indians as well. Lulu purchases a copy of the painting for her new apartment at the Senior Citizens, noting that everyone owned it, "whether they liked Kashpaw and wanted to venerate his youth, or did not like him and therefore made fun of his naked leap." The painting evokes widely varying attitudes, and comes to symbolize both white and Indian ambivalence.

Nector's offers ultimately teach him something. Out of humiliation comes the determination to survive. Nector vows to fool that pitiful old woman who painted his death in the plunge down to the rock-strewn stream: "I'd hold my breath when I hit and let the current pull me toward the surface, around jagged rocks. I wouldn't fight it, and in that way I'd get to shore," he imagines. Nector survives by letting the current take him where it will. He can handle only one thing at a time. He wants to sit against a tree and watch the cows, but he is drawn into tribal politics without his intention: "I had to speed where I was took." There is both humor and pathos in Nector's situation, split as he is between Lulu and Marie.

There is tender humor with an ironic turn in Nector's first encounter with Marie. In the comedy of a chance meeting, Nector loses his way, weakened by her "tight plush acceptance, graceful movements, little jabs that lead me underneath her skirt where she is slick, warm, silk." On his way to the convent, where he hopes to sell the two geese he and Eli have shot, Nector dreams of Lulu and his plans for meeting her that night. When Marie comes down the hill straight from her duel with Leopolda, her fork-stabbed hand wrapped in a pillowcase emblazoned with the initials SHC, and into Nector's path, he challenges her. His hasty observation of Marie leads him to think she must have stolen the sisters' linen, and he wonders, ironically, what else she may have hidden beneath her skirt. His calculations are way off. He misreads the signs of Marie's flight from the convent. Trapped by his desire to earn a possible reward from the nuns for returning stolen goods, perhaps a chalice, from Marie Lazarre, "the youngest daughter of horse-thieving drunks," Nector is caught by Marie, whose wounded hand he cannot let go. In their sexual encounter on the hill, in full view of the convent, Nector is bound to Marie. His plans to buy the French-style wedding band for Lulu are thwarted.

There is human comedy as well in Nector's midlife crisis. He contemplates the passing of time, the accumulation of babies that he and Marie have produced and taken in: "Seventeen Years of married life and come-and-go children." Suddenly aware of a diminishing self, Nector begins to think of Lulu. Enlisting her help to deliver commodity butter on the reservation, Nector is out-maneuvered once again by a woman. Lulu drives him up to the lookout in her Nash Ambassador Custom automobile, complete with air conditioning, where they resume a relationship broken off years before by Nector's marriage to Marie. Nector, "middle-aged butter mover," has somehow been transformed into "the young hard-muscled man who thrilled and sparked her so long ago," and not entirely by his own intent.

The love medicine of the Chippewa provides another humorous instance of human vanity in the hands of Lipsha Morrissey. In an interview with Jan George, Erdrich says that humor is a tribal trademark: "The Chippewa have the best sense of humor of any group of people I've ever known." In the depiction of Lipsha as the wise fool, Erdrich creates the would-be trickster, the trickster gone off the trickster's tangent, an even more ridiculous version of the mythical trickster.

Lipsha, like the original trickster from Chippewa myth, Naanabozho, who was cared for by his grandmother, Nokomis, is raised by his foster grandmother, Marie. As the son of Gerry Nanapush, he inherits the tricky heart that keeps him out of military service, but as modern version of trickster, Lipsha loses the touch. Many times he tries to use the gifts that he believes have come down to him but fails to carry out his healing power. In his practice of love medicine, he tries to bring Marie and Nector back together with the frozen heart of a turkey bought from the Red Owl grocery store and blessed by himself at the holy water font at the convent. When Nector chokes on the cooked heart and Marie collapses from the shock of Nector's death, Lipsha begins to gain an understanding of love, and comforts his grandmother by reassuring her that Nector loved her "over time and distance," but he died so quickly he never got the chance to tell her. Though his grandmother doesn't believe his explanation, she does believe in Lipsha. In that way Lipsha regains some belief in himself.

In *The Bingo Palace,* joining with Lyman Lamartine, Lipsha participates in a secularized version of the vision quest that parodies the sacred. His visions consist of Big Macs and the retreat of the Chippewa to their beginnings: "In my mind's eye I see us Chippewa jumping back into the Big Shell that spawned us." He dreams of eluding Lyman, he and Shawnee Ray and Redford sailing off in the shell, leaving Lyman, contender for Shawnee's affection and also Redford's father, to watch until they disappear into space. Alternating between bouts of loneliness and movie scenes replayed in his head, Lipsha ends his vision quest visited by a skunk that shuts down his senses and sends Xavier Toose, his instructor in the quest, into attacks of laughter.

Trickster prevails in all cultures. In the myths of the Chippewa, Manobozho is the chief trickster. His name has many variants—Naanabozho, Nanapush, Nanabush, and Wenebojo, to name a few. There are literally hundreds of stories about him. He is a complex being who was the youngest son of the union of Epingishmook, the West, and a virgin mother named Winonah. Left an orphan, he was brought up by his grandmother, Nokomis. According to Basil Johnston, Nanapush could be both foolish and wise; he was a teacher who instructed in the art of healing, and he possessed the greatest of human virtues: kindness. Although known as a peacemaker, he also has an evil side, being capable of deceit, trickery, and lewdness. Trickster can change shape, cross existing borders, and subvert existing systems. Erdrich incorporates the idea of trickster in several of her characters, Nanapush in *Tracks* being the most obvious. Gerry Nanapush, his grandson through Lulu, and Lulu herself qualify for trickster status as well.

According to Lulu, Gerry's delicate energy and capacity to change his shape testify that he is a Nanapush man, the son of trickster—whom she identifies as Old Man Pillager, her mother's cousin Moses—although he bears the name of Nanapush, self-appointed grandfather to Lulu, to whom he gave his name in baptism. As trickster, master subverter of systems, Gerry will not be contained in a white man's jail. Over and over again he breaks out of prison. According to Albertine, "He boasted that no steel or concrete shitbarn could hold a Chippewa, and he had eellike

properties in spite of his enormous size." Myth springs up around Gerry. Once he had squirmed into a six-foot-thick prison wall and vanished. In true trickster fashion, Gerry rubs his belly for luck and escapes, appearing at Dot Adare's door, giving her a less than lucky assignment: "Hiding a six-foot-plus, two-hundred-and-fifty-pound Indian in the middle of a town that doesn't like Indians in the first place isn't easy." In another escape, he folds himself into the trunk of the Firebird bought by King with June's life-insurance money, and is rescued by Lipsha as his breath is about to give out.

Trickster's appetite is notoriously voracious. Gerry follows the pattern as he consumes "stacks of pork chops, whole fryers, thick steaks," tossing the bones out the window, heedless of the neighbors, who eventually complain and bring the law to his door. In her daydreams, Albertine pictures Dot and Gerry in Dot's trailer house, both hungry: "Heads swaying, clasped hands swinging between them like hooded trunks, they moved through the kitchen feeding casually from boxes and bags on the counters, like ponderous animals alone in the forest."

Possessing trickster's sexual prowess, Gerry manages to have sexual relations with Dot in a far corner of a state prison visiting room, away from the closed-circuit television camera's lens: "Through a hole ripped in her pantyhose and a hole ripped in Gerry's jeans they somehow managed to join and, miraculously, to conceive." Albertine imagines the two of them in the trailer settling themselves on Dot's king-size bed: "They rubbed together, locking and unlocking their parts. They set the trailer rocking on its cement-block-and-plywood foundation and the tremors spread, causing cups to fall, plates to shatter in the china hutches of their more established neighbors." The baby that comes of their union feeds voraciously, too, nursing for hours, refusing to be satisfied with pacifiers.

Like trickster, Gerry has a penchant for getting

into trouble. When he is caught on the Pine Ridge Reservation, he resists arrest, shooting and killing a state trooper. He is sent to the control unit of the federal prison in Marion, Illinois, "where no touching is allowed, where the voice is carried by phone, glances meet through sheets of Plexiglas, and no children will ever be engendered." Still, Gerry always manages to escape, usually when he is being transferred to another institution.

Constantly defying social order, in *The Bingo Palace* Gerry finds the trickster's luck again when, with some weighty assistance from Lulu's influence on the tribe, he is transferred from Illinois to a maximum-security prison in Minnesota. He survives a plane crash during a snowstorm, and even sends a call for assistance to his son, Lipsha, who steals a getaway car with him. In the chase over the snow, reminiscent of the snowstorm in which June had perished, Gerry, following a vision of June in her blue Firebird, leaves the road. Lipsha watches his father go to June: "It isn't that he doesn't care for me, I know that, it's just that his own want is too deep to resist." In this case, trickster escapes myth and enters the realm of human need.

Gerry's mother, Lulu, as female trickster and strong woman, possesses personal power and transcends conventional expectations. In the traditional dance and trill that she exhibits for the news cameras, Lulu demonstrates that she knows how to subvert the system. She leads the federal marshals first one way and then another as they question her about where her son has gone. Having taken him over the Canadian border, Lulu feigns confusion and memory loss, even fainting, proving more than a match for the investigators, who "spent a long time questioning a fish in the river, they spent a longer time talking to a turtle in its shell, they tried to intimidate a female badger guarding the mouth of its den and then, to fool an old lady coyote who trotted wide of the marks her pups had left." In true trickster fashion, Lulu leads first one way and then another, finally triumphing in gained time that allows Gerry to make his escape and in her victorious show of ceremony in a grand exit in full Chippewa regalia.

Lulu's independence of mind and body resonates in a poem from *Jacklight,* "The Lady in the Pink Mustang." Like the lady in the pink Mustang, Lulu has established a place for herself where she can move in either direction:

> She is always at that place, seen from behind,
> motionless, torn forward, living in a zone
> all her own. It is like she has burned right through
>   time,
> the brand, the mark, owning the woman who bears
>   it.

Lulu owns herself in her relationships with assorted husbands and lovers. Lulu explains in *Love Medicine* that she "was in love with the whole world and all that lived in its rainy arms."

Lulu is as audacious as the blue jay, in *The Blue Jay's Dance,* that defies the attacking hawk, continuing to dance, "hopping forward, hornpiping up and down with tiny leaps, all of its feathers on end to increase its size." Fierce and shrieking, the jay amazes and confuses the hawk into a puzzled retreat. In a similar outrage, in *Love Medicine,* Lulu confronts the tribe as business interests move to take her land. She threatens to name all the fathers of her children unless she is granted her home and the land it stands on. When the house is burned, Lulu and her boys camp out on the land until the tribe builds a government crackerbox house for them on a "strip of land rightfully repurchased from a white farmer." In their common defiance, Lulu, the blue jay, and the Chippewa face the enemy and endure. In refusing to move from her land, Lulu reminds the reader of the U.S. government policy that sent Chippewas from east of the Great Lakes westward to the prairie in the 1800s.

* * *

Erdrich's women are powerful. Some, like Marie Kashpaw, turn experience into helping and healing—themselves and others; others, like her daughter Zelda, resist experience and defer healing. There is transforming energy in Marie's raising a family of five children, molding Nector into tribal chairman, and proving to the world that she has risen above the ''dirty'' Lazarres from whom she came. Marie knows evil, for she has faced it in the drunken lives of her mother and father and in the fraud of Sister Leopolda. She meets evil in what happened to her sister's child, June, who came to her hardly able to stand up, ''starved bones, a shank of black strings,'' a creature of the woods who ''had sucked on pine sap and grazed grass and nipped buds like a deer.''

In *Love Medicine,* Marie's ambition takes her first to the convent, where she intends to be worshiped by the nuns: ''I'd be carved in pure gold. With ruby lips. And my toenails would be little pink ocean shells, which they would have to stoop down off their high horse to kiss.'' Escaping from Leopolda with a burned back and a pierced hand, Marie uses that experience to mold Nector into tribal chairman. Peeling potatoes, scrubbing floors, and churning butter, Marie plots Nector's future, relying on her own strength: ''I don't pray. When I was young, I vowed I never would be caught begging God. If I want something I get it for myself.'' In claiming a respected role for herself in the community, Marie has transformed herself from a ''dirty'' Lazarre into a proud mother and the wife of a tribal official. In the process of self-transformation, she has learned to empathize. Even though she has barely enough to feed her children, she takes in June, just as she would later take in June's son, Lipsha. She can feel pity for Leopolda although it is mixed with a need to prove that she has not been condemned to the life of raising Indian brats that Leopolda had predicted.

As Marie helps others to survive, she too gets past the hurt of being left by Nector for Lulu. When Zelda brings her the note Nector left under the sugar jar, telling her he loves Lulu, Marie feels powerless, not even recognizing her own response, which is so far beyond anger. She describes a feeling of transcendence, of not being in her own body. Then she regains herself by falling back on potato peeling—''enough . . . to feed every man, woman, child of the Chippewas''—and floor waxing. Marie steps away from the sting, overcoming the hurt of being abandoned. In her vision of herself she is still Marie, Star of the Sea. She would be there intact when they stripped the wax off her floor! Returning the note to the table, this time placing it under the salt, Marie lets Nector wonder about her reaction to his announcement of love for Lulu. Did she get the note? Does she know? Marie never tells. She uses what she learned from her experience with Leopolda: ''I put my hand through what scared him. I held it out there for him. And when he took it with all the strength of his arms, I pulled him in.''

In *The Bingo Palace,* although Marie's daughter Zelda has inherited her mother's energy, it is without transforming power. Lipsha dreads the single-minded control that he feels surrounding him in Zelda's presence: ''When women age into their power, no wind can upset them, no hand turn aside their knowledge; no fact can deflect their point of view. It is like that with the woman I was raised to think of as sister and call aunt in respect.'' Zelda, who needs outlets for her enormous supply of energy, turns her talents to engineering the marriage of Lyman Lamartine and Shawnee Ray Toose. She insinuates herself into their lives by caring for their son, Redford. Lipsha knows that he figures in Zelda's calculations as a device to get the wedding date moved up. He is to be the designated third element—a catalyst that will bring about the union of Shawnee Ray and Lyman. Any excess energy Zelda has, she expends caring for Redford, making sure he does not go back to Shawnee's sisters, whom she considers unfit to raise children.

Zelda has cultivated a history of goodness that begins with giving up Xavier Toose, whom she had resisted despite loving him ''with a secret unkilled feeling stronger than acids, unquenched, a coal fire set inside of her and running through each vein with a steady heat.'' Lighting candles to the saints to help her overcome her passion for Xavier Toose, Zelda refused him regularly in order to save herself for a white man who would take her away from the reservation to the city. She diverted the energy containing her passion to marry Swede Johnson, from off reservation. Their child Albertine arrived prematurely, and Swede went AWOL from the army, never to be seen again. Repressing her sexuality, Zelda subsequently channeled her energy into good works to build a public reputation. She intended never to be subject to love.

Remembering the fire that her father, Nector, started at Lulu's house, Zelda vows to exist without love ''in the dark cell of her body.'' Reminiscent of the crazed self-mortification of Pauline in *Tracks,* she becomes ''capable of denying herself everything tender, unspoken, sweet, generous, and desperate.'' And after thirty years' abstinence from feeling, Zelda feels desire rock her body, desire that drives her to Xavier Toose.

Albertine, child of Zelda's loveless marriage, bears the scars of her mother's life. She understands that she will need enormous support from a husband or lover because she has been emotionally deprived. Restlessly ambitious, Albertine finds power in learning to heal in the way that she herself needs healing. Deciding to become a doctor has enabled Albertine to gain perspective on her own experience. She remembers crawling under the quilts of her mother's bed but never daring to ''grab her tight.'' Once, running away from home to the city, Albertine lay in bed with a man she hated; later she comes to realize ''that the desperation with which she gave in to his touch has been no more than a child's wish to crawl closer to the side of her mother.'' Albertine uses her knowledge of her own need to point out the needs of others. She reminds her mother of Shawnee's right to arrange her life as she wishes—to go back to school and take Redford with her. She lets Lipsha know that he must straighten out his own life before he involves Shawnee in it.

Mothering is an important issue in Erdrich's life and her art. She and Michael Dorris have three daughters and they have adopted three children as well, according to her ''Dedication and Household Map'' in *The Blue Jay's Dance.* Erdrich is very concerned with what it means to be a parent, and this book is intended to add to her daughters' memories. She considers mothering ''a subtle art whose rhythm we collect and learn, as much from one another as from instinct.'' Mothers collectively form a sacred alliance—a group that identifies the struggle common to all mothers. Outwardly they look secure in their knowledge of mothering, but as she talks with other mothers, Erdrich comes to recognize her own daily task of hanging on ''to the tiger tail of children's, husband's, parents', and siblings' lives while at the same time saving a little core of self in our own, just enough to live by.''

One measure of women's power in Erdrich's novels is expressed in the capacity to mother. Denied or misdirected sexual energy results in unsuccessful mothering. For example, Zelda's passionless life draws out Albertine's need. Pauline Puyat's loveless union with Napoleon Morrissey brings forth Marie, a daughter whom she finds repulsive and whom she gives to someone else to raise.

In *The Bingo Palace,* June could not be a mother to him, Lipsha reasons, because her own pain was too deep. As he contemplates how he was saved from drowning, he reaches back to the darkness in the bottom of the slough, where he feels his mother's touch and connects with the truth of her action in releasing him to the water.

> Pain comes to us from deep back, from where it grew in the human body. Pain sucks more pain into it, we don't know why. It lives, and we harbor its weight. When the worst comes, we will not act the opposite. We will do what we were taught, we who learnt our lessons in the dead light. We pass them on. We hurt, and hurt others, in a circular motion.

June, denied love by her own mother, has refused Marie's mother love; she chooses instead to live with Eli, who could chew the pine sap, as she had done. She cannot give emotionally to her husband, Gordie, or to her sons, Lipsha and King. The hurt is passed on.

Fleur's mothering loses strength when she fears her personal power has dried up. She sends Lulu away to boarding school, an act that alienates daughter from mother. Lulu laments her loss of a mother: "I never grew from the curve of my mother's arms. I still wanted to anchor myself against her. But she had tore herself away from the run of my life like a riverbank. She had vanished, a great surrounding shore, leaving me to spill out alone." As she becomes more like Fleur, her need for her grows, especially when Nector begins to look at her. In the search for a mother, Lulu goes to Moses Pillager, Fleur's cousin, from whom she learns both the bitterness and the sweetness of love. Still, the rift between Lulu and Fleur never heals, the price of leaving a child retold to Lulu by Nanapush in *Tracks.*

Despite not being mothered, both Marie and Lulu know how to be mothers. Brought into the world by cooking spoons and quickly given over to Bernadette Morrissey, who turns her over to the Lazarres, Marie raises her own children, laments the ones that die, and takes in Lipsha and June. She becomes the solid rock, the matriarch of an expanding family. Although Lulu's boys are not the center of her life, she keeps them together on her plot of land, watches them grow up, and is proud of them.

In *The Beet Queen* mothering is foregrounded in the contrast between a woman who has been mothered successfully and one who has been abandoned by her mother. Celestine James speaks of her mother's dying early and being cared for by her older sister Isabel, who supports Celestine and her brother Russell until she "married into a Sioux family and moved down to South Dakota." Celestine is able to raise Dot, devoting time and energy to her care despite the trying circumstance of dealing with Mary Adare, a motherless woman who wants to intervene in Dot's upbringing.

In Erdrich's novels, women become mothers to other women through the common experience of birthing. The power they hold over life establishes a strong kinship among women. Margaret Kashpaw's offices at Lulu's birth secure a bond with Fleur, whose delivery of Lulu is precipitated by the sudden appearance of a bear. The suggestion is that Margaret earned her traditional name, Rushes Bear, by confronting the bear face-to-face, thereby linking her to the power of the natural world. In the expanded version of *Love Medicine,* female connections empower and comfort Marie as she gives birth to her last child assisted by Margaret and Fleur, whose knowledge of the old medicines is needed to help direct Marie's difficult labor. Women adapt to each other's need in Erdrich's novels.

Adapting successfully means finding a new way to live without giving up the self, but it can also mean giving up the self. In *Tracks,* Nanapush survives disease and starvation by talking, by telling a story. When he was the last one of his family left during the year of the sickness, he kept talking: "Death could not get a word in edgewise, grew discouraged, and traveled on." So he joins with Fleur and Margaret, putting together a family from the remnants of families. He thinks like animals; he can track deer back to where they were born. He coaches Eli in the hunt for deer and in the pursuit of Fleur. He survives the invasion of the land around Lake Matchimanito because he accepts the fact that the land will be sold. He understands the transience of power:

> Power dies, power goes under and gutters out, ungraspable. It is momentary, quick of flight and liable to deceive. As soon as you rely on the possession it is gone. Forget that it ever existed, and it returns. I never made the mistake of thinking that I owned my own strength, that was my secret. And so I never was alone in my failures. I was never to blame entirely when all was lost, when my desperate cures had no effect on the suffering of those I loved.

Like Nanapush, whom she calls Uncle, Lulu survives because she has the same transcending power. In *Love Medicine,* she admits to crying the only tears that she would ever cry in her life on the school bus that took her away from the reservation. Lulu understands the encumbrances of the body: "How come we've got these bodies? They are frail supports for what we feel. There are times I get so hemmed in by my arms and legs I look forward to getting past them. As though death will set me free like a traveling cloud." Lulu is able to transcend the past in her relationship with Marie. She discovers the way another woman feels for the first time. In bathing Lulu's eyes with drops, Marie puts the tears back. They mourn Nector together.

Critical appraisal of Erdrich's work has ranged from open acceptance of its innovative form and testament to the Chippewa tribal people to guarded concern about narrative method and suspicion regarding the further marginalization of Native Americans. With its multiple-narrator format, *Love Medicine* is considered by many reviewers to be strongly connected to the oral tradition of storytelling. The multivoiced structure and the involvement of the reader in reconciling the often competing versions of the stories have stimulated considerable critical response. In its departure from the pattern of other contem-

porary Native American novels, *Love Medicine* has been noted for its concentration on community gossip instead of on the oral tradition and ritual associated with novels like N. Scott Momaday's *House Made of Dawn* and Leslie Marmon Silko's *Ceremony.* Instability of family, a dominant theme in both *Love Medicine* and *The Beet Queen,* begins in *Tracks.* The fluctuation of the term "family" is considered by Linda Ainsworth to be an apt metaphor for *Love Medicine,* and it is perpetuated in the novels that follow.

There are both speaking and nonspeaking voices in Erdrich's novels. Named narrators alternate with unidentified third-person narrators, and, in the case of *The Bingo Palace,* a community chorus. Stories change as tellers change. There are no narrators privileged to tell an authentic version of the story. Time is not always chronological; events loop around and fall back on themselves in unpredictable patterns. The novels speak to each other; the reader must play a role in the connecting of story lines. In the expanded version of *Love Medicine,* Erdrich forges the links that align events and develop character to bring the novels to the status of epic.

Tracks employs a dual narrator structure and a linear chronology. Nanapush and Pauline challenge one another's authority, leaving the reader to piece the story together. They agree only on what they have seen of the crazed behavior of creatures driven to the edge of life. Nanapush describes the buffalo dwindling, feeding on each other's flesh, and Pauline reports the same behavior in human beings crowding the new road of death, their numbers dwindling from influenza and consumption. They agree on the decimation of the tribe.

Love Medicine in its first version has seven named narrators: Marie, Nector, Albertine, Lulu, Lyman, Lipsha, and Howard Kashpaw. An unnamed teller recounts the story of June's death in the opening chapter. Another objective narrator tells the story of Lulu's eight sons. The middle chapter, "A Bridge," relates Albertine and Henry Lamartine's meetings in Fargo, and in the chapter "Crown of Thorns," another third-person narrator chronicles Gordie Kashpaw's hallucinations about his wife, June. All the narrators contribute some information about June, but Marie Kashpaw, Gordie, Albertine, and Lipsha are the most concerned about the meaning of her life and her place in the family.

In the revision of *Love Medicine* (1993), Erdrich clarified the chain of events that occurred when Nector met Marie on her way down the hill from the convent. She did not intend that their sexual encounter be interpreted as a rape, as some readers had done. When Marie tells Nector that she has had better, Nector's words indicate that no force has been used: "I know that isn't true because we haven't done anything yet. She just doesn't know what comes next."

There are four new chapters in the expanded version, each of which helps to make needed connections among the novels. "The Island," narrated by Lulu, gives her reaction to Marie's marriage to Nector, and her return to the reservation from boarding school. In a section added to "The Beads," Marie becomes connected to Rushes Bear when she assists at the birth of Marie's last child. Marie's role as mother is further developed in "Resurrection," in which she deals with Gordie's advanced alcoholic hallucinating. This chapter also provides a sense of the futility of Gordie and June's marriage. The chapters "The Tomahawk Factory" and "Lyman's Luck" give more dimension to Lyman's character, especially with regard to his devastation at his brother's death, and also set up his role as gambling entrepreneur in *The Bingo Palace*.

There is a more definite pattern to the narrative structure in *The Beet Queen,* in that the chapters are narrated by the main characters in the first person and their narrations are followed by a neutral consciousness that has gained entry into the consciousness of each character. The novel begins with a third-person account of Mary and Karl's separation on a cold spring morning in 1932, followed by Mary's full first-person account of how the family was left by Adelaide. Establishing the pattern of narration, the third part of the 1932 chapter is related by an impersonal third-person narrator who tells what happened to Karl when he was cut loose from the family. In this way a community of voices speak as one and as individuals.

In a departure from the alternating narrator pattern, *The Bingo Palace* contains ten chapters narrated by Lipsha Morrissey. There is a community chorus that speaks in the first person plural, and there is an account of the fortunes of Lyman, Fleur, June, Gerry, Albertine, Shawnee, Zelda, and Redford, as well as Lulu, rendered by an omniscient narrator. The novel begins and ends with the community voices, undesignated in time.

Louise Erdrich resists being labeled a Native American writer although she declares in an interview with Hertha Wong that it is very important to her "to be known as having been from the Turtle Mountain Chippewa and from North Dakota." Whether she writes about Indians or their white neighbors, Erdrich strives to depict human transcendence in all four novels as well as in her nonfiction. She is concerned about showing that tribal culture endures in new forms even as Indians are pushed to the margins of society by the dominant culture. Community voices join to tell the remembered stories. The loss of tribal land chronicled in *Tracks* has not diminished personal identity and human connections. That human beings endure despite holocaust is the overriding message in all of Erdrich's work.

Trickster goes on defying social order just as he did in Ojibwa myth. Mothers succeed and fail as they have always done. For every June and Adelaide, there is a Marie and Celestine. The absurdity of existence spills over in the trials of

Lipsha, the wise fool. Through it all, Indians have not been annihilated—that is Erdrich's message of hope.

Selected Bibliography

WORKS OF LOUISE ERDRICH

FICTION

Love Medicine. New York: Holt, Rinehart and Winston, 1984. New and exp. ed. New York: Henry Holt, 1993.

The Beet Queen. New York: Henry Holt, 1986.

Tracks. New York: Henry Holt, 1988.

The Crown of Columbus. New York: HarperCollins, 1991. Written with Michael Dorris.

Route Two. Northridge, Cal.: Lord John Press, 1991. Written with Michael Dorris.

The Bingo Palace. New York: HarperCollins, 1994.

NONFICTION

Imagination. Westerville, Ohio: Charles E. Merrill, 1981.

"Where I Ought to Be: A Writer's Sense of Place." *New York Times Book Review,* July 28, 1985, pp. 1, 23–24.

The Blue Jay's Dance: A Birth Year. New York: HarperCollins, 1995.

POETRY

Jacklight. New York: Holt, Rinehart and Winston, 1984.

Baptism of Desire. New York: Harper & Row, 1989.

CRITICAL STUDIES

REVIEWS

Ainsworth, Linda. Review of *Love Medicine. Studies in American Indian Literatures,* 9:24–29 (Winter 1985).

Banks, Russell. "Border Country." Review of *The Beet Queen. Nation,* November 1, 1986, pp. 460–463.

Bennett, Sarah. Review of *The Bingo Palace. Studies in American Indian Literatures,* 6:83–88 (Fall 1994).

———. Review of *Love Medicine: New and Expanded Version. Studies in American Indian Literatures,* 7:112–118 (Spring 1995).

Bruckner, D. J. R. Review of *Love Medicine. New York Times,* December 20, 1984, C21.

Jahner, Elaine. Review of *Love Medicine. Parabola: The Magazine of Myth and Tradition,* 10:96, 98, 100 (Summer 1985).

———. Review of *Jacklight. Studies In American Indian Literatures,* 9:29–34 (Winter 1985).

Kinney, Jeanne. Review of *Love Medicine. Best Sellers,* 44:324–325 (December 1984).

Lewis, Robert W. Review of *Love Medicine. American Indian Culture and Research Journal,* 9, no. 4:113–116 (1985).

Messud, Claire. "Redeeming the Tribe." A Review of *The Bingo Palace. Times Literary Supplement,* June 17, 1994, p. 23.

Nelson, John S. "*Beat Queen* Traces Delicate Web of Family Ties." *Wichita* (Kansas) *Eagle Beacon,* October 5, 1986, p. WE6.

Owens, Louis. "Acts of Recovery: The American Indian Novel in the 80s." Essay review of *The Beet Queen. Western American Literature,* 22:53–57 (May 1987).

Portles, Marco. "People with Holes in Their Lives." Review of *Love Medicine. New York Times Book Review,* December 23, 1984, p. 6.

Sands, Kathleen M. Review of *Love Medicine. Studies in American Indian Literatures,* 9:12–24 (Winter 1985).

Silko, Leslie Marmon. "Here's an Odd Artifact for the Fairy-Tale Shelf." Review of *The Beet Queen. Impact/Albuquerque Journal Magazine,* October 7, 1986, pp. 10–11. Reprinted in *Studies in American Indian Literatures,* 10:178–184 (Fall 1986).

Simon, Linda. "Small Gestures: Large Patterns." Review of *The Beet Queen. Commonweal,* October 24, 1986, pp. 565–566.

Strouse, Jean. Review of *Tracks. New York Times Book Review,* October 2, 1988, pp. 40–42.

Tyler, Anne. "After *Love Medicine,* a Still Better Novel from Erdrich." Review of *The Beet Queen.* (Raleigh, N.C.) *News and Observer,* August 31, 1986, p. 4D.

Vecsey, Christopher. "Revenge of the Chippewa

Witch.'' Review of *Tracks. Commonweal,* November 4, 1988, pp. 596–98.

CRITICISM

Bevis, William. ''Native American Novels: Homing In.'' In *Recovering the Word: Essays on Native American Literature.* Edited by Brian Swann and Arnold Krupat. Berkeley: University of California Press, 1987. Pp. 580–620.

Castillo, Susan Pérez. ''Postmodernism, Native American Literature and the Real: The Silko–Erdrich Controversy.'' *Massachusetts Review,* 32:285–294 (Summer 1991).

Flavin, Louise. ''Louise Erdrich's *Love Medicine:* Loving over Time and Distance.'' *Critique* 31:55–64 (Fall 1989).

———. ''Gender Construction Amid Family Dissolution in Louise Erdrich's *The Beet Queen.*'' *Studies in American Indian Literatures,* 7:17–24 (Summer 1995).

Gleason, William. '' 'Her Laugh an Ace': The Function of Humor in Louise Erdrich's *Love Medicine.*'' *American Indian Culture and Research Journal,* 11, no. 3:51–73 (1987).

Harris, Patricia, and David Lyon. ''The Fine Art of Collaboration.'' *Boston Globe Magazine,* November 15, 1987, pp. 58–62.

Lincoln, Kenneth. '' 'Bring Her Home': Louise Erdrich.'' In his *Indi'n Humor: Bicultural Play in Native America.* New York: Oxford University Press, 1993. Pp. 205–253.

Magalaner, Marvin. ''Louise Erdrich: Of Cars, Time, and the River.'' In *American Women Writing Fiction: Memory, Identity, Family, Space.* Edited by Mickey Pearlman. Lexington: University Press of Kentucky, 1989. Pp. 95–112.

McKenzie, James. ''Lipsha's Good Road Home: The Revival of Chippewa Culture in *Love Medicine.*'' *American Indian Culture and Research Journal,* 10, no. 3:53–63 (1986).

Peterson, Nancy. ''History, Postmodernism, and Louise Erdrich's *Tracks.*'' *Publications of the Modern Language Association,* 109:982–994 (October 1994).

Rainwater, Catherine. ''Reading between Worlds: Narrativity in the Fiction of Louise Erdrich.'' *American Literature,* 62:405–420 (September 1990).

Silberman, Robert. ''Opening the Text: *Love Medicine* and the Return of the Native American Woman.'' In *Narrative Chance: Postmodern Discourse on Na-* *tive American Literatures.* Edited by Gerald Vizenor. Albuquerque: University of New Mexico Press, 1989. Pp. 101–120.

Slack, John S. ''The Comic Savior: The Dominance of the Trickster in Louise Erdrich's *Love Medicine.*'' *North Dakota Quarterly,* 61:118–129 (Summer 1993).

Woodward, Pauline G. *New Tribal Forms: Community in Louise Erdrich's Fiction.* Ph.D. dissertation, Tufts University, 1991. Ann Arbor, Mich.: Copyright, 1991. Order number 9126146.

———. ''Chance in *The Beet Queen:* New Ways to Find a Family.'' *ARIEL: A Review of International English Literature,* 26, no. 2:109–127 (April 1995).

STUDIES OF THE CHIPPEWA

Camp, Gregory S. ''Working Out Their Own Salvation: The Allotment of Land in Severalty and the Turtle Mountain Chippewa Band, 1870–1920,'' *American Indian Culture and Research Journal,* 14, no. 2:19–38 (1990).

Densmore, Frances. *Chippewa Customs.* Washington D.C.: U.S. Government Printing Office, 1929. New York: Johnson Reprint, 1970.

Helbig, Alethea K. *Nanabozhoo: Giver of Life.* Brighton, Mich.: Green Oak, 1987.

Johnston, Basil. *Ojibway Ceremonies.* Lincoln: University of Nebraska Press, 1982.

Schneider, Mary Jane. *North Dakota Indians: An Introduction.* Dubuque, Iowa: Kendall, Hunt, 1986.

Vizenor, Gerald. *The Everlasting Sky: New Voices from the People Named the Chippewa.* New York: Crowell-Collier, 1972.

———. *Interior Landscapes: Autobiographies, Myths, and Metaphors.* Minneapolis: University of Minnesota Press, 1990.

INTERVIEWS

Bonetti, Kay. *Interview with Louise Erdrich.* American Prose Library, 1986. Audiotape, fifty minutes.

Bruchac, Joseph. ''Whatever Is Really Yours: An Interview with Louise Erdrich.'' In his *Survival This Way: Interviews with American Indian Poets.* Tucson: Sun Tracks/University of Arizona Press, 1987. Pp. 73–86.

Chavkin, Nancy Feyl, and Allan Chavkin. ''An Interview with Louise Erdrich.'' In *Conversations with Louise Erdrich & Michael Dorris.* Edited by Allan Chavkin and Nancy Feyl Chavkin. Jackson: University Press of Mississippi, 1994. Pp. 220–253.

Coltelli, Laura. ''Louise Erdrich and Michael Dorris.'' In her *Winged Words: Native American Writers Speak.* Lincoln: University of Nebraska Press, 1990. Pp. 41–52.

George, Jan. ''Interview with Louise Erdrich.'' *North Dakota Quarterly,* 53:240–246 (Spring 1985).

Moyers, Bill. ''Louise Erdrich and Michael Dorris.'' In *Bill Moyers' World of Ideas.* Audiotape transcript. New York: Journal Graphics, November 14, 1988.

Pearlman, Mickey. ''Louise Erdrich.'' In *Inter/View: Talks With America's Writing Women.* Edited by Mickey Pearlman and Katharine Usher Henderson. Lexington: University Press of Kentucky, 1990. Pp. 143–148.

Wong, Hertha D. ''An Interview with Louise Erdrich and Michael Dorris.'' *North Dakota Quarterly,* 55:196–218 (Winter 1987).

—PAULINE GROETZ WOODWARD

William Gaddis

1922—

ALTHOUGH HE PUBLISHED only four novels prior to 1995, William Gaddis achieved the critical status of a major writer. His first book, *The Recognitions* (1955), remains one of the most widely discussed and acclaimed works of postwar fiction, while his more recent work, which began to appear in 1975 after a twenty-year hiatus, extended his range and consolidated his reputation as one of our foremost satirical novelists. His brilliant ear for dialogue, his grasp of the complexities of contemporary life, and his distinctive use of ironic drama made him an attractive model for younger fiction writers, including Joseph McElroy and Thomas Pynchon (whose *V.* [1963] and *Gravity's Rainbow* [1973] surely owe a great deal to the intricate speech rhythms and black humor of *The Recognitions*).

Gaddis has generally refrained from autobiographical commentary because he is by nature a private person and because he feels that "one thing said leaves others equally significant unsaid." The outline of his life before the publication of *The Recognitions* is simple enough and appears in the introduction to John Kuehl and Steven Moore's *In Recognition of William Gaddis* (1984). William Thomas Gaddis was born in Manhattan on December 29, 1922; an only child, he lived on Long Island until he was five. His family owned property in Massapequa, which would later provide the shabby-genteel setting for the Bast residence in *J R* (1975) and the Crease house in *A Frolic of His Own* (1994). The boarding school Gaddis then attended for eight years in Berlin, Connecticut, is described in *J R* by Jack Gibbs: "A place up, small school nobody's ever heard of in Connecticut up near Hartford, probably not even there any ..." The loneliness Gibbs mentions may derive from Gaddis' own experience: "—End of the day alone on that train, lights coming on in those little Connecticut towns stop and stare out at an empty street corner dry cheese sandwich charge you a dollar wouldn't even put butter on it." Gaddis attended public school for the eighth grade and went to high school on Long Island, where like Wyatt Gwyon in *The Recognitions* he contracted erythema grave, a disease the curing of which led to a kidney disorder, keeping him out of World War II. He entered Harvard in 1941, but dropped out for a year because of the kidney problem; in 1943 he joined the *Harvard Lampoon* staff and edited the publication, later becoming its president. His publications in the *Lampoon* constitute a long and varied list, including film reviews, fiction, essays, plays, and verse parodies. Though little of this work displays any sign of Gaddis' virtuosity as a mature writer, the *Lampoon* provided him with an opportunity to test his range, voice, and interests.

In 1945 Gaddis got into trouble with the Cambridge police, and his name appeared in the paper. Consequently, a dean told him to resign from the college, so he left without earning a degree. During his brief postwar residence in Greenwich Village that followed, Gaddis entered the world of artists, writers, and critics, gathering material he would work into his first novel and discovering what would become topics in his work: the failure of the artist to portray America adequately, and the failure of America to support and appreciate its artists. After more than a year working as a fact checker at the *New Yorker*, he traveled to Mexico, Panama, and Costa Rica before going back to New York in 1948. After a brief stay and disappointing love affair with the painter Sheri Martinelli, he left in frustration for Europe and North Africa. In Spain, he met Robert Graves and read *The White Goddess* (1948); in Paris, he wrote radio programs for UNESCO and a brief article titled "Stop Player. Joke No. 4" for the *Atlantic*. He returned to New York in 1951.

During these busy years of self-exile he managed to write most of *The Recognitions*, beginning with a brief sketch written when he first returned to New York. A draft of the second chapter of the novel appeared in the first issue of *New World Writing* in April 1952. In New York, Gaddis wrote for a government publication until receiving a contract and an advance for *The Recognitions*. Near Montgomery, New York, Gaddis spent the winter of 1952–1953 completing the first draft. After another winter of revision, *The Recognitions* was accepted at Harcourt, Brace, shepherded by Robert Giroux through the editing process, and finally published on March 10, 1955. It received more than fifty reviews, but only two or three appreciated the novel's magnitude and power. (Gaddis would later parody some of the more inept reviews in *J R*.) Despite the efforts of dedicated readers like "Jack Green," a pseudonymous amateur journalist who

devoted three issues of his magazine to examining the foolish reviews of *The Recognitions,* the novel nearly disappeared into obscurity.

Though decidedly not an autobiographical novel, and though Gaddis has said, "The question of autobiographical sources in fiction has always seemed to me one of the more tiresome going," *The Recognitions* draws upon actual events and people, including the author. In the summer of 1948, Gaddis habitually wore a white Panama suit, as Otto Pivner does, and he traveled for two years in Spain, as Reverend Gwyon does. He also used Martinelli as a model for Esme.

The Recognitions takes its title from the third-century *Clementine Recognitions,* which has been called the first Christian novel, according to Gaddis in the Abádi-Nagy interview, adding, "(I remember thinking mine was going to be the last one)." Gaddis' first novel is encyclopedic in scope, densely textured, and inexhaustibly interesting. An outline of the plot, however helpful, cannot begin to convey the density and power of the work, but it does suggest the breadth of Gaddis' thematic grasp. *The Recognitions* opens soon after World War I when Reverend Gwyon and his wife, Camilla, after six years of marriage, leave their young son, Wyatt, at home in a New England small town and sail from Boston to Spain on vacation. On shipboard, Camilla, stricken with appendicitis, dies when Frank Sinisterra, a counterfeiter posing as a ship's surgeon, clumsily operates on her (for which he is sentenced to prison). Alone in Spain, where he has buried his wife in the cemetery of San Zwingli, Reverend Gwyon, after various travels, enters the Franciscan Real Monasterio de Nuestra Señora de la Otra Vez. There he falls ill and hallucinates the touch of his dead wife.

Back in New England the following spring, Reverend Gwyon, his sister, May, and Wyatt, now four, resume their lives. Aunt May is a religious fanatic who cannot understand her brother's scholarly vagaries or her nephew's stubborn individualism. As the years pass, Wyatt develops a talent for drawing, which his aunt deplores as a form of idolatry. After her death during his adolescence, Wyatt suffers a mysterious illness. Conventional medicine fails to control the illness, so his father attempts to cure him by performing a pagan ritual involving the sacrifice of a Barbary ape, and succeeds.

Wyatt spends his convalescence painting. Two of his works from these months help shape the plot of the novel. One is a copy he begins of the Hieronymus Bosch tabletop painting, *Seven Deadly Sins* that was illegally brought back, like the Barbary ape, by Reverend Gwyon from Europe. The other is an unfinished portrait of his mother made from a photograph taken before her marriage.

Wyatt attends divinity school for a year, but then decides to study art in Europe. To finance his trip he finishes the copy of the Bosch and sells the original to Recktall Brown, who will later employ Wyatt as an art forger. From Munich, Wyatt writes to his father and explains that his inherited guilt (for the death of his mother) and his contempt for Christianity have rendered him unfit for the ministry. Reverend Gwyon, alone now with a retarded serving girl, loses himself in studies of paganism, focusing particularly on Mithraism, a rival to early Christianity.

After three years in Paris, Wyatt finds himself disgusted by the fashionable art world. Because he refuses to share his sales with an art critic named Crémer, his show fails and he cannot sell his work. When he discovers that his Memling imitation has been sold as authentic, he abandons Paris for New York and spends several years in unspecified activities. Seven or eight years later, still in New York City, he marries Esther and works as a draftsman, occasionally designing bridges which his supervisor, Benny, claims as his own. Wyatt also restores paintings, but has avoided original work since the failure of his

Paris show. Esther and Wyatt's relationship suffers when they meet Otto Pivner, a playwright and recent Harvard graduate, as Esther soon begins an affair with him. Wyatt in further disgust quits both his job and his marriage and agrees to forge paintings for Recktall Brown. Otto moves in with Esther. After this point in the novel, Wyatt loses his name and henceforth is only ''he'' or, in the last few chapters, Stephen, a variant on the name in a stolen passport and an acknowledgment of his own martyrdom.

Otto works on a banana plantation in Central America for half of the year to finance his writing. He is writing a play called *The Vanity of Time,* a title he found in Wyatt's copy of Reverend Gwyon's funeral sermon for Aunt May. Otto plans to return to New York with his play completed and his arm in a black sling (he has suffered no actual injury), for which he expects due sympathy. When he does return in December, he attends a Greenwich Village party at which a new painting by Max Schling is unveiled. This work apparently consists of a mounted workshirt complete with grease stain. At this party most of the novel's other characters appear, including Agnes Deigh, a literary agent; Hannah, a beer-drinking artist attracted to Stanley, a Catholic composer of organ music who presciently fears being buried alive; Anselm, a poet obsessed with and contemptuous of religion; Maude and Arny Munk, a childless couple looking for a child to adopt; Herschel, a homosexual political writer; Ed Feasley, who attended Harvard with Otto; Mr. Feddle, who writes poetry and publishes it in vanity presses; and Esme (possibly named, with considerable irony, after a character in a J. D. Salinger short story, ''For Esme, with Love and Squalor''), who is a manic-depressive heroin addict, poet, and model involved with Chaby, Frank Sinisterra's son. Otto takes Esme home from the party and falls in love with her.

Esme models for Wyatt and falls in love with him, and the quadrangle of Otto, Esther, Esme, and Wyatt develops. Wyatt's career as forger becomes complicated by Basil Valentine, a critic and undercover agent who authenticates the forgeries but who maintains a more complicated view of art and forgery than Brown does. Valentine takes advantage of a growing friendship with Wyatt by planning to have him forge a painting by Hubert van Eyck, though Wyatt never actually does so. Meanwhile, Agnes Deigh rejects Otto's play, which is rumored to have been plagiarized; Ed Feasley and Otto steal an amputated leg from a hospital morgue (the leg belonged to Stanley's mother); and Stanley more or less avoids seduction by Agnes only to find that rumors report him to have slept with Hannah.

Again attempting to shed his guilt and disgust, Wyatt returns to New England to resume his divinity studies. Wyatt finds that his father now worships Mithras, while his grandfather mistakes Wyatt's father for Prester John, and the retarded servant girl believes him to be the Second Coming of Christ. In the most dramatic moment of the book, Wyatt, as lightning crashes into the barn, demands that his father tell him if he, Wyatt, is *"the man for whom Christ died?"* The Reverend Gwyon cannot answer. Disappointed, Wyatt returns to New York.

Otto continues to pursue Esme, who attempts suicide to escape the squalor of her life. Frank Sinisterra, now out of prison again, resumes his counterfeiting schemes. He meets Otto in a bar and mistakes him for the person to whom he is supposed to pass five thousand counterfeit dollars. Otto, who mistakes Sinisterra for his own father, finds himself unexpectedly rich. However, Sinisterra discovers his mistake, and with the intended contact person follows Otto as he gives money to Stanley and Anselm, buys nude photographs of Esme, and is arrested for soliciting an undercover policewoman.

Wyatt decides to expose his role in Brown's fraudulent dealings and tells Valentine he plans to do so at Brown's Christmas party, which coincides with Esther's, which in turn largely replays the earlier Greenwich Village party. Afterward, Stanley, the devout Catholic, tries to buy a drink with a counterfeit twenty and is arrested. Though the two parties expose many of the characters' foibles, including plagiarism and sexual inadequacies, Wyatt does not successfully reveal the forgeries because Valentine has destroyed the evidence. The plan becomes moot, however, when Brown, having drunkenly climbed into a suit of armor, tumbles downstairs to his death.

On Christmas, Reverend Gwyon performs a Mithraic ceremony in his church. Taken to an asylum, he ends up crucified by one of the other patients. The minister who has replaced him sends his ashes to the monastery in Spain. Otto flees the country with his counterfeit money and returns to Central America, where he actually breaks his arm and earns his sling. Stanley, out of jail, prepares to go to Italy to play his organ concerto in the church at Fenestrula. Wyatt, Frank Sinisterra, Basil Valentine, Esme, and other characters also sail for Europe, for different reasons.

In Spain, Sinisterra, under the name Mr. Yák, goes to San Zwingli to obtain a corpse. Wyatt also has gone there to see the place where his mother lies entombed. When Sinisterra realizes that this is the young man whose mother he had accidentally killed while posing as a surgeon, he takes charge of Wyatt, giving him a Swiss passport bearing the name ''Stephan Asche.'' Sinisterra's motives are mixed: he feels actual guilt over Wyatt's mother's death, but nonetheless uses Wyatt to further a counterfeiting scheme—preparing a fake mummy to sell to someone Sinisterra believes to be an Egyptologist but who is actually an assassin on the trail of the real Mr. Yák. As it turns out, Sinisterra steals the corpse of a little girl destined for sainthood, while the corpse of Wyatt's mother, mistaken for that of the little girl, has already gone to Rome for canonization.

At the end of the novel, Wyatt, now calling himself Stephen, resides at the Real Monasterio restoring paintings by completely scraping off the paint to expose the original canvas or wood. Otto works as a doctor's assistant in Barbados. Ed Feasley supervises a number of mental patients boarding at his father's estate. Anselm publishes his confessions and denounces his former friends. Esme decides to become a nun, though she proposes marriage to Valentine, who rejects the idea. She dies from a staph infection. Sinisterra also dies, having been murdered by the hit man posing as an Egyptologist. After hearing of Esme's death, Stanley attempts to play his concerto at Fenestrula on Easter Sunday. However, ignorant of Italian, he fails to follow the priest's orders not to use the bass notes. He pulls out all the stops and begins to play. The resulting vibrations cause the old church to collapse, killing him. The closing page of the novel focuses on the survival of Stanley's music: "it is still spoken of, when it is noted, with high regard, though seldom played."

Countless minor episodes, abrupt shifts of scene, many minor characters, telegraphic and fragmented episodes, and dozens of allusions to obscure literature, arcane mythology, and religion make *The Recognitions* a challenge even for sophisticated readers. Among the novel's subjects are the quest for identity, the role of the artist in a society that values art of the past far more than art of the present, and the difficulty of determining fakery in a society lacking clear ethical and moral standards. Wyatt Gwyon, as artist, forger, and would-be priest, traces his identity full circle back to the monastery where his father retreated after his mother's death, and traces art back to its origin as potential, as blank canvas and bare wood. Gaddis dramatizes the contemporary desire to discover primary identity by returning to origins, or to places of primal significance. Nearly every character seems to be in some sort of identity crisis. The act of recognition, if authentic, would be

one of self-recognition, which Gaddis considers almost impossible to obtain either in a culture as uncertain and corrupt as ours or in a foreign place where understanding comes with great difficulty, if at all. The lesson of Stanley's fate is a grim one; Gaddis' novel may well be an imperative to abandon the search for absolutes, such as religious certainty and unquestioning love, both in life and in art.

The book has fascinated and bemused critics with its grim humor and air of finality. Gregory Comnes argues that "*The Recognitions* demonstrates the essential alterity of the world . . . by forcing the reader to acknowledge and accept the inherent ambiguity limiting any systematized approach to understanding." Perhaps the quest for identity itself is at fault; perhaps an unstable world precludes the possibility of a stable identity. Comnes goes on to point out that the novel depicts "three conflicting mythic systems of order: Christianity, technological science, and 'alchemical' art." These systems fail to provide substance or certitude because they are too easily counterfeited and thus partisan to doubt and skepticism.

Most critics have agreed that alchemy plays an important role in the novel. Comnes notes how closely alchemy is linked to art, representing "the transformational power of Wyatt's artistic imagination," while Steven Moore argues in his introduction to *A Reader's Guide to William Gaddis's The Recognitions* (1982) that "alchemy plays a role of major importance both in unifying the symbolic elements and referential material . . . and in providing a spiritual 'plot' to complement (and justify) the narrative of the novel." *The Recognitions* includes two pages openly dealing with alchemy (pp. 131–132), as well as numerous references, which Moore in his *Reader's Guide* carefully traces to their sources. Yet one might argue that the real value of alchemy in this novel is as an example of a bogus art that encourages fakery, since surely however often the references occur they hardly constitute a strong enough motif to unify the elements of so diffuse a novel. Wyatt's quest for authenticity and redemption might well seem alchemical, but in the end the only gold he discovers is actually base: the raw canvas or wood beneath the ancient paintings he despoils at the monastery. Nevertheless, Comnes seems correct in arguing that the novel uses alchemy to expose Christianity as a conspiracy against the mysteries of life. Perhaps Mithraism, too, better serves the mysteries, though the ironic fate of Wyatt's father demonstrates the danger of such archaic explorations.

Other critics have approached *The Recognitions* as a study of the role of art in contemporary society rather than as an identity quest. Joseph Salemi, for example, argues that the novel is concerned with exploring the extremities of experience and intellect required to generate an art adequate to the complex realities of contemporary life. He notes that the novel uses "reality" and "art" as mutual metaphors, indulges in numerous comments about its own style and complexity, and is quite judgmental about appropriate models of art from the past. Further, he seizes upon Stanley's argument that "the devil is the father of false art" as an ethical statement, claiming that "the creation of ["genuine"] art is an act of atonement . . . not only for false art, but for false life as well." Thus when the church collapses on Stanley, it represents the collapse of false art in the reverberations of Stanley's true art of atonement.

The Recognitions is a compendium of literary allusion. Various critics have cited sources in the work of Rainer Maria Rilke, T. S. Eliot, the Bible, Friedrich Nietzsche, André Gide, St. John of the Cross, Vincent van Gogh's letters, and in nonliterary work such as the music of Mozart and the paintings of Rogier van der Weyden, though Gaddis dismisses such allusion hunting as "a distraction." Aside from merely identifying allusions, however, some critics have determined that they are intrinsic to the structure of the work. Miriam Fuchs argues, for instance, "Another way to discover the central idea of this novel is to go beyond its dizzying surface to the work of T. S. Eliot. Wyatt's development can be viewed in the context of *The Four Quartets* [1943], while the civilization that crumbles around him can be viewed in the context of *The Waste Land* [1922]." Not only does this analysis point to the sophistication of the novel, but it demonstrates how central its issues are to twentieth-century literature.

Generally critics have agreed that a central theme in *The Recognitions* is the problem of distinguishing between the counterfeit and the genuine, both in art and in life. Gaddis' great novel of black humor fully recreates a world in which this problem assumes innumerable dimensions and shadings. With such complexity comes a kind of timeless flexibility. Although *The Recognitions* remains difficult—its dense plotting and abrupt, often fragmented, dialogue still challenge the casual reader—the novel may seem less intimidating than when first published, since its themes have become more familiar, and its critique of the degradation of culture and language remains as urgent as ever.

In the years following its publication, *The Recognitions* slowly made its way into the literary consciousness, as the introduction to Kuehl and Moore's book makes clear. Even some of the reviewers who were initially puzzled or dismayed by it began to understand its significance within a few years. In 1957, for instance, Anthony West named it "the most interesting and remarkable novel written by a young American in the last twenty-five years." Two years later Norman Mailer in *Advertisements for Myself* advertised Gaddis with a favorable if patronizing mention. Meridian issued a paperback edition in 1962. This bore numerous corrections, many by Jack Green, and though it received few reviews, being a reprint, most were very favorable. Green wrote and paid for a full-page advertisement in the *Village Voice* on March 29, 1962, to promote both *The Recognitions* and his own publication "fire the bastards." The Meridian edition sold well—almost nine thousand copies. That same year Gaddis' novel appeared for the first time in England, though many British critics found it obnoxiously complex and oblique. Gaddis meanwhile had begun and abandoned several new literary projects. As he listed them in a 1962 letter, they included

> A novel on business begun and dropped in about '57; a novel begun, rebuilt into an impossibly long play (very rear guard, Socrates in the US Civil War), shelved 1960; current obsession with expanding prospects of programmed society & automation in the arts which may bring an advance, a commitment, even an escape from the tomb of the 9-to-5.

Eventually these projects, like Gaddis' paid work of this period, would find a place in *J R* in the work of the characters Jack Gibbs and Thomas Eigen. An actual fragment of the play, *Once at Antietam,* also appears in this novel.

Kuehl and Moore describe Gaddis' paid employment over these years as including writing for school television for the Ford Foundation, a project which collapsed in 1963, and public relations work for Pfizer International, a pharmaceutical firm that appears in *J R* as Nobili. In 1964 Gaddis traveled to Belgium to make a documentary film for the army on the Battle of the Bulge. The sardonic world of *J R* places these vocation efforts in perspective. Meanwhile *The Recognitions* had become nearly forgotten. Though an academic essay on it appeared in 1965, it merely tried to draw a parallel between Gaddis' novel and *Ulysses* (1922), which does neither work justice (Gaddis even denies having read *Ulysses*). Occasionally critics reviewing novels clearly indebted to Gaddis' work, such as Joseph McElroy's *A Smuggler's Bible* (1966),

would mention *The Recognitions* as an example of critical and public neglect. An Italian translation appeared in 1967 and received favorable reviews, but a German translation fell through. Lois Cantor featured Gaddis in a 1968 article titled "Ten Neglected American Writers Who Deserve to Be Better Known." The profile notes that "Gaddis lives in Croton-on-Hudson, N.Y.," where he "supports himself, 'however feebly,' with industrial and corporate writing" and was working on his second novel, presumably *J R*. Interestingly, Gaddis is quoted as saying, "among friends, literary gossip and money are pretty much all we do talk about." And Cantor notes admiringly, "As editor of the Harvard *Lampoon,* he once leaped out a window into a net, completely sauced, without suffering a scratch." In conclusion, the profile quotes Gaddis on his identity as a writer: "You just have to decide—or have it forced on you—whether you're a craftsman or a commercial writer. I wouldn't want to compete with Leon Uris if it should come to that."

Despite these years of neglect, failing marriage (to Pat Black, with whom he had two children, Sarah and Matthew), and discouraging jobs, Gaddis worked steadily on *J R*. According to Kuehl and Moore, the early seventies saw his reputation begin to extend beyond the smallest literary circles, with the publication of excerpts from the new novel, articles by important critics such as David Madden and Tony Tanner, and a French translation of *The Recognitions*. The publication of *J R* on October 29, 1975, by Knopf in hardcover and paperback editions seemed to assure that reputation. The new book went through three printings in five months, hardly a best-seller but impressive for such a difficult work. In contrast to the petulant reviews of *The Recognitions,* the reviews of *J R* were generally positive. A few reviewers, like William H. Pritchard in the *Hudson Review,* disliked the book (Pritchard even boasted that he was unable to finish it), and other reviewers were puzzled, but John W. Aldridge in *The Saturday Review,* George Stade in the *New York Times Book Review,* Elizabeth Fox-Genovese in the *New Republic,* Thomas LeClair in *Commonweal,* and Gilbert Sorrentino in *Partisan Review* were inspired by Gaddis' book to write masterful reviews.

J R refuses the sort of narrative and structural coherence that makes it possible to summarize a novel with any degree of accuracy. Despite the generally favorable reviews, even so experienced a critic as George Steiner classed *J R* as an "unreadable book [that] will humiliate, confound, and rout the reader." However, the main thrust of the novel is clear enough. Finance and art offer competing systems of value; both, however, are fraudulent insofar as they claim to present complete pictures of the world. The central plot revolves around the growth and collapse of a financial holding company called the J R Family of Companies. This paper empire is founded by J R Vansant ("J R" means junior, Gaddis has said), an eleven-year-old boy who follows instructions gathered during a class trip with his sixth-grade teacher, Amy Jourbet, to a Wall Street investment firm. J R's peculiar career begins when he cheats his classmates out of their interest in the single share of stock the class has purchased and wins a minor shareholder's suit. He writes away for samples of odd products, buys a million surplus picnic forks from the navy, and sells them to the army. His headquarters consist of phone booths beside the boys' toilet, in a candy store, and in the Museum of Natural History.

J R's complex affairs eventually draw in the Greenwich Village artists and bohemians who appeared in *The Recognitions,* now twenty years older. So caught up in their business affairs are these characters that they can no longer accomplish anything else. Typical of these frustrated artists is Edward Bast, a composer in residence at J R's school, who finds himself entangled in the empire's machinations and, even more hope-

lessly, in its language, which is almost entirely about money and financial manipulations, but also includes radio dialogue, transcribed video images, and other montage effects. Another character, Jack Gibbs, a sixth-grade science teacher who is a drunk and a gambler, struggles to write an impossible book entitled *Agapē, Agape,* which deals with "order and disorder more of a, sort of a social history of mechanization and the arts, the destructive element." An alienated friend of Gibbs, Tom Eigen, once published a book like *The Recognitions* but has become (like Gaddis himself) a corporate speechwriter. He, his wife, Marian, and several other failed artists live in an apartment that Bast, at the request of J R, makes the headquarters of the J R Family of Corporations. The male characters share a comic immaturity, sometimes expressed in inappropriate sexual desires, while the women seem trapped by the artistic and social failure of the men. The weakest woman character, Rhoda, who becomes the mistress of Bast, Jack Gibbs, and Al the mailman-guitarist, embodies the humiliation that awaits the woman who embraces the fraudulent world of the men.

J R pressures Bast into fronting for him, since he needs an adult to sign papers. Only Bast understands that J R is a financial genius—the other adults work for Bast, assuming that he is the shrewd manipulator in charge. Following a few general principles about capitalism and finance, J R with Bast's aid as amanuensis and front not only creates a huge holding company but virtually enslaves the other characters. Although he comes to believe his publicist's description of him as "a man of vision," in the end J R finds himself trapped in a lonely and disappointing situation. He complains to Bast, whom he has used until Bast's original, weak personality has almost disappeared, "Everybody's trying to use me!" Finally, following hostile stock-market manipulations, his empire in ruins, J R himself seems to admit that entropy and disorder have won out: "I had these here big plans you know hey? I mean not just for me for the both of us. . . .''

Most of the novel consists of fragments of dialogue, harangues, and jargon spoken by various characters warped by the exigencies of high finance. Gaddis has carefully effaced the narrator, ''obliging the thing to stand on its own, take its own chances,'' as he said in the Kuehl and Moore interview. Scene flows into scene with little if any delineation. The style is not a flow of consciousness, however, since no single mind could absorb this bulk of fragmented information, and no definable narrator intrudes. No speech by any character maintains sufficient integrity to serve as a moment of rest, order, or even intelligibility. In fact, for long stretches the only means of identifying characters is by the peculiarities of their speech, so the reader must learn to identify the cast by its idiosyncrasies of phrasing or vocabulary.

The thematic concerns, however, are more explicit than the plot. The depredations of greed spawned the novel, according to Gaddis, who in the Kuehl and Moore interview confessed, ''J R was started as a story which quickly proved unsatisfactory, inspired . . . by the postwar desecration of the Long Island village of Massapequa where my family had had property since around 1910, take a look at it now and you'll see all the book's worst hopes realized.'' Capitalist logic controls the world of J R and desecrates everything it touches, even the school he attends and the lives of the struggling Bohemian artists. ''There's a market for everything,'' Coach Vogel says of drug-free urine sold on the black market to those worried about random testing. Not the love of money but the fear of it propels those characters who fail, unlike J R, to understand how capitalism works.

The financial empire created by J R is itself like a novel: a paper empire. Founded on credit, this empire totters along for hundreds of pages, generating huge paper profits for J R. By purchasing stock on margin, writing letters, and garnering shares and dividends without any capital investment, he shapes a massive holding company that is both worthless (''wallpaper,'' as Wall Street calls such holdings) and worth a theoretical fortune. Like the novel, money is a form of discourse and must be interpreted to be understood. J R misreads his own paper, seizes upon what ''ragged ribbons of newspaper, magazine pages torn jagged,'' say about his paper empire, and generally loses his ability to interpret and manipulate the world around him. Gaddis' target is not only the abstract problem of order versus disorder but the very concrete and yet very fragile construct of finance in a late capitalist economy.

In such an economy, the stability of the monetary system reflects the degree of coherence in society. According to Gaddis, that coherence is decidedly lacking, perhaps due in part to the belief that paper bears inherent worth. He suggests this criticism in the opening dialogue of the novel, a reminiscence of two elderly sisters (the aunts of Edward Bast):

—Money . . . ? in a voice that rustled.
—Paper, yes.
—And we'd never seen it. Paper money.
—We never saw paper money till we came east.
—It looked so strange the first time we saw it. Lifeless.
—You couldn't believe it was worth a thing.
—Not after Father jingling his change.

The comic identification of money, the human voice, and paper suggests that, as in *The Recognitions,* the value of anything—money, music, literature, human relationships—will be difficult, if not impossible, to determine. Not only do fraud, mendacity, and misunderstanding rustle throughout contemporary life with the frequency and intellectual coherence of dollar bills, but paper, like people, presents a pliable, fragile, and deceptive surface on which almost anything can be inscribed. In *J R,* for example, financial chicanery involving the manipulation of the U.S. Government and a small African nation will produce a massive profit for Typhon International at the cost of the U.S. taxpayer. Typhon proposes, essentially, that taxpayers assume all cost and risk for the corporation to operate an ore processing plant to sell cobalt to the U.S. government:

> For the purposes of cobalt stockpiling, national security and so forth and so forth, that during the life of this contract as stated in clause one supra the government hereby agrees to purchase from Typhon International five point two thousand tons of contained cobalt annually, at the guaranteed price of four dollars sixty seven cents per pound, now. Down in seven. In order to expedite this and so forth and so forth the government agrees to advance to Typhon International the sum of thirty-nine point seven million dollars to construct a smaltite processing plant for the extraction of contained cobalt and then down in eleven, the government agrees to sell, at cost, to the processing plant to be erected operated and so forth by Typhon International in the country of Gandia, sufficient smaltite ore . . .

Gaddis' fascination with corporate and legal language centers on the way contractual terminology conceals or at least renders respectable business practices that through deception amount to outright theft.

The deception most central to *J R* is the development of the paper empire J R creates with nothing but credit. It perfectly mirrors corporate empires of Wall Street in the book, like the Diamond Cable–Typhon International group. Although Wall Street turns on J R and crushes his fragile corporation, he refuses to cease his manipulations because he correctly perceives that he has been operating according to the standards and practices of corporate America. The only problem with the J R Family of Corporations is that it cannot sustain credibility as effectively as some of the more mature but equally fraudulent corporations sanctified by being listed on the major exchanges. His vision of the U.S. as a cred-

ulous money-driven perversion of nationhood coincides, though crazily, with the author's. J R is justified in not being able to distinguish deception from authenticity. In this regard, *J R,* like *The Recognitions,* challenges the status of art and particularly the novel in a society that can neither depend on fact nor intelligently make use of fiction. Though not as obviously encyclopedic as *The Recognitions, J R* extends and develops the earlier novel's focus on fraud and forgery and the consequences for the world of art. But rather than focus on the problem of the relationship of the author to the work, a problem that looms large in *The Recognitions, J R* concerns itself with the problem of audience. J R cannot understand the difference between his paper empire and the real empires of Wall Street because there is no important difference.

A difference between *The Recognitions* and *J R,* however, and perhaps a mark of Gaddis' development, is the acknowledgment that encyclopedic fictions can no longer fulfill their former role in contemporary culture. Among the products generated by the paper empire is a children's encyclopedia, which supposedly is "doing extremely well even though it seems to be teeming with inaccuracies." And Jack Gibbs, we learn, once sold encyclopedias to work his way through Harvard, and his self-critique has an authorial air about it: "must have thought I could, like Diderot good God how I ever thought I could do it." The authorial arrogance required to write so comprehensive a book seems to have faded both in the world of *J R* and in Gaddis himself. And, if not for the relatively simple narrative that would shape his next novel, *Carpenter's Gothic* (1985), it would be easy to concur with the critics who claim that *J R* marks the liberation of the novel not only from comprehensiveness but from narrative itself, that basic element of order we seem to expect in fiction.

Yet in tracing the rise and fall of the J R Family of Corporations, Gaddis does generate a narrative so simple it becomes almost invisible yet is sufficient to tie the novel together, to make it readable and memorable as a distinct entity with beginning, middle, and end. Some reviewers, of course, faced with a textual complexity they found uncongenial and indifferent to their standards of concision and directness, claimed the book lacked focus, a guiding intelligence, and control. Many reviewers and readers, though, accepting the difficulty of the book, its subtle changes of scene, and its lack of chapter divisions, found *J R* not only readable but engrossing. *J R* appeared a year after the Avon reissue of *The Recognitions* as a mass-market paperback, so perhaps the good reviews of the new book intended to atone for the neglect of the earlier one, which was proclaimed, in retrospect, a masterpiece. But *J R* made its own way, winning the National Book Award in 1976 and remaining in print as of 1995. It so clearly and accurately argues its critique of our money-dazzled culture that thematic clarity to some extent alleviates its narrative murkiness, and the uncompromised integrity of its artistry, in which seemingly chaotic but uncannily amusing dialogue perfectly mocks the fractured discourses of an age of instant communication, impresses even puzzled readers.

In accepting the National Book Award for *J R,* Gaddis insisted that

> a writer should be read and not heard, let alone seen. I think this is because there seems so often today to be a tendency to put the person in the place of his or her work, to turn the creative artist into a performing one, to find what a writer says about writing somehow more valid, or more real, than the writing itself.

Except for two valuable interviews published in *The Review of Contemporary Fiction* and *The Paris Review,* Gaddis, despite his contemporary fame, has resisted commenting on his work or on the state of writing in general, and except for spending 1977 as distinguished visiting professor at Bard College has been living a quiet life in a former carriage barn in Wainscott, Long Island, and in New York City. A Guggenheim Fellowship (1981) and a MacArthur Foundation Fellowship (1982) helped finance the writing of his next book, which appeared ten years after *J R* and was thought by some reviewers to represent a diminution of his abilities.

Carpenter's Gothic is the most immediately accessible of Gaddis' novels in terms of scale and narrative. Gaddis in the Abádi-Nagy interview claims to have written the book as a series of ''problems'' he hoped to solve in ''style and technique and form'':

> I wanted to write a shorter book, one which observes the unities of time and place to the point that everything, even though it expands into the world, takes place in one house, and a country house at that, with a small number of characters, in a short span of time.

The plot, although complex, follows an inner logic of development, with dramatic motivation and cause and effect at least suggested in the dialogue. The single setting and smaller cast make for a conventionally manageable text in that no unaccountable spatial leaps and few unaccountable shifts in dramatis personae occur. Furthermore, the descriptive passages, more numerous and imagistic than in the other novels, provide a more fully depicted setting as well as breaks from the otherwise characteristically relentless dialogue.

However, the vision of the novel is disconcerting because it reverses conventional ethical patterns and grants success and fulfillment to its greediest, most unfeeling character, Paul Booth, and destruction to its most sympathetic character, Elizabeth, his wife. The couple has rented a house in the style known as ''Carpenter Gothic'' (the correct architectural description, as one character points out), north of New York City near the Hudson. Paul, a Vietnam veteran, works as a media consultant for the Reverend Elton Ude. Paul's primary task is to prepare meretricious media events to promote various religious and fund-raising events revolving around the Reverend's crusade against the evil powers infiltrating America. He also has to concern himself with an indictment for racketeering and bribery. Furthermore, Paul has implicated Elizabeth in his schemes, sending her to a fraudulent doctor, for example, to abet his claim that injuries she has suffered in an airline crash have caused him "conjugal distress." Because she cannot discuss her husband's lack of integrity with him or anyone else, she confides in her unfinished, ongoing novel.

Their visitors generate the plot, which the reader must piece together (from dialogue). This process of making sense is exemplified by Paul's frustration at trying to understand the scheme he promotes with his media manipulations, by Elizabeth's vague perception of the trajectory of her moral confusion and eventual failure, and most clearly by a climactic dialogue between Elizabeth and McCandless, the landlord. Elizabeth's brother, Billy, lives a nomadic sixties lifestyle and drops in to criticize her for her relationships with what he calls "These real inferior types." McCandless, a mysterious geologist, drops by frequently for purposes of his own, which include seducing Elizabeth. He is a hypocrite, on the one hand frequently raving about the excesses of government, the hypocrisy of religion, and the inanity of society, on the other hand having recently sold survey maps to the CIA through his old friend Lester, maps that will be used to further corrupt the military governments of Africa and will help precipitate the geopolitical apocalypse at the end of the novel.

One night Paul comes home with a serious knife wound inflicted by a young black man who might have been a mugger but apparently was an assassin dispatched by the Reverend Ude or the Vorakers company. Paul knows too much about Ude and Voraker's illegal international scheming, and the Reverend may have decided to have him killed. Besides, Paul is plotting against the Reverend and has paid a young man to assassinate him. The event seemed to induce in Paul a flashback to Vietnam, and he killed his assailant. At this point in the novel, everything the Reverend Ude has worked for seems in jeopardy as Grimes, CEO of Vorakers, attempts to force the U.S. government to intervene in East Africa. A senator on a fact-finding mission dies when his airplane is shot down—Billy is also aboard. In the tense atmosphere of these events, Elizabeth and McCandless come together in the novel's climactic scene. McCandless wants to take her away with him, but she resists and engages him in a dialogue that begins when she blames McCandless for Billy's death, claiming that his account of American exploitation had inspired Billy to go to Africa to see it for himself. Gradually Elizabeth begins to understand that McCandless' grasp of the situation is deeply flawed. He doesn't even realize that Paul had been forced to kill a man who tried to assassinate him but thinks instead that Elizabeth's husband is merely a wanton murderer. McCandless, when corrected by Elizabeth, still fails to trace the plot unfolding about him, dismissing it as "madness . . . just madness." Elizabeth begins to grasp the role of human responsibility in these apparently chaotic events. McCandless wants to take her with him to South America, leaving his various treacheries behind, but Elizabeth, accusing him of simpleminded apocalypticism, resists. McCandless, in the end, agrees to try to do something to halt the impending disaster.

Whether Elizabeth would have run off with him remains uncertain. After he leaves, she finds her house in disarray and McCandless' ex-wife at the door. Elizabeth has a brief discussion with her in which Mrs. McCandless suggests that her husband had been in a mental hospital and that his experiences in Africa may be imaginary.

Alone again, Elizabeth rushes in her kitchen, apparently stumbles, strikes her temple on a corner of the table, and dies in a fetal position as the phone rings. Reported in bold headline as "HEIRESS SLAIN IN SWANK SUBURB," her death is misinterpreted by the police, because of the disorder of her house, as murder by an interrupted burglar. (In *A Frolic of His Own* Christine asserts that Elizabeth died of a heart attack after striking her head, and that the maid after finding the body stole the household money and checkbook, leading the police to assume a burglary.) This error mirrors McCandless' misreading of Paul's killing of the young black man and cruelly suggests that Elizabeth was doomed to atone for the earlier death.

At Elizabeth's funeral, her bereaved husband attempts to seduce her best friend, using the same line he had used on Elizabeth, claiming in the last moments of the novel, "I've always been crazy about the back of your neck." And just before the funeral a heavy black newspaper headline announces, "10K 'DEMO' BOMB OFF AFRICA COAST," suggesting how McCandless' sellout and Paul's by now highly profitable scheming have led the world on the path to destruction.

Like Gaddis' other novels, *Carpenter's Gothic* is self-reflexive, self-parodying, and concerned with the contemporary failings and dubious future of both literature and life. Gaddis seems to suggest that the making of art is essentially derivative, particularly as carpenter Gothic is a derivative pattern-book architectural style. The house itself is the novel in that it contains the characters and shapes the plot, a randomly constructed "patchwork of conceits, borrowings, deceptions, the inside's a hodgepodge of good intentions like one last ridiculous effort at something worth doing even on this small a scale." Elizabeth tries to resist despair, but her fate suggests how futile is resistance to entropy and chaos, and the explosion off the coast of Africa not only suggests a coming apocalypse but an ironic return to human origin.

Most readers and reviewers missed what Gaddis in the Abádi-Nagy interview calls "the scheme of the book": "the book of Genesis emerging from the fiery holocaust that created the Great Rift Valley from Lebanon down through Israel, down through the Red Sea and all the way down East Africa, as where man was born, where he emerged." The apocalyptic element in the novel constitutes a structural device, one source of the urgency of the language and of the sense of doom hanging over what could otherwise seem a reckless veering from the domestic to the remote world of multinational corporate conspiracy.

Unlike *The Recognitions* and *J R, Carpenter's Gothic* does not offer extensive rhetorical or narrational complexities that challenge the reader to discover in textuality the order the portrayed world lacks. Consequently, reviews and critics have generally found it the bleakest of Gaddis' novels, despite its characteristically bizarre humor. As Gregory Comnes argues,

> Because it does not contain the aesthetic complexities present in the earlier novels, *Carpenter's Gothic* does not lend itself to transformation into something that says to its readers, "Learn how to manage and transform the chaos and negativity within me so that you can learn to manage and transform the same discontinuity in the real world." Instead, this novel speaks to the reader of the limits of aesthetic mediation, enacting in narrative the fact that sometimes aesthetic, coherent solutions are simply not possible.

Perhaps because *Carpenter's Gothic* refuted those critics who had read *J R* as liberating the novel from narrative, it did not generate critical speculation about Gaddis' future work in the way the two earlier novels had. But some reviewers, finding *Carpenter's Gothic* to lack the admirable qualities of the previous books, thought Gaddis had depleted his creative resources and would not write another work of the intensity of *The Recognitions* and *J R*. They would be proven wrong nine years later when *A Frolic of His Own* appeared.

The language of the law has proven to be an irresistible medium for Gaddis. "Justice?—You get justice in the next world, in this world you have law," says Harry, husband of Oscar Crease's stepsister in *A Frolic of His Own*. This novel embraces the collusion of law and money in America, and lovingly explores the absurdity and obfuscation of legal language as a symptom of the general decline of language. It also continues Gaddis' exploration of corruption and materialism, both in the contemporary time and, somewhat ironically, in the Civil War era. Oscar is a college instructor and playwright who, as the book opens, lies in the hospital after having managed to run himself over with his own car, a small, red Japanese model called the Sosumi. The "frolic" of the title is "a longwinded play about his grandfather" titled *Once at Antietam* (the title of an unfinished play by Gaddis), which has apparently been pirated by Constantine Kiester, a Hollywood producer, to make a gory blockbuster called *The Blood in the Red White and Blue*. Much of the novel concerns itself with Oscar's efforts to sue Kiester. However, many other legal entanglements occur; one of the most amusing involves a dog trapped in a complex public sculpture in Tatamount, Virginia. Other suits are about a wrongful death during baptism in the Pee Dee River (the defendant is Reverend Ude, who seems to have survived the apocalypse in *Carpenter's Gothic*) and a trademark violation that has the Episcopal Church suing Pepsico ("Pepsi Cola" is an anagram for "Episcopal"). Various jurists, most importantly Oscar's father, the elderly federal judge Thomas Crease, contribute wheezy or whimsical legal rulings to the text.

Oscar's wealthy stepsister, Christina, and her doomed attorney husband, Harry Lutz, visit Oscar in the hospital, as do several other characters, including Lily, his flighty young lover, who is also involved in various legal difficulties, and his insurance agent, who is properly bemused by Oscar's account of his accident. Following the complete text of the legal decision handed down by Oscar's father on the dog-in-sculpture case, a masterpiece of addled legal reasoning, the scene shifts to the Long Island mansion where most of the rest of the novel occurs. Tired of Oscar's attempts to persuade him to sue the Hollywood producer on his behalf, Harry directs Oscar to another legal firm, and the new lawyer, an African American named Harold Basie (Oscar wanted a Jewish lawyer), attempts to make something of the case. As the novel gradually presents us with the actual text of the play, a scene or two at a time, Basie prepares and actually files a complaint on Oscar's behalf. But when the attorney hired by Kiester arrives to take a deposition from Oscar, it turns out that parts of his play strongly resemble passages from Eugene O'Neill's *Mourning Becomes Electra* (1931) and from Plato's *Republic,* thus complicating the lawsuit and demonstrating, as *The Recognitions* does, how complex is the problem of originality in art.

Oscar, predictably, loses his suit; he is also served with a summons in the Sosumi lawsuit he has initiated. Basie, perhaps as predictably, is not an attorney at all but an imposter, an actor who learned his trade in prison. Although Basie took and passed the New York bar exam (on his second try), he never attended law school but learned as a jailhouse lawyer to manipulate the legal system. Meanwhile, lightning strikes the sculpture, killing the dog and therefore shifting the ground of one of the lawsuits in Thomas Crease's jurisdiction. One of those suits involves the Reverend Ude (who seems to have survived the apocalypse of *Carpenter's Gothic*), who, it seems, has drowned a boy while baptizing him.

Jawaharlal Madhar Pai (often referred to as Mr. Mudpye), the attorney from Harry's firm who represented Kiester, shows up at Oscar's house with his assistant, Trish. He and Oscar engage in a long and rather compelling discussion of the play, but the reader suspects that Mr. Mudpye is probing for information to use in the appeal. Harry gets into a driving incident that results in yet another suit. Trish describes the death of Elizabeth (in *Carpenter's Gothic*), arguing that Paul, whom she refers to as "that brutish man," murdered her. Christina corrects her friend, reminding her that the death was an accident. However, this death from a previous novel foreshadows those to come.

Now the court of appeals, approving a brief written (we later learn) by Thomas Crease, reverses the verdict in Oscar's suit against Kiester and rules that Oscar is entitled to all the profits from *The Blood in the Red White and Blue*. Consequently, Mr. Mudpye loses his position at Harry's law firm and blames Oscar, claiming that the Creases have conspired against him. The victory is short-lived, however. Just as the Eugene O'Neill estate files suit against both Oscar and Kiester for copyright infringement, Thomas Crease dies at the age of ninety-seven. Then Oscar's award is reduced by a court-appointed master and set at only twenty percent of the profits of the film. *The Blood in the Red White and Blue* now appears on television, and Harry (showing signs of illness), Lily, and Oscar watch it together.

Thomas Crease had appointed his law clerk as his executor, so the elderly man appears with the judge's ashes and settles into the library for a long stay. From now on the death scenes mount up—a dog, tropical fish, and finally Harry. Christina blames this series of fatalities on the law clerk—"with those ashes and his black sock and the snakes"—but actually the law has killed Harry, just as it kills everything it touches. Oscar is reminded of this when he receives the final award for his lawsuit. In a remarkable feat of accounting, the producers prove that despite the film's 370-million-dollar gross it actually lost eighteen million, an outcome that recalls the Jarndyce and Jarndyce suit in Dickens' *Bleak House* (1852–1853). Consequently, Oscar receives less than the two hundred thousand dollars once offered as an out-of-court settlement. At almost the same moment Lily discovers that her breast implants have ruptured and threaten to leak silicone throughout her body.

With a flourish of paperwork Mr. Gribble arrives to try to settle the auto lawsuit, which has become, he explains to Oscar, "a suit between who you are and who you think you are." It seems that the suit now involves the auto dealer, wholesaler, manufacturer, and parts vendors, most of whom are affiliated with overseas subsidiaries of American corporations. Lily, however, aggressively deals with Mr. Gribble and gets him to agree to a generous medical settlement for Oscar, finally concluding this foolish suit. In a final irony, Oscar discovers by examining old family papers that he has based his play, and his vision of his ancestry, on false premises. He concludes, "I've been lied to all my life." In response, Lily motivates him to restore his death-stricken aquarium, a modest but eloquent gesture toward recuperation.

The book winds down with a flurry of mishaps. After Lily has her faulty implants removed, Christina discovers that the elderly law clerk has executed the judge's estate in such a way that she and Oscar retain only the house. Furthermore, she learns that Harry's half-million-dollar life insurance policy named his firm, not Christina, as beneficiary. The book concludes oddly, with a glimpse of Oscar and Christina's childhood together, as he leaps from behind a door and tickles her breathless.

A Frolic of His Own is Gaddis' most orderly and accessible book, sacrificing neither complexity nor scope to achieve its clarity. The topic of law proves an exceptionally rich source of black humor, and Gaddis' familiar themes of corruption and the decay of language here touch the lives of more or less ordinary people. Oscar's suit embodies a direct confrontation between corporate America and the individual, while Harry's death from overwork demonstrates how the accepted standards of success can destroy intelligent and well-meaning people. As is typical of Gaddis' work, dialogue shapes the narrative, but in a particularly witty and focused manner. Like *J R* and *Carpenter's Gothic, A Frolic of His Own* in avoiding interior monologue achieves a degree of dramatic purity uncommon in the contemporary novel. Though it sharply delineates the psychological processes of its characters, it does so entirely through dialogue and action. This perfection of Gaddis' characteristic style and technique did not go unnoticed. The book earned extensive and generally very favorable reviews, including front-page notices in the *New York Times Book Review* and *Book World,* and lengthy articles in the *New York Review of Books, Los Angeles Times Book Review,* and other prominent newspapers and journals. It also won the 1994 National Book Award in fiction.

Gaddis' novels make greater demands than many readers can or wish to meet, but nonetheless they have attracted a dedicated group of admirers and a considerable amount of serious criticism. Few novelists have presented so comprehensive and dramatic a view of the social and economic problems of their age. And fewer still have at the same time convincingly linked those problems to the anxiety and despair of the individual confronted by a world indifferent to his or her existence. Gaddis' sensibility was formed in the era of existentialism, when the conflict between the public world and the private self seemed the most essential of themes, and expressed itself in *The Recognitions;* his three later novels demonstrate how this conflict, still unresolved, has become a part of corporate society, fueling a new consumerism and reliance on law and the state. Gaddis writes with an ear for dialogue perhaps unmatched by any other contemporary novelist, but it may be his startling depictions of individuals crushed by urban culture or helplessly adrift in the corporate imagination that make his work so compelling.

Selected Bibliography

WORKS OF WILLIAM GADDIS

NOVELS

The Recognitions. New York: Harcourt, Brace, 1955; with corrections, New York: Meridian, 1962; New York: Avon, 1974; with corrections, New York: Penguin, 1985; with corrections and an introduction by William H. Gass, New York: Penguin, 1993.

J R. New York: Knopf, 1975; with corrections, New York: Penguin, 1985; with corrections and an introduction by Frederick R. Karl, New York: Penguin, 1993.

Carpenter's Gothic. New York: Viking, 1985; with corrections, New York: Penguin, 1986.

A Frolic of His Own. New York: Poseidon Press, 1994.

CONTRIBUTIONS TO BOOKS AND PERIODICALS

" 'Stop Player. Joke No. 4.' " In Steven Moore, *A Reader's Guide to William Gaddis's* The Recognitions. Pp. 299–301. First published in *Atlantic,* July 1951, pp. 92–93.

"Les Chemin des ânes." *New World Writing,* 1:210–222 (April 1952).

"From *The Recognitions.*" In *Writers in Revolt,* edited by Richard Seaver, Terry Southern, and Alexander Trocchi, New York: Frederick Fell, 1963; New York: Berkley, 1965. Pp. 225–249.

"J. R. or the Boy Inside." *Dutton Review,* no. 1:5–68 (1970).

"Untitled Fragment from Another Damned, Thick, Square Book." *Antaeus,* 13/14:98–105 (Spring–Summer 1974).

"Nobody Grew but the Business." *Harper's,* June 1975, pp. 47–54, 59–66.

"In the Zone." In Steven Moore, *A Reader's Guide to William Gaddis's* The Recognitions. Pp. 301–304. First published in *New York Times,* March 13, 1978, p. A21.

"Szyrk v. Village of Tatamount et al." *New Yorker,* October 12, 1978, pp. 44–50.

"The Rush for Second Place." *Harper's,* April 1981, pp. 31–39.

[On *The Recognitions*]. In Steven Moore, *A Reader's Guide to William Gaddis's* The Recognitions. Pp. 298–299.

"Trickle-Up Economics: J R Goes to Washington." *New York Times Book Review,* October 25, 1987, p. 29.

SPEECH

"Acceptance Speech for the National Book Award in Fiction for *J R*," National Institute of Arts and Letters, April 21, 1976.

BIOGRAPHICAL AND CRITICAL STUDIES

Aldridge, John W. *The American Novel and the Way We Live Now.* New York: Oxford University Press, 1983. Pp. 46–52, 148.

Bakker, J. "The End of Individualism." *Dutch Quarterly Review of Anglo-American Letters,* 7:286–304 (1977).

Banning, Charles Leslie. "William Gaddis's *J R:* The Organization of Chaos and the Chaos of Organization." *Paunch,* 42/43:153–165 (December 1975).

Benstock, Bernard. "On William Gaddis: The Recognition of James Joyce." *Wisconsin Studies in Contemporary Literature,* 6:177–189 (Summer 1965).

Black, Joel Dana. "The Paper Empires and Empirical Fictions of William Gaddis." *Review of Contemporary Fiction,* 2:22–31 (Summer 1982).

Boccia, Michael. "—What Did You Say Mister Gaddis? Form in William Gaddis's *J R*." *Review of Contemporary Fiction,* 2:40–44 (Summer 1982).

Cantor, Lois. "Ten Neglected American Writers Who Deserve to Be Better Known." *Book World* (*Washington Post/Chicago Tribune*), June 2, 1968, 6.

Comnes, Gregory. *The Ethics of Indeterminacy in the Novels of William Gaddis.* Gainesville: University Press of Florida, 1994.

Eckley, Grace. "Exorcising the Demon Forgery, or the Forging of Pure Gold in Gaddis's *The Recognitions*." In *Literature and the Occult.* Edited by Luanne Frank. Arlington: University of Texas Press, 1977. Pp. 125–136.

Fuchs, Miriam. " 'il miglior fabbro': Gaddis' Debt to T. S. Eliot." In *In Recognition of William Gaddis.* Edited by John Kuehl and Steven Moore. Pp. 92–105.

Green, Jack. "fire the bastards!" (parts 1–3). *newspaper,* nos. 12–14:1–76 (February 24, August 25, November 10, 1962).

———. *Fire the Bastards.* Normal, Ill.: Dalkey Archive, 1992.

Guzlowski, John Z. "Hollow Gestures and Empty Words: Inconsequential Action and Dialogue in Recent American Novels." *Markham Review,* 12:21–26 (Winter 1983).

———. "Masks and Maskings in Hawkes, Gaddis, Barth, and Pynchon." *Journal of Evolutionary Psychology,* 4:214–226 (Fall 1983).

———. "No More Sea Changes: Hawkes, Pynchon, Gaddis, and Barth." *Critique: Studies in Modern Fiction,* 23:48–60 (Winter 1981–1982).

Johnston, John H. *Carnival of Repetition: Gaddis's* The Recognitions *and Postmodern Theory.* Philadelphia: University of Pennsylvania Press, 1990.

Koenig, David. "The Writing of *The Recognitions*." In *In Recognition of William Gaddis.* Edited by John Kuehl and Steven Moore. Pp. 20–31.

Koenig, Peter William. "Recognizing Gaddis's *Recognitions*." *Contemporary Literature,* 16:61–72 (Winter 1975).

Kuehl, John, and Steven Moore, eds. *In Recognition of William Gaddis.* Syracuse: Syracuse University Press, 1984.

LaCapra, Dominick. "Singed Phoenix and Gift of Tongues: William Gaddis's *The Recognitions*." *Diacritics,* 16:33–47 (Winter 1986).

Lathrop, Kathleen L. "Comic-Ironic Parallels in William Gaddis's *The Recognitions*." *Review of Contemporary Fiction,* 2:32–40 (Summer 1982).

LeClair, Thomas. "William Gaddis, *J R,* & the Art of Excess." *Modern Fiction Studies,* 27:587–600 (Winter 1981–1982).

Leverence, John. "Gaddis Anagnorisis." In *In Recognition of William Gaddis.* Edited by John Kuehl and Steven Moore. Pp. 32–45. First published in *Itinerary,* no. 3:49–62 (Summer 1977).

Madden, David. "On William Gaddis's *The Recognitions*." In *Rediscoveries.* Edited by David Madden. New York: Crown, 1971. Pp. 291–304.

Malmgren, Carl D. "William Gaddis's *J R:* The Novel of Babel." *Review of Contemporary Fiction,* 2:7–12 (Summer 1982).

Martin, Robert A. "The Five Recognitions of William Gaddis." *Notes on Contemporary Literature,* 15:3–5 (January 1985).

Martin, Stephen-Paul. "Vulnerability and Aggression: Characters and Objects in *The Recognitions*." *Review of Contemporary Fiction,* 2:45–50 (Summer 1982).

Moore, Steven. "Chronological Difficulties in the Novels of William Gaddis." *Critique: Studies in Modern Fiction,* 22:79–81 (1980).

————. *A Reader's Guide to William Gaddis's* The Recognitions. Lincoln: University of Nebraska Press, 1982.

————. *William Gaddis.* Boston: Twayne, 1989.

————. "William Gaddis: A Selected Bibliography." *Review of Contemporary Fiction,* 2:55–56 (Summer 1982).

" 'Nothing but Darkness and Talk?': Writers' Symposium on Traditional Values and Iconoclastic Fiction." *Critique: Studies in Contemporary Fiction,* 31:233–255 (Summer 1990).

Safer, Elaine B. *The Contemporary American Comic Epic: The Novels of Barth, Pynchon, Gaddis, and Kesey.* Detroit: Wayne State University Press, 1988.

Salemi, Joseph S. "To Soar in Atonement: Art as Expiation in Gaddis's *The Recognitions*." In *In Recognition of William Gaddis.* Edited by John Kuehl and Steven Moore. Pp. 46–57. First published in *Novel,* 10:127–136 (Winter 1977).

Sawyer, Tom. "False Gold to Forge: The Forger behind Wyatt Gwyon." *Review of Contemporary Fiction,* 2:50–54 (Summer 1982).

Stark, John. "William Gaddis: Just Recognition." *Hollins Critic,* 14:1–12 (April 1977).

Steiner, George. "Books: Crossed Lines." *The New Yorker,* January 26, 1976, pp. 106–109

Strehle, Susan. "Disclosing Time: William Gaddis's *J R.*" In *In Recognition of William Gaddis.* Edited by John Kuehl and Steven Moore. Pp. 119–134. First published in *Journal of Narrative Technique,* 12:1–14 (Winter 1982).

Tabbi, Joseph. "The Cybernetic Metaphor in William Gaddis's *J R. ANQ,* 2:147–151 (October 1989).

Tanner, Tony. *City of Words: American Fiction 1950–1970.* New York: Harper & Row, 1971. Pp. 393–400.

Weisenburger, Steven. "Contra Naturam?: Usury in William Gaddis's *J R.*" *Genre,* 13:93–109 (Spring 1980).

————. "Paper Currencies: Reading William Gaddis." In *In Recognition of William Gaddis.* Edited by John Kuehl and Steven Moore. Pp. 147–161. First published in *Review of Contemporary Fiction,* 2:12–22 (Summer 1982).

INTERVIEWS

Kuehl, John, and Steven Moore. "An Interview with William Gaddis." *Review of Contemporary Fiction,* 2:4–6 (Summer 1982).

Abádi-Nagy, Zoltán. "The Art of Fiction CI: William Gaddis." *Paris Review,* 105:54–89 (Winter 1987).

—WILLIAM DORESKI

Mary Gordon

1949—

*T*O TRACK THE evolution of Mary Gordon's themes and genre interests across two decades is also to discover a trail of critic's labels. Cited regularly as one of her generation's finest writers, Gordon also has been described as a Catholic writer, a feminist writer, a "collective contemporary American Mother," a neorealist novelist, and a master novelist of both the Irish Catholic immigrant subculture and the family saga genre. As early as 1980, Gordon was discussed as a moral novelist "on the verge of moving into the company of writers such as William Golding, Bernard Malamud, Walker Percy and Samuel Beckett." A decade later and under the rubric of essayist-novelist, she was placed alongside George Eliot, William Thackeray, Nathaniel Hawthorne, Mary McCarthy, Salmon Rushdie, and V. S. Naipaul, all novelists whose prowess includes critical essays on literature, art, politics, and religion.

Gordon resists labels of any stripe, especially "Catholic writer." In 1995 she insisted,

> in all honesty, I have to call myself a "woman writer." I won't call myself "a Catholic writer." That's too limiting. . . . it makes me sound like this Graham Greene, Evelyn Waugh, Flannery O'Connor . . . I feel no affinity. I don't feel that was how I was formed. But I do think I was formed as a writer by my femaleness.

When pushed by interviewers to describe her work, Gordon usually resorts to understate-ment that tends to have an autobiographical context:

> I don't think I write about things that are trivial. I had a fortunate background in that I was exposed in a real sense to the "complicatedness" of peoples' lives. On the other hand, the working-class people around me in my Long Island community led seemingly straightforward lives, yet they had a rich inner religious life. It taught me to look a little below the surface.

The critical and commercial success of Gordon's first novel, *Final Payments* (1978), confirmed her virtuosity at expressing in prose the depths of peoples' lives. Eighteen years later, in a memoir-biography Gordon recognizes as being somehow pivotal in her career, *The Shadow Man* (1996) exemplifies what Margaret Drabble has described as Gordon's use of "mutually exclusive ways of being and of seeing" to reach "for a sense of wholeness, for the possibility of inclusion rather than exclusion, for a way of connecting the different passages of existence."

This quest has been a subtext of her four novels, three novellas, collections of essays and short stories, and several dozen other publications that also reflect Gordon's shifting preoccupations with Catholicism, immigrants, and other writers and writing, art, film, ethics, and feminism. Her general subject has been women, men, and children within enclosed circles of love, enmity, and loss. Gordon brings much of this together in *The Shadow Man* and reaffirms with almost harrowing candor her early introduction to "the 'complicatedness' of peoples' lives," including her own, which began on December 8, 1949, in Far Rockaway, New York.

Mary Catherine Gordon's birth was greeted as something of a miracle because her forty-one-year old mother had been crippled by polio since childhood. The only child of David and Anna Gagliano Gordon, Mary grew up in Valley Stream, an Irish Catholic working-class suburb on Long Island where, during the first seven years of her life, she recalls "waiting for my father to be recognized as the man he was, the man he and I (but not my mother) knew him to be. My mother thought he was a failure. Unlike her father, her brothers, he could not make a living. She could." Working as a legal secretary, Anna was the family's breadwinner just as her father had predicted in 1947 when she married David, an unemployed writer whose publishing schemes habitually folded after a few issues. Their marriage was cross-cultural, like that of Anna's Irish-born mother and Sicilian-born father. David, a Lithuanian Jew who had moved to New York from Ohio during the Depression, had become an archconservative convert to Catholicism in 1937, a conversion due in part to his support of Generalissimo Francisco Franco in Spain. The couple was brought together by their shared commitment to a serious religious life. That, their humor, and their daughter gradually became their only intimate bonds. From young Mary's vantage point, her parents represented disparate worlds. On the one hand was the pragmatic, peasant-stock parochialism of her mother and her mother's large family. From her witty, tough-minded mother, Gordon learned a certain intellectual precision, a preoccupation with what she has called "dailiness," and the ability to remember jokes, stories, and conversations. On the other

hand was her intellectual father, who taught her to read at age three and taught her the Latin Mass at age five and French at age six; who let Mary choose the plot structures and characters for her bedtime stories; and who inscribed in seven languages, "To my daughter, Mary Catherine, with love from her father. I love you." in a copy of Robert Louis Stevenson's *A Child's Garden of Verses*.

In a pattern that would mark New York City as his daughter's "real" home, David Gordon often took Mary into Manhattan, where they shared his visits to potential backers for his publishing schemes, lunches in the theater district, and films at Radio City Music Hall. In 1956, when David Gordon had a massive heart attack at the New York Public Library and died a month later, seven-year-old Mary was shunted into her mother's world and her widowed grandmother's home in Valley Stream. The rest of Mary Gordon's childhood and youth was circumscribed by her mother's family, neighborhood, and Irish Catholic parish, and by the poorly staffed, crowded parochial schools she attended.

Deciding at age eight that she wanted to be a writing nun, Gordon began turning out religious treatises on prayer and the Trinity as well as her first poems. Two years later, in a lined notebook, Gordon began a biography of her father with the sentence: "My father had one of the greatest minds I have ever known." After twenty-eight pages, the project trails off. The pages show a straining for facts; it was not until 1994 that Gordon uncovered information that undermined everything he had told her and her mother—facts about his age, his country and town of birth, his family, his education, and his travels. Left unaltered were her father's singular devotion to his daughter, whom he once told he loved more than God, his religious commitment, and his publications. The anti-Semitic and antimodernist vitriol of the latter posed a dilemma that Mary Gordon did not confront until her 1985 essay "David" and did not resolve until 1996 in *The Shadow Man*. However, long before she knew about her father's immigration to and self-fabrications in the United States, her fourth novel, *The Other Side* (1989)—as well as several essays, short stories, and interviews—had attacked myths surrounding immigrant success, prejudice against Jews, and the anti-intellectualism of the American Catholic Church, in general, and of Irish Catholics, in particular.

She learned about these myths and prejudices firsthand from her mother's family, whose members, sometimes kiddingly but more often pejoratively, called Gordon "her father's daughter," meaning outsider, intellectual, and Jew. In 1967 Gordon's stubborn resolve and what she describes as her mother's feeling "a great mandate from my father to take my intellectual life seriously" got her back to Manhattan and to Barnard College, where her mentors were Anne Prescott, Janice Farrar Thaddeus, and Elizabeth Hardwick. Hardwick was the first person to insist that Gordon was a fiction writer, not a poet—advice that augmented her response to Virginia Woolf's writing. Gordon recalls, "I remember the phrase in *Mrs. Dalloway* that did it to me: 'trophies of nuts and roses.' There was a click like the snap of a broken bone; for something in me broke, broke apart."

Gordon attempted her first work of fiction in 1973 while completing a collection of poetry for a master's degree in writing at Syracuse University. That attempt was a short story based on a verbal exchange with James Brain, a British-born anthropologist and a professor at the State University of New York College at New Paltz, whose fieldwork centered on Tanzania. Brain and Gordon married in 1974. In 1973, Gordon enrolled in the doctoral program at Syracuse University and began research for her dissertation on Virginia Woolf. Encouraged by the stylistic and technical models of Woolf and Elizabeth Bowen and by the contemporary moral tone and subject matter of Margaret Drabble, Gordon also began work on

her first novel in 1974, the same year she wrote "Now I Am Married," a short story that became her first published fiction in 1975 and her first prizewinner. A year later, Gordon was befriended in London by Margaret Drabble, who introduced the twenty-six-year-old writer to Peter Matson, Drabble's agent and, subsequently, Gordon's.

Gordon separated from Jim Brain in 1977. Years later, she would admit that in her 1982 short story "Safe" (in *Temporary Shelter*, 1987) Brain was reflected in the narrator's account of her first husband: "[he] thought of me as if I were colonial Africa: a vast, dark, natural resource, capable, possibly, of civilization. As it turns out, I did not want his civilization—a tendency colonialists have discovered to their sorrow." In light of Gordon's acknowledgment of the autobiographical element in the story and the fact that she fell in love in 1977 with Arthur Cash, it is interesting to read the paragraph in "Safe" where the narrator, after making love with her second husband, muses,

> Because of this, because of what I feel for him, what he feels for me, of what we do, can do, have done together in this bed, I left another husband. Broke all sorts of laws: the state's, the church's. Caused a good man pain. And yet it has turned out well. Everyone is happier than ever. I do not understand this.

In 1979, Gordon divorced Brain and married Cash, a biographer of Laurence Sterne and a professor of English at New Paltz. Their marriage marked a decisively happy resolution to the preceding year, when the pending divorce had cast a shadow on even the reception given Mary Gordon's first novel, *Final Payments*.

The novel's success caught Gordon by surprise. She remembers asking Anne Freedgood, her editor at Random House, "Do you think there's a chance I'll get reviewed in the *New York Times*?" Reviews appeared in major newspapers, magazines, and journals throughout the country. Then the novel was named one of the outstanding books of 1978 by the *New York Times Book Review*, was nominated for the New York Critics Circle Award, and received the 1979 Janet Heidinger Kafka Prize for best novel written by an American woman. By 1980, it had been published in eight languages.

Final Payments surprised critics as well, a reaction Nan Robertson underscored in the *New York Times*: ''All of a sudden, this first novel called 'Final Payments' has surged up out of the 'me generation' of self-absorbed, navel-contemplating dropout American children, and has knocked the critics for a loop.'' The plot itself was not the surprise. The story begins at the funeral of Joe Moore, an archconservative Catholic intellectual who has been cared for by his daughter, Isabel, during his last eleven, stroke-ridden years. Determined to ''invent an existence'' for herself, thirty-year-old Isabel leaves their parochial neighborhood and Queens to pursue her adulthood and a job. After a confused affair with her best friend's husband, she falls in love with Hugh Slade, who is a fine person but who is also a married man. When publicly humiliated by Hugh's wife, Isabel recoils from her new life, breaking off contact with Hugh and her friends. She tries to emulate her earlier life by taking care of the one person she has always despised, Margaret Casey, the former housekeeper for her father. After months of physical neglect and psychological numbness, Isabel gives Margaret her inheritance and reclaims her own life.

On the most basic level, the plot resembles that of many other novels; its use of a closed–open–reclosed–reopened sequence would not in itself attract critical interest. Critics were struck, instead, by Gordon's remarkable mastery of language, her parochial and metaphoric treatments of Catholicism, and her tapping into one of our society's best-hidden arenas of confusion—sacrifice.

Final Payments is the work of an accomplished, rather than an apprentice, writer who mixes lyrical, logical, and comedic prose with an intense moral seriousness. Clues to her syntactical sophistication fill the three sentences of the novel's opening paragraph:

> My father's funeral was full of priests. Our house had always been full of priests, talking to my father, asking his advice, spending the night or the week, leaving their black shaving kits on the top of the toilet tank, expecting linen towels for their hands. A priest's care for his hands is his one allowable vanity.

The first deceptively quiet sentence, with its alliteration, suggests Gordon's risk taking, her poetic ear, and the emotional import of the novel's subsequent plot. The accreting precision of the second sentence's details and the wavelike repetition of short phrases begin a boiling motion below the quiet surface that culminates in the pithy wisdom of the third sentence, an example of Gordon's penchant for aphorisms.

Her attention to sentence and paragraph rhythms and to metaphors and similes reflects Gordon's thorough training as a poet. Many sentence sequences, in fact, could easily be divided into poetic lines that rise, fall, and push forward. Gordon also excels in brisk exchanges of logic and debate that break off suddenly, leaving behind palpable resonances. Especially characteristic of *Final Payments* is Gordon's employment of a venerable British tradition of comic fiction—represented by such writers as Jane Austen, Charles Dickens, George Meredith, and James Joyce—in which comedy and religion are intimately linked. For example, Gordon's characters Isabel, Eleanor, and Liz maintain their lifelong friendships through a web of jokes, satire, and profanities drawn from their shared parochial schooling and religious training. As adults they no longer practice their religion, but their comedic treatment of faith acts as its replacement, a surrogacy that all three depend on in relational and psychological crises. Even though Isabel worries privately about ''some hollowness, some wrongness'' in these comedic mediations, the three women trust humor's complex ability to bridge and to heal. A memorable example appears in the novel's final scene, in which Eleanor and Liz arrive before dawn to take Isabel away from Margaret's house and from Isabel's self-destructive reenactment of religious sacrifice. As Isabel walks in a daze toward the car, Liz delivers the ludic salvation: ''Who did your hair? Annette Funicello?''

Gordon suggests that ''the comedy of Catholic life . . . comes, of course, like all other comedy, from the gap between the ideal and the real.'' The novelistic potential spanning this gap is only one of the gifts she absorbed from Catholicism, which, in her words, serves as a ''metaphoric rubric'' for her first two novels. While describing the novelistic advantages of her early introduction to the diverse rhythms, imagery, literature, and participants of the Mass, Gordon also has pointed out,

> One of the greatest treasures a novelist can have is a secret world which he or she can open up to his or her reader. When I turned from poetry to fiction in my mid-twenties, I had a natural subject—the secrets of the Catholic world. And since the door had not been very widely opened before I got there, I was a natural.

Along with her use of language, part of the excitement generated by Gordon's first novel was due to her unfashionable decision to open up parochial Catholicism. Mikhail Bakhtin has suggested that ''A sealed-off interest group, caste or class, existing within an internally unitary and unchanging core of its own, cannot serve as socially productive soil for the development of the novel'' unless that core is ''shifted somehow from its state of internal balance and self-sufficiency.'' His qualification directs us to Gordon's keen sense of novelistic opportunity in the shifting of Catholicism's tectonic plates after Vatican Council II, with its significant changes in the liturgy and language of the Mass and the sacraments, its ecumenism, and its emphases on lay participation and on socioeconomic and political problems. Her novel addresses this gap between preconciliar and postconciliar worldviews.

At the same time, Gordon's exploration of sacrifice captures some of the profound contemporary confusions that drive private and public tendencies toward self-sacrifice and self-destruction. Such confusions have long been recognized; some fifty years ago, for example, the literary theorists Max Horkheimer and Theodor Adorno insisted that ''the history of civilization is the history of the introversion of the sacrifice.'' Throughout *Final Payments* as well as her second and third novels, Gordon addresses the intricate properties of and introverted dangers within sacrifice. The history of sacrifice with Judeo-Christian rituals, scriptures, and traditions forms the larger context of her explorations. Gordon focuses on Roman Catholic traditions of sacrifice involving celibacy, fasting, silence, and the Eucharist; the church's deprivileging of the Virgin Mary's sexuality, and thus all women's sexuality; and the church's designation of women to roles as supportive servants to male authority and the parish community.

Final Payments opens and closes with overt gestures of sacrifice: Isabel's devoted, eleven-year period of caring for her invalid father and her failed attempt to care for Margaret, to whom she subsequently gives her inheritance. Gordon's attention to these gestures and their recipients reveals an astute understanding of the dual nature of sacrifice. As Roberto Calasso had observed, ''The basis of sacrifice lies in the fact that each one of us is two, not one. . . . The revelation of the sacrificial stratagem—that sacrificer and victim are two persons, not one—is the dazzling, ultimate revelation concerning our selves, concerning our double eye.'' Gordon's most dramatic demonstration of this kind of ''double eye'' begins with Isabel's retreat from verbal and sexual expression (thus embodying vows of silence and celibacy) to take care of Margaret whose ''unattractiveness and stupidity,'' by contrast, had clarified Isabel's earliest sense of herself: ''I always knew who I was; I was not Margaret.'' At Margaret's house, however, Isabel sacrifices not only her adult autonomy; she also sacrifices her own attractiveness and intelligence. In what Maud Ellmann describes as Isabel's ''gynophagous relationship with Margaret,'' Isabel internalizes Margaret; she in effect, ''devours'' Margaret through eating binges, weight gain, a terrible haircut, and a retreat into lethargy and sleep. As Isabel recognizes when she looks at herself in the mirror, she has become Margaret, the one person she has always loathed physically, intellectually, and emotionally.

By taking on Margaret's selfhood and body, Isabel demonstrates her unresolved grief for her father, for his faith and parochial world, and for the clarity she had felt while caring for him. Her self-persecutory sacrifice for Margaret clearly parodies her earlier sacrifice through a misguided embodiment of Christ's sacrifice and the Eucharist. In effect, Isabel's fat blocks her acceptance of her father's death and of the complexity of adult relationships. As Isabel recognizes, she must shed the fat, giving up both her father's and Margaret's bodies in order to rejoin Hugh. Isabel's struggle with this decision is an example of Gordon's feminist attention to the intricate ways in which women's roles, sexuality, and desirability are conflated with male authority. By leaving Margaret's house, Isabel takes a first step toward a more inclusive wholeness; it is the kind of open-ended resolution that also appears in Gordon's next two novels.

The publication in 1980 of *The Company of Women* coincided with the birth of Mary Gordon and Arthur Cash's first child, Anna Gordon Cash, a coincidence mentioned, along with Gordon's unmistakable joy, in several interviews at the time. The novel earned Gordon a second Janet Heidinger Kafka Prize and generated prominent critical and commercial attention. Not unexpectedly, comparisons with Gordon's first novel filled the reviews, which were much more mixed than those for *Final Payments*. While even the most laudatory reviews criticized the novel's middle section, critics were divided about the thematic continuity and technical achievement in *The Company of Women*, which is more somber than its predecessor and a far more intense exploration of preconciliar and postconciliar world views.

The novel's working title, *Fields of Force*, suggests the multiple agencies—on the one hand, religious faith and rituals, a Catholic priest and female friendships, and on the other, the turbulent 1960s, a Columbia University professor, and sexuality—that drive the novel's plot, structure, imagery, and themes. Within each of these fields or systems, Gordon deploys radical standards of authority, obedience, and faith that must be ultimately reexamined in terms of truth and love. The movement from systems and standards to reexamination parallels the novel's epigraph: twenty-one lines from ''The Common Life'' by W. H. Auden, Gordon's favorite poet.

Organized around the years 1963, 1969–1970, and 1977, the novel spans fourteen years in the lives of Felicitas Maria Taylor (from age fourteen to twenty-eight); an ultratraditionalist priest, Father Cyprian Leonard; and a group of five working women, including Felicitas' mother, Charlotte Taylor (a character based on Gordon's mother, to whom the novel is dedicated), Elizabeth McCullough, Clare Leary, Mary Rose (née Costello), and Muriel Fisher. As in Gordon's first novel, the plot moves through a closed–opened–reclosed–reopened sequence. Part one (1963) introduces the closed company of women and

Father Cyprian, a circle of religious devotion that is already something of an anomaly in parish life. Gordon lays out the history of their individual and collected lives, including the childhood and youth of the novel's protagonist, Felicitas, the only child in their circle and upon whom the group places its hopes. In part two (1969–1970) the circle is forced open by Felicitas, who tries to establish a life outside the group by attending Columbia University and participating in its cultural life. Her attempts end in double enclosures. The first constitutes a radical, secular mirror image of the Cyprian circle: Felicitas moves into the apartment-commune of her professor and first lover, Robert Cavendish, and his sexual and political female groupies, one of whom has his child. Then Felicitas, when pregnant by either Robert or their neighbor Richard, goes to an illegal abortion clinic but changes her mind and returns to her mother's home. Part three (1977) is an unexpected reopening revealed in seven first-person monologues that also signal Gordon's innovative shift from third-person narration. Almost the entire Cyprian group is now living in Orano, New York, and Felicitas, trying to build a different sort of life for herself and her young daughter, Linda, within the now-aging group, has decided to marry a quiet, steady, local man, Leo Byrne.

In a 1988 interview, Gordon mentioned that someone had made an offer for the movie rights to *The Company of Women* with the proviso that, at the end of the movie, Felicitas and young Linda would go back to New York. To prefer that ending, Gordon protested, was to miss "the whole point of the book in a very radical way. It's not *An Unmarried Woman* [1978]. It's not somebody who goes through a rough patch and pulls herself up by her boot straps and goes and works for *Ms.* And most people do have severely limited lives." Both sides of this exchange reveal the novel's exploration of limitations, in particular, those created by extreme systems and standards of authority.

One of Gordon's central feminist preoccupations in the novel is women's unquestioning abdication of responsibility to male authority—in the form of father figures, priests, lovers, professors, and the male-dominated institutions each represents. Gordon recognizes the comfort and assistance Father Cyprian has given to his five women devotees, and she has elsewhere emphasized, "The positive side of people like Cyprian is that they stand for a kind of absolute standard and passion and uncompromisingness and some notion of the ideal. Without which I think life is very impoverished." However, Gordon shows that it is through her adult women characters' surrender of their and young Felicitas' lives to Cyprian that very real damage occurs. In addition, Gordon uses Felicitas' pregnancy to address specific, pragmatic limitations that women faced in the pre-pill and pre-legal-abortion context of the 1960s "sexual revolution."

Gordon extends her commentary on authority by showing that men's unquestioning presumption of authority and adherence to authoritative structures invariably restrict their own lives. This aspect of *The Company of Women* and Gordon's other novels may seem less significant than their presentation of the difficulties and limitations women often face in life, such as the decisions women have to make about sexuality, marriage, careers, motherhood, and, most important, personhood. Gordon, moreover, introduces such issues in tandem with questions about the moral and spiritual dimensions of contemporary women's lives. Nevertheless, Gordon's warnings about authority are clearly intended for men as well; no male character in her novels demonstrates this more thoroughly than Father Cyprian whose life and career shatter because he is immovably devoted to the absolute authority and rigor of the pre-Vatican II priesthood.

At Felicitas' baptism, one of her three godmothers had joked that the virgin martyr's name given the infant offered "some hope for ordinary human happiness.'' There was, however, nothing ordinary in the love and expectations surrounding the child. As an adult, Felicitas recognizes, ''Adoration is addictive. It is also corrupting; there is no way out of it except a radical life''— which is not what she wants for her daughter, Linda. In the seven monologues of part three, Gordon ultimately gives preference to ordinary, rather than radical, human happiness and thus the women's humane practicality, humor, and daily celebrations of life and love. Late in life, even Cyprian recognizes,

> I have had to be struck down by age and sickness to feel the great richness of the ardent, the extraordinary love I live among. I have had to learn ordinary happiness, and from ordinary happiness, the first real peace of my life, my life which I had wanted full of splendor.

Both *The Company of Women* and *Final Payments* reflect Gordon's ability to transform rituals and patterns observed and memorized in childhood into multivalent fictional structures. As anthropologist Victor Turner reminds us, ''When we act in everyday life, . . . we act in frames we have wrested from the genres of cultural performance. . . . when we enter whatever theatre our lives allow us, we have already learned how strange and many-layered every life is, how extraordinary the ordinary.''

Gordon began work on *Men and Angels* (1985) shortly before her daughter was born in 1980 and completed it a year after the 1983 birth of her second child, a son, David Dess Gordon Cash, whose youth continues to be well-documented in Gordon's articles and essays. While the shift from Catholicism to motherhood in Gordon's novelistic focus seems natural, it was carefully chosen. As she asked an audience at the Boston Public Library in 1985, ''Who has written seriously about the inner world of mothers?'' In several interviews, Gordon detailed what led

to the appearances in the novel of the world of art and a non-Catholic religious fanatic. The latter, she explained, represents an interest in ''the perversion of the religious impulse,'' adding, ''I had used the religious impulse differently in other books.''

In her primary focus on motherhood, Gordon once again circumvented conventions of subject matter observed by most contemporary novelists of her rank. In addition, her thematic development of motherhood ignores postmodernism, which, according to Judie Newman, ''has tended to offer only games for the boys.'' Responses to such decisions can be galling, as Gordon soon recognized: ''to write about women and children is to be immediately ghettoized,'' particularly if ''you take a man out of the central focus.''

Gordon's third novel does just that. Michael, the husband of Anne Foster, one of the novel's two protagonists, has left his family behind in Selby, a New England college town, to begin a sabbatical year in Europe. The novel thus focuses on Anne, her passionate devotion to their two children, and Laura Post, an unattractive, young, fundamentalist fanatic who becomes the children's au pair and who sees in Anne a surrogate mother. Like many of the novel's other characters, both women were rejected by their mothers, and like Isabel in *Final Payments* and Felicitas in *The Company of Women*, both attempt to invent compensatory existences for themselves: Anne in an obsessively devoted motherhood, Laura in a religious fanaticism that denies human love. The tension between obsessive constructs and rejection in this novel make it Gordon's most powerful study of *caritas* (self-sacrificing love or charity).

Anne Foster's research as an art historian adds an important third female presence: the deceased Caroline Watson, a fin de siècle, American-born painter whom Gordon created from the lives, careers, letters, and journals of painters Cecilia Beaux, Mary Cassatt, Suzanne Valadon, and fPaula Modersohn-Becker. Caroline Watson's letters and journals add a third voice to Anne's and Laura's alternating, third-person narrations. Gordon also develops another of several surrogate mother-daughter pairings in Anne and the deceased painter, whose professional struggles as a woman confirm Anne's own experiences. The pair reflects what Judie Newman describes as "a double-mothering": Watson's life and work make it possible for Anne to establish a scholarly reputation; reflexively, Anne's work brings the forgotten painter back to life, an effort Anne thinks about in maternal terms.

Gordon incrementally links such mothering to rejection and death. For example, while poring through the painter's journals, Anne is disturbed to discover Watson's candid rejection of her young son, whom the mother considered unlovable and who eventually drank himself to death. Anne is even more disturbed by her own rejection of the desperately needy Laura, whose presence Anne views as a poison contaminating her home and corrupting her self-image as a good person. What began as Anne's characteristic charity (in hiring the disquieting Laura) darkens to equity, then decency, and finally hatred. Anne's descriptions of these stages draw attention to the reversal process that Gordon has set into motion: Laura's dark spirit lightens in direct proportion to the tension that results from Anne's increasingly difficult gestures of kindness. But for Laura, these gestures are proof of Anne's love. When the au pair's negligence almost kills the children, Anne, enraged, abruptly fires Laura, who responds with equal decisiveness: "She would cut her hands just at the wrists. The cut would be in the name of Anne. . . . so Anne would see how much she loved her." And Laura begins, certain of entering proudly into "the light of God's own countenance." Conversely, in discovering Laura's body, Anne is plunged into the dark knowledge that her closed heart has driven the young woman to her death.

This reversal is so well controlled that Gordon's readers are pushed through their own reversal process, an achievement Walter Clemons summarizes precisely: "Most of the way through *Men and Angels* we're so partial to Anne that we want Laura exposed and punished. At the end we have to revise judgment. We're made to ache for Laura. This change in feeling is the work of a humane, masterly novelist."

After Laura's suicide, Gordon adds a close examination of Anne, the survivor, who, despite her inherent goodness, has always worried about being good. Yet Anne has willfully sacrificed Laura to protect her children and her "safe" family, all of whom are altered by Laura's death and by Anne's and her young son's discovery of Laura's body. By the end of the novel's epilogue, which some critics feel is unnecessary, even melodramatic, Gordon has stripped Anne of hubris. Anne has learned that motherhood is "not all of life" and that her and her family's lives must encompass the dead Laura, Anne's career, ambiguities, and even violence. Human love, she recognizes, must be lived in the midst of, not safely apart from, the "beautiful," "terrible" world. As Margaret Drabble's review of the novel admits, the novel "disturbs, rather than reassures, for it demonstrates that family life itself, that safest, most traditional, most approved of female choices, is not a sanctuary: it is, perpetually, a dangerous place."

By the time *Temporary Shelter* (1987) was published, a number of Gordon's short stories were already in anthologies, and the story "The Only Son of the Doctor" had won an O. Henry Award (1983). For the collection, Gordon put together twenty published and unpublished short stories from the many she had written during the preceding twelve years. In reviewing *Temporary Shelter*, Paul Gray suggests that "Gordon's formidable reputation has not been won through short stories." But then he adds a crucial revision: "At least until now." Within a year of its publication, the collection appeared in Dutch and Japanese translations; in 1990, Gallimard released its French translation.

Although Gordon's three novels had already demonstrated her interest in a conflicted ambience, the collection confirms Gordon's ability to sustain both a constant and an unsettling pressure, which, as Christopher Lehmann-Haupt points out, is "a matter of art, for Ms. Gordon always strives for a point of view that simultaneously envisions the peace and catastrophe implicit in her material." Gordon's balancing act of "peace and catastrophe" is reflected in the tension between the words "shelter" and "temporary." What unites the stories thematically is human loneliness and an awareness that nothing or no one can assuage this condition permanently. The characters who come to understand this truth include children, adult sons and daughters, wives, young mothers, émigrés, widows, divorcées, and elderly persons. In various lengths and narrative voices, their stories unfold within often-layered oppositions such as: female-male; child-adult / parent; Jew-Catholic; Catholic-Protestant; immigrant-established; crippled–non-crippled; underprivileged-privileged; and unsophisticated-sophisticated.

In these and other dichotomies, we recognize a mosaic of preoccupations that characterize all four of Gordon's novels as well her later memoir-biography. The collection's stories concerning parents and children are cases in point. Five of the stories, for instance, reflect Gordon's interest in "bad mother / parent" types. In the superb title story, "Temporary Shelter," Gordon creates a contradictory duality between an uncouth "bad mother" (who tells her son too much, too early about harsh realities and limits) and a refined "good father" (who tells his daughter and surrogate son too little, too late.) Similarly, the story "Billy" shows how a mother's protectiveness of and obsessive candor with her young son maim

his entire life. On the other hand, the "good mothers" who narrate the stories "The Imagination of Disaster" and "Safe" are reminiscent of the fiercely protective Anne Foster in *Men and Angels*. In "The Murderer Guest," Gordon reverses the pattern and allows a child to narrate a terror of invasive violence.

Other stories (such as, "The Magician's Wife" and "Mrs. Cassidy's Last Year") revolve around parents whose love for each other excludes their child. The latter story, published in 1983, contains a nucleus of parental neglect and damage around which Gordon eventually developed her fourth novel, *The Other Side* (1989). Like these two stories, "The Only Son of the Doctor" makes a circuitous approach to neglect, in this case, an obsessively philanthropic father's neglect of his son, whose rebellion is as inevitable as those of Isabel and Felicitas, who, in *Final Payments* and *The Company of Women*, respectively, react in extreme ways to unlivable, radically exclusive love and standards.

Each story in the collection and those written subsequently reveal a distinctive strategy. Gordon habitually sets out a barrage of details, usually disparate, and then, without warning, parries their impact. This device simultaneously delays and intensifies the plot's unfolding. When the time arrives for the recognition scene (the sudden understanding of the story's events and dilemmas), Gordon delivers it in an intense sequence in which she usually still manages to encapsulate disparate details.

This is a part of what Gordon describes as "the craft of concealment" in "The Writing Lesson," the story about writing a story with which she concludes *Temporary Shelter*. Gordon's decision to put this didactic story at the end of the collection is both calculated and risky. But the risk was worth taking, for as Christopher Lehmann-Haupt points out, " 'A Writing Lesson' . . . could just as well have been called 'A Reading Lesson.' " The story is, in fact, more valuable to Gordon's readers that to those who solely want to write well. The most helpful instructions have to do with learning to follow her craft of fictional clues, understatement, and delaying mechanisms; her control of paired and triadic characters; and, certainly, her use of details. Gordon's final instructions in the story suggest a methodology for fiction writing and reading as well as for explication and analysis: "Once you have decided upon the path of your narrative and have understood its implications, go back to the beginning of the story. Describe the house."

In *The Other Side* (1989), Gordon's fourth novel, one of its younger characters demonstrates that this methodology can also be applied to the narrative of one's life. After years of observing the four generations of his Irish American family, the grandson of the novel's main protagonists finds a phrase to describe them all: "the house of Atreus," the mythical Greek dynasty whose internecine behavior includes fratricide and cannibalism. When Dan MacNamara visits Ireland and the respective hometowns of his great-grandparents and his immigrant grandparents, he replaces the ancient metaphor for his dysfunctional family with a medical one: The MacNamaras "could never be happy, any of them, coming from people like the Irish. Unhappiness was bred into the bone, a message in the blood, a code of weakness. The sickle-cell anemia of the Irish: they had to thwart joy in their lives."

This startling assertion is confirmed by each of the twenty-odd MacNamaras. Moreover, it is intimately linked to Gordon's primary agenda for *The Other Side*, which is to debunk myths that have cloaked immigrant experiences and opportunities in the United States, especially those about Irish Catholics. Gordon's treatment of immigration and the Irish is searingly unsentimental, even though it is informed by a personal agenda. In 1985, during the early research stage of *The Other Side* (then titled *The Rose Tree*),

she commented to Walter Clemons, "I think I'm probably of the last generation to feel itself slightly apart from the American mainstream. If I take my children to Ellis Island . . . they won't feel quite the way I do when I see it. I want to write about that before it entirely disappears." During another interview that year, Gordon suddenly asked Herbert Mitgang, "Have you ever been to Ellis Island? My grandmother arrived there at the age of 17. It's a chilling, moving place today."

The novel's structure and language reflect both expanding ambitions and innovative restraints that differentiate it from its predecessors. For *The Other Side* Gordon adopts a five-part structure unlike her earlier triadic organizations. The lengths of the parts and the thirty-four chapters are markedly irregular. Likewise, the narrative voices shift from chapter to chapter, with some chapters employing as many as five narrators. Yet there are two gravitational centers within the narratives: Gordon anchors the multigenerational, alternating voices in parts one, three, and five around the independent voices in part two (three long chapters are given to the voice of Ellen MacNamara, the matriarch and driving force of the family) and part four (one long chapter narrated by Vincent MacNamara, the patriarch of the family). The result is an unsettling, unsmiling, transatlantic family portrait.

Employing a technique akin to montage, Gordon only gradually fits together the individual immigrations of Ellen Costelloe and her future husband, Vincent MacNamara, their Irish childhoods and families, their initial experiences in America, and their subsequent work, marriage, friends, politics, religion, and progeny. Two static devices—the Aristotelian unities of time and place—frame the family's evolution across the seven decades of Ellen's and Vincent's American experiences: the story unfolds within a twenty-four-hour time span on August 14, 1985, at 128 Linden Street in Queens Village, New

York, which had been Ellen and Vincent's home for sixty-three years. There, all four generations are gathering around ninety-year-old Ellen's deathbed. They await eighty-nine-year-old Vincent's return from a convalescent home to fulfill his long-ago promise to Ellen: she could die in her own home with Vincent at her side.

The date is the story's (and Gordon's) most remarkable irony, the significance of which only Vincent vaguely recalls but does not mention. In the Catholic Church calendar, August 14 is a day of vigil, the day before the Feast of the Assumption, which celebrates the bodily ascension of the Virgin Mary into heaven after her death. Gordon, in effect, has set up an ironic contrast between the vigil in Queens and the vigil for the Queen of Heaven. The latter is just the sort of observance that Ellen, in her total repudiation of Catholicism, might have mocked savagely had she been able to speak coherently. Moreover, the dying Ellen's foulmouthed ragings and her actions as a young woman and as a mother are an absolute contradiction of the Virgin Mary's model of gentle humility, maternal love, and serene death.

Thus Gordon opens up a charged arena, in which unarticulated and articulated repudiations of transatlantic, religious, and cultural traditions are linked to anger and death and, more importantly, to what one kills within oneself and others during life. The familial vigil provides a circular context of grief, anger, and unrealized hopes within which Gordon challenges a core of myths and superficial assumptions about immigrant assimilation into the American mainstream. Gordon's repudiation of facile immigration is most fully expressed through the character of Ellen MacNamara, whose radical belligerence against homogeneity and whose strength, intelligence, rage, love, and damage cast long shadows across her life, her husband's, and three generations of their family.

Gordon's description of Ellen's shattered childhood and youth in Ireland underscores the fact that many immigrants were crushed even before they boarded the ships, and such damage was the invisible, immigrant cargo (what John B. Breslin has described as "the blight in their baggage") that they unloaded on "the other side." Ellen's repudiation of her heritage debunks the nostalgia-for-the-home-country myths; scoffing at fellow immigrants who want to take their children to see Ireland, Ellen habitually insists, "What would I go for? . . . none of that 'I'll Take You Home Again Kathleen' cod for me, thank you. That's my husband's department. Say the word 'bog' only and he's drowning in the water of his tears." In Vincent's contrasting sentiments and more particularly in his hopeful approach to America despite a harrowing childhood, we recognize a continued inquiry into ambiguity that Gordon began in the epilogue of *Men and Angels*. There, Anne Foster finally recognizes that there is no predicting how children will respond to rejection and calamity: "children throve or starved, and no one knew why, or what killed or saved."

Another contradiction within *The Other Side* is perhaps the novel's most threatening premise: the immigrants Ellen and Vincent MacNamara are (damage notwithstanding) much stronger and more significant than their American-born progeny. It is a premise that attracted critical attention. For example, while puzzling over "whether it is a failure in Gordon's art or a mark of it, and of her keen sociological insight," David Toolan observes, "the farther we get from Ellen's moon and Vincent's sun along the line of descent, the more that energy dissipates." Alice Bloom, on the other hand, has no such reservations; in the midst of praising Gordon's expertise in creating a twenty-character, family portrait gallery, Bloom suggests,

> for each life, a whole America is painted in, beginning with immigrant life in New York, early union organizing, two world wars, the Depression, holding the family together despite all, up to a new

slacker America of divorce, scattered households, weaker characters, more money but far less sense, much less beauty.

The understatement and general restraint of Gordon's language in this family portrait suggest a major change in her style. Judith Thurman astutely notes, "Gordon's sentences used to be better than her novels, like the kind of lavish hair which outrivals a woman's face. But the prose of 'The Other Side' is matter-of-fact . . . more precisely, its poetic lushness has been suppressed." While not entirely suppressed, Gordon's lyrical talent is reined in, and its appearances are far more irregular. In its place, Gordon sometimes employs the kind of ludic flashes found in her first novel. Another stylistic change is the accelerated pace of contrasts between staccato phrasing and lyricism in Gordon's monologues and dialogues. Many other passages, however, reflect a syntactical evenness that represents another innovation in Gordon's work and aids in the rapid exposition of a great many details.

It is the accretion of such details that makes the novel's conclusion so devastating. Ellen's dying, like her immigration, like many of her offspring's living, is one of inarticulate rage. Looking at the beautiful, translucent skin of her forehead, one of the family members gathered around her bed thinks, "you would expect the brain beneath this bone and skin to be serene. But it is not." When Vincent arrives, Ellen recognizes his step, and the story ends. Gordon leaves us to face the implications of the immigrant "brain beneath this [novel's] bone and skin," which is not serene in America, which was not serene in Europe.

The Other Side was followed by Gordon's collection *Good Boys and Dead Girls and Other Essays* (1991). A year earlier, the same year she received a Barnard Woman of Achievement Award from her alma mater, Gordon had been appointed Millicent C. McIntosh Professor of Writing at Barnard College and an adjunct professor of writing in Columbia University's graduate school. While this entailed a split life between Manhattan and New Paltz, Gordon was overjoyed to be back in her beloved milieu (documented in her 1994 article "Coming Home") and to share its advantages with her children, advantages evident when her daughter's acting debut in a Brearley School production of *The Heidi Chronicles* was featured in a 1995 article by Wendy Wasserstein for the *New Yorker*. The move, however, was complicated by Gordon's having to place her now physically and mentally incapacitated mother in a nursing home in Manhattan. It was not until some five years after the completion of her collection that Gordon addressed her mother's decline in her unsparingly candid essay "My Mother Is Speaking from the Desert," a 1995 feature essay in the *New York Times Magazine*.

As a reviewer for the *Economist* describes them, the twenty-eight pieces in Gordon's 1991 collection reflect the diverse ways in which her "fierce intelligence copes with the shifting surfaces of modern life." The selections themselves came from a wealth of possibilities. Between 1978 and the middle of 1995, Gordon published some fifty-seven essays and articles; eight important introductions, prefaces, or forewords to editions of works by other writers; and some thirty reviews, most of them appearing in the *New York Times Book Review* and the *New York Review of Books*.

The essays, reviews, articles, and journal entries that make up the three-part collection confirm Gordon's command of a nuanced repertoire of analytical and creative skills. Equally clear is a self-imposed mandate for candid inquiry. Like many of the writers who attract her attention, Gordon does not presume to give definitive answers, but she is bent on raising pivotal questions.

Part one of the collection concerns other writers and writing itself while part two groups together essays and articles on Catholicism, Irish Catholics, immigration, and women's struggles (including her own) as writers and artists or with ethical dilemmas such as abortion. Part three, "Parts of a Journal," offers highly charged fragments of autobiography, art and film criticism, and theology. The collection's finale, "The Gospel According to Saint Mark," represents a surprising hermeneutical exercise that is informed by Gordon's theological curiosity, her literary acumen, and her honesty, which is evident in the opening passage: "To write of this subject in this way is to acknowledge my place among the noninnocent." Gordon brings a similar combination to her 1993 essay on anger, written for a *New York Times Book Review* series on the deadly sins, and to her 1992 essay "Explaining Evil," in which she approaches one of the knottiest problems in human inquiry and parenting by considering her childhood and that of her children.

Gordon's power in addressing such issues is evident throughout parts two and three of the *Good Boys and Dead Girls* collection, but her treatment of writers and writing deservedly attracted the most critical attention. This is due in part to the logical and linguistic virtuosity with which she fashions her criticism—these essays reveal her own skills as well as elucidate other writers' work. Similarly, Gordon's selections and analyses of novelists' works often echo preoccupations in her own work: strangely isolated children or adults, Catholicism, the Irish, women as writers or readers or in fiction, and the art of discourse itself.

Gordon's interest in the difficulties of contemporary discourse and in writers' searches for and obsessions with language, fuels many of the section's essays, particularly those on works by Christa Wolf, Ingeborg Bachmann, David Plante, Edith Wharton, and Mary McCarthy. The same is true for her essays on Zelda Fitzgerald (1992),

James Joyce (1994), and Katherine Anne Porter (1995). But because Gordon views Wolf's novel *Accident / A Day's News* as "a model of passionate engagement" (and thus fundamentally similar to her own work), this review offers an unusually succinct summary of both her criticism and fiction. Gordon first examines the language and methodology that allow Wolf to ground "her most abstract notions in concrete life." Then Gordon approaches the protagonist's obsession with the connections between language and human inventiveness and destructiveness, connections underscored by her waiting for news about the Chernobyl disaster and about her brother's surgery. After building up a remarkable catalog of the novel's questions, Gordon pivots to the protagonist's most essential inquiry (directed to her brother, who is about to undergo brain surgery): "Is it worthwhile, brother, staking one's life on being able to express oneself ever more precisely, discernibly, unmistakably?" This question informs Gordon's view of Wolf: "These are exactly the things on which Christa Wolf stakes her life. She uses language as if her life depended upon finding the connections among the conflicting elements that make up the whole of life." One could easily apply this description to Gordon's own work as well as to her professional commitment to write about other writers' and artists' work; it is as if her life and theirs depended on it.

Reviewing the 1991 collection, Doris Earnshaw emphasizes that Gordon's essays show "the range possible to the modern woman writer," a range Gordon continues to expand. As she was putting the collection together, Gordon was expanding her repertoire of genres in fiction. *The Rest of Life: Three Novellas* was published in 1993, the year Gordon was awarded a Guggenheim Fellowship and a year after she had received a Lila Wallace–Reader's Digest Writers' Award.

When asked about the genre shift, Gordon explained, "I think that *The Other Side* was an enormous structural labor; it really kind of wore me out for a larger structure. So, I wanted something that was more compressed, more lyric in its impulse, and actually more poetic and not so dependent on author or structure.'' Responding to a suggestion that the novellas also reflect a technical shifting, she continued, ''I'm probably more open to less linear, less thoroughly rational ways of structuring.'' This is borne out in the nonchronological flow of the three female protagonists' individual narratives. Clearly, each plot is episodic and ambiguous, representing what Gordon describes as ''permeability.''

The three conclusions exemplify the controlled ambiguity. At the end of ''Immaculate Man,'' the first unnamed protagonist admits, ''He holds me in his arms here on the street, the rue Jacob in Paris. 'I'll never leave you,' he says again. I believe him. But I don't know for how long.'' In ''Living at Home,'' the final musings of the second protagonist (also unnamed) augment those of the first: ''I am lying beside him [Lauro] now. . . . It is neither night nor morning. . . . But very soon he'll be awake. And then, I don't know what will happen.'' Finally, in ''The Rest of Life,'' Paola, the seventy-eight-year-old protagonist, with a lifetime of unresolved ambiguity suddenly behind her, walks back toward her hotel in Turin, Italy: ''The doorman says, 'Your son, his friend, are waiting.' Yes, thank you, she says. *Sì, grazie.*'' These words represent a resolution to the entire collection. In short, the novellas are not disparate; they form a deliberately crafted whole. It is only on the surface that they seem autonomous.

The first concerns a forty-eight-year-old social worker (and divorced mother of two teenagers) and her unexpected relationship with Father Clement (Frank) Buckley, the last active priest of a disbanded order, who directs a women's shelter. Her ignorance about his religious faith and tradition equals his sexual inexperience, but their relationship and his profound appreciation of her middle-aged body transform both of their lives. Although she fears he will eventually prefer a more needy and attractive type of woman, Frank is her final, definitive love.

The middle novella's unnamed, forty-five-year-old protagonist lives with Lauro, a fifty-seven-year-old, Italian-born correspondent who is compulsively interested in third world trouble spots. A child of Jewish parents who left Germany in 1935, the British-born protagonist (previously married three times and the mother of two almost-grown sons) is a respected psychiatrist who directs a London school for autistic children. Knowing that he is her final love, she is terrified when Lauro leaves on dangerous assignments; yet, they share this need for ''entrances and exits'' in which their relationship and London flat serve as their oasis.

The final novella opens and closes in 1991 in Italy, where Paola, the Turin-born protagonist, has returned after more than six decades. In 1928, after her sixteen-year-old lover's suicide, her adored father did not defend her from public and familial scorn and instead sent her to relatives in America. Paola never saw her father again, and she has never divulged (not even to her Sicilian-American husband or her sons) her secret of betrayal, shame, and guilt. Only when she revisits the scene of Leo Calvi's suicide can she weep for his death, for their childish suicide pact, for her life-long anguish. Finally understanding that ''the dead, being one and many, knew there was nothing to forgive'' and experiencing emotional buoyancy for the first time since 1928, Paola goes back to her hotel to begin the rest of her life.

On the most obvious level, the novellas are linked in several ways: similar lengths, contemporary settings, intimate venues, and the protagonists' stage of life (middle age and older). Another link is the protagonists' present or past relationships with men; these relationships add an intensity to their lives that Janette Turner Hospital has described as a "supernova" that, despite its risk, gives meaning to ordinary life.

The less-apparent similarities between the protagonists are, however, equally significant. All three have children with whom they have good relationships; each abhors behavior toward children that might damage, shame, or isolate them; all three have worked as professionals to restore constituents' lives, bodies, and minds; each has consciously modeled her life in contrast to that of another woman or a parent; the central man in each protagonist's life represents a fundamentally unshareable other world, whether it be the priesthood, third world trouble spots, or death; all three women articulate deep uncertainties about these relationships; yet neither the two middle-aged women nor the older Paola want to remarry or envision themselves in another love relationship.

Moreover, each protagonist has a penchant for living in the present and for a certain candid modesty in her private musings. Of particular consequence is the women's preoccupation with the meaning and implication of words in their lives and the lives of others. Whether italicized or not, seemingly inevitable or surprising, word emphases fill the novellas' pages, and in them we discover Gordon's finest links between her protagonists and between the novellas. All three narrators are highly conscious of how they tell their own, most intimate story; they are also aware of the implied, and sometimes acknowledged, reader of their story. These venerable novelistic devices, in turn, serve Gordon's larger purpose of questioning language itself and its arbitrary connections with perceived realities and selfhood. It is an indication of Gordon's skill that one or two words can summarize each of the protagonists' lives. For the first protagonist, what has formed her lover's life and what now dictates their life together comes down to "all that." For the second, the entire conscious and unconscious shaping of her adult life was simply "all this." And for Paola, sixty-three years of her life were

determined by the tragedy, "It." Gordon thus emphasizes that words are necessary to what and how we know about ourselves, one another, and events. The stories in *The Rest of Life* are Gordon's reminders that personhood is one's spoken and unspoken language, that both personhood and language are inherently ambiguous, that they are "mated, but in the way of our age, partial."

Gordon's later book, *The Shadow Man* (1996), begins with an extended address, "To the Reader." This introduction establishes the circumstances and investigatory processes of her project in which Gordon, after decades of avoidance, confronts painful facts about her father, who died when she was seven. The (auto)biographical project is, in her words, "a journey of discovery and loss, of loss and re-creation, of the shedding of illusion and the taking on of what might be another illusion, but one of my own. I was looking for my father."

The introduction also includes a partial provenance of the work. This listing of sources only hints at the essays, short stories, novels, articles, and interviews in which Gordon previously addressed themes and events found in *The Shadow Man*. Both the introduction and the book conclude with reaffirmations of love for her father. Between these two points, Gordon engages in a sort of struggle to the death; how to reconcile a man whose writing was either "mad or evil" with her adored and adoring father, a man whose self-fabrications, which Gordon discovered during 1994, threaten her self-perceptions? *The Shadow Man* suggests, if not a turning point in Gordon's career, then a distinctive, circular moment in which her life and family and her parents' lives and families come together under the full scrutiny of her critical, aesthetic, moral, and emotional judgment.

Gordon recognized her first nonfiction book as being somehow "pivotal" in her career. In a 1995 interview, she explained, "I think it brings a lot of preoccupations together. 'Traces them' is the word—'tracks them,' " yet in an early draft of the book's introduction Gordon admitted to uncertainty about the book's genre. After listing biography, autobiography, memoir, and cultural history, she declared, "None of them hits the mark." She later affirmed the "memoir-biography" tag.

The book's goal is similar to that found in the poem Gordon used as the epigraph for *The Company of Women*, "The Common Life" by W. H. Auden, Gordon's favorite poet. Like Auden, Gordon sets herself the task of weighing truth against love in the midst of human complexity. In the first chapter, "Knowing My Father," Gordon begins with her father's heart attack and death in 1957, which split her life "into the part when my father was alive and the part that he was not" and into two self-appointed quests: remembering her father and obeying the laws of the Catholic Church, whose belief in transubstantiation (the transformation of bread and wine into the body and blood of Christ) also offered her a model for transforming her "father's history" into "one of the Lives of the Saints."

The chapter turns to others' memories of her father and then to her own, four of which she has held on to as extended, silent films. These memories, as well as kept and lost objects of her father, offer no solace: the "invention and interpretation" within memory cannot be trusted, and her ongoing habits of losing prized objects and of getting lost confirm "lostness" as her "most true, most fixed, most natural home." Gordon admits the "impossibility of knowing what happened to or with the dead," and yet the chapter concludes with the challenge she sets for herself in the book's subsequent chapters: "The task's impossibility doesn't mean I'm spared the obligation to take it on."

In the second chapter, "Reading My Father," Gordon assumes a complex persona of scholar-researcher, artist, and critic, as well as daughter, to confront her father's publications. She moves through his children's magazines; through his one success, *Hot Dog*, a soft-core girlie magazine; through the anti-Semitic vitriol and bizarre slants of his essays; through a poem in memory of his mother; and through archconservative articles and radiant meditations in Catholic journals. She stops only after rereading letters she and her father exchanged during the last month of his life in Bellevue Hospital.

Gordon recognizes unexpected conflicts embedded within these words. Most significantly, his words inform what Gordon describes as "the making of ME," "the formation of the way I know myself as who I am, different from others." She also realizes that to read his words carefully is to permanently alter the way in which she perceives her adored father: "I can't silence the voice that is hateful to me. . . . It isn't that I wouldn't like to. But I can't." This is further conflicted by Gordon's knowledge that she is "a writer because he was one" and that "he does not allow me, the reading daughter, the writing daughter, a place of rest."

The third chapter, "Tracking My Father: In The Archives," documents Gordon's research in Manhattan and Ohio. The man who emerges is someone she scarcely recognizes. David Gordon, in fact, was not born in Lorain, Ohio, in 1899; he arrived in Baltimore as a Yiddish-speaking six-year-old who had been born in 1894 in Vilna (now called Vilnius), Lithuania. He was not an only child; he had three sisters. Of his immigrant family, barely a trace of information, achievement, or happiness remains. More problematic to his writer-daughter is his education. Instead of attending the University of Pennsylvania and Harvard, as he claimed, he had dropped out of high school to work for the railroad. Moreover, he had never gone to France and England during the twenties. David Gordon's self-fabrications create for his daughter a profoundly sad portrait of immigrant struggle, of self-taught intellectualism, of a young, intelligent Jewish boy who was determined to "pass" in a world of Gentile power.

Gordon divides the fourth chapter into two

parts, neither of which has a precedent in her writing. As a polyphonic interrogation and defense of David Gordon, it is the most risk-filled chapter of this memoir-biography. In the longer first part, which is divided into fourteen sections, Gordon attempts to place her father—an anti-Semitic Jew and a Catholic—within the context of his generation, more specifically, within a generation influenced by the anti-Semitic rhetoric of Henry Roth, H. L. Mencken, Bernard Berenson, and Ezra Pound. Litanies of facts alternate with trials, dreams, and police sketches. Each in its turn breaks down. In the last section, Gordon is alone with searing facts that must be faced and written about, but this desolation contains its contradiction: her words replace her father's. She gives him a new name and place. Gordon realizes that she has, in effect, given birth to her own father; she writes, "This man owes me his life, and he will live forever." In part two, she employs the habit that cemented their seven years together and that informed her professional life: she tells him stories "that will allow us to know who we are."

The final chapter begins with the unsparingly candid description of the continuing decline of Gordon's mother, the essay "My Mother Is Speaking from the Desert" that first appeared as a 1995 feature essay (accompanied by full-page and smaller photographs) in the *New York Times Magazine*. Gordon confirms in the book's introduction the ironic timing of her mother's decline, "At the very time I was engaging in this project of memory and discovery, my mother's mind was shutting down." Gordon elsewhere has admitted that the essay in some ways "was an exposing act to my mother and to myself." Nevertheless, for the sake of others facing such painful realities, she decided, "it was important to speak truthfully about all the ambivalence—to me, the wild ambivalence—that one feels about this kind of degeneration."

The second part of the chapter (the memoir-biography's conclusion) is, like Gordon's de-scription of Christa Wolf's work, "a model of passionate engagement." It is about her decision to have her father's body disinterred from its unmarked place in the Gagliano family plot. Journal entries detail each step: the purchase of a Gordon-Cash cemetery plot, legal intricacies surrounding disinterments and reburials, plans for the reburial service, transportation, food, and clothes. The reburial, along with its documentation in the memoir-biography, is a daughter's extravagant gesture, the likes of which is rarely seen outside myth, opera, or scripture. Yet Gordon wisely concludes in quiet dailiness. Over breakfast, she shares with her son, David, a hard-won certainty: "Love is stronger than death."

Her son's response—"You should write that down before you forget"—is, as Gordon intended, a richly ironic final sentence for *The Shadow Man*. The sentence invites a retrograde review of Gordon's intrinsically bonded life and work. Such a review might move first to 1988 and her essay "I Can't Stand Your Books: A Writer Goes Home," which concludes with Gordon's holding her infant son and determining (after an uncle's funeral and after enduring a barrage of familial insults about her novels): "one thing's for sure I would write about it"; second, to 1977 and her short story "The Thorn," in which a young daughter tries desperately to retain a sharp memory of her dead father; third, to 1959 and Gordon as a ten-year-old trying to bring words and her father to life on the pages of her school notebook: "My father had one of the greatest minds I have ever known"; then finally, to 1955 and the copy of Robert Louis Stevenson's *A Child's Garden of Verses*, inscribed in seven languages that tell Gordon, "To my daughter, Mary Catherine, with love from her father. I love you."

That daughter became a respected and successful writer, critic, and scholar whose first important female protagonist, Isabel Moore (*Final Payments*, 1978), also learned that her beloved's words were written on her body, mind, and life.

As Isabel and *The Shadow Man* affirm, it is a risk-filled business to respond to that metaphorical reality. Despite the risk, Gordon's multi-genred obsession with language and its profound implications in people's lives forms the core of her first two decades as a writer.

Gordon's habitual manipulation of (auto)biographical material across traditional genres may prove to be one of her most radical innovations. An interesting case of genre ambivalence is Gordon's autobiographical essay ''The Important Houses'' (1992), which was included in *Best American Short Stories 1993* despite Gordon's forthright explanation of its genre (reaffirmed in the collection's contributors' notes).

Gordon herself has no interest in discussing demarcations between fact and fiction or life and art; she insists that ''the question of whether there is a different method for fiction and non-fiction . . . is the kind of thing that makes me want to take to my bed with the vapors.'' Vapors are, in truth, anathema to Mary Gordon's personality and work. In 1994, some eleven months before completing *The Shadow Man*, she already had sketched out characters and plots for a fifth novel, *Pearl*, and three more novellas. If, as Gordon has suggested, *The Shadow Man* marks a pivot in her career, her next works warrant, at the very least, the attention her past work has received.

Selected Bibliography

WORKS OF MARY GORDON

NOVELS AND NOVELLAS
Final Payments. New York: Random House, 1978.
The Company of Women. New York: Random House, 1980.
Men and Angels. New York: Random House, 1985.
The Other Side. New York: Viking, 1989.
The Rest of Life: Three Novellas. New York: Viking, 1993.

COLLECTIONS OF SHORT STORIES AND ESSAYS
Temporary Shelter. New York: Random House, 1987.
Good Boys and Dead Girls and Other Essays. New York: Viking, 1991.

MEMOIR-BIOGRAPHY
The Shadow Man. New York: Random House, 1996.

ARTICLES AND OTHER PROSE
''Now I Am Married.'' *Virginia Quarterly Review*, 51:380–400 (Summer 1975).
''The Unexpected Things I Learned from the Woman Who Talked Back to the Pope.'' *Ms.*, July / August 1982, pp. 65–67, 69.
''My Father's Daughter.'' *Mademoiselle*, May 19, 1985, pp. 184–185, 250, 252.
''Growing Up Catholic and Creative.'' *U. S. News & World Report*, October 5, 1987, 74.
''The Irish Catholic Church.'' In *Once a Catholic: Prominent Catholics and Ex-Catholics Discuss the Influence of the Church on Their Lives and Work*. Edited by Peter Occhiogrosso. Boston: Houghton Mifflin, 1987. Pp. 65–78.
''At the Kirks'.'' *Grand Street*, 9:41–53 (Winter 1990).
''Separation.'' *Antaeus*, Nos. 64/65:208–217 (Spring–Autumn 1990). Also in *Best American Short Stories 1991*. Selected by Alice Adams with Katrina Kenison. Boston: Houghton Mifflin, 1991. Pp. 184–193.
''The Silent Drama in Vuillard's Rooms.'' *New York Times*, May 13, 1990, section 2, pp. 1, 38.
''Born to Love'' [on Gwen John]. *Art & Antiques*, April 1992, pp. 60–65.
''The Important Houses.'' *New Yorker*, September 28, 1992, pp. 34–45. Also in *Best American Short Stories 1993*. Edited by Louise Erdrich with Katrina Kenison. Boston: Houghton Mifflin, 1993. Pp. 335–358.
''Introduction.'' In *Zelda Fitzgerald: The Collected Writings*. Edited by Matthew J. Bruccoli. New York: Collier, 1992. Pp. xv–xxvii.
''The Myth of the Tough Dame.'' *Mirabella*, November 1992, pp. 102–108.

''The Deadly Sins / Anger: The Fascination Begins in the Mouth.'' *New York Times Book Review*, June 13, 1993, pp. 3, 31.

''Coming Home.'' *US Air Magazine*, November 1994, p. 136.

''George Eliot, Dorothea, and Me: Rereading (and Rereading) 'Middlemarch.' '' *New York Times Book Review*, May 8, 1994, 3, 26.

Introduction to James Joyce's ''The Dead.'' In *You've Got to Read This: Contemporary American Writers Introduce Stories that Held Them in Awe.* Edited by Ron Hansen and Jim Shepard. New York: Harper, 1994. Pp. 284–286.

''The Angel of Malignity: The Cold Beauty of Katherine Anne Porter.'' *New York Times Book Review*, April 16, 1995, pp. 17–19.

''My Mother is Speaking from the Desert'' [feature essay]. *New York Times Magazine*, March 19, 1995, pp. 44–49, 60, 63, 69, 70.

POETRY

''On Trying to Telephone California,'' ''To a Doctor,'' ''Nancy Creighton (1814–59),'' ''The Dead Ladies,'' and ''Quite a Comedown.'' In *New American Poetry.* Edited by Richard Monaco. New York: McGraw-Hill, 1973. Pp. 74–80.

''To a Cow.'' *American Review*, 16:106 (February 1973).

''Poem for the End of the Year.'' *New York Review of Books*, December 17, 1981, p. 46.

''Wedding Photograph: June 1921.'' *Times Literary Supplement*, December 25, 1981, p. 1501.

''Reading Auden while Nursing My Daughter.'' *New Statesman*, June 18, 1982, p. 22.

''On the Death of Laurence Sterne.'' In 1984 limited edition broadside printed by the Laurence Sterne Trust, Shandy Hall, Coxwold, York, England.

''A Reading Problem.'' *Global City Review*, Fall 1994, pp. 69–70.

BIBLIOGRAPHIES

Bennett, Alma. ''Selected Bibliography.'' In *Mary Gordon.* New York: Twayne, 1996.

Mahon, John W. ''A Bibliography of Writings by Mary Gordon'' and ''A Bibliography of Writings about Mary Gordon.'' In *American Women Writing Fiction: Memory, Identity, Family, Space.* Edited

by Mickey Pearlman. Lexington: University Press of Kentucky, 1989. Pp. 60–67.

BIOGRAPHICAL AND CRITICAL STUDIES

Auchard, John. ''Mary Gordon.'' In *Dictionary of Literary Biography: American Novelists since World War II*, 2d ser., vol. 6. Detroit: Gale, 1980. Pp. 109–112.

Baumann, Paul. ''A Search for the 'Unfettered Self.'' *Commonweal*, May 17, 1991, pp. 327–331.

Bennett, Alma. *Mary Gordon.* New York: Twayne, 1996.

Ellmann, Maud. *The Hunger Artists: Starving, Writing, and Imprisonment.* Cambridge, Mass.: Harvard University Press, 1993. Pp. 49–53.

Gandolfo, Anita. *Testing the Faith: The New Catholic Fiction in America.* Westport, Conn.: Greenwood Press, 1992. Pp. 8, 20–21, 163 ff.

Goldsworthy, Joan. ''Mary Gordon.'' In *Contemporary Authors, New Revision Series*, vol. 44. Detroit: Gale, 1994. Pp. 162–165.

Kolbenschlag, Madonna. ''Man, Woman, Catholic I.'' *America*, July 4–11, 1981, pp. 4–6.

Mahon, Ellen Macleod. ''The Displaced Balance: Mary Gordon's *Men and Angels.*'' In *Mother Puzzles: Daughters and Mothers in Contemporary American Literature.* Edited by Mickey Pearlman. Westport, Conn.: Greenwood Press, 1989. Pp. 91–99.

Mahon, John W. ''Mary Gordon: The Struggle with Love.'' In *American Women Writing Fiction: Memory, Identity, Family, Space.* Edited by Mickey Pearlman. Lexington: University Press of Kentucky, 1989. Pp. 46–60.

''Mary Gordon.'' In *Contemporary Literary Criticism*, vol. 13. Detroit: Gale, 1980. Pp. 249–251.

''Mary Gordon.'' In *Contemporary Literary Criticism*, vol. 22. Detroit: Gale, 1982. Pp. 184–188.

''Mary Gordon.'' In *World Authors 1975–1980.* Edited by Vineta Colby. New York: H. W. Wilson, 1985. Pp. 275–277.

Martin, Wendy. ''Passions and Provocations.'' *New York Times Book Review*, April 28, 1991, p. 9.

May, John R. ''Mary Gordon.'' In *Dictionary of Literary Biography Yearbook: 1981.* Edited by Karen L. Rood, Jean W. Ross, and Richard Ziegfeld. Detroit: Gale, 1992. Pp. 81–85.

Morey, Ann-Janine. ''Beyond Updike: Incarnated

Love in the Novels of Mary Gordon.'' *Christian Century*, November 20, 1985, pp. 1059–1063.

Neary, John M. ''Mary Gordon's *Final Payments*: A Romance of the One True Language.'' *Essays in Literature*, 17:94–110 (Spring 1990).

Newman, Judie. ''Telling a Woman's Story: Fiction as Biography and Biography as Fiction in Mary Gordon's *Men and Angels* and Alison Lurie's *The Truth about Lorin Jones*.'' In *Neo-Realism in Contemporary American Fiction* (Postmodern Studies 5). Edited by Kristiaan Versluys. Amsterdam: Rodopi, 1992. Pp. 171–192.

Perry, Ruth. ''Mary Gordon's Mother.'' In *Narrating Mothers: Theorizing Maternal Subjectivities*. Edited by Brenda O. Daly and Maureen T. Reddy. Knoxville: University of Tennessee Press, 1991. Pp. 209–221.

Ragen, Brian Abel. ''Mary Gordon.'' In *The Oxford Companion to Women's Writing in the United States*. Edited by Cathy N. Davidson and Linda Wagner-Martin. New York: Oxford University Press, 1995. Pp. 358–359.

Seabury, Marcia Bundy. ''Of Belief and Unbelief: The Novels of Mary Gordon.'' *Christianity and Literature*, 40:37–55 (Autumn 1990).

Sipper, Ralph B. ''Five Women . . . and a Priest.'' *Los Angeles Times Book Review*, February 22, 1981, pp. 1, 11.

Suleiman, Susan Rubin. ''On Maternal Splitting: A Propos of Mary Gordon's *Men and Angels*.'' *Signs: Journal of Women in Culture and Society*, 14: 25–41 (Autumn 1988).

Versical, David. ''Mary Gordon.'' In *Contemporary Authors*, vol. 102. Detroit: Gale, 1981. Pp. 223–225.

Ward, Catherine. ''Wake Homes: Four Modern Novels of the Irish-American Family.'' *Eire-Ireland: A Journal of Irish Studies*, 26:78–91 (Summer 1991).

Ward, Susan. ''In Search of 'Ordinary Human Happiness': Rebellion and Affirmation in Mary Gordon's Novels.'' In *Faith of a (Woman) Writer*. Edited by Alice Kessler-Harris and William McBrien. Westport, Conn.: Greenwood Press, 1988. Pp. 303–308.

INTERVIEWS

Bannon, Barbara A. ''PW Interviews Mary Gordon.'' *Publishers Weekly*, February 6, 1981, pp. 274–275.

Bennett, Alma. ''Conversations with Mary Gordon.'' *South Carolina Review*, 28:3–36 (Fall 1995).

Bolotin, Susan. ''Moral Aerobics.'' *Vogue*, April 1985, pp. 232, 234.

Clemons, Walter. ''Ah, They're On to Me.'' *Newsweek*, April 1, 1985, p. 75.

Cooper-Clark, Diana. ''An Interview with Mary Gordon.'' *Commonweal*, May 9, 1980, pp. 270–273.

Gorman, Trisha. ''CA Interview.'' In *Contemporary Authors*, vol. 102. Detroit: Gale, 1981. P. 225.

Hunnewell, Susannah. ''What It's Like to Live in a Female Body.'' *New York Times Book Review*, August 8, 1993, p. 25.

Keyishian, M. Deiter. ''Radical Damage: An Interview with Mary Gordon.'' *Literary Review*, 32:69–82 (Fall 1988).

Milhaven, Annie Lally. ''Mary Gordon.'' In *The Inside Stories: 13 Valiant Women Challenging the Church*. Edited by Annie Lally Milhaven. Mystic, Conn.: Twenty-Third Publications, 1987. Pp. 101–118.

Robertson, Nan. ''A Young Author Probes Old Themes.'' *New York Times*, May 31, 1978, pp. C1, C8.

Samway, Patrick H. ''An Interview with Mary Gordon.'' *America*, May 14, 1994, pp. 12–15.

Schreiber, Le Anne. ''A Talk with Mary Gordon.'' *New York Times Book Review*, February 15, 1981, pp. 26–28.

Wachtel, Eleanor. ''Mary Gordon.'' In *Writers and Company: In Conversation with CBS Radio's Eleanor Wachtel*. Toronto: Knopf, 1993. Pp. 262–272.

White, Edmund. ''Talking with Mary Gordon.'' *Washington Post Book World*, April 9, 1978, pp. E1, E4.

—ALMA BENNETT

Paula Gunn Allen

1939—

*A*T THE FULCRUM of Paula Gunn Allen's poetry, fiction, and scholarship is the figure of a tiny but powerful creature who lives in the shadows, who spins stories to ensure the survival of the people, and who sustains with her intricate web the reciprocal relationships linking specific geographic places, the communities that inhabit them, and the creative forces of the universe:

> Out of her body she extruded
> shining wire, life, and wove the light
> on the void.
> . . . . . .
> After her,
> the women and the men weave blankets into tales
>   of life,
> memories of light and ladders,
> infinity-eyes, and rain.
> After her I sit on my laddered rain-bearing rug
> and mend the tear with string.
>
> "Grandmother," from *Coyote's Daylight Trip*
>   (1978)

As Gunn Allen, who claims Laguna Pueblo and Sioux ancestry, explains in an essay titled "Where I Come from Is Like This" (in *The Sacred Hoop: Recovering the Feminine in American Indian Traditions,* 1986), it is Grandmother Spider "who brought the light, who gave us weaving and medicine, who gave us life." Known also as Thought Woman, this sometimes female, sometimes androgynous mythic creator appears in mul-

tiple guises in the songs, rituals, and stories of several American Indian oral literatures. She resurfaces in the writings of many contemporary Native American authors, including Marilou Awiakta (Cherokee), Joseph Bruchac (Abenaki), Simon Ortiz (Acoma Pueblo), and Gunn Allen's cousin, Leslie Marmon Silko (Laguna Pueblo). Gunn Allen's own work, like the web spun by Tse che nako in a Laguna creation story, insists upon interconnections. Pulling together oral and written traditions from different tribal cultures, she creates threads in her scholarship, poetry, and fiction linking Native American storytellers across generations, time, and place.

In the titular essay of *The Sacred Hoop,* Gunn Allen comments, "At base, every story, every song, every ceremony tells the Indian that each creature is part of a living whole and that all parts of that whole are related to one another by virtue of their participation in the whole of being." She argues in "Where I Come from Is Like This" that the "web of identity that long held tribal people secure ... gradually [became] weakened and torn" in the fifteenth century, when Europeans began colonizing the Americas. Contemporary Native American writers resurrect and transform old stories and spiritual practices to avert "the complete destruction of the web, the ultimate disruption of tribal ways." The text that opens this essay, Gunn Allen's often-anthologized poem

"Grandmother" (from *Coyote's Daylight Trip,* 1978), suggests that recuperating lost tribal values and practices, or "mend[ing] the tear with string," requires not only connecting one's craft to traditional Pueblo arts, such as weaving and storytelling, but also creating new patterns. By emphasizing cultural context and continuity in Native American literature, Gunn Allen bridges seemingly irreconcilable differences between American Indian, European, reservation, urban, spiritual, academic, contemporary, and traditional perspectives.

A creative writer, scholar, and teacher, Gunn Allen earned acclaim as an essential figure in Native American women's literature. In the early seventies, her poetry appeared in the first major anthologies of contemporary Native American writing, establishing her as an important voice in the surge of literary activity referred to as the Native American Renaissance. Her *The Woman Who Owned the Shadows* (1983) was the first novel focusing on a Native American woman published by a Native American woman in fifty years. She is perhaps most recognized for *The Sacred Hoop: Recovering the Feminine in American Indian Traditions* (1986), a landmark collection of essays that interweaves personal, historical, and literary critical perspectives to assert the resilience of Native women's spiritual traditions. In 1989, she edited *Spider Woman's Granddaughters: Traditional Tales and Contemporary Writings by Native American Women,* the first collection of traditional and contemporary stories by Native American women. In addition, she published more than six volumes of poetry and dozens of articles, edited two other anthologies of Native American literature, contributed to numerous anthologies aimed at both academic and nonacademic audiences, and taught at major universities, including Stanford and the University of California at Berkeley. The recipient of many awards and fellowships, including a fellowship from the National Endowment for the Arts and an American Book Award from the Before Columbus

Foundation, Gunn Allen was in the mid-1990s a professor in the English Department at the University of California at Los Angeles and the mother of three grown children. She commuted between Albuquerque and Malibu and gave frequent readings and interviews, covering topics ranging from nuclear power to hypocrisy and racism in the women's movement and among lesbians. She continued to create new patterns, to push against mainstream preconceptions and categories.

Gunn Allen's versatility and her commitment to recognizing women's roles in Native American traditions derived, in part, from the polyglot and matrilineal culture in which she was raised. She was born October 24, 1939, in Albuquerque and grew up in Cubero, New Mexico, a small Spanish-land-grant town between the Laguna and Acoma Pueblo reservations. She pointed out that it is located at a crossroads and that the Laguna Pueblo have long included and intermarried with different peoples. The confluence of cultures, languages, and religious traditions that characterized her childhood led her often to refer to herself as a "multicultural event." Her Laguna Pueblo-Sioux-Scottish American mother spoke English and Mexican Spanish. Her father, twice-elected lieutenant governor of New Mexico and the first Lebanese American to hold a high political office in the United States, grew up speaking Spanish and Arabic. Various members of her family followed Presbyterian, Lutheran, Roman Catholic, Maronite, Jewish, and American Indian religious traditions. As she explains in Joseph Bruchac's anthology *Songs from This Earth on Turtle's Back: Contemporary American Indian Poetry* (1983), these multiple influences can make her, and her writing, difficult to categorize:

> When you're a halfbreed, a daughter of both Laguna and Lebanon; when you're raised in Cubero where almost everyone speaks Spanish, New Mexico style; when your granddaddy is Jewish from Germany—not Orthodox, not Reformed, just born

of Jews; when your whole family's lives are obscure in America, revised, disappeared; when you think Main Street is a small dusty road that winds its way Uptown—to the rest of the small village you call home; when only one of the five languages your family converses in is English—you're bound to be a bit challenging to understand.

While Gunn Allen's life and work reveal a range of cross-cultural sensibilities, she remained firmly connected to her mother's Laguna Pueblo culture, which she termed "the last gynocracy on earth." In Laguna Pueblo traditions, important deities are female, and women are accorded powerful positions in society. Gunn Allen's writing interweaves her mother's and grandmothers' stories, memories, and unofficial versions of history with traditional stories of Corn Woman, Yellow Woman, and Thought Woman. As James Ruppert notes in his 1994 essay, "Paula Gunn Allen," "Both the land which delineates Laguna sacred cosmology and Pueblo cultural traditions have continued to form the bedrock of her understanding of the world and her place in it."

The stories and the particular landscape Gunn Allen came to know as a child function as a matrix for her writing—a place for her to travel out from and come back to, again and again. When Gunn Allen talked about her upbringing, she frequently started with the land and road outside her childhood home. In "The Autobiography of a Confluence," she identifies "The land, the family, the road" as "three themes that haunt my mind and form my muse." She comments that the road from her childhood headed in one direction past her grandmother's house and up toward the mountain and tall rock mesas. In the other direction, the road traveled alongside "the Arroyo, a deep cavernous slit in the earth," meandering past her great-grandfather's trading post toward Laguna and then on toward the highway and the urban world. Gunn Allen remarked to Bruchac that throughout her life, she continued to move in both directions: "Where Cubero is, is between civilization and wilderness; and the

choice for me is: Which way do I go? The resolution for me is that I don't take either choice. I stay in the middle of both."

Like stories, and like the road, the Laguna Pueblo landscape conveys motion. As Gunn Allen explains in "Iyani: It Goes This Way" (in Geary Hobson's *The Remembered Earth: An Anthology of Contemporary Native American Literature,* 1979), identification with the land is "embedded in Native American life and culture in the Southwest." Landscape is not viewed as "a setting for our affairs, a resource, . . . or the ever-present 'Other' which supplies us with a sense of 'I,' " but rather, as part of a dynamic equilibrium shaping both human and nonhuman events. The rain clouds carry the Shiwana, the spirits of the ancestors: "The old ones come . . . to participate in the eternal living being of the land/people as rain. The gods come from the skies and mountain peaks to participate in this immutable gestalt." In an interview with Annie O. Esturoy, Gunn Allen observed that people are the background against which the land enacts *her* drama, rather than the other way around, and that the landscape includes not only the mountains but also the rainstorms.

Along with respect for Laguna Pueblo stories and perspectives, Gunn Allen inherited from her mother and grandmother the pride, anger, and sense of loss that often accompany the choice to claim an American Indian identity. Her mother frequently repeated the injunction she had been told by Gunn Allen's grandmother to "Never forget that you're Indian!" instilling in both women a fierce determination to resist "being engulfed" by mainstream culture. The poem "Dear World" (collected in *Skins and Bones: Poems 1979–1987,* 1988), which is about Gunn Allen's mother, addresses the dilemma faced by mixed-blood American Indians:

> I know you can't make peace
> being Indian and white.
> They cancel each other out.

The speaker explains, "There are historical reasons / for this." In *The Sacred Hoop*'s "A Stranger in My Own Life: Alienation in American Indian Poetry and Prose," Gunn Allen comments, "The breed (whether by parentage or acculturation to non-Indian society) is an Indian who is not an Indian . . . the consciousness of this makes [mixed bloods] seem alien to traditional Indians while making them feel alien among whites." In that collection's "Answering the Deer: Genocide and Continuance in the Poetry of American Indian Women," she attributes the sense of estrangement experienced by both mixed-blood and full-blood Indians to the history of assimilation, relocation, and forced removal that resulted in a "tiny subpopulation" of people who actively claim their American Indian identities. Under such conditions, the choice to identify as an American Indian requires a resolute act of will and must be reinforced by support networks, education, and role models.

Although Gunn Allen valued her own mainstream education, she also recognized it as a force that, like the nineteenth-century boarding schools that punished Indian children for speaking tribal languages, afforded contemporary Native Americans few opportunities to claim their cultural heritage. Her own mixed heritage became a focus of her work and an essential component of the cultural resources she hoped to provide for younger generations of Native Americans, resources that were lacking in her own formal education. "You have to have your reality reflected back, or you think you're not real," she told the Maidu-Koyangkauwi poet Janice Gould, "And then you're damaged forever." In her interview with Eysturoy, she said she offers her students advice she received from her mother: "you must accept all your identities . . . nobody has the right to take them away from you."

When Gunn Allen was six, she went to a Catholic boarding school in Albuquerque, and, as she put it, the Sisters of Charity took over her education. She attended Catholic schools until she was seventeen, returning to Cubero for summers and vacations. Her writing sometimes uses Christian images or echoes the sounds of the Latin Mass. In *Shadow Country*'s "Easter Sunday: Recollection" (1982), for example, the speaker remembers,

> the endless kneeling
> the dust-filled sky, the cold, unending wind,
> the somber certitude of loss and guilt and grief.

She was encouraged to read widely at home and at school. "There's not a lot of illiteracy [where I come from]," she reported in an interview with Bruchac. "When the Bookmobile comes out to the Laguna villages, it doesn't get to half of them before it's empty." In high school, she became infatuated with the works of Gertrude Stein and instructed her mother to buy everything she could find by Stein. In an interview with Donna Perry, Gunn Allen said that she credited Stein in the acknowledgments to her first novel because "I couldn't have found the rhythms I found in *The Woman Who Owned the Shadows,* which I borrowed from legend, unless I had Stein's rhythms inside me. She fractured the language, which then enabled me to do that in my way."

After high school, Gunn Allen intermittently attended the Colorado Women's College and the University of New Mexico. During this time she also married and raised two children. She took her first poetry seminar with Robert Creeley at the University of New Mexico, when, as she reported, she was still "this frightened little housewife from Grants, New Mexico, bedecked in a beehive hairdo." She acknowledged Creeley as a major influence, along with Charles Olson and Allen Ginsberg. She was also inspired by the protest movements of the 1960s, but felt her options as an activist were limited by her responsibilities as a mother. "To some extent I became a writer because I had these babies and couldn't just go and do anything I wanted," she told Eysturoy. She decided to finish her undergraduate education at the University of Oregon, where she received a B.A. in English in 1966 and an M.F.A. in creative writing two years later.

In 1968, the publication of Kiowa writer N. Scott Momaday's *House Made of Dawn* proved a life-altering event for Gunn Allen. As a displaced, mixed-blood student in Eugene, Oregon, she found herself missing her community and her landscape. "I was dreadfully alone and dreadfully suicidal," she said to Bruchac. Her parents sent her a new book by a family acquaintance; grounded in American Indian oral traditions, the novel told of the ritual healing of a mixed-blood Southwesterner. On numerous occasions Gunn Allen asserted that *House Made of Dawn* "saved my life." "I wouldn't be writing now if Momaday hadn't done that book. I would have died." Reading Momaday allowed her to see that she was not alone. "If I was crazy at least fifty thousand people out there were just as nutty in exactly the same way I was, so it was okay," she joked. The book also returned her land to her. "Eugene, Oregon is nothing like *Cubero,*" she emphasized. "Part of what I was going through was land sickness—loss of land." It offered her a prototype and a direction for her own writing. She explained to Laura Coltelli, "I had no models. There was no such thing as Native American writing, contemporary writing, then—not that I knew of."

After obtaining her M.F.A., Gunn Allen returned to Albuquerque and entered the Ph.D. program in English at the University of New Mexico. When she informed the graduate dean that she wished to focus on Native American literature, he answered that there was no such thing. To the extent that literature can be defined as a field of study sanctioned by institutions of higher education, his response was accurate. As Lucy Maddox observes in her 1993 essay "Native American Poetry," "Only within the last few years has Native American writing attracted sufficient notice to earn it a distinct place in texts devoted to American literature or in the curricula of academic departments where American literature is taught." However, Momaday's novel, which was awarded a Pulitzer Prize in 1969, helped to change the atmosphere in which the Native American writer could exist. Like Gunn Allen, other Native American writers began to feel that they were not alone. As Maddox explains, the success of Momaday's novel "opened up the possibility that the American public might be receptive to Native American writing and, more important, that publishers might recognize the existence of a commercially viable market for Native writing."

Like Momaday, Gunn Allen played a pivotal role in securing the literary establishment's recognition of new Native American writers and scholars. While completing her doctoral studies at the University of New Mexico, she taught at several schools, including San Diego State University, the College of San Mateo, and the California State University at San Francisco. During these years, she helped to found the Association for Studies in American Indian Literature, a professional organization that continues to provide a forum for scholars and writers. In 1975, she filed her dissertation on Pueblo emergence stories titled "Sipapu: A Cultural Perspective," earning a Ph.D. in American Studies with a special emphasis in Native American Literature.

Gunn Allen's growing professional commitment to Native American literature coincided with an outburst of political activity on the part of many Native Americans of her generation, marked, in part, by the founding of the American Indian Movement (AIM) in 1968; the publication of Standing Rock Sioux Vine Deloria Jr.'s "Indian Manifesto," *Custer Died for Your Sins,* in 1969; and the occupation of Alcatraz Island in 1969 and of Wounded Knee in 1973. As Maddox observes, "these events signaled, on the one hand, a new determination on the part of many Native Americans to articulate their own concerns in their own voices, and, on the other hand, an increased interest on the part of non-Indian Americans in listening to those voices." In her capacity as a scholar and teacher, Gunn Allen acted as a mediator for those voices, providing a context in which they could begin to be heard and understood through careful and responsible study. As she explains in *Studies in American Indian Literature: Critical Essays and Course Designs* (1983), "When Americans cannot view American Indians as people with histories, cultures, customs, and understandings worthy of study and dispassionate observation, they ignore the real plight of too many Indian people who must go without jobs, food, decent housing, or, far too often, the simple human right to survive."

Working with other scholars, Gunn Allen set about to integrate American Indian literary traditions into the study of American literature at every level. *Studies in American Indian Literature,* which she edited, developed from the 1977 Modern Language Association–National Endowment for the Humanities Summer Seminar on American Indian Literature. This indispensable reference book provides guidelines for broad survey courses, as well as suggestions for the specialized study necessary to approach "a realistic understanding of literatures that represent several hundred different tribes and cover several thousand years." Susan Fraiman summarizes the book's agenda and achievement: "part theoretical text, part hands-on study guide, and part reformist curriculum guide, [this] book clearly demonstrates that Native American Literatures have emerged as integral to the discipline of American Literature(s)." Continuing in the mid-1990s to be the standard introduction to the field, it features articles and bibliographies by prominent writers and scholars, including Linda Hogan and A. LaVonne Brown Ruoff. Gunn Allen contributed two important essays: "The Sacred Hoop: A Contemporary Perspective," which discusses Native American literature within the context of ceremonial conceptions of time and space, and "The Feminine Landscape of Leslie Marmon Silko's *Ceremony,*" which uses the principles outlined in "The Sacred Hoop" to contextualize Silko's novel.

In the late 1970s and early 1980s, Gunn Allen's promotion of fellow Native American poets, as well as her prodigious publication of her own poetry and literary commentaries, helped to secure both a community and an audience for those she called "contemporary tribal singers." In eight years, she published five volumes of poetry: *The Blind Lion* (1974), *Coyote's Daylight Trip* (1978), *A Cannon between My Knees* (1981), *Star Child* (1981), and *Shadow Country* (1982). She also edited *A, A Journal of Contemporary Literature's* 1978 special issue on Native women of New Mexico and wrote several essays discussing poetry by Native American women. For her these literary activities contribute to the cultural survival of Native American peoples. In *The Sacred Hoop*'s "Angry Women Are Building: Issues and Struggles Facing American Indian Women Today," she specifies some causes of cultural genocide: "sometimes violent and always virulent racist attitudes and behaviors directed against us by an entertainment and educational system that wants only one thing from Indians: our silence, our invisibility, and our collective death." If reading Momaday's novel saved Gunn Allen's life because it figuratively returned her home and its landscape to her, her mentoring and critical work, in turn, encouraged other Native American women writers to claim their own tribal and spiritual landscapes. In an autobiographical essay titled "You *Can* Go Home Again," Athabascan poet Mary TallMountain pays tribute to Gunn Allen as the "friend and tutor" who "honed my unskilled talent into the great gift of wordsmithing.'' ''In one of my quick clips of vision,'' Tall-Mountain writes, ''Paula and I are caught changeless, sitting still and rapt, Indian women bound by the enduring thread of a common dream, a powerful purpose.''

In *The Sacred Hoop*'s ''Answering the Deer,'' Gunn Allen describes the purpose of contemporary Native American women's poetry as both practical and spiritual: to bear historic witness to ''the real possibility of total extinction'' and yet enact ''the oldest tribal ceremonial theme,'' that of transformation and renewal. Gunn Allen's essay articulates the complex negotiations attained by poets who must balance the ''despairing reality'' of loss, alienation, and rage with ''the hope that continued existence requires.'' Her attentive, elegant readings of poems by Leslie Marmon Silko, Linda Hogan (Chickasaw/Choctaw), Elizabeth Cook-Lynn (Crow-Creek-Sioux), Joy Harjo (Creek), and others demonstrate the vigor and resilience of the theme of regeneration. She identifies humor as the vital element, ''reconciling the tradition of continuance, bonding, and celebration with the stark facts of racial destruction.'' Coyote tales, for example, provide a metaphor for ''all the foolishness and the anger that have characterized American Indian life in the centuries since invasion.''

Gunn Allen's own poetry uses regeneration motifs to register the effects of colonization while affirming the vitality of tribal traditions. As Helen Jaskoski notes, the complex image of spider-weaver-poet and other metaphors of androgyny and creativity in ''Grandmother'' are the result of a cultural literacy that is particularly Laguna Pueblo, but also includes Walt Whitman's ''A Noiseless Patient Spider'' as well as a traditional Tewa poem, the ''Song of the Sky Loom.'' Many of Gunn Allen's poems forge connections between Euro-American, American Indian, and other poetic traditions. Critics have observed that her early poems reveal a craftsmanship similar to that of Creeley and other Black Mountain poets.

In interviews, Gunn Allen acknowledged the influence of these and other poets, including Judy Grahn, John Keats, Denise Levertov, Audre Lorde, Adrienne Rich, and William Carlos Williams. In addition to writing, she cited the importance of music, including the Arabic chants of her Lebanese father, the country-western ballads of the Southwest, the musical structure of Mozart, and the rhythm of pueblo hunting songs.

While Paula Gunn Allen's poetry draws on multiple genres and traditions, it continually returns to the landscapes of the Southwest and the spiritual values of Native American traditions. She spoke to Bruchac of ''a sorrow and a grievingness'' that permeates her poetry's attempt to reconcile ''all the places that I am.'' This ''hauntedness'' is particularly noticeable in *Shadow Country,* where many poems speak of ''going home,'' either literally or in one's imagination. Several poems reveal facets of the contemporary life of a modern, urban, professional American Indian woman. Yet they remain grounded in the oral heritage, history, dreams, spirituality, and memories of the Laguna Pueblo people. As Maddox explains,

> the voices of ''the old ones,'' both the human voices of her Laguna family and the spirit voices that speak in and through the landscape near Laguna, are perhaps the most real presences in Allen's poetry, even though the poems track her movement through the parts of contemporary America, especially its cities, that seem the most hostile to the old voices.

The first poem in *Shadow Country,* ''Creation Story,'' recounts the Laguna Keres origin myth, ''an emergence story'' of moving from the fourth world into the fifth that invokes ''Iyetiko,'' corn mother and sister to Grandmother Spider. It provides a corollary for the images of movement, loss, and searching that characterize poems with titles like ''Los Angeles, 1980,'' ''American Apocalypse,'' or ''Words for a Bike-Racing, Osprey-Chasing Wine-Drunk Squaw Man.'' Although the emphasis varies from one poem to the next, most interfuse mythic, personal, and historical meanings. The intensely autobiographical ''On the Street: Monument'' laments the death of one of the poet's twin sons and, at the same time, talks back to Marxist theorists. ''The Warrior,'' dedicated to the Navajo soldier Ira Hayes, offers a somber corrective to official history in its portrayal of ritual sacrifice. The cowboy dancers in ''Durango Suite,'' a poem dedicated to Gunn Allen's father, stomp toward each other with coyote bravado. The final section of *Shadow Country,* titled ''Medicine Song,'' focuses on women. Several poems, such as ''Womanwork'' and ''The Beautiful Woman Who Sings,'' honor the resourcefulness and endurance of Native American women. The cycle ''Suiciding(ed) Indian Women'' testifies to the painful conditions of the lives of Indian women. It mourns the abandonment of Corn Woman, who was sent away long ago by men who, preferring gambling to ''necessary dancing'' and other traditional responsibilities, ''put women out of the center.'' This poem refers to Gunn Allen's own experience of displacement and near suicide, links this contemporary experience to the historical experiences of Indian women, and anticipates the ''gynocentric'' perspective she will articulate in her collection of essays, *The Sacred Hoop.*

Folklorists use the term ''cycles'' to refer to a number of stories—whether told, chanted, or sung—that cluster around a more or less central theme and often feature a specific cast of characters and events. Perhaps it is not surprising that Gunn Allen arranges the poems in *Shadow Country* to function something like story cycles. However, Gunn Allen identifies a similar dynamic in contemporary Native American novels, including her *The Woman Who Owned the Shadows.* In an anecdote appearing in *Spider Woman's Granddaughters: Traditional Tales and Contemporary Writings by Native American*

Women (1989) that comments on the history of the Native American novel, she reports that at an early Modern Language Association seminar on American Indian literature, the ''germane and humorous question'' was asked, ''Do Indians write novels?'' ''We literary people in the session laughed,'' she reports, ''recognizing the quixotic nature of [this] query and our situation.'' She goes on to say that the Native American writers in the room ''had to ask ourselves if we were traitors to our Indianness. Maybe we were so assimilated, so un-Indian, that we were doing white folks' work and didn't realize it!'' Nevertheless, Gunn Allen answers, ''Yes, Indians do novels. And nowadays some of us write them. Writing them in the phonetic alphabet is the new part, that and the name. The rest of it, however, is as old as the hills, from which we take our sense of who we are.''

In her critical writings on the Native American novel, Gunn Allen introduces the notion of ''ceremonial time,'' which she contrasts to an evolutionary or progressive sense of events unfolding in history. She observes that unlike typical Western narratives that require conflict-and-resolution-driven plots, American Indian literature relies on non-linear, nonchronological structures derived from ritual-based traditions. Because the few nineteenth-century novels written by American Indian writers had to capitulate to Western narrative structures in order to get published at all, she explains, they necessarily portrayed the Indian as a tragic victim. Early American Indian fiction was thus concerned with unredeemed and unredeemable forces of alienation, colonization, genocide, and hopelessness. *House Made of Dawn,* the first nonchronological, ritual-centered novel written by a Native American, connects the literary genre of the novel to American Indian oral traditions, creating a fusion between narrative forms thought to be incompatible prior to its publication. Gunn Allen was one of the first scholars to identify the non-linear, nonliterary structures that enable and compel the contemporary Native American novel. In addition, she noted other important features that characterize Native American novels written since the 1960s, such as a focus on a mixed-blood protagonist; the recurrence of shifting modes of identity; and the convergence of personal, familial, and mythic stories.

As A. LaVonne Brown Ruoff observes, Gunn Allen's autobiographical novel, *The Woman Who Owned the Shadows,* brings a feminist perspective to the ritual quest Gunn Allen recognizes in the works of other American Indian writers. Gunn Allen identifies woman lore, generation, regeneration, and continuance as the novel's central themes. She describes the main character as a woman made up of qualities drawn from her grandmother, mother, and herself. This protagonist, who feels at home neither in the Southwest nor in San Francisco, recovers from a nervous breakdown, the death of her infant son, divorce, and near suicide by recognizing a place for herself in the old stories. Educated at a convent school, Ephanie Atencio grows up removed from tribal influence: she "had forgotten how to spin dreams, imaginings about her life, her future self, her present delights. Had cut herself off from the sweet spring of her own being." As an adult, she flees her childhood community because of the effects of Western society and history: Indian males beat their wives and children, persecute homosexuals, murder their neighbors, and drink themselves to death. In San Francisco, she feels uneasy in the urban American Indian community and uncomfortable in the company of white women who look to her for the wisdom they believe she must innately own as a Native American. But Ephanie learns the art of remembering, she establishes a connection with the Grandmother's spirit, who eventually helps her to understand that her life and the lives of her mother and grandmother parallel the tribal narratives. She recovers her past, her place, and therefore her identity. As Gunn Allen commented to Donna Perry, "It is only when [Ephanie] goes back and recognizes all that pain and that she is Indian and that she has told all these lies to herself that she discovers who she is. She has to go back and retell her stories and then she can reclaim herself." At the end of the novel, Ephanie tells her story to her white lover, Teresa, in an invitation to make new connections.

Critic Annette Van Dyke points out that for the Lagunas, storytelling often functions as a ceremony for curing, and she suggests that the novel's conclusion continues this tradition. *The Woman Who Owned the Shadows* is structured by a series of prologues that form a story cycle describing Thought Woman, her sisters, and the twin war gods. Other traditional stories, including the Iroquois creation story "The Woman Who Fell From the Sky" and the Keres "Yellow Woman" stories, circulate through the text. These emblems from a verifiable oral tradition are interwoven with "artifacts" of a writing-based culture, including personal letters, a divorce settlement, and notes from a therapist.

In this way the novel resituates the old stories even as it offers new ways to interpret familiar institutions in the dominant culture such as post offices, courthouses, and doctors' offices. Thematically, it addresses the protagonist's intensely personal odyssey in relation to larger political events, such as the U.S. government's forced detainment and relocation of Navajo prisoners during the "Indian wars," and later the forced internment of Japanese American citizens during World War II. In addition, Gunn Allen self-consciously incorporated components from literary modernism into her novel. As she commented to Janice Gould, "American Indian writers use ... tropes that come directly out of the Native world, out of our tradition and historical senses; and also out of being very contemporary, modern members of the Native community. But we also use tropes and structures that come directly from American letters, and beyond that from the continent and England.'' Gunn Allen was pleased that *The Woman Who Owned the Shadows* was well-received in university courses of American literature, and she was especially heartened by the response it received in American Indian communities. In interviews, she noted that although she intended to speak to the dilemma of the mixed-blood woman, several full-blood American Indian students said that it spoke to them as well.

In her interview with Eysturoy, Gunn Allen commented that *The Sacred Hoop: Recovering the Feminine in American Indian Traditions* picks up where *The Woman Who Owned the Shadows* ends. It ''is about recovery, recovery of ourselves.'' First published in 1986 and reissued in 1992, this collection pulls together seventeen essays written between 1975 and 1985 that, together, articulate the central concerns in Gunn Allen's work, including the influence of ceremony on contemporary Indian literature, the crucial role of Native American women in sustaining American Indian cultural traditions, the challenges faced by a mixed-blood writer, and the place of feminist and lesbian perspectives in Native American studies. Although the essays have been classified as literary criticism, anthropology, history, theology, and cultural theory, they are written in a direct, accessible style. Gunn Allen made a conscious choice to use the personal voice. She calls attention to her subjective knowledge in part to counteract the supposed objectivity of anthropologists and folklorists. Throughout the collection, she retells stories and recasts ideas, embodying the arguments she sets forth about the way stories in an oral tradition shift or change according to the audience, purpose, or time frame in which they are presented. This repeating and intertwining of personal, theoretical, literary, and historical observations, in turn, opens up questions not often considered in literary criticism and analysis. She examines not only the initial colonial/patriarchal responses to Native American women but also the lingering, and often devastating, effects of colonialism on the everyday lives of Native American women.

The Sacred Hoop, like much of Gunn Allen's work, celebrates the ability of American Indians to endure, in part, by reviving woman- and ritual-centered spiritual traditions denounced by missionaries and outlawed by the federal government. Her conviction, noted in Bruchac's *Songs from This Earth on Turtle's Back,* ''that transformation is not only possible through proper use of language, but is inherent to it'' and that ''Language, like a woman, can bring into being what was not in being'' is reflected in the section titles of the book. The first section, ''The Ways of Our Grandmothers,'' includes the essays ''Grandmother of the Sun: Ritual Gynocracy in Native America'' and ''When Women Throw Down Bundles: Strong Women Make Strong Nations''; it provides an overview of female deities in Native American traditions, a history of American Indian women, and some of the family and tribal stories shaping Gunn Allen's own life. The second section, ''The Word Warriors,'' presents studies of traditional and contemporary American Indian literatures. The third section, ''Pushing Up the Sky,'' reflects Gunn Allen's concerns with contemporary women's lives, including her involvement in the feminist movement, American Indian women's movements, and lesbian feminism.

The latter discussions, especially, highlight aspects of mainstream (white) feminism's vexed relation to the roles and experiences of Native American women, as well as those of other women of color. In several respects, the publication of *The Sacred Hoop* initiated discussion of the relation between feminist and Native American studies. Despite the rapid developments in both academic fields over the past decade, *The Sacred Hoop* is a text non-Indian feminist scholars continue to draw upon in their approaches to Native American texts and issues. In her essay "Who Is Your Mother? Red Roots of White Feminism" Gunn Allen argues "the feminist idea of power as it ideally accrues to women stems from tribal sources." Pointing to the traditional power and status of Iroquois matrons and asserting that the United States's constitutional system of government is based on the Iroquois confederacy, Gunn Allen attacks the propensity of patriarchal historians to misread and ignore women's roles. Other essays in the collection demonstrate the ambivalence experienced by Native American women in the face of white feminism.

In "Kochinnenako in Academe: Three Approaches to Interpreting a Keres Indian Tale," Gunn Allen addresses typical limits of white feminist interpretation. She first presents a version of the Keres Yellow Woman tale transcribed by her mother's uncle, John Gunn, after he collected it from a Keres-speaking informant. She contrasts the "classist, conflict-centered patriarchal assumptions" of this version with a hypothetical "Feminist-Tribal Interpretation," which provides "a traditionally tribal, nonracist, feminist understanding of traditional and contemporary American Indian life." In between these two interpretations, she includes a traditional "Keres Interpretation" that does not focus on women and a "non-Keres feminist" reading of the story. She imagines that a white feminist interpretation such as the latter would conclude, inaccurately, that the story was about the low status of women in tribal cultures and the violence enacted on them by men. She notes ways in which mainstream feminist and Native American perspectives are not always contiguous, and warns mainstream feminists to be aware of the limits, blindnesses, and racist and classist tendencies of their approaches. In this way, *The Sacred Hoop* encouraged white feminist awareness of issues in Native American culture even as it articulated the resistance to white feminism that women of color began voicing in the 1970s and 1980s.

Critics have taken issue with what they see as Gunn Allen's "essentialism"—the assumption that those with the same ancestry, the same biological "essence," share the same identity and experience—an approach they consider to be reductive. In *Keeping Slug Woman Alive: A Holistic Approach to American Indian Texts* (1993), Greg Sarris (Kashaya Pomo) criticizes Gunn Allen for generalizing across tribal cultures and histories, and for not taking sufficient account of her own cultural position as a critic. Sarris suggests that in *The Sacred Hoop* Gunn Allen may have diminished the complexity and power of the stories and points of view she includes. Similarly, Osage scholar Robert Allen Warrior's study *Tribal Secrets: Recovering American Indian Intellectual Traditions* (1995) associates the ideas Gunn Allen puts forth in *The Sacred Hoop* with other "appeals to essentialized world views" that present American Indian culture as "part of a global consciousness shared by all indigenous people in all periods of history." Warrior identifies these ideas as characteristic of American Indian critical writing of the mid-1980s and notes how Native women critics are now dissenting from "both the essentialist feminism of Allen and the complete dismissal of Euro-American feminism of other Native women."

Other critics, however, such as Gerald Vizenor, Kenneth Lincoln, and Sagari Dhairyam, detect strategic irony and mockery in Gunn Allen's self-presentation as an American Indian and in her generalizations about Indian and lesbian identities. Drawing on postcolonial and cultural theory, Dhairyam describes Gunn Allen's focus on "body/experience" as one of the many "paradoxes which shape Allen's signature." The sustained critical engagement with issues raised in *The Sacred Hoop* makes clear the importance of Gunn Allen's work to growing fields of feminist, lesbian, and multicultural studies, as well as to Native American studies. Even critics who contest some of her arguments also recognize, depend upon, and build on the work she began. In addition to Sarris, critics and historians such as Timothy Sweet, Siobhan Senier, M. Annette Jaimes (Juaneño-Yaqui), and Theresa Halsey (Standing Rock Sioux) have developed ideas Gunn Allen first articulated in *The Sacred Hoop.*

The questions raised by one of the last essays in *The Sacred Hoop*, ''Hwame, Koshkalaka, and the Rest: Lesbians in American Indian Cultures,'' have in a similar manner exposed tensions between Native American and lesbian and gay literary and cultural interpretations. In this piece, Gunn Allen sets lesbianism ''within a larger social and spiritual tribal context'' and comments on the ways that the lack of attention to lesbianism in ethnographic studies of Native Americans assumes lesbianism to be an ''individual aberration that . . . has nothing to do with tribal life in general.'' Gunn Allen adopts the Lakota term *koskalaka,* translated as ''young man'' or ''woman who doesn't want to marry,'' and retranslates it as ''dyke.'' She likewise takes up the term *winkte*— the *koskalaka's* male counterpart—and explains that both were seen to possess magical, mysterious, and sacred ''medicine power.'' She asserts that lesbians, especially, ''did exist widely in tribal cultures'' and goes on to say, ''Indeed, same-sex relationships may have been the norm for primary pair-bonding.''

Her poetry and short fiction frequently elaborate on these views and have appeared in collections that represent lesbians, gays, and women of color. Her poem ''Some Like Indians Endure,'' for example, demonstrates her ability to bridge these different communities. The poem begins, ''i have in my mind that / dykes are indians / they're a lot like indians / they used to live as tribes . . .'' It continues, ''like indians   dykes / are supposed to die out / or forget / or drink all the time.'' The poem ends by noting, ''they don't anyway— —even / though the worst happens'' ''they remember and they / stay . . . / because the stars / remember / and the persistent stubborn grass / of

the earth.'' Judy Grahn, who was Gunn Allen's partner at the time, printed this poem in *Another Mother Tongue: Gay Words, Gay Worlds* (1984); it is the opening poem, functioning as an invocation of sorts, in Will Roscoe's *Living the Spirit: A Gay American Indian Anthology* (1988); and it appears in Gloria Anzaldúa's *Making Face, Making Soul: Haciendo Caras, Creative and Critical Perspectives by Feminists of Color* (1990). Selections of Gunn Allen's work-in-progress *Raven's Road,* which she described to Coltelli as ''a medicine-dyke novel,'' appear in *Living the Spirit,* in Bennett L. Singer's *Growing Up Gay: A Literary Anthology* (1993), and in other collections of lesbian and gay writing.

A number of gay critics use Gunn Allen's comparisons and assertions as a catalyst for their own work, most notably Walter L. Williams in his *The Spirit and the Flesh: Sexual Diversity in American Indian Culture* (1986). Others, such as Ann-Louise Keating and Dhairyam, find in Gunn Allen's writings a positive model for lesbian women of color. Some critics, however, claim that Native American culture has been made inappropriately available to gay and lesbian activists. Gunn Allen herself, in a 1989 review of *The Spirit and the Flesh,* expresses discomfort at the way Williams' ''exploration of traditional roles of those he has decided to identify as 'berdache' serves to bolster his sense of the acceptability of gayness.'' The figure of the ''berdache''—a term first used by French explorers to describe male Indians who specialized in the work of women and formed emotional and sexual relationships with other men—has been used by both non-Native and Native groups, following the work of Williams and others, to provide a history of American homosexuality as a basis for promoting gay rights. Gunn Allen points out, ''Too often native people's attitudes, beliefs and religious practices are used in greater America to authorize its own proclivities, and this use seldom redounds to the benefit of the native people.'' In a 1992 essay titled "American Indian Women: At the Center of Indigenous Resistance in Contemporary North America," Jaimes and Halsey take Gunn Allen to task for enabling studies such as Williams'. They suggest that Gunn Allen's "sweeping exaggeration" about the frequency of same-sex relationships "has been seized upon by those seeking to deploy their own version of 'noble savage' mythology for political purposes."

In the late 1980s and early 1990s, Gunn Allen continued the commitment to traditional and contemporary Native American women that emerges in *The Sacred Hoop.* In that collection's closing essay, titled "Stealing the Thunder: Future Visions for American Indian Women, Tribes, and Literary Studies," she observes that because there have been no great and noble women to complement figures like Red Cloud, Black Elk, or Lame Deer "in that essentially literary cultural memory called tradition, there is no sense of the part that women have played in tribal life either in the past or today." She then conjectures,

> But let us suppose that among the true heroes were and are many women. Suppose the names of Molly Brant, Magnus, Pocahontas, Sacagawea, Malinalli, Nancy Ward, Sara Winnemucca, and scores of others were the names that came to mind when we thought of the noble and sacred past of the tribes. Suppose that when we heard the tribal deities referred to we thought of Thought Woman, Sky Woman, Cihuacoatyl, Selu—that theirs was the name of god, the Great Spirit.

In her recent poetry and through her publication of anthologies of writing by Native American women, Gunn Allen has worked to make this supposition a reality. She foregrounds and recontextualizes the stories and histories of contemporary Indian women, legendary historical figures, and deities.

Gunn Allen's 1988 volume of poetry, *Skins and Bones,* is divided into three categories: "Songs of Tradition," "Songs of Colonization," and "Songs of Generation." These song-poems recast women like "Eve the Fox"; Sacagawea, "The One Who Skins Cats"; and "Molly Brant, Iroquois Matron" as warriors, pathfinders, and wily survivors. Their wry, ironic tone is a comment on the ways in which these legendary/historical figures were recorded in history as traitors to their people. In monologues that become dialogues, Gunn Allen's women warriors answer back to the ethnologists, historians, husbands, white women, and other figures who excoriated, exoticized, or silenced them. In "Pocahontas to Her English Husband, John Rolfe," the speaker transforms herself from a "hostage" of Christian, European culture into a powerful tricksterlike woman who not only controls her own death but also brings about the death that awaits the descendants of European culture. The poem focuses not, as one might expect from the title, on Pocahontas' love for her husband, but rather on her teaching him to plant tobacco. His perception of this source of sacred power in many tribal traditions as a source of gold will have dire consequences:

> Tobacco. / It is not without irony that by this crop / your descendants die, for other / powers than you know / take part in this and all things.

The poem thus criticizes the depiction of Pocahontas by Charles Larson in the epigraph as the victim of a "white dream—a dream of cultural superiority." This poem and others evoke a complex, transformative response to a world out of balance and the effects of forced separation and loss.

In the 1980s, Gunn Allen's poetry became widely anthologized. It appears in mainstream collections like *Harper's Anthology of 20th Century Native American Poetry* (1988, edited by Duane Niatum [Klallam]) and Norton's *New Worlds of Literature* (1989, edited by Jerome Beaty and

J. Paul Hunter). The literary critic Cynthia Franklin has discussed the emergence in the 1980s of specialized and multigenre anthologies, describing them as "a privileged site for marginalized groups of women to theorize and put into practice communities founded upon a powerful but inherently unstable politics of identity." Yet anthologization brings with it a problem of interpretation. While stories and writers are thus given more widespread and mainstream attention, the contexts that gave rise to them disappear. Native American critics in particular have cautioned that anthologies add another degree of separation to stories that often have already been removed from an oral, tribal storytelling tradition.

Well aware of these problems, Gunn Allen points out that publishing practices and interpretive paradigms that ignore or minimize tribal traditions result in "aesthetic colonization" and "intellectual apartheid." In her own publications, she intervenes in these practices by acknowledging cross-cultural tensions and iniquities, breaking down distinctions between literary genres, and promoting "tribal aesthetics." Throughout her work, she emphasized the importance of performance, infusing her writings with features of oral traditions and relying frequently on the spoken word. She gave frequent public presentations of her poetry, drawing large audiences at major universities, city coffee shops, academic conferences, and Native American community colleges and high schools. In response to Katharyn Aal's question whether she prefers giving a reading or having a group of poems published, Gunn Allen claimed she'd "much rather do a reading." She said that, as a writer who draws on various oral traditions, she needs to "see what her audience hears." She uses her body, voice, and face to convey meaning, and she "listens" to her audience, relying on their responses to direct her performance. To some degree, she took on the role of the storyteller who chooses her words in response to the audience's needs.

As part of the effort to usher Native American literature into the mainstream, Gunn Allen edited three anthologies of primary material: *Spider Woman's Granddaughters: Traditional Tales and Contemporary Writing by Native American Women* (1989), *Grandmothers of the Light: A Medicine Woman's Sourcebook* (1991), and *Voice of the Turtle: American Indian Literature 1900–1970* (1994). In each volume, she extracts the content from previously published selections, such as "as-told-to" ethnologies or nineteenth-century novels, and reorganizes them into sequences that reflect and establish tribal oral traditions. She further contextualizes the works she includes by providing background on the political and social histories that inform them, identifying particular Native American tribal affiliations and traditions. In addition to accessible introductions that establish evaluative guidelines for Native American literature as a whole, she includes prefaces to the sections within each volume and to each entry. Each anthology also contains extensive bibliographies, glossaries, and biographical backgrounds on the contributors.

Spider Woman's Granddaughters collects stories from diverse and often difficult-to-find ethnographic sources, previously unpublished autobiographical pieces by new writers, and excerpts from longer works of published fiction in support of Gunn Allen's proposition that American Indian women "spend each day aware that we live in a war zone." The introduction examines the relationship between tribal literature and the experience of conquest, and also proposes critical parameters for a fuller understanding of the stories. The anthology is divided into three sections, each of which reveals the ways that literature by Native American women redefines popular conceptions of warfare. In "The Warriors," the stories redress stereotypes of Native Americans as "bloodthirsty savages howling down in vengeance upon helpless white settlers," as well as portrayals of brave warriors as "noble victims of white depredation.'' The pieces in ''The Casualties'' explore the relationship between victimizers in the earlier stories, evil spirit people, and contemporary victimizers, such as whites in general or the Roman Catholic church in particular. ''The Resistance'' demonstrates that traditional and contemporary stories alike express the powers of wonder, of right understanding of ritual events, and of endurance. Perhaps most significantly, Gunn Allen arranges the individual pieces within each section to reveal the continuity between old stories, ''as-told-to'' nineteenth-century stories, and contemporary writings. For example, she places ''told-to-people'' renditions of traditional stories alongside contemporary writers' ''told-to-the-page'' stories. Thus Delia Oshogay's rendition of the traditional Chippewa (Anishinabeg) story ''Oshkikwe's Baby'' prefigures the story's rearticulation in Louise Erdrich's short story ''American Horse.''

Spider Woman's Granddaughters met with generally widespread enthusiasm. Ursula K. Le Guin, in the *New York Times Book Review*, called the book's implications ''exhilarating,'' noting the ''intelligent passion'' with which the stories are written and commenting on the ''esthetic wholeness'' of the volume itself. In addition to being chosen as a *New York Times Book Review* ''Notable Book of 1989,'' it was awarded an American Book Award from the Before Columbus Foundation, a Susan Koppelman Award from the Women's Caucus of the Popular and American Culture Association, and the Santa Cruz Native American Literature Prize, all in 1990.

Gunn Allen's 1991 collection, *Grandmothers of the Light,* conveys a highly personal exploration of American Indian oral traditions. In this volume, Gunn Allen turns from ''gynocracy,'' the female-based social system she coined in *The Sacred Hoop,* to ''cosmogyny,'' a term she defines as connoting ''an ordered universe arranged in harmony with gynocratic principles.'' She explores the mysteries of women's power in Native American societies by retelling the tribal myths that surround them. They are the stories that, Gunn Allen says, ''have served as my guides and as my sourcebook as I navigate the perilous journey along the path that marks the boundary between the mundane world and the world of spirit.'' As Choctaw scholar Clara Sue Kidwell notes in a review that appeared in the *American Indian Quarterly,* Gunn Allen plays ''the role of a contemporary spiderwoman, a creative force. Like Indian weavers and storytellers among tribes today, she creates new forms and embellishments on traditional themes.'' In these ''Goddess'' stories Gunn Allen thus revisits and interweaves stories that have become familiar in her work. Grandmother Spider, for example, appears in ''A Hot Time,'' a humorous commentary ''on the supposed infirmities of old age.''

Although some reviews celebrated the evocative language and woman-centered focus in *Grandmothers of the Light,* it received a more guarded response than Gunn Allen's other works. Kidwell calls Gunn Allen's interpretive weavings of traditional myths ''intriguing'' and revealing of ''the humor that gives insight into the deeper meaning of the tales,'' but determines that ''they are also problematic in that Allen appropriates an essential Native American identity to legitimate her stories.'' She goes on to call the book ''dangerous'' because it may lead readers, especially feminist readers, to regard Gunn Allen's ''tales as some kind of authentic 'truth.' '' The volume also raised questions about the publication of sacred materials, questions Gunn Allen herself raised elsewhere in relation to Silko's novel *Ceremony.*

Although Gunn Allen celebrated *Ceremony's* ''feminine landscape'' in a well-known article that appeared in both *Studies in American Indian Literature* and *The Sacred Hoop,* in a 1990 article titled ''Special Problems in Teaching Leslie Marmon Silko's *Ceremony,*'' published in the

American Indian Quarterly, she criticizes Silko's use of a clan story to structure *Ceremony.* According to tribal mores, she explains, certain stories are never meant to leave the tribe. Drawing on lessons she learned as a child raised in a Laguna Pueblo community, she warns that "telling the old stories, revealing the old ways can only lead to disaster." She strongly urges caution in the teaching of students who exhibit more enthusiasm than sensitivity, and she takes a particularly strong stance in regard to scholarly research: "I could no more do (or sanction) the kind of ceremonial investigation of *Ceremony* done by some researchers than I could slit my mother's throat. Even seeing some of it published makes my skin crawl." Some critics note that, in collecting sacred stories drawn from many American tribal traditions in *Grandmothers of the Light,* Gunn Allen appears to be doing exactly this kind of investigation. Jana Sequoya (Chickasaw), for example, considers Gunn Allen's own appropriations of sacred material for the commercial market "a practice that she apparently did not forego following her critique of that practice."

Gunn Allen's 1994 anthology, *Voice of the Turtle,* is the first of a projected two-volume collection of Native American narrative literature of the past one hundred years. Its fundamental theme, Gunn Allen writes, is the transformations that Native Americans have experienced. Its selections, from seventeen Native American writers, include short stories, sketches, parts of novels and autobiographies, and traditional tales. The foreword provides a useful overview of Native American literature. In a note to the readers, Gunn Allen requests that they approach the excerpts from longer works, not as incomplete fragments, but "as one of many interconnecting portions of the vast Native Narrative Tradition." She explains that reading the book "should be as much as possible like participating in storytelling sessions over several weeks." The second volume, also under Gunn Allen's editorship, will examine literature published since 1970.

While Gunn Allen repeatedly asserted that the Native narrative tradition reshapes, challenges, and invigorates the field of American literary studies, she also insisted upon its political significance. When asked about the history of genocide of Native Americans, Gunn Allen argued that it continued, not just on a cultural level, as in the "soul-theft" that occurs when baskets are placed in museums or sacred burial sites are converted into golf courses, but also on the level of literal survival. She discussed the killing of Indians in Guatemala, Mexico, and Argentina; the forced sterilization of Indian women and men; the fact that on death row in the United States, in proportion to the population, American Indian men outnumber every other group; and the devastating effects of fetal alcohol syndrome. At the same time, she noted the continuation of American Indian activism, applauded the building of coalitions, and supported the recognition that the British, Scottish, Welsh, and Irish cultures are ethnic like the Pueblo, the Lakota, and the Cherokee. Gunn Allen's 1992 preface to the reissued *Sacred Hoop* addresses the increasingly rapid recuperation of American Indian culture and tradition, the pan-tribal economic and environmental issues that the five-hundredth anniversary of the landing of Columbus forced many to confront, and the child welfare issues confronting Indian community leaders. In her continued exploration of a women's rituals and spirituality, she began to write about menopause and the powers and positions of women as they grow older, in Native American contexts and the world over.

Gunn Allen's interest in nuclear technology, a theme that emerged frequently in her work in the early 1990s, consolidates the concerns listed above in a forceful manner. In the mid-1990s she was collaborating with feminist scholar Jane Caputi to produce an anthology titled *The*

Heart of Knowledge: American Indians on the Bomb. Gunn Allen's interest in nuclear power and radiation, like that of other Native American writers, grew out of the disastrous consequences of uranium mining in her own community. As Caputi notes in her essay "The Heart of Knowledge: Nuclear Themes in Native American Thought and Literature," not only was the atom bomb developed on Pueblo lands, but uranium milling on Laguna and Navajo lands has led to dire health and economic conditions. Furthermore, the problems of the atomic industry are not limited to Southwestern Native Americans: "Because Indian Reservations often are located in undeveloped and economically depressed areas, they have become prime targets for test sites and waste dumps . . . American Indians (as well as other indigenous peoples worldwide) have been, often unknowingly, on the front lines of atomic development." Gunn Allen and other Native American writers, such as Marilou Awiakta, Leslie Marmon Silko, and Gunn Allen's sister, Carol Anne Sanchez, offer apocalyptic visions of a prophesied return-to-balance of the world. These writings function not only as an expression of tribal resistance to exploitation but also as part of a movement to reclaim the powers of technology.

Raven's Road, the novel Gunn Allen in the mid-1990s had been working on for over a decade, weaves conceptions of nuclear technology into its central concerns. In one scene, excerpted in Mary Dougherty Bartlett's *The New Native American Novel: Works in Progress* (1986), two mixed-blood women position themselves to witness an above-ground test of the atomic bomb. When the test starts, Raven, the title character, remembers incredulously that what she saw in the bomb was "An old woman, . . . I remember now. I saw an old woman's face." Gunn Allen commented to Coltelli that this novel redresses the cold-war

attitude of "Oh look, they're going to kill us" with the tribal attitude of "Look, the grandmother is coming." As she explained in an interview with Gould, "I believe that there's something terribly sacred about the bomb, and about nuclear power. I'm exploring the possibility that maybe it isn't the isotopes that kill, but our terrible disrespect for this ancient grandmother goddess who walks among us again." She adds in Caputi's *Gossips, Gorgons, and Crones: The Fates of the Earth* (1993) that this association of the atomic bomb with the Laguna creation story of Thought Woman, or Grandmother Spider, has been circulating in stories around Laguna that portray the bomb as something Thought Woman breathed into being, just as she breathed into being her two sisters, Iyatiku and Naotsete: "Uranium was first mined at Laguna, and the form it comes in is called yellowcake. . . . I can't help thinking that Iyatiku, who is Corn Woman, is associated with all this and that yellowcake is associated with yellow Corn Woman. Around Laguna they say she's come back, and they say it with respect to the bomb."

According to Caputi's "The Heart of Knowledge," Gunn Allen's approach recalls the atom's "repressed sacred/gynocentric face" and thereby removes it "from its immurement in male supremacist language, sexuality, and religion." Nevertheless, Gunn Allen told Perry that she anticipated *Raven's Road* would receive criticism from "white liberals" for its nuclear stance and for its treatment of other issues, including alcoholism, drug abuse, and "power tripping" within the feminist community. She explained her role as that of a third-world woman writer who must challenge each of her many audiences. She surmised, "Maybe by the turn of the century [Native American writers and their colonizers] can have a real dialogue about the past—not just, 'You're guilty,' or 'How awful,' but a real dialogue about what happened and what is still happening."

Selected Bibliography

WORKS OF PAULA GUNN ALLEN

POETRY

The Blind Lion. Berkeley, Cal.: Thorp Springs, 1974.

Coyote's Daylight Trip. Albuquerque, N. Mex.: La Confluencia, 1978.

A Cannon between My Knees. New York: Strawberry, 1981.

Star Child. Marvin, S. Dak.: Blue Cloud Quarterly, 1981.

Shadow Country. Los Angeles: University of California Press, 1982. Foreword by Kenneth Lincoln.

Wyrds. San Francisco: Taurean Horn, 1987.

Skins and Bones: Poems 1979–1987. Albuquerque, N. Mex.: West End, 1988.

"Grandmother." In *New Worlds of Literature.* Edited by Jerome Beaty and J. Paul Hunter. New York: Norton, 1989. Pp. 264–265.

"Some Like Indians Endure." In *Making Face, Making Soul: Haciendo Caras, Creative and Critical Perspectives by Feminists of Color.* Edited by Gloria Anzaldúa. San Francisco: aunt lute, 1990. Pp. 298–301.

PROSE

"The Mythopoetic Vision in Native American Literature." *American Indian Culture and Research Journal,* 1, no. 1:3–13 (1974).

"Sipapu: A Cultural Perspective." Ph.D. dissertation, University of New Mexico, 1975.

"The Sacred Hoop: A Contemporary Indian Perspective on American Indian Literature." In *Literature of the American Indians: Views and Interpretations.* Edited by Abraham Chapman. New York: New American Library, 1975. Pp. 111–135. Reprinted in *Studies in American Indian Literature.* Edited by Paula Gunn Allen. New York: Modern Language Association, 1983. Pp. 3–22. Reprinted in *The Sacred Hoop: Recovering the Feminine in American Indian Traditions.* Boston: Beacon, 1986. Pp. 54–75.

"A Stranger in My Own Life: Alienation in Contemporary Native American Prose and Poetry." *Studies in American Indian Literature,* 2, no. 4:1–10 (Winter 1978) and 3, no. 2:16–23 (Spring 1979). Expanded and revised in *MELUS,* 7, no. 2:3–19 (Summer 1980). Reprinted in *The Sacred Hoop:*

Recovering The Feminine In American Indian Traditions. Boston: Beacon, 1986. Pp. 127–146.

"The Psychological Landscape of *Ceremony.*" *American Indian Quarterly* 5, no. 1:7–12 (1979). Expanded and revised as "The Feminine Landscape of Leslie Marmon Silko's *Ceremony.*" In *Studies in American Indian Literature.* Edited by Paula Gunn Allen. New York: Modern Language Association, 1983. Pp. 127–133. Reprinted in *The Sacred Hoop: Recovering the Feminine in American Indian Traditions.* Boston: Beacon, 1986. Pp. 118–126.

"Beloved Women: The American Indian Lesbian." *Conditions* 7:67–87 (1981). Revised and expanded as "*Hwame, Koshkalaka,* and the Rest: Lesbians in American Indian Cultures." In *The Sacred Hoop: Recovering the Feminine in American Indian Traditions.* Boston: Beacon, 1986. Pp. 245–261.

"The Grace That Remains: American Indian Women's Literature." *Book Forum,* 5, no. 3:376–382 (1981). Reprinted as *American Indians Today.* New York: Horizon, 1982.

"Answering the Deer: Genocide and Continuance in American Indian Women's Poetry." *American Indian Culture and Research Journal,* 6, no. 1 (1982). Reprinted in *The Sacred Hoop: Recovering the Feminine in American Indian Traditions.* Boston: Beacon, 1986. Pp. 155–164.

"Chee Dostoyevsky Rides the Reservation: Contemporary American Indian Fiction, 1967–1980." In *The History of Western American Literature.* Edited by Thomas J. Lyon. Lincoln: University of Nebraska Press, 1983.

"This Wilderness in My Blood: Spiritual Foundations of the Poetry of Five American Indian Women." In *Coyote Was Here.* Edited by Bo Schöler. Aarhus, Denmark: Seklos, 1984. Pp. 95–115. Reprinted in *The Sacred Hoop: Recovering the Feminine in American Indian Traditions.* Boston: Beacon, 1986. Pp. 165–183.

The Woman Who Owned the Shadows. San Francisco: Spinsters, Ink, 1983; aunt lute, 1994.

"All the Good Indians." In *The 60s without Apology.* Edited by Sohnya Sayres, Anders Stephanson, Stanley Aronowitz, and Fredric Jameson. Minneapolis: University of Minnesota Press, 1984. Pp. 226–229.

"Red Roots of White Feminism." In *Learning Our Way: Essays on Feminist Education.* Edited by Sandra Potter and Charlotte Bunch. Trumansburg, N.Y.: The Crossing Press, 1983. Reprinted as "Who Is Your Mother? Red Roots of White Feminism." *Sinister Wisdom,* 25:34–46 (1984). Reprinted in *The Sacred Hoop: Recovering the Feminine in American Indian Traditions.* Boston: Beacon, 1986. Pp. 209–221.

"Kochinnenako in Academe: Three Approaches to Interpreting a Keres Indian Tale." *North Dakota Quarterly,* 53, no. 2:84–106 (Spring 1985). Reprinted in *The Sacred Hoop: Recovering the Feminine in American Indian Traditions.* Boston: Beacon, 1986. Pp. 222–244.

Raven's Road (excerpt). In *The New Native American Novel: Works in Progress.* Edited by Mary Dougherty Bartlett. Albuquerque: University of New Mexico Press, 1986.

"Whose Dream Is This Anyway? Remythologizing and Self-definition in Contemporary American Indian Fiction." In *Literature and the Visual Arts in Contemporary Society.* Edited by Suzanne Ferguson and Barbara Groselclose. Coumbus: Ohio State University Press, 1985. Pp. 95–122. Reprinted in *The Sacred Hoop: Recovering the Feminine in American Indian Traditions.* Boston: Beacon, 1986. Pp. 76–101.

The Sacred Hoop: Recovering the Feminine in American Indian Traditions. Boston: Beacon, 1986; Beacon, 1992.

"American Indian Fiction, 1968–1983." In *A Literary History of the American West.* Edited by J. Golden Taylor and Thomas J. Lyon. Fort Worth: Texas Christian University Press, 1987. Pp. 1058–1066.

"The Autobiography of a Confluence." In *I Tell You Now: Autobiographical Essays by Native American Writers.* Edited by Brian Swann and Arnold Krupat. Lincoln: University of Nebraska Press, 1987. Pp. 141–154.

"Bringing Home the Fact: Tradition and Continuity in the Imagination." In *Recovering the Word: Essays on Native American Literature.* Edited by Brian Swann and Arnold Krupat. Berkeley: University of California Press, 1987. Pp. 563–579.

"Earthly Relations, Carnal Knowledge: Southwestern American Indian Women Writers and Landscape" (with Patricia Clark Smith). In *The Desert Is No Lady: Southwestern Landscapes in Women's Writing and Art.* Edited by Vera Norwood and Janice Monk. New Haven: Yale University Press, 1987. Pp. 174–196.

"America's Founding Mothers: Our Native American Roots." *Utne Reader,* March–April 1989, pp. 108–109.

Review of *The Spirit and The Flesh: Sexual Diversity in American Indian Culture,* by Walter L. Williams. *American Indian Quarterly,* 13:109–110 (Winter 1989).

"What I Do When I Write . . ." *Woman's Review of Books,* 6:23 (July 1989).

"Special Problems in Teaching Leslie Marmon Silko's *Ceremony.*" *American Indian Quarterly,* 14:379–386 (Fall 1990).

"Voice of the First Mother." *Ms.,* September–October 1990, pp. 25–26.

"The Woman I Love Is a Planet, The Planet I Love Is a Tree." In *Reweaving the World: The Emergence of Ecofeminism.* Edited by Irene Diamond and Gloria Feman Orenstein. San Francisco: Sierra Club, 1990. Pp. 52–57.

"My Lebanon." In *Roots and Branches: Contemporary Essays by West Coast Writers.* Edited by Howard Junker. San Francisco: Mercury House, 1991. Pp. 97–109.

" 'Border' Studies: The Intersection of Gender and Color." In *Introduction to Scholarship in Modern Languages and Literature.* Edited by Joseph Gibaldi. Pp. 303–319. New York: Modern Language Association, 1992. Pp. 303–319.

"The Business of Columbus" (with Lee Francis III and the assistance of Mary Allen Francis). In *Columbus and Beyond: Views from Native Americans.* Edited by Randolph Jorgen. Tucson: Southwest Parks and Monuments Association, 1992. Pp. 56–62.

"Skywoman and Her Sisters." *Ms.,* September–October 1992, pp. 22–26.

"Going Home, December 1992." In *A Circle of Nations: Voices and Visions of American Indians.* Edited by John Gattuso. Hillsboro, Ore.: Beyond Words Publishers, 1993.

"Introduction." *Gossips, Gorgons, and Crones: The Fates of the Earth,* by Jane Caputi. Santa Fe: Bear and Company Publishing, 1993.

"Spirit Woman." In *Earth Song, Sky Spirit: Short Stories of the Contemporary Native American Experience.* Edited by Clifford E. Trafzer. New York: Doubleday, 1993. Pp. 245–255.

Raven's Road (excerpt). In *Growing Up Gay/Growing Up Lesbian: A Literary Anthology.* Edited by Bennett L. Singer. New York: New Press, 1994.

ANTHOLOGIES THAT FEATURE MULTIPLE WORKS BY PAULA GUNN ALLEN

Four Indian Poets. Edited by John R. Milton. Vermillion: University of South Dakota Press, 1974.

The Remembered Earth: An Anthology of Contemporary Native American Literature. Edited by Geary Hobsen (Cherokee). Albuquerque, N. Mex.: Red Earth, 1979.

Shantih, 4, no. 2, special issue on Native American literature (1979). Edited by Brian Swann.

The Third Woman: Minority Women Writers of the United States. Edited by Dexter Fisher [Alice Poindexter]. Boston: Houghton Mifflin, 1980.

"Native American Women." *Frontiers,* 6, special issue (Fall 1981). Edited by Linda Hogan (Chickasaw).

Songs from This Earth on Turtle's Back: Contemporary American Indian Poetry. Edited by Joseph Bruchac (Abenaki). Greenfield Center, New York: Greenfield Review, 1983.

A Gathering of Spirit. Edited by Beth Brant (Mohawk). Rockland, Maine: Sinister Wisdom, 1984.

That's What She Said: Contemporary Poetry and Fiction by Native American Women. Edited by Rayna Green (Cherokee). Bloomington: Indiana University Press, 1984.

New and Old Voices of Wah'Kon-Tah. Edited by Robert K. Dodge and Joseph B. McCullough. New York: International Publishers, 1985.

Harper's Anthology of Twentieth Century Native American Poetry. Edited by Duane Niatum (Klallam). San Francisco: Harper & Row, 1988.

Living the Spirit: A Gay American Indian Anthology. Edited by Will Roscoe. New York: Saint Martin's, 1988.

WORKS EDITED BY PAULA GUNN ALLEN

"Native Women of New Mexico." *A, A Journal of Contemporary Literature,* 3, special issue:13 (Fall 1978).

Studies in American Indian Literature: Critical Essays and Course Designs. New York: Modern Language Association, 1983.

Spider Woman's Granddaughters: Traditional Tales and Contemporary Writing by Native American Women. Boston: Beacon, 1989.

Grandmothers of the Light: A Medicine Woman's Sourcebook. Boston: Beacon Press, 1991.

Voice of the Turtle: American Indian Literature 1900–1970. New York: Ballantine, 1994.

CRITICAL STUDIES AND OTHER WORKS CITED

Awiakta, Marilou. *Selu: Seeking the Corn-Mother's Wisdom.* Golden, Colo.: Fulcrum, 1993.

Bataille, Gretchen M., and Kathleen Mullen Sands. *American Indian Women: Telling Their Lives.* Lincoln: University of Nebraska Press, 1984.

Bredin, Renae. " 'Becoming Minor': Reading *The Woman Who Owned the Shadows.*" *Studies in American Indian Literatures,* 2d ser., 6:36–50 (Winter 1994).

Caputi, Jane. "The Heart of Knowledge: Nuclear Themes in Native American Thought and Literature." *American Indian Culture and Research Journal,* 16:1–27 (1992).

———. *Gossips, Gorgons, and Crones: The Fates of the Earth.* Santa Fe: Bear and Company, 1993.

Chapman, Mary. " 'The Belly of This Story': Storytelling and Symbolic Birth in Native American Fiction." *Studies in American Indian Literatures,* 2d ser., 7:3–16 (Summer 1995).

Dhairyam, Sagari. " 'A House of Difference': Constructions of the Lesbian Poet in Audre Lorde, Adrienne Rich, and Paula Gunn Allen." Ph.D. dissertation, University of Illinois at Urbana-Champaign, 1993.

Fraiman, Susan. Review of *Studies in American Indian Literature: Critical Essays and Course Descriptions.* Edited by Paula Gunn Allen. *Studies in American Indian Literatures,* 9:131–135 (Summer 1985).

Franklin, Cynthia. "Writing Women's Communities: Identity Politics and Multi-Genre Anthologies, 1980–1990." Ph.D. dissertation, University of California, Berkeley, 1994.

Gould, Janice (Maidu-Koyangkauwi). "American Indian Women's Poetry: Strategies of Rage and Hope." *Signs: Journal of Women in Culture and Society,* 20:797–817 (Summer 1995).

Grahn, Judy. *Another Mother Tongue: Gay Words, Gay Worlds.* Boston: Beacon, 1984.

Green, Rayna (Cherokee). *Native American Women: A Contextual Bibliography.* Bloomington: Indiana University Press, 1983.

Gunn, John M. *Schat-Chen: History, Traditions, and Narratives of the Queres Indians of Laguna and Acoma.* Albuquerque, N. Mex.: Albright & Anderson, 1917.

Hanson, Elizabeth I. *Paula Gunn Allen.* Boise, Idaho: Boise State University, 1990.

Herzog, Kristin. Review of *Spider Woman's Granddaughters: Traditional Tales and Contemporary Writing by Native American Women.* Edited by Paula Gunn Allen. *Studies in American Indian Literatures.* 2d ser., 2:23–26 (Fall 1990).

Holford, Vanessa. "Re Membering Ephanie: A Woman's Re-Creation of Self in Paul Gunn Allen's *The Woman Who Owned the Shadows.*" *Studies in American Indian Literatures,* 2d ser., 6:99–113 (Spring 1994).

Jahner, Elaine. "A Laddered, Rain-bearing Rug: Paula Gunn Allen's Poetry." In *Women and Western American Literature.* Edited by Helen Stauffer and Susan Rosowski. Troy, N.Y.: Whitson, 1982. Pp. 311–326.

———. "Climbing a Sacred Ladder: Technique in the Poetry of Paula Gunn Allen." *Studies in American Indian Literatures,* 7:76–80 (Fall 1983).

Jaimes, M. Annette (Juaneño-Yaqui) with Theresa Halsey (Standing Rock Sioux). "American Indian Women: At the Center of Indigenous Resistance in Contemporary North America." In *The State of Native America: Genocide, Colonization, and Resistance.* Edited by M. Annette Jaimes. Boston: South End, 1992. Pp. 311–344.

Jaskoski, Helen. "Allen's *Grandmother.*" *Explicator,* 50:247–249 (Summer 1992).

Keating, AnneLouise. "Myth Smashers, Myth Makers: (Re) Visionary Techniques in the Works of Paula Gunn Allen, Gloria Anzaldúa, and Audre Lorde." In *Critical Essays: Gay and Lesbian Writers of Color.* Edited by Emmanuel S. Nelson. New York: Haworth Press, 1993. Pp. 73–95. Copublished simultaneously in the *Journal of Homosexuality,* 26:73–95 (1993).

Kidwell, Clara Sue (Choctaw). Review of *Grandmothers of the Light: A Medicine Woman's Handbook,* by Paula Gunn Allen. *American Indian Quarterly,* 17:278–279 (Spring 1993).

Koolish, Lynda. "The Bones of This Body Say, Dance: Self-Empowerment in Contemporary Poetry by Women of Color." In *A Gift of Tongues: Critical Challenges in Contemporary American Poetry.* Edited by Marie Harris and Kathleen Aguero. Athens: University of Georgia Press, 1987. Pp. 1–56.

Le Guin, Ursula K. Review of *Spider Woman's Granddaughters: Traditional Tales and Contemporary Writing by Native American Women.* Edited by Paula Gunn Allen. *New York Times Book Review,* Sunday, May 14, 1989, sec. 7, p. 15.

Lincoln, Kenneth. *Native American Renaissance.* Los Angeles, Calif.: University of California Press, 1983.

———. *Indi'n Humor: Bicultural Play in Native America.* New York: Oxford University Press, 1993.

Lowe, John. "Cantas Encantadas: Paula Gunn Allen's *Shadow Country.*" *Studies in American Indian Literatures,* 7:56–65 (Fall 1983).

Maddox, Lucy. "Native American Poetry." In *The Columbia History of American Poetry.* Edited by Jay Parini and Brett C. Millier. New York: Columbia University Press, 1993. Pp. 728–749.

Ruoff, A. LaVonne Brown. Review of *The Woman Who Owned the Shadows,* by Paula Gunn Allen. *Studies in American Indian Literatures,* 7:65–69 (Fall 1983).

———. *American Indian Literatures: An Introduction, Bibliographic Review, and Selected Bibliography.* New York: Modern Language Association, 1990.

———. *Literature of the American Indian.* New York: Chelsea House, 1991.

Ruppert, James. "Paula Gunn Allen." In *Dictionary of Native American Literature.* Edited by Andrew Wiget. New York: Garland, 1994. Pp. 395–399.

———. "Paula Gunn Allen and Joy Harjo: Closing the Distance Between Personal and Mythic Space." *American Indian Quarterly,* 7, no. 1:27–40 (1983).

St. Clair, Janet. "Uneasy Ethnocentrism: Recent Works of Allen, Silko, and Hogan." *Studies in American Indian Literatures,* 2d ser., 6:83–98 (Spring 1994).

Sarris, Greg (Kashaya Pomo). *Keeping Slug Woman Alive: A Holistic Approach to American Indian Texts.* Berkeley: University of California Press, 1993.

Senier, Siobhan. "A Zuni Raconteur Dons the Junco Shirt: Gender and Narrative Style in the Story of Coyote and Junco." *American Literature,* 66:223–238 (June 1994). Reprinted in *Subject and Citizens: Nation, Race, and Gender from Orookoko to Anita Hall.* Edited by Michael Moon and Cathy N. Davidson. Durham, N.C.: Duke University Press, 1995. Pp. 417–432.

Sequoya, Jana (Chickasaw). "How (!) Is an Indian?: A Contest of Stories." In *New Voices in Native American Literary Criticism.* Edited by Arnold Krupat. Washington, D.C.: Smithsonian Institution, 1993. Pp. 453–473.

Sevillano, Mando. "Interpreting Native American Literature: An Archetypal Approach." *American Indian Culture and Research Journal*, 10, no. 1:1–12 (1986).

Sprayberry, Sandra. Review of *Grandmothers of the Light: A Medicine Woman's Sourcebook*, by Paula Gunn Allen. *Studies in American Indian Literatures*, 2d ser., 6:71–73 (Fall 1994).

Sweet, Timothy. "Masculinity and Self-Performance in the *Life of Black Hawk*." *American Literature*, 65:475–499 (September 1993). Reprinted in *Subject and Citizens: Nation, Race, and Gender from Orookoko to Anita Hall*. Edited by Michael Moon and Cathy N. Davison. Durham, N.C.: Duke University Press, 1995. Pp. 219–243.

TallMountain, Mary (Athabascan). "Paula Gunn Allen's 'The One Who Skins Cats': An Inquiry Into Spiritedness." *Studies in American Indian Literatures*, 7:69–75 (Fall 1983); 2d ser., 5:34–38 (Summer 1993).

———. "You *Can* Go Home Again." In *I Tell You Now: Autobiographical Essays by Native American Writers*. Edited by Brian Swann and Arnold Krupat. Lincoln: University of Nebraska Press, 1987. Pp. 1–13.

Van Dyke, Annette. "The Journey Back to Female Roots: A Laguna Pueblo Model." In *Lesbian Texts and Contexts: Radical Revisions*. Edited by Karla Jay and Joanne Glasgow. New York: New York University Press, 1990. Pp. 339–354.

Vizenor, Gerald. *Manifest Manners: Postindian Warriors of Survivance*. Hanover: Wesleyan University Press, 1994.

Warrior, Robert Allen (Osage). *Tribal Secrets: Recovering American Indian Intellectual Traditions*. Minneapolis: University of Minnesota Press, 1995.

Williams, Walter L. *The Spirit and the Flesh: Sexual Diversity in American Indian Culture*. Boston: Beacon, 1986.

INTERVIEWS

Aal, Katharyn Machan. "Writing as an Indian Woman: An Interview with Paula Gunn Allen." *North Dakota Quarterly*, 57:148–161 (Spring 1989).

Ballinger, Franchot, and Brian Swann. "A MELUS Interview: Paula Gunn Allen." *MELUS*, 10:3–25 (Summer 1983).

Bruchac, Joseph (Abenaki). "I Climb the Mesas in My Dreams: An Interview with Paula Gunn Allen." In his *Survival This Way: Interviews with American Indian Poets*. Tucson: Sun Tracks and the University of Arizona Press, 1987. Pp. 1–21.

Caputi, Jane. "Interview with Paula Gunn Allen." *Trivia*, 16:50–67 (1990).

Coltelli, Laura. In *Winged Words: American Indian Writers Speak*. Lincoln: University of Nebraska Press, 1990. Pp. 10–39.

Eysturoy, Annie O. In *This Is about Vision: Interviews with Southwestern Writers*. Edited by William Balassi, John F. Crawford, and Annie O. Eysturoy. Albuquerque: University of New Mexico Press, 1990. Pp. 94–107.

Gould, Janice (Maidu-Koyangkauwi). "An Interview with Paula Gunn Allen." *Hembra* 3:8–9 (September 1993).

Paula Gunn Allen: Interview, Paper, and Discussion. Los Angeles: KPFA, 1982. Video produced by Elouise Healie.

Perry, Donna. *Backtalk: Women Writers Speak Out / Interviews by Donna Perry*. New Brunswick, N.J.: Rutgers University Press, 1993. Pp. 1–18.

Phillips, Adam. "Where I Come from, God Is a Woman: An Interview with Paula Gunn Allen." *Whole Earth Review*, 74:44–47 (Spring 1992).

Smith, Lucinda Irwin. "Paula Gunn Allen." *Women Who Write*, volume II. New York: Simon & Schuster, 1994. Pp. 129–137.

The Key Is Remembering: Poetry and Interviews by Native American Women (Linda Hogan, Mary TallMountain, Wendy Rose, Paula Gunn Allen, Joy Harjo, Diane Burns). New York: Art, Incorporated, 1982. Tapes for radio produced by Helen Thorington.

—LAUREN MULLER WITH JACQUELINE SHEA MURPHY

Dashiell Hammett

1894–1961

*D*ASHIELL HAMMETT WAS the first great realist of American crime fiction. Starting out in an era of artificial and anglicized mystery novels, Hammett brought the genre into line with his own experience of crime and punishment as a Pinkerton detective in the years just before and after World War I. His terse, ironic prose brought a new voice to American realism and spawned a school of "hard-boiled" fiction that remains influential today. Hammett's literary legacy, however, is inseparable from the myth surrounding his life. Hammett himself encouraged this confusion, advertising his Pinkerton career on book jackets as a marker of authenticity. His later life became mythic as well: the wild years in Hollywood, when he threw away money faster than he earned it; his stoical refusal to answer questions during a government anticommunist trial in 1951; and the prison sentence he served as a result of not answering. In the end celebrity was not kind to Hammett. He had hoped to move beyond the detective formula to write a more serious (if less popular) naturalistic fiction. But his audience fell in love with the hard-boiled image: they drowned him in money and adulation, and he lacked the strength and discipline to move on. Like F. Scott Fitzgerald, Hammett was to some extent a victim of his own success, and so the more serious work that might have sustained him in later years was stillborn.

Nonetheless, Hammett's achievement is an important one. When he began writing in the early 1920s, detective fiction was an escapist genre. Agatha Christie, Dorothy Sayers, Anthony Berkeley, and S. S. Van Dine—to name only the best— were writing a kind of puzzle-fiction, clever but formulaic. Often set in grand English country houses full of domestics, these novels reek of nostalgia for a world that was rapidly disappearing. Nothing could have been farther from the world Hammett knew. Starting out with little formal education, he had suffered illness and poverty and had two children, with little hope of supporting them, by his mid-twenties. Above all, his experience as a detective gave him a deeper knowledge of crime than any other author of the period. In "The Simple Art of Murder" (1944), Raymond Chandler wrote that Hammett "gave murder back to the kind of people that commit it for reasons, not just to provide a corpse; and with the means at hand, not hand-wrought dueling pistols, curare, and tropical fish."

Hammett's realism brought the literature of crime back to its roots. Long before Arthur Conan Doyle domesticated the genre, some of the best writers of the nineteenth century—Edgar Allan Poe, Charles Dickens, and Wilkie Collins— were producing detective fiction. Joseph Conrad joined them with *The Secret Agent,* and Graham Greene and a few other modernists made regular forays into the genre. Hammett cleared away the cobwebs in the detective novel, reviving the documentary impulses that had fueled it from the beginning. At his best, he extended the genre into the realm of modernism, competing with acknowledged American masters like Hemingway and Faulkner. His influence can be seen in the barren prose of "dirty realist" writers like Raymond Carver and Richard Ford. But Hammett's significance is not confined to "serious" fiction. He started out as a pulp writer, drawing on the indigenous American tradition of the dime novel, with its cheap but invincible heroes and cardboard villains. Like the cowboy and the comic strip superhero, the hard-boiled detective answered a need for modern warriors, men of action who would stand up to crime and corruption. Hammett's legacy in popular culture can be measured not only by the popularity of the movies *The Maltese Falcon* and *The Thin Man* but in the continuing vitality of the genre he helped create: the crime novel.

Samuel Dashiell Hammett was born on May 27, 1894, in a farmhouse in southern Maryland. His father, Richard Thomas Hammett, was an alcoholic, moving the family to Philadelphia and then Baltimore for a succession of low-paying jobs: farmer, streetcar conductor, clerk. Hammett's mother, Annie Bond Dashiell Hammett, was fastidious and proud, insisting that her son's middle name be pronounced with the accent on the second syllable in honor of her French ancestry. After Hammett had completed a single semester of high school his father forced him to withdraw and help support the family. Thereafter Hammett held several jobs, none of which lasted. As a messenger boy at the Baltimore and Ohio Railroad he was chronically late until the boss called him into his office to fire him. As he left, the boss called him back to give him a second chance if he would promise never to be late again. Hammett thanked him and refused, because he knew he could not keep the promise. This kind of honesty and willpower, flashing out from behind a taciturn facade, often surprised Hammett's friends. Several decades later a doctor told Hammett he would die if he did not stop drinking. No one expected a change. But Hammett gave his word that he would stop—and kept it.

In 1915 Hammett replied to an obscure want ad in a Baltimore newspaper and was soon hired as an operative at the Pinkerton National Detective Agency. Pinkerton's was the largest private law enforcement agency in the United States. It was founded in 1850 by Alan Pinkerton, a famously tough Scotsman who rode shotgun on stages while chasing thieves and coined the phrase "private eye." The motto of the Pinkerton Agency was "we never sleep." James Wright, the short, tough-talking assistant manager at the Baltimore office who was to become the model for the Continental Op, taught Hammett the art of detection. Shadowing a suspect—a young op's chief task—required enormous patience, often with no action or results for weeks at a time. The hours were long and the pay was only moderate, but Hammett liked it and worked hard, gaining a reputation as a good agent.

In 1918 Hammett joined the army and was assigned to the 154th Depot Brigade at Camp Mead, Maryland, fifteen miles from his family's home. He trained as an ambulance driver but soon became sick with influenza and spent the next eight months in and out of the hospital. In May 1919 he was diagnosed with intractable tuberculosis and discharged. For a year he lived as an invalid at his parents' home, working part-time for Pinkerton's. In May 1920 Hammett went west to start again and landed a job at the Pinkerton office in Spokane. He traveled through the West, shadowing con men and miners, swindlers and murderers. In late 1920 his TB acted up again and he checked into the Cushman sanatorium in Tacoma, where he began an affair with a twenty-three-year-old nurse named Josephine Annis Nolan. They had little in common, but when "Jose" got pregnant, Hammett agreed to marry her. In the summer of 1921 they settled in San Francisco; their daughter Mary Jane was born a few months later, on October 16th. (A second daughter, Josephine Rebecca, called "Jo," was born on May 24, 1926.) San Francisco was infested with crime and corruption in the twenties, so the opportunities for private investigation were spectacular. Hammett worked part-time for the Pinkerton Agency, playing a role in several well-known celebrity cases. But by the end of the year TB forced him to quit, and Hammett and his family barely managed to survive on his twenty-dollars-per-month disability pension. Hammett was able to work part-time writing ad copy for a jeweler named Albert Samuels, and he began writing fiction for the first time.

The *Smart Set*, the fashionable magazine edited by H. L. Mencken and George Jean Nathan, published Hammett's first one-hundred-word sketch, "The Parthian Shot," in October 1922. As his health recovered, Hammett wrote more frequently, despite the poor pay (a penny a word). He was drawn to the seriousness and glamour of magazines like the *Smart Set* and soon recognized that his own experience was a literary asset. "From the Memoirs of a Private Detective," published in the March 1923 *Smart Set,* already bears some traces of the restrained, ironic voice Hammett would develop later. He had not read Hemingway, but the parallel between their styles is strong:

> A man whom I was shadowing went out into the country for a walk one Sunday afternoon and lost his bearings completely. I had to direct him back to the city. . . .

> In 1917, in Washington, D.C., I met a young lady who did not remark that my work must be very interesting. . . .

> I know a man who once stole a Ferris-wheel.

Detective fiction was just entering what the mystery writer and critic Julian Symons has called the Golden Age. The genre was immensely popular, and critics were formulating rules of crime and detection that precluded any serious treatment of character, passion, or politics. Reaction was inevitable, if only because writers prefer not to do the same thing for very long. *Black Mask,* founded in 1920 by Mencken and Nathan to help pay for the *Smart Set,* published detective stories with baroque titles like "The Uncanny Voice" and "The Jest Ironic." But late in 1922 *Black Mask* acquired new owners and a new editor. In December they published a fifteen-hundred-word story, called "The Road Home," by one "Peter Collinson." In criminal slang a "Peter Collins" was a nobody. "Nobody's son": Hammett used the name as a private joke, hoping to keep his real name for poetry. His stories appeared frequently in *Black Mask* and other pulp magazines. (A number of these stories were later republished. "Arson Plus" and a story from 1923, "Slippery Fingers," were collected in the 1951 volume, *Woman in the Dark.*)

Within a year of publishing "Arson Plus," Hammett was using his own name and had developed the character that would dominate his fiction for the rest of the decade. Short, heavyset but strong, thirty-five years old (later he is forty), the Continental Op is never addressed by name. "I didn't deliberately keep him nameless," Hammett wrote later, "but he got through 'Arson Plus' and 'Slippery Fingers' without needing a name, so I suppose I may as well let him run along that way. He's more or less of a type, and I'm not sure that he's entitled to a name." Hammett's Op was set in deliberate contrast to the leading "type" of *Black Mask* fiction, Carroll John Daly's Race Williams. Williams was tall, handsome, tough-talking, and invincible. "I do a little honest shooting on the side," he says in one story, but "I never bumped a guy off what didn't need it." The Continental Op's attitude was similar, but he was far less predictable than Williams.

Unlike most fictional detectives, the Op is not charismatic. Balding and overweight, he complains about back trouble and paperwork. Nor is he the chivalrous knight of Raymond Chandler's novels. He is often rude, even cruel—though never gratuitously so. In "The Scorched Face" (1925)—reprinted in the collection called *The Big Knockover* (1966)—the Op insists on questioning a man whose wife has just committed suicide. When the man objects, the Op thinks: "I felt sorry for this young man whose wife had killed herself. Apart from that, I had work to do. I tightened the screws." Sometimes the Op blames the Old Man, boss of the Continental Detective Agency. But when his own safety is threatened, the Op's survivalist nature is made clear, as in a story found in *The Continental Op* (1974), "The Whosis Kid," which was originally published in 1925. At a critical juncture in "The Whosis Kid," the Op remarks:

> For myself, I counted on coming through all in one piece. Few men *get* killed. Most of those who meet sudden ends *get themselves* killed. I've had twenty years of experience at dodging that. I can count on being one of the survivors of whatever blow-up there is. And I hope to take most of the other survivors for a ride.

Hammett developed a distinctive style without seeming to do so because he wrote, as Raymond Chandler has observed, in "a language not supposed to be capable of such refinements." Like his Op, Hammett disliked extravagant or excessive language. In another story that appears in *The Continental Op,* "The Girl with Silver Eyes" (1924), the Op's client is an overwrought, Anglophile and poet named Burke Pangburn who represents everything that Hammett disliked in fiction. The Op lets Pangburn talk at first, then cuts him short: "The phrases '*victim of foul play,*' '*into a trap*' and so on began to flow hysterically

out again . . . Finally I got him quieted down and, sandwiched in between occasional emotional outbursts, got a story out of him that amounted to this. . . ." What the Op does not tell us is that Pangburn sounds like an Agatha Christie novel. When he translates Pangburn's story into his own terse prose, Hammett is enacting a small victory for his own fictional techniques over those of the old school. Something similar occurs fairly often in Hammett's stories whenever the Op filters more garrulous talkers through his own laconic voice. When the action starts, Hammett's prose conveys it in sharp, staccato rhythms: "We crashed down on dead Billie. I twisted around, kicking the Frenchman's face. Loosened one arm. Caught one of his. His other hand gouged at my face. . . ." Verbs sustain the energy of a passage like this. Scene changes are rapid, linking the dialogue that forms the meat of the story.

Like Hemingway, who developed a similar prose style during these years, Hammett furnished his hero with a "code" of behavior to which he adheres with resolute stoicism. Criminals offer bribes, women offer their bodies, but the Op's fidelity to his calling never wavers. The stories from 1924 and 1925 highlight the code and set forth two themes that persist throughout Hammett's work: wealth corrupts, and women are dangerous. The first often involves characters who are children of the rich, whose lack of discipline leads to all kinds of trouble. Several of the Op stories are "wandering daughter jobs," in which rich girls flirt with criminals and put the Op in danger. The second theme appears in "The House in Turk Street" (1924), another story republished in *The Continental Op.* Here the Op meets a woman with "smoke-gray eyes that were set too far apart for trustworthiness—though not for beauty." The Op supposes, "Her red mouth laughed at me, exposing the edges of little sharp animal teeth. She was as beautiful as the devil, and twice as dangerous." In "The Girl with the Silver Eyes" a gorgeous murderess tries to break the Op's resistance: ''Men have loved me and, doing what I liked with them, I have found men contemptible. And then comes this little fat detective whose name I don't know, and he acts as if I were a hag—an old squaw. Can I help then being piqued into some sort of feeling for him?'' These women never fool the Op; nor would their successor, Brigid O'Shaughnessy, fool Sam Spade in *The Maltese Falcon* (1930).

The Op is based in San Francisco, but he travels more widely as his adventures go on. In ''Corkscrew'' (1925), collected in *The Big Knockover,* the Op goes to Arizona to fight old-style badmen. (*Black Mask,* where the story was published originally, printed westerns as well as detective stories.) In ''Dead Yellow Women'' (1925), one of Hammett's best stories, which may also be found in *The Big Knockover,* the Op goes to Chinatown in San Francisco to investigate murders at the seaside mansion of Lillian Shan, a beautiful Chinese American. To do so he must deal with Chang Li Ching, an underworld boss who speaks in a parody of court-Chinese (''If the Terror of Evildoers will honor one of my deplorable chairs by resting his divine body on it, I can assure him the chair shall be burned afterward. . . .'') The Op replies in the same language, but never turns his back to Chang Li Ching. In ''The Gutting of Couffignal'' (1925), another story in *The Big Knockover,* the Op takes on crime on a larger scale. The setting is Couffignal, an island in San Pablo Bay near San Francisco inhabited by ''well-fed old gentlemen who, the profits they took from the world with both hands in their younger days now stowed away at safe percentages, have bought into the island colony so they may spend what is left of their lives nursing their livers and improving their golf among their kind.'' The owners are asking for it—or so the Op implies—and they get it when a group of expatriate Russians with machine guns tries to loot the entire island. The Op stops them, but

without any undue respect for his wealthy clients.

In 1926 *Black Mask* got a new editor, a former bayonet instructor and diplomat named Joseph Thompson Shaw. ''Cap'' Shaw had no experience as an editor, but he recognized at once the kind of fiction he wanted. He wrote to Hammett, asking him to extend the Op's range and write a novel. Hammett replied at once: ''You've hit on exactly what I've been thinking about and working toward. As I see it, the approach I have in mind has never been attempted. The field is unscratched and wide open.'' Shaw proved an exceptional editor, nursing a whole school of crime writers including Raymond Chandler, Carroll John Daly, Erle Stanley Gardner, Raoul Whitfield, and others.

In 1927 Hammett took Shaw's suggestion, moving toward longer and more ambitious work with two linked stories, ''The Big Knockover'' and ''$106,000 Blood Money,'' later incorporated into the 1943 novel *$106,000 Blood Money.* (The two stories were reprinted in their original form in *The Big Knockover.*) In ''The Big Knockover'' the Op works with a reckless young op named Jack Counihan who serves to highlight the Op's worn resilience. The cynicism of the Old Man, boss of the Continental, begins to sound like a warning to the Op:

> Fifty years of crook-hunting for the Continental had emptied him of everything except brains and a soft-spoken, gently smiling shell of politeness that was the same whether things went good or bad—and meant as little at one time as another. We who worked under him were proud of his cold-bloodedness.

Jack and the Op shadow a virtual army of thugs in the wake of an enormous bank heist, and the crooks proceed to slaughter each other. The story is lean and well-plotted, despite some tinny rhetoric from the Op (''The room was as black as an honest politician's prospects''). The climactic fight scene, in a dark speakeasy crowded with criminals, is superb: "It was a swell bag of nails. Swing right, swing left, kick, swing right, swing left, kick. Don't hesitate, don't look for targets. God will see that there's always a mug there for your gun or blackjack to sock, a belly for your foot."

In the sequel, "$106,000 Blood Money," the mastermind of the bank robbery and subsequent murders is loose. The reward money draws a self-made bootlegger from Mexico named Tom-Tom Carey:

> Tall, wide-shouldered, thick-chested, thin-bellied, he would add up to say a hundred and ninety pounds. His swarthy face was hard as a fist, but there was nothing ill-humored in it. It was the face of a man of forty-something who lived life raw and thrived on it. His blue clothes were good and he wore them well.

The Op likes Tom-Tom and agrees to work with him on the search. Jack Counihan, however, the Op's fellow detective and (not coincidentally) the spoiled son of a rich man, has been suspect from the beginning. In the finale the Op catches Jack out in a conspiracy with the enemy and forces him to confess. "The prospect of all that money completely devastated my morals," says Jack. But the Op isn't fooled, and he points to the real reason for Jack's betrayal: "You met the girl and were too soft to turn her in. But your vanity—your pride in looking at yourself as a pretty cold proposition—wouldn't let you admit it even to yourself. You had to have a hard-boiled front." With this neat turn, the Op brings a new level of self-consciousness to the story and to the "hard-boiled" tradition. He also provokes Jack into drawing his gun. Tom-Tom shoots Jack to save the Op; another detective (unaware of Jack's treachery) shoots Tom-Tom. The Op's reaction: "I stepped over Jack's body, went into the room, knelt beside the swarthy man. He squirmed, tried to say something, died before he could get it out.

I waited until my face was straight before I stood up."

Clearly, the Op's sympathies are with Tom-Tom, who would never give in to sentiment, as Jack has, but is nonetheless capable of generous action. Fake toughness is distinguished from the real thing. But even the Op's genuine toughness comes to seem, at the end of the story, like a kind of brutal expediency. The Op, as it turns out, has orchestrated the entire closing scene. He makes this report to the Old Man: " 'It happened that way,' I said deliberately. 'I played the cards so we would get the benefit of the breaks—but it just happened that way.' " The Old Man just smiles. The Op has saved him from the trouble of dealing with a treacherous employee; no one else knew about Jack's deal with the criminals. In the end, even the Op seems worn out by the heartlessness his trade enforces. " 'I'm going to take a couple of weeks off,' I said from the door. I felt tired, washed out."

In late 1927 Hammett began writing his first full-length novel, *Red Harvest* (which was published in 1929). The narrator is still the Op, but the scale is larger: a whole western city erupting into gang warfare. Hammett had larger ambitions for the story, too. After the fourth installment was published in *Black Mask* Hammett sent "Poisonville" (the provisional title) to Knopf. Blanche Knopf, who edited the mystery series, wrote back within weeks that she had "read POISONVILLE with a great deal of interest." She argued that the violence should be reduced—but added, "There is no question whatever that we are keen about the mss, and with the necessary changes, I think that it would have a good chance." Within a few days Hammett returned all his revisions with another letter divulging his ambitions as a writer:

> I'm one of the few—if there are any more—people moderately literate who take the detective story seriously. I don't mean that I necessarily take my own or anybody else's seriously—but the

detective story as a form. Some day somebody's going to make ''literature'' of it (Ford's GOOD SOLDIER wouldn't have needed much altering to have been a detective story), and I'm selfish enough to have my hopes, however slight the evident justification may be.

Behind the forced modesty of these lines, one can sense the dawning exultation of a writer who has found his voice and is just discovering an audience. Hammett was on his way.

Red Harvest is based on Hammett's work in Anaconda, Montana, in the early 1920s, shadowing unionized miners for the Pinkerton Agency. Years later, as a member of the American Communist Party, Hammett must have seen some irony in his having played this particular role. At the time it was just a job. The Industrial Workers of the World (''the Wobblies'') had called strikes before the war. Anaconda (where Jose Hammett grew up) was a company town just outside Butte; the Anaconda mine owners brought in strikebreakers, gunmen, and Pinkerton detectives to stem the union tide. By the time Hammett arrived, the Wobblies were nearly gone, but the crooks remained, running local bootlegging and gambling operations.

This is the world that formed the basis for Personville, or as the inhabitants call it, ''Poisonville,'' the setting of *Red Harvest*. The Op comes to town at the behest of Donald Willsson, a reformist newspaper editor and son of the man who owns the town—the mines, the banks, the newspapers, the government. The Op finds his client dead in the street and soon discovers that Personville is really run by the gangsters old Elihu Willsson hired years before to knock out the unions. The bedridden Elihu, an icon of impotent rage, summons the Op and howls at him. The Op's response is typical: '' 'What's the use of getting poetic about it?' I growled. 'If you've got a fairly honest piece of work to be done in my line, and you want to pay a decent price, maybe I'll take it on. But a lot of foolishness about

smoking rats and pig-pens doesn't mean anything to me.' '' Elihu puts up the money. When he changes his mind, it is too late: the Op is angry. The local police chief, Noonan, has tried to kill the Op. The Op decides to carry out his mission and does it with a sense of violent retribution that is lacking in most of Hammett's stories. The Op's method is to set the criminal factions against each other (as he does in ''Corkscrew'') and watch as they fight it out. He throws a wrench into local gambling operations and stirs up old vendettas with the help of Dinah Brand, a sort of freelance gangsters' moll who will do anything for money and has information on all the major players. The result is a crescendo of violence, a small-scale apocalypse—stabbings, shootings, bombings—until the town seems to be on fire. Even the Op seems to be losing control, giving way to the poison. He confesses to Dinah after arranging a ''peace conference'' designed to set the gangsters at one another's throats: ''I've arranged a killing or two in my time, when they were necessary. But this is the first time I've ever got the fever. It's this damned burg. You can't go straight here.'' The next morning, after a night of gin and laudanum and furious dreams, the Op wakes up on the floor, his hand grasping an ice pick that is buried in Dinah Brand's chest. Even he doesn't know at first whether he killed her or not.

In the end the Op escapes, leaving the city ''all nice and clean and ready to go to the dogs again.'' He has masterminded an orgy of violence; all the gangsters are dead. His success is partly a measure of his refusal to take bribes or give in to Dinah Brand's seductions. But it is impossible to see in this novel the chivalric pattern that critics have often discerned in Hammett's fiction and in the fiction of other detective writers. The Op is no knight, and the order he restores (temporarily) to Personville can hardly be called justice. André Gide called the book ''the last word in atrocity, cynicism, and horror'' and thought the dialogue equal to the best in Hemingway. Many American critics agreed, and the English poet Robert Graves was to look back on *Red Harvest* as "an acknowledged literary landmark."

The Dain Curse (1929) is a more self-conscious novel than *Red Harvest* and, in some ways, a less satisfying one. It was a product of conflicting impulses. Hammett had written to Blanche Knopf in 1928 that he wanted to "try adapting the stream-of-consciousness method, conveniently modified, to a detective story, carrying the reader along with the detective . . . letting the solution break on both of them together." At the same time Hammett was eager to sell material to Hollywood, and he knew that film required that he maintain a more conventional approach. The result is a stilted, somewhat ridiculous plot with an eccentric novelist figure behind it, the half-crazed Owen Fitzstephan.

Like several of Hammett's stories, *The Dain Curse* starts out as a "wandering daughter job": the Op is looking for the mysterious Gabrielle Leggett. But in other ways Hammett makes significant breaks with his usual form: set in the suburbs rather than the city, the story lacks gangsters and clear motives. Like Gabrielle's father Edgar Leggett, who escapes from Devil's Island to become a fastidious scientist and expatriate, Hammett moves into new territory with *The Dain Curse*. The novel begins with a diamond theft that leads to Edgar Leggett's death and the revelation of the "Dain curse" that plagues his family. In the second part of the book Hammett breaks new ground by describing Gabrielle's involvement with the Cult of the Holy Grail (a plot development that was based on Hammett's own experience with religious mania in California). The Op confers all along with his friend, the novelist Fitzstephan, who has helped him with a previous case. Fitzstephan always argues for mystery and the literary qualities of the case—against the Op's hard-boiled empiricism. Fitzstephan complains:

"You'd reduce the Dain curse, then, to a primitive strain in the blood?"

"To less than that, to words in an angry woman's mouth."

"It's fellows like you that take all the color out of life."

This argument indicates the novel's concern with perception and reality. Most of the main characters are either crazy or drugged, and the Op must sort out their confusions as well as the crime. In the end, the Op's explanation to Gabrielle has less to do with justice or emotion than with interpretation: "Thinking's a dizzy business, a matter of catching as many of those foggy glimpses as you can and fitting them together the best you can."

In the final section the Op recognizes that the Dain curse is the work of a single mind—Fitzstephan's. He explains the curse to Gabrielle and helps her to withdraw from a heroin addiction. But he cannot explain his generosity to her, even when she presses him. He tells her: "I'm twice your age, sister; an old man. I'm damned if I'll make a chump of myself by telling you why I did it, why it was neither revolting nor disgusting, why I'd do it again and be glad of the chance." Perhaps the Op has had a similar experience with drug withdrawal; we don't know. It seems more likely that he is merely hiding behind the pretense of hidden feelings as he ties up the loose ends. He knows Gabrielle wants some display of affection, and he wants—as always—to get the job done; so he placates her. His paramount rule of conduct is to avoid intimacy, particularly with women. Fitzstephan, after all, is driven to madness by love of Gabrielle, and all her other suitors and advisers die. The Op will not repeat their mistake. Like the Old Man, the Op appears in this novel to have lost touch with any sort of feeling; he has seen too much.

If *The Dain Curse* presses up against the conventions with which Hammett had worked previously, *The Maltese Falcon* adapts those same conventions skillfully. The Op is gone, and in his place is a charismatic private eye whose moral status is ambiguous from the first description: he looks "rather pleasantly like a blond satan." Sam Spade, as Hammett later put it, "had no original. He is a dream man in the sense that he is what most of the private detectives I worked with would like to have been and what quite a few of them in their cockier moments thought they approached." Spade is self-reliant, brave, and ruthless, but not without feelings. His energy makes the book implicitly theatrical; one critic has called *The Maltese Falcon* "a series of brilliant dialogues." The prose is as lean as ever and the characterizations are superb. Hammett sensed all this. In June 1929, after running the novel in *Black Mask,* he wrote to Harry Block, his editor at Knopf:

> I started *The Maltese Falcon* on its way to you by express last Friday, the fourteenth. I'm fairly confident that it is by far the best thing I've done so far, and I hope you'll think so too. . . . Though I hadn't anything of the sort in mind while doing it, I think now that it could very easily be turned into a play. . . . Another thing: if you use The Falcon will you go a little easy on the editing? While I wouldn't go to the stake in defense of my system of punctuation, I do rather like it and I think it goes with my system of sentence structure.

As it turned out, Knopf's primary objection was to the sexual language in the novel. Here Hammett managed to fool all his editors with the word "gunsel," which they left in, thinking it meant a hired gunman. Most readers still make the same assumption, even if they recognize that Wilmer—the gunman in question—is also a boy kept by the homosexual Joel Cairo.

The plot of *The Maltese Falcon* is admirably lean and simple. It begins, like many of Hammett's stories, with a beautiful woman and an unsolved murder. It ends, in a nice touch of symmetry, with the revelation that the woman and the murder are linked: something Spade has known all along. In between lies the ostensible subject of the book. The search for the priceless falcon, and the ruthless greed it elicits from everyone who knows about it, has been seen as a parable about materialism. But avarice and cruelty are part of the fabric of almost all Hammett's work, and the falcon is really just a pretext, a tidbit of romantic history Hammett uses to fuel the story. The fact that the falcon turns out to be fake is less significant than it is funny. The falcon is a kind of metaphor for plot. We need something lurid to draw us in, but once the characters become real to us we can toss it out; it's made of lead. This metafictional reading becomes more plausible in light of Hammett's confession to James Thurber that *The Maltese Falcon* had been inspired by Henry James's *The Wings of the Dove,* another subtly ironic novel about what people will do for money. In any case, the real force behind the story is not the loot but Sam Spade himself, who commands our attention like no other Hammett character.

Spade's magnetism derives partly from his moral ambiguity. He plays along with the deceptions and postures of Brigid, Gutman, and Cairo, and we are never sure where he stands in relation to law and order. Early in the novel, after his partner Archer is killed, Archer's wife (with whom he has had an affair) asks him if he committed the murder; the police have similar suspicions. Later, Spade manages to play Brigid and the others off against one another by keeping them in the dark about his own corruptibility. He admits this strategy to Brigid: "Don't be too sure I'm as crooked as I'm supposed to be. That kind of reputation might be good business—bringing in high-priced jobs and making it easier to deal with the enemy." But to treat even this claim as a full confession would be misguided. The best hiding places, as Edgar Allan Poe would have it, are those in plain sight. Most of what Spade says is infected with irony, including the intimacy with which he calls Brigid (and Effie Perine) "angel" and "darling." Sexual ethics have changed since Hammett's day, but it is still shocking to see Spade sleep with Brigid, then ransack her apartment and return to his place in time to rouse her with breakfast. Throughout the novel, Spade's motives remain intriguingly unclear: What will he get out of his involvement with Brigid? What drives him? The only answer comes in the form of a seemingly irrelevant story Spade tells Brigid while they are waiting for Joel Cairo. It concerns a man named Flitcraft, a successful real estate salesman who disappears one day without any warning, leaving behind his wife and children. Five years later he is seen in a nearby city, and Spade, then working for a local detective agency, is assigned to find him. He discovers Flitcraft living a life identical to the old one but with a new name, new job, new wife and children. Flitcraft explains that on the day of his disappearance he had been passing an office building when a falling beam came within inches of killing him. He might easily have been killed, and the recognition changes him: "The life he knew was a clean orderly sane responsible affair. Now a falling beam had shown him that life was fundamentally none of these things." He becomes convinced that he is "out of step" with life and that he has to take action: if "life could be ended for him at random by a falling beam . . . he would change his life at random by simply going away." In the end, though, he falls back into his old patterns. Spade explains that Flitcraft "adjusted himself to beams falling, and then no more of them fell, and he adjusted himself to them not falling."

This story is the thematic center of the novel, and it makes Hammett's vision continuous with the naturalism of early twentieth-century writers like Stephen Crane and Theodore Dreiser. Spade does not comment on the story he tells, but his feelings about it are clear in the telling. "He knew then," Spade says of Flitcraft, "that men died at haphazard like that, and lived only while blind chance spared them." The story's contextual meaning is clear enough, too. When Spade finishes telling it, Brigid plays with his suit buttons and coyly urges him to trust her. "Don't let's confuse things," he tells her. "You don't have to trust me, anyhow, as long as you can persuade me to trust you." Spade lives in a world in which beams fall, and he will not be taken in. But Brigid doesn't get it—or perhaps she trusts that her beauty will win out over Spade's philosophy. Their dance of mutual suspicion and desire is at the heart of the novel and brings it to its climax with some of Hammett's finest writing.

Spade has been called a heartless hero, incapable of intimacy. It is true that he seems to value masculine toughness and independence above all things, even in women: when Effie Perine proves her mettle Spade tells her, "You're a damned good man, sister." But to see Spade as utterly emotionless, as some critics do, is to miss out entirely on the dramatic tension of the final scene. Neither Spade nor Brigid says anything substantially new here; she continues to appeal to Spade's emotions while he stubbornly holds to his logic. But underneath the dialogue, the reader can see, Spade's resistance is stretched to the breaking point. This tension manifests itself, as in Hemingway, through what is not said rather than through what is. When the scene begins, Spade's face is red, his palms sweating. After he forces Brigid to admit that she murdered his partner Archer, Spade's face turns "pale." When Spade first threatens to turn Brigid in, his face is "yellow-white" and his voice has alternated from flat to harsh to tender to "soft, gentle." She challenges him, and then, we're told, "his yellow-white face was damp with sweat and though he held his smile he could not hold softness in his voice." When Brigid protests that she loves him and he loves her, "His eyes were becoming bloodshot." Soon afterward, "blood streaked Spade's eyeballs now and his long-held smile had become a frightful grimace." In the closing sequence his voice is hoarse. "His wet yellow face was set hard and deeply lined. His eyes burned madly."

Despite Spade's masterful control of the outcome, the undertone of this final dialogue suggests that he is working under enormous internal strain. He *does* want Brigid, but he knows that he cannot trust her. He must hold to the discipline of his code, not because of the law but because giving in blindly to emotion would be weakness. "I won't play the sap for you," he tells Brigid. Spade is a survivor, like the Continental Op. But the stakes of his drama are far higher than the Op's ever were. Critics have generally agreed about this: Hammett had reached a new peak with *The Maltese Falcon.* Joseph T. Shaw, introducing the serial version of the novel to *Black Mask* readers, was effusive: "In all of my experience I have never encountered a story as intense, as gripping or powerful as this one." The *New Republic* granted it the "absolute distinction of real art."

Hammett had been living separately from his wife and children since 1927, because of his TB. By 1929, when the *Falcon* appeared serially in *Black Mask,* he had a permanent girlfriend named Nell Martin, a writer who—like Hammett—had pursued several careers: law student, actress, migrant worker. She dedicated her book *Lovers Should Marry* to him, and he dedicated *The Glass Key* (1931) to her. They made plans to move to New York together, and Hammett encouraged Jose and the children to move to Los Angeles, where Jose had relatives. Despite the instability, these years appear to have been the happiest and most productive in Hammett's life. Although he had some trouble finishing *The Glass Key* after the move to New York, he was still on the rise, eager to prove that he could make serious fiction out of his hard-boiled materials.

With *The Glass Key* Hammett abandoned the detective format altogether. Yet many critics consider it his best work; for Julian Symons it is "the peak of the crime writer's art in the twentieth century." Certainly Hammett's writing is at its best, with all the obtrusively conventional tags of the *Black Mask* school cleaned out. The setting is a kind of large-scale Poisonville. The story centers on Ned Beaumont, an unfathomably tough right-hand man to the gang boss Paul Madvig. Beaumont is not physically strong, but he "can stand anything," and he proves it several times in the course of the novel, undergoing beatings and risking his life repeatedly. Like the Op's Old Man, Beaumont is known for his survivor's wits; he jokes that he was wrong "once back in 1912 . . . I forget what it was about." And like Sam Spade, he is without illusions. When Janet Henry asks why Beaumont seems to despise her, he corrects her: " 'I don't despise you,' he said irritably, not turning to face her. 'Whatever you've done you've paid for and been paid for and that goes for all of us.' " For Beaumont, Janet's emotional responses are "riddles," not worth thinking about. He is a political fixer, a man of action. Mere words—whether Janet's sentimentalities or the "necessary" lies of politics—are meaningless to him. Beyond the level of action Beaumont barely seems to exist; his inner life is a mystery. Hammett sustains the sense of mystery by describing Beaumont as if he were an object: "Spots of color appeared in Ned Beaumont's lean cheeks. . . . Ned Beaumont's face lost its animation, became a slightly sullen mask. . . . Amusement glinted for a moment in Ned Beaumont's face and vanished." In prose like this Hammett achieves the ultimate in what his critics have called the "objective method," and he does so consistently throughout the novel. This method renders Beaumont's motives invisible to us; we only get to see how he appears on the surface.

The narrative voice of *The Glass Key* tracks Beaumont's activities with extraordinary care and with a kind of formality: he is always addressed by his full name, "Ned Beaumont." In contrast, the other characters call him ''Ned'' or ''Beaumont,'' and all of them, as this subtle detail leads one to expect, end up underestimating him. (Needless to say, critics run the same risk.) We see more than any of the other characters do, but we have no access to Ned's thoughts. We watch as he goes to New York to extort a gambling debt from his thuggish bookie; endures a near-fatal series of beatings at the hands of Shad O'Rory, Madvig's former underboss; saves Madvig from political death (and probable imprisonment) by preventing the newspapers from printing allegations that he has murdered Senator Henry's son Taylor. Finally we watch Ned take on a detective's role, eliciting the truth from the senator in the presence of his horrified daughter Janet: the senator has actually killed his own son.

In the end, Janet's horror at what her father has done forces her into Beaumont's arms. The novel ends as they go away together. Yet she barely knows him. The only clue we have to any intimacy between them is the dream sequence that gives the novel its title. Janet tells Beaumont that she has dreamt that she is lost in the forest with him, tired and starving. They find a house and see through the window a table piled with delicious food. They find the key and open the door only to find deadly snakes all over the floor. They slam the door shut. Ned suggests that they open the door and hide, letting the snakes run out. They do just that, then lock the door behind them and eat to their hearts' content. After hearing about this dream, Ned expresses doubt about the happy ending. Later, as the novel ends, Janet admits to him that she had made that part up. In the real dream, the key was glass. When they opened the door it shattered, and the snakes attacked them.

Critics generally take this dream to be about intimacy or sex: what Janet wants but is frightened of, too. The same goes for Beaumont, who is just as incapable of intimacy as all Hammett's heroes. On this level, *The Glass Key* is a novel of limited interest, stunted (like all Hammett's fiction) by a failure to transcend the tough guy's indifference to emotion. In the words of Robert Edenbaum: ''The Hammett mask is never lifted; the Hammett character never lets you inside. Instead of the potential despair of Hemingway, Hammett gives you unimpaired control and machinelike efficiency.'' There is some truth to this criticism with regard to Hammett's work as a whole, but it does not suffice as a comment on *The Glass Key*. We *do* in fact know something about Beaumont's inner life. He is a compulsive gambler, with a gambler's superstitious reverence for his luck. When Madvig asks him why he is so keen to chase down the bookie who stole his winnings, he answers:

> Listen, Paul: it's not only the money . . . it would be the same if it was five bucks. . . . What good am I if my luck's gone? Then I cop, or think I do, and I'm all right again. I can take my tail out from between my legs and feel that I'm a person again and not just something that's being kicked around. The money's important enough, but it's not the real thing. It's what losing and losing does to me.

When Beaumont returns with the money he is once again ''a clear-eyed tall erect man . . . In color and line his face was hale. His stride was long and elastic.'' Luck means everything to Beaumont. Like Sam Spade, Beaumont lives in a world of falling beams, but he lacks Spade's ability to master events. He can only hope for a better roll of the dice. When Janet Henry asks him if he believes in dreams, Beaumont replies: ''I don't believe in anything, but I'm too much of a gambler not to be affected by a lot of things.'' Paul Madvig has pulled him out of a bad losing streak, and he is grateful. But during the course of the novel he loses something more important than money: his friendship with Paul. The two men fight when Paul refuses to take Beaumont's advice about how to deal with Shad O'Rory. Beaumont begins to suspect that Paul is hiding the truth about Taylor Henry's death from him; finally he knows it, and they fight again. The death of this friendship is the real substance of *The Glass Key*.

The title of the book, like that of *The Maltese Falcon,* is misleading, a false clue. The dream of the key, after all, is Janet's; it can hardly be taken as an emblem of Beaumont's emotional life. His relationship with Janet Henry is almost meaningless. In the end, when she begs him to take her away to New York, he is reluctant: "He blinked at her. 'Do you really want to go or are you just being hysterical?' he asked. Her face was crimson by then. Before she could speak he said: 'It doesn't make any difference. I'll take you if you want to go.' " Shortly afterward Madvig arrives, and his feelings for Beaumont almost break the bounds of manly decorum: "Madvig cleared his throat violently. 'I don't want to be a God-damned fool,' he said, 'but I'd like to think that whether you went or stayed you weren't holding anything against me, Ned.' " Beaumont reassures him, and then Paul begs him once more to stay. Ned says there is no bad blood, but he has to go. Then he reveals that Janet is going with him:

> Madvig's lips parted. He looked dumbly at Ned Beaumont and as he looked the blood went out of his face again. When his face was quite bloodless he mumbled something of which only the word "luck" could be understood, turned clumsily around, went to the door, opened it, and went out, leaving it open behind him.
>
> Janet Henry looked at Ned Beaumont. He stared fixedly at the door.

These are the final words of the novel. They make it clear that Janet is little more than a gesture between the two men, a convenient way to make an ending. Ned Beaumont's loyalty and "luck" once belonged to Paul, but now that is over. *The Glass Key* is primarily a story about male friendship. It was also Hammett's favorite among his novels.

By the time *The Glass Key* was published in 1931 Hammett was already a minor celebrity, with reviews of his books appearing frequently in the press. But Dorothy Parker, writing in the *New Yorker,* dismissed Ned Beaumont as a character who "can in no way stack up against the mag-

nificent Spade, with whom, after reading *The Maltese Falcon,* I went mooning about in a daze of love such as I had not known for any character in literature since I encountered Sir Launcelot. . . ." This review is typical of Hammett's reception by serious critics. They did not want to hear about his interest in Henry James. For them he was a primitive, a working-class tough with real detective experience and the scars to prove it. They were infatuated with his image and blind to the fact that he had been trying for years to transcend mere tough-guy writing. But Hammett had no time to savor the irony: he was negotiating with David O. Selznick for a very lucrative job at Paramount, and in the spring of 1931 he moved to Hollywood. Some of the friends he had made in New York followed him: Dorothy Parker, Alan Campbell, Herbert Asbury, S. J. and Laura Perelman. Hammett's star was rising, and he was making real money for the first time. Free of all obligations (he had left Nell Martin in New York) and surrounded by young starlets, he lived a reckless life of hard drinking and womanizing. He also met Lillian Hellman, who later became one of the most celebrated playwrights of her time. He was to love her faithfully, though not conventionally, for the rest of his life. She was twenty-four and married; he was thirty-six and just coming off a five-day drunk. "When I first met Dash," she later wrote in *An Unfinished Woman* (1969),

> he had written four of [his] five novels and was the hottest thing in Hollywood and New York . . . it was of extra interest to those who collect people that the ex-detective who had bad cuts on his legs and an indentation on his head from being scrappy with criminals was gentle in manner, well educated, elegant to look at . . . and spent so much money on women that they would have liked him even if he had been none of the good things.

For the next year or so, shuttling back and forth from Los Angeles to New York City with Hellman, drinking heavily, he worked intermittently on his next novel.

*   *   *

The Thin Man (1934) grew directly out of Hammett's newfound celebrity and his life with Hellman. In this novel the world of crime and corruption, once the basis of Hammett's fiction, recedes to the status of an amusing sideshow of criminals with names like Shep Morelli and Studsy Burke. Nick Charles, the novel's protagonist, is a reluctant detective, drawn away from his life of glamorous dissipation by an unsolvable murder involving Herbert Macaulay, whose life Nick saved in the war, and Mimi Wynant, an ex-lover. But real crime is less important in *The Thin Man* than the general atmosphere of drunkenness and sexual innuendo. Mimi tries to buy Nick with her body, and her daughter Dorothy is constantly collapsing on Nick's hotel couch, in a half-conscious, girlish effort to possess him. Hammett got into some trouble with *The Thin Man,* thanks to the reference to sex in the following passage. Nora says,

> "Tell me something, Nick. Tell me the truth: when you were wrestling with Mimi, didn't you have an erection?"
> "Oh, a little."
> She laughed and got up from the floor. "If you aren't a disgusting old lecher," she said.

Redbook bowdlerized this passage before serializing *The Thin Man.* Knopf, however, took out an ad in the *New York Times* in which Alfred Knopf was quoted as saying, "I don't believe the question on page 192 of Dashiell Hammett's *The Thin Man* has had the slightest influence upon the sale of the book."

Indecent language is not the only crime in the novel. The entire Wynant family is perverse and manipulative, and Macaulay turns out to be a murderer who tries to kill the very man who once saved his life. But none of this seems to matter much. The pointed irony of Hammett's previous novels is replaced, in *The Thin Man,* by the aimless irony of drunken cocktail-party banter. For the first time, murder seems out of place in a

Hammett novel, the solution contrived. In a mere two pages, Nick reveals (with the help of police chief Guild) that Wynant has been dead for months and that Macaulay, the murderer, has been faking Wynant's letters. Nick knocks the fleeing culprit, Macaulay, out cold. That takes care of the murder, but it hardly resolves the questions raised by the rest of the book, as Nick's wife Nora herself observes:

> "What do you think will happen to Mimi and Dorothy and Gilbert now?"
> "Nothing new. They'll go on being Mimi and Dorothy and Gilbert just as you and I will go on being us and the Quinns will go on being the Quinns. Murder doesn't round out anybody's life except the murdered's and sometimes the murderer's."
> "That may be," Nora said, "but it's all pretty unsatisfactory."

This is how the novel ends. Many readers agree with Nora; *The Thin Man* is probably the weakest of Hammett's novels. With each of his previous books Hammett had refined his technique, moving steadily away from the pulp formulas that got him started. But *The Thin Man,* despite its new subject matter, seems stale and uninventive. It has one redeeming feature: Nick and Nora. Their dialogue has a warmth and energy that keeps the story alive. Early on, for example, Nick narrates the following:

> Nora sighed. "I wish you were sober enough to talk to." She leaned over to take a sip of my drink. "I'll give you your Christmas present now if you'll give me mine."
> I shook my head. "At breakfast."
> "But it's Christmas now."
> "Breakfast."
> "Whatever you're giving me," she said, "I hope I don't like it."
> "You'll have to keep them anyway, because the man at the Aquarium said he positively wouldn't take them back. He said they'd already bitten the tails off the—"
> "It wouldn't hurt you any to find out if you can help her, would it? She's got so much confidence in you, Nicky."

"Everybody trusts Greeks."

"Please."

"You just want to poke your nose into things that—"

"I meant to ask you: did his wife know the Wolf girl was his mistress?"

This kind of dialogue, as Hammett later said, was inspired by his relationship with Hellman, who used to try to make him take up detective work again (as Nora does Nick) so that she could tag along. Nick and Nora's banter translated well into the 1934 film version of *The Thin Man*, starring William Powell and Myrna Loy. The seamier aspects of the novel—including Nick and Nora's nonstop drinking—dissipate in the film's atmosphere of flippant comedy and charm.

In 1934 Hammett published what was to be his last fiction. His income in that year was about $80,000, and it remained near $100,000 for the next six years, largely from screenwriting and royalties for film versions of his earlier work. He was also paid $500 a week by Hearst's King Features for *Secret Agent X-9*, a comic strip version of the generic tough-guy story. Fame and fortune appear to have destroyed Hammett's discipline and ambition together. He lived a life of unparalleled debauchery, drinking, and womanizing almost constantly. He ignored his wife and children, broke almost every contract he signed, and left unpaid bills and debts everywhere—despite all his income. Lillian Hellman took a romantic view of Hammett's spending, arguing (in one of her memoirs) that he just "didn't care about money." A more plausible explanation came from Hammett's friend Nunnally Johnson, who wrote:

> From the day I met Hammett . . . his behavior could be accounted for only by an assumption that he had no expectation of being alive much beyond Thursday. . . . Even allowing for the exuberance of youthfulness and the headiness of the certain approach of success, not to mention the daffiness of the twenties, no one could have spent himself and

his money with such recklessness who expected to be alive much longer.

In early 1936, increasingly out of control, under investigation by both the IRS and the California tax authorities, Hammett spent several weeks detoxing at the Lenox Hill Hospital in New York. While there he read Marx for the first time, and his political life began. Later he was to call himself a Marxist and to support the American Communist Party for many years; but he remained skeptical, and as Garry Wills has written, "The worst thing one could have wished on the mousy world of Communist ideologues in America was a dozen more Hammetts." Hammett also helped support the Spanish Republicans, a popular cause in Hollywood, and gave speeches for the Screen Writers Guild. In 1939 Hammett's MGM contract ended with *Another Thin Man*, the third in the *Thin Man* series and the last one he would work on. In 1941 Hammett's fame flared for the last time with John Huston's version of *The Maltese Falcon*, probably the best film of a Hammett book ever made. (Several critics have called it the best screen adaptation of any novel.) Huston, who had never directed a Hollywood feature before, won Warners initial approval with his superb screenplay adaptation of the novel. He removed the Flitcraft story, but otherwise kept the dialogue from the novel largely intact. At a few points he even managed to improve it. As Spade holds the lead falcon, in Huston's version, one of the cops asks him what it is, and Spade replies: "The stuff that dreams are made of." The film retains much of the dramatic tension one finds in the book, and the casting is excellent: Humphrey Bogart as Spade, Sydney Greenstreet as Gutman, Peter Lorre as Cairo, Elisha Cook as Wilmer. Mary Astor as Brigid is the one weak link. Overall, the film was a magnificent success.

In 1942 Hammett was accepted into the army, to Lillian Hellman's horror and his own deep satisfaction. He spent most of his time on a remote island in the Aleutians, where the men looked up to him (they called him "Sam"), and he edited a military newspaper. He appears to have enjoyed the war, perhaps in part because it offered him discipline and an excuse for not writing. After his release he taught intermittently at the Marxist-oriented Jefferson School of Social Science in New York, and spent time at Hellman's farm in Westchester County.

In 1951 Hammett was sentenced to six months in prison when he refused to give the names of contributors to a bail fund that had been used to free several Communists on trial for conspiracy. Lillian Hellman has suggested that Hammett's stand in the matter was heroic. Certainly Hammett was brave, and probably he acted on principle. But he did not know the names of the other contributors; he could have avoided the sentence by admitting as much. When he emerged from jail he had been effectively blacklisted, his radio shows canceled and his books out of print. The government held a lien on all his income, thanks to $100,000 of unpaid taxes dating to 1943. He scraped by, living in a borrowed cottage in Katonah, New York, until his death on January 10, 1961.

Hammett's last fictional effort, abandoned in 1952 or 1953 and collected in *The Big Knockover* (Lillian Hellman's edition of the stories), was called "Tulip." It describes an older man (it is clearly a self-portrait) being visited by a war buddy named Tulip who wants "Pop" to write about his life. Pop's explanation is a kind of apologia for Hammett's failure to write anything during his later years, and it is painful to read. It is ironic as well, because Hammett's life has been the inspiration for fiction, film, and myth ever since he died. And the genre he helped to create has never been stronger. Writers like Elmore Leonard and George Higgins stand in a direct line of influence from Hammett, and though their work is billed as "crime fiction" in drugstores and on best-seller lists, it is reviewed (and some

of it published) in the *New Yorker* too. The boundary between popular fiction and serious literature is more permeable than ever before. It may even be argued that Hammett's influence extends to film directors like Martin Scorsese and Quentin Tarantino, whose careers are based on the enduring American fascination with crime. Dashiell Hammett, who took pulp fiction and made it into art, deserves to be remembered as a godfather to all those who do so today.

Selected Bibliography

WORKS OF DASHIELL HAMMETT

NOVELS
Red Harvest. New York: Knopf, 1929.
The Dain Curse. New York: Knopf, 1929.
The Maltese Falcon. New York: Knopf, 1930.
The Glass Key. New York: Knopf, 1931.
The Thin Man. New York: Knopf, 1934.
$106,000 Blood Money. New York: Spivak, 1943.

COLLECTED SHORT STORIES
The Adventures of Sam Spade and Other Stories. New York: Spivak, 1944.
The Continental Op. New York: Spivak, 1945.
The Return of the Continental Op. New York: Spivak, 1945.
Hammett Homicides. Edited by Ellery Queen. New York: Spivak, 1946.
Dead Yellow Women. Edited by Ellery Queen. New York: Spivak, 1947.
Nightmare Town. Edited by Ellery Queen. New York: American Mercury, 1948.
The Creeping Siamese. Edited by Ellery Queen. New York: Spivak, 1950.
Woman in the Dark. Edited by Ellery Queen. New York: Spivak, 1951.
A Man Named Thin and Other Stories. Edited by Ellery Queen. New York: Ferman, 1962.

The Big Knockover. Edited by Lillian Hellman. New York: Random House, 1966.

The Continental Op. Edited by Steven Marcus. New York: Random House, 1974.

MISCELLANEOUS

"The Parthian Shot." *Smart Set,* 69 (October 1922).

"The Master Mind." *Smart Set,* 70 (January 1923).

"From the Memoirs of a Private Detective." *Smart Set,* 70 (March 1923).

"In Defence of the Sex Story." *Writer's Digest,* 4 (June 1924).

"Finger-Prints." *Black Mask,* 8 (June 1925).

Secret Agent X-9: Book One. Philadelphia: McKay, 1934.

Secret Agent X-9: Book Two. Philadelphia: McKay, 1934.

The Battle of the Aleutians. Captions by Robert Colodny. Adak, Alaska: Intelligence section, Field Force Headquarters, Adak, 1944.

BIBLIOGRAPHIES

Layman, Richard. *Dashiell Hammett: A Descriptive Bibliography.* Pittsburgh: University of Pittsburgh Press, 1979.

Nolan, William F. "The Hammett Checklist Revisited." *Armchair Detective,* 6 (August 1973).

―――. "Revisiting the Revisited Hammett Checklist." *Armchair Detective,* 9 (October 1976).

BIOGRAPHICAL AND CRITICAL STUDIES

Chandler, Raymond. "The Simple Art of Murder." *Atlantic Monthly* (December 1944).

Edenbaum, Robert I. "The Poetics of the Private Eye: The Novels of Dashiell Hammett." In *Tough Guy Writers of the Thirties.* Edited by David Madden. Carbondale: Southern Illinois University Press, 1968. Pp. 80–103.

Grella, George. "The Wings of the Falcon and the Maltese Dove." In *A Question of Quality.* Edited by L. Filler. Bowling Green, Ohio: Bowling Green University Popular Press, 1976. Pp. 108–114.

Hellman, Lillian. *An Unfinished Woman—A Memoir.* Boston: Little, Brown, 1969.

―――. *Pentimento: A Book of Portraits.* Boston: Little, Brown, 1973.

―――. *Scoundrel Time.* Boston: Little, Brown, 1976.

Johnson, Diane. *Dashiell Hammett: A Life.* New York: Random House, 1983.

Layman, Richard. *Shadow Man: The Life of Dashiell Hammett.* New York: Harcourt Brace Jovanovich, 1981.

Macdonald, Ross. "Homage to Dashiell Hammett." In *Self-Portrait: Ceaselessly into the Past.* Santa Barbara, Calif.: Capra, 1981. Pp. 109–122.

Malin, Irving. "Focus on *The Maltese Falcon:* The Metaphysical Falcon." In *Tough Guy Writers of the Thirties.* Edited by David Madden. Carbondale: Southern Illinois University Press, 1968. Pp. 104–110.

Marling, William. *Dashiell Hammett.* Boston: Twayne, 1983.

Nolan, William F. *Dashiell Hammett: A Casebook.* Santa Barbara: McNally & Loftin, 1969.

―――. *Hammett: A Life at the Edge.* New York: Congdon & Weed, 1983.

Skinner, Robert E. *The Hard-Boiled Explicator: A Guide to the Study of Dashiell Hammett, Raymond Chandler, and Ross Macdonald.* Metuchen, N.J.: Scarecrow, 1985.

Symons, Julian. *Bloody Murder.* London: Faber and Faber, 1972.

―――. *Dashiell Hammett.* New York: Harcourt Brace Jovanovich, 1985.

—ROBERT WORTH

Lorraine Hansberry
1930–1965

WHEN LORRAINE HANSBERRY'S *A Raisin in the Sun* received the 1959 New York Drama Critics Circle Award for Best Play of the Year (in competition with works by Eugene O'Neill, Tennessee Williams, and Archibald MacLeish) and placed its author in the record books as the youngest American, fifth woman, and first African American to win this honor, some critics grumbled that the chief motivation for this decision was to recognize an African American. However, most critics today would agree that Hansberry's work belongs in the highest rank of modern American dramas, alongside O'Neill's *Long Day's Journey into Night* (1956), Williams' *A Streetcar Named Desire* (1947), and Arthur Miller's *Death of a Salesman* (1949). Its acute, complex blending of personal and social vision, its ability to embody key issues of its time while illuminating their importance for all time, its insight into the extraordinary qualities of ordinary people, and its wisdom, humanity, and unobtrusive poetry place it firmly within this elite group. Moreover, Hansberry's play redefines domestic realism by incorporating more than three centuries of African American history and struggle presented through a multigenerational, multidimensional perspective. Subtly yet effectively merging realism with symbolism and thought-provoking experimentalism, Hansberry's play simultaneously expands the audience's theatrical

and social visions. Similarly, while Hansberry composed the play with an appreciative eye to Western culture and dramatic tradition, she also infused it with both a formal and thematic tribute to African culture.

Hansberry's other major works, including *The Sign in Sidney Brustein's Window* (1964, her only other play produced during her lifetime), the posthumously produced *Les Blancs* (produced in 1970), and the still-unproduced television play *The Drinking Gourd* and play *What Use Are Flowers?*, have remained more controversial in terms of both their content and quality, with some critics even asserting that she was a one-play dramatist. However, many of her critics would agree that all her dramas incorporate the same extraordinary breadth and clarity of vision, intellectual integrity, excoriating wit, complex characterization, quietly innovative style and form, and abiding concern for all humanity. A hallmark of Hansberry's work is that, although she was among the most thoroughly committed political and social writers, she never failed to place her ideas and beliefs in the widest possible human context and, like Sean O'Casey and Bertolt Brecht, to make her art a means of providing her audiences with new perspectives rather than restricting them with narrow ideological concerns.

A full judgment cannot yet be made on Hansberry's work since much of it remains unknown to the public. Although her unproduced screenplay for *A Raisin in the Sun,* which differs strikingly from both the play and the screenplay of the film starring Sidney Poitier and Claudia McNeil (1961), was finally published in 1992, her equally well-written and important screenplay based on Jacques Roumain's *Gouverneurs de la Rosée* (1944) has yet to appear either on the screen or in print. Hansberry's former husband and literary executor, Robert Nemiroff, was editing her nearly completed novel, *All the Dark and Beautiful Warriors,* when he died in 1991, so it too awaits publication, though it will probably appear within the next few years. And these two extraordinary works are only the tip of Hansberry's unpublished legacy, which includes completed or nearly completed plays, essays (such as her lengthy, thoughtful feminist review of Simone de Beauvoir's *The Second Sex* [1949–1950]), short stories, poems, journals, and letters (both public and private). This legacy and the list of her unfinished (often barely begun) projects— including plays and operas based on the ancient Egyptian ruler Akhenaton, the eighteenth-century feminist Mary Wollstonecraft, the Haitian liberator Toussaint-Louverture, and Oliver La Farge's Navajo character Laughing Boy— exhibit not only the astonishing range of her interests and intellect but also the immensity of our loss by her early death at thirty-four.

Lorraine Vivian Hansberry was born on May 19, 1930, to a highly prominent family in Chicago's African American community. Wealthy by black standards of the time, comfortably middle class by white, both of her parents were very active socially, attracting to their home many of their most important black contemporaries, such as Paul Robeson, Duke Ellington, and Joe Louis. They were also profoundly involved in politics. Her mother, Nannie Perry, who had been trained as a teacher at Tennessee Agricultural and Industrial University, was a community leader and ward committeewoman. When she was barely into her childhood, Lorraine gained an awareness of world racial politics that never left her from her mother's ferocious denunciation of the Pope for blessing the Italian troops on their way to fight the Ethiopians, an awareness that was heightened by newsreels showing the Africans with spears trying to stand up to Italians with guns. Lorraine's father, Carl Augustus Hansberry, who had built up a successful real estate business, served as a U.S. marshal, ran as a Republican for Congress, and contributed time, effort, and money to the National Association for the Advancement of Colored People (NAACP) and the Urban League. His greatest lesson to her about racial pride and determined resistance came when he decided to challenge Chicago's restrictive covenants, the agreements among white real estate dealers that segregated the city into all-white and all-black sections. To do so, he surreptitiously bought a house in an area reserved for whites—at the time, a jailable offense. He then moved his family in and carried on a legal battle all the way to the U.S. Supreme Court to establish his claim to it. While he was arguing his case with the help of the NAACP's legal team, a hostile white mob surrounded the house; eight-year-old Lorraine almost lost her life when a concrete slab thrown through the window nearly hit her. An armed guard hired by her parents dispersed the mob, and Lorraine later witnessed her mother prowling the house at night with a loaded gun to protect the family, a scene she used in her first draft of *A Raisin in the Sun* (her final draft excluded it because she ended her narrative at an earlier point).

After losing initially in the Illinois courts, the Hansberry family was evicted from its new home. Unfortunately, Carl Hansberry's ultimate victory in the landmark 1940 *Hansberry v. Lee* Supreme Court decision declaring restrictive covenants illegal proved equally embittering since in practice such covenants continued. Discouraged by his inability to make significant changes in the United States' racist system and by his two sons' problems with military discrimination (Carl Jr. served in a segregated unit during World War II and Perry protested against a draft that incorporated segregation), Hansberry decided in 1945 to move the family to Mexico, though he died there from a cerebral hemorrhage before completing his plans.

Carl Hansberry's choice of Mexico rather than Africa for relocation reflected his relative lack of interest in Africa. In contrast, Lorraine's uncle, William Leo Hansberry, taught African history at Howard University and helped inspire Lorraine's own powerful sense of affinity with Africa. As one of the first African American scholars to investigate African antiquity, he made a profound contribution to the development of the field and attracted many African students to his classes, some of whom, like Kwame Nkrumah of Ghana and Nnamdi Azikewe and Julius Nkize of Nigeria, were involved in resistance movements to European colonialism and would eventually become leaders of their newly independent countries. On his visits to Lorraine's family, William Hansberry often brought such students along with him, and one or more of them may have provided the inspiration for her African character, Joseph Asagai, in *A Raisin in the Sun*.

In 1947, the year in which she was elected president of the debating society at Englewood High School, she, along with other middle-class, well-behaved black students, observed a mob of striking white students answering shouted insults with shouted rebuttals. Her diffidence was abruptly altered, not only for the moment but for the rest of her life, by the arrival of working-class black students from nearby high schools who had heard about the rioting whites and felt that this racist insult must be answered in the strongest possible terms, with physical resistance. Her sympathy was then wholly with the fighters.

After her graduation from high school in 1948, she attended the University of Wisconsin at Madison, experiencing further problems with discrimination but discovering a new way to fight back—through drama. She was so strongly affected by a production of Sean O'Casey's *Juno and the Paycock* (1924), whose human and humane treatment of the Irish rebellion against British oppression reminded her intensely of the situation of American blacks, that she decided to write her own version of the vision she shared with O'Casey, a version that would, of course, draw upon her individual memories and knowledge.

Unhappy with her life at the university and the bulk of her studies there, Hansberry moved to New York in 1950 and began her active involvement with the struggle for social change by working for *Freedom,* the radical newspaper founded by Paul Robeson, who had been a visitor at her parents' home. Starting as a reporter in 1951 covering stories on colonialism, poverty, racism, and a host of domestic and world events as well as reviewing books and dramas by blacks, Hansberry became an associate editor in 1952. During 1952, she also served as Paul Robeson's representative at the Intercontinental Peace Congress in Uruguay after his passport request was denied. This was a difficult mission because she had both to evade the notice of those officials who had opposed Robeson's participation and to fly on a plane that was nearly downed by a storm, an experience so distressing to her that she could never bear to fly again. The year 1952 took on an added, even greater significance when, while covering a demonstration against sports discrimination at New York University, she met Robert Barron Nemiroff, a white graduate student of Russian Jewish heritage whom she subsequently dated and married. On the night of their wedding in 1953, they delayed their celebration to take part in a demonstration to protest the impending execution of Julius and Ethel Rosenberg, who had been convicted (many believed falsely) of treason.

Shortly before starting at *Freedom*, Hansberry had taken a course on short story writing during her "two erratic months" at the New School for Social Research, and she composed stories as well as poetry and plays while writing articles and reviews for the newspaper. She quit *Freedom* in 1953 to spend more time on creative writing because she considered her writing the most effective contribution she could make to the social and political conflicts of her time. From 1953 to 1956 she worked on three plays while holding a succession of less-absorbing jobs, such as tagger for the garment fur industry, typist, production assistant for a theatrical company (a job she promptly quit when she discovered her primary duty was to fetch coffee), staff member of *Sing Out* magazine, program director at an interracial summer camp, teacher at the Marxist-oriented Jefferson School for Social Science (where she had previously studied African history and culture under W. E. B. Du Bois), and recreation leader at the Federation for the Handicapped.

Hansberry's writing goals were strongly supported by Nemiroff, who was an aspiring writer himself. While Hansberry was holding down her series of odd jobs, he did the same, working as part-time typist, copywriter, waiter, Multilith operator, and reader. After graduating from New York University, he became promotions director of Avon Books. In 1956, he and his friend Burt D'Lugoff wrote a hit folk song, "Cindy, Oh, Cindy," and he used this financial success to allow Hansberry to concentrate full-time on her writing. During this year, Nemiroff also began work running a music publishing firm for their mutual friend Philip Rose.

Once freed from the necessity of doing other work, Hansberry moved from a variety of projects—including a novel, some plays, and an opera, which she had been working on simultaneously—to one project that soon absorbed all her energy, a play originally titled *The Crystal Stair* and later called *A Raisin in the Sun.* After completing the play, she read it to her husband, Burt D'Lugoff, and Philip Rose and was astonished when Rose announced that he wanted to option her work for production on Broadway. Although neither he nor coproducer David J. Cogan had ever tackled Broadway before, they found a number of small investors willing to share their risk (after the major Broadway producers declined to invest in a play about African American life) and arranged for tryouts in New Haven, Philadelphia, and Chicago to convince some Broadway theater owner to take a chance on their project. The success of the tryouts, particularly in Philadelphia, convinced the Shubert chain to offer them the Ethel Barrymore Theatre.

A Raisin in the Sun opened on March 11, 1959, with a cast that read like a Who's Who of the black theater in days to come, including Sidney Poitier, Claudia McNeil, Ruby Dee, Diana Sands, Louis Gossett Jr., Ivan Dixon, Glynn Turman, Douglas Turner Ward, and Lonne Elder III (Ossie Davis Jr. later replaced Poitier in the lead); Lloyd Richards set precedent as the first black director on Broadway. Receiving favorable reviews from the vitally important New York critics and enthusiastic responses from audiences, drawing a vastly greater number of blacks into the theater than ever before while attracting a substantial number of whites as well, Hansberry's drama became an overnight success and two months later won the New York Drama Critics Circle Award for best play. It had a highly successful run of 538 performances and made Hansberry a celebrity.

The play focuses on the legacy of Big Walter Younger, both the material bequest of the insurance money paid on his death and his spiritual heritage. Each surviving member of his family has dreams about what to do with the money, dreams that reflect the unfulfilled hopes of African Americans through many generations. His son, Walter Lee Jr., wants to go into business; his daughter, Beneatha, wants an education and the chance to serve humanity; his wife, Lena, now the head of the family, wants to hold them all together, to find a decent house in a decent neighborhood, and to provide her grandson (Walter Lee's son), Travis, the living space that the adults in the family had not had the opportunity to experience. Lena uses part of the money to buy a house in a "white neighborhood," a purchase made possible by the removal of the restrictive covenants Carl Hansberry had fought. When the white neighbors try to buy them out, the family honors Big Walter's spiritual bequest of racial pride and courage in the face of oppression by deciding to move into the hostile neighborhood, prepared to face whatever struggle awaits them, rather than, as Lena puts it, taking money "that was a way of telling us we wasn't fit to walk the earth."

Within this framework, Hansberry deftly depicts the diversity of the black community. Walter Lee's materialistic goals, fixated on his becoming part-owner of a liquor store, are met head-on by Lena's religious objections to selling liquor. Lena's Christianity is further confronted by Beneatha's atheistic humanism. Beneatha's exuberant embracing of her African heritage contrasts with a rich black boyfriend's unconvincing contempt for all things African and her sister-in-law Ruth's more legitimate refusal to accept only African music as righteous and abandon jazz and the blues as "assimilationist junk." Even at the end, after the family has shown its unity in the face of white insults and threats, Walter Lee and Beneatha walk off arguing, fiercely but playfully, about whether Beneatha should marry her idealistic African suitor, Joseph Asagai, or a man with money, an argument showing that Walter has retained his materialistic views while learning that racial pride and family should come first. Throughout the play, this African American di-

versity stands in marked contrast to the white community's insistence on conformity.

The language of the characters reveals a similar diversity. Lena, Walter, Ruth, and Travis all customarily use Black English Vernacular, as in Walter's comment "He just going to have to start getting up earlier" or Travis' statement "This is the morning we supposed to bring the fifty cents to school." In contrast, Beneatha, who is attending college, speaks a more educated version of English mixed with youthful slang, as in the coupling of her assertion "Brother is a flip" with her explanation "Brother isn't really crazy yet—he—he's an elaborate neurotic." The sole African, the college-educated Asagai, speaks a highly formal English with an unusually large vocabulary and almost no colloquialisms.

Hansberry's attentiveness to language adds greatly to the surface realism of her play, a realism that led some of her early critics to regard her approach to drama as old-fashioned. But she detested the photographic type of writing that tries to portray life exactly as it is and insisted that realism ought to show the possible alongside the actual. One of the best examples of her flexible approach to realism ocurs when Walter Lee, drunk, finds his sister playing African music, jumps up on a table, and speaks as an African leader calling his people to war. His language then is far different from his everyday vernacular: "Do you hear the screeching of the cocks in yonder hills beyond where the chiefs meet in council for the coming of the mighty war." This humorous scene, which has never jarred audiences or even critics into disbelief, expresses both the eloquence of the African oral tradition and the difference between the elevated position of warrior Walter Lee would have held in African society had his ancestors been permitted to remain there and his contemporary, degraded position as a chauffeur in American society. Thus, Hansberry's realism works to reveal Walter's potential courage and nobility, qualities that are fully confirmed by the ending, alongside the oppressing actuality of his circumstances.

It is important to note, however, that Hansberry did not find eloquence only in elevated formal language, such as the traditional African call to war or Joseph Asagai's more modern, idealistic metaphors about progress and struggle. Like Sean O'Casey, she had a keen ear for the poetry and wisdom in the vernacular. The most memorable and moving passage in her play is given by Lena in her working-class African American speech patterns when Beneatha, appalled by Walter's despairing decision to accept the whites' offer for the house (a decision he will shortly reverse), tells her mother that she no longer considers Walter her brother:

> Child, when do you think is the time to love somebody the most? . . . It's when he's at his lowest and can't believe in hisself 'cause the world done whipped him so! When you starts measuring somebody, measure him right, child, measure him right. Make sure you done taken into account what hills and valleys he come through before he got to wherever he is.

This speech, wholly in the vernacular, has a powerful rhythm that reinforces the emotion, a pattern of repetition that focuses on a central idea and complements the simple, stirringly appropriate imagery. With its arousing, measured tones expressing painfully gained knowledge, Lena's speech urges Beneatha and the audience not only to reevaluate Walter Lee's character and behavior but also to see the speaker herself, all African Americans, and, by extension, all humanity in the light of compassion. This passage shows clearly how Hansberry was able simultaneously to make a social and political statement concerning the African American situation in African American speech and to touch the universal as fully as have the renowned dramatists of the past and those great works of folk art, the spirituals.

* * *

Hansberry's sudden ascension to fame appealed to both her fun-loving side, exemplified by the humor that shines in even her bleakest works, and her desire for a platform from which to speak out on the issues that disturbed her most, including racism, colonialism, sexism, nuclear warfare, Joseph McCarthy's communist witch hunting, and worldwide oppression in its myriad forms. She delighted in the many unsolicited letters that came to her and tried to answer all of them, including those that were hostile to her ideas. Her frequent appearances on radio and television talk shows gave her ample opportunities to display her sharp wit and even sharper intellect. With a sympathetic interviewer like Studs Terkel, she could develop her thoughts in comfort and depth, assured that every nuance was understood and appreciated. However, with an acerbic, confrontational interviewer like Mike Wallace, she stood her ground against innuendo and ideas she considered misleading and presented her own views forcefully and cogently. For example, when Wallace attacked the supposed bestiality of the Mau Mau revolutionaries in Kenya, she asserted that the violence of the oppressed should not be judged in the same way as the violence of the oppressor and that the primary guilt for all the violence there lay with the British colonial government, a viewpoint she would later develop artistically in her African play, *Les Blancs*.

In a 1959 speech titled "The Negro Writer and His Roots: Toward a New Romanticism" made at a conference sponsored by the American Society of African Culture, Hansberry argued, as she would on many occasions, that all art makes social statements, though works embodying conventional ideas are seldom discussed in terms of their social content whereas those offering radical views are stigmatized as propaganda. Her own intention was to make the strongest and most insightful social statement she could while consistently striving for the highest artistry. As this artistic credo implies, social commitment was primary in both her life and her art. While her essay also delineated and praised the most notable aspects of African American culture—its speech and its music, those aspects that scholars such as Stephen Henderson and Houston Baker Jr. later pointed to as definitive—Hansberry also insisted that black writers must participate in the intellectual life and strife of the general culture.

The major exception to her open commitments was her lesbianism. At the time she was writing, even the progressive social movements with which she identified were openly hostile to homosexuality, and the gay liberation movement did not yet exist. She had no strongly committed group or community with which to unite in order to strive for social change concerning her sexual orientation, as she did in her fight against racial and gender oppression. She did, however, write letters to the two existing homophile publications, *One* and *The Ladder*, signed either L. N. and L. H. N., which stressed her awareness of the linkage between all forms of oppression and particularly between women's issues and homosexual issues. In addition, she included complex minor homosexual characters in two of her major plays, *The Sign in Sidney Brustein's Window* and *Les Blancs*, and dealt more centrally with the lesbian and homosexual experience in some pseudonymously published short stories and unpublished plays. Eventually her lesbianism also led her to separate from Robert Nemiroff (their physical relationship had already ended in 1959), though their respect for each other's intellect and aesthetic judgment enabled them to continue to collaborate creatively.

In 1960, to commemorate the Civil War centennial, producer-director Dore Schary planned to commission five original ninety-minute television plays for the National Broadcasting Company and approached Hansberry to write the first one—on slavery. After receiving Schary's assurance that she could be "frank" in her treatment of the subject, Hansberry did extensive research, culled her memories of slavery stories told her by her mother and grandmother, delved into her imagination and knowledge of society and individual psychology, and created *The Drinking Gourd*. Although Schary himself admired it, Hansberry's television play proved too controversial for National Broadcasting Company executives, and the entire project was canceled. In 1972, Robert Nemiroff included it in the posthumous *Les Blancs: The Collected Last Plays of Lorraine Hansberry*, but by 1995 there had been no televised version.

The Drinking Gourd is a three-tiered tragedy and social indictment. The message, spelled out by a narrator who is pointedly not identified with a particular region, is that the Civil War was necessary to eliminate slavery because this destructive system "has already cost us, as a nation, too much of our soul." Carefully constructed and fully attuned to human complexity, Hansberry's play supports this thesis through an exploration of the devastating effects of slavery on the white plantation masters and the poor whites as well as on the slaves.

The cost to the soul of Hiram Sweet, the owner of a large plantation, is that he has taken his role as "master" too seriously and is unprepared for the loss of control that comes from both his illness (which appears to be, appropriately, a heart condition) and the very system that seemed to grant him all his power. He has been a "humane" master, forcing his slaves to do only nine and a half hours of unpaid labor a day, but is confronted with the painful decision of either following his fellow slave owners' pattern of overworking their slaves to the point of killing some of them (such deaths and subsequent replacements being cost-effective) or watching all he has set into place fall apart through his inability to compete. Like Oedipus, his ambition and arrogance have been bolstered by his belief that he has been a benefactor to his community (which, in Sweet's case, consists first and foremost of his family and slaves—he regards the latter as children). However, again like Oedipus, his confidence in himself is undermined by the discovery that he is a spiritual blight on the people of that community. Fond of Rissa, one of the four slaves who originally helped him to build up the plantation, Hiram must face her unforgiving anger when his son nearly destroys her son, and he dies crying for help from her and the other slaves, which they refuse to give, despite his supposed benevolence toward all of them.

Everett Sweet, the weak son of a too-strong father, is caught in an intolerable and unresolvable dilemma; he wants to earn his father's respect by making a financial success through running the plantation with methods that his father considers abhorrent. Taking advantage of his father's illness, Everett runs the plantation in the ''modern'' way of harshness and increasing demands on the slaves only to find himself forced to commit the unforgivable act of punishing the one slave his father wanted most to protect, Rissa's son Hannibal. This act not only provokes his father's rage against him but also leads indirectly to his father's death, something that Everett would never have wished to occur since he genuinely loves his father in spite of their differences.

The blight on the soul of Zeb Dudley, a poor white farmer unable to compete in the plantation system, causes him even more pain than the blight on the Sweets' souls causes them. Although he is encouraged by a friend to migrate west, where he would still have a chance to make an honest living by farming, Zeb has been deluded by the meretricious values of his society, which hold up Hiram Sweet as a model for success; he prefers to accept Everett's offer of a position as slave driver in the hope that he can build up a stake to buy slaves of his own. Zeb too would like to be a big plantation owner and knows that Hiram did not start out wealthy. A more disturbing and engaging

motivation is his profound concern for his children, who are close to dying from starvation. He is misled by his desire for independence and security, however, as Everett is only looking for an instrument with which to perform his will. The full horror of his situation comes home to him when Everett requires him to put Hannibal's eyes out as the soul-price exacted for continuing in his position. While Hansberry always applauds characters who emerge from crises strengthened in their will to struggle for what they are convinced is right (thereby becoming moral forces for change), she also sympathizes with characters who give in to overwhelming social pressures, emphasizing the vulnerability of morality when it contradicts the social will.

The most ravaged victims of slavery are, inevitably, the slaves. Forced to sacrifice their labor, their families, and their hopes and dreams for the benefit of others, they gain nothing of value from the system, though some, like Hiram's driver, Coffin, foolishly betray others for the token advantages offered by their masters to house slaves, drivers, and informers. Under such a system, Hannibal, a man fully as ambitious as the Sweets and Zeb Dudley, prefers to be lazy and recalcitrant rather than put forth an effort that will be reaped by a man whom he in no way recognizes as his master. His ambition instead takes the path of seeking knowledge through reading and writing, accomplishments legally prohibited to slaves. This is the great ''crime'' for which Everett Sweet has Hannibal's eyes put out. At the end, though, his blind eyes continue to see more than those of his would-be masters, and his body contains an indomitable spirit bent on heading for the North where the struggle is being waged to set men like him free. He, his timid girlfriend, Sarah (now holding a rifle procured for them by Rissa), and a young boy named Joshua are on their way to a Promised Land which, like the biblical Israel, must be fought for. Together, they embody what is left of the soul in this greed-driven, soul-devouring system.

Given the considerable success of the stage version of *A Raisin in the Sun,* it was nearly inevitable that a movie version would be made. However, as she was well aware of the travesties of African American life Hollywood had presented in the past, Hansberry insisted on retaining the right to do the screenplay herself. Unfortunately, this immersed her once again in controversy and censorship.

Alert to the differences between stage and screen, Hansberry hoped to move the Younger family out of the apartment, in which the entire action of the play takes place, and stage new scenes in the Chicago area focusing on the individual family members. These included one in which Lena fights with a South Side market clerk over high-priced ancient apples, leading her to take the bus across town to a supermarket and pass the house in a white neighborhood that she decides to buy. In another new scene, Walter talks to a white liquor store owner named Herman who is sympathetic toward Walter but insensitive to his dream of owning a store; Walter then meets his associates in the liquor store deal, Bobo and the confidence man Willy Harris, in a bar where they mock those whites whom they believe want to keep them from competing. The strongest of the new scenes, however, is one in which a street-corner speaker talks about those blacks who ask whites for a job and get only a broom in reply, asking why blacks have been disinherited and where are the businesses they should have had and the opportunities they need. The presence of Walter in the crowd underlines the relevance of the speech to his circumstances, and that of the revolutionary African student, Asagai, adds further meaning to the words.

Of these and other new scenes, virtually nothing remained in the version filmed by Columbia Pictures in 1961. The Columbia executives, like those at NBC, feared offending large segments of the moviegoing public and even cut out parts of the original play, such as (eyeing the European market) the references to British and French colonialism, in their efforts to keep the work as safe and profitable as possible. Nevertheless, Hansberry was able to retain enough of the content and spirit of her play to make the movie a landmark in the portrayal of African American life on the screen and to deserve the Gary Cooper Award (for "outstanding human values") it received at the Cannes Film Festival that year. A more representative treatment of the play is the 1989 televised American Playhouse version, starring Danny Glover and Esther Rolle and containing almost an hour more of material than the original movie; it demonstrates just how powerful the play could be on film. The huge critical success of the American Playhouse version, however, will probably discourage potential producers and directors from attempting another filming for some time to come. Still, in 1992, Hansberry's original, unfilmed screenplay was published in a version edited by Robert Nemiroff from her first two drafts, so that readers could at least imagine the movie that she wanted to make, readers that may include a committed producer and a gifted director.

After her experience with Columbia Pictures, Hansberry was leery of offers from major studios. However, when a small independent film company approached her to adapt Jacques Roumain's *Gouverneurs de la Rosée* (English language publication in 1947 as *Masters of the Dew*), she readily accepted because of her respect for Roumain's work and her hope that she would be freer to develop her cinematic artistry this time. However, when she had completed her third draft, a polished, producible version though she planned further revisions, a contract dispute centering on a clash between her artistic vision and that of the producers led to the end of the project. This final draft should eventually be published as it is one of Hansberry's finest works.

In preparing her adaptation, Hansberry adhered fairly closely to the basic plot of Roumain's novel. She also retained and reinforced Roumain's socialist vision, portraying the peasants' struggle with oppressors and nature sympathetically and forcefully. She felt, however, that some of the characters were thinly developed and needed to be fleshed out.

While increasing the complexity of all the characters, Hansberry concentrated most on Annaise and Delira, the lover and the mother respectively of the central character, Manuel. As Hansberry reconceived them, both of the women became much stronger figures. Annaise was transformed from a totally adoring female, ready to applaud her lover's every aim and utterance, into a woman who can pretend to be submissive when it suits her but supports only those actions she agrees with and insists on being treated with respect. Considerably more independent than Roumain's Annaise, Hansberry's creation remains a woman of her place and time, honoring her elders and deeming her only real chance at power is through influencing the man she loves. Hansberry's Delira is a believer in both Christianity and African religion, and she has other basic similarities with Roumain's character. However, in her final confrontation with Hilarion, the people's exploiter, Hansberry's Delira demonstrates an added measure of determination and guile that Roumain's character lacks.

Hansberry's other major departure from Roumain is in the dialogue. She decided against the type of consciously poetic speech that her friend Langston Hughes and Mercer Cook had reproduced so admirably in their translation of the novel because she felt that this way of speaking would be awkward in the mouths of American actors. While her simpler, less formal language contains, as all her writing does, poetic rhythms and imagery, Hansberry regarded film as primarily a visual medium and constructed her screenplay in line with her belief that the best poetic effects it could attain were through visual imagery. As a highly circumspect artist, Hansberry always strove to make the fullest use of the special qualities of whatever medium she was working in.

In 1962, Hansberry mobilized support for the Student Nonviolent Coordinating Committee's efforts to end racial segregation and denounced the repressive tactics of the House Un-American Activities Committee. However, the situation that probably disturbed her most at this time was the Cuban missile crisis, during which worldwide nuclear annihilation seemed imminent. At the same time, she was preoccupied with the despairing vision of Samuel Beckett and other dramatists of the theater of the absurd, which pictured the world as pointless, irrational, ridiculous, and trivial. The result of all these concerns was her short play *What Use Are Flowers?* (collected in *Les Blancs*).

The basic situation in *What Use Are Flowers?* is the result of atomic confrontation. After a nuclear holocaust, a hermit and a group of children discover each other as the sole survivors, and the hermit attempts to make them understand and respect civilization. The play is also about Hansberry's confrontation with nihilism. The hermit's role as reluctant teacher gave her the chance to address the issues highlighted by Beckett in *Waiting for Godot*. While she, like Beckett, held no belief in a personal God or in any preordained values and order in the universe, she believed that human beings could impose their own meaning on life, and even though she often felt a despair akin to Beckett's, she refused to surrender to it. In her play, the hermit, like his creator, is brought again and again to the brink of giving up on the children (and in effect on humanity) as they seem to throw away his lessons and their future in petty, envious, self-destructive squabbles; yet each time he manages, often just barely, to find a reason to continue helping them.

In contrast to Beckett's play, which disorients and ferociously questions an audience's beliefs in time, identity, history, language, and reason, Hansberry's work pays respect to the slow, agonizing accumulation of these stabilizing and progressive concepts as the essence of civilization and the only viable defense against madness and annihilation. Beckett's characters wait, seemingly an eternity (though who can tell since time has no meaning?), for something, anything, to illuminate their lives, and at the end they are still waiting. Hansberry's hermit, who had turned his back on civilization only to find himself its last representative, gives the language-less foundlings names, tortuously builds up their vocabularies, helps them to see one boy's rediscovery of the wheel as progress, introduces them to reason as a hedge against the self-destructive release of emotions, and enables them to have a chance, however frail and continuously endangered, at constructing a history. He also teaches the children to move behond a utilitarian vision of life and recognize that "the uses of flowers were infinite."

In 1963, Hansberry faced the onset of cancer, though she was never told the nature of her illness. Despite frequent sickness and hospitalization for tests, she continued to work for the causes she believed in. On May 24, Hansberry joined her friend James Baldwin and other prominent blacks, along with a few whites, at a widely publicized meeting with Attorney General Robert Kennedy concerning the contemporary racial conflicts. Hansberry forcefully added her voice to the others' attempts to make Kennedy see the need for his brother, President John F. Kennedy, to intervene more visibly in the crisis and make a symbolic gesture that would demonstrate his solidarity with the civil rights activists. When the youngest of Baldwin's party, black activist Je-

rome Smith, infuriated Kennedy by saying he would never be willing to fight for America, Hansberry urged the Attorney General to reconsider his anger since, in her eyes, Smith, who was putting his life on the line in the struggle to desegregate the South, was the most important member of the group. Less than a month afterward, Hansberry chaired a meeting to raise funds for the Student Nonviolent Coordinating Committee and later prepared the text for a collection of photographs, *The Movement: Documentary of a Struggle for Equality,* which would be published in 1964 to further benefit the organization.

Along with her social commitments, Hansberry maintained her commitment to her art with a variety of projects, including *Les Blancs,* the African play Robert Nemiroff would bring to fruition after her death, and *The Sign in Sidney Brustein's Window,* her last play to be produced on Broadway in her lifetime. Despite Nemiroff's continuing involvement with her work, he and Hansberry formalized their separation with a divorce on March 10, 1964, though they told only their close friends and family and continued to see each other until the day she died.

During 1964, she was frequently hospitalized as her cancer spread, though she exerted all the willpower and energy she had left to continue to support the causes she cared so much about. In May, she struggled out of her hospital bed to deliver a speech for the winners of the United Negro College Fund writing contest; it contained the now-famous phrase, "to be young, gifted, and Black." June found Hansberry leaving her sickbed again to participate in the Town Hall debate between militant black artists—including Amiri Baraka, John Oliver Killens, and Paule Marshall—and three white liberals on "The Black Revolution and the White Backlash." In opposition to her fellow black debaters, Hansberry affirmed that leadership should not be based on color and that she would prefer the leadership of whites like John Brown who were willing to give their lives in the cause of black liberation to that of a traitorous black like Moishe Tshombe, the African leader responsible for the death of the anticolonialist Patrice Lumumba. What was needed most, she argued, was for white liberals to stop being liberal and become American radicals. The effort she made simply to attend the debate represents the kind of commitment she called for.

Hansberry was often hospitalized as her cancer advanced, but she managed to complete *The Sign in Sidney Brustein's Window* and participate in its staging at Broadway's Longacre Theatre, where it opened on October 15, 1964. The producers were Robert Nemiroff and Burt D'Lugoff. In early October, Hansberry moved to the Hotel Victoria to be near the production and frequently needed a wheelchair to attend the rehearsals.

While Hansberry's drama received more favorable than unfavorable reviews, it did not obtain the large number of raves usually needed for a Broadway play to survive. Many critics applauded its ambitiousness, wit, humanity, insight, and intelligence, yet also considered it talky, overloaded with characters and plot, and a bit incoherent. A handful of critics, notably those from *Newsweek* and *Women's Wear Daily,* attacked what they viewed as its mean-spiritedness, sordidness, and triviality. That the play ran for 101 performances in spite of the death knell tolled by mixed reviews is a theatrical miracle. An extraordinary number of people—ministers, civil rights activists, actors, politicians, theatergoers from every conceivable background—donated time, effort, money, and enthusiasm to keep it going. But this outpouring of love for the play—and the playwright—was finally halted on January 12, 1965, the day Lorraine Hansberry died.

The central thread that holds *The Sign in Sidney Brustein's Window* together is the character of Sidney Brustein. In "An Author's Reflections: Willie Loman, Walter Younger, and He Who Must Live," Hansberry argues, "Fine plays tend to utilize one big fat character who runs right through the middle of the structure," and chides herself for having failed to develop such a character in *A Raisin in the Sun,* though it could be argued that part of the strength of her play is the way she made the entire Younger family the protagonist. Consciously or unconsciously, however, Hansberry made sure that no one could make a similar criticism about her second major play. Sidney Brustein never leaves the stage, and it is his response to every person and issue surrounding him that is the heart of the story.

Sidney is a Jewish intellectual living in New York's Greenwich Village, a place that attracts a huge variety of people, and his home is the cultural center of the play. His wife, Iris, is, in Sidney's words, the "only Greco-Gaelic-Indian hillbilly in captivity," and his friends and acquaintances include the African American Alton Scales, the Irish American Wally O'Hara, and the Italian American Sal Peretti. The social and moral range of the characters entering Sidney's home matches that of the ethnic range: Iris' sister Mavis is "The Mother Middleclass itself"; her other sister, Gloria, is a call girl; Sidney's brother, Manny, is a successful businessman; his neighbor David Ragin is a sponging playwright. Sidney is the ethical center of the play. This does not mean that he is always right in his judgments, as he is a character who grows, but rather it means that he is the character who learns the most about self and world and that what he learns is the main message of the play.

At the play's outset, Sidney, after many years of marching and petitioning for every cause that aroused his intellectual sympathy, has retreated from all commitments, though he remains a busybody. During this retreat, he takes tranquilizers for the ulcer occasioned by his continuing pain over social injustices; he notes that when his ancestors, the Maccabees, saw evil they raised their swords against it, something that is no longer acceptable behavior: "One does not *smite* evil any more: one holds one's gut, thus—and takes a pill.'' While starting up a newspaper, Sidney initially has sympathy for the position of his painter friend Max, who believes in art for art's sake, but eventually moves to a position closer to that of Alton, an ex-communist who continues to regard art as a weapon in the struggle against oppression. After convincing Sidney to permit him to editorialize about Sal's death by drug overdose, Alton also gets him to support their friend Wally, who is running for local office as a reform candidate opposing the use of their community as a narcotics drop. At the end Sidney is ravaged both by one more incident involving drugs (Gloria's suicide using ''goofball pills'') and by the discovery that Wally is owned by the drug interests. This combination of events leads the descendant of the Maccabees to warn his friend Wally that he and others who had campaigned for him will return to the streets ''more seasoned, more cynical, tougher, harder to fool—and therefore, less likely to quit.'' No longer permitting tranquilizers of any type to lessen his commitment, Sidney has gone beyond being a white liberal to becoming an American radical.

One of the liberal causes that Sidney dedicated himself to was the fight against prejudice. As a Jew, he has experienced anti-Semitism firsthand, including that of his sister-in-law Mavis. However, he has not only opposed the prejudice against his own group but also championed other oppressed groups, including blacks, and tells the homosexual David Ragin that if he wants to start up a petition against the sex laws he'll sign it. Nevertheless, Sidney retains some prejudices of his own. In one of the most startling and moving scenes in the play, Sidney discovers some dimensions to Mavis that he never dreamed existed and, to his amazement, ends up applauding the strengths and insight of this woman whom he had thought embodied all the middle-class obtuseness, moral complacency, and pettiness he loathed. In addition, Sidney has been a male chauvinist, forcing his wife to fit into the role of

mountain girl that he wants her to play whenever he retreats from spiritually toxic city life into a Thoreau-like fantasy of living in a pure, mountain atmosphere. Iris leaves him in order to search for the sense of self he has helped her to lose and only returns to him at the end of the play, after despair, guilt, and intense soul-searching render him capable of treating her as a partner rather than an appendage. Self-alteration is clearly the hardest but most necessary type of change, and it is only when experience has fully transformed and radicalized him that Sidney has a real hope of making a moral impact on the society around him. Sidney comes to recognize ''that the earth turns and men change every day . . . and that people wanna be better than they are.''

It is significant that the crisis of overwhelming despair that prepares Sidney for his rise to a higher level of struggle is expressed in the form of a miniature theater of the absurd drama. Earlier, Sidney had challenged David's absurdist approach to drama with his humanist aesthetic and had confidently pointed to the ''stars'' of his dramatic dream team, Euripides and Shakespeare. However, when he realizes that his desire to oppose corruption has led him to support a corrupt politician (Wally), Sidney engages in a drunken Samuel Beckett–Eugène Ionesco-inspired absurdist orgy of fragmented language with David and Gloria, who is shattered because Alton called off their engagement after learning she had been a prostitute. However, once he lifts himself out of despair, though not out of the pain and guilt he feels for having contributed to Gloria's despair and subsequent suicide, he reaches a new level of engaged humanism and expresses himself in coherent and even poetic language. Absurdism is thus presented as a stage of awareness that may well touch important truths but must ultimately be transcended for humanity to survive and progress.

Perhaps the most painful insight Sidney must cope with is that a person may be a victim in one context and an oppressor in another, or sometimes even both simultaneously. He himself both endured prejudice as a Jew and acted oppressively as a male. Alton's example is even more complex. His rejection of Gloria after discovering she had been a call girl is triggered in part by his bitter memories of how his father, a railroad porter, had hated "the white man's leavings" brought home by Alton's mother, a maid. But for Alton to consider Gloria merely as "white man's leavings" and to refuse even to talk to her because she is white betrays both the great extent to which he has been wounded by racism and the traces of responsive racism in himself, something that he loathes with his head even while he finds himself unable to relinquish it in his heart. Nevertheless, Hansberry makes it clear that even in a complicated case like this it is possible to distinguish right from wrong, and she stresses the need to root out every bit of inhumanity in oneself for the sake of humanity as a whole.

Despite the dedication and enthusiasm of the many people who fought to keep the play alive, it is doubtful that *The Sign in Sidney Brustein's Window* will ever touch the masses as *A Raisin in the Sun* did. Hansberry chose to portray an intellectual in all his complexity, and a full appreciation of this work requires more than one viewing and a considerable degree of erudition, as Sidney and his friends refer appropriately and often wittily to art, philosophy, music (jazz, classical, and folk), anthropology, literature from all areas and eras, and a host of other sophisticated topics. Yet its humanity, humor, warmth, and poetry will surely continue to be appreciated. Hansberry's spirit may perhaps be best represented by the two poetic speeches made by Sidney that were placed on Hansberry's grave marker:

> I *care!* I care about it all. It takes too much energy *not* to care. Yesterday I counted twenty-six gray hairs in the top of my head—all from trying *not* to care.

> The "why" of why we are here is an intrigue for adolescents; the "how" is what must command the living. Which is why I have lately become an insurgent again.

Hansberry designated her former husband as her literary executor, and he devoted the twenty-six years that remained of his life to making the public aware of her worth and keeping her works alive. He performed this service with great dedication, intelligence, and verve. His approach to this task was that of an admiring fellow artist, and most of what he did was creative. For example, his 1969 play, *To Be Young, Gifted, and Black: Lorraine Hansberry in Her Own Words*, set forth an overview of Hansberry's life and conveyed her philosophy and spirit through insightful juxtapositions of selections from her published and unpublished plays, poems, novel, essays, speeches, interviews, letters, and diaries. Its twelve-month run off-Broadway at the Cherry Lane Theater and subsequent touring productions greatly excited audiences about Hansberry. In 1970, taking advantage of this fervor, Nemiroff published a much more extensive compilation of Hansberry's autobiographical, social, and creative writing using the same title.

The year 1970 also saw the production at Broadway's Longacre Theatre of Hansberry's African play, *Les Blancs*, in a version edited and brought to fruition by Nemiroff. Since the work in putting together a polished final draft of the play required considerably more than editing, though the essential concepts, characterizations, and speeches were Hansberry's, the produced and published version should be regarded as an artistic collaboration between Hansberry and Nemiroff.

Les Blancs is fully attuned to the harsh realities experienced by people living under colonialism and neocolonialism, including the brutalization and frenzied theft by foreigners of their history, wealth, and cultural life, the distorted image of their struggle for independence placed in the world press by those whom they are struggling against, and the brainwashing given to the most receptive young minds by the exploiter's educational system so that "native" control even in a nominally independent country would still mean foreign control. The sharply divided reviews of this play, like the sharply divided audiences, seemed to be responding more to the subject matter than to the artistry with which the subject matter had been presented, though it required artistry to arouse such a high level of emotion both for and against.

The play revolves around what the Ghanaian novelist Aiy Kwei Armah affirmed in *Two Thousand Seasons* (1973) to be the African ethical imperative: reciprocity or giving and taking in equal measure. For Hansberry, as for Armah, the European colonizers violated this precept by taking everything of value in Africa for themselves (Hansberry's land-seizing colonizer Major Rice even rapes the wife of a chief) and offering only the mind-controlling pseudo-gifts of European education and religion in return. At the other extreme in *Les Blancs,* the Reverend Torvald Neilsen's attempt to follow the Christian ethic of giving without any desire to receive in his mission to the Africans, modeled on that of the world-famous philosopher and philanthropist Albert Schweitzer, is revealed to be founded on the arrogant assumption that the Africans have nothing valuable spiritually or culturally to give him in return.

In contrast, a truly reciprocal relationship between a European and an African is formed by Mme. Neilsen, Torvald's wife, and Aquah, the chief's wife who died giving birth to Major Rice's child by rape. Mme. Neilsen recounts to Charlie Morris, a visiting American journalist, that Aquah was her ''dearest friend'' in Africa and had taught her ''the drums and to speak the language of the Kwi people,'' whereas she taught Aquah some English and French. Neilsen, like Schweitzer, never bothers to learn any African language.

Mme. Neilsen also has a reciprocal relationship with the chief's son Tshembe Matoseh, the play's protagonist, in which each displays great affection for the other and has an equal interest in the other's feelings, thoughts, and culture. In fact, after Aquah's death, Mme. Neilsen becomes a second mother to Tshembe.

The most important reciprocal relationship, however, is the one tortuously worked out between Charlie Morris and Tshembe. Curious about Tshembe's supposed radical stance, Charlie initiates the dialogue between them on the assumption that he is prepared to exchange ideas with the African, but soon he reveals that he is carrying around a bagful of fixed beliefs and prefers lecturing to listening. Only at the end, after his firsthand experiences have confirmed what Tshembe told him about the vastness of the social injustices perpetrated by the colonizers, can Charlie honestly tell Tshembe, ''I've heard you,'' and shake hands meaningfully with him. In this moment, Charlie, like Sidney, has changed from white liberal to American radical.

Tshembe, for his part, is not as radical as Charlie assumed at the outset. Though filled with rage over the fate of his country, Tshembe's verbal denunciations are no longer backed by actions. In fact, he resides now in England with a white wife and son and has only returned for his father's funeral. Even after being summoned by a woman warrior embodying the spirit of his people to join the resistance, goaded by his biting exchanges with Charlie to shed his illusions and hypocrisies, and stunned by the revelation that his father had formed the resistance, Tshembe continues to hesitate until his Hamlet-like delay causes the death of a resistance leader. Preparing to act at last as his father's son, Tshembe can then meet Charlie on the common ground of their mutual radicalization, a transformation that each has helped to assist in the other. Their final reciprocal relationship, like that of Sidney and Iris Brustein, is clearly the product of growth in both characters.

Although staggeringly huge efforts and sacrifices may be required to achieve them, diverse cultures or even whole civilizations need to hammer out reciprocal relationships between themselves as individuals do. As Tshembe affirms,

"Europe—in spite of all her crimes—has been a great and glorious star in the night. Other stars shone before it—and will again with it," and there is no doubt he considers Africa one of these stars.

In 1972, Nemiroff published *Les Blancs: The Collected Last Plays of Lorraine Hansberry,* which includes *The Drinking Gourd, What Use Are Flowers?,* and his own vibrantly written, informative, and insightful critical backgrounds for each play. In 1974, he and Charlotte Zaltzberg wrote the book for the musical *Raisin,* which they based not only on the original Broadway version of *A Raisin in the Sun* but also on deleted but exciting material from previous drafts. In reshaping the play for a new medium, Nemiroff and Zaltzberg treated the material as flexibly as Hansberry herself had in the unproduced screenplays. *Raisin* won both the 1974 Tony Award and the 1974 Grammy Award for Best Broadway Show Album. Every time *A Raisin in the Sun* or *Les Blancs* was published in a new edition, Nemiroff took the opportunity to add valuable material from the drafts so that the most recent editions became the most comprehensive. He also did this with new productions of the plays, and one reason for the superiority of the 1989 American Playhouse version of *A Raisin in the Sun* over previous ones is the power added by material Hansberry had had to forgo due to considerations of time and money.

Prior to his death from cancer at age sixty-one, Nemiroff completed the editing of the published version of Hansberry's screenplay for *A Raisin in the Sun,* planned a collection of her essays which would have included "Queer Beer" (an unpublished work about homosexuals), and did extensive editing on her uncompleted novel, *All the Dark and Beautiful Warriors.* The debt all those who appreciate Hansberry's work owe to Nemiroff is immense.

*   *   *

Hansberry left two drafts of *All the Dark and Beautiful Warriors,* which probably comprise about two-thirds of the novel. Excerpts from it are included in *To Be Young, Gifted, and Black,* and portions have been published in the *Village Voice, TriQuarterly,* and *Southern Exposure.* Covering a period of thirty years, it focuses on Candace Braithwaite, whose experiences growing up in an upper-middle-class black family in Chicago resemble Hansberry's, and Denmark Vesey "Son" Williams, who comes from a farming family in Tennessee. Though their backgrounds are different, they display similar patterns of conformity and rebellion in the development of their characters. Eventually, after having been radicalized by experience, a transformation usually undergone by Hansberry's strongest characters, Candace and Son become involved with one another and take part in the Civil Rights Movement. Although the published portions of the novel reveal some influence by Richard Wright and Ralph Ellison, they also demonstrate that Hansberry was putting her artistic stamp on fiction as she had on drama.

Selected Bibliography

WORKS OF LORRAINE HANSBERRY

PLAYS, SCREENPLAYS, AND MUSICALS (first editions)

A Raisin in the Sun. New York: Random House, 1959.

The Sign in Sidney Brustein's Window. New York: Random House, 1965.

To Be Young, Gifted, and Black. Adapted by Robert Nemiroff. New York: Samuel French, 1971.

Les Blancs: The Collected Last Plays of Lorraine Hansberry. Edited by Robert Nemiroff. New York: Random House, 1972. Includes *The Drinking Gourd* and *What Use Are Flowers?*

Raisin. New York: Samuel French, 1978. Musical version of *A Raisin in the Sun* with book by Robert Nemiroff and Charlotte Zaltzberg, music by Judd Woldin and lyrics by Robert Brittan.

A Raisin in the Sun: The Unfilmed Original Screenplay. Edited by Robert Nemiroff. New York: Plume, 1992.

PLAYS

(Later, more extensive editions used as the sources for quotations in this text)

Lorraine Hansberry: The Collected Last Plays. New York: New American Library, 1983.

A Raisin in the Sun (Expanded Twenty-fifth Anniversary Edition) and The Sign in Sidney Brustein's Window. Edited by Robert Nemiroff. New York: New American Library, 1987.

A Raisin in the Sun: The Complete Original Version. New York: New American Library, 1988.

Les Blancs: The Collected Last Plays. Edited by Robert Nemiroff. New York: Vintage, 1994. Includes *The Drinking Gourd* and *What Use Are Flowers?*

AUTOBIOGRAPHICAL COLLATION

To Be Young, Gifted, and Black: Lorraine Hansberry in Her Own Words. Adapted by Robert Nemiroff. Englewood Cliffs, N.J.: Prentice-Hall, 1969; New York: New American Library, 1970.

PHOTOTEXT

The Movement: Documentary of a Struggle for Equality. New York: Simon & Schuster, 1964.

UNCOLLECTED PROSE

Letter signed L. N. *The Ladder,* 1, no. 1 (1957): 26–30.

"An Author's Reflections: Willie Loman, Walter Younger, and He Who Must Live." *Village Voice,* August 12, 1959, pp. 7–8.

"Stanley Gleason and the Lights that Must Not Die." *New York Times,* January 17, 1960, sec. 10, pp. 11–14.

"On Summer." *Playbill,* June 27, 1960, pp. 3, 25–27.

"This Complex of Womanhood." *Ebony,* August 1960, p. 40.

"Images and Essences: 1961 Dialogue with an Uncolored Egghead Containing Wholesome Intentions and Some Sass." *Urbanite,* 1:10–11, 36 (May 1961).

"Genet, Mailer, and the New Paternalism." *Village Voice,* June 1, 1961, pp. 10, 14–15.

"The American Theatre Needs Desegregating, Too." *Negro Digest,* 10:28–33 (June 1961).

"A Challenge to Artists." *Freedomways,* 3:33–35 (Winter 1963).

"The Shakespearean Experience." *Show,* 4:80–81, 102 (February 1964).

"The Black Revolution and the White Backlash" (transcript of the Town Hall Forum). *National Guardian,* 4 July 1964, 5–9.

"The Nation Needs Your Gifts." *Negro Digest,* 13:26–29 (August 1964).

"The Scars of the Ghetto." *Monthly Review,* 16:588–591 (February 1965).

"The Legacy of W. E. B. Du Bois." *Freedomways,* 5:19–20 (Winter 1965).

"Original Prospectus for the John Brown Memorial Theatre of Harlem." *Black Scholar,* 10:14–15 (July–August 1979).

"The Negro Writer and His Roots: Towards a New Romanticism." *Black Scholar,* 12:2–12 (March–April 1981).

"On Arthur Miller, Marilyn Monroe, and 'Guilt.' " In *Women in Theatre: Compassion & Hope.* Edited by Karen Malpede. New York: Drama Book Publishsers, 1983. Pp. 173–176.

"All the Dark and Beautiful Warriors." *Village Voice,* August 16, 1983, pp. 1, 11–16, 18–19.

"From *All the Dark and Beautiful Warriors.*" *Tri-Quarterly,* 60:35–60 (Spring/Summer 1984).

"The Buck Williams Tennessee Memorial Association" (portion of *All the Dark and Beautiful Warriors*). *Southern Exposure,* 12:28–31 (September/October 1984).

ARCHIVES AND BIBLIOGRAPHIES

The Hansberry archives are held by the Schomburg Center for Research in Black Culture in New York City.

Arata, Ester S., and Nicholas John Rotoli. *Black American Playwrights, 1800 to the Present: A Bibliography.* Metuchen, N.J.: Scarecrow, 1976.

Kaiser, Ernest, and Robert Nemiroff. "A *Lorraine Hansberry* Bibliography." *Freedomways,* 19:285–304 (Fourth Quarter 1979).

Kolin, Philip C. *American Playwrights since 1945: A*

Research Survey of Scholarship, Criticism, and Performance. New York: Greenwood, 1989.

Rush, Theressa G., Carol F. Myers, and Esther S. Arata. *Black American Writers Past and Present: A Biographical and Bibliographical Dictionary.* Metuchen, N.J.: Scarecrow, 1975.

Williams, Ora. *American Black Women in the Arts and Social Sciences: A Bibliographic Survey.* Metuchen, N.J.: Scarecrow, 1973.

BIOGRAPHICAL AND CRITICAL STUDIES

Abramson, Doris E. *Negro Playwrights in the American Theatre 1925–1959.* New York: Columbia University Press, 1969. Pp. 239–254, 263–266.

Bigsby, C. W. E. *Confrontation and Commitment: A Study of Contemporary American Drama, 1959–1966.* London: MacGibbon & Kee, 1967; Columbia: University of Missouri Press, 1968. Pp. 156–173 and passim.

Bond, Jean Carey, ed. *Freedomways,* 19 (special Hansberry issue, Fourth Quarter 1979).

Brown, Lloyd W. "Lorraine Hansberry as Ironist: A Reappraisal of *A Raisin in the Sun.*" *Journal of Black Studies,* 4:237–247 (March 1974).

Brown-Guillory, Elizabeth. *Their Place on the Stage: Black Women Playwrights in America.* New York: Greenwood Press, 1988.

Carter, Steven R. *Hansberry's Drama: Commitment amid Complexity.* Urbana: University of Illinois Press, 1991.

———. "Images of Men in Lorraine Hansberry's Writing." *Black American Literature Forum,* 19: 160–162 (Winter 1985).

———. "Lorraine Hansberry." In *Concise Dictionary of Literary Biography: The New Consciousness, 1941–1968.* Detroit, Mich.: Gale Research, 1987. Pp. 244–258.

Cheney, Anne. *Lorraine Hansberry.* Boston: Twayne Publishers, 1984.

Cruse, Harold. "Lorraine Hansberry." In *The Crisis of the Negro Intellectual.* New York: William Morrow, 1967. Pp. 267–284.

Fabre, Genevieve. *Drumbeats, Masks, and Metaphor: Contemporary Afro-American Theatre.* Cambridge, Mass.: Harvard University Press, 1983.

Farrison, W. Edward. "Lorraine Hansberry's Last Dramas." *College Language Association Journal,* 16:188–197 (December 1972).

Friedman, Sharon. "Feminism as Theme in Twentieth-Century American Women's Drama." *American Studies,* 25:69–89 (Spring 1984).

Gomez, Jewelle L. "Lorraine Hansberry: Uncommon Warrior." In *Reading Black, Reading Feminist: A Critical Anthology.* Edited by Henry Louis Gates Jr. New York: Meridian, 1990. Pp. 307–317.

Grant, Robert H. "Lorraine Hansberry: The Playwright as Warrior-Intellect." *DAI,* 82-22 (1984), p. 634.

Hairston, Loyle. "Lorraine Hansberry—Portrait of an Angry Young Writer." *Crisis,* 86:123–124, 126, 128 (April 1979).

Holtan, Orley I. "Sidney Brustein and the Plight of the American Intellectual." *Players,* 46:222–225 (June–July 1971).

Isaacs, Harold R. *The New World of Negro Americans.* New York: John Day, 1963.

Keyssar, Helene. *The Curtain and the Veil: Strategies in Black Drama.* New York: Burt Franklin, 1981.

———. *Feminist Theatre.* New York: Grove, 1985. Pp. 32–36.

Lewis, Allan. *American Plays and Playwrights of the Contemporary Theatre.* New York: Crown Publishers, 1965. Pp. 112, 252, 257.

Marre, Diana: "Lorraine Hansberry (1930–1965): Playwright, Activist." In *Notable Black American Women.* Edited by Jessie Carney Smith. Detroit, Mich.: Gale Research, 1992. Pp. 452–457.

Miller, Jordan Y. "Lorraine Hansberry." In *The Black American Writer.* Vol. 2. Edited by C. W. E. Bigsby. Deland, Fla.: Everett/Edwards, 1969. Pp. 157–170.

Mitchell, Loften. *Black Drama: The Story of the American Negro in the Theatre.* New York: Hawthorn Books, 1967.

Ness, David. "Lorraine Hansberry's *Les Blancs:* The Victory of the Man Who Must." *Freedomways,* 13:294–306 (Fourth Quarter 1973).

———. "*The Sign in Sidney Brustein's Window:* A Black Playwright Looks at White America." *Freedomways,* 11:359–366 (Fourth Quarter 1971).

Potter, Vilma R. "New Politics, New Mothers." *College Language Association Journal.* 16:247–255 (December 1972).

Scheader, Catherine. *They Found a Way: Lorraine Hansberry.* Chicago: Children's Press, 1978.

Schiff, Ellen. *From Stereotype to Metaphor: The Jew in Contemporary Drama.* Albany: State University of New York Press, 1982. Pp. 155–160.

Washington, Charles J. "*A Raisin in the Sun* Revisited." *Black American Literature Forum.* 22:109–124 (Spring 1988).

Weales, Gerald. *American Drama since World War II.* New York: Harcourt, Brace & World, 1962.

———. *The Jumping-Off Point: American Drama in the 1960s.* London: Macmillan, 1969. Pp. 117–122.

Wilkerson, Margaret B. "Lorraine Hansberry: Artist, Activist, Feminist." In *Women in American Theatre.* Edited by Helen Krich Chinoy and Linda Walsh Jenkins. Revised and expanded edition. New York: Theatre Communications Group, 1987. Pp. 180–185.

———. "Hansberry, Lorraine Vivian." In *Black Women in America: An Historical Encyclopedia.* Vol. 1. Edited by Darlene Clark Hine. Brooklyn, N.Y.: Carlson, 1993. Pp. 524–529.

———. "The Dark Vision of Lorraine Hansberry: Excerpts from a Literary Biography." *Massachusetts Review,* 28:642–650 (Winter 1987).

———. "The Sighted Eyes and Feeling Heart of Lorraine Hansberry." *Black American Literature Forum,* 17:8–13 (Spring 1983).

Williams, Mance. *Black Theatre in the 1960s and 1970s: A Historical-Critical Analysis of the Movement.* Westport, Conn.: Greenwood Press, 1985.

INTERVIEWS

Fisher, Diane. "Miss Hansberry & Bobby K.: Birthweight Low, Jobs Few, Death Comes Early." *Village Voice,* June 6, 1963, pp. 3, 9.

Hammel, Faye. "A Playwright, a Promise." *Cue,* February 28, 1959, pp. 20, 43.

Poston, Ted. "We Have So Much to Say." *New York Post,* March 22, 1959, Magazine section, p. 2.

Robertson, Nan. "Dramatist against Odds." *New York Times,* March 8, 1959, sec. 2 (Arts and Leisure), p. 3. (This attributes quotations to Hansberry that she denied saying; her letter of correction to the *Times* was never published).

Ross, Don. "Lorraine Hansberry Interviewed: 'Whites Dreadfully Ignorant of Negro Life.' " *New York Herald-Tribune,* March 12, 1960, sec. 4, p. 3.

Terkel, Studs. "Make New Sounds: Studs Terkel Interviews Lorraine Hansberry." *American Theatre,* 1:5–8, 41 (November 1984). 5–8, 41.

"Village Intellectual Revealed." *New York Times,* October 31, 1964, sec. 2 pp. 1, 3.

White, E. B. "The Talk of the Town: Playwright." *New Yorker,* May 9, 1959, pp. 33–35.

Wallace, Mike. "The Beauty of Things Black—Towards Total Liberation: An Interview with Mike Wallace, May 8, 1959." In *Lorraine Hansberry Speaks Out: Art and the Black Revolution.* Caedmon TC 1352.

Willis, Ellen. "We Hitch Our Wagons." *Mademoiselle,* August 1960, p. 315.

AUDIOVISUAL MATERIALS

A Raisin in the Sun. Directed by Daniel Petrie. Screenplay by Lorraine Hansberry. Columbia, 1961. 128 min.

A Raisin in the Sun. Directed by Bill Duke. American Playhouse, 1989. 171 min.

Lorraine Hansberry: The Black Experience in the Creation of Drama. Princeton, N.J.: Films for the Humanities, 1976. Filmstrip (FFH 128).

Lorraine Hansberry Speaks Out: Art and the Black Revolution. Selected and edited by Robert Nemiroff. Caedmon TC 1352. (Includes interview with Mike Wallace, May 8, 1959).

—STEVEN R. CARTER

Joseph Heller

1923—

JOSEPH HELLER HAS earned a wide public reputation as the coiner of "catch-22," a phrase that not only captures the absurdist flavor of bureaucratic double-shuffles within the imaginative world of his novel but also transcends the strictures of time and circumstance to become a telling emblem for the decades since *Catch-22* (1961) was originally published. In much the same way that Franz Kafka's haunting image of modern man squirming uncertainly beneath authority's thumb has given rise to the all-purpose adjective "kafkaesque," Heller's destabilization of language results in a darkly comic vision immediately recognizable as uniquely his own.

That we do not identify this imaginative world as "Hellerian" is probably just as well, for critical labels make Heller uncomfortable. Take "black humor," for example. As a description of the grimly funny turn that certain American writers took in the 1960s (one thinks of Bruce Jay Friedman, Terry Southern, John Barth, Philip Roth, and, of course, Heller), the term had merit, even if it was ultimately longer on convenience than accuracy; but in a 1972 interview with Richard Sale Heller took pains to make it clear that he was *not* a black humorist: "First of all, I don't like the term 'black humor.' I like to think of it as sour sarcasm or ugly satire. I don't like comedy for the sake of comedy."

In the same interview Heller goes on to point out that he cut some 175 typewritten pages from the original draft of *Catch-22* because they were only of a humorous nature and did not contribute to what he called "the feeling of absurdity." He also changed the original title of his novel—"Catch-18"—because the publisher felt it would suffer from confusion with, and comparison to, Leon Uris' *Mila 18* (1961). With an irony all too familiar in American letters, Uris has largely faded from the literary scene (in the early 1960s, he was still riding the considerable waves generated by *Exodus* [1958]), while Heller continues to be the object of popular and critical attention. Even more ironic perhaps is the fact that Heller's jerry-built title is much more reflective of the doubling one finds in the novel—everything from deliberately comic repetition to a character who "sees everything twice"—than his original title.

Heller poured his World War II experiences and a long apprenticeship writing short fiction into his bulky first novel. Excess, energy, and, perhaps most of all, playfulness are its most obvious hallmarks. Unmoored from the constraints of realism, *Catch-22* became a joke book (of sorts) for all seasons, one peppered with allusions high and low and with jokes aimed at groundlings as well as literary insiders. Thus, the near rhymes in such character names as Chaplain

Tappman or Yossarian the Assyrian coexist with speculations about what the letters *T* and *S* in Eliot's name really stand for or how one might reverse Washington Irving's moniker for comic effect. A gargantuan list of Milo Minderbinder's purchases include cork from New York, shoes from Toulouse, ham from Siam, and, most ingeniously, most polysyllabically, tangerines from New Orleans.

Heller's essential spirit is seriocomic, at once Shakespearian in its range and cartoonish in its excesses. Imagining a character named Major Major might be funny, but it will not pack the comic punch, much less the satiric commentary, that comes with the re-redoubling of Major Major Major Major. Much the same effect occurs when readers encounter clichés in the full glory of their shallowness: "Men," Colonel Cargill tells the enlisted men under his command, "you're American officers. The officers of no other army in the world can make that statement. Think about it." Or when an earnest effort to construct a multipurpose letter backfires comically: "Dear Mrs., Miss, or Mr. and Mrs. Daneeka: Words cannot express the deep personal grief I experienced when your husband, son, father or brother was killed, wounded, or reported missing in action." Words, indeed, cannot express the proper emotion because language no longer works, and it is this breakdown of communication, what critic Judith Ruderman in her book *Joseph Heller* calls the "farce—as well as the tragedy—of miscommunication," that becomes *Catch-22*'s abiding technique.

To recognize that words create the smoke screens and elegantly designed closed systems behind which malevolence hides is to become nervous, edgy, and, most of all, isolated. Clevinger is a character who steadfastly refuses to be budged from innocence. He believes in both the System and the words it uses to justify itself. When Yossarian worries that "they're trying to kill me," Clevinger assures him that it is not personal, and that he should not take it as such: "They're shooting at *everyone*. . . . They're trying to kill everyone." Yossarian, however, is hardly consoled. "What difference does that make?" he asks, especially when Clevinger later "flies into a cloud," never to return.

Innocence is one of the defining preoccupations of our national literature, and nowhere does this observation seem truer than in American fiction about war. Henry Fleming, the protagonist of *The Red Badge of Courage* (1895), Stephen Crane's impressionistic account of one soldier's experiences in the Civil War, moves from grand expectations to grim reality. Instead of struggle on an epical scale, he is forced to confront the smoke, confusion, and mortality of actual battles and, in the process, to reassess romantic illusion against the sterner tests of manhood. In the twentieth century, Fleming's journey of learning was reenacted many times over as young recruits discovered that the reality of the Great War called the romanticism of recruiting slogans and patriotic songs into question. Two novels published in 1929 proved especially memorable: Erich Maria Remarque's *All Quiet on the Western Front* describes World War I from the perspective of a doomed German soldier, while Ernest Hemingway's *Farewell to Arms* focuses on a young American ambulance driver caught up in the Italian retreat at Caporetto. Despite important differences in style, what these two novels dramatize is perhaps the existential truth of combat life—namely, it is nasty, brutish, and often very, very short.

It is no small wonder, then, that Hemingway's protagonist, Frederic Henry, ends up with a decided preference for the "concrete names of villages, the numbers of roads, the names of rivers, the numbers of regiments and the dates." These objectified facts do not lie, and more important, they do not kill. By contrast, abstract words, such as "glory, honor, courage, or hallow," do. That is why Henry concludes that the rhetoric of recruiting posters is ''obscene'' and, moreover, why the typical Hemingway character puts his faith in the unsullied purity of sensation—what makes one feel good, what makes one feel bad, what chills and what warms.

Catch-22's extraordinary achievement can be measured in terms of its radical departure from the conventions that had governed previous war novels. Unlike Norman Mailer's *Naked and the Dead* (1948), which added a self-consciously political dimension to older naturalistic formulas of man versus machine, Heller realized that initiations appropriate to the World War I novel were neither appropriate to nor required in a novel about World War II. One could, in effect, *begin* where the serious fiction of the earlier war had ended. Thus, Yossarian, Heller's quixotic, anxious protagonist, shares few of the illusions that the protagonists of the earlier novels, including Mailer's, must overcome. While his predecessors move toward disillusionment, Yossarian knows at the outset that the enemy is out to kill him. One of the ways his creator knows it is from such novels as *A Farewell to Arms*, *All Quiet on the Western Front*, and *The Naked and the Dead*. What Yossarian does not know, however, is the bizarre, mind-bending forms that the ''enemy'' can take.

Ultimately, Heller's protagonist discovers the deadly truth about language being power because those who bend words to their will also construct a world in which sanity no longer has a fighting chance. That is the special genius of catch-22, an elegant instance of language at its most insidious:

> There was only one catch and that was Catch-22, which specified that a concern for one's own safety in the face of dangers that were real and immediate was the process of a rational mind. Orr was crazy and could be grounded. All he had to do was ask; and as soon as he did, he would no longer be crazy and would have to fly more missions. Orr would be crazy to fly more missions and sane if he didn't, but if he was sane he had to fly them. If he flew them he was crazy and didn't have to; but if he didn't want to he was sane and had to. Yos-

sarian was moved very deeply by the absolute simplicity of this clause of Catch-22 and let out a respectful whistle.
> ''That's some catch, that Catch-22,'' he observed.
> ''It is the best there is,'' Doc Daneeka agreed.

Heller takes special delight in turning conventions upside down and then establishing bizarre comic ''realities'' in their place. Some, like catch-22, have a death-haunted look about them, while others initially look more innocent—but the net result of this pursuit of excess is the hope that it might lead to sober wisdom. Thus, Colonel Cargill is described as a man who was once a very bad marketing executive. How bad? He was ''so awful a marketing executive that his services were much sought after by firms eager to establish losses for tax purposes. . . . Colonel Cargill could be relied on to run the most prosperous enterprise into the ground. He was a self-made man who owed his lack of success to nobody.'' Heller's verbal irony calls a wide range of assumptions into question, but none more so than the bureaucratic, willful obfuscation that turns military uniforms into shrouds. In this sense, every seemingly comic diversion—whether by exaggeration or strategic inversion—leads back to the dark absurdity of catch-22 itself.

It is no surprise that Heller's protagonist lets out a respectful whistle when he first grasps the enormous power of catch-22. Yossarian is at once an enigma and an everyman, a rebel whose bizarre behaviors unsettle his fellow airmen as well as a thoroughly representative figure of their plight. What gives him both distinction and style, however, is the comic lengths he will go to bonk convention on the beezer. Yossarian's idea of a good joke is to write letters to everyone he knows telling them that he is going on a dangerous mission: '' 'They asked for volunteers. It's very dangerous, but someone has to do it. I'll write you the instant I get back.' And he had not written to anyone since.''

Or while confined to the hospital and when forced to censor the letters of enlisted men, Yossarian hits upon a comically subversive strategy that turns boredom into high jinks:

> Death to all modifiers, he declared one day, and out of every letter that passed through his hands went every adverb and every adjective. The next day he made war on articles. He reached a much higher plane of creativity the following day when he blacked out everything in the letters but *a, an* and *the*. That erected more dynamic intralinear tensions, he felt, and in just about every case left a message far more universal.

The absurdity of Yossarian's "dynamic intralinear tensions" not only reduplicates the chaotic spirit of catch-22—albeit in a milder, less life-threatening form—but also demonstrates just how contagious its perverted "logic" can be. In one permutation or another, the virus spreads through the island of Pianosa, first by severing meaning from language, and then by separating language from reality.

The complicated, interlocking strands of Heller's comic seriousness and serious comedy were probably formed in the crucible of his Coney Island childhood. Long before he became a serious reader, life had made Heller savvy and street-smart, suspicious and skeptical. No doubt the Jewish American ethos of that time and place made its own contribution, but Heller would probably have become the author of *Catch-22* without them. He was born on May 1, 1923, to Russian Jewish immigrant parents, Isaac and Lena Heller, in the Coney Island section of Brooklyn. Of the five boroughs that make up New York City, Brooklyn has been at once the launching pad and source of nostalgia for a wide variety of Jewish American writer intellectuals, including Bernard Malamud, Alfred Kazin, and Norman Podhoretz. Coney Island's major thoroughfare, Surf Avenue, runs one block north of the Boardwalk along the Atlantic Ocean, which featured in its heyday arcades, amusement rides (the Steeplechase being the most famous), and food stands hawking chocolate egg creams (made from chocolate syrup, milk, and seltzer), candied apples, and Nathan's famous foot-long hot dogs.

With the possible exception of Nathan's and the Steeplechase, Coney Island's best-known historical landmark was probably the Half Moon Hotel, where Murder, Incorporated's Abe ("Kid Twist") Reles met his untimely death (he was unceremoniously tossed from one of its windows). Largely populated by Jews and Italians, Coney Island on hot summer days teemed with New Yorkers who made their way to Surf Avenue via trolleys or elevated trains. The result was often as loud as it was certainly vivid: the Yiddish or Italian of an older generation counterposed against the Brooklynese of their children. No doubt some found daily life in Coney Island to be suffocatingly parochial; others regarded it as the very essence of neighborhood warmth. But what cannot be doubted is the feisty democratic spirit Heller found there or the ways that its complicated textures were forever stamped on his heart, mind, and ear.

Closing Time (1994) includes vivid accounts of this largely Jewish enclave, one many critics feel is largely responsible for the street-smart, skeptical turn that his writings often take. Whatever the mixture of autobiography and imagination in this work, some facts about Heller's early years are indisputable. His father, a bakery-truck driver, died following a botched operation when Heller was five years old, and his mother and older brother were forced to deal with the harsh economic realities that played themselves out against the larger backdrop of Coney Island's carefree, carnival atmosphere. The contrast could hardly have gone unnoticed by the young Heller.

He attended Coney Island's public schools and, after graduating from high school in 1941, worked briefly in an insurance company (as did

Robert Slocum, the protagonist of *Something Happened* [1974]) and as a blacksmith's helper in the Norfolk Navy Yard before enlisting in the United States Army Air Corps in October 1942. During the war, Heller, a bombardier, watched a fellow aviator die of wounds, and that clearly traumatic episode ultimately took the form of the death of a character in *Catch-22*, Snowden, whose entrails ooze through his flak jacket as he moans about being cold. Heller's lifelong opposition to war can be traced to this incident.

Discharged in 1945, he married Shirley Held, also a Brooklyn native. A daughter, Erica, was born in 1952 and a son, Theodore, in 1956. In 1945, Heller took advantage of the GI Bill by enrolling at the University of Southern California. His California sojourn, however, was a short-lived one. In 1946 he transferred to New York University, where he majored in English. Elected to Phi Beta Kappa in the same year in which he received his B.A. (1948), Heller continued his education at Columbia University, earning his M.A. in 1949. Named a Fulbright scholar, he spent the 1949–1950 school year at Oxford University, where he continued his studies in English literature.

The fiction-writing bug bit Heller early. As a youngster, he had submitted stories to the *New York Daily News*, *Liberty*, and *Collier's*—predictably enough without success, but also without discouragement. Between 1945 and 1950, Heller wrote some twenty-five short stories, of which eight eventually were published. Many of the early short stories were exercises in imitation, efforts to duplicate the rhythms and thematic concerns of Irwin Shaw, John O'Hara, and, perhaps most of all, Hemingway. Looking back at those times and short stories in a 1985 interview with Charles Ruas, Heller makes it clear just how hit-and-miss his attempts at fiction were: "I didn't have any concept of what I should write. . . . I would read a story in a magazine like *Good Housekeeping* or *Women's Home Com-panion*, and then I would try to write a story for them. I was not very good at it."

Nonetheless, some of these efforts bore fruit. The Marvin B. Winkler of "Bookies, Beware!" and "The Art of Keeping Your Mouth Shut" becomes a partial model for Milo Minderbinder, while the unpublished "Polar Bear" contains early evidence of Heller's self-negating sentences and his penchant for spinning out statements that dutifully deny the meaning they have just advanced: "It was impossible not to like him—but I had achieved the impossible before. I succeeded in loathing him, particularly since he renewed our friendship by apologizing for his knavery at our party."

Ultimately, Heller's talents as a writer outstripped his considerable abilities as a student, and with stories published in such prestigious magazines as *Esquire* and *Atlantic*, it was just a matter of time until Heller became a full-time professional. In his case, the decade between 1950 and 1960 represented this span of time—years spent as an instructor at Pennsylvania State College (1950–1952), an advertising copywriter for *Time* (1952–1956) and *Look* (1956–1958), and a promotion manager at *McCall's* (1958–1961). He continued to write short fiction and movie scripts (under the pseudonym Max Orange) during this period and the experiences he amassed in corporate America later resurfaced in *Something Happened*, a darkly comic novel about the competition, anxiety, and domestic malaise that characterizes midlevel executives.

All the while, Heller worked on draft after draft of the novel that changed his life as well as contemporary American fiction: *Catch-22*. In its central metaphor and the layering of its comic implications, Heller's vision formed a nearly perfect union with his technique. But the achievement, great as it surely was, did not come without a cost. Heller's subsequent fiction was held (often unmercifully) against the high standard of *Catch-22*. After its publication, he did occasional stints as a visiting writer at Yale and the City College of New York, but always on his terms and within his specialty. The days of teaching freshman composition were over, as were the years when he ground out ad copy on deadline and to specification.

Catch-22 begins, significantly enough, in the base hospital rather than on the battlefield, with the hapless Yossarian caught in an ill-defined, anxiety-producing, and wildly comic middle ground: he has a liver condition that is not quite jaundice and not quite *not* jaundice. As the Yiddish of Heller's childhood would have it, he is *nit ahin, nit aher,* neither here nor there: "The doctors were puzzled by the fact that it wasn't quite jaundice. If it became jaundice they could treat it. If it didn't become jaundice and went away they could discharge him. But this just being short of jaundice all the time confused them." Yossarian's odd liver ailment is, among other things, an echo of Prometheus and the punishment he received for bringing fire to mankind (his liver was plucked out by an eagle, only to regrow and be consumed again the following day). It is hardly surprising that Yossarian, put-upon by the small print of procedures and the small minds who administer the rules, quickly became the iconic figure for those who came of age in the counter-cultural 1960s. Ostensibly, *Catch-22* may have been about the waning days of World War II, but it gradually emerged as an etiquette book for oppositional manners as well as an extended trope for the war in Vietnam.

In *Catch-22*, Heller explores the widening gap between expectation and result, between truth and illusion. Yossarian's doctors are perplexed because his liver won't cooperate with their need for precision, but that, as vaudeville comics liked to put it, is only the beginning: language per se refuses to stand still. Confusion is perhaps the defining condition on Pianosa. The effect is akin to the chaos that the Marx Brothers inflicted on

everything from stuffy college campuses (in *Horse Feathers*) to small European countries (in *Duck Soup*), but with this important difference: Heller is less interested in piling one outrageous pun onto another than he is in undermining the relationship between word and object, language and meaning. In the Marx Brothers films, the result is comic anarchy as immigrant energy overwhelms a WASP establishment; for Heller, comic wordplay leads (often quite literally) to dead ends. Small wonder that Yossarian collects evidence of linguistic mismanagement or that he comes to appreciate the elegant effectiveness of catch-22.

That logic is turned on its head is perhaps the most obvious dimension of Heller's comic method, but on a deeper, more insidious level, words have the power both to murder and create—as happens when the LePage Glue Gun apparently materializes out of the thin air of its comic naming or when an absurdist notion, such as "tight bomb clusters," begins to take on a life of its own. Such stretchers, leg-pulls, and tall tales (related with matter-of-factness and the straightest of faces) have their origin in the whoppers that humorists of the old Southwest spun out during the nineteenth century. In his memoir, *No Laughing Matter* (1986), Heller makes it clear that he takes great delight in his considerable talent as a raconteur; what *Catch-22* demonstrates is that, taken together, his yarns have the seriousness that serious literature requires. Put a slightly different way, in traditional war novels, soldiers have died for more. Now they perish for decidedly less, as they go laughing to the gallows.

In *American Fictions, 1940–1980*, Frederick R. Karl suggests that Heller often works by "defining or suggesting elements through the negative" and, further, that *Catch-22* is an "expanded litotes, that form of understatement and irony in which something is expressed by way of the negative of its opposite." Thus, Major Major's father takes full advantage of a governmental bureaucracy that seems as nonsensical as anything hatched in the military-industrial complex:

> The government paid him well for every bushel of alfalfa he did not grow. The more alfalfa he did not grow, the more money the government gave him, and he spent every penny he didn't earn on new land to increase the amount of alfalfa he did not produce. Major Major's father worked without rest at not growing alfalfa.

In such a world, knowing that officers like eggs for breakfast is enough to set Milo Minderbinder's global trading company into motion. He is savvy enough to know how it is possible to buy a Malta egg for five cents, sell it for three cents, and still make a profit. The running gag of Milo's economic formula seems, at first glance, to have been cut from the same absurdist cloth that characterizes the relationship between officers and enlisted men, but in this case the absurdity is built upon Milo being on both sides of the transaction simultaneously. He is at once buyer and seller; all he needs to do is commandeer Air Force planes and then keep the trading fast and furious. Milo's increasingly elaborate scam works on the same pyramid principle that cons a great number of Peters to pay precious few Pauls. In such operations, the base must increase exponentially—that is, until one literally runs out of numbers, and the edifice collapses. In Milo's case, the military-industrial complex can absorb losses on a fantastic scale, especially as the officer's mess moves from fresh eggs to increasingly elaborate four-star meals. In the process, Heller stretches his portrait of the enlisted man who is not above war profiteering so that Milo becomes yet another example of how the grotesque can become normalized.

The horrible "secret" that Yossarian learns as Snowden dies in his arms ("Man was matter. . . . Drop him out of a window and he'll fall. Set fire to him and he'll burn. Bury him and he'll rot like

other kinds of garbage'') is precariously balanced against Yossarian's discovery late in the novel that Orr—the spirit of alternatives in the novel, the "or"—has survived his crash landing and is sitting out the war in Sweden: "Don't you understand [Yossarian insists]—he planned it that way from the beginning. He even practiced getting shot down. He rehearsed for it on every mission he flew. And I wouldn't go with him! . . . Now I understand what he was trying to tell me." Armed with the fresh perspective called hope, Yossarian sets off for Sweden. No matter that he is only inches from the revenge-seeking knife of Nately's whore (who imagines, incorrectly, that Yossarian is responsible for her lover Nately's death), no matter that he is, at best, a shaky recruit to Orr's commonsensical pragmatism; at least he knows that catch-22 can be beaten. For who would accuse Orr of consciously going AWOL, who would charge him with "rehearsing" crash landings, and, most of all, who could imagine him rowing to Sweden using a "tiny little blue oar"? It is all too absurd, too outlandish—even for those who manipulate language until the result is catch-22. But that is precisely what Orr did.

Critics have been divided about *Catch-22*'s dizzying repetitions and seemingly disjointed narrative. As Heller told Paul Krassner in a 1962 interview: "If they *don't* like the book, it's repetitious; if they *like* it, it has a recurring and cyclical structure, like the theme in a Beethoven symphony." Even those readers who cannot give a fig about the novel's chronology—a matter Heller took some care to shape into shapelessness—never forget such memorable minor characters as Milo Minderbinder, Chief White Halfoat, Chaplain Tappman, Major ———— de Coverly, Colonel Cathcart, Major Major, and perhaps most haunting of all, Snowden.

Yossarian and *Catch-22* are loosely based on Heller and his own experiences as a World War II bombardier, but in the novel Heller did what he could to distance himself from autobiography. Thus, Yossarian makes much of the fact that he is Assyrian—extinct already, as the running rhyming joke about his name would have it—rather than Jewish. Like Robert Slocum of *Something Happened*, another novel seemingly close to Heller's biographical pulse, Yossarian is a comic mouthpiece for his creator. His protest emanates from a conviction that life's double-shuffles are what grind us to death.

Those who have followed Heller's long trail of crotchets and increasingly unsuccessful fictions have been at a loss to explain—much less to justify—what can only be described as a decline. Granted, there was *Something Happened*, arguably Heller's *other* great novel, but there was also the long, souring arc that gave us *Good As Gold* (1979), *God Knows* (1984), *Picture This* (1988), and *Closing Time*. Put charitably, Heller's fiction has a nervous, anxious edge, as if the social order, and especially its language, were shifting so rapidly, so absurdly, that any discoveries a protagonist might make are not likely to come in time. Into the teeth of the storm of modern society Heller hurls one-liners. Put more critically, Heller's fiction is yet another prolonged demonstration of how American humorists begin as comedians and end up as scolds. Mark Twain is the condition writ large, especially during his last bitter years, when he donned the robes of moral philosopher and broke his lifelong rule about not manifestly teaching and preaching.

Heller has *always* been a railer. Moreover, like Twain, he has also been a novelist uncomfortable with Jamesian dictates about how a well-crafted piece of fiction ought to look and act. In *Catch-22*, comic energy of a high order carries the day. Other than literary critics, few care whether the escalating number of required bombing missions is consistent throughout the novel's plotline or whether essentially the same formula used to describe Doc Daneeka ("He was a very neat, clean man whose idea of a good time was to sulk") could be trotted out some fifty pages later to describe Major Major's father (he "was a sober God-fearing man whose idea of a good joke was to lie about his age"). In the 1960s, *Catch-22* "played our song" as few novels did.

Future decades and subsequent Heller novels were another story. The generation that laughed out loud as Milo Minderbinder's empire became ever more comically entangled did not know quite what to do when Heller's portrait of suburban angst hit closer to home. Bob Slocum, the jittery protagonist of *Something Happened*, "gets the willies" whenever he sees a closed door, so fearful is he of what those behind the door might be saying about him—or worse, hatching against him. Even though Slocum is a successful company man whose fears are largely unfounded, Slocum's defining characteristic is dread. "Something" is going to happen that will affect him adversely. Even paranoiacs, we are told, can have real enemies.

Heller teases us with the notion that the figure in Slocum's tortured imagination resides in his past (perhaps an oedipal complex or a traumatic primal scene), but such explanations are too facile by half. Slocum is, in fact, the very essence of the ordinary, a homegrown variant of Hannah Arendt's famous phrase, "banality of evil." Granted, Slocum is hardly a Nazi; he does not carry out his marching orders in a death camp. But he *is* one of those craven, faceless sorts who fully participates in the rituals of corporate dehumanization. Moreover, readers soon suspect that that is what makes him both "one of us" and the monster we hold at arm's length. Even Heller himself was not immune from such speculation. In a 1974 interview with George Plimpton, he confesses that although he "told several people while . . . writing the book that Slocum was possibly the most contemptible character in literature," by the time he had finished he "began feeling sorry for him."

One can understand such seemingly contradictory judgments because who, after all, could fail to empathize with Slocum, who realized early that

> I would never have broad shoulders and huge biceps, or be good enough, tall enough, strong enough, or brave enough to become an All-American football player or champion prizefighter, the sad, discouraging realization that no matter what it was in life I ever tried to do, there would always be somebody close by who would be able to do it much better.

Yet, if the sheer competitiveness of modern life can plunge even moderately thoughtful people into gloominess, what is one to make of the elaborate arithmetic Slocum packs into his "chain of fears":

> In the office in which I work there are five people of whom I am afraid. Each of these five people is afraid of four people (excluding overlaps), for a total of twenty, and each of these twenty people is afraid of six people, making a total of one hundred and twenty people who are feared by at least one person. Each of these one hundred and twenty people is afraid of the other one hundred and nineteen, and all of these one hundred and forty-five people are afraid of the twelve men at the top who helped found and build the company and now own and direct it.

If the net effect is not quite kafkaesque, it is, nonetheless, a considerable improvement over the more conventional portrait of corporate America provided in novels such as Sloan Wilson's *The Man in the Gray Flannel Suit* (1955). Heller's novel has more grit and more interest as literature than Wilson's largely sociological study of the death of the individual soul in corporate life.

In its best, most chillingly familiar moments, *Something Happened* is a novel of contemporary manners, one as unsparing in candor as it is meticulous in detail. Consider, for example, the way that Heller uses the myth of Oedipus as a way of focusing (or fixating) on the death of a son. Un-

like the haunting death of Snowden, around which the narrative of *Catch-22* revolves, we move by inches toward the heartbreaking moment when Slocum literally squeezes the life out of his son in a desperate attempt to save him. Moreover, the novel itself, as James Mellard points out in his essay "*Something Happened*: The Imaginary, the Symbolic, and the Discourse of the Family," resists Freudian readings. Slocum's self-conscious use of Freudian allusions actually causes the reader to look beyond Freud for the "real" source of his neurotic behavior. Instead, Heller's emphasis falls on the juxtaposition of sounds as they contribute to the meaning of words as well as on the juxtaposition of interlocking narratives about Slocum's childhood, his lost son, and echoes of Oedipus. The net effect is what J. Hillis Miller calls the Quaker Oats box effect:

> When a novel presents a fiction within a fiction [the technical term is *reflexivity*], the reality at the beginning and ending of this series tends to be assimilated into and to appear as itself a fiction. . . . A real Quaker Oats box is fictionalized when it bears a picture of a Quaker Oats box which in turn bears a picture of a Quaker Oats box, and so on indefinitely, in an endless play of imagination and reality.

But even here, in a novel many Heller buffs feel may yet outlast the formidable competition of *Catch-22*, there are foreshadowings of the screeds that follow. However much Slocum's domestic turmoil may or may not resemble Heller's own (Heller insists, in interviews, that it does not), there is little doubt about the source of the voice one hears in the following lamentations:

> The world is winding down. You can't get good bread anymore even in good restaurants (you get commercial rolls), and there are few good restaurants. Melons don't ripen, grapes are sour. . . . Butter tastes like the printed paper it's wrapped in. Whipped cream comes in aerosol bombs and isn't whipped and isn't cream. . . . From sea to shining

sea the country is filling with slag, shale, and used-up automobile tires. The fruited plain is coated with insecticide and chemical fertilizers.

When the novel gets stuck or begins to bore, Heller fires off a well-turned tirade. He does this at stray moments in *Something Happened* and then with increasingly longer swatches in novels such as *Good As Gold*, *God Knows*, and *Picture This*. Not surprisingly, the result pulls his fictions in several competing directions. *Good As Gold*, for example, begins as the effort—probably ill-advised—of its protagonist, Bruce Gold, to write a book about the Jewish experience in America. Gold's heart clearly isn't in the project. Neither, apparently, is Heller's, for he means to show that academic hustlers are really not so different from the likes of the entrepreneurial Milo Minderbinder or the corporate toady Bob Slocum. So far so good, even if most of the "gold" in Heller's theme—and Professor Gold's projected book—has long ago been played out. It at least gave Heller the chance to elbow large slabs of remembrances of Coney Island past into his novel and to write a few Jewish family dinner scenes that can hold their own with the best of this strain of American fiction.

The difficulties appear when the plotlines of *Good As Gold* multiply faster than Heller is able to keep them under control. There are, for example, the long narrative patches of Gold among the Washington, D.C., politicos (where, not surprisingly, we learn that obfuscation and double-talk have been raised to a high, self-serving art) and an even longer, thoroughly undisguised effort on Heller's part to bring down Henry Kissinger. Gold/Heller begins by quoting liberally, and verbatim, from statements in the press—Kissinger on power, on acquiring wealth, on Vietnam, on the Middle East—and then fantasizes about writing yet another book (*The Little Prussian*) that would include not only copious examples of Kissinger "Teuton his own horn" but also the shocking charge that he is not Jewish:

Gold was prepared to develop the thesis that Kissinger was not a Jew in a book of Kissinger "memoirs" he was positive would excite attention and hoped [would] earn him at least a discernible fraction of the *parnusseh* [living] Kissinger was raking in from his own memoirs. . . . In Gold's conservative opinion, Kissinger would not be recalled in history as a Bismarck, Metternich, or Castlereagh but as an odious *shlump* [sad sack] who made war gladly and did not often exude much of that legendary sympathy for weakness and suffering with which Jews regularly were credited.

Novels written in the white heat of political outrage, such as Philip Roth's *Our Gang* (1971) or Robert Coover's *The Public Burning* (1977), initially divide readers into those who enjoy seeing their enemies skewered and those who insist on fair play, but only the truest of true believers bother to turn their pages after the battle has moved elsewhere. *Good As Gold* is especially disappointing because there really *is* a significant novel about the Jewish experience in America hidden within the fatty folds of the political polemic. It is not quite that Gold is, as one character puts it, a "*shonda* [disgrace] to your race," but rather that neither Gold nor Heller stayed the aesthetic course.

God Knows is, if anything, worse—reminding us of what Mark Twain's Connecticut Yankee said about an interminably bad performance by King Arthur's court jester:

I think I never heard so many old played out jokes strung together in my life. . . . It seemed peculiarly sad to sit here, thirteen hundred years before I was born and listen again to poor, flat worm-eaten jokes that had given me the dry gripes when I was a boy.

For all its shows of biblical knowledge and moments of stylistic dazzle (Heller seems incapable of writing a dull page or lackluster paragraph), one cannot quite escape the feeling that *God Knows* turns King David's kvetching into a cheesy lounge act. At one point God insists that he never promised to "make sense": "I'll give milk. I'll give honey. Not sense."

Like Slocum in *Something Happened*, King David, Heller's protagonist-narrator, may be anchored in the terrible physicality of the present—one characterized by a chill that even the luscious Abishag cannot thaw—and his narrative perspective is as free-flowing, as associative as Slocum's. David's father figures (Jesse, Saul, and God) have abandoned him, and in this sense Heller's novel is another prolonged cry for justice. Acting as his own best advocate, David puts it this way:

> Wherever Saul sent me to fight, I went. And the better I was able to serve him in war against the Philistines, the greater grew his envious and furious suspicions that I was slated to replace him and was scheming already to do so. Was that fair? Was it my fault people liked me?

Saul, or at least *David*'s Saul, is a study in pathology, a man given to powerful, unpredictable swings of mood: one moment taking David to his bosom, the next plotting to take his life. Indeed, "there were times, it seemed, when he wanted to kill just about everyone, everyone, even his natural son Jonathan." David's extended monologue is, among other things, an effort to explain, to justify, above all, to *tell* his side of the story.

King David's "story" contains generous portions of stand-up comedy: "To the goyim He gives bacon, sweet pork, juicy sirloin, and rare ribs of beef. To us He gives a pastrami." But for all the wisecracks and filler (Bathsheba inventing bloomers or Abishag whipping up a round of tacos in the royal kitchen), *God Knows* is more than an endless string of one-liners. The two events that matter centrally to David are the precipitous way that God will often withdraw his favor (thus occasioning Saul's murderous rages) and his galling habit of punishing fathers by destroying their sons. In the special "theater" David's monologue creates, he casts himself as a man not only put upon by circumstance but also

more sinned against than sinning. "Is it *my* fault?" he asks repeatedly, and rhetorically. But then again, Heller's specialty has always been verbal theater—in this case, everything from the interplay of a wide variety of languages (the elevated diction of the King James Bible, David's earthy Yiddish, Oxford English, even passages that echo Gilbert and Sullivan) to the assorted roles that such minor characters as Nathan, Uriah, and the doomed Tamar play.

Still, one cannot entirely escape feeling that the "best lines" in *God Knows* are to be found in Chronicles, Judges, and, most of all, 1 and 2 Samuel rather than in Heller's imaginative send-ups. The notable exception occurs in the novel's final paragraphs, when Heller returns us to an aging King David who can no longer be warmed, much less sexually aroused, by Abishag. He may take careful notice of her powdered arms and legs, her fragrant mouth, but his mind is elsewhere: "I am thinking of God now, and I am thinking of Saul." Moreover, what he sees, as if in a vision, is the image of an eager, bright-eyed boy who was once upon a time himself: "One bare knee of his is bent to the ground, and he is holding in his lap a lyre with eight strings. The apparition has come to play for me." Unfortunately, the moment, touching in its delicacy, cannot be sustained, for Abishag interrupts it "without noise, wearing only a vivid scarf." King David's final lines say it all, about the alienation and emptiness, the estrangement and odd yearning, that has become his lot: "I want my God back; and they send me a girl."

No Laughing Matter—an account of Heller's scary bout with Guillain-Barré syndrome (GBS)—has the look of life imitating art. Heller suffered his first attack (December 12, 1981) at a time when he was in the middle of writing *God Knows*, a chronicle of and by a protagonist who is so weak he can hardly get out of bed. A similar condition struck the author of *No Laughing Mat-*

ter, not as an affliction of old age or as just punishment for a sinful life, but unexpectedly, mysteriously, "existentially."

Heller is hardly the first author to have the "surprises" of art give him or her cause for reflection, but in Heller's case, *No Laughing Matter* represents a significant change from the imaginative excess that had become his trademark. Not only was he writing about himself without the aesthetic distancing that serious fiction depends upon, but, more important, he also was chained to the facts of his medical history. To turn the story of how he was rendered the helpless victim of a sudden and debilitating nerve disorder into a memoir that fans of *Catch-22* could admire was a risky proposition. He somehow had to avoid writing yet another sentimental, uplifting tale of how pluck ultimately carried the day.

There were other, more technical problems as well. While it is true that a book such as *No Laughing Matter* surely required Heller to write clear paragraphs about his condition and the increasingly complicated medical procedures it occasioned, it is equally true that the book ultimately had to be more than a tale of survival. Keeping self-pity out (important as that was) could not be sufficient; the real issue became what Heller would put *in*. The decision to share chapters, and differing perspectives, with Speed Vogel (Heller's longtime friend and a wonderfully comic doppelgänger) was something of a masterstroke. It allows for long stretches of comic relief as Vogel describes Heller's hospital room crowded with the likes of the cutup Mel Brooks or the *Godfather* (1969) author Mario Puzo while Vogel holds down the fort back at Heller's apartment. The book's title, a cliché of the first water that its coauthors exploit for ironic effect, sets the tone for much of the high jinks to follow. Granted, the result is not a novel, nor is it a substantial contribution to American letters, but the insider's account of Heller's troubles—his

bout with GBS as well as with the divorce lawyers out to pick him clean—makes for an intriguing read.

Unfortunately, one could not make the same claim with regard to *Picture This*, Heller's tedious exercise in deconstructing Rembrandt's *Aristotle Contemplating the Bust of Homer*. One can fairly describe its ambience as that of an extended meditation on all manner of things— the life of Rembrandt and the death of Socrates, the rise of the Netherlands and the fall of Athens, what is real versus what is illusion, and, perhaps most of all, how money, then and now, talks:

> To Aristotle contemplating the bust of Homer, the continuing preoccupation of the world with making money was an enigma he was not even aware he was unable to decipher. . . . Homer begged and Rembrandt went bankrupt. Aristotle, who had money for books, his school and his museum, could not have bought this painting of himself.
> Rembrandt could not afford a Rembrandt.

Heller was always partial to the oxymoronic (in *Picture This*, we hear much about paintings that are, for example, "an authentic imitation of a Hellenic reproduction") as well as to the possibilities that open up when one pushes an observation to its logical absurdity. In this sense, Rembrandt's painting is for Heller what a found object (say, an interesting piece of driftwood) is to certain contemporary poets, namely, the objectification of a worldview. That things are not as they seem—that the bust in question is not of Homer, nor is the representation of Aristotle really Aristotle—becomes merely the tip of a much larger iceberg. For Heller, *nothing* is as it appears, although if the Big Lie is repeated long enough, not only is illusion regarded as the truth, but people are also perfectly happy to pony up enormous amounts of money for it.

Meanwhile, Socrates would have laughed at "this imitation on canvas in color of this copy in plaster or stone of an imitation in marble of the likeness of a man whom nobody we know of had ever seen and of whose existence there is no reliable written or oral verification.'' Moreover, Socrates would have insisted on the close relationship between the writing of comedy and the writing of tragedy. Here, Heller's source is Plato's *Symposium*, a work in which (as *Picture This* puts it) ''Socrates was busy compelling these two prize-winning playwrights [Aristophanes and Agathon] to acknowledge that a man who could write a comedy could also write a tragedy, and that the true artist in tragedy was an artist in comedy too.'' Heller is correct about Socrates, but he is even more revealing about his own aesthetic aims.

In its argument—namely, that the more things change, the more they remain the same—*Picture This* has ambition and scope, enormous effort, and not a few examples of the dazzling cadences and satiric wit associated with Heller at his novelistic best. But it is also true that the book is awash with large chunks of material lifted virtually unchanged from the Socratic dialogues and Plato's *Laws,* from Aristotle and Thucydides, from political histories of seventeenth-century Holland and biographies of Rembrandt van Rijn. As David Seed points out in *The Fiction of Joseph Heller*, ''at one point Heller will meditate on money; at another he will mimic a chronicler; and at yet another he will condense a Platonic dialogue and then suddenly shift it into burlesque.'' How could such a novel *not* collapse under the accumulated weight of its cultural references and rapidly shifting narrative techniques?

Moreover, *Picture This* is not only about imitation, as Plato and Aristotle defined the term, but is also itself an imitation of an imitation of an imitation. The novel, in short, offers up more information about the Age of Pericles, Rembrandt's tangled finances, and the strange odyssey that brought *Aristotle Contemplating the Bust of Homer* to the auction block than it does about the painting per se. One way to describe a novel such as *Picture This* is to call it reflexive, meaning that it unfolds as an onion skin or a Chinese box nestling inside yet another Chinese box. Another would be to call attention to the novel's self-consciousness about the fictionality of fiction. Either way, however, the fact remains that both Rembrandt's portrait and Heller's book are effectively cancelled out in the process.

Closing Time, Heller's effort to reclaim a prominence that had been slipping away since the publication of *Catch-22,* is yet another example of the brave tethered to the foolish. It is brave because the novel has sprawl and narrative energy, and it is foolish because it only encourages comparison with its classic predecessor, and ultimately loses. *Closing Time* is, in short, a sequel, one reuniting a handful of *Catch-22*'s survivors some fifty years later as they deal with their bodies' decay and plots even wider and more insidious than those which energized Heller's first novel. This time, however, Heller adds Jewish characters, including himself, who add large dashes of growing up in Coney Island to the mix. Even more important, *Closing Time* is a novel in which Heller eschews the distancing masks of his earlier fiction and speaks to readers as if they were his contemporaries. As such, *Catch-22*'s sequel is less an exercise in the absurdist imagination than a sobering reflection on death as quotidian fact. As Sammy Singer puts it: ''People I know are already dying and others I've known are already dead.'' To the specter of Snowden, Heller now adds a cast of dozens.

The result is a novel with more ambition than cohesion. Heller has always been longer on the pyrotechnics of style than on unfolding a conventional story line, but one suspects that tracing the complicated twists and turns of *Closing Time's* plot will drive even his most devoted fans to despair. What can one say about a novel in which the comically pathetic Chaplain A. T.

Tappman from *Catch-22* now finds himself passing heavy water (it takes two people to lift an eyedropper full) and in which Milo Minderbinder, *Catch-22*'s war profiteer par excellence, has evolved into a weapons dealer who threatens to join forces with Dr. Strangelove (yes, *the* Dr. Strangelove, essentially the same darkly comic character of Stanley Kubrick's film of the same name) in the world's ultimate smashup?

In Heller's words, *Closing Time* is his "summing up," one that begins (as did *Catch-22*) with Yossarian—worried as ever—in a hospital bed:

> In the middle of his second week in the hospital, Yossarian dreamed of his mother, and he knew again that he was going to die. The doctors were upset when he gave them the news.
> "We can't find anything wrong," they told him.
> "Keep looking," he instructed.
> "You're in perfect health."
> "Just wait," he advised.

Closing Time has a number of moments that evoke the nervous wackiness of Heller's first novel, and none more so than those that expose the double-talk and inveterate lying that, for Heller, constitute so much of contemporary life. Here, for example, is his riff on the comic possibilities to be found in the Freedom of Information Act:

> The Freedom of Information Act, the chaplain explained, was a federal regulation obliging government agencies to release all information they had to anyone who made application for it, except information they had that they did not want to release.
>
> And because of this one catch in the Freedom of Information Act, Yossarian had subsequently found out, they were technically not compelled to release any information at all. Hundreds of thousands of pages each week went out regularly to applicants with everything blacked out on them but punctuation marks, prepositions, and conjunctions.

Unfortunately, such moments, sprightly as they are, do not balance the overly long sections devoted to the netherworld hidden in the bowels of the Port Authority bus terminal or Heller's straining efforts to work erudite allusions to Thomas Mann's *Death in Venice* (1912) or Richard Wagner's *Ring* cycle into the fabric of his own fiction. What these self-conscious embroideries come to are variations of what Kurt Vonnegut calls the "mythic dimensions" of such novels as *Catch-22* and *Something Happened*. In this case, however, the myths surrounding the aging protagonists bring few consolations, for the peace that Yossarian so desperately wished for has proved disappointing, if not downright stultifying. Moreover, the World War II veterans who join Yossarian share a sense that Henry Thoreau was right about the special grief of coming to the end of one's life only to realize that one hasn't lived. Leo Tolstoy's Ivan Illyich comes to roughly the same conclusion. Only the war captures their collective imagination, for it was only during the war that, ironically enough, they had been truly alive.

Small wonder, then, that so much of contemporary life is fraught with bile for Yossarian and his friends, as they find sons uninterested, wives out of touch, and nonveteran friends bored. In *Closing Time*, Yossarian—now Major John Yossarian, retired—has not only aged but has also entered the human condition in ways that were not part of *Catch-22*'s territory, in which the escalating number of required missions grew, but always with the sense that such sorties were curiously cut off from time and cultural circumstances. The war against the Nazis is less important, and certainly less deadly, than the internal struggles Yossarian has with catch-22. In such a world, it takes all one's energy to "live forever or die in the attempt."

By contrast, *Closing Time* unfolds against the backdrop of historical actuality and Yossarian's gradual replacement of gestures of rebellion with those of accommodation. In short, this Yossarian has lost his innocence, and in this sense he is more akin to Bob Slocum than to the Yossarian we cheered onward in *Catch-22.* He is the novelistic equivalent of poet Wallace Stevens' phrase "an emptiness that would be filled." Unfortunately, his efforts to achieve an authentic self that might have turned into an existential desire, and then into a life-affirming direction, fall victim to his cynical understanding of the world. Even the possibility that Melissa MacIntosh, an "attractive floor nurse with the pretty face and the magnificent ass who was openly drawn to Yossarian, despite his years," might rekindle his old fires hardly leads to a romantic subplot. The problem lies squarely with Yossarian, and his hapless situation is not helped by the elaborate Wagnerian detour in which he imagines himself as Siegfried and casts Melissa as Brünnhilde. True enough, they eventually make love in the (significantly named) old Time-Life building, but memory so reconfigures the event that the novel's central quest, its "Rhine journey," points to the murky past rather than a bright future.

Granted, Heller gets a certain comic mileage out of the layerings of cultural material, but what they finally come to is flight: Yossarian, in short, runs, just as he did at the end of *Catch-22,* but without the inspiring spirit of Orr, who beat the system at its own game. Instead, in *Closing Time,* Yossarian flies to Kenosha, Wisconsin (one of the many places that Tappmann has been held in government custody) and then to Washington, D.C.—only to have Milo present him with a $500,000 commission check for keeping his scam about a secret fighter plane afloat. The complicated plotlines are often as hard to follow as they are to fathom, but readers of *Catch-22* know already that all Yossarian's roads eventually lead to the hospital—because that is where he goes for survival, rest and recreation, and, most of all, refuge from reality's relentless assaults.

What changes in *Closing Time* is Yossarian's adaptability. He becomes something of a chameleon, which was Slocum's corporate strategy and strongest suit. Working for Milo Minderbinder's

M & M E & A, Yossarian unconsciously assumes its outlook: scheming for the marriage of Minderbinder's son into the wealthy, high society Maxon family, with the wedding to be held in the Port Authority Bus Terminal (with actors playing the roles of the prostitutes, pimps, and assorted homeless who are typically found there); selling Milo's Sub-Supersonic Invisible and Noiseless Defensive Second-Strike Offensive Attack Bomber to the government, knowing full well that it doesn't work; and even advising his son, Michael, a commercial artist, that ethical qualms about designing visuals for sales presentations are out of place: "You're only being asked to draw a picture of the plane, not to fly the fucking thing or launch an attack. . . . [Milo and Associates] don't care now if it works or not. All they want is the money."

In an echo of what Donald Trump would call the "art of the deal," Yossarian *deals.* Proposals must be proposed (and then accepted), and aviators must fly (and possibly crash), but in such ever-spiraling circles, the sounds of entropy are deafening, the whispers of consolation nearly extinct—and not just for Heller's aging soldiers, but for his readers as well. Humor, or at least what readers of *Catch-22* took for humor, ends up on the casualty list. As one character puts it to Yossarian (she might well have been speaking of Heller himself): "You sound so bitter these days. You used to be funnier."

By contrast, the extended portraits of Lew Rabinowitz and Sammy Singer may well be worth the price of admission, for they return Heller to the Coney Island of his childhood and to the memories that stand in stark contrast to those produced by the horrors of war:

> There was a two-cent "deposit" charged on every small soda bottle, a nickel on sodas of larger size that sold for ten cents, and none of the members in all of the families on that West Thirty-first Street block were inattentive to the value of those empty soda bottles. You could buy things of value for two

pennies then. Sometimes as kids we'd go treasure hunting for deposit bottles in likely places on the beach. We would turn them in for cash at the Steinberg candy store right on my street at the corner of Surf Avenue and use the coins to play poker or twenty-one for pennies once we knew how, or spend them at once on things to eat. For two cents you could buy a nice-sized block of Nestlé's or Hershey's chocolate, a couple of pretzels or frozen twists, or, in the fall, a good piece of the halvah we all went crazy about for a while.

Singer is a particularly lively addition to the crew of *Catch-22*, now reassembled in the sequel, for he reminds us of Yossarian at his loopy, insidiously subversive best. Here, for example, is a representative passage in which Korn's laws are added to the repertoire of absurdities huddling beneath catch-22's wide umbrella:

> under Korn's laws, the only ones ever permitted to question anything were those who never did. But he put me [Sammy] to work tutoring others with simple examples from algebra and geometry in the reasons one must always shoot well ahead of a target moving in relation to you—and in order to shoot ahead of a plane moving in relation to you had to shoot behind. If a plane is so many yards away and a cartridge travels at so many yards per second, how many seconds will it take for your cartridge to reach it? If the plane is traveling at so many feet per second, how many feet will it travel by the time the bullet reaches it? They saw it in practice in the hours we spent skeet shooting and firing on the gunnery range from a moving truck. But though I taught it and knew it, even I had trouble with the principle that you fired ahead of a plane coming in on attack by always aiming behind it, between the target and your tail, because of the forward airspeed of the bullets from your own plane and the swerving path that plane would have to follow to fire in front of you.

Added together, the biographical portraits of Singer, Rabinowitz, and little "Joey" Heller tell us a good deal about the Jewish ethos that produced the writer we know as Joseph Heller. They also account, at least in part, for his unyielding rage against all that is duplicitous and destructive in the world he encountered beyond Coney Island's protective folds. No doubt a satirist such as Heller needs exasperation and anger to fuel his creative juices, but such a writer also needs control and craft if the resulting novel is to have coherence and imaginative force. As was the case in *Good As Gold*, *Closing Time* is, in effect, "several" novels, each working against the grain of the other, and none of them quite adding up to the power Heller unleashed with *Catch-22*.

Ironically enough, reading Heller's first novel is one of the ways we first sensed civilization's long decline and fall and the body's losing battle with entropy. In this respect, *Closing Time*'s sour vision of the apocalypse just around the corner seems like so much old wine poured into new bottles:

> Another oil tanker had broken up. There was radiation. Garbage. Pesticides, toxic waste, and free enterprise. There were enemies of abortion who wished to inflict the death penalty on everyone who was not pro-life. There was mediocrity in government, and self-interest too. There was trouble in Israel. . . . Nothing made sense and neither did everything else.

Heller is not alone in harboring the illusion that history itself will end when he does, but the impulse hardly justifies his effort to move from the death of Snowden in *Catch-22* to the Sturm und Drang of *Closing Time*. Given the reverence with which *Catch-22* is rightly held, *any* sequel would have constituted an enormous risk. In flashes, *Closing Time* reminds us that language creates an absurdist reality—and that this shadow world can wreak its own brand of destruction. So when we read about Milo Minderbinder's latest efforts to manipulate the military-industrial complex, the lunacy has a familiar ring. Heller is, of course, largely responsible for this general perception. He taught us how to read the contemporary world, even as we laughed at the verbal gymnastics of his style. For this he deserves both credit and our enduring thanks.

Selected Bibliography

WORKS OF JOSEPH HELLER

NOVELS

Catch-22. New York: Simon & Schuster, 1961.
Something Happened. New York: Knopf, 1974.
Good As Gold. New York: Simon & Schuster, 1979.
God Knows. New York: Knopf, 1984.
Picture This. New York: Putnam, 1988.
Closing Time. New York: Simon & Schuster, 1994.

PLAYS

We Bombed in New Haven. New York: DeHa, 1969.
Catch-22: A Dramatization. New York: Delacorte Press, 1973.
Clevinger's Trial. In *The Best Short Plays of 1976.* Edited by Stanley Richards. Radnor, Pa.: Chilton Book, 1977.

SCREENPLAYS

Sex and the Single Girl. Warner Brothers, 1964. Screenplay by Heller and David R. Schwartz.
Dirty Dingus Magee. Metro-Goldwyn-Mayer, 1970. Screenplay by Heller and Tom and Frank Waldman.

ESSAYS AND SHORT FICTION

"I Don't Love You Any More." *Story,* September/October 1945, pp. 40–45.
"Bookies, Beware!" *Esquire,* May 1947, p. 98.
"Castle of Snow." *Atlantic Monthly,* March 1948, pp. 52–55.
"Girl from Greenwich." *Esquire,* June 1948, pp. 40–41, 142–143.
"A Man Called Flute." *Atlantic Monthly,* August 1948, pp. 66–70.
"Catch-18." *New World Writing,* 7:204–214 (April 1955).
"McAdam's Log." *Gentleman's Quarterly,* December 1959, pp. 112, 166–176, 178.
"Too Timid to Damn, Too Stingy to Applaud." *New Republic,* July 30, 1962, pp. 23–26.
"World Full of Great Cities." In *Nelson Algren's Own Book of Lonesome Monsters.* Edited by Nelson Algren. New York: Lancer, 1964.

"Catch-22 Revisited." *Holiday,* April 1967, pp. 44–61.
"How I Found James Bond, Lost My Self-Respect and Almost Made $150,000 in My Spare Time." *Holiday,* June 1967, pp. 123–130.
"Love, Dad." *Playboy,* December 1969, pp. 180–182, 348.
"I *Am* the Bombardier!" *New York Times Magazine,* May 7, 1995, p. 61.

ARCHIVES AND BIBLIOGRAPHIES

Keegan, Brenda M. *Joseph Heller: A Reference Guide.* Boston: G. K. Hall, 1978.
Heller's papers are housed in the Brandeis University Heller Collection.

MEMOIR

No Laughing Matter. With Speed Vogel. New York: Putnam, 1986.

BIOGRAPHICAL AND CRITICAL STUDIES

Berryman, Charles. "Heller's Gold." *Chicago Review,* 32, no. 4:108–118.
Blues, Thomas. "The Moral Structure of *Catch-22.*" *Studies in the Novel,* 3:64–79 (Spring 1971).
Burhans, Clinton S., Jr. "Spindrift and the Sea: Structural Patterns and Unifying Elements in *Catch-22.*" *Twentieth Century Literature,* 19:239–250 (October 1973).
Costa, Richard Hauer. "Notes from a Dark Heller: Bob Slocum and the Underground Man." *Texas Studies in Literature and Language,* 23:159–182 (Summer 1981).
Davis, Gary W. "*Catch-22* and the Language of Discontinuity." *Novel,* 12:66–77 (Fall 1978).
Doskow, Minna. "The Night Journey in *Catch-22.*" *Twentieth Century Literature,* 12:186–193 (January 1967).
LeClair, Thomas. "Joseph Heller, *Something Happened,* and the Art of Excess." *Studies in American Fiction,* 9:245–260 (Autumn 1981).
Lowin, Joseph. "The Jewish Art of Joseph Heller." *Jewish Book Annual,* 43:141–153 (1985–1986).

MacDonald, James L. "I See Everything Twice!: The Structure of Joseph Heller's *Catch-22.*" *University Review,* 34:175–180 (March 1968).

Merrill, Robert. "The Structure and Meaning of *Catch-22.*" *Studies in American Fiction,* 14:139–152 (Autumn 1986).

———. *Joseph Heller.* Boston: Twayne, 1987.

Miller, Wayne Charles. "Ethnic Identity As Moral Focus: A Reading of Joseph Heller's *Good As Gold.*" MELUS 6:3–17 (1979).

Nagel, James. "*Catch-22* and Angry Humor: A Study of the Normative Values of Satire." *Studies in American Humor,* 1:99–106 (1974).

———. ed. *Critical Essays on "Catch-22."* Encino, Calif.: Dickenson, 1974.

———. "Joseph Heller and the University." *College Literature,* 10:16–27 (1983).

———. ed. *Critical Essays on Joseph Heller.* Boston: G. K. Hall, 1984.

Nelson, Thomas Allen. "Theme and Structure in *Catch-22.*" *Renascence* 23:173–182 (Summer 1971).

Pinsker, Sanford. *Understanding Joseph Heller.* Columbia: University of South Carolina Press, 1991.

Ruderman, Judith. "Upside-Down in *Good As Gold*: Moishe Kapoyer as Muse." *Modern Jewish Studies Annual,* 5:55–63 (Fall 1984).

———. *Joseph Heller.* New York: Continuum, 1991.

Sebouhian, George. "From Abraham and Isaac to Bob Slocum and My Boy: Why Fathers Kill Their Sons." *Twentieth Century Literature,* 27:43–52 (Spring 1981).

Seed, David. *The Fiction of Joseph Heller: Against the Grain.* New York: St. Martin's Press, 1989.

Seltzer, Leon F. "Milo's 'Culpable Innocence': Absurdity as Moral Insanity in *Catch-22.*" *Papers on Language and Literature,* 15:290–310 (Summer 1979).

Sniderman, Stephen L. " 'It Was All Yossarian's Fault': Power and Responsibility in *Catch-22.*" *Twentieth Century Literature,* 19:251–258 (October 1973).

Strehle Klemtner, Susan. " 'A Permanent Game of Excuses': Determinism in Heller's *Something Happened.*" *Modern Fiction Studies,* 24:550–556 (Winter 1978–1979).

Thomas, W. K. "The Mythic Dimension of *Catch-22.*" *Texas Studies in Literature and Language,* 15:189–198 (Spring 1973).

———. " 'What Difference Does It Make': Logic in *Catch-22.*" *Dalhousie Review,* 50:488–495 (Winter 1970–1971).

Tucker, Lindsey. "Entropy and Information Theory in Heller's *Something Happened.*" *Contemporary Literature,* 25, no. 3:323–340.

Way, Brian. "Formal Experiment and Social Discontent: Joseph Heller's *Catch-22.*" *Journal of American Studies,* 2:253–270 (October 1968).

INTERVIEWS

Krassner, Paul. "An Impolite Interview with Joseph Heller." *The Realist* (November 1962). P. 283.

Ruas, Charles. *Conversations with American Writers.* New York: Knopf, 1985.

Sorkin, Adam J., ed. *Conversations with Joseph Heller.* Jackson: University Press of Mississippi, 1993. Includes interviews conducted by George Plimpton and Richard B. Sale.

—SANFORD PINSKER

Linda Hogan

1947–

NATIVE AMERICAN POET, novelist, and essayist Linda Hogan displays in both her life and writing the flux and energies of the late twentieth century. Motifs of history and conflict, identity and mutability, and the precariousness of human life in the future permeate her work. Much of Hogan's writing reflects as inner dialogue in which she comes to terms with her Chickasaw ancestry and its effect on her as a woman in the late twentieth century, as an indigenous person in the context of the history of colonialism, and as a concerned environmentalist searching for a land ethic. Her work acquires its power in the highly personal and idiosyncratic inflections of her narrative voice. While Hogan participates in the debates about identity that enliven contemporary literature—seeing herself as a member of women's and working class communities as well as the Chickasaw community—her literary orientation is most strongly defined by her Native American heritage.

Hogan's work can be roughly divided into three periods. In her earliest work, she focuses on issues of identity. She later writes about her connections to her family and history. In the third period her work is concerned with the global community. Sketching a general model for a writer's development in a conversation with Patricia Smith, Hogan gives us an outline for assessing her own growth: ''In our human development we begin with ourselves and move outward toward rela-tionship, and in writing work, it seems to be the same, that most writers begin with their own identity, with autobiography, and then move out toward family, friends, environment, country, world.'' Hogan, too begins with herself. Her earliest poetry, collected in *Calling Myself Home* (1978), *Daughters, I Love You* (1981), *Eclipse* (1983), and *Seeing through the Sun* (1985), was written in the 1970s and 1980s; these poems often take as their subject her life as a working woman with a mixed-blood heritage. Her work from the mid-1980s, including the poems in *Savings* (1988) and the short stories in *That Horse* (1985), moves outward thematically and examines her identity in relation to her family, to the dominant culture, and to history, culminating in the novel *Mean Spirit* (1990). Her work from the 1990s continues to explore the themes of identity and history, but in a more global context, focusing on the dangers of environmental devastation and human alienation from the natural world. Her collection of poetry *The Book of Medicines* (1993), her novel *Solar Storms* (1995), and her collection of natural history essays entitled *Dwellings: A Spiritual History of the Living World* (1995) reflect how Hogan's vision grew without sacrificing the qualities of intimacy and immediacy that mark her work.

In order to best understand Hogan's writing, students of Native American literature must put aside the usual critical and interpretative conventions applied to most other kinds of literature and pay attention to firsthand accounts of her experience, her resources, and her intentions. Rather than distancing themselves from the author in order to view the work objectively, readers should give heed to the connections between Hogan's life and work and think about how her particular experience as a woman with mixed-blood ancestry influenced her poetry, fiction, and essays. The best information about why Hogan writes what she does comes from Hogan herself, especially in the many interviews she has given and in the autobiographical content that can be gleaned from her work.

Hogan was born Linda Henderson in Denver, Colorado, in 1947 and spent her childhood living wherever her father's work took the family. Her father, a veteran of the Korean War was, at different times in Hogan's childhood, a carpenter, ranch hand, and soldier; the family farm in Oklahoma had been lost during the Depression, and, like many rural Americans, Hogan's family was forced to live on the fringes of city life and culture. Even when the Depression ended, the hardships it created did not. However, her father's Chickasaw ancestry and connection to southern Oklahoma gave his family's somewhat itinerant life a center and home. Hogan refers often to Oklahoma in her writing, and in the interview with Smith, she observes:

> I think my connection to Oklahoma is maybe not even a birth connection; that doesn't seem to make sense. But my identity with family is there, with Chickasaw people and land, and maybe my idea of what a home is, is *there,* is south-central Oklahoma. . . . I think Oklahoma was where magic lived for me, and still does, in the fireflies, and in the breezy motion of trees, and the stillness.

On her mother's side, Hogan is descended from Nebraska pioneers and she has commented that while that side of her family was busy conquering the frontier, the Chickasaw side was being driven off their homelands, suffering the removal to Oklahoma that many tribes from the southeastern United States endured.

This mixed-blood heritage often situates Hogan and her writing outside the dominant culture. In some ways, this position was an advantage for Hogan, giving her a different perspective from which to view the world. She claims, in an interview with Joseph Bruchac, that from her Chickasaw grandparents she " 'learned everything,'. . . that there is a better and alternative way to exist in the world, better ways to love, to take care of life." In other ways, this heritage was one of poverty and lack of privilege, especially in terms of education. She explains to Smith:

> As I grew up, education wasn't valued. We had different values from the dominant society, and I'm now seeing that the values of mid-America are difficult and painful ones—and are the source of dislocation and stress for people. I didn't read when I was young. I wasn't interested in literature, but I did listen to stories.

The values acquired through her Chickasaw grandparents sustained Hogan and she eventually found her way to writing, through somewhat nontraditional channels.

The vitality of Hogan's poetry and fiction comes from the powerful connection she maintains between her work and the world about which she writes. Many Western literary traditions do not emphasize the importance of the relationship between the writer and the world, preferring to understand the writer's work as the product of autonomous genius, distanced from the world. Hogan sees herself apart from this Western tradition. As part of the Native American community, Hogan participates in the oral tradition with her literary endeavors. In the oral tradition, the storyteller's words have a restorative function; they heal and unite the community. A traditional storyteller, or shaman, tells a story to make something happen, to bring about a needed change. Hogan shared with Bo Schöler that she writes to effect change. Poetry ''makes me change; it makes other people change. When you read something that is really put together well, something unresolved in the heart or psyche moves toward resolution and wholeness. It's magic.'' Literary language, for Hogan, takes on the power of healing, in the manner of the sacred words of the Native American oral tradition. Apparent in Hogan's work is an ever widening circle of healing. She initially writes for herself, then for her family and Native American community, and finally for the global community.

In combining oral and written traditions, Hogan has laden her work with responsibility. She has an oracular sense of her duties as a poet and novelist. Literature, according to Hogan, has the power of revelation; she observes to Schöler that literature ''takes a fact or an event, even an imagined one, and it makes truth out of it. Prose is a process of uncovering, of getting to the bare, unstated facts of living.'' Often more interested in substance than form, Hogan has moved with grace and agility across genres—writing poetry, drama, essays, and fiction. Drawing on the past and concerned for the future, she perceives her task to be one of uncovering a number of truths, about the way to live with ourselves, the way to live with each other, and the way to live in the world.

Throughout her life, Hogan spent a great deal of time in the Oklahoma land of her Chickasaw ancestry, but she never made her home there. Perhaps because of this distance from her family's place of origin, Hogan needed to confirm her Native American identity and explore those beginnings. When she started writing, she tells Bruchac:

I was living in Washington, D.C., a sort of suburban kind of life, and I had a great deal of difficulty just trying to put the early life of moving back and forth between rural Oklahoma and working-class Denver together with that one. . . . The poetry writing was very important to me. It was a way of trying to define who I was in an environment that felt foreign.

Her writing became so important to her, in fact, that she went back to school in the mid-1970s (after having dropped out of high school at age fifteen and later obtaining her GED in California) and took a creative writing class at the University of Maryland. She later completed her undergraduate degree and went on for her M.A. at the University of Colorado (1979). These early poems of self-definition and assertion became part of her first published collections, *Calling Myself Home* and *Daughters, I Love You.*

In her earliest work, Hogan confronts issues of identity and experiences a process of self-revelation through writing. These poems document both the discovery of a self labeled with multiple identities and the importance of restoring an inner unity. Through writing, she could heal the divisiveness of those labels—mixed blood, Chickasaw, white—and nurture the wholeness of herself, a motivation that gave her artistic process greater urgency. She tells Bruchac: ''There is a life deep inside me that always asserts itself. It is the dark and damp, the wet imagery of my beginnings. Return. A sort of deep structure to myself, the framework. It insists on being written and refuses to give me peace unless I follow its urges.'' The inadequacy of racial tags to represent who she is spurs Hogan's earliest poetry. Because she lives in a world that distorts her ''framework,'' that confuses her identity, she attempts to release her genuine self, that ''deep life,'' in her writing.

We can hear Hogan's attempt to gain access to that ''deep structure'' of her true self, or core identity, in several of these poems. Images of blood and bone represent the inner self revealed; such images are found in "Finding Beads," from *Calling Myself Home:*

> Beads made of bone, our vertebrae,
> arms and legs
> strung together beneath skin.

Hogan imagines a human rosary pieced together with bone, transforming her search for identity into prayer, earnestly longing to know exactly who she is. She reduces herself in "Water Rising," from *Eclipse,* to "just lungs, heart / and skin." With this froglike image, she reverses evolution in order to return to her origins and understand her identity. In a later poem, "In So Many Dark Rooms," from *Seeing through the Sun,* she confronts her inner life with fewer doubts about who she is:

> I am not afraid of my skeleton.
> It is a good souvenir of life
> dancing inside an old shawl of flesh.

In this poem, her core self begins to be a partner in her "dance" of life rather than being out of step with whom she believes herself to be.

Hogan's desire to find an identity that is deeply rooted and authentic comes, perhaps, from her mixed-blood ancestry. On being mixed blood, she observes in "The Two Lives": "I am aware of the fact that as a light-skinned Indian person I am seen as a person of betweens, as a person of divided directions." Hogan struggles against internalizing this message of being a split person, at odds with herself. In her short story "Aunt Moon's Young Man," her narrator recalls her feelings about being mixed blood while growing up: "Our blood was mixed like Heinz 57, and I always thought of purebloods as better than us." Rather than accepting this feeling of inferiority, Hogan works to reclaim her multiple heritage as

a source of power, as she explains in her interview with Schöler:

> If you live on the boundaries between cultures, you are both of those cultures, and neither of those cultures, and you can move with great mobility in any direction you want. . . . In my life I have felt myself to be judged by both groups, and I've had to struggle for a balance that's beyond that judgment. It makes for strength and for character. Or characters, I should say.

Being either and neither gives Hogan a liminal role, that of the translator or go-between, a burdensome task at times, in that such a position can so often be misunderstood or be the cause of rejection from both communities. However, Hogan has not been greatly concerned with this danger; she tells Carol Miller: "If Indian communities don't like me, if white communities don't like me, that could mean I can have more artistic freedom." In this early poetry, Hogan works at reclaiming her mixed-blood identity and finding her liminal persona as a writer liberating.

Hogan's early poetry enacts autobiographical processes of reconciliation. She uses poetic language to deal with the responsibility of bearing the past, present, and future of both sides of the cultural conflict in her blood. She discovers the necessity of abandoning the outside world's perception of her identity as a self divided, in order to find wholeness. In "Leaving," from *Calling Myself Home,* Hogan asserts her unified self and portrays the verbal healing process: "Good-bye, divisions of people: . . . All my people are weeping / when I step out of my old skin." Hogan reconciles her divided ancestry by giving birth to herself through language, an act that has costs to her relationships but also confirms her survival.

While such a poem suggests that Hogan wants to put the past behind her, many of these early poems speak of the past being preserved intact within her less carefully formed self, as if her body were amber and the past the primordial insect within. The image of amber is one Hogan uses repeatedly and powerfully in the poem "Turtle," from *Calling Myself Home:*

> We are amber,
> the small animals
> are gold inside us.

Hogan's sense of the value of the past as it lives within her reveals her sense of the continuity of her Chickasaw heritage. The "small animals" of her ancestors reside within her without contradiction. In "The Sand Roses," from *Seeing through the Sun,* she writes that

> we hear voices
> in the solar plexus
> the heart
> the ancient ones that burn inside us.

She reconciles the mixed-blood heritage that she was told would tear her apart by situating her Native American ancestry in the center of her being. Yet, as some of this early poetry reveals, she feels her life connected not only to the past but to the future as well.

Children, her own and others, appear often in Hogan's work, reflecting her concern for the future and those who will inherit the world her generation has left for them. Her hope for the next generation and the future they hold is articulated in "Blessing the Children," from *Daughters, I Love You,* when she tells her adopted Lakota Sioux daughters that she "made tobacco prayers" for them. But this hope is countered by an awareness of the fragility of life, particularly the lives of children, in whom so much is invested. She writes in the title poem of the same volume: "How quickly we could vanish, / your skin nothing." In this poem, her narrative voice expresses the fear of nuclear annihilation and the potential loss of entire generations, a fear made personal when she beholds with great tenderness her daughters' bodies. Hogan's concern for future generations is related to her quest for a unified self. Divisions in the present make weak foundations for the future. The knowledge that the security of the next generation rests on her own stability gives Hogan greater motivation to write through the processes of self-reconciliation.

The tenuous hold she has on the future, the hold the past has on her: these conditions make honoring life in the present even more important for Hogan. Aware of the fragility of life, Hogan attempts to distill a moment of clarity amid the images of Hiroshima in "Disappearances," from *Daughters, I Love You:*

> This moment the world continues.
> I pour coffee into a cup my sister made
> and count blessings, two daughters
> sleeping with open mouths.

She affirms the perfection of the isolated moment by contemplating her connections to her past through the artifact of family and savoring her link to the future, represented by her daughters. By weaving together past and future, she transforms the present into something solid enough to be cupped in her hand, tangible and complete. The tensions and fears that pull at the present moment are stilled as later in the same poem she affirms: "It is a good thing to be alive." In these largely autobiographical poems, Hogan affirms not only her own life but also the goodness of living. The simple act of drinking a cup of coffee becomes, for Hogan, a celebratory ritual.

Being audience to Hogan's early poetry is to participate in this ritual of self-reclamation. This process is guided by her powerful autobiographical narrative voice, a voice that becomes both elastic and sure as she develops as a poet. The reader is invited to take part in Hogan's healing as she addresses us directly, making us part of her inner conversation. In "The Truth Is," from *Seeing through the Sun,* she writes:

In my left pocket a Chickasaw hand
rests on the bone of the pelvis.
In my right pocket
a white hand. Don't worry. It's mine.

As she assures her audience of her unified identity, she also reassures herself in her ongoing work of healing, because, as she states in the same poem,

the truth is
we are crowded together
and knock against each other at night.
We want amnesty.

This work of reconciliation is continuous, she confides to her readers, needing repeated buttressing with the language of healing. Near the poem's conclusion, her narrative voice is inflected with humor and confidence as she states in her aside to herself: "Girl, I say, / it is dangerous to be a woman of two countries." In spite of the danger, Hogan is unwilling to relinquish her citizenship in either state as she draws on the power of her liminality to create the vibrant voice of this poetry.

The mixed-blood identity that was the source of the sense of dislocation that urged Hogan to begin writing takes on wider significance as Hogan's work matures. She realizes that hers is an often untold story and she understands the importance her story has for those who share her marginality. She tells Smith:

I, as an Indian woman, from a non middle-class background, on the margin, not a member of the dominant culture—I need to speak what my struggle has been, and offer the strength of that survival to keep us all moving together, to offer back my own words. This means to speak about what it's like to be of mixed blood, to have suffered losses, to have not been educated, to have worked primarily at working-class jobs until fairly recently—*and* to have worked as a writer.

Hogan writes not simply for her own development but also to articulate the stories that have been ignored or silenced by poverty, cultural assimilation, and racism. She writes in "Houses," from *Eclipse,* that the only thing she possesses, that her people have possessed in their poverty, is the desire to speak:

Nothing . . . belongs to us
except this searching for words
to say again what has been said
and not heard.

In her poem "To Light," from *Seeing through the Sun,* she reminds her readers:

We have stories
as old as the great seas
breaking through the chest,
flying out the mouth,
noisy tongues that once were silenced,
all the oceans we contain
coming to light.

Writing autobiographically, then, is not merely self-reflection on her own maturation processes but a statement of cultural survival told to those who share her culture and to those who do not, available as a message of hope or defiance, depending on the reader's position.

Hogan is aware of but puzzled by the radical nature of such writing, asking in "The Two Lives": "Why is it that telling our lives is a subversive thing to do?" The subversiveness of Hogan's poetics does not come from radical political rhetoric, but rather from her conscious disassociation from Western literary traditions, in which poetry that is a locus for change or a call for justice is dismissed as topical. Contrary to what these traditions dictate, her passion for poetry comes from its ability to move its readers to action. In an interview in the *Missouri Review,* she recalls: "When I discovered poetry I fell in love with it. I thought it was the most incredible thing in the world. It was not only a language, it was an emotion. It was something that moved me, and that I believed could affect change.'' The autobiographical content of Hogan's poetry charges it with emotions that can ''affect change,'' for in telling her life, Hogan tells of loss, dislocation, and the history of injustice.

Hogan's late entry into a literary education made her suspicious of formal poetry yet also freed her to read and write apart from Western literary traditions. Her early experiences with poetry in her late twenties challenged her to forgo some preconceived notions about the dead language of poets. She tells Schöler:

> I had never read contemporary poetry. I thought all poetry was written by dead people, and, that it all had to do with ravens that say ''Never more.''... One day I started writing. Then I got a hold of the collected works of Rexroth...and I thought, ''Wow, I could write like that; you don't have to rhyme or anything.''

Her introduction to contemporary free verse liberated her from the compulsions of traditional forms and gave her permission to write the poetry of her own life.

Early in her career, she claims in the interview with Schöler, form took a secondary position to content in her work: ''I have so much I want to say—I'm always wanting to put things into language—that I don't have time to go back and experiment with form.'' Hogan perceives the preoccupation with poetic form to be a matter of empty manipulation of words, stating in the interview with Bruchac: ''I feel that poetry is a process of uncovering our real knowledge. To manipulate the language merely via the intellect takes away the strength of the poem.'' According to Hogan, poetry is the language of revelation and revolution: how poetry affects the reader matters more to her than the structural details of poetry. Rather than using poetic language to explore aesthetic values, she uses it to address her responsibility as a poet; in ''The Two Lives'' she writes:

I thought of the best ways to use words, how great was my responsibility to transmit words, ideas, and acts by which we could live with liberation, love, self-respect, good humor, and joy. In learning that, I also had to offer up our pain and grief and sorrow, because I know that denial and repression are the greatest hindrances to liberation and growth.

The values with which she loads her poetry are those of survival and cultural sustenance; she uses language to represent the possibilities of life.

It would be inaccurate to state, however, that Hogan's early work was not influenced by Western literary traditions. Free verse itself has a long history in Western poetics, as do the image-propelled stanzas on which Hogan's work so often relies. From the metaphysical poets to the imagists to many contemporary writers, the importance of image as the main vehicle of emotion in Western poetry should not be underplayed. For Hogan, image has incantatory power, giving her readers the ability to imagine what was previously unimaginable. In her critical essay ''Who Puts Together,'' she writes: ''The ability to say, in poetic form, that which is unspeakable, to create and hold an image in the mind, gives language its power. What is spoken is seen.'' Poetic language, cast in images, can heal the reader through its ability to make what is normally understood by intuition more tangible. Hogan also says in the same essay: ''The potential of language to heal and restore lies in its ability to open the mind and to make the world visible, uniting all things into wholeness.'' Even though choosing the correct image for such an act of restoration requires a kind of formal precision, Hogan's purpose rarely allows her readers simply to revel in the beauty of her language, but instead asks us to use the power of beauty to renew language, charge emotion, and bring about change.

While it is important to understand Hogan's connection to Western literary traditions, it is equally helpful to delineate her relationship to other contemporary Native American writers and

Native American literary traditions. Many of Hogan's colleagues in the Native American literary community share a mixed-blood heritage and draw on their multiple points of origin to perform the task of translation between cultures. Like Hogan, they perceive this fin-de-siècle culture in which they write to be a precarious one. Their work often asks readers to reflect on the danger of cultural division and the power of cultural difference when it is respected and honored.

These writers often draw on both the oral traditions of their Native American ancestry and the narrative strategies of the modern and postmodern novel in order to depict themes of dislocation, alienation, and cultural genocide. The novels of N. Scott Momaday, James Welch, and Simon Ortiz move the reader between cultures, asking them to share the split vision of their protagonists. However, not all Native American writing has such a bleak outlook; many Native American women writers, including Hogan, emphasize survival and resilience rather than death and loss in their work. For example, the poetry of Joy Harjo and Luci Tapahonso and the fiction of Paula Gunn Allen and Louise Erdrich attest to the resources of courage, love, and humor that are as much a part of Native American culture as the history of suffering.

The Native American literary critic Louis Owens has commented in *Other Destinies: Understanding the American Indian Novel* that the visionary motifs of contemporary Native American literature will remain out of reach to anyone who does not take the trouble to learn about the tribal cultures of its authors: "And just as [T. S.] Eliot—looking forthrightly toward Europe—attempted to piece together the cultural and mythological resources needed in a time of deracination and despair, Native American writers are offering a way of looking at the world that is new to Western culture." Along with Hogan, Native American writers like Leslie Marmon Silko, James Welch, and Gerald Vizenor, among others, articulate a vision that Owens calls "holistic, ecological . . . one that places essential value upon the totality of existence, making humanity equal to all elements but superior to none and giving humankind crucial responsibility for the care of the world we inhabit." These writers broaden the boundaries of their communities in order to share, via their literary work, values that can bring about healing in a troubled world. As Hogan's writing expands beyond the autobiographical concerns of self-restoration, she, too, gives more attention to the healing of a larger community.

During the 1980s Hogan's work took a subtle turn; as her narrative voice gained more power and confidence, she turned with this newfound clarity to address new genres and themes. While concern for the land and people of the places she calls home permeates her earlier works, this concern, in her middle period, expands into themes of preserving community. In the poetry collected in *Savings,* the short stories of *That Horse,* and her first novel, *Mean Spirit,* Hogan more consciously draws on her connection to the oral tradition and Native American history. Similarly, while Hogan's early poetry is often narrative, giving her readers full stories as well as sketches of emotion, she later shifts into writing fiction as well, widening the range of her narrative voice into character and plot. Fiction allows Hogan to move outside her own experience. Her narrative voice, while often maintaining its autobiographical orientation, develops a communal quality. As Hogan's interests become more focused on the community beyond the borders of her identity, so does her means of expression.

What seems to have enabled Hogan to make this transition is her exploration of Native American oral history, oral literature, and materials related to the healing tradition. In the early 1980s, she studied the oral tradition with a Tribal Historical Scholarship and a Newberry Library

Fellowship. Hogan's early work points to an awareness of her relationship to these traditions; she has often observed that she came from a family of storytellers and, in a way, that the oral tradition shaped her earliest understanding of narrative as a communal and multivoiced event. She tells Miller: "While I don't know if what my dad and family and my grandmother spoke was what you would call the oral tradition, I knew that they were important stories and that they had to be documented. It's our lives." However, during this middle period, she articulates her relationship to the oral tradition more clearly, making it more central to her writing. In "Who Puts Together," she remarks that in "the American Indian oral tradition . . . words function as part of the poetic processes of creation, transformation, .and restoration." The oral tradition cannot be understood in aesthetic terms only, nor can its influence on Hogan's writing be analyzed in a purely structural manner. Rather, readers must pay attention to how Hogan incorporates the oral tradition's function as both an expression of individual creativity and communal spirituality in her writing as she, as a writer, turns outward from her own healing to projects focused on the community.

In Hogan's early poetry, her audience is privileged to eavesdrop on her reflections, to overhear her inner dialogue. With the maturation of her narrative voice, she speaks to her audience directly. For example, she instructs us to shake up our lives in "Morning with Broken Window," from *Savings:* "So rip your gray dress at the seams, / tear things apart." She urges us to renew ourselves and shed our lethargy through action. Because she believes poetry can effect change, Hogan takes on the responsibility of maintaining, restoring, and creating values in her work that would lead to the survival of indigenous peoples and the ecological network that supports them. Like the storyteller of the oral tradition, Hogan is present to her readers in these

writings, looking them in the eye, as it were, so they will listen.

The oral tradition that Hogan draws on often uses storytelling as a remedial response for the ills of the community. A particular story can be told to remind its listeners of the morals that should guide them or, even more pointedly, can be directed at someone who has broken with the traditions that hold the community together with the intent of bringing that person back within the community's borders. Although these stories change over time as the community changes, they preserve the values that serve as a constant. Such stories, while not necessarily "true," frequently contain the "truth" of how the community should live.

Hogan's poetry and fiction of this period frequently address this notion of truth. For example, she is concerned that stories of Native American people do not rely on romanticized notions of "Indians"—living in tepees or hunting with bows and arrows—but include things that matter to the contemporary Native American community. In the introduction to her short story "Crow," in *That Horse* she complains that "there are never enough stories about who we are now." Rejecting the Indian of American myth, she writes in "Crow" about "real life," about pickup trucks, bumper stickers that read Pilgrim Go Home, and the loneliness of the elderly. The truth Hogan depicts in this particular short story is the reality of rural poverty, its dignified transformation through the humor and love of an Indian elder, and the importance for the young people of this story of not neglecting the elder or what she can teach them. The truth of a Native American identity, according to Hogan, has little to do with traditional regalia but everything to do with traditional values.

Her poetry of this period is similarly concerned with notions of the truth. In "Neighbors," from *Savings,* she warns her readers, "This is the truth, not just a poem." Poetry, like fiction, bears the responsibility of representing the reality of Native American life, of letting Hogan's readers discover the power of the values of Native American culture. It is important to remember that for Hogan words themselves have the power to heal, words themselves are the vehicle of revelation. Later in the same poem she reminds her readers: "This is a poem and not just the truth." Like the listeners of the oral tradition, Hogan's audience cannot simply dissect her work for a message but must participate in the language. She wants her readers to pay attention to the affective power of poetic language. For Hogan, the images themselves can enact the transformations that lead her readers to an understanding of the truth.

This notion of the power of poetry to change its audience connects Hogan strongly to the spiritual aspect of the Native American oral tradition. Hogan writes in "The Two Lives": "Poetry is a large spiritual undertaking. So are stories, in the telling and the listening. So is being a mother and a caretaker of animals and trees." The oral tradition does not clearly distinguish between what is sacred and what is ordinary, allowing stories to move fluidly in and out of both realms. Poetry, following in this tradition, can function as prayer, and writing can become a spiritual undertaking. A prayer of thanksgiving appears in "Elk Song," also in *Savings:*

> We give thanks
> to deer, otter,
> the great fish
> and birds that fly over
> and are our bones and skin.

Hogan acknowledges, in this poem-prayer, the interconnections between the human and animal communities, enfleshing her gratitude in the image of the last line. Reading the poem grants her audience membership in this community united by the word "we." Hogan's readers are included in her prayer and are permitted to merge with the plurality of her narrative voice.

Emerging in this poetry is a stronger sense of a communal narrative voice: Hogan's autobiographical "I" more and more often becomes "we" in the poems collected in *Savings.* While the boundaries of this communal voice are often expansive enough to include her readers, Hogan's confirmation of her Native American identity in her earlier work makes it clear that "we" refers specifically to her Chickasaw people. The narrator of her short story "Making Do" reveals that as Chickasaws "We make art out of our loss." Yet any reader who has experienced loss can participate in Hogan's work.

This "we" remembers pain. In "What I Think," Hogan observes that "our lives break / like windows from a flying stone." "We" also speaks defiantly in "Those Who Thunder" to those who would break its spirit, saying that "we won't put up with hard words and low wages / one more day." Finally, her communal narrative voice calls on endurance in "The Lost Girls": "We go on / or we don't." Connecting with her tribal identity allows Hogan to become more than herself. She is able to find strength by sharing her heritage of loss, defiance, and endurance in her poetry and can deal with subjects that are too difficult to speak about when carried alone.

Hogan's writing also serves the community by enjoying the importance of celebration, passion, and play. As she tells Smith: "These [communal] responsibilities shouldn't be taken so seriously by writers, by women, as to take away passion, and joy, and play." The Native American oral tradition, burdened as it is with the solemn task of preserving the community, is often full of earthy humor and an appreciation for the physical side of human life. The balance of both speaking the truth and partaking in play is also evident in Hogan's work. In the same poem that addresses the value of endurance, "The Lost Girls," her narrative "I" returns to playfully remark: "I'm going to laugh and weep tonight, / quit all my jobs and I mean it this time.'' Jubilant and high-spirited, Hogan's narrative voice attests to the value of balancing high moral purpose with no moral purpose. Poetry shadowed by a monotone of moral lessons would quickly lose its vitality. Wisely, Hogan preserves her poetics of challenge and change by allowing her readers to experience a full range of emotion.

In her novel *Mean Spirit,* which is something of a culmination of this period in her work, humor leavens the often difficult histories and environmental concerns that permeate the text. Ona Neck, a relatively insignificant character in terms of the plot, provides many humorous asides, making the enjoyment of human foolishness as much a part of living as love and tragedy. In the face of murder and conspiracy, Ona is asked to help watch the sacred fire of the Indian people; annoyed at being bothered, she grumbles, ''Everyone's always getting killed.'' Ona's presence in the novel serves as a reminder that sustaining the moral imperative of the communal tradition cannot come at the cost of the humanity of that community in all its needs, as small as they may seem. Speaking of *Mean Spirit* to the *Missouri Review,* Hogan observes: ''The humor was always there also, because even in desperate situations people are human. They still do funny things, and they still have their obsessions and habits.'' For Hogan, there is no contradiction in writing of mirth and tragedy on the same page— the full dimensions of her characters come from the intersection of comic and solemn elements, reflecting the mixed boundaries of these qualities in human experience.

Hogan frequently crosses boundaries in her writing. The divisions between genres seem almost permeable in her work because she feels that the task of her writing is not to be a poet or a novelist, but to tell needed stories. She tells the *Missouri Review:*

> If you feel like the material you're working with really has to be told, that people's survival and wholeness somehow depends on it, then you're committed to getting the material out in whatever form it will be. If you're committed to being a ''poet,'' whatever that is, or a ''fiction writer,'' then you're trying to find material that you can pull into your category.

Her shift from writing poetry to writing fiction in this middle stage is one such crossing. Hogan found her way to fiction not only through her study of the oral tradition but also through drama; her play, ''A Piece of Moon,'' won the Five Civilized Tribes Museum Playwright Award in 1980. Although it was never published, it was produced in Oklahoma in 1981. Her experience in writing the play allowed her to think about character in a different way than poetry did and allowed her to tell different stories. In her fiction, her narrative voice adopts concerns beyond the issues of her identity, looking at what history asks of her and what the communities of which she is a member need.

Hogan's fiction includes shifts across literary genres as well, blurring the edges of myth and truth, oral tradition and contemporary fiction. She tells Schöler, ''Fiction may be a dance along the razor's edge of paradox.'' Paradox creates the tension that pulls at fiction, giving it energy and momentum. The tension that propels *Mean Spirit* is produced by her combination of a murder-mystery plot with the history of the Oklahoma oil and land scandals committed against the Osage tribe in the 1920s. Scattering bodies and clues throughout the novel, Hogan evokes the page-turning appeal of the popular whodunit, but with this difference: she mixes a radical interpretation of a previously silenced history with the mystery. She studied the FBI files on this scandalous period of United States history and included many of the events, personalities, and situations recorded there.

But Hogan does not merely recite a history of greed and violence in *Mean Spirit.* Fact rubs against imagination, producing yet another shift across genre, as she wraps the events of the novel in images most akin to those found in the magic realism of late-twentieth-century Latin American writers. The novel opens with the image of dawn coming to the Osage townspeople who are sleeping outside to avoid the heat of the summer, where "four-posters rested in cornfields that were lying fallow." The startling displacement of the everyday found in this opening scene reminds Hogan's readers to be awake to the extraordinary, to put aside their understanding of history and listen to her story in order to hear history retold. (Hogan did receive some criticism for her imaginative retelling of history, in part because the ownership of such history can be a sensitive issue with Native American people. There were those who felt that as a Chickasaw, Hogan should not have told Osage history. Other Native American writers have been similarly criticized about ownership issues, more often because they included in their work aspects of oral tradition that some tribal members felt belonged only to the tribe. So often in the past, ethnologists "stole" stories without fully understanding how to handle the sacred materials. Native American writers who give away their people's stories are sometimes seen as betraying the trust of their people. Unlike the oral tradition, the history Hogan tells in *Mean Spirit* reached into the lives of many non-Osage people as well, including her own Chickasaw ancestors.)

The transformation of a narrative through its retelling is integral to the oral tradition, in which stories bend and shift with each storyteller and audience, yet retain qualities of each previous retelling. The authorship of the stories of the oral tradition is communal and the narrative voice of *Mean Spirit* participates in this sense of communality. The narrative is told from multiple consciousnesses and diverse perspectives, revealing the layers of the history that concern Hogan. She incorporates the oral voice of historical narratives in order to shift the emphasis of this history to meet the needs of the present audience. She adds her own voice to an already multivoiced history.

It is appropriate that *Mean Spirit* is told communally because it is a story very much about community, about caring for community. Hogan expands the conversation she began with the animal, plant, and mineral worlds in her poetry. There is no hierarchy of value in this community, only a sense of the irreplaceable value of each being to each other being. She makes it clear that she shares the Native American sense of community, whose borders include not only family and tribe but also animal- and plant-people as well as the very land on which they live.

The Oklahoma land that is so important to her identity functions almost as a character in *Mean Spirit*, receiving care and abuse and giving in kind. Like other Native American people, Hogan feels that she is the land and the land is she; she tells Bruchac: "I think my umbilical cord is buried there [in Oklahoma]. Everything there, the land, is the oldest part of me and the wisest. The part that can survive." The Oklahoma land teaches the reader, in particular, about the value of patience and endurance and about the vast repercussions of a little nurturing or abuse. What Hogan wants her readers to learn from the "deep and dreaming voice of the land" in *Mean Spirit* is the tremendous responsibility we have of caretaking the earth.

Caretaking is a major theme of *Mean Spirit*, in more ways than one. Hogan's main characters, Belle Graycloud and Michael Horse, are primarily caretakers; Belle's tasks are oriented toward caring for life in the present, while Horse's work focuses more on the abstract issues of caring for the past and the future. Hogan tells Smith: "I consider caretaking the basic work of living on earth." Her work as a wildlife rehabilitation volunteer has been an important outlet for Hogan's sense of responsibility as a caretaker, but her writing permits her to act as a caretaker as well.

Mean Spirit solidifies Hogan's notion that writing is a form of caretaking, because she reaches out to her community of readers in much the same way that Belle and Horse care for the novel's community.

Belle Graycloud's caretaking revolves primarily around her family and her neighbors, but also includes the plant and animal communities that surround her; much of the novel takes place around her kitchen table, where she provides food, talk, and coffee for her large family and anyone else who passes through her home. When her neighbor Grace Blanket is murdered, Belle takes in Grace's daughter, Nola, to live as part of her family. When another neighbor, Jim Josh, complains about his chronically sore feet, Belle packs up her herbs and pays him a visit. Belle extends this comfort and protection beyond her human family. As a beekeeper, she understands the delicate balance caretaking requires, nurturing her hives in exchange for the honey they provide, sharing with the bees a symbiotic relationship. In her cornfield, she feeds sprouting corn plants with her prayers. Her presence is a nurturing one and she understands the power within each living thing.

Like Belle, Michael Horse also functions as a caretaker, but his duties are somewhat more abstract. Informed by his dreams of prophesy, he is able to foresee and forewarn his neighbors of dangers. He can predict the weather and divine water underground; these gifts are part of the continual conversation he engages in with his environment, which is interrupted when the subterranean current of oil is brought to the surface. The prospecting of oil gives rise to conflicts between the Anglo and Indian communities and disrupts the voice of the land, causing Horse to lose his ability to dream and prophesy. Throughout the novel, he is plagued by the failure of these gifts; however, Horse never fails in his duty as the keeper of the tribal fire.

Like Belle and Horse, Hogan uses her novel to do some caretaking of her own. Speaking to Miller about her intended audience, she observes: "I always try to write what would have integrity for the people, and also I don't want to exclude anybody, to not allow access to what I'm working on. I don't want anybody to be damaged or hurt by it." By sharing with her readers the values that she acquired from her Chickasaw grandparents who taught her to care for the planet, she expands the borders of her Native community and provides her readers with the means of preserving the future of the human world.

Hogan has often reiterated her feelings about the importance of caretaking in her writing and interviews; she tells Laura Coltelli: "If you believe that the earth, and all living things, and all stones are sacred, your responsibility really is to protect those things. I do believe that's our duty, to be custodians of the planet." Hogan's vision of the human role in and responsibility toward the rest of the planet challenges her readers to imagine an environmental ethic of caretaking. A world bereft of such values is a very grim one, as *Mean Spirit* demonstrates. Without the caretaking of Belle Graycloud and Michael Horse, *Mean Spirit* would be a painful novel; their humane acts offset, to some degree, the relentless violence and oil-hungry greed that dominate much of the text.

Like much of Hogan's poetry, *Mean Spirit* belongs to a tradition different from that of most contemporary fiction. Her lack of moral ambiguity situates this novel in the tradition of the American political novel of the 1930s, yet her values clearly belong to the Native American community. She confirms this moral clarity in her interview with Schöler:

From the time I was a child, I knew that some things are always wrong, and some things are always right. If you caretake life, and pay close attention to your duty to take care of the planet and of one another, it's always right. If you kill animals, are cruel, injure others, or create bombs, it's always wrong. There are very few things that are clear-cut in life, but those things have no crazy edges.

While there may be room for paradox in fiction, the values that transcend fiction are, for Hogan, perfectly clear.

These values speak to Hogan's hope for the future; in spite of the cruelty and destruction that she documents in *Mean Spirit,* the novel has a strong sense of generational survival. The orphaned and pregnant Nola, after enduring a disastrous teenage marriage, returns to the safety of her mother's former home with the "Hill people." They are a branch of the Osage tribe who, according to Hogan's retelling, eschewed modern convenience and government intervention and held fast to the traditional ways of the tribe, sheltering themselves from the modern world by concealing themselves in the hills. At the novel's end, Nola gives birth to her baby, an emblem of the future, in the security of the Hill community, an emblem of the past. The future has a chance of survival, Hogan indicates, when it is safeguarded by the past.

Hogan's view of the symbiosis of the past and the future is tied to her sense of history and the importance of making it come alive in the present. *Mean Spirit* does just that, cataloging the broken bodies and broken promises of a painful era in Native American history as well as documenting real—not romanticized—Native American life in the 1920s. The murders and swindles endured by the Oklahoma Indians that Hogan culled from the FBI files are balanced with her memories of family stories from that time. She tells Miller that these stories were a "part of my own family history, . . . so they were really a part of my life." Hogan draws on these memories to show Native American life as an amalgamation of the traditional ways of the Native Americans with those of their Anglo neighbors. Cars, dance marathons, and stylish hats share the page with traditional values that emphasize the importance of hospital-ity, communal ownership, and non-Christian spirituality. For the Native American community of the novel, the traditional past merges with the present, changed yet intact.

History lives in *Mean Spirit* in order to give the next generation a chance of survival. Hogan notes, to the *Missouri Review,* that she sees her "everyday life in a historical context. We are living in the midst of history; it's important that somebody keeps records." Keeping records preserves the histories that enliven the future. In her poem "Two of Hearts," from *Savings,* she writes: "But I never forget / to recite history." Only when history is forgotten, untold, or repressed will the future be threatened.

By sharing Native American histories with her non–Native American readers in *Mean Spirit,* Hogan expands the borders of community and begins to approach the more global perspective found in her later writing. Her caretaking work as a writer evolves into serving the global community. She tells Smith:

> I ask myself how best to let my words serve. I know that part of that is to take a global perspective, because I see what's happening in the world, and others see, and our combined voices are a chorus, a movement toward life. They are a protest against human-imposed suffering.

While Hogan has been concerned with speaking out against suffering since her earliest poetry, in her collection of poetry *The Book of Medicines,* her second novel, *Solar Storms,* and her collection of natural history essays in *Dwellings,* she no longer limits the borders of her commitment "toward life" to her own life, her family, or the Native American community. However, her narrative voice remains personal in the three texts; dealing with abstract issues like justice and goodness does not dilute the power of her autobiographical presence or the immediacy of her narrative voice.

Hogan's global perspective is often a historical one; she tells forgotten histories in order to protect the future. In "The Two Lives" she writes: "Telling our lives is important, for those who come after us, for those who will see our experience as part of their own historical struggle. I think of my work as part of the history of our tribe and as part of the history of colonization everywhere." This history is often a harsh one, documenting losses and struggle more often than victory and peace. Her poem "Return: Buffalo," in *The Book of Medicines,* speaks to

> the people I have loved
> who fell
> into the straight, unhealed
> line of history.

Imagined as an unyielding blade, this history eviscerates the citizens of the present community because it has been silenced. In Hogan's poetics, healing comes from participating in imaginative language; the community can be healed by hearing its story.

However, to tell history is to somehow relive it, in all its pain and suffering. The paradox of this suffering is the theme of Hogan's first section of *The Book of Medicines,* a long poem entitled "The History of Red." Red is the color of birth, violence, death, and rebirth, a cycle of hope and struggle in which everyone must find their place in order to survive:

> We are all burning
> red, inseparable fires
> the living have crawled
> and climbed through
> in order to live
> so nothing will be left
> for death at the end.

Only when individual struggle, pain, and loss are placed in the context of history, connected to the anguished lives of others, and transformed into "inseparable fires" is death defeated. Then the future is created, umbilically connected to a past that is not isolated and forgotten but alive in the present.

Hogan entitles the second part of *The Book of Medicines* "Hunger"; and it chronicles a history of lack and desire shared by Native and non-Native peoples alike. Concerned with more than the material hungers that are so often the lot of Native American peoples in contemporary culture, she addresses the vast spiritual emptiness of the dominant culture and the consequent parasitical nature of its hunger. She explains to Miller how burdensome the expectations of the non-Indian audience can be:

> They are so unreasonable, they're so needy in what they want from an Indian person. Some are so uncomfortable with their need that it's impossible for them to be full of their own lives. A lot of people have needs that go so deep there's nothing that can ever fill them, it's like a bottomless well.

Destructive and limitless, this form of human need perpetuates its own emptiness. Hogan's imagery in this volume looks at the damage caused by this "bottomless" hunger and refers to several of the very real issues of crisis in the modern world: nuclear destruction, ecological disaster, and the losses of aboriginal peoples and cultures. As with much of her earlier work, there are no moral ambiguities in this volume in terms of the way one should respond to human pain; Hogan's vision consistently attempts to balance justice with compassion. However, the boundary between victim and victimizer is not always so clear, since everyone, in Hogan's vision, endures suffering.

In Hogan's poetic retelling of history, hunger is unleashed on the world with the first ships of colonization. In the title poem,

> Hunger crosses oceans.
> It loses its milk teeth.
> It sits on the ship and cries.

Hogan personifies hunger as a slave child taken in the Middle Passage (the transport of slavery from Africa to the Americas), an emblem of suffering and want. Both victim and victimizer mature in this cycle of endless need and unquenchable desire. Such desire creates powerlessness, which Hogan captures mercilessly in "Harvesters of Night and Water." The sexuality of the image of

> tiny men,
> with impotent nets
> limp as poverty

underscores how the desire for mastery becomes the very means by which those with power become undone. Hunger cuts us off from history, turns us against nature, and isolates us from each other. In "Bear," Hogan looks with irony at how the fear that hunger creates can misguide us when she says,

> We are safe
> from the bear
> and we have each other,
> we have each other to fear.

In this collection of poetry, Hogan views the values of the dominant culture in an unforgiving light.

More clearly than in her earlier work, Hogan is at pains to reject these values in *The Book of Medicines*. In the poem "Mountain Lion," she writes: "Two worlds cannot live / inside a single vision." At this stage of her development as a writer, Hogan has unequivocally chosen Native American values. Her need to choose the world of her Chickasaw grandparents coincides with her success as a poet, novelist, and critic that found her a home in academia—she has taught at the University of Colorado since 1987. Perhaps this position of privilege made choosing the traditional values of her Native American heritage an obvious one, a powerful way of fortifying herself against subtle co-optation by the values of the dominant culture and maintaining the moral purpose in her work.

However, Hogan has not entirely rejected the dominant culture from which the "white hand" in her pocket was born. Rather, she more specifically grounds herself in her traditional values in order to reach across the cultural divide. In "Crossings," she speaks of "a place at the center of the earth / where one ocean dissolves inside the other"—a place where difference can merge. The image of this still "center of the earth" suggests that the meeting ground for difference is in a spiritual or mythical dimension. Similarly, the notion of two oceans suggests that the differences between cultures are fluid and need not confront each other with sharp edges. What both cultures need, according to Hogan, is healing.

Healing is what Hogan offers in the third part of this volume of poetry, called, like the book's title, "The Book of Medicines"; she extends healing to the Native American cultures, who have forgotten their traditional wisdom, and to the dominant culture, which never learned the lessons of Native American culture. Healing comes with connection and communion—to each other and every aspect of the world—and with, as she says in "Carry," "something stronger, / older, deeper." With healing, Hogan assures her readers, comes the possibility of resurrection and the promise for the future.

Literature, Hogan tells the *Missouri Review,* is "a descent into something older, deeper and more powerful than our everyday being or reality." Literature offers the possibility of finding that mythic location of merging and emergence, the "center of the earth" that she speaks of in "Crossings." Thus, the healing that Hogan holds out to her readers is not merely a metaphor, but, she believes, comes to them through the very act of reading, of engaging in poetic language. In "Who Puts Together," she explains how the poet traditionally serves the community as a healer: "A singer, writer, or healer is able to unite the internal with the external. . . . The words of prose or poetry function like an opening of the self into the universe and the reciprocal funneling of the universe into the self." Healing through poetry happens when boundaries blur, when the border guards leave their posts and worlds of inner and outer, self and other, meet and merge. This imagery is apparent in the early poetry as well. In "Wall Songs," from *Seeing through the Sun*, Hogan imagines this blurring of boundaries:

> Let them [walls] be
> made of the mysteries further in
> in the heart, joined with the lives of all,
> all bridges of flesh,
> all singing,
> all covering the wounded land
> showing again, again
> that boundaries are all lies.

With "The Book of Medicines," this hope is far less tentative; she is more certain of the necessity of making those wounding divisions whole.

In order to create wholeness, Hogan draws on the healing traditions of her Native American ancestry. She has often commented on the powerful presence of her father's parents in her life and the importance of her relationship with her grandmother. In *Calling Myself Home*, she writes, in "Heritage," of her grandmother's knowledge of tobacco medicine, which, she said, "would purge your body of poisons." Hogan calls on her vital connection with her grandmother again in "The Book of Medicines," imagining her as one of a chorus of traditional singers in "The Grandmother Songs." Rather than making a single body whole, however, these grandmothers remake the world:

> The grandmothers
> keep following the creation
> that opens before them
> as they sing.

The past world sings the future world into existence. Hogan's connection to her past via her grandmother permits her to remake the world with her poetic acts, her song.

Just as communion with the past will make the future a hopeful possibility, so will communion with the natural world. Hogan asks her readers, in "The Bricks," to imagine this world as conscious and alive, to listen to

> a forest dreaming
> inside every wall,
> wanting to send out
> a passionate tendril of life.

Again, Hogan wants to break boundaries and obscure borders: the dead wall of bricks contains its own passionate reunion with what is "stronger, deeper, older." She poetically calls on the past of the old forest and the future of the seed to dissolve all divisions.

Hogan asks her readers to listen to the voice of the living planet in order finally to obtain communion with themselves, with their own "center of the earth." This voice comes not only from the outside but also from within. In "Partings," the earth gives Hogan this message: "Believe the medicine of your own hand." Hogan suggests that her readers can heal themselves; even more, the power they contain can bring healing to others as well.

As the medicine that came from Hogan's hand, the poetry in this volume is potent. Much denser than her earlier poetry, the poetry in *The Book of Medicines* coils image around image. While the first two sections build a vocabulary of the woundedness of the world through nuclear devastation, environmental rape, and other acts of human cruelty, the final section transforms these images of Hiroshima, the slaughter of whales, and the abuse of children into hope. The suggestiveness of the single word titles, like "Drum," gives us a boundary-less sense of language as the meanings of words slide evocatively through memory; ''drum'' is the pulse of the earth, of the human heart, and the rhythm of the sacred songs of oral tradition. By wrapping her poetry around remembered goodness and calling on the simple acts of nurture from traditional ways of her Chickasaw ancestors, Hogan puts her medicine to work.

Hogan's second novel, *Solar Storms,* takes as its theme the possibilities of healing with the medicine of one's own hand. Angel Jensen, the novel's protagonist and its central consciousness, discovers this power within herself. She returns to the far north territory of her childhood at the age of seventeen, after having been horribly scarred and abused by her mother, then moved from one foster home to the next. Desperately in need of healing, Angel chooses to return, she says, to the ''watery places in order to unravel my mind and set straight what I had lost.'' She comes to Adam's Rib, a spit of land in the Boundary Waters between Canada and Minnesota, in search of her great-grandmother Agnes, her great-great-grandmother Dora Rouge, and Bush, the Chickasaw woman who adopted Angel's mother and raised Angel when she was a young girl.

Like so much of Hogan's writing, *Solar Storms* is not merely fiction but the truth, a retelling of history. Speaking to the *Missouri Review* about the connection between history and fiction, Hogan observes: ''Fiction is a vertical descent; it's a drop into an event or into history or into the depths of some kind of meaning in order to understand humans, and to somehow decipher what history speaks, the story beneath the story.'' Angel's search for her own identity through and against the mother who abused and abandoned her is connected to the struggle of the Cree people for control of their lives and land. Hogan frequently brings these inner and outer worlds together in her writings; as she tells Bruchac: ''For me . . . the spiritual and the political are very united.'' In her second novel, she sets Angel's personal, spiritual journey against a backdrop of corporate greed and government betrayal, retelling the little-known history of the damming of the Boundary Waters for a hydroelectric power plant in the 1970s.

Just as Angel is a victim of her own history of abuse, as her mother was, as her grandmother was, this abuse is not random and psychotic, as Hogan writes it, but the direct result of a history of poverty and persecution endured by indigenous people. Angel wants to retrieve her past, to know who she is and where she came from. She wants to read the scars on her face like a map to the secret of her identity. But, she tells us, ''I didn't know then that what I really wanted none of us would ever have. I wanted an unbroken line between me and the past. I wanted not to be fragments and pieces left behind by fur traders, soldiers, priests and schools.'' Angel discovers, in the course of the novel, that her scars will never disappear, but that she will become her true self and a whole woman in spite of her brokenness. Seeing the remnants of her people pulling humanity from their fragmented lives teaches her that she can do without that ''unbroken line.''

Angel's self-discovery occurs on the journey north she takes with her family of women to protest the building of the dam. She finds comfort in the cheerful frailty of Dora Rouge, in the earthy mysticism of Agnes, in the quiet strength of Bush, who had tried so hard to protect Angel from her own mother. As they travel north together by foot and canoe, Angel is physically and emotionally challenged by the wildness of the interior of the Boundary Waters. But, she muses, ''never . . . was life so good, were women more wonderful.'' Hogan tells a women's story of self-reliance forged in the company of other women, and Angel, a troubled teenager at the novel's beginning, emerges a resourceful and intelligent young woman when they reach their destination.

Angel's maturation in the wilderness takes place because the deep waters and forests of this landscape show her that the straight lines she longs for, the clarity she desires in her life, have no antecedent in the wild. She gives herself over to the "spell of the wilderness." With new eyes, she sees that in the wilderness, "everything merged and united. There were no sharp distinctions left between darkness and light." Earlier in the novel, Angel reflects on the power of liminality and how the loss of boundaries could lead to a vision of the truth; she realizes that life with her newfound family has given her a new kind of knowledge: "I began to form a kind of knowing at Adam's Rib. I began to feel that if we had no separate words for inside and out and there were no boundaries between them, no walls, no skin, you would see me." Like so much of Hogan's previous writing, *Solar Storms* asks readers to reflect on the power of liminality and the potential this in-between world has for breaking down walls and healing the larger world with its demands for definition and order.

Angel herself becomes an agent of healing, within her own family and in the larger community as well. She is able to face her mother and forgive her as her mother lies dying. She enacts that forgiveness by adopting and loving her little half-sister, an infant who had begun the same cycle of abuse that Angel endured but who is saved by the intervention of their mother's death. Like the baby in Nola's arms at the end of *Mean Spirit,* this child, little Aurora, represents the future, the new day for which she is named.

As with much of her previous work, Hogan tells us through Angel's reassuring narrative voice that it is not futile to place hope in the future, in spite of the losses suffered. And *Solar Storms* documents those losses, too: Agnes dies on the journey north; Tulik and the other Native peoples who are their relations and friends, facing the apex of the struggle over the land, are violently persecuted for their defense of their homeland; and the land is devastated by the calculations and miscalculations of those who attempt to gain control of the waters. But the losses are not the whole story; Angel, Bush, and Dora Rouge contribute to an indigenous people's struggle that succeeds in forestalling the building of the power plant. Angel recounts at the novel's conclusion:

> Our belated victory was the end of something. That one fracture was healed, one crack mended, one piece back in place. Yes, the pieces were infinite and worn as broken pots, and our human pain was deep, but we'd thrown an anchor into the future and followed the rope to the end of it.

While Angel never finds all the missing pieces of her life in the space of the novel, her calm, reflective narrative voice, which looks back on these events from some centered place in the present, assures Hogan's readers that, indeed, the future is worth securing.

Solar Storms fits Hogan's ever-widening trajectory of concern, recovering the history of struggle of the Cree people in the 1970s and placing that struggle in the global perspective of the need to protect and care for the planet. Perhaps the farthest reaching of these later, globally conceived works is her collection of natural history essays, entitled *Dwellings.* In these essays, Hogan writes a literature of values that addresses the sacredness of the planet and the consciousness of all creation. Yet she does not pontificate in these works; instead, she reflects, with some humility, on her varied experiences with the extraordinary and commonplace in the natural world.

As in much of Hogan's earlier work, she does not hedge about her values here; again, some things are always right, some things always wrong. This clarity of values does not make for misleading oversimplification, as is often the case. In fact, what fascinates Hogan is the paradox of the human relation to the world that has eluded human control. She observes in "Waking Up the Rake" that "we are the embodiment of a paradox. We are the wounders and we are the healers.'' Unlike so many environmental preachers, she finds herself as culpable as the rest of humanity in the damaging of the planet.

But Hogan wants to move beyond that paradox, not to be caught in an intellectual whirlpool of inactivity. Her words reflect on the power of beauty and mystery to move humanity beyond what it already believes. In her essay ''The Feathers,'' she writes about being touched by ''sacred reason, different from ordinary reason, that is linked to forces of nature.'' Such reason might be called instinct in animals or intuition in humans, but Hogan connects it to the ability to let go of human limitations in order to experience that powerful liminality she has written about so often, a liminality that moves her onto the plane of the sacred in the traditional spirituality of her Native American heritage.

If we are able to understand ourselves and our place in the natural world differently, Hogan suggests, then we may be able to act differently as well. Hogan's spirituality, as she represents it in these essays, calls for movement and change, which demand action and require work. In her essay ''Waking Up the Rake,'' she reflects on work as prayer: ''Work is the country of hands, and they want to live there in the dailiness of it, the repetition that is time's language of prayer, a common tongue.'' It is her work in raking the cages of eagles and owls at the wildlife rehabilitation clinic that she refers to specifically here, but Hogan is also asking her readers to transform the rhythms of their bodies to the dance of healing.

In an unassuming way, the essays in *Dwellings* compose a call to action, to protest environmental devastation and heal the planet as a way of ensuring the future. In insisting on the need we have for the natural world and waking us up to this need, Hogan follows a long line of American nature writers, from Henry David Thoreau to Barry Lopez. Like Thoreau, she has an essay entitled ''Walking.'' In his essay, Thoreau calls on his mid-nineteenth-century readers to value wildness as a virtue, both the wildness of the forest and that of the human spirit. Hogan transforms Thoreau's wildness into that sense of ''older, stronger, deeper'' that she has written of previously: ''Walking, I am listening to a deeper way. Suddenly all my ancestors are behind me. Be still, they say. Watch and listen. You are the result of the love of thousands.'' While Thoreau speaks of removal and spiritual distance from a culture that will confine the spirit, Hogan uses her own sense of the past to reflect on the liberation made possible by her connection to a realm of history and love.

It is fruitful to consider Hogan's body of work in this light: transforming the traditions of the dominant culture that inform her work with traditions of her own. Keeping alive the intent of the oral traditions of her Chickasaw grandparents in her work, she changes what poetry can do, what a novel can do, and simultaneously asks her audience to change as well. As the boundaries of Hogan's healing circle expand from self, to her family and Native American community, to the global community, she finally is also writing for the future, for the healing of the boundaries between human culture and the natural world. From her poetry of identity to her novels of transformative history, from the individualism of autobiography to communally conceived oral tradition, Hogan's work asks readers to reconsider the perspective from which they view the world and to reexamine their relationship to it and to each other.

Hogan's position as a mixed-blood writer places her in a position between worlds and gives her the power to see beyond the boundaries that divide us. Sharing Hogan's perspective are some of her favorite creatures, bats. What she has to say about bats as emblems of liminality gives us insight into what power she ascribes to her own liminal being. In *Mean Spirit,* she writes of ''the double world of bats with their whistling songs and their lives in the cool and deep darkness.'' Like the bats, mixed bloods perceive the world differently, seeing double. In *Dwellings,* she writes that bats ''live in double worlds of many kinds'' and that they ''are intermediaries between our world and the next.'' Hogan is similarly positioned, using her writing to travel between our world and not the afterlife, but the future. Her special vision permits her to imagine a world without boundaries and limits, and she shares this possibility with her readers.

Selected Bibliography

WORKS OF LINDA HOGAN

NOVELS
Mean Spirit. New York: Atheneum, 1990.
Solar Storms. New York: Scribners, 1995.

SHORT STORIES
''New Shoes.'' In *Earth Power Coming: Short Fiction in Native American Literature.* Edited by Simon Ortiz. Tsaile, Ariz.: Navajo Community College Press, 1983. Pp. 3–20.
''Meeting.'' In *The Stories We Hold Secret: Tales of Women's Spiritual Development.* Edited by Carol Bruchac, Linda Hogan, and Judith McDaniel. Greenfield Center, N.Y.: Greenfield Review Press, 1985. Pp. 279–283.
That Horse. Acoma Pueblo: Pueblo of Acoma Press, 1985.
''Making Do.'' In *Spider Woman's Granddaughters: Traditional Tales and Contemporary Writing by Native American Women.* Edited by Paula Gunn Allen. Boston: Beacon, 1989.
''Aunt Moon's Young Man.'' In *Talking Leaves: Contemporary Native American Short Stories.* Edited by Craig Leslie. New York: Laurel, 1991. Pp. 147–169.

POETRY
Calling Myself Home. Greenfield Center, N.Y.: Greenfield Review Press, 1978.

Daughters, I Love You. Denver: Laretto Heights College Research Center on Women, 1981.
''The Diary of Amanda McFadden.'' In *That's What She Said: Contemporary Poetry and Fiction by Native American Women.* Edited by Rayna Green. Bloomington: Indiana University Press, 1984.
Eclipse. Los Angeles: American Indian Studies Center (UCLA), 1983.
Seeing through the Sun. Amherst: University of Massachusetts Press, 1985.
Savings. Minneapolis: Coffee House Press, 1988.
The Book of Medicines. Minneapolis: Coffee House Press, 1993.

COLLECTED WORKS
Red Clay: Poems and Stories. Greenfield Center, N.Y.: Greenfield Review Press, 1991. Reissued poems from *Calling Myself Home* and stories from *That Horse.*

ESSAYS AND CRITICISM
''Who Puts Together.'' In *Studies in American Indian Literature.* Edited by Paula Gunn Allen. New York: Modern Language Association, 1983.
''Women: Doing and Being.'' In *Stories We Hold Secret: Tales of Women's Spiritual Development.* Edited by Carol Bruchac, Linda Hogan, and Judith McDaniel. Greenfield Center, N.Y.: Greenfield Review Press, 1986. Pp. ix–xvi.
''The Two Lives.'' In *I Tell You Now: Autobiographical Essays by Native American Writers.* Edited by Brian Swann and Arnold Krupat. Lincoln: University of Nebraska Press, 1987. Pp. 231–249.
Dwellings: A Spiritual History of the Living World. New York: Norton, 1995.

CRITICAL STUDIES

Ackerberg, Peggy Maddux. ''Breaking Boundaries: Writing Past Gender, Genre, and Genocide in Linda Hogan.'' *Studies in American Indian Literatures,* 6:7–14 (Fall 1994).
Allen, Paula Gunn. *The Sacred Hoop: Recovering the Feminine in American Indian Traditions.* Boston: Beacon Press, 1986.
Bell, Betty Louise. ''Linda Hogan's Lessons in Making-Do.'' *Studies in American Indian Literatures,* 6:3–6 (Fall 1994).

Blair, Elizabeth. "The Politics of Place in Linda Hogan's *Mean Spirit.*" *Studies in American Indian Literatures,* 6:15–22 (Fall 1994).

Carew-Miller, Anna. "Caretaking and the Work of the Text in Linda Hogan's *Mean Spirit.*" *Studies in American Indian Literatures,* 6:37–48 (Fall 1994).

Casteel, Alix. "Dark Wealth in Linda Hogan's *Mean Spirit.*" *Studies in American Indian Literatures,* 6:49–68 (Fall 1994).

Lincoln, Kenneth. *Indi'n Humor: Bicultural Play in Native America.* New York: Oxford University Press, 1993.

Musher, Andrea. "Showdown at Sorrow Cave: Bat Medicine and the Spirit of Resistance in *Mean Spirit.*" *Studies in American Indian Literatures,* 6:23–36 (Fall 1994).

Owens, Louis. *Other Destinies: Understanding the American Indian Novel.* Norman: University of Oklahoma Press, 1992.

INTERVIEWS

Bruchac, Joseph. "To Take Care of Life." In his *Survival This Way: Interviews with American Indian Poets.* Tucson: Sun Tracks and the University of Arizona Press, 1987. Pp. 119–133.

Coltelli, Laura. "Linda Hogan." In her *Winged Words: American Indian Writers Speak.* Lincoln: University of Nebraska Press, 1990. Pp. 71–86.

"Everything Has a Spirit." (video recording). Denver: Front Range Educational Media, 1993.

"Interview with Linda Hogan." *Missouri Review,* 17, no. 2:109–134 (1994).

Miller, Carol. "The Story Is Brimming Around: An Interview with Linda Hogan." *Studies in American Indian Literatures,* 2:1–9 (Winter 1990).

Schöler, Bo. "A Heart Made out of Crickets: An Interview with Linda Hogan." *Journal of Ethnic Studies,* 16:107–117 (Spring 1988).

Smith, Patricia Clark. "Linda Hogan." In *This Is about Vision: Interviews with Southwestern Writers.* Edited by William Balassi, John F. Crawford, and Annie O. Eysturoy. Albuquerque: University of New Mexico Press, 1990. Pp. 141–155.

Thorington, Helen. "Interview with Linda Hogan." *The Key Is Remembering: Poetry and Interviews with Native American Women.* (audiotape). New York: Art, Inc., 1982.

—ANNA CAREW-MILLER